Defending Your Digital Assets
Against Hackers, Crackers, Spies and Thieves

Randall K. Nichols

Daniel J. Ryan

Julie J.C.H. Ryan

McGraw-Hill
New York   San Francisco   Washington, D.C.
Auckland   Bogotá   Caracas   Lisbon   London
Madrid   Mexico City   Milan   Montreal   New Delhi
San Juan   Singapore   Sydney   Tokyo   Toronto

McGraw-Hill

A Division of The McGraw-Hill Companies

Copyright © 2000 by The McGraw-Hill Companies, Inc. All rights reserved. Printed in the United States of America. Except as permitted under the United States Copyright Act of 1976, no part of this publication may be reproduced or distributed in any form or by any means, or stored in a data base or retrieval system, without the prior written permission of the publisher.

1 2 3 4 5 6 7 8 9 0   AGM/AGM   9 0 4 3 2 1 0 9

ISBN 0-07-212285-4

The executive editor for this book was Steven Elliot, the managing editor was Jennifer Perillo, the editing supervisor was Penny Linskey, and the production supervisor was Claire Stanley. It was set in Century Schoolbook by Victoria Khavkina of McGraw-Hill's Desktop Composition Unit, in cooperation with Spring Point Publishing Services.

Throughout this book, trademarked names are used. Rather than put a trademark symbol after every occurrence of a trademarked name, we use names in an editorial fashion only, and to the benefit of the trademark owner, with no intention of infringement of the trademark. Where such designations appear in this book, they have been printed with initial caps.

Printed and bound by Quebecor Martinsburg.

This book is printed on recycled, acid-free paper containing a minimum of 50% recycled, de-inked fiber.

From Randy Nichols

To: Montine, Kent, Robin, Phillip, Diana and my
    pumpkin Michelle—the Bear is back!
To: Gladys and Chuck—I thought you guys retired.
To: My Grandkids—Ryan, Kara and Brandon, take
    the future in your hands.
To: WITZEND and Waldo T. Boyd, two of the best
    editors in the country.

From Dan and Julie Ryan

To: Mom & Dad; R, C & G; Chris, Alleen, & Jake;
    Andy; Jon & Sandy.

Contents

Preface

Information Trends

Three information trends, evident in our world, which make this book necessary are: 1) a huge amount of valuable information is being created, stored, processed, and communicated using computers and computer-based systems and networks, 2) computers are increasingly interconnected, creating new pathways to valuable information assets, and 3) threats to information assets are becoming more widespread and more sophisticated.

These three trends have influenced significant developments in three diverse computer security areas: 1) Infocrimes and Digital Espionage (DE), 2) Information Security (INFOSEC) and 3) Information Warfare (IW). This book studies the interrelationships and technologies associated with each area.

Infocrimes and Digital Espionage

Infocrime refers to any crime where the criminal target is *information*. **Digital Espionage (DE)** is the *specific intent infocrime* of attacking, by computer means, personal, commercial or government information systems and assets for the purpose of theft, misappropriation, destruction, and disinformation for personal or political gain. This crime has become an enormous problem with the growth of the Internet. The authors' definition of *Digital Espionage* represents a compendium of activities. *DE* is really a **family** of *specific intent infocrimes*. Some examples of DE cases prosecuted under the 1996 computer crime statute, 18 U.S.C § 1030 include:

- Eugene E. Kashpureff for unleashing software on the Internet that interrupted service for tens of thousands of Internet users worldwide.
- Israeli citizen for hacking United States (including Whitehouse.gov) and Israeli computers.
- A chief computer network program designer for a $10 million extortion scheme based on a computer bomb.
- A juvenile hacker who cut off communications at the FAA tower at a regional airport.

■ Reuters's indictment for digital espionage of rival Bloomberg's operating code worth $millions.

According to 1999 FBI crime statistics, the DOD and other government computer using offices are attacked up to a hundred times a day. One particularly irritating mode of DE is the use of malicious viruses and code. One virus researcher has catalogued over 53,000 virus signatures by "families" and their variants. He has shown how a search of the Internet would yield at least four different free "automatic" virus making kits that require little brainpower to activate and unleash for malicious purposes. Commercial sites are "easy pickings" for the experienced computer criminal.

The Players

Computers are everywhere and they affect everything we do. As long as there have been computers, there have been **hackers.** Until recently being a hacker was not considered a dirty word. Now hackers are mild peppers compared to **crackers.** The difference is that hackers are performing break-ins for the thrill of it and crackers are breaking in for the profit of it. In the 21st century, we can expect that all fraud against property will be perpetrated by computer means. **Thieves** do not need to enter our homes to steal. Everything we own, invest, bank, or hold title to is referenced on our personal computers or computer databanks of the organizations with whom we do business. And then we have traditional **spies.** Their targets may be any of a variety of personal, commercial or government treasures.

No matter what we call them—*hackers, crackers, spies,* or *thieves*—they are breaking the law and violating your property and rights. It is your responsibility and duty to stop them! It is your right to protect your personal data, your computers, or your organization's information. We trust this book will provide tools to assist you in meeting these security goals.

INFOSEC Countermeasures

Digital Espionage can be thwarted by the *appropriate* and *effective* use of *INFOSEC* technologies. INFOSEC is a maturing science that has broad ranging applications in business and government. Every commercial venture that either markets its products internationally or uses computer networks for global communications and customer services must be concerned with protecting its assets and its customers' information from a wide variety of attacks. This concern is increased when the Internet is the primary communications medium.

At one time the sole province of government and military concerns, INFOSEC technologies have expanded in many directions and dimensions: recreational, scientific, biometric, educational, tactical, strategic, and global. The well-informed company (and government) recognizes the value that INFOSEC adds to the security of its computer information assets. Unfortunately, only a minority of corporate managers has deployed INFOSEC tools to protect their company computer communications and databases. This trend seems to be reversing dramatically as businesses expand into global markets and the cost of installing appropriate computer security systems decreases.

Information Warfare

Information warfare (IW) operations consist of those actions intended to protect, destroy, exploit, corrupt, or deny information or information resources to achieve a significant advantage over an enemy. IW is based on the value of a target and the cost to destroy or disable it. IW involves much more than computer and computer networks. It encompasses information in any form and transmitted over any media. IW includes operations against information, support systems, hardware, software and people. It is arguably more damaging than conventional warfare.

The purview of IW is very large. The concepts of information security, INFOSEC weapons, intelligence, countermeasures and policy need to be applied to the more global view of national security. A systems methodology to analyze the effects of various security contributions is required to affect information warfare in terms of the enemy's decision cycle. Information targets and the resulting countermeasures indicated to the defender have value and their risk assessment may be politically, technologically or behaviorally based. A model to view the overlapping technologies of OSI, practical implementation and available services in the cyberspace battlefield is studied.

The Rationale for this Book

Productivity, and hence competitiveness, is inextricably tied to computer connectivity, so we are increasingly vulnerable to the corruption, destruction, or exploitation of our valuable information assets and systems. Electronic access to vast amounts of data and critical infrastructure control is now possible from almost anywhere in the world. We are past the point of knowing the identity of everyone to whom our systems are connected. The sheer volume of data in our information systems makes these systems increasingly vulnerable and potentially lucrative targets for disgruntled employees, foreign intelligence services, hackers and terrorists, and competing commercial interests. We are only in the early stages of applying and understanding the new information technologies across our society and many questions remain unanswered. Neither the ethics that define acceptable behavior on-line for an Internet society nor the legal structures that would punish misbehavior have been fully developed.

The threat to our information and systems continues to grow. The threat is no longer limited to high school computer geeks. Criminals use systems and networks to steal valuable information to sell, or just eliminate the middlemen and illicitly enter the computers of banks and other financial institutions, and steal the money directly. Criminal hackers, using bogus wire transfers to offshore banks where the money can be retrieved with less risk, have transferred millions of dollars.

Today, information technology is evolving at a faster rate than information security technology. Technological advances in optical communications, for example, have led to unprecedented improvements in communications. Hair-thin strands of silica glass have spawned a communications revolution. A similar picture can be drawn for the computer industry where personal computer and workstation-based technology is reported to roll over every eighteen months. In fact, the technology is so fast paced that system designers can barely complete system design calculations before the manufacturer wants to update certain specifications. Databases, operating environments, and even operating systems are being distributed across networks.

These technological transformations have resulted in improved network services, performance, reliability, and availability as well as significantly reduced operating costs due to the more efficient utilization of network resources. And—most important to this discussion—interoperability of dissimilar computers in multi-vendor environments is paving the way for transparent information sharing capabilities and a globally integrated information infrastructure.

Unfortunately, testing and validation of the security of large systems can take years. The technologies and architectures, which were advancing the state-of-the-art when existing security policies were written, are now obsolete. Methods carefully crafted to secure computers that stood alone have been shown to be wholly inadequate when computers are networked.

In addition to the natural evolution of information technology, we are also undergoing a revolution that is creating unprecedented security challenges for information systems. For example, the development and operation of massive parallel processing and neural networks, artificial intelligence systems, and multimedia environments present problems beyond any that formed our current information systems security experience base. Policies and standards applying to data formats and data labeling must be reviewed and adjusted as necessary to incorporate the necessary information systems security. Standards for security labeling of voice and video notes and files are needed. Doctrines for manipulating and combining formats have yet to be developed.

There is also a natural opposition between security management and network management. Network managers need to know who is using the system and how they are using it. They need to know where data is coming from and where it is going, and at what rates, in order to maximize the efficiency of their networks. Security managers—recognizing the value of such information to those who would corrupt, exploit or destroy our information assets and systems—prefer these things to be confidential. These requirements are difficult to reconcile.

High technology is readily available on the open market and so is appearing in the hands of narcotics traffickers and terrorists. The technology needed by these miscreants is not very expensive, and the understanding needed to use the technology in support of illicit goals is available at the undergraduate levels of our universities. Even governments are getting into the field, using the capabilities developed during the cold war to obtain information from business travelers to pass to local competitors. Developing the capability to commit infocrime or infoterrorism or to wage infowar is much less expensive than developing nuclear, chemical or biological weapons of mass destruction. These new threats have considerable disposable income behind them that can be applied, from co-opting our authorized users in gaining access to our confidential information, to attacks against our technology-based national infrastructure.

Fortunately, we are not helpless. We have powerful INFOSEC tools, such as cryptography, to help us protect information that is being stored on our computers or which is being transferred across our networks. For those times when we cannot use cryptography to protect our information assets—mostly when we are creating or working with them on-line—we have computer science to help us build and operate systems and networks. These systems deny illicit access to those who would misuse or destroy our data, and help us detect intrusions by outsiders or abuses by those who have been granted authorized access to some information or systems. Further, that same science can facilitate corrective action and recovery from attacks.

Target Audience

Defending Your Digital Assets Against Hackers, Crackers, Spies and Thieves is aimed at the manager and policy maker, not the specialist. It was written for the benefit of commercial and government managers and policy-level executives who must exercise *due diligence* in protecting the valuable information assets and systems upon which their organizations depend. Aimed at the information-technology practitioner, it is valuable to CIO's, operations managers, technology managers, agency directors, military commanders, network managers, database managers, programmers, analysts, EDI planners and other professionals charged with applying appropriate INFOSEC countermeasures to stop all forms of Digital Espionage. This book is suitable for a first year graduate course in computer security, for computers in business courses and for Engineering/MBA programs. There are plenty of resources in the bibliography, URL references, and textual leads to further reading.

Benefits to the Reader

Defending Your Digital Assets Against Hackers, Crackers, Spies and Thieves will provide the reader with an appreciation of the nature and extent of the threat to information assets and systems and an understanding of the:

- Nature and scope of the problems that arise because of our increasing dependence on automated on-line information systems
- Steps that can and should be taken to abate the risks encountered when on-line operations are adopted as part of an organization's technology infrastructure
- Processes used to protect information assets from disclosure, misuse, alteration, or destruction
- Application of risk management to making key decisions about the application of scarce resources to information assurance
- Security architectures that can be used in designing and implementing systems that protect the confidentiality, integrity, and availability of valuable information assets
- Issues associated with managing and operating systems designed to protect trade secrets and confidential business information from industrial spies, organized criminals, and infoterrorists
- Practical countermeasures that can be used to protect information assets from digital attacks

Defending Your Digital Assets Against Hackers, Crackers, Spies and Thieves covers INFOSEC, security policy, risk management, enterprise continuity planning processes, cryptography, protocols, key management, public key infrastructure (PKI), virtual private networks, certificate authorities and digital signatures technologies for identification, authentication and authorization on the world wide web, secure electronic commerce, biometrics and digital warfare.

The book provides resources for applying INFOSEC to protect private, commercial and government computer systems.

Plan of the Book

There is a calculated momentum to this book. PART 1 introduces the surprising range and level of *Digital Espionage* against commercial and government computer systems. PART 2 presents the theoretical foundations of *INFOSEC* technology and shows its relevance to the protection of economic and military operations. Among the topics presented are risk management, security policy, privacy and security verification of computer systems and networks. PART 3 should be of special interest to managers who have the authority to make the vital security decisions required to protect their organizations. PART 3 is the core group of chapters defining INFOSEC practical countermeasures. It discusses cryptography, public key systems, access control, digital signatures and certificate authorities, procedures for permission management, identification, authentication and authorization on the World Wide Web, virtual private networks (VPN), and biometrics. PART 4 discusses the enterprise management process before, during and after a digital attack. Special attention is devoted to protecting the web server. PART 5 expands the concept of DE and INFOSEC principles to the global arena and information warfare (IW) operations. It discusses the requirements of information warfare, weapons and methods of employment. The process of building trust on-line through a Public Key Infrastructure (PKI) is reviewed in depth. Finally, as an expansion to Chapter 7 privacy issues, the authors look at politics of cryptography, one of the technology pillars of INFOSEC. The Appendices cover information technology, legal statutes and political issues, digital signatures, certificate authorities, Executive Orders, U.S. Title 18 Code, and compare virtual private networks (VPNs).

PART 1: Digital Espionage, Warfare, and Information Security (INFOSEC)

PART 1 introduces the family of *infocrimes* that constitute *Digital Espionage* and their relationship to the restricted implementation of information security (INFOSEC) technologies. This is covered in two chapters:

1. **Introduction to Digital Espionage:** This chapter introduces key topics: digital espionage (DE), scope of computer crime, infocrime, problems in jurisdiction and identity, digital warfare, anatomy of the computer crime and criminal factors relating to computer crime and countermeasures thereof, prosecution tools and encryption.

2. **Foundations of Information Security (INFOSEC)**—Chapter 2 develops the theoretical acceptable foundation of information security, such as confidentiality, integrity, availability; relevance of information security to economic and military operations; the consequences of failure to maintain INFOSEC goals. Donn Parker's brilliant extensions to the traditional INFOSEC theory are reviewed.

PART 2: INFOSEC Concepts

PART 2 presents the INFOSEC concepts of risk management, information security policy, privacy, intellectual capital and multilevel secure systems.

3. **Risk Management and the Architecture of Information Security (INFOSEC)**—Chapter 3 discusses risk management, threats and reducing vulnerability of information systems.

4. **Information Security Policy**—Chapter 4 argues for establishing an effective security policy for the nation and organizations. It discusses information classification management and the requirement for standards of due diligence.

5. **Privacy in a Knowledge-Based Economy**—Chapter 5 explores the tradeoffs of information security with our notions of privacy.

6. **Security Verification of Systems and Networks**—Chapter 6 presents the cost/benefits and requirements for accreditation, evaluation and certification for multi-level secure systems.

PART 3: Practical Countermeasures

INFOSEC is a family of technologies used as countermeasures against digital invasions and espionage. The six chapters of PART 3 present practical countermeasures:

7. **Cryptography**—Chapter 7 presents modern cryptography concepts, key management, Public Key Infrastructure (PKI), and comparison of the well-known RSA and elliptic curve cryptography (ECC) public key technologies. Hardware and software implementation issues are discussed.

8. **Access Control—Two Views**—Chapter 8 reviews the access control mechanisms normally used to limit access to systems and networks as well as audit people.

9. **Digital Signatures and Certification Authorities—Technology, Policy, and Legal Issues**—Chapter 9 covers the complex topic of digital signatures and certificate authorities used for authentication of computer systems and users.

10. **Permissions Management: Identification, Authentication, and Authorization (PMIAA)**—Chapter 10 is dedicated to per-

missions management and identification, authentication and authorization for secure commerce. It discusses protection systems and secure electronic commerce on the World Wide Web. Web site vulnerability, Internet and on-line systems, attacks, countermeasures, deployment, transaction security and technologies are explored.

11. **Virtual Private Networks**—This chapter discusses the use, standards, and security of VPN technologies for secure point-to-point and remote to host communications. It covers VPN implementation hurdles of performance, authentication/key management, fault tolerance, reliable transport, network placement, addressing/routing, administrative management, and interoperability.

12. **Biometric Countermeasures**—Chapter 12 compares eleven different biometric technologies and their use as secondary countermeasures.

PART 4: Enterprise Continuity Planning

PART 4 acknowledges that Digital Espionage against commercial and government computer information assets is prevalent. It discusses the management of defending against attacks during the process.

13. **Before the Attack: Protect and Detect**—Chapter 13 covers the process of vulnerability assessment, countermeasures, backups and beta sites, anti-viral measures, training and awareness, auditing and monitoring information transactions, system and network security management, encryption, and liaison with law enforcement and intelligence communities.

14. **During and After the Attack; Special Consideration—The Web Server**—Chapter 14 looks at the manager in the heat of the attack. It discusses system and network triage and reconstituting capability at a backup location. Protection of the web server is critical because it is a prime target.

PART 5: Order of Battle

PART 5 scales the DE/INFOSEC process to the level of war—INFOWAR. It adds the dimension of building trust online via a public-key infrastructure (PKI) and assesses the politics associated with implementation of and exportation of encryption systems on U.S. industry.

15. **The Big Picture**—Chapter 15 combines the concepts of information security, INFOSEC countermeasures and policy. It applies them to the more global view of National security. A systems methodology to analyze the effects of various securities contributions is presented.

16. **Information Warfare**—Chapter 16 discusses the IW, cyberspace environment, and implications for conventional war strategies. Chapter 16 discusses information warfare in terms of the enemy's decision cycle. It looks at the way value is assigned to information targets and the resulting countermeasures indicated to the defender. Risk assessment may be politically, technologically or behaviorally based.

17. **Information Warfare Weapons, Intelligence and the Cyberspace Environment**—Chapter 17 is a fascinating look at the weapons, intelligence and cyberspace environment for IW. A multi-dimensional model of the services (telecommunications, radio, cellular communications, personal communications systems, paging, mobile satellite services, very small aperture terminals and direct TV) is overlayed with the theoretical OSI framework and practical hardware implementations.

18. **Methods of Employment**—Chapter 18 continues the discussion by adding planning targeting and deployment issues for effective IW. The focus is on the unique features of IW. It looks at deployment issues such as targeting, Cyberwar Integrated Operations Plan (CIOP), candidate targets, intelligence preparation, comprehensive strategic information, weapons capabilities, metric for success, possible enemies, phases of conflict, and uniqueness of IW.

19. **Public Key Infrastructure: Building Trust Online**—Chapter 19 investigates the application, management and policy considerations for building trust on line using a Public Key Infrastructure (PKI). It switches to the government wide effort to deploy a functional PKI infrastructure by 2001. There is a serious effort to build trust online; however, the challenges of workable standards and interoperable equipment have not been fully solved.

20. **Cryptographic Politics: Encryption Export Law and Its Impact on U.S. Industry**—Chapter 20 recognizes the contribution that cryptography plays in the scheme of both government and

commercial computer countermeasures. Cryptography exists in a particularly active political environment. On 16 September 1999, Clinton ordered the export controls on cryptography [after 3 years of tightening efforts] to be relaxed. A review of the laws governing cryptography and their impact on U.S industry is presented.

The Appendices cover INFOSEC technology, Executive Orders, electronic signatures, certificate authorities, criminal statutes, and offer a comparison of commercial VPN offerings.

Internet Mailing List

An Internet mailing list has been set up through COMSEC Solutions, LLC so that managers who want to keep current or instructors using this book can exchange information, suggestions, and questions with each other and the authors. To subscribe, send an e-mail message to InfoDE@COMSEC-Solutions.com with a message body of "subscribe Digital-Espionage." Further instructions will be returned for posting messages and receiving updates.

Acknowledgments

Books such as this are the products of contributions by many people, not just the musings of the authors. *Defending Your Digital Assets: Against Hackers, Crackers, Spies, and Thieves* has benefited from review by numerous experts in the field, who gave generously of their time and expertise. The following people reviewed all or part of the manuscript: William E. Baugh, Jr., Vice President and General Manager, Advanced Network Technologies and Security for SAIC; Dorothy Denning, Professor of INFOSEC Technology at Georgetown University; Jules M. Price (WITZ END), an expert on cipher technology; Charles M. Thatcher, Distinguished Professor of Chemical Engineering, University of Arkansas; Scott Inch, Associate Professor of Advanced Mathematics, Bloomsburg University; Jim Lewis, Director of Cryptographic Export Policy for the Bureau of Export Administration; Phillip Zimmermam, internationally known cryptographer and inventor of PGP; Cindy Cohn, attorney for Professor Daniel J. Bernstein; Waldo T. Boyd, senior editor, owner of Creative Writing, Pty. and senior cryptographer; Donn B. Parker, author of *Fighting Computer Crime;* Mark Zaid, Attorney at Law for the James Madison Project; Arthur W. Coviello, Jr., President of RSA Security, Inc.; Sandra Toms Lapedis, Director of Communications for RSA; Andrew Brown, Director of Marketing at RSA; Elizabeth M. Nichols, CFO for COMSEC Solutions; Kevin V. Shannon, Executive Vice President and Damian Fozard, CEO of InvisiMail; and Penny Linskey, supervising editor; Jennifer Perillo, managing editor, and Steven Elliot, senior executive editor for McGraw Hill Professional Books.

Several of Professor Nichols' students from his 1999 graduate course in *Cryptographic Systems: Application, Management and Policy* at The George Washington University assisted with Chapters 19 and 20 and Appendix 16. We are grateful for the dedicated and enthusiastic assistance from Charlene Fareira, Mike Ross, Jim Luczka, Cornellis Ramey, Shafat Khan, Bill Kimbrough, Lynn Kinch, John Allen, Sami Mousa, Terry May, Harry Watson, Alexx Bahouri, Joan L. Bowers, Rebecca Catey, Chad Smith, and Joseph Wojsznski.

Among the many we have to thank, special recognition is due Nina Stewart, Tony Oettinger, Bob Morris, Devolyn Arnold, and Tom Rona who provided much of the inspiration that fostered our thinking. Mike McChesney, Steve Kent, and Steve Walker helped shape our understanding of the technologies and the business implications of their use. William Perry, as Secretary of Defense, and R. James Woolsey, as the

Director of Central Intelligence, had the foresight and courage to charter the Joint DoD-DCI Security Commission, which explored the depths and breadths of the subject matter. Bill Stasior, Larry Wright, Fred Demech, and Larry Clarke provided opportunities and encouragement to us. Jim Morgan has been a friend, colleague, mentor, supporter and constructive critic for years. Finally, Montine Nichols deserves a commendation for her help on the Glossary and References and patience during the writing of this book. To these and many others we may have failed to give appropriate credit, we are grateful for their relevant ideas, advice and counsel. Any mistakes or errors are, of course, our own. Please advise the authors of errors by e-mail to *DE@comsec-solutions.com* and we will do our best to correct the errors and publish an errata list on the *www.COMSEC-Solutions.com* listserver.

Best to all,

Randy Nichols
Professor, The George Washington University
and
President
COMSEC Solutions, LLC
Cryptographic / Anti-Virus / Biometric Countermeasures
Email: *Rnichols@COMSEC-Solutions.com*
Website: http://*www.comsec-solutions.com*
Carlisle, Pennsylvania
December 1999

Dan Ryan, Esq.
E-mail: *danryan@danjryan.com*
Website: *http*://www.danryan.com
Annapolis, Maryland
December 1999

Julie J.C.H. Ryan
President
Wyndrose Technical Group
E-mail: *JulieRyan@julieryan.com*
Website: *http://www.julieryan.com*
Annapolis, Maryland
December 1999

List of Contributors

The authors express their gratitude to the talented review team who contributed so much of their time and expertise to make this book a success. With deep respect, we present the qualifications of our teammates.

Authors

Randall K. Nichols

Randy Nichols (Supervising Author/Editor) formed COMSEC Solutions, LLC in 1997 [www.comsec-solutions.com]. He has 35 years of experience in a variety of leadership roles in cryptography and computer applications in the engineering, consulting, construction, and chemicals industries. COMSEC Solutions provides INFOSEC support to more than 200 commercial, educational and U.S. government clients. In addition to CEO duties for COMSEC Solutions, Nichols serves as Series Editor for Encryption and INFOSEC for McGraw Hill Professional Books and lectures at the prestigious The George Washington University in Washington, DC.

Defending Your Digital Assets Against Hackers, Crackers, Spies and Thieves is Nichols' fourth book on the subjects of cryptography and INFOSEC countermeasures. Nichols' previous books, *The ICSA Guide to Cryptography* (McGraw-Hill Professional Books, 1998, ISBN 0-07-913759-8) and *Classical Cryptography Course, Volumes I and II* (Aegean Park Press, 1995, ISBN 0-89412-263-0 and 1996, ISBN 0-89412-264-9, respectively) have gained recognition and industry respect for both Nichols and COMSEC Solutions.

Professor Nichols teaches graduate level Cryptography and Systems Applications Management and Policy at The George Washington University in Washington, D.C. He has taught cryptography at the FBI National Academy in Quantico, VA. Mr. Nichols is a professional speaker and regularly presents material at professional conferences, national technology meetings, schools and client in-house locations on INFOCRIME/INFOSEC/INFOWAR.

Nichols previously served as Technology Director of Cryptography and Biometrics for the International Computer Security Association (ICSA). Nichols (a.k.a. LANAKI) has served as President and Vice President of the American Cryptogram Association (ACA). He has been the Aristocrats'

Department Editor for the ACA's bimonthly publication "The Cryptogram," since 1985.

Nichols holds BSChE and MSChE degrees from Tulane University and Texas A & M University, respectively, and an MBA from University of Houston. In 1995, Nichols was awarded a 2nd DAN (Black Belt) by the American and Korean Tae Kwon Do Moo Duk Kwan Associations.

Daniel J. Ryan

Daniel J. Ryan is a lawyer, businessman, and educator. Prior to entering private practice, he served as Corporate Vice President of Science Applications International Corporation with responsibility for information security for Government customers and commercial clients who operate worldwide and must create, store, process, and communicate sensitive information and engage in electronic commerce. At SAIC he developed and provided security products and services for use in assessing security capabilities and limitations of client systems and networks, designing or re-engineering client systems and networks to ensure security, enhancing protection through a balanced mix of security technologies, detecting intrusions or abuses, and reacting effectively to attacks to prevent or limit damage.

Prior to assuming his current position, Mr. Ryan served as Executive Assistant to the Director of Central Intelligence with primary responsibility as Executive Secretary and Staff Director for the Joint DoD-DCI Security Commission. Earlier, he was Director of Information Systems Security for the Office of the Secretary of Defense serving as the principal technical advisor to the Secretary of Defense, the ASD (C3I) and the DASD (CI & SCM) for all aspects of information security. He developed information security policy for the Department of Defense and managed the creation, operation and maintenance of secure computers, systems and networks. His specific areas of responsibility spanned information systems security (INFOSEC), including classification management, communications security (COMSEC) and cryptology, computer security (COMPUSEC) and transmission security (TRANSEC), as well as TEMPEST, technical security countermeasures (TSCM), operational security (OPSEC), port security, overflight security and counterimagery.

In private industry, he was a Principal at Booz•Allen & Hamilton where he served as a consultant in the areas of strategic and program planning, system operations and coordination, data processing and telecommunications. At Bolt Beranek & Newman, he supplied secure wide-area telecommunications networks to Government and commercial clients. He represented the Los Angeles-based Systems Development

Division of TRW in Washington, D.C., and he was Director of Electronic Warfare Advanced Programs at Litton's AMECOM Division. He headed a systems engineering section at Hughes Aircraft Company where he was responsible for the design, development and implementation of data processing systems. He began his career at the National Security Agency.

Mr. Ryan received his Bachelor of Science degree in Mathematics from Tulane University in New Orleans, Louisiana, a Master of Arts degree in Mathematics from the University of Maryland, a Master of Business Administration degree from California State University and the degree of Juris Doctor from the University of Maryland. He is admitted to the Bar in the State of Maryland and the District of Columbia, and has been admitted to practice in the United States District Court, the United States Tax Court, and the Supreme Court of the United States. He has been Certified by the United States Government as a Professional in the fields of Data Systems Analysis, Mathematics and Cryptologic Mathematics.

Julie J. C. H. Ryan

Julie J. C. H. Ryan began her career as an intelligence officer after graduating from the Air Force Academy in 1982. She transitioned from active duty Air Force to civilian service with the Defense Intelligence Agency, where she served as an all-source intelligence analyst studying the capabilities, intentions and expertise of Soviet Union and Warsaw Pact military forces in the areas of C3, EW, and C3 countermeasures (C3CM). Her work at DIA included supporting the early attempts to understand how to develop multi-level secure computer systems; including directing and monitoring the design, development, and delivery of secure data bases. Her responsibilities spanned budget and program management techniques, system design and engineering practices, data base design, intelligence data requirements, information security concepts, user capabilities and knowledge base, and human engineering. From that experience, Julie developed an abiding interest in enterprise-wide security solutions, creating and deploying an appropriate mixture of technologies, tools, and procedures to address the security requirements of information assets and systems.

Since leaving government service, Julie Ryan has continued working in security engineering. At Sterling Federal Systems she performed comparative functional, technical and cost feasibility analyses of possible alternative system implementations for the Intelligence Community and the military services. At Booz & Hamilton, she served as a special consultant to highly classified Government programs, performing technical analyses, test and system engineering, and long-range strategic planning. At Welkin Associates, she assisted in advanced systems design and development for national- and theater-level requirements satisfaction, including architecture studies and investigations of new and unique uses for emerging technologies in secure information management, data processing and product distribution. For TRW, Julie served as an Information Warfare specialist, coordinating Information Warfare-related activities horizontally across the lines of businesses, networking applicable capabilities and competencies, and participating in strategic planning processes. She prepared white papers, briefings and publications on Information Warfare for both internal educational and strategic planning purposes as well as for customer briefings and work proposals. These included an Information Order of Battle concept briefing, a concept exploration of intelligence support to information warfare.

Julie participated as a Member of the Naval Studies Board of the National Academy of Sciences in studying technology implications to warfare and national security applications. She also supports the Assistant Secretary of Defense (C3I) in Information Warfare studies, evaluations and planning.

Julie currently serves as President of the Wyndrose Technical Group, Inc., a company providing information technology and security consulting services. She specializes in security systems engineering, creating solutions for specific operational environments based on realistic assessments of the organization's security requirements. Having received a Masters Degree from Eastern Michigan University's College of Technology, she is now pursuing a Doctor of Science from the Engineering Management and Systems Engineering Department of the School of Engineering and Applied Sciences (SEAS), George Washington University. Julie teaches graduate-level classes in engineering and technology for GWU and is researching information security management practices for her dissertation.

Randy Nichols

Dan Ryan

Julie J.C.H. Ryan

COMSEC Solutions Review Team

Waldo T. Boyd

Waldo was not always President of Creative Writing, Inc. [wboyd@net-dex.com] or vigorously editing *Defending Your Digital Assets Against Hackers, Crackers, Spies and Thieves.* The U.S. Navy lopped off Waldo's blond curls at age 18 and converted his 80 wpm typing into radio operating in 1936. After attending technical and engineering schools, he was assigned to Sydney University (Australia) ECM labs (electronic countermeasures) for research in crypto, underwater, aircraft, ship and sub ECM. Since his Secret clearance required line officer or else, he left the ranks to become a Warrant Radar Electrician.

Waldo resigned his commission in 1947, and became tech writer and teacher of ECM to Air Force officers as a civilian, Berlin Airlift. He spent nine years at Aerojet-General Rocket-Engine plants as manager technical manuals dept, produced over 100 missile tech manuals on Titan and other systems. Edited magnetic air and undersea detection manuals under contract for U.S. Air Force, computer texts, wrote six books for Simon & Schuster, H. W. Sams, etc., general and youth readership. Wrote weekly science articles for two syndicates. "Retired" at age 62—he continues to write and edit selectively to the present day.

His publication credits include seven titles:

Your Career in the Aerospace Industry, Julian Messner Div., Simon & Schuster, 1966 (Jr. Lit. Guild Selection).

Your Career in Oceanology, Simon & Schuster, 1969

Oceanologia (Spanish Edition) Brazil, 1969

The World of Cryogenics, G.P. Putnam's Sons, N.Y., 1970

The World of Energy Storage, Ibid, 1977

Fiber Optics with Experiments, Howard W. Sams, Ind., 1982

Fiber Optics (Japanese Edition), Tokyo, 1984

Cryptology and the Personal Computer, Aegean Press, L.A., 1986

Computer Cryptology: Beyond Decoder Rings, Prentice-Hall, 1988

And 2000 articles in *Popular Science Monthly*; *Popular Electronics*; *Popular Mechanics*; *Think* (IBM); *Western Fruit Grower*; *Harvest Years*; *London Times*; *The Foreman's Letter*; *Supervisor's Letter*; *Business Management*; *Cable TV Magazine*; *Ham Radio*; *73 Magazine*; *80-Micro*; *80-US*; *Hot Coco*; *Advanced Computing*; *Fate*; *OfficeSystems96*; *Weekly Syndicated Science Column*; and many others.

Jules M. Price

Jules M. Price (WITZ END) has been a Senior Cryptographer with the ACA since 1950 and has solved over 10,000 cryptograms. Only a few people in the world, since 1929, have obtained that ranking, which signals expertise in nearly 75 different classical cipher systems. In his other life, he is a Professional Engineer, and as Vice President, Chief Engineer and Project Manager, he has directly involved in the construction of multi-million dollar projects ranging from highways and bridges to colleges, schools, hospitals, and Shea Stadium (home of the New York Mets.) WITZ END was the chief reviewer for the successful *ICSA Guide To Cryptography,* published by McGraw Hill in 1998. His long experience with building plans and specifications has given him a razor sharp eye for details. For this talent, he was chosen as a primary reviewer for this book.

Charles M. Thatcher

Chuck Thatcher joined COMSEC Solutions in 1998 as Vice President in charge of Research and Development. He has more than 33 years of experience in mathematical modeling, systems analysis, computer simulation, optimization and applications programming.

Dr. Thatcher is the principal author of *Digital Computer Programming: Logic and Language* by Addison-Wesley Publishing Co., 1967, and *Fundamentals of Chemical Engineering* by Charles E. Merrill Books, Inc., 1962. Numerous papers, technical reports, patents, and commercial computer programs are credited to Dr. Thatcher.

Dr. Thatcher was the Distinguished Professor of Chemical Engineering and Alcoa Aluminum Company Chair at the University of Arkansas, 1970-1992. He was awarded his Ph.D. (ChE) from the University of Michigan in 1955.

Scott Inch

Scott Inch earned a B.S. in Mathematics in 1986 from Bloomsburg University, a M.S. in Mathematics in 1988 and a Ph.D. in Applied Mathematics in 1992 from Virginia Polytechnic Institute and State University. His areas of specialty are control theory, integro-partial differential equations, and energy decay in viscoelastic and thermo-viscoelastic rods. Dr. Inch is currently an Associate Professor in the Department of

Mathematics, Computer Science and Statistics at Bloomsburg University. He has always been interested in cryptology and now gets to teach it.

Mark Zaid

Mark S. Zaid is a solo practitioner in Washington, D.C., specializing in litigation and lobbying on matters relating to international transactions, torts and crimes, national security, foreign sovereign and diplomatic immunity, defamation (plaintiff) and the Freedom of Information/Privacy Acts.

Through his practice Mr. Zaid often represents former/current federal employees, intelligence officers, Whistleblowers and others who have grievances or have been wronged by agencies of the United States Government or foreign governments.

Mr. Zaid is the Executive Director of the James Madison Project, a Washington, D.C.-based non-profit, with the primary purpose of educating the public on issues relating to intelligence gathering and operations, secrecy policies, national security and government wrongdoing.

In connection with his legal practice on international and national security matters, Mr. Zaid has testified before, or provided testimony to, a variety of governmental bodies including the Department of Energy and subcommittees of the Senate Judiciary Committee, the Senate Governmental Affairs Committee, the House Judiciary Committee, and the House Government Reform Committee.

A 1992 graduate of Albany Law School of Union University in New York, where he served as an Associate Editor of the Albany Law Review, he completed his undergraduate education (cum laude) in 1989 at the University of Rochester, New York with honors in Political Science and high honors in History. Mr. Zaid is a member of the Bars of New York State, Connecticut, the District of Columbia, and several federal courts.

Elizabeth M. Nichols

Elizabeth M. Nichols joined COMSEC Solutions in 1998 as General Manager in charge of Finance, Accounting and Public Relations. In 1999, she was promoted to the post of CFO, adding to her duties Auditing, Taxes, Capital Expenditures, and Human Relations.

Mrs. Nichols came to COMSEC Solutions with 23 years of management and field experience in "stat" laboratory and hospital administration. She has developed policies and security procedures for major hospitals and schools such as Humana Hospital, LabCorp and University of Arkansas Medical School at Little Rock.

The Glossary, Appendices and final copy edit for *Defending Your Digital Assets Against Hackers, Crackers, Spies and Thieves* were developed, inspected, and tenaciously prepared by Mrs. Nichols.

Mrs. Nichols was granted a BSMT from University of Arkansas in 1976.

Christopher R. Ryan

Christopher Ryan is an information security expert with Ernst & Young, specializing in the evaluation and deployment of public key infrastructures. Prior to joining Ernst & Young, he was an information engineer at Science Applications International Corporation. He has a B.S. in Computer Science from the University of Maryland.

Foreword

The authors' broad backgrounds of practice and academia allowed them to seamlessly present the most current state of information protection and vulnerabilities in an easy to understand, but documented treatise. The cases presented are real, topical and flow with the theme of the subject matter presented. They tell you the risks, examine the cases where people and systems have fallen victim and tell you the remedy.

The work begins with discussion of foundation and structure of information protection and reviews the consequences of failure to protect information. An interesting discussion of the tools that are available to protect against cyberthreats complete this area of discussion.

Countermeasures and protections are presented and include relevant tools such as encryption, access control, authentication, and digital signatures. The authors discuss private networks and the challenges inherent in end-to-end security of communications. Public key infrastructure and management are treated well and in detail.

Contingency planning, recovery, and practical directions are provided for those who have been attacked and damaged by hackers or malicious code insertion. Readers will understand to a much greater detail what has happened and what to do. Then in scholarly but interesting detail Information Warfare and the Politics of the subject are analyzed and observed. These weapons, their use, and potential are explained and range from viruses and malicious code to RF weapons that destroy circuits and components.

Readers will find the approach the authors have taken is one of best business practices, combined with a systems approach to the problem of information security. The book is designed for readers, who operate at the executive, policy or managerial level and who have some responsibility for protection of the organization's information assets, intellectual property and systems. Content presented is equally valuable to both commercial and government managers.

This work provides a reasoned approach to making sound decisions about how to expend resources, often scarce, to achieve a balanced multidisciplinary approach. The search is for the security required at an affordable price to the organization. Three basic processes are used in defining and developing a program of protection: protection, detection and correction. Risk management rather than risk avoidance, provides the methodology for applying cost-benefit and Return on income analyses.

The extensive appendices provide source information on information technology, legal and political issues now in the cyberspace.

Defending Your Digital Assets: Against Hackers, Crackers, Spies, and Thieves is a joint effort by three experienced information security professionals.

Randall K. Nichols is President of COMSEC Solutions and author of three previous titles on cryptography. He recently served as Technology Director of Cryptography and Biometrics for the International Computer Security Association (ICSA). Nichols is considered an expert on cryptanalysis and INFOSEC countermeasures. Nichols lectures on cryptography policy and systems management at the prestigious The George Washington University.

Daniel J. Ryan is an attorney, businessman, and educator who has served in private industry, including as Corporate VP of SAIC, and in the public sector, as Executive Assistant to the DCI. He is an Adjunct Professor of Information Security and Internet Law for The George Washington University and James Madison University.

Julie J. C. H. Ryan is President of Wyndrose Technical Group, providing security engineering and knowledge management consulting to commercial and government clients. She is an Adjunct Professor with The George Washington University in the Engineering Management and Systems Engineering Department of the School of Engineering and Applied Sciences.

WILLIAM E. BAUGH, JR.
MCLEAN, VA. USA
16 NOVEMBER 1999

About William E. Baugh, Jr.
Mr. Baugh is a senior executive in a Fortune 500 company, an Attorney, and a Director or Advisor to companies involved in Information Security and Intellectual Property Protection. He is active in both National, and International Telecommunications fraud remediation, signal theft, piracy, and network security. He has published a number of articles on Information Security, Encryption and Crime in Cyberspace. He has testified before the United States Congress as an invited expert on encryption and information protection and periodically comments to the National Media. Before entering private industry, he served as Assistant Director of the Federal Bureau of Investigation, responsible for Information Resources and Technology, retiring after 26 years of service. Mr. Baugh has offices in McLean, Virginia, and Savannah, Georgia.

Foreword

Welcome to the inaugural book from RSA Press! From our participation in technical and legislative policy to hosting the world's foremost security conference, RSA Security has continually sought to educate the world on e-security issues, technologies and futures. Now, we are pleased to extend this same tradition through our new line of RSA Press books. We believe that the industry as a whole can advance more quickly with an open exchange of information and through education on the security issues that are shaping today's online marketplace.

RSA Security's nearly two decades of hands-on experience in the e-security realm make us uniquely suited to be a trusted source for information on the latest e-security trends and issues. With the proliferation of the Internet and revolutionary e-business practices, there has never been a more critical need for sophisticated security technologies and solutions - and for trustworthy information about e-security. RSA Press books can help your company move safely into the new and rewarding arena of electronic business, by providing relevant and unbiased information to guide you around the potential dangers of doing business in the networked world. Whether you are an enterprise IT manager, an application developer, a CEO, CIO or an end user of computer technologies, titles from RSA Press will be available to answer your questions and address your concerns about reaping the benefits of e-commerce while minimizing the risks involved with doing so.

As our first published title, *Defending Your Digital Assets Against Hackers, Crackers, Spies and Thieves* provides a solid foundation for information security professionals to learn about the methods of protecting their organizations' most precious assets: data. Network data has become increasingly valuable in today's public and private sectors, and most information that's accessible from a network is not as secure as it should be. *Defending Your Digital Assets Against Hackers, Crackers, Spies and Thieves* discusses the growing vulnerabilities associated with doing business online and offers detailed explanations and advice on how to prevent future attacks, detect attacks in progress, and quickly recover business operations.

We hope you enjoy this inaugural work, and welcome your comments, criticism and ideas for future RSA Press books. Please visit our Web site at *http://www.rsasecurity.com* for more information about RSA Security, or find us at *http://www.rsasecurity.com/rsapress/* to learn more about RSA Press.

ARTHUR W. COVIELLO, JR.
PRESIDENT
RSA SECURITY INC.

PART 1

Digital Espionage, Warfare, and Information Security (INFOSEC)

In Chapter 1, the interesting concepts of *Digital Espionage* and *Digital Warfare* are introduced. The family of computer security countermeasures known as INFOSEC is discussed. All computer information is vulnerable to a variety of attacks. A primary theme of this book is that information security (INFOSEC) countermeasures are reasonable and prudent technologies to thwart *Digital Espionage* and *Infocrimes* perpetuated by a host of bad guys we encounter: *Hackers, Crackers, Spies,* and *Thieves.* As a corollary, poorly implemented INFOSEC technologies provide fertile ground for the practice of *Digital Espionage* in corporate and military theaters. We attempt to profile the computer criminal and present some primary tools that investigators have at their disposal to prosecute them. Since encryption is a primary weapon in the INFOSEC arsenal, it is introduced at this junction.

In Chapter 2, traditional INFOSEC goals are persented. We review some of the serious consequences that occur when INFOSEC technologies are inappropriately applied. Finally, Donn Parker's brilliant extensions to the traditional INFOSEC theory are reviewed.

CHAPTER 1

Introduction to
Digital Espionage

Digital Espionage (DE)—What It Is and What It Represents

Infocrime refers to any crime where the criminal target is *information*. *Digital espionage* (DE) is the *specific-intent infocrime* of attacking, by computer means, personal, commercial, or government information systems and assets for the purpose of theft, misappropriation, destruction, and disinformation for personal or political gain. This crime has become an enormous problem with the growth of the Internet. The authors' definition of digital espionage represents a compendium of activities. DE is really a *family* of specific-intent infocrimes. The logical questions are as follows: how big is the family, what really is a computer crime, why and how does it occur, and most importantly, how does one prevent a computer crime from occurring? How important is it that the main thrust of the attack is against information assets?

The advent and growth of the Internet has made digital espionage a real and potential danger of enormous magnitude. The average computer user is still blissfully unaware of this danger, but digital espionage has already begun to affect the general public, as well as corporations and government agencies. Corporate management has also been slow to recognize and react to the specter of digital espionage. Most existing security systems reflect a concern for short-term profit or reaction to a specific breach of security in the past. The need to educate employees about the protection of intellectual property is rarely seen as a high-priority item. Many security initiatives are delayed until the manager is dealing with crisis rather than appropriate planning and security policies. Each new security crisis usually induces a similar limited reaction, without any consideration of the more general problem within which any one incident is only an immediate example.

Scope of Computer Crime (Infocrime)

The scope of computer crime is difficult to quantify. Public reports have estimated that computer crime costs us between $500 million and $10 billion per year.[1] A survey performed jointly by the Computer Security Institute (CSI) and the Federal Bureau of Investigation's Computer

Crime Division found that nearly half of the 5000 companies, federal institutions, and universities polled experienced computer security breaches within the past 12 months. These attacks ranged from unauthorized access by employees to break-ins by unknown intruders. The study found that:[2]

- The problem is growing.
- The greatest problem is insider attacks.
- Identified computer crime accounted for over $100 million in losses in 1996.

In addition, a WarRoom Research, Inc. survey of 236 respondents showed major underreporting of security incidences related to computers:[3]

- 6.8 percent always reported intrusion
- 30.2 percent only report if anonymous
- 21.7 percent only report if everyone else did
- 37.4 percent only report if required by law
- 3.9 percent only report for "other reasons, including protect self"

According to a recent U.S. Department of Justice presentation,[4] some examples of systems and facilities that were seriously hit are as follows:

- U.S. Marshals system—Alaska
- U.S. District Court system—Seattle
- NASA attack—Houston
- Military systems—Gulf War
- Organ Transplant Hospital—Italy
- Power companies
- 911 systems

Furthermore, in 1996 the National Security Agency (NSA) reported over 250 intrusions into DoD systems. The consequences from these computer attacks were labeled as *devastating*.

Research by Barbara D. Ritchey at the University of Houston presents another view: computer crimes account for losses of more than $1 billion annually and those computer criminals manifest themselves in many forms, including coworkers, competitors, and "crackers."[5] The Computer Security Institute of San Francisco also surveyed 242 separate Fortune 500 companies concerning Internet security and found that in 1995 only 12 percent of the companies reported losses as a result of system penetration totaling losses of $50 million. In terms of dollar value, the average theft costs a company $450,000 for each incident.

In 1996, *Information Week* magazine conducted its third annual survey in conjunction with Ernst and Young. The survey queried 1290 respondents, almost one-half of which said they suffered a financial loss related to information security in the last two years. At least 20 percent of the 1290 respondents stated their information security losses came to more than $1 million each. Additional loss information acquired from the Ernst and Young survey is that one in four U.S. companies has been a victim of computer crime, with losses ranging from $1 billion to $15 billion.[6]

From 1990 through 1995, the number of computers in the world increased tenfold, from 10 million to 100 million. In 1990, 15 percent of the computers were networked, and by 1995, 50 percent, or almost 50 million computers, were hooked together. From 1995 to 1999 the number of connected computers is estimated to have grown to over 250 million.

Theft of trade secrets is one of the most serious threats facing business today. The latest CSI/FBI Computer Crime and Security Study, released in March 1999, found that of the 12 types of computer crime and misuse, theft of proprietary information had the greatest reported financial losses for the period 1997 to 1999. According to the survey, more than $42 million worth of trade secrets were stolen from 64 organizations that were able to quantify their losses from this type of breach.[7] Reported losses in 1998 ranged from $500 to $500,000. Penetration attacks by "outside" sources were 18 percent of the organizations reporting in 1997 and 21 percent of those reporting in 1998.[8]

The Federal Computer Incident Response Center reported 244 incidents involving government sites from October 1996 through October 1997. Of those, 92 (38 percent) were intrusion incidents, 83 (34 percent) were probes, 37 (15 percent) were computer viruses, 22 (9 percent) were e-mail incidents, 4 (2 percent) were denial of service incidents, 2 (1 percent) were malicious code incidents, 2 were misuse incidents, and 2 were scams. One particularly sensitive intrusion ran over several months and involved more than 10,000 hosts. Hackers gained root access in several of the incidents.[9]

The National Police Agency of Japan received reports of 946 cases involving hacking during the first six months of 1997. This was a 25 percent increase over the first six months in 1996. The Australian Computer Emergency Response Team reported a 220 percent increase in hacker attacks from 1996 to 1997.[10]

Networking has helped technology increase exponentially. With these cultural changes, the need for heightened security has also increased. A computer criminal formerly was able to attack systems at only one location, giving administrators the advantage of protecting one site. In today's client/server environment, network administrators are fighting a very different battle. They are subject to attacks at every access point on their network, from a modem port to a laptop on an airplane headed for Paris. The Internet poses its own share of unique problems in that never before have so many computers been hooked together.[11]

The Criminal Playground

Computer crimes take several forms including sabotage, revenge, vandalism, theft, eavesdropping, and even "data diddling," or the unauthorized altering of data before, during, or after it is input into a computer system. Computers can be used to commit such crimes as credit card fraud, counterfeiting, bank embezzlement, and theft of secret documents. The physical theft of a disk storing 2.8 MB of intellectual data is considered data theft. Logging into a computer account with restricted access and being caught there or purposely leaving evidence in the form of a message with an explanation of what has been done are examples of data diddling. A traveling employee who leaves his or her computer unattended while on an airplane, only to discover an empty drive slot to the tune of lost billing information, marketing plans, and/or customer data, can be considered inattentive, but this type of incident is steadily increasing.

Another type of computer crime involves electronic funds transfer or embezzlement. The first person convicted under the Computer Fraud and Abuse Act was Robert T. Morris Jr., who, as a Cornell graduate student, introduced a "worm" into the Internet. These "worms" float freely through the computer environment, attacking programs in a manner similar to viruses. Some would consider this an act of vandalism. By multiplying, the worm interfered with approximately 6200 computers. Morris was sentenced to three years' probation, ordered to pay a $10,000 fine, required to perform 40 hours of community service, and required to pay $91 per month to cover his probation supervision.

Computers can play three different roles in criminal activity. First, computers can be *targets* of an offense; for example, a hacker tries to steal information from or damage a computer or computer network. Other examples of this behavior include vandalism of Web sites and the introduction of viruses into computers.

Second, computers can be *tools* in the commission of a traditional offense, for instance, to create and transmit child pornography. COMSEC

Solutions composed an interesting list wherein the computer was used as a tool to facilitate the following crimes:[12]

- Drug trade
- Illegal telemarketing
- Fraud, especially false invoices
- Intellectual property theft
- "True face" or ID theft and misrepresentation
- Espionage, both industrial and national
- Conventional terrorism and crimes
- Electronic terrorism and crime
- Electronic stalking
- Electronic harassment of ex-spouses
- Inventory of child pornography
- Bookmaking
- Contract repudiation on the Internet
- Cannabis smuggling
- Date rape
- Gang crimes, especially weapons violations
- Organized crime
- Armed robbery simulation
- Copycat crimes
- Pyramid schemes
- DoS (denial of service) attacks
- Exposure or blackmail schemes
- Revenge and solicitation to murder of spouses
- Hate crimes
- Web site defacement (automated)

Third, computers can be *incidental* to the offense, but still significant for law enforcement purposes. For example, many drug dealers now store their records on computers, which raises difficult forensic and evidentiary issues that are different from paper records.

In addition, a single computer could be used in all three ways. For example, a hacker might use his or her computer to gain unauthorized access to an Internet service provider ("target") such as America Online, and then use that access to illegally distribute ("tool") copyrighted software stored on the ISP's computer-server hard drive ("incidental"). COMSEC Solutions composed another interesting list where the computer was an incidental part of computer crime. These included hacking, data theft, diddling, alteration and destruction, especially involving financial or medical records, spreading viruses or malicious code, misuse of credit and business information, theft of services, and finally, denial of service.

Internet service providers (ISPs) and large financial institutions are not the only organizations that should be concerned about computer crime. Hackers can affect individual citizens directly or through the person's ISP by compromising the confidentiality and integrity of personal and financial information. In one case, a hacker from Germany gained complete control of an ISP server in Miami and captured all the credit card information maintained about the service's subscribers. The hacker then threatened to destroy the system and distribute all the credit card numbers unless the ISP paid a ransom. German authorities arrested the hacker when he tried to collect the money. Had he been quiet, he could have used the stolen credit card numbers to defraud thousands of consumers.[13]

Government records, like any other records, can be susceptible to a network attack if they are stored on a networked computer system without proper protections. In Seattle, two hackers pleaded guilty to penetrating the U.S. District Court system, an intrusion that gave them access to confidential and even sealed information. In carrying out their attack, they used supercomputers at the Seattle-based Boeing Computer Center to crack the courthouse system's password file. If Boeing had not reported the intrusion to law enforcement, the district court system administrator would not have known the system was compromised.[14]

The computer can also be a powerful tool for consumer fraud. The Internet can provide a con artist with an unprecedented ability to reach millions of potential victims. As far back as December 1994, the Justice Department indicted two individuals for fraud on the Internet. Among other things, these persons had placed advertisements on the Internet promising victims valuable goods upon payment of money. But the defendants never had access to the goods and never intended to deliver them to their victims. Both pleaded guilty to wire fraud.[15]

Personal computers can be used to engage in new and unique kinds of consumer fraud never before possible. In one interesting case, two hackers in Los Angeles pleaded guilty to computer crimes committed to ensure they would win prizes given away by local radio stations. When the stations announced that they would award prizes to a particular caller—for example, the ninth caller—the hackers manipulated the local telephone switching network to ensure that the winning call was their own. Their prizes included two Porsche automobiles and $30,000 in cash. Both miscreants received substantial jail terms.[16]

In another interesting case that raises novel issues, a federal court in New York granted the Federal Trade Commission's request for a temporary restraining order to shut down an alleged scam on the World Wide Web. According to the FTC's complaint, people who visited pornographic Web sites were told they had to download a special computer program to view the sites. Unknown to them, the program secretly rerouted their phone calls from their own local Internet provider to a phone number in Moldova, a former Soviet republic, for which a charge of more than $2 a minute could be billed. According to the FTC, more than 800,000 minutes of calling time were billed to U.S. customers.[17]

Internet crimes can be addressed proactively and reactively. Fraudulent activity over the Internet, like other kinds of crimes, can be prevented to some extent by increased consumer education. People must bring the same common sense to bear on their decisions in cyberspace as they do in the physical world. They should realize that a World Wide Web site can be created at relatively low cost and can look completely reputable even if it is not. The user should invest time and energy to investigate the legitimacy of parties with whom they interact over the Web. Just as with other consumer transactions, we should be careful about where and to whom we provide our credit card numbers. The legal maxim *caveat emptor* ("let the buyer beware"), which dates back to the early sixteenth century, applies with full force in the computer age.

The public can also be protected by vigorous law enforcement. Many consumer-oriented Internet crimes, such as fraud or harassment, can be prosecuted using traditional statutory tools, such as wire fraud. Congress substantially strengthened the laws against computer crime in the National Information Infrastructure Protection Act of 1996. The law contains 11 separate provisions designed to protect the confidentiality, integrity, and availability of data and systems.

Novel Challenges: Jurisdiction and Identity

The Internet presents novel challenges for law enforcement. Two particularly difficult issues for law enforcement are *identification* and *jurisdiction*.

One of the benefits of the global Internet is its ability to bring people together, regardless of where in the world they are located. Boundaries are virtual, not real. This can sometimes have a subtle impact for law enforcement. For example, to buy a book, you used to drive to the local bookstore and have a face-to-face transaction; if the bookseller cheated you, you went to the local police. But the Internet can make it easier and cheaper for a consumer to make purchases, without even leaving his or her home, from a distributor based in a different state or even a different country. And if the consumer pays by credit card or, in the future, electronic cash, and then the book never arrives, this simple transaction may become a matter for the federal or even international law enforcement community, rather than a local matter. There are issues of *trust* that concern both the merchant and the customer.

The Internet makes interstate and international crime significantly easier in a number of respects. For example, a fraudulent telemarketing scheme might be extremely difficult to execute on a global basis because of the cost of international telephone calls, the difficulty of identifying suitable international victims, and the more mundane problem of planning calls across numerous time zones.[18] But the Internet enables scam artists to victimize consumers all over the world in simple and inexpensive ways. An offshore World Wide Web site offering the sale of fictitious goods may attract U.S. consumers who can "shop" at the site without incurring international phone charges, who can be contacted through e-mail messages, and who may not even know that the supposed merchant is overseas. The Moldova phone scam demonstrates the relative ease with which more-complex international crimes may be perpetrated. In such a global environment, not only are international crimes more likely, but some consumer fraud cases traditionally handled by state and local authorities may require federal action.

Another fundamental issue facing law enforcement involves proving a criminal's identity in a networked environment. In all crimes—especially information-based infocrimes—the defendant's guilt must be proved beyond a reasonable doubt, but global networks lack effective identification mechanisms. Individuals on the Internet can be anonymous, and even those individuals who identify themselves can adopt false identities by providing inaccurate biographical information and misleading screen names. Even if a criminal does not intentionally use anonymity as a shield, it is easy to see how difficult it could be for law enforcement to prove who was actually sitting at the keyboard and committing the illegal act. This is particularly true because identifiable physical attributes such as fingerprints, voices, or faces are absent from cyberspace, and there are few mechanisms for proving identity in an electronic environment.

A related problem arises with the identity of the victim. With increasing frequency, policymakers are appropriately seeking to protect certain classes of citizens, most notably minors, from unsuitable materials. But if individuals requesting information can remain anonymous or identify themselves as adults, how can the flow of materials be restricted? Similarly, if adults can self-identify as children and lure real children into dangerous situations, how can these victims be protected? In 1999, Congress, in response to this problem, enacted the Communications Decency Act. The act did not pass its first federal court challenge. The federal court found the act to be exceedingly vague.

One area that raises both identification and jurisdictional issues is Internet gambling. The Internet offers several advantages for gambling businesses. First, electronic communications, such as electronic mail, allow for simple record keeping. Second, the Internet is far cheaper than long-distance and international telephone service. Third, many software packages make it easy to operate consumer businesses over the Internet. Use of the Internet for gambling—as well as for other illegal activities such as money laundering—could increase substantially as the use of "electronic cash" becomes more commonplace.[19]

Existing federal law governs gambling on the Internet. Interstate gambling by the use of any wire communication facility, including the Internet, is illegal unless the gambling activity is legal in both states. Even where gambling is legal, it is legal only for adults. Therefore, the legality of gambling depends critically on both the location and the age of the participants, neither of which can be verified reliably through current network mechanisms, especially when the participants are not willing to cooperate. Congress has already established the National Gambling Impact Study Commission to study a variety of issues, including "the interstate and international effects of gambling by electronic means, including the use of interactive technologies and the Internet."[20]

Digital Warfare

Certain futurists predict that the next U.S. war will involve the injection of malicious code into Pentagon computers and the blitzing of telecommunication and financial networks through use of a modem. This information war can be conducted by attacks on software in lieu of hardware, such as targeting the Federal Reserve software versus the Federal Reserve headquarters building, taking power grids off-line in Kosovo rather than bombing a hydroelectric plant, crashing the air traffic control computers instead of hijacking a plane, activating a virus within SPADOC (Space Defense Operations Center) computers or NORAD/USSPACECOM I & W (the Integrated Warning Division at the U.S. Space Command Headquarters in Cheyenne Mountain, Colorado, responsible for alert, warning, and verification of potential hostile space-related events), and blinding satellite communications versus theft of a nuclear weapon.

Approximately 33 countries are perfecting information war attack strategies, and the U.S. Department of Defense is developing combat viruses, logic bombs, electromagnetic pulse weapons, and other classified technology designed to "fry" circuit boards, crash networks, and alter an enemy's weapons control software so that bombs miss their intended targets. The outlay in the Department of Defense's information security budget is approximately one-twentieth the cost of a B-2 bomber.[21]

Of several possibilities, Dr. Dorothy Denning describes a future warfare scenario in which military operations take place almost exclusively in cyberspace. Under this scenario, wars will be fought without armed forces. Instead, trained military hackers will break into the enemy's critical infrastructures, remotely disabling communications, command, and control systems that support governmental and military operations. Operations might also target key civilian and commercial systems, such as banking and finance, telecommunications, air traffic control, and power supply. At present, however, there is no evidence to support the notion that a country's infrastructures could be so disabled by hacking that a government would surrender to a foreign power or alter its policies. The fallout from such an attack and how it would affect the decision-making systems of the enemy are unknown. Launching it would require considerable knowledge about target systems and interconnectivities.[22] (Recognize that this is a primary motive for digital espionage activities. Note the interesting line between the criminal aspect of DE and the military offensive, hence sanctioned, use of DE. In the first case you go to jail. In the second case, you are decorated or if you are on the opposing side, you go to jail.) As a counterpoint, DE activities against U.S. national security information are a serious crime.

The Digital Espionage Family

Focusing on computer-related and computer-facilitated crime issues in the following, we have slightly amended the U.S. Department of Justice

(USDOJ) Criminal Division's view; the digital espionage family has been broadly divided into:

Computer-Related Crime
- Intrusion or malicious hacking
- Theft of service
- Denial of service (DoS)

Computer-Facilitated Crime
- Espionage: theft of national security information
- Economic espionage: theft of trade secrets
- Worldwide distribution of pornography and its associated kidnapping and/or physical molestation
- Fraud, including pyramid schemes and bait and switch schemes
- Theft and embezzlement

The rationale behind this familial ordering is the potential for financial loss. The potential is enormous. The USDOJ recorded at least two cases that incurred multimillion dollar losses.[23] Computer-related crimes catch the public with their eyes closed—for example, the California radio contest mentioned previously.[24] Banks and securities firms will tell you that information about money or the movement of money is more valuable than money itself. It is also the measure that allows for successful prosecution of computer-related crimes.[25] The value and movement of money is used to comply with evidentiary requirements of the various federal statutes.

Portrait of the Computer Criminal—Targets of Opportunity

Computer criminals manifest themselves in many forms. Many company security officers believe that the weakest element in the computer cycle is the disgruntled or simply lazy employee. Conversely, the preeminent danger to a company's intellectual property (trade secrets, R & D plans, pricing lists, customer information) is other companies. "Competitors are the single greatest threat in computer crime," according to Richard Power of Computer Security Institute in San Francisco. Insiders steal corporate data to boost their income. Competitors may be the primary threat, but the insiders perform the dirty work.

A CSI/FBI survey found that insiders were involved in 46 percent of electronic espionage cases. When trying to identify the insider who has perpetrated a fraud, look for the disgruntled employee who is making points for himself or herself with a future employer. The American Society for Industrial Security (ASIS) estimates the loss from theft of intellectual property to the U.S. industry to be approximately $2 billion per month.[26]

Numbers like the previous example may leave the manager cold. They are not personal enough. During the writing of this book, one interviewee at a large company, who required anonymity, gave a different point of view:

If someone steals our manager's personalized pen set, given to him by the president for success of our division in sales, every employee hears about it and security for the area is substantially upgraded. But when someone steals from our computer [network] key documents for marketing of [a new toy], which may or may not be successful via a campaign with a fast food chain, and *valued by accounting at five million*, based on labor costs and equipment depreciation, et cetera, you will be lucky if you get to talk to the manager's secretary. You will be even luckier if he springs for some intrusion detection software, and luckier still if he approves the *ten thousand* needed to install VPN [virtual private network] secure gateways between our trading partners and customer sites. And, bringing the security solution to him makes me the prime suspect.[27]

As long as there have been computers, there have been *hackers*. Until recently being a hacker was not considered a dirty word. Now hackers are mild peppers compared to *crackers*. The difference is that hackers are performing break-ins for the thrill of it, and crackers are breaking in for the financial rewards involved.

This is not the only way in which computer crimes occur. Some *thieves,* on the other hand, do not bother to break into the computer via the hacker method; they just steal the entire hardware ensemble, server and all. Organized gangs are known to steal chips and components. Traditionally, computer chips have been stolen from suppliers and assemblers that would have the chips on hand. Criminals are now stealing computer chips by dismantling the computer to get them or carrying off the entire computer.

And then we have the traditional *spies*. Their targets may be any of a variety of treasures: SIOPS (Single Integrated Operational Plans—used to tie together military nuclear weapons and regional plans from the Atlantic, the Pacific, and Europe), commercial marketing plans, military or diplomatic ESI (Extremely Sensitive Information), or personal data on political or sports figures, and so on. No matter what we call them— hackers, crackers, spies, or thieves—they are breaking the law and violating your property and rights. It is your responsibility and duty to stop them. It is your right to protect your personal data, your computers, your company's data, or your organization's information. We trust this book will provide some tools to assist you to achieve these security goals.

Another type of "computer criminal" are *Tiger Teams*. These are teams assembled by the U.S. Army to perform *legal* and *permitted* surprise attacks on computer systems to test the security of the systems and support structures. One researcher reports that in one year tiger teams attacked 8932 systems and penetrated 7860 of them. Only 390 of these attacks were detected and 19 reported.

Tiger teams are also hired by private industries to break into their computers to test their security programs. The main problem in computer crimes is not the crime itself but the detection of the break-in because there are few tools to trace the criminal's path through the network. Tiger teams have been around since the 1960s when the NSA used them to check the security of its own computer systems. NSA's judgment of the results was mixed because the problem was a moving target and solutions found were temporary.[28]

The perceived anonymity of the act of computer crime and the huge financial gain involved lead individuals to do things that they would not normally do. The belief that they will not be detected is the basis for many crimes. An otherwise upstanding executive would not dream of looking into the briefcase of a competitor but has no problem perusing their computer files. As more and more global businesses join the World Wide Web, the motive to commit computer crimes increases. Companies that spend billions on research and development, which if performed successfully by a competitor would allow the competitor to catapult ahead in technology, are especially susceptible.

Network administrators are another source for the rise in computer crimes. Many individuals blame the Internet and new connections that create back doors for crackers, but professional hackers who test networks say that security is too lax due to the network administrator's complacency.

Failure to monitor security programs that are implemented allow crackers to infiltrate and often remain undetected. The former coworker, now referred to as an ex-employee, poses a unique threat. The termination of an employee, disgruntled or otherwise, is too often handled by a manager who fails to notify the network administrator. This oversight creates a huge hole through which that ex-employee could breach security.

Social engineering—that is, contacting company employees and acquiring sensitive information by posing as a friendly—is often employed by computer criminals to gain important information such as passwords. Annual reports for companies are a wealth of information when looking for connections. Much like a burglar guesses the combination to a safe by viewing how long it takes to open between turns or numbers, a computer cracker can read the cryptographic key by timing the computer as it decrypts a message.

Other threats to networks include firewall and system probing, network file systems application attacks, vendor default password attacks, spoofing attacks, sniffing attacks, easy-to-guess password compromise, destructive computer viruses, prefix scanning, and Trojan horses. Programs that were initially built for the network security specialists are now being used by crackers to break into networks. "Crack," a brute-force program, was designed for network security officers to test for easy-to-guess passwords. This program attacks the computer by trying every dictionary word as a possible password.

The network file, which is used to share files between systems, is exploited through well-known vulnerabilities. Crackers use vendor-installed passwords to infiltrate systems. "Spoofing" involves faking the Internet Protocol (IP) address to appear as if a friendly computer is involved. "Sniffing" is literally a program that sniffs all traffic on a network to collect authorized passwords. "Prefix scanning" involves scanning telephone company phone lines for modem lines. This detection is especially damaging because most modem lines bypass firewalls and security. Trojan horse programs are also aptly named. This is a program that will install "backdoor" programs, allowing unrestricted access into the internal systems by bypassing the monitoring and auditing process. Crackers inform other crackers of the existence of these programs via Web sites.

Mainframe computer security was relatively simple in that the physically large disk drives were secured behind locked doors and direct access could be denied to the attackers. In the current client/server environment, physical and information security is complex. More individuals than before have access to the server where programs and data are stored. Laptop computers, which in some cases are more powerful than old mainframes, fly around the world with businesspeople. Internet connections, if connected to the company's main server, pose an original challenge in that literally millions of people are able to access the computer. Computer systems that cannot provide adequate information security to protect data from intruders are not acceptable. Surveys produce huge estimates of dollar losses resulting from system penetration, but the truth of the matter is that these figures represent only a small portion of the actual losses, because the average business usually is not aware of the penetration and therefore has no idea the store is being robbed.

The USDOJ Criminal Division suggests that computer criminals intrude because of their curiosity or pride in their ability to use the computer as a gateway or launching pad for more-advanced attacks; their ability to destroy things, such as rerouting calls (including 911) and shutting down power systems in order to cause mayhem in a hospital; their desire to eliminate or destroy personnel data (in one case, convincing the VA that a soldier was dead when in fact he was very much alive—and, we suspect, pretty angry); and finally, their ability to commit digital espionage against industrial, national, or personal targets.[29]

Portrait of the Computer Criminal—Who Are They?

It would be nice if we could identify the computer criminal by traits. In general terms we can. Let's start with the hacker. According to J.P. Barlow, "When a hacker perceives a computer or an automated information system (AIS) is poorly protected, he sees a challenge. Hacking to him is an art. He perceives himself as having an obligation to break into any system that can be broken into."[30] Peter Pitorri, an expert in counterespionage, presents this portrait of a typical hacker, based on Barlow's original work:[31]

Portrait of a Hacker, Circa 1991

- Lacking in moral values
- Well educated
- Male
- Between 15 and 37 years of age
- Lacking in self-esteem
- Passively resistant to authority
- Disdainful of the law
- Disdainful of the rights of others
- Disdainful of loyalty
- Devious
- Narrow minded, finely focused
- Introverted

- Highly intelligent
- Patient
- Social deviate, in that he seems incapable of empathy, genuineness, warmth, defined personal goals, and respect for societal norms
- Usually an authorized user of the system he has attacked.

Pitorri concludes that persons fitting this profile represent a clear and present threat to the firm that employs them.

In May 1999, COMSEC Solutions, a cryptographic, anti-virus, and biometrics countermeasures firm, presented its own research at the FBI National Academy at Quantico, Virginia:[32]

Typical Profile of the Corporate Computer Criminal

- Male, white, young (19 to 30 years of age)
- Has no prior record
- Identifies with technology, not his employer
- Employed in information systems or accounting
- Bright, clever, self-confident, adventurous
- Accepts challenges and is motivated by them
- Feels exploited by his employer and wants to get even
- Does not intend to hurt people, just feels cold indifference to his employer
- Believes that deceiving the establishment is fair game
- Uses drugs or alcohol
- Feels resentment for having been passed over for promotion
- Feels resentment due to pay inequality with peers and friends
- Believes the challenge is to beat the system, although not necessarily for monetary reward
- Has a proclivity for high living
- Has financial pressures
- Is divorced (sometimes multiple)
- Has a desire to impress a new boyfriend or girlfriend (especially for homosexual relationships)
- Is chronically late—especially with reports

These profiles are based on known cases, and the traits represent an analysis of identified repeating factors. Lest we encourage the idea that this is an exact science, we refer the reader to several additional sources: *Fighting Computer Crime* by Donn B. Parker, *Information Warfare and Security* by Dorothy E. Dennings, *Corporate Espionage* by Ira Winkler, and *Corporate Intelligence and Espionage* by Richard Eells and Peter Nehemkis.[33,34,35,36] The interested reader will soon find that the profiles are not straightforward; human interactions and motivations are very complex. It is also interesting that as of this writing, no females have been charged with the commission of a newsworthy computer crime.

Motive, Opportunity, Means, and Method (MOMM)

In the twenty-first century almost all crime against property will be perpetrated within computer systems—hence, the name *computer crime* or, more descriptively, *infocrime*. Many other crimes, even violent ones, will be controlled or directed by computers, because computers play the central role in storing and processing the assets of individuals and organizations and in directing the activities of enterprises. Exactly what the term "computer crime" encompasses can be hard to pin down. There are 50 states, as many different laws, and at least as many definitions. And there are federal laws that do not coincide with the state laws, and international laws that do not address the virtual boundaries that exist with computer crimes. Along with confusing politics and legal definitions, organizational victims generally do not want to prosecute the perpetrator because of adverse public relations. Some companies, stinging from a theft or break-in of their computer systems, actually pay the bad guy to keep his mouth shut and to show them how he did it. Computer crime is difficult to prosecute because the offenders generally know a great deal more about computer technology than do prosecutors and judges. However, this is changing.

In 1996 the USDOJ formed the Computer Crime and Intellectual Property Section (CCIPS) to neutralize the problem. The section works with a coordinator for computer and telecommunications in each U.S. attorney general's office. The FBI created the Computer Investigations and Infrastructure Threat Assessment Center (CIITAC), in 1996, adding six computer crime squads in New York, Washington, DC, Seattle, San Francisco, Los Angeles, and Boston, and a seventh in Dallas in 1998.

Every FBI field office now employs a CIITAC agent. They also have forensic computer examination personnel in most field offices and a special team at Quantico, Virginia.

Investigators who will prosecute a computer crime normally look for motive, opportunity, means, and method (MOMM). *Motive* includes personal causation, such as economic, ideological, egocentric, or psychotic. *Opportunity* usually refers to a lapse in system controls (such as internal or access controls) or management controls (such as rewards, ethics, or trust) that permits penetration of the system. *Means* refers to the ability to compromise controls, personnel, and technology. *Methods* may include falsifying or destroying input, throughput, and output, as well as time and access logs.

Let's elaborate upon the material behind COMSEC Solutions' Typical Profile of the Corporate Computer Criminal. The following list presents several factors that invite or encourage computer crime in established corporations:

Factors that Encourage Computer Crime—Motivations

- Inadequate rewards: pay, fringe benefits, bonuses, incentives, perquisites, job security, enrichment, promotional opportunities
- Inadequate management controls: failure to communicate minimum standards of performance or on-the-job personal behavior
- Ambiguity in job roles, relationships, responsibilities, authority, and accountability
- Inadequate reinforcement or performance feedback
- Lack of recognition for service, good work, longevity, and effort
- Lack of recognition for truly outstanding performance
- Delayed or no performance feedback
- Delayed discussions about performance inadequacies or behaviors
- Failure to counsel or mentor when performance is below expectations
- Lack of job challenge or rotation
- Inadequate management support
- Lack of adequate resources meeting minimum requirements
- Failure to audit, inspect, or follow through to ensure compliance with company goals and norms
- Tolerance of antisocial behavior such as alcohol or drugs

- Fostering hostility, interdepartmental competitiveness, or bias in selection, promotion, or pay

The following lists add the dimensions of personal inducement and prevention:

Factors that Enhance the Probability of Computer Crime—Personal Inducements

- Inadequate standards of recruitment and vetting [British term that means to subject a person to an appraisal via a background investigation]
- Inadequate orientation and training on security matters
- Unresolved financial or social problems
- Failure to, for sensitive positions, screen and verify past employment, education, financial reliability, and character
- Job-related stress or anxiety

Factors that Discourage Computer Crime—Prevention

- Separation or rotation of duties
- Periodic audit and surprise inspections
- Clear written statements of policy and procedures
- Encryption hash totals and digital signatures (discussed in Chapters 7 and 9)
- Internal accounting controls: dual signature authorities, dollar budget limits, renewable check authority
- Offline entry controls and limits

The following lists add the dimensions of access controls and detection systems:

Factors that Discourage Computer Crime—Access Controls

- Identification defenses: key or card inserts, passwords, code phrases, challenge-response; exclusion and lock-out; time activator,
- Forced password length rather than user choice and frequent changes
- Authentication defenses: random personal data, biometrics, including voice, palm, iris, and/or fingerprint recognition
- Level of authority access permissions
- Need to know by using Special Compartmented Information (SCI)

Factors that Discourage Computer Crime—Detection

Exception Logging Systems
- Out-of-sequence runs and entries
- Improper order of priority of runs and entries
- Aborted runs and entries
- Out-of-pattern transactions: too high/low/many/often/few unusual file accesses
- Wrong password, entry code parity, and redundancy checks against repeated attempts to gain access improperly

Management Info Systems
- Monitoring operational performance levels for variations from plans and standards, deviations from accepted or mandated policy and procedures, and deviations from past quantitative relationships or performance norms

Intelligence Gathering
- Monitoring employee attitudes, values, and job satisfaction levels
- Soliciting random feedback from customers, vendors, and suppliers for evidence of dissatisfaction, inefficiency, and inconsistency with policies, corruption, or dishonesty by employees.

Computer criminals commit their crimes when opportunity equates to knowledge and access. Hackers have a surprising level of knowledge of communications protocols, applications programs, operating systems, database and file management systems, and accounting procedures. Access can be either physical or electronic and is the most important element in the equation. The following lists explain technical and malicious code attacks that may be used to gain access and then extend the access into the system. A good description of each of these attacks can be found in Diane E. Levine's seminal paper, "Virus and Related Threats to Computer Security," in *Computer Security Handbook*.[37]

Methodology—Obtain Access

- Masquerading as a user or being falsely identified and authenticated as a network hardware device
- Forging of credentials and passwords
- Port scanning
- War dialing

- Wiretapping
- Optical spying
- Installing bugs
- Reading electromagnetic emanations
- Scavenging outputs
- Simulating targets
- Keystroke stealing
- Deception
- Corruption of programs or database
- Guessing and dictionary attacks
- Object reuse
- Exploiting insecure terminal
- Piggybacking a valid job
- Tailgating
- Between-the-lines entry
- Exploiting bugs and getting user identification

Once the intruder has access, he or she exploits it to gain privileges. Then the intruder uses the access to destroy data. The following lists explain the process in more detail:

Extending Access

- Browsing
- Covert channeling
- Trap-door entries
- Back doors—using bypass programs
- Superzapping with utility programs to violate controls
- Becoming a "superuser" and attacking the network "root" structure
- Synchronous attacks in privileged mode
- Brute-force password attack
- Social engineering

The following list focuses on the data or internal systems destruction:

Scrutinizing, Changing, and Destroying Data

- Trojan horse

- Viruses such as Melissa, Chernobal, and Papa
- Flash2 and CIH viruses wich attack computer hardware, not just its software
- Macro and variant with encrypted signatures
- Worms and logic bombs
- Stealth programs
- IP spoofing and TCP sequencing

The criminal needs to erase his or her steps. The following list points to a few well-known approaches to destroying evidence of one's presence:

Erasing the Evidence

- Changing the clock(s)
- Using superuser privileges
- Erasing the audit trail
- Redirecting the audit data (tactical delay)
- Archiving the change-data sets (tactical delay)
- Altering the logs to frame a legitimate user

In general, security countermeasures to computer crime fall into three areas: (1) computer and terminal access controls, (2) data communications controls, and (3) improvements to environment and policy. The following lists show some of the popular countermeasures and security maxims for these three control areas:

Security Countermeasures to Computer Crime Computer and Terminal Access Controls

- Passwords (alpha and numeric)
- Compartmentalization
- Error lockout
- Voiceprint recognition
- Fingerprint recognition
- Palm geometry
- Magnetic card accesses
- Automatic shutoff
- Time lock
- Modem callback

- Random personal information
- Challenge and response
- PIN numbers with magnetic card as proof of identity
- Personal signature recognition—light pen

Security Countermeasures to Computer Crime Data Communication Controls

- Cryptographic transmission and storage of data
- Scramblers
- Dial-back devices—access after terminal ID or user ID
- Passwords and authority verification
- Logs kept and monitored.
- Aborts and alarm mode monitoring
- Online monitoring by security personnel

Security Countermeasures to Computer Crime Environment and Policy

Environment

- Requirement: Clear and explicit policies with respect to proper and authorized use of computers and sanctions for abuses thereof
- Accounting controls
- Defensive countermeasures to ward off attacks and intrusions by outsiders
- Internal controls
- Supervision of employees with computer responsibilities
- Laws against criminal acts committed by computer and against computers
- Stabilization of the current laws
- Education of computer users about security and privacy of information
- Computer auditing methods
- Hardware and software protection
- Telecommunications systems protection
- Physical security of computer centers
- Proprietary information protection methods
- Personnel policies; rewards, standards, confidentiality agreements, nondisclosure agreements

- Teamwork
- Have in place a set of security related maintenance procedures to keep the network running smoothly such as backups and ISO Security Standards

Security Policy Maxims
- No security is 100 percent effective—anything can be overcome
- Those responsible for security policy should have a basic understanding of networks; password and authentication mechanisms; remote access
- Use balanced approach to risk management
- Use products that are based on industry standards
- Use countermeasures in depth
- Look for the weakest link in your armor.
- Improve employee awareness

Like many businesses, the intelligence community consists of a number of discrete organizations that perform distinct missions for overlapping sets of customers. Under the Intelligence Systems Board (ISB), headed in 1994 by Director Steven T. Schanzer, a team of CIA experts developed INTELINK. INTELINK is a secure, private collection of networks implemented on existing government and commercial communications networks. These networks employ Web-based technology, use established protocols, and are protected by firewalls to prevent external use. INTELINK captures the essence of current advanced network technology and applies it to the production, use, and dissemination of classified and unclassified multimedia data among the nation's intelligence resources. INTELINK is patterned after the global Internet. The following list presents some of the key elements of the INTELINK security strategy:[38]

INTELINK Security Strategy

- Strong authentication (two-way challenge/response)
- End-to-end confidentiality (integrity of data during transmission)
- Enhanced access control
- Community of interest (COI) for most sensitive materials
- Network auditing and monitoring: logging, analysis, and reporting
- Single sign-on
- Transparent security to user

- Secure collaboration
- Security management infrastructure
- Encryption, key management, certificate management, COIs, CRLs (certificate revocation list)
- SSL (Secure Sockets Layer protocol) with initial authentication, message privacy, and ensured data integrity

Prosecution Tools

The authors apologize for being a little informal with defining terminology. We have intertwined *digital* and *computer* and have given a broad definition to *espionage*, mapping it to a family of crimes. We have suggested that the main target is information—hence, the term *infocrime*. In addition, we have presented DE as a specific intent crime—one has to specifically intend to do this crime; negligence does not fall into our initial definition. We have little respect for hackers, crackers, spies, or thieves or for the damage they do in society. We support making their profession less profitable by prosecuting them. Computer crime falls under the jurisdiction of the U.S. Department of Justice (USDOJ).

Fortunately, Congress has provided USDOJ prosecutors with six serious tools to slow the tide. The following list sets forth the six main U.S. statutes used in the prosecution of computer crimes.[39,40,41,42,43,44]

- Computer Fraud and Abuse Act, 18 U.S.C. 1030
- Economic Espionage Act, 18 U.S.C. 1831, to 1839
- Trafficking in Fraudulent Access Devices, 18 U.S.C 1029
- Wire Fraud, 18 U.S.C. 1343
- Wiretap Act, 18 U.S.C. 2511
- Access to Stored Electronic Communications, 18 U.S.C. 2701

Computer Fraud and Abuse Act, 18 U.S.C. 1030

The strongest prosecutorial tool is the Computer Fraud and Abuse Act. Section 1030 covers fraud and related activity in connection with computers. The act was extensively amended in October 1996. It protects confidentiality, integrity, and availability of data and computer systems. It prohibits using unauthorized access to computers to commit seven crimes: espionage, access to unauthorized information, access to nonpublic government computers, fraud by computer, damage to computer, trafficking in stolen passwords, and threats to damage a computer. The act covers "protected computers," which are exclusively or shared by a financial institution or the U.S. government or used in interstate or foreign commerce or communications.

Two key terms in this act are *exceeding authorized access*, which applies to any authorized user—also called "insiders" on the system—who accesses or alters information that he is not permitted to alter, and *without access*—an "outsider" who breaks in and uses the computer for any purpose. In parts of statute, the penalty may depend on whether you are an insider or outsider to the system. *Damage* is defined as any impairment to the integrity or availability of data, a program, system, or information, causing a loss of $5000 or more in a 12-month period; or impairment of medical records or data; or causing personal physical injury; or threatening public health or safety.

The act protects national security information and specifically prohibits accessing computer without or in excess of authority, obtaining national security information that could be used to injure the U.S., and communicating or attempting to communicate that information to someone not entitled to receive it. Maximum penalties specified under this act are 10 years in prison (20 years for second violation) and a $250,000 fine. This act is similar to 18 U.S.C. 793(e), which prohibits obtaining national defense information from any source and communicating or attempting to communicate it in any manner.

The act protects information from anyone intentionally accessing a computer without permission in excess of authorization and thereby obtaining information from a financial record or a credit report, a federal agency, or a "protected computer" if conduct involves an interstate or foreign communication. It protects confidentiality of computer data from *being read, even if not downloaded* (e.g., browsing National Crime Investigation Computer data).

The act prohibits intentional trespass in a U.S. government computer. It prohibits accessing any nonpublic computer of a department or agency if not authorized to access any computer of that department or agency. In addition, the act prohibits knowingly causing the transmission of a "program, information, code, or command" and as a result of such conduct, intentionally causing damage (without authorization) to a protected computer. It applies to insiders or outsiders. It further prohibits intentionally accessing a protected computer without authorization and causing any damage negligently or otherwise.

Economic Espionage Act, 18 U.S.C. 1831 to 1839

The Economic Espionage Act became effective as of October 11, 1996. It was originally aimed at stopping foreign theft of U.S. information. It criminalizes on a federal level the theft of trade secrets. It has two main provisions that cover state-sponsored (1831) and commercial (1832) thefts.

A Section 1831 violation occurs if a defendant stole—or without authorization of owner, obtained, destroyed, or conveyed—information; that the defendant knew was proprietary or a trade secret, and that the defendant knew would benefit, or was intended to benefit, a foreign government, instrumentality, or agent.

A Section 1832 violation applies the same elements of Section 1831 and adds that the defendant intended to convert the trade secret to the economic benefit of someone besides the owner, the defendant knew or intended that the owner of the trade secret would be injured, and the trade secret was related to a product that was produced or placed in interstate or foreign commerce.

Trafficking in Fraudulent Access Devices, 18 U.S.C 1029

Section 1029 of the Trafficking in Fraudulent Access Devices applies to fraud and related activities in connection with access devices. A person is in violation of this title if he or she, with intent to defraud, produces, uses, or traffics in one or more counterfeit access devices, in order to effect transactions aggregating $1000 or more in a year; or knowingly and with intent to defraud uses, produces, traffics in, has control or custody of, or possesses a telecommunications instrument that has been modified or altered to obtain unauthorized use of telecommunications services; or knowingly and with intent to defraud uses, produces, traffics in, has control or custody of, or possesses the following:

- A scanning receiver,

- Hardware or software used for altering or modifying telecommunications instruments to obtain unauthorized access to telecommunications services, or

- Without the authorization of the credit card system member or its agent, knowingly and with intent to defraud causes or arranges for another person to present to the member or its agent, for payment, one or more evidences or records of transactions made by an access device; shall, if the offense affects interstate or foreign commerce be in violation of this title.

A fine under this title is twice the value obtained by the offense, or imprisonment for not more than 15 years.

Wire Fraud, 18 U.S.C. 1343

Section 1343 covers fraud perpetrated by means of wire, radio, or television. It states that anyone who devises any scheme to defraud for obtaining money or property by means of false or fraudulent pretenses, representations, or promises, or who transmits or causes to be transmitted by means of wire, radio, or television communication in interstate or foreign commerce, any writings, signs, signals, pictures, or sounds for the purpose of executing such scheme or artifice, shall be fined, imprisoned not more than five years, or both. If the violation affects a financial institution, that person shall be fined not more than $1,000,000 or imprisoned not more than 30 years, or both.

Wiretap Act, 18 U.S.C. 2511

Section 2511 of the Wiretap Act prohibits interception and disclosure of wire, oral, or electronic communications. Complex elements of a 2511 violation include the intentional interception of any wire, oral, or electronic communication or the use of any electronic, mechanical, or other device to intercept any oral communication when the device is affixed to, or otherwise transmits a signal through, a wire, cable, or other like connection used in wire communication, or when the device transmits communications by radio or interferes with the transmission of wire communication, and intentionally discloses contents of any wire, oral, or electronic communication. It also covers the knowledge that the information was obtained through the interception of a wire, oral, or electronic communication.

It is further unlawful to use a pen register or a trap and trace device (without authority). It is unlawful to intercept wire or electronic communication that is scrambled, encrypted, or transmitted using modulation techniques, the essential parameters of which have been withheld from the public with the intention of preserving the privacy of communication, such as:

- Radio portion of a cellular telephone communication, a cordless telephone communication that is transmitted between the cordless telephone handset and the base unit, a public land mobile radio service communication, or a paging service communication

- Interception of a satellite transmission (encrypted or scrambled)

Punishment specified under this act includes a minimum of $500 for each violation and jail terms dependent on circumstances and damages.

Access to Stored Electronic Communications, 18 U.S.C. 2701

Section 2701 of the Access to Stored Electronic Communications Act makes it unlawful to access stored communications where one intentionally accesses without authorization a facility through which an electronic communication service is provided; or intentionally exceeds an authorization to access that facility; and thereby obtains, alters, or prevents authorized access to a wire or electronic communication while it is in electronic storage in the system. The punishment for an offense committed for purposes of commercial advantage, malicious destruction or damage, or private commercial gain is up to two years in jail.

Investigation

Given the legal tools in the preceding lists, investigators would be concerned with several questions. How did they get in? What did they do? How do we identify them? How do we catch them?

In this chapter we've specified some of the methods of intrusion.

Additionally, we have defined the profile for the typical attacker. Attackers generally are skilled (capable of writing the automated attack tools) or nonskilled (tool users). Both have ties to the underground. The professional attacker is hard to detect and is not tied to the underground. The outside attacker uses techniques as indicated earlier in this chapter. After the attack, the nonprofessional might access e-mail, or files, use the system as an attack platform, share information with buddies, and create back doors, install Trojans horses, and sniffers. The professional gets in, gets the data, gets out, and leaves no tracks.

Detecting an intrusion can be done by: (1) user notices (rare), (2) system administrator notices, (3) anomaly in system log, (4) system crashes, (5) receiving a call from another system admin, or (6) reading about it in the daily news or Usenet (definitely not good).

The bad guy can conceal his or her identity on the Internet in many ways: (1) screen name can be changed each session, (2) IP address can be spoofed so header information is wrong, (3) an anonymizer can be used, (4) anonymous remailers can be used, and (5) compromised accounts can be used.

Investigators obtain evidence in several ways using real-time interception through monitoring the ISP, keystrokes, and e-mail; by court order (a.k.a. "T3"); by subpoena of the subscriber; by review of log files, transactional data, usage history, and cell phone calls; by "Reasonable and Articulable Facts Order" (18 U.S.C. 2703 (d); and by search warrant on unopened mail on the ISP server.[45]

A Word about Encryption

Software or hardware may use a mathematical algorithm to scramble (encrypt) bits of data sent or stored on computer networks. The key to the cipher is a string of numbers or characters. The stronger the algorithm and the longer and more chaotic or random makeup of the string, the more difficult it is to break.

The length of the key is measured in bits, the number of digits in the key. For most encryption techniques in use today, the bit length combined with the rendomness of the key can be used as an approximation of the strength of an encryption program. Longer bit length does not guarantee greater security; a poorly designed security program could be invaded without the invader's making a brute force attack on the key (a *brute-force attack* consists of trying all the possible keys in hopes of finding the one that works). But longer bit length usually (assuming true randomness of the bits) means stronger encryption.

Two types of encryption systems are employed. The symmetric or private key cipher uses a secret key for both encipherment and decipherment. Sender and receiver both have the same encrypting/decrypting transformation and use the identical secret key. Drawbacks of this method include: (1) the secret key must be transmitted in a separate medium between recipients, (2) the secret key might be revealed and affect full system compromise, and (3) the key may be used to forge a document in the sender's name.

The development of public key encryption from 1974 to 1975 solved this problem. There are two keys: a public key and a private key that are mathematically related. The relationship between the two keys is a nearly insoluble mathematical problem. The public key is available to everyone who desires to communicate; the private key is never given to anyone and is held very confidentially by its owner. The sender of a message uses the recipient's public key to encrypt the message. The recipient uses his or her private key to decipher the message. Only the user's private key can decrypt the message.

Public key cryptography permits the use of digital signatures of a message to uniquely identify the message sender. The sender encrypts a small portion of the message called the *hash* or *MAC* (message authentication code) with his or her private key and the message with the public key of the recipient. The recipient uses his private key to decrypt the message and the user's public key to decrypt and verify the sender's signature. Public key cryptography allows for rigorous authentication. Authentication is as important as confidentiality as a security goal when either financial and/or Internet transactions are considered. Public key cryptography can be used to secure public infrastructure communications, because authentication of users can be performed without revealing users' secret keys.

Pressure to regulate the use of strong encryption comes from law enforcement interests.[46] Encryption represents one of the biggest challenges to law enforcement because of its use by criminals. Law enforcement is able to crack the weak and older encryption (publicly announced as about 56 bits) but without key recovery (an entrenched battle with academic, industry, and public interests is ongoing). Law enforcement loses the ability to solve crime in a timely fashion. To law enforcement, basically encryption is a double-edged sword: If law enforcement *can't* crack it, the criminal may escape punishment. If law enforcement *can* crack it, the criminal is uniquely tied to the evidence.

What almost all law enforcement interests want is key escrow or key-recovery mandates. Under this system, people who use encryption must file their secret keys with the government or a third party, or include decoding information along with the message without their knowledge. Law enforcement interests want access to the stored messages and their real-time transmission.

A national debate has ensued over the use and export of strong encryption. Law enforcement interests support legislation that would force U.S. citizens and residents to give the government access to their keys. However, export controls and government-prescribed key recovery has not kept strong encryption out of the hands of criminals and terrorists, because technology is available worldwide without key-recovery features. Efforts under the Clinton administration have failed to convince either the U.S. Congress or other countries of the requirement. In March 1999, even France, who had an oppressive lock on encryption technologies for their citizens, removed restrictions from 128-bit encryption use.

A June 10, 1999 study by Lance Hoffman at George Washington University found 805 hardware and software products incorporating cryptography manufactured in 35 countries outside the United States. In addition, 167 foreign cryptographic products use strong encryption algorithms, and 512 foreign companies manufacture or distribute cryptographic products in at least 67 countries outside the United States.[47]

Probably the most interesting case in the pipeline is Bernstein v. Department of Justice. On May 6, 1999, a federal appeals court confirmed that all source code is a form of expression protected by the First Amendment. The Bernstein case involved a challenge to the federal regulations restricting the export of software, which includes strong encryption. The Bureau of Export Administration (BXA) is in near shock, and this is their response verbatim:

May 6 Court Decision in Bernstein Encryption Case

You may have read about a recent court decision regarding encryption exports. Please be advised that this decision does not mean that encryption products may be exported without regard to the Export Administration Regulations (EAR). Regardless of how the decision might be interpreted, the decision is subject to a stay. This stay is in effect for at least 45 days. (See Department of Justice press release.)

On May 6, the U.S. Court of Appeals for the Ninth Circuit rendered a decision in Bernstein v. the United States Department of Justice. Professor Daniel Bernstein filed suit against the U.S. Government after he was notified by the State Department that his "Snuffle" encryption program was subject to the

International Traffic in Arms Regulations (ITAR) and would require an export license to post the source code on the Internet. Bernstein subsequently amended his petition to challenge the controls on encryption products maintained under the EAR after President Clinton placed encryption exports under the Commerce Department's jurisdiction in 1996. In a 2-1 decision, the Ninth Circuit court upheld the district court's decision that the regulation of Bernstein's export of his "Snuffle" program "constitute[s] an impermissible prior restraint on speech."

Exporters should be aware that the decision does not affect the applicability of the EAR to exports and reexports of encryption hardware and software products or encryption technology. This includes controls on the export of encryption software in source code. The EAR remains in effect for these items. The Commerce Department will apprise exporters of any changes to the encryption controls.[48]

The Department of Justice statement shows more balance, but they are clearly not happy about the decision. The next strategic decision that must be made after it fails a rehearing (requested by President Clinton) by the federal court is to take the case to the Supreme Court. A loss here would be final, and BXA employees would need to update their résumés. Here is the DOJ statement verbatim:

Department of Justice Statement On Ninth Circuit Court of Appeals Decision in Encryption

On May 6, a three judge panel of the United States Court of Appeals for the Ninth Circuit in San Francisco issued a decision in a case involving government controls on encryption exports. The Department of Commerce and the Department of Justice are currently reviewing the Ninth Circuit's decision in Daniel Bernstein v. United States Department of Justice and United States Department of Commerce. We are considering possible avenues for further review, including seeking a rehearing of the appeal en banc in the Ninth Circuit.

The regulations controlling the export of encryption products currently remain in full effect. The Ninth Circuit's decision will not take effect until the court issues its mandate, which will not occur for at least 45 days. If the government asks the Ninth Circuit to rehear the appeal during that time, the mandate will not issue until after the Ninth Circuit has acted on the government's request.

The district court injunction in this case relating to the encryption export regulations has been stayed by orders issued earlier by the district court and the Ninth Circuit, and the stays of the injunction remain in effect until the mandate issues. Accordingly, all persons who wish to engage in encryption export activity, including the posting or other distribution of encryption software on the Internet, must still comply with the export licensing requirements of the Export Administration Regulations, administered by the U.S. Department of Commerce's Bureau of Export administration (BXA).

Information about the regulations is available at the BXA website at www.bxa.doc.gov. 99-178[49]

Electronic eavesdropping methods allow law enforcement officers to legally compromise privacy. Privacy activists argue that law enforcement already has many technologies available to them that can be used as alternatives to wiretaps. Alternatives not defeated by the use of encryption, include:

- Improved call-tracing methods
- Surveillance with infrared scanners
- Aerial surveillance
- Bugging
- Filtering that picks certain voices or keywords out of the babble of telecommunications traffic, formerly precluded by the sheer volume of calls
- Supersensitive satellite photography that lets the police peer into windows or identify a license plate from 20 miles up in the sky
- Vast electronic databases [many combined]
- Plaintext readers such as Tempest, which read text appearing on computer screens through closed doors and walls as we type
- Laser light beams that allow conversations to be deduced from vibrations of the windowpane
- Credit card transactions, e-mail, Internet transactions, and clickstream data are all easy to intercept or subject to other electronic surveillance methods.

Whitfield Diffie summarizes the privacy case as follows: "Throughout history, the science of cryptography repeatedly advanced beyond the ability of cryptanalysts to crack the codes. Law enforcement has always had the right to try to decipher encrypted messages; they never had a practical or constitutional guarantee of success. The government's right to search one's house does not entail a power to forbid people to hide things."[50]

Do not count the USDOJ or BXA out of the game. Congress has usually supported their requirements. It is easy to see the USDOJ position; it is in the tough job of catching the bad guys who have up-to-date communication tools. Vice President Al Gore's recent call for balance to keep encryption out of the hands of terrorists and criminals is a noble request. It may be difficult to achieve in a world (outside of the United States) that does not share our policy or views.

Wrap-Up

The scope of a *family* of crimes under the title of *Digital Espionage* has been identified and classified. The MOMM of computer crimes and the tools that investigators, such as the USDOJ, may use to stop computer crime in situ have been reviewed. Since targets of computer crime tend to be information-based, *infocrimes* have an enormous financial impact. Because of its overall effectiveness, a point-of the-pin look at encryption and the political environment in which it exists was introduced. The authors contend that computer crimes and digital espionage occur because of a failure to provide appropriate information security (INFOSEC) countermeasures in organizations. Chapter 2 introduces the concept of INFOSEC and risk and applies it in a more global scope. Subsequent chapters introduce due diligence implementation of INFOSEC technologies.

Notes

1. Statement of Robert S. Litt, Deputy Assistant Attorney General, U.S. Department of Justice, Criminal Division, before the Subcommittee on Social Security, Senate Ways and Means Committee, United States Senate, Washington, DC, 20530, May 6, 1997.

2. Ibid. (CSI, the Computer Security Institute, is a leading security training organization that publishes surveys and reports such as computer crime and information security program assessment. It jointly works with the FBI on its annual surveys. Their Web site is at *http://www.gocsi.com/homepage.shtml.*)

3. Zwillinger, Marc J., "Investigation and Prosecution of Computer Crime," Computer Crime and Intellectual Property Section Criminal Division, U.S. Department of Justice, 4 November 1998, *http://www.amc.army.mil/amc/ci/ nov4a/tsld005.htm.* Also, WarRoom Research is a firm specializing in business and competitive intelligence. Their Web site is at *http://www.warroomresearch.com.*

4. Ibid.

5. Ritchey, Barbara D. DISC6341, Professor Hirschheim, "Computer Crimes and How to Prevent Them," *http://disc.cba.uh.edu/~rhirsch/fall96/barba.htm.*

6. Violino, Bob. "Your Worst Nightmare," *Information Week*, February 1996,

34-36.

7. Ritchey, op. cit.

8. Edwards, Owen, "Hackers from Hell," *Forbes ASAP Supplement*, October 1995, 182.

9. Denning, Dorothy E., "Who's Stealing Your Information," *Information Security*, April 1999, 29.

10. Ibid.

11. DeYoung, H. Garrett, "Thieves Among Us," *Industry Week*, Vol. 245, June 1996, 12-16.

12. Nichols, Randall K., COMSEC Solutions presentation to FBI Security CIITA agents, Quantico, VA, 27 May 1999. (COMSEC Solutions is a leading cryptographic, anti-virus and biometric countermeasures firm. Their Web site is at *http://www.comsec-solutions.com*.

13. Litt, op. cit.

14. Ibid.

15. Litt, op. cit. On February 22, 1993, the two defendants were sentenced to 5 years' probation, $30,000 restitution (joint and several), and 250 hours of community service. As a condition of probation, both hackers were restricted from owning or using a computer without permission from the probation officer.

16. Ibid.

17. Ibid.

18. Ritchey, op. cit.

19. Litt, op. cit.

20. Ibid.

21. Denning, op. cit.

22. Ibid.

23. Zwillinger, op. cit.

24. Litt, op. cit. One of the two was sentenced to incarceration of 15 months', and 36 months' probation, while the other was sentenced to 60 months' probation. Restitution was ordered jointly in the amount of $32,000.

25. Litt, op. cit. See United States v. Peterson, 98 F.3d 502, 504 (9th Cir. 1996), upholding two-level enhancement under sentencing guidelines for use of special skill to facilitate crimes, including crime described in text.

26. Ritchey, op. cit.

27. Interview, 3 March 1999.

28. Ritchey, op. cit.

29. Zwillinger, op. cit.

30. Pitorri, Peter, *Counterespionage for American Business*, (Oxford, Great Britain: Butterworth-Heinemann, 1998).

31. Barlow, J. P., et al., Forum: "Is Computer Hacking a Crime?" *Harper's Magazine*, March 1990, 46-57.

32. Nichols, op. cit.

33. Parker, Donn B., *Fighting Computer Crime* (New York: Wiley, 1999).

34. Denning, Dorothy, *Information Warfare and Security*, (Reading, Mass.: Addison Wesley, 1999).

35. Winkler, Ira, *Corporate Espionage*, (Rocklin, Calif.: Prima Publications, 1997).

36. Eells, Richard, and Peter Nehemkis, *Corporate Intelligence and Espionage*,

(Indianapolis: Macmillan, 1984).

37. Levine, Diane E., "Virus and Related Threats to Computer Security," *Computer Security Handbook*, ed. Arthur E. Hutt, Seymour Bosworth, and Douglas B. Hoyt (New York: Wiley, 1995).

38. Martin, Frederick Thomas, *Top Secret Intranet: How the U.S. Intelligence Built INTELINK* (Upper Saddle River, NJ: Prentice-Hall, 1997).

39. 18 U.S.C. 1030, *http://mailer.fsu.edu/~btf1553/ccrr/federal.htm*.

40. 18 U.S.C. 1831-1839, *http://mailer.fsu.edu/~btf1553/ccrr/federal.htm*.

41. 18 U.S.C. 1029, *http://mailer.fsu.edu/~btf1553/ccrr/federal.htm*.

42. 18 U.S.C. 1343, *http://mailer.fsu.edu/~btf1553/ccrr/federal.htm*.

43. 18 U.S.C. 2511, *http://mailer.fsu.edu/~btf1553/ccrr/federal.htm*.

44. 18 U.S.C. 2701, *http://mailer.fsu.edu/~btf1553/ccrr/federal.htm*.

45. Zwillinger, op. cit.

46. Singleton, Solveig, "Policy Analysis: Encryption Policy for the 21st Century," *http://www.cato.org/pubs/pas/pa-325es.html*.

47. Hoffman, Lance J., et al., "Growing Development of Foreign Encryption Products in the Face of U.S. Export Regulations," Report No. GWU-CPI-1999-02, June 10, 1999.

48. BXA Press release, June 1 1999, *www.bxa.doc.gov/encryption/state.htm*. Superseded by statement of Office of the White House Press Secretary, *Administration Announces New Approach to Encryption,* September 16, 1999, *www.bxa.doc.gov/encryption/whpr99.htm*. See also BXA FAQ on update to encryption policy, September 16, 1999.

49. U.S. Department of Justice statement on Ninth Circuit Court of Appeals Decision in Encryption Case, May 7, 1999, *www.usdoj.gov/opa/pr/1999/may/178civ.htm*.

50. Diffie, Whitfield and Susan Landau, *Privacy on the Line: The Politics of Wiretapping and Encryption* (Cambridge, Mass.: MIT Press, 1998, 6.

CHAPTER 2

Foundations of Information Security (INFOSEC)

Introduction

In Chapter 1, we defined *digital espionage* as a *specific-intent infocrime* associated with information technology and information processing industries. Because information has value, it has become an attractive target for criminals. Information about individuals can be used to their detriment in ways that extend from extortion and blackmail to expropriation of their bank and credit card accounts. A new type of infocriminal has emerged whose crimes are specific to the theft, misuse, storage, destruction, or transfer of information. The impact of digital espionage is not limited, however, to individuals. Businesses suffer losses that run into billions of dollars annually from the digital theft of their secrets through exploitation of their intellectual capital and other information assets. Attacks on business secrets come from individuals and organized criminal groups and through industrial espionage by competing firms.

Secrets are not the only targets of infocriminals. From motives ranging from juvenile mischief to monetary gain, irreparable harm can be caused if the reliability or availability of information assets can be brought into question. What would be the cost to an organization to re-create its personnel and payroll records if these were compromised or destroyed? At what cost would a bank have to re-create a single day's transaction records if a hacker or infocriminal destroyed them? How much liability would a hospital incur if its patient records were compromised or lost, and how much more in human tragedy if the computer programs and databases it uses to dispense drugs to patients were illicitly changed? As we shall see, several firms have already had to answer these questions.

Digital espionage is not, unfortunately, the end of the problems posed by the theft, misuse, disclosure, or destruction of information assets. For the same reasons that other terrorists attack the tangible assets of nations and high-visibility institutions, *infoterrorists* find intangible information assets attractive targets. Moreover, the nature of our information networks and the relative ease of access to them make such targets especially attractive. They can be attacked from afar, according infoterrorists less risk of detection and apprehension than arises in attacks on tangible targets where physical access is required, like the World Trade Center or the Federal Building in Oklahoma City.

At the far end of the scale from the individual criminal stealing another individual's secrets for personal gain lies the possibility of nations attacking the information infrastructure of other nations by digital warfare. *Digital warfare* is a form of the more general effort of infowar. Our networks, extending as they do worldwide, provide access to the systems and information that in their totality make up the information infrastructure supporting our country's economy and many of its most important activities. This cyberspace of interconnected networks and the information it carries is already recognized as a battlefield of the future. Information weapons based on today's computer viruses, logic bombs, and Trojan horses will attack and defend at electronic speeds using strategies and tactics aimed at crippling or destroying another nation's capacity to fight, to produce, or to compete in the marketplace. Digital warfare technology is capable of deciding the outcomes of geopolitical confrontations without firing a single bullet or missile or taking the life of even one soldier.

Protecting ourselves and our information assets from spies (military, political, or industrial), infocriminals, infoterrorists, and the possibility of infowar is the function of information security, or *INFOSEC*. INFOSEC is traditionally composed of the technologies and methods we use to protect the confidentiality, integrity, and availability of information and the computers, systems, and networks that create, process, store, and communicate our information. **Digital espionage occurs where there has been a failure or breach of INFOSEC.** Digital warfare exploits breaches of applied information security on a large scale. To produce effective countermeasures against infocrimes caused by digital espionage, we must understand how to apply INFOSEC protection to information assets and systems.

Traditional Foundation of Information Security

INFOSEC didn't arise with the advent of computers. It is traceable to the dawn of writing in the hieroglyphics of the pharaohs. Today, however, it is intimately tied to the evolution and use of information technology. To comprehend INFOSEC, we need to understand how systems create, store, use, and communicate information and in what ways these systems are vulnerable to exploitation. We must become aware of the threats posed to our information assets and systems, and ferret into view the capabilities of those who would exploit our weaknesses. We can then devise a means to protect our systems and data.

Based on INFOSEC principles, our computers are designed, implemented, and operated to ensure that only authorized persons can gain access to confidential data, can modify or destroy information assets, or can affect our ability to find and use information when and where it is needed. The computers that make up our communications networks employ complex cryptography to ensure that only the intended recipients of messages can read them and that we can verify the transmission and receipt of messages. Current technology, together with appropriate policies and procedures, can do much to safeguard our systems and the information they contain. Where the technology is evolving at a rate that is creating gaps in our ability to provide needed protection, we will explore possibilities for correcting the resulting shortfalls.

The purpose of information security that most INFOSEC practitioners identify is to preserve the three elements: *confidentiality, integrity* and *availability*.

Confidentiality

The first questions that must be answered in protecting information are these:

- What information needs to be protected?
- How much protection is needed?
- For how long must protection be effective?

Most people understand the value of and need for secrecy. Throughout history premature disclosure of military and diplomatic information has had grave consequences for nations. More recently, the need to protect individual privacy has become apparent. Certain communications of a personal nature could be embarrassing if disclosed. Medical and legal institutions depend upon privileged communications. Business secrets must be protected in a competitive economy. More recently, it has become obvious that economic secrets alone or in aggregate may be used to a country or region's detriment in the international marketplace. How valuable would a miscreant find the knowledge of the price of gold that would be fixed publicly an hour or two later, or soon-to-be-posted crop statistics before they become public knowledge? Even geological, littoral, or environmental information may need protection.

Integrity

The need to protect the integrity of information is equally important, even when confidentiality is not an issue. Information that cannot be trusted is worse than useless; it costs money and time to create and store, but provides no benefit. A database that is only slightly tainted may require extensive resources to correct and validate, if it is possible to recover it at all. We must therefore ask, "What information must be protected from illicit modification or destruction, how much of such protection is needed, and for how long?"

Availability

Similarly, information that is not available when required is of no use, even if its confidentiality is secure and its integrity intact. Systems and networks that are not on-line when needed not only represent a waste of their cost, but people and companies that depend on them may be irreparably damaged by operational shutdowns or loss of revenue if their systems and information assets cannot be reached. How readily must our information be available? Must it be accessible in minutes? Hours? Days? And if, as is surely often the case, more protection costs more money or burdens other scarce resources, how much protection can we afford? An effective denial of service (DoS) attack, which interrupts critical information to an organization, can be very costly.

Economic Effects

Information systems security has both direct and indirect economic consequences. Protecting information and systems can be expensive. There may be real and significant costs if we fail to adequately protect our information assets, resulting in loss of confidentiality, integrity, or availability. Because we are highly dependent on our ability to readily retrieve, process, analyze, and communicate information, we are highly vulnerable to its misuse, corruption, or loss. While exact figures are not available, estimates of economic losses due to failures of information systems security run into billions of dollars each year. In extreme—but not completely improbable—cases, the economic consequences of the failure to protect information could directly affect the well being and security of our nation. Conversely, by ensuring integrity and availability, and confidentiality as appropriate, we can enhance the likelihood of diplomatic success, increase the power of our fighting forces, and provide a substantial competitive advantage to our country's commerce and economy.

The Relevance of Information Security

It is easy to understand the relevance of protecting tangible assets, such as the gold in Fort Knox, the deed to a house, or pictures of your parents when they were young. These are all things that exist in one form and in one place. They can be indexed, tracked, and monitored. Their loss or destruction can be valued. It is less likely that the relevance of protecting information assets from theft, loss, destruction, or manipulation will be immediately evident. If a text file is stolen, it's only a copy of the file that's gone and the original still exists. How can that loss be assigned value for insurance purposes or as threat to the enterprise? Thinking of the text file as the plans for the next-generation miracle drug can help put this loss in a more understandable light. A lost copy of such valuable information both endangers the enterprise operations, in that market advantage has been compromised, and dilutes the intrinsic value of the information itself.

Two short discussions will bring these considerations into sharper focus. The first is an exploration of the effects of information security on the economy. The second explores these concerns relative to their effect upon the social health of the nation.

Effects on the Economy

On August 23, 1992, Hurricane Andrew unleashed 120-mph winds on South Florida, with devastating results. Eighteen schools were destroyed. One hundred and fifty public housing buildings were severely damaged. Thirty-one libraries had to be closed. Forty fire stations were ruined. Eighty-seven thousand homes were damaged from significantly to beyond repair, and over $1 billion in crops and livestock were lost. Hurricane Andrew then crossed the Gulf of Mexico and struck Louisiana with less, but still damaging, force. Estimates to rebuild ran from three to five years, with a total cost of between $30 and $40 billion.

The United States has the largest economy of any nation in the world; Hurricane Andrew was not a knockout blow, nor an even crippling one— but neither was it inconsequential. An even larger disaster, one that could do long-lasting or permanent damage to the economy, could reach a high level of concern for the United States' economic security among the world's nations. A larger storm, a high Richter scale earthquake in a densely populated area, or a failure of information systems security could produce such a calamity.

Consequences of Failure to Maintain Confidentiality

Some information is meant to be available to everyone. Journalists, librarians, publishers, and teachers make careers of providing public access to a wide variety of data, employing many media. Some information is intended to be shared only with a select audience. Such information might be of a personal nature or not considered to be of wide interest, or which might, perhaps, be embarrassing if generally known. Some kinds of information could be dangerous to the person or group who owns it if it were widely distributed. This could include business information that might be used by competitors to the detriment of the organization to which the information applies. "Privileged" information, like that between doctors and their patients or attorneys and their clients, is protected in order to encourage free and open communications within protected circles. The national security and law enforcement communities protect the identities of agents or informers. And, of course, military and diplomatic information is carefully protected in the national interest.

Disclosure of some sensitive information might result in embarrassment or inconvenience. At the other extreme, disclosure of classified information could have serious detrimental consequences for delicate diplomatic negotiations, markedly degrade the effectiveness of expensive high-technology surveillance or weapons systems, or impair the success of military operations. For each of these cases, and at points between, there are potentially significant economic consequences of failure to protect the confidentiality of information. In some of the worst-possible cases, our high-technology surveillance and reconnaissance systems could be rendered useless—or worse, misleading—if their capabilities and limitations were known. Billions of dollars would have been wasted on their development, bad decisions made based on tainted information they gathered, and tragically, lives of U.S. personnel needlessly lost.

As the Cold War and the threat of nuclear confrontation fades, technological and economic intelligence takes on increasing importance. While the Commonwealth of Independent States remains a region of great concern, there is increasing awareness of the dangers inherent in technology transfer to third-world nations and the proliferation of nuclear, chemical, and biological weapons and associated delivery systems. Certain technical information developed in this country and by our allies' enables us to build and operate highly accurate weapons of mass destruction, such as those used in the Gulf War. Potential compromise of this information is of gravest concern.

Knowledge about our smart-weapons systems could result in their being avoided or met with effective countermeasures, so that billions of dollars in development, production, and operations costs would have been spent for no gain, and battles or wars lost. On the commercial front, loss of confidential information concerning financial and trade issues or proprietary technological developments of commercial importance could harm our country by reducing our competitive edge. Information about environmental conditions and natural resources may also need protection.

A threat might come not only from our former enemies but also in unexpected ways from our erstwhile friends. The French intelligence service, Direction Generale de la Securitie Exterieure (DGSE), has been found using the traditional espionage techniques, originally developed to spy on the Soviet bloc, to obtain trade secrets from foreign business executives traveling to and in France. Trade secrets so garnered have been passed to French industrial firms, which have used them to vie successfully for competitive awards. Other foreign intelligence services have also mounted operations aimed at obtaining U.S. technology secrets. Techniques employed range from intercepting fax, voice, and telex communications to bugging hotel rooms and aircraft seats, from stealing a company's trash to bribing its employees. Failure to protect the confidentiality of our information assets can all too easily mount to staggering sums. Opportunities and contracts lost to foreign competitors mean reduced revenues, worsening trade balances, increasing unemployment, and a declining standard of living.

Consequences of Failure to Maintain Integrity

While the economic consequences of loss of confidentiality may be severe, loss of information or degradation of its value may be even more catastrophic. In 1985, a New York bank had software problems that resulted in modifications to its transaction records. To cover its accounts while diagnosing and correcting the problem, the bank had to borrow over $23 million, at a cost of $5.6 million in interest. Loss of the integrity of databases, software, and systems in all sectors of the economy can have both economic and safety consequences.

Consider that the air traffic control system, stock transactions, financial records, currency exchanges, Internet communications, telephone switching, credit records, credit card transactions, management information systems, office automation systems, the space program, the railroad system, hospital systems that monitor patients and dispense drugs, manufacturing process control systems, newspapers and publishing, the insurance industry, power distribution, and utilities all depend on computers. The law enforcement community also relies heavily on the integrity of information and information processing systems.

Integrity of information can be threatened by physical destruction of the systems that create, process, and communicate information, or destruction or erasure of the media containing the information. Destructive programs called "logic bombs" may be placed in data processing systems and networks, where they lie in wait for either a specified set of conditions or the passage of a specified length of time. Then they "wake up" and destroy the information in the computer or its data storage peripherals.

There is the case of a young programmer who placed a logic bomb in his company's personnel system. The malicious program checked periodically to see if his name was still on the list of employees. When he was terminated, his name was removed from the list, and the logic bomb destroyed the company's personnel records. In another case, on April 11, 1980, many IBM 4341 mainframe computers shut down due to a logic bomb that had been planted by an unhappy employee. In yet another instance, a medical center lost nearly 40 percent of its data to malicious software.

Computer viruses may also destroy data. The news media has widely reported the discovery of the Michelangelo virus, a time bomb set to go off on March 6 (Michelangelo's birthday) of any year and destroy the contents of a personal computer's hard disk. Thousands of viruses are known, many of which destroy data, and more are appearing at the estimated rate of 12 per day. As our systems become more interconnected and interoperable, the question becomes not whether your system will become infected, but how soon and how often. Over $100 million was spent by U.S. industry to avoid the effects of the Datacrime virus scheduled to wreak its destruction on Columbus Day in 1989. The U.S. Congress spent over $100,000 to repair the effects of a single virus attack. In 1991, it is estimated that viruses caused $1.077 billion's worth of damage. The widespread and rapid proliferation of personal computers in homes, offices, and schools prevents a precise measure of the actual damage.

Malicious programs that corrupt or destroy information may not simply delete files or erase disks. In one case, the manager of research and development altered the management information system used to guide a major corporation so that the data displayed in the president's spreadsheets was changed by a subtle percentage. The R&D manager anticipated that the president, relying on his computerized analyses, would make a series of bad decisions and be forced to resign, and the R&D manager might then logically be chosen to replace him. As it turned out, the malicious code was detected, and it was the R&D manager who lost his job.

Such attacks are especially hard to detect. One datum might be changed at random every few days. Slight changes are not as obvious as missing files or mangled data would be, yet could cause as much or more damage in the long run. Surreptitious alterations occurring over long periods of time may defeat periodic backup processes, since each succeeding backup incorporates collectively the preceding alterations. Enormous amounts of money and time may be required to re-create a corrupted database, if it is possible to repair the damage at all.

Consequences of Denial of Availability

Most people don't think about, and many are unaware of, the fact that our telephone system—the public utility switched network—is in reality a computer system. When we pick up our handset to make a call, it isn't obvious that modern phones are themselves computers that are connected to other computers for local calls via the local switching office, and from there via trunk circuits to other switching offices around the world. With the exception of a dwindling number of rapidly disappearing electromechanical switches in low-density rural areas, all switching and control functions are carried out by computers. En route between switching computers, calls may traverse copper wires, coaxial cables, microwave radio links, fiber-optic cables, and satellite up- and down-links. Despite this complexity, the phone system in the United States is one of the most reliable systems in the world. Even so, at 2:25 P.M. Monday afternoon, January 15, 1990, the AT&T long-distance network comprising 114 switching centers, each containing a main and a backup computer to ensure that the system could handle every conceivable problem, began to falter. Within minutes, more than half of all calls being attempted by AT&T customers were answered by a recorded message informing the caller that, "All circuits are busy. Please try again later." Not until 11:30 P.M., some nine hours later, would the network return to normal service.

The economic consequences were significant. AT&T estimates that it cost the company $75 million in lost calls alone. Of 138 million long-distance and 800-number calls, some 70 million were rejected by the faulty system. Many of those calls were business-related. Failure to connect cost those businesses directly due to orders not placed and operations delayed or halted. There were indirect costs as well due to decreased efficiency and productivity. Some businesses, like the New York Stock Exchange, had made arrangements for backup service and so were less affected; other businesses, which had not had the foresight to buy backup service, were out of business or severely set back. Airlines, hotels, and car rental companies lost reservations. Phoned catalog orders were not placed. Service companies could not support their customers. Undoubtedly, some of the revenue those companies lost was gained by other companies that didn't use AT&T, but some were lost forever. The total economic consequences are probably unknowable.

Unfortunately, the January 1990 incident was not an isolated case. On June 10, 1991, more than a million Pacific Bell customers in the Los Angeles Basin lost phone service for 90 minutes. Soon thereafter, on June 26 and 27 of the same year, 10 million phones in four widely separated U.S. cities went down. More millions of dollars were lost.

In the networked world of general computer systems and networks, there are analogies to the outages of the telephone system. The Internet is a worldwide network consisting of over 5000 subnets, each of which connects from one to dozens of computers and terminals to any other user on the Net.

On November 2, 1988, a small program appeared on computers connected to the Internet. This program was a "worm"—a program (much like the computer viruses that have been widely publicized) that makes copies of itself and sends those copies along to other computers on a network. The copies make copies in turn and send them along, and the copies make copies, and so on. The result is like a chain reaction in nuclear physics, and in short order the network was so busy creating and sending copies of the worm that it couldn't do anything else. In a wide area network like the Internet upon which thousands depend, the consequences were serious indeed. When the Internet worm struck, it was immediately feared that the program might be a Trojan horse, an apparently innocent program that contained destructive code to be activated at some later time or date. Others were concerned that the worm was placed into the net by an enemy power, either to compromise or destroy information or to disrupt services. Many system operators were so concerned that they shut down their computers and brought all usage, including their research and communications, to a stop. Some of the computers were down for most of the following week, with attendant economic consequences.

Fortunately, the Internet worm was not a Trojan horse type of logic weapon. It clogged up the Internet and denied the benefits of the Net to many of its users, but the program was basically benign, the result of a graduate student's research that got out of hand. Even so, the economic damages resulting from the denial of service are impressive. One estimate of the damage reached $116 million, with up to 6000 computers affected. Damage estimates at individual sites ranged from $200 to over $50,000.

Until the attack of the Internet worm, no one had seen such a widespread network infection, but in fact, the damages were small in comparison with what they might have been had two developments been true at the time:

- First, today there are many more computers and more of them are interconnected on networks, so damages would now be more widely spread and their total sum higher. The proliferation of computers and networks since 1988 has been exponential in scale. The damage consequent to a similar incident today would be catastrophic; the damage five years from now would be unimaginable.

- Second, the Internet worm was not designed to compromise or destroy information, but merely to replicate. Had it been designed to destroy data, the economic consequences of the worm attack could have reached many times its actual level.

Stealing Service

Beyond the direct and indirect consequences of failures of information systems security in protecting confidentiality, integrity, and availability, both fraud and theft are related security problems. Computer crime may be costing the economy as much as $50 billion annually—more than Hurricane Andrew each year—and the total is growing.

"Phone phreaks" are hackers who specialize in understanding and manipulating telephone systems. In addition to the danger that they will inadvertently or deliberately shut down all or part of the phone system, phreaks steal services, either by fooling the system into thinking that no charge is necessary or by having their charges appear on someone else's bill. Telephone industry losses to phreaks approached $2 billion in 1992.

Credit card fraud is another form of information systems security failure. Lost or stolen credit cards, together with fraudulent use of misappropriated credit card account numbers, cost credit card companies over $1 billion per year. While much of this loss might be avoided with improved information security, the credit card companies treat such losses as simply a cost of doing business. The losses are quietly passed along to their customers in the form of higher rates, and the country's economy is the loser.

Still another form of loss occurs when unauthorized users steal computer time. In 1991, computer hackers cost the United States economy more that $164 million. One hacker logged up a significant amount of stolen computer time on a supercomputer by breaking into the system and playing computer games. In another case, over half of the logons to an unprotected government computer were unauthorized. Two-thirds of the same system's use time was by users who didn't have valid accounts. Assuming that the system was sized based upon experience, the system became three times as large as was needed to perform the actual work for which it was intended. Millions of tax dollars could have been saved by buying a system properly sized for the projected legitimate work. Resultant increased operational and maintenance costs dwarf the original investment and more than offset the cost of the computer security that would be needed to prevent unauthorized use.

Economic Impact

Information systems security has a monetary value. The government and private industry together spend billions of dollars for communications security, computer security, and physical security of information and information processing systems and personnel security in order to protect information assets. However, the cost to our economy of not securing our systems and protecting our information is already high and is potentially much higher. Individual instances of failure of confidentiality, integrity, or availability have cost hundreds of millions, and the additive costs of failures are astronomical.

In the past, the diversity of our systems and networks has protected us, at a cost to productivity that we cannot sustain if we are to continue to be competitive in world markets. But greater connectivity and greater interoperability mean greater vulnerability, both to accidents and to malicious attack. In the worst cases, the entire economy could be damaged and the country consequently put at risk.

The challenge is great. Fortunately, technology, together with well-planned and executed security procedures, can ensure the confidentiality, integrity, and availability of our information assets. As part of the global village, we will then be able to safely share in the rich exchange of information needed to support competitive economic activity.

Impact on Military Operations and Geopolitics

Karl von Clausewitz wrote a statement that has been translated into English as: "War is the continuation of politics by other means." The implication of this phrase is that there is a continuum of activities that together make up the group dynamics of governance and sovereignty. A crucial piece of this continuum of activities is the role of the armed forces in protecting and defending the interests and property of the community as a whole. The relationships between information, information security, and that continuum of activities that includes both politics and military operations are very closely interwoven.

The importance of information security to military operations cannot be overstated. The Russian failure at Tannenberg in August of 1914 occasioned the complete destruction of two Russian armies by a single German army half their combined size. This decisive victory was the direct result of the interception and exploitation of Russian communications, which were broadcast totally in the *clear* as the battle progressed. The German commanders knew exactly what the Russian plans and orders were, often before the Russian officers received them from their own command. The Russians had failed to distribute military ciphers and the associated keys, so neighboring units within each army could not communicate securely, much less could the two armies coordinate a complex pincher surprise attack. In the end, 30,000 Russians were killed or declared missing, 100,000 were captured, one of the two Russian armies was devastated and the other one simply ceased to exist, all at the guns of the smaller but more mobile German army with its infinitely more secure communications.

As David Kahn writes, "The case was clear-cut. Interception of unenciphered communications had awarded the Germans their triumph."[1] The message of Tannenberg to military commanders could not be clearer: "Be sure of your information security or you lose." Commanders and military theoreticians had, in fact, understood the importance of information security for centuries. Aeneas the Tactician of Greece described a system of cryptography in one of the earliest books on military science, *On the Defense of Fortified Places*. The Spartans used military cryptography as early as the fifth century B.C. Later, Julius Caesar tells, in his *Gallic Wars*, of using enciphered messages, and Suetonius implies that the Caesars routinely exchanged secret messages with their military commanders.[2]

Military history between the Gallic wars and the World Wars cites thousands of examples of the use of cryptography and many, many cases illustrating the power of cryptanalysis in resolving battles, crises, and even the course of wars. Consider the fall of Réalmont to Henry II of Bourbon, Prince of Condé. When, during his siege, Condé had a secret message from the town intercepted and decrypted that reported the town's desperate need for munitions, he simply returned the deciphered message, and the town surrendered. The incident captured the attention of Cardinal Richelieu, who found cryptography to be admirably suited to the political and diplomatic games in which he engaged on behalf of the French court. This led to the hiring of Antoine Rossignol, a superb cryptographer of the day, by the king and the renaissance of modern cryptography as an enabling technology for geopolitical intrigues as well as military victories.[3]

As the history of World War II has been declassified in the half century since its conclusion, it has become increasingly clear that information security failures of the Axis powers and cryptanalytic successes of the Allies provided an overwhelming advantage to the latter and contributed significantly, if not decisively, to the outcome. For example,

Japanese policy stressed the importance of communications security, but their practices and procedures implementing that security were slipshod. Consequently, Admiral Nimitz knew as much about the Japanese plans for the Battle of Midway as did many of the captains of the Japanese warships that were to participate in what could have been the completing victory for the Japanese in the drive that began at Pearl Harbor to control the Western Pacific. Nimitz was able to use the advantage of surprise that Yamamoto depended upon but lost to American cryptanalysts. This cost the Japanese the battle, forced them to shift from an offensive to a defensive strategy, and turned the tide of the war. John Keegan says that Midway "restored a Naval equilibrium in the Pacific in 1942."[4] Admiral Edwin Layton says, "Midway proved to mark the beginning of the ebb tide for Japanese naval power in the Pacific."[5] Kahn calls Midway a cryptologic victory "more crucial to the course of history than any other [cipher] solution except that of the Zimmermann telegram."[6]

Apologizing in advance for the oversimplification, we can see in these examples the broad outline of the influence of information security on modern world history. The Russians lost at Tannenberg, starting them on a downward path that led ultimately to the fall of the tsars, the ascent of communism and its subjugation of almost half the world, and 50 years of Cold War. Conversely, the American win at Midway stopped the Japanese juggernaut, turned the Allied strategic position in the Pacific theater from defensive to offensive, and led eventually to victory. It positioned the United States to protect the freedoms of half of the world in the ensuing Cold War and ultimately to win the Cold War. In each case, a key element was the information security failure of one side and the successful exploitation of that failure by the other. Little wonder that information security is deemed so important to military operations, or that codes and ciphers, cryptographic keys, and information security technologies occupy such a central place in the essential elements of information that comprise the highest-value targets for military intelligence. Also little wonder that the technologies supporting information security play so often in the nightmares of military counterintelligence officers.

Information Security and Military Intelligence

Information security and military intelligence can be viewed, in some ways, as two sides of the same coin. This is not a matter of logical necessity, but of historical consequence. Notwithstanding the commonly held view among the natural fiber "espiocrats" at CIA and INR (State Department— Bureau of Intelligence and Research) that "military intelligence is to intelligence as military music is to music,"[7] the soldier's and sailor's deep understanding of the value of signals intelligence and communications security has led to significant investments by the military in information security technologies, including the mathematical disciplines of cryptography and cryptanalysis and those arts' love affairs with computers.

Computers are designed to limit access to confidential data. Communications networks employ mathematically rigorous cryptography to ensure that only the intended recipients of messages can read them. As modern communications systems have evolved, they have increasingly become computer-based networks. The existing infrastructure of computer expertise and technology in the military cryptologic community provided a natural forum for the evolution of information security to its modern level. It is composed of both communications security and computer security, with associated related disciplines. Information security has consequently found a comfortable home in the military and, especially, since shortly after the end of World War II, at the National Security Agency, within the defense establishment.

But just as military intelligence is not congruent with intelligence, information security is not synonymous with protection of the secrecy of military and diplomatic information. In its modern form, information security encompasses integrity and availability protections as well as privacy protections. Loss of the integrity of databases, software, and systems can have profound consequences.

For the military, calling up the reserves to respond to crises or war requires complete and accurate data on personnel, equipment, plans, contingencies, and logistics, just as calling up the reserves depends upon the public switched telephone network and the nation's transportation system, both directly and completely dependent on computers.

The integrity of information can be threatened by the physical destruction of the systems that create, process, and communicate information, or by the destruction or erasure of the media containing the information. In the case of military organizations, the cost may extend beyond the organization to the country the military is charged with defending. These additional dimensions of integrity and availability are not as well understood today as is protection of confidentiality, but they take on deep significance in the context of protecting the National Information Infrastructure (NII) against infoterrorism and information warfare, subjects to which we now turn.

Information Warfare

Information warfare is much discussed but as yet not well understood. In its defensive form, it is essentially congruent with the discipline of information security as practiced by those who seek to protect information rather than computers per se. Defensive information warfare is about the protection of confidentiality, integrity, and availability of information assets on the battlefield, throughout the theater of operations, and "back in the world." Its tools, informed by intelligence and counterintelligence, are composed of a similar mix of cryptography and trusted computer science to that used to protect in peacetime the national information infrastructure, the computer and network resources of the private sector and academia, and the personal computers of the citizens.

The field is evolving rapidly due to increased reliance on computers to create, store, process, and communicate information, and to increased connectivity among computers being so used. The basic outlines of the technical discipline have been thoroughly explored, and so the problems are problems of speed and scale rather than of fundamental definitions and applications.

The offensive form of information warfare, on the other hand, is something truly new. Information warfare—or infowar—is, first of all, warfare. It is part of military operations, not of military intelligence or counterintelligence. It is related to, but not part of, other types of military operations characterized by information exchange and manipulation, such as psychological operation (PSYOPS) or electronic warfare. It is certainly not espionage using networks for access to desirable information, nor is it information terrorism, nor computer crime, and it is surely not hacking. These are all interesting and dangerous phenomena that individuals, corporations, and governments face today, but they are not infowar. There is danger in defining infowar too broadly, resulting in ambiguity, confusion, and squabbles for control of missions and budgets. In infowar, computers and networks are the battlefield, computer programs are the weapons, and information assets are the targets.

The Joint Security Commission has said:

> Networks are already recognized as a battlefield of the future. Information weapons will attack and defend at electronic speeds using strategies and tactics yet to be perfected. This technology is capable of deciding the outcome of geopolitical crises without the firing of a single weapon.[8]

Infowar is, then, the application of destructive force on a large scale against information assets and systems for geopolitical purposes. This distinction is vital and determines the appropriate response options and responding agencies in an information crisis. Without that distinction, one quickly finds oneself mired in the prospect of sending the Department of Defense against a single teenage hacker.

Remember that when Rick Ames was discovered to be spying for the Russians, the United States did not respond with armed retaliation by the Defense Department, but with criminal proceedings under the auspices of the Department of Justice. When the World Trade Center was bombed, the FBI responded, not the military services. Make no mistake, there are real issues here, including the problems of knowing that an infowar attack is underway, of ascertaining the scope of that attack, and of quickly bringing to bear effective responses.

These are, however, questions that can only be resolved after an appropriate framework of policies, practices, and procedures has been established, a framework that is only just beginning to evolve. Defining the World Trade Center attack as infowar merely because information assets were attacked as a consequence serves no management purpose and detracts from the systematic protection of assets and prosecution of those who would commit such acts of terror.

It should not be surprising that infowar, being a new type of warfare, should not yet have a full complement of strategies, tactics, and doctrines, supported by appropriate logistics and exercised routinely in preparation for crises and the outbreak of hostilities. From the days of runners carrying news of battles and their outcomes over the plains of Greece, through the eras of signal fires, semaphores and carrier pigeons, to today's use of encrypted satellite transmissions, information has always been a crucial component of military decision making. Information is vital to the formulation and execution of effective battle plans. All other things being equal, more timely, accurate, and complete information is essential to winning in battle. This is so thoroughly understood by our military that it is a fundamental part of our strategic and tactical planning processes. This is, however, "information-based warfare," not infowar as we have defined it. It is warfare informed and enhanced by critical information, but the weapons are guns, tanks, ships, and planes, not computer viruses and logic bombs, and the battlefields are silicon in the form of sand rather than in the form of computer chips.

The concept of information-based warfare recognizes the dependence of armed forces on information and systems that can rapidly and securely provide that information to decision makers, and understands the need to maintain and enhance one's own information while denying that advantage to the enemy. In information-based warfare, better, faster, and more complete information provides an advantage in applying conventional or strategic forces. In infowar, the information networks become the battlefields and information itself becomes both the weapon and the target.

The notion of information-based warfare would be easily recognized by Sun Tzu, Alexander the Great, Genghis Kahn, von Clausewitz, or Dwight David Eisenhower. What would be an innovation to these masters of strategy would be the notion of information as a separate area of warfare independent of guns, ships, tanks, and bombs.

This concept of information warfare as opposed to information-based warfare is being examined, studied, and explored by many of the world's strategic thinkers from Moscow to Teheran and from Beijing to Chiapas. We have ample examples of innovations and fundamental changes to warfare. In World War I, the new paradigm of air warfare began to be explored. At first, planes were observation platforms only. Then someone decided that leaflets and bombs could be dropped from them. Eventually (after a number of pilots shot down their own planes by disintegrating their propellers), synchronized guns made air-to-air combat possible. Later, as World War II progressed, a new battlefield—the electromagnetic spectrum—was discovered, and the "wizard war" was born, now called electronic warfare. If it seemed like sorcery to the scientists and engineers who invented it, imagine how incomprehensible it was to the cavalry and infantry soldiers whose training and experience centered on more tactile dimensions of combat.

Two decades ago the need to incorporate the role of space into warfare became apparent. Infowar is facing and must stand up to the same sorts of challenges faced by air, electronic, and space warfare as they evolved, and we will see and participate in the consideration, consolidation, and eventual mastery of this new dimension of warfare.

Decision Making and the Control of Information Operations

Since information warfare is warfare, it is properly in the domain of operations rather than that of intelligence. Unfortunately, in the domain of information warfare, the skills and technologies needed to conduct information operations have been developed primarily by the intelligence community to support espionage using computers and networks to gain access to important intelligence information. The intelligence community justly claims that its intelligence officers are ideally suited to initiate and conduct attacks in cyberspace, since they are already positioned to do so by virtue of their military intelligence activities. Moreover, revealing to the operational community the vulnerabilities being exploited for espionage purposes would increase the risk of disclosure and would jeopardize not only the intelligence activities but also the access required to conduct a successful offensive information warfare operation. Best leave the planning and execution of information warfare operations in the hands of the intelligence community.

But history has shown that it is not a good idea to have control of operations in the hands of the intelligence community. Let us return to the situation that faced Admiral Nimitz in April of 1943 when American cryptanalysts intercepted and decoded a Japanese message detailing the itinerary of Admiral Isoroku Yamamoto. Yamamoto was the dominant officer in the World War II Japanese Navy, and the opportunity provided by the message to shoot down Yamamoto's plane would both demoralize the Japanese and revenge the United States for the attack on Pearl Harbor that Yamamoto had conceived. Yamamoto's death would be a major victory for the Americans. There was, however, a serious problem. If the Americans were successful in shooting down Yamamoto, there was a danger that the Japanese would become suspicious that the Allies were reading their messages and that their codes were compromised, as in fact they were. If the Japanese changed their codes, the Allies might not be able to break the new codes quickly, and valuable intelligence information would be lost. Nimitz, the operational commander, elected to take the risk, although he minimized the danger by creating a cover story that coastwatchers had detected the flight.[9] Would the decision have been the same if the intelligence community were making it? The logic is straightforward: If you lose access, you lose intelligence information, and without that information, operations must be conducted blindly. The result is increased losses of lives and equipment. Believing fervently in the value of their products, and having no direct responsibility for the success or failure of operations but ultimate responsibility for continuing to provide intelligence information, intelligence officers would be hard-pressed to risk access. Their imperatives, even when acting in the best of faith, make weighing possible loss of access against operational gains difficult or impossible.

It is also vital that information warfare be fully integrated into the battle plans created, practiced, and executed by operational commanders. Unity of command and control is essential to the successful execution of modern military operations with air, land, sea, space, electromagnetic, and cyberspace dimensions. All things considered, it is probably best that information warfare should be left in the province of warriors, not intelligence officers.

Political Impact

Information security is in opposition to military intelligence. The first seeks to protect the confidentiality, integrity, and availability of information assets, while the second seeks to gain access to and steal such of those information assets as may be valuable for military purposes. History teaches us that there is a clear imperative in information security, or equivalently in defensive information warfare: "Be sure of your information security or you lose." In the extreme case of warfare in the new dimension of information systems and networks, defensive information warfare seeks to protect both military secrets and the information infrastructure both in the theater of operations and back at home. Offensive infowar attacks the information assets and systems of the enemy, using logic weapons across networks as part of a coherent battle plan that incorporates operation in the information dimension with operations on land and sea, in the air, and across the electromagnetic spectrum. Our warriors are beginning to develop the strategies and tactics to successfully exploit this new dimension of warfare.

Modern Foundation of Information Security

We close this chapter with reference to (and our recommendation to read) Donn B. Parker's brilliant paper, "Restating the Foundation of Information Security,"[10] in which he argues that INFOSEC must provide for six elements, not three. These are as follows:

- Authenticity
- Utility
- Possession
- Confidentiality
- Integrity
- Availability

Parker suggests that the currently acceptable foundation of security calls only for the preservation of:

- Confidentiality
- Integrity
- Availability

of information from:

- Disclosure
- Modification
- Destruction
- Use

by:

- Prevention
- Detection
- Recovery

to:

- Reduce loss, or
- Reduce risk of loss.

Parker presents loss scenarios that support his framework. His most interesting case is for the inclusion of possession of information. Although it is similar to confidentiality, there is a legal difference between owning data and possessing it. Stealing information may be different than stealing the ownership of the information. This difference is experienced in different ways depending on whether it is government or business that is in the driver's seat. These differences make clear why employee clearances, the principle of need-to-know, mandatory access control, classification of information, and cryptography are typically most important government controls, whereas the owner, custodian, and user accountability principle involves four typically most important business controls:

- Need to withhold
- Discretionary access control
- Copyright and patent
- Digital signatures

Parker's paper presents a rigorous foundation of information security. He presents his framework in terms of abusive acts, nine functions, and four goals. His framework calls for the preservation of the following:

- Availability
- Utility
- Integrity
- Authenticity
- Confidentiality
- Possession of information

from accidental or intentional:

- Destruction
- Interference
- Use of false data
- Modification or replacement
- Misrepresentation or repudiation
- Misuse or failure to use
- Access
- Observation or disclosure
- Copying, stealing, or endangerment

by:

- Avoidance
- Deterrence
- Prevention
- Detection
- Mitigation
- Transference
- Sanction
- Recovery
- Correction

to:

- Meet a standard of due care
- Avoid loss

- Reduce loss
- Eliminate loss[11]

The concept of meeting "a standard of due care" or "with due diligence" is very important to business as a defense against lawsuits. It will be covered in more detail in the discussion of information security policy in Chapter 4. We find Parker's arguments convincing.

Wrap-Up

Information security technologies (INFOSEC) have traditionally been identified with preservation of the three elements of confidentiality, integrity, and availability. Failure to maintain any of these three elements has economic, political, and social consequences. Because information has value, it has become an attractive target for criminals. Based on INFOSEC principals, our computers are designed, implemented, and operated to ensure that only authorized persons can gain access to our confidential data, can modify or destroy our information assets, or can deny access to our information when legitimately needed. The traditional INFOSEC design may not be enough to counter modern-day computer threats. INFOSEC practitioners must be concerned with the additional elements of authenticity, possession, and utility to reduce loss and to meet a standard of due care to protect our information assets.

Notes

1. Kahn, David, *The Codebreakers: The Story of Secret Writing* (London: Weidenfield and Nicholson, 1967), 627.
2. Ibid., 82-84. Historical note: The Caesars that Suetonius was talking about were Julius and his nephew Augustus. Not all the Caesars exchanged coded messages with their military commanders. And Julius did not exchange them with Augustus because Julius was dead when Augustus ascended the throne. Before that he was not privy to "Godly information."
3. Ibid., 157 ff.
4. Keegan, John, *A History of Warfare* (New York: Alfred A. Knopf, 1993) 377.
5. Layton, RADM Edwin T., et al., *And I Was There* (New York: William Morrow, 1985) 448.
6. Kahn, op. cit., 573.
7. Codevilla, Angelo, *Informing Statecraft: Intelligence for a New Century* (New York: Maxwell Millian International, 1992) 192.

8. "Redefining Security," A report by the Joint Security Commission to the Secretary of Defense and the Director of Central Intelligence, 28 February 1994, 103.

9. Kahn, op. cit., 595-601.

10. Parker, D. B., Proceedings of the 14th National Computer Security Conference, 1991. See also Parker, D.B., *Fighting Computer Crime*, Wiley, 1998, Chapter 10.

11. Ibid.

PART 2

INFOSEC
Concepts

In the following four chapters that make up Part 2, we explore the important INFOSEC concepts of risk, security policy, intellectual capital, individual privacy, and finally, evaluation/certification of computer systems and networks. Part 2 defines the theoretical basis for the practical countermeasures presented in Part 3.

CHAPTER 3

Risk Management and Architecture of Information Security (INFOSEC)

Risk is inherent in life. As it is the antithesis of security, we naturally strive to eliminate risk. As worthy as that goal is, however, we learn with experience that complete elimination is never possible. Even if it were possible to eliminate all risk, the cost of achieving that total risk avoidance would have to be compared against the cost of the possible losses resulting from having accepted rather than having eliminated risk. The results of such an analysis could include pragmatic decisions as to whether achieving risk avoidance at such cost was reasonable. Applying reason in choosing how much risk we can accept and, hence, how much security we can afford is known as *risk management*.

Thinking about Risk

It is useful in thinking about risk management to use a tentative "relationship." This is not, of course, a mathematical equation for use in making quantitative determinations of risk level. It is an algorithm for use in thinking about the factors that enter into risk management and in assessing the qualitative level of danger posed in a given situation.

Consider the following statement:[1]

$$\text{Level of Risk} = \frac{(\text{Threat} \times \text{Vulnerability})}{\text{Countermeasures}} \times \text{Impact}$$

Natural disasters represent very real dangers to people, facilities, equipment, inventory, and other assets, including information and information systems, and have to be considered by managers as part of the larger issue of disaster planning, as we discuss later. Reliability and the steps necessary to allow for and deal with reliability failures are also risk management issues for managers. In information systems security and Infowar, however, we use the word *threat* in describing a more limited component of risk. For these purposes, threats are posed by organizations or individuals who both intend us harm and have the capability to accomplish their objectives. These types of threats and measures that may be taken to reduce or eliminate the risks they create comprise one of the principal themes of this book. They may take the form of computer hackers, criminals, industrial or state-sponsored spies, enemy armed forces, terrorists, psychotics, drug lords or saboteurs. Their organizations may be formal, as are foreign armies or intelligence services, or informal, like the terrorist group that attacked the World Trade Center or hacker groups like the Legion of Doom or Chaos.

Threats to our information or to our computer processing and communications systems may be from outsiders seeking access to our information assets, but more often they are insiders—white-collar criminals, disgruntled employees harboring real or imagined grievances, or traitors who turn over their country's secrets for money or ideological incentives. Unfortunately, in real-world security situations, threats do not occur one at a time, or even independently.

Vulnerability

Vulnerabilities are characteristics of our situations, systems, or facilities that can be exploited by a *threat* to do us harm. A vulnerability for which there is no *credible threat* does not require a response by security processes. Examples of vulnerabilities include structural weaknesses of buildings located near earthquake fault zones, weak passwords on our computers and networks, easily penetrated facilities, nonvetted personnel, or operations carried out such that outsiders can detect their existence and analyze their objectives. Careful attention to the design of facilities and systems can reduce or eliminate vulnerabilities. Locks and barriers can be strengthened, fences raised, alarms and monitors installed, computer systems and networks upgraded to incorporate security features, sprinkler systems installed, and a wealth of other features, devices, and procedures implemented to reduce vulnerabilities.

Threats

Managers must consider the possible consequences of attacks from a wide variety of threats. Each attack may act on a tangential vulnerability. Many exploitation attempts go unrecognized. Often threats to information and information systems are paired with a specific line of attack or set of vulnerabilities. A threat that has no vulnerability creates no risk. It is useful to deal with threat-vulnerability pairings in the risk management process. There is need to recognize that there is no one-to-one correspondence, so we cannot depend upon elimination of a vulnerability to neutralize a threat, or elimination of a threat to mean that vulnerability can be tolerated safely. The numerator of our equation is, therefore, a sum of threat-vulnerability products, where any given threat or vulnerability may occur in more than one product. Any threat with no associated vulnerability or vulnerability with no threat results in a zero addition to risk, simplifying the analysis.

Countermeasures

Countermeasures may abate the danger even if there are malevolent and capable threats as well as vulnerabilities, which can be exploited by those threats. All else being equal, more countermeasures mean less risk, so countermeasures appear in the denominator in our algorithm. Guards can be hired, personnel may be subjected to background investigations or polygraph examinations, badges may be used to identify authorized personnel, procedures may be implemented in our computer systems and networks to back up databases and to enforce sound password practices, and so forth. Such countermeasures reduce the likelihood of a successful attack and so lessen risk. To distinguish between a vulnerability and a countermeasure, consider the former a consequence of system design and the latter the means available to overcome or mask the vulnerability.

Impact

The *impact* of a successful attack depends upon the *value* of the target. If the impact of a security failure is small, allocation of scarce and expensive resources to security systems and processes can also be small. For example, the loss of some routine office correspondence might occasion little concern. Conversely, the consequences of some security failures can be exceptionally dire. Failure of the public switched network that carries our telephone and computer communications could be devastating to the nation's economy. The use of nuclear, chemical or biological weapons by terrorists, penetration of our cryptographic systems by foreign intelligence services, or foreknowledge of our strategic and tactical war plans by our enemies could have consequences for our country too severe to permit the smallest relaxation of security, even if such threats are relatively unlikely and the cost of protection is high. Obviously, as the value of the target rises, the impact of a successful attack goes up as well, and so our sense of risk increases. Consequently, *impact is a force multiplier in our algorithm*.

It is not always possible to evaluate in any quantitative sense the factors in the risk management algorithm. The cost of some countermeasures like alarm systems or insurance may be easily determined, although acquiring information about the true cost of countermeasures and allocating those costs among various security functions turns out to be surprisingly difficult using current methods of accounting. What portion of the cost of a wall is attributable to security rather than structural necessity? If guards were not needed to protect information and information systems, would they still be needed to protect employees from criminal intruders? If computers that are shielded against emission of potentially compromising radiation are an option, are both cases (with and without shielding) costed independently and compared, and would the shielding still be needed to protect the system against incoming radiation from the environment (nearby airport radars can cause problems in unshielded wireless receivers, for example) or deliberate attacks by infoterrorists using high-energy laser beams or electromagnetic pulse (EMP) weapons? Even if it were easy to determine the cost of potential countermeasures, the likelihood of the threat being successful, the extent of our vulnerabilities, and the impact of a possible loss are at best uncertain. As with most management problems, insufficient information makes security decisions more of an art form and less of a science.

This uncertainty is a contributing cause of our tendency to rely on risk avoidance. By assuming the threat to be capable, intense, and competent, by valuing our potential targets highly, and by conservatively estimating uncertainties, we reduce risk management to: "What are our vulnerabilities and how much do countermeasures cost to eliminate them?" The management problem is, "How much money can I spend and where can I spend it most wisely?" In most cases, fortunately, it is possible to do better. It is often sufficient to bind the problem, even when exact figures are not available. By careful analysis, we may be able to estimate the value of each factor in our equation and balance the risk of loss or damage against the costs of countermeasures and select a mix that provides adequate protection without excessive cost.

Ultimately, the risk management process is about making decisions. The impact of a successful attack and the level of risk that is acceptable in any given situation are fundamental policy decisions.

The threat is whatever it is, and while it may be abated, controlled, or subdued by appropriate countermeasures, it is beyond the direct control of the security process. The process must focus, accordingly, on vulnerabilities and countermeasures. *Vulnerabilities are design issues and must be addressed during the design, development, fabrication, and implemen-*

tation of our facilities, equipment, systems, and networks. Although the distinction is not always certain, *countermeasures are less needed due to the characteristics of our systems than of their environments and the ways in which we use them.* Typically, to make any asset less vulnerable raises its cost, not just in the design and development phase but also due to more-extensive validation and testing to ensure the functionality and utility of security features, and in the application of countermeasures during the operation and maintenance phase as well.

A Model for Cost-Effective Risk Management

A fundamental problem of risk management, then, is to link the choice of design characteristics and that countermeasures to threat and impact, in order to create a *cost-effective balance*, that achieves an acceptable level of risk. Such a process might work as follows:

1. *Assess the impact of loss of or damage to the potential target.* While the impact of the loss of a family member as a parent is beyond measure, the economic value of the member as a wage earner can be estimated as part of the process of deciding the amount of life insurance to purchase. The economic impact of crime or destruction by fires in a city can be determined as part of the process of sizing police and fire departments. The impact of loss of a technological lead on battlefield effectiveness can be specified.

   Not all impacts are economic, of course. Loss of sovereignty through war or destruction of civilization in a strategic nuclear exchange is beyond calculation. On a lesser scale, the political and diplomatic impacts of damage or destruction of some assets must be considered—for example, when an embassy is overrun as happened in Teheran. Such considerations are often of necessity subjective and qualitative rather than quantitative in nature.

   Specify the level of risk of damage or destruction that is acceptable. This may well be the most difficult part of the process. None of us contemplates easily the loss of our loved ones or of our own life. At the other end of the scale, the destruction resulting from nuclear war is unthinkable. In between, addressing loss or destruction in terms of acceptability seems cold-hearted and unfeeling.

2. *Identify and characterize the threat.* The leaders of our country, diplomats and military commanders, intelligence and counterintelligence officers, who constantly seek to understand the capabilities, intentions, and activities of our enemies perform this function. The damage that can be caused by accident, disease, or natural forces such as earthquakes, hurricanes, tornadoes, fires, or floods is known. Criminal behavior can be described and predicted. Terrorist groups have been studied, and their activities have been cataloged.

3. *Analyze vulnerabilities.* For individuals, dietary and exercise regimens can reduce vulnerability to some health threats. Fire and intrusion alarms can detect problems and alert response teams. Computer systems and networks can be designed to be less vulnerable to hacker attacks. In military and intelligence situations, both offensive and defensive specialists need to be consulted in order to understand how attacks might be initiated. Where potential improvements that may reduce vulnerabilities are identified, the cost of their implementation must be estimated.

4. *Specify countermeasures.* Where vulnerabilities are inherent or cost too much to eliminate during the design and development of facilities or systems, countermeasures must be selected to reduce risk to an acceptable level. Access to facilities can be controlled. Use of computers and networks can be monitored or audited. Personnel can be vetted to various degrees. Not all countermeasures need be used if some lesser mix will reduce risk to an acceptable level. Costs of each type of countermeasure must be estimated to determine the most cost-effective mix.

5. *Allow for uncertainties.* None of the factors in the risk management equation is absolute. No threat is infinitely capable and always lucky. No system is without vulnerability. No countermeasure is completely effective, and short of complete destruction, the impact of damage to an asset is problematic. Risk management requires the realistic assessment of uncertainties, erring on neither conservative nor optimistic sides.

In practice, the estimations needed in applying such a risk management process are accomplished in gross terms. Threat level or uncertainty may be assessed as high or low. Impact may be designated as severe or moderate. This gross quantification of factors in the risk management equation allows the design attributes used to reduce vulnerabilities and the countermeasures to be grouped so that they can be applied consistently throughout large organizations. The previous analysis of impact, threat, and acceptable risk ultimately leads the manager to appropriate decisions regarding reducing vulnerability and application of effective countermeasures.

Understanding and Estimating Threat

That there is real danger to information assets and systems is beyond question. No one who reads the newspapers or pays attention to the other journalistic media can have missed such stories as the denial of service attacks against the Internet (November 2, 1988) or against the law firm that breached netiquette by posting an advertisement on a large number of newsgroups and was forced off the Net by the resulting flood of protesting e-mail. Or found a virus on a PC. Or noted the net attack on Citibank that allegedly resulted in $2.8 million in illicit funds transfers, although Citibank claims that only about $400,000 was not recovered (Reuters, August 18, 1995). Or read Cliff Stoll's fascinating description in his book *The Cuckoo's Egg* (1989) of the tracking and capture of German hackers funded by the KGB to break into United States government computers. Nevertheless, we must ask just how severe the danger truly is? How widespread are such attacks? How much damage do they do? Are technology improvements diminishing the problem? And is there potentially an information Pearl Harbor in our future?

Computer Viruses

Consider the problem of computer viruses. It is estimated by the International Computer Security Association in 1999 that there are some 6000 or more viruses in circulation and that 71 percent of all corporate networks have been infected.[2] Viruses are so pervasive that they have been detected in shrinkware software shipped directly from the manufacturer. New ones crop up at a rate that exceeds 20 per week. The question is not so much "Will you get a virus?" as "When will you get a virus?" But so what? Why not just get an antivirus software package?

Viruses are just programs, of course, and so can be detected by looking for *characteristic sequences of instructions* that comprise either the part of the program that makes copies and sends them along to spread the infection or the part that does the dirty work—the *payload*—that displays an annoying message or destroys your data. And therein lies a problem. The antiviral software has to have been taught to recognize the instruction string, or *signature,* of the virus in order to be able to detect it. A new virus will not be detected at all unless, as occasionally happens, the programmer just used an old virus and changed the payload. That's what happened when the "Stoned" virus, which displayed a message recommending legalization of marijuana, was mutated into "Michelangelo," which destroys data on March 6, the painter's birthday. Of course, antiviral software can be updated as new viruses or new versions of old viruses are discovered, but it's always a game of catch-up, and even those who take care to upgrade often will not be completely safe.

Programmers who create viruses keep up with the state of the art in antiviral software and constantly improve their malicious technology. We are now seeing viruses that are encrypted to escape detection. Other viruses use compression technology to make transmission easier and recognition more difficult. Since the order in which instructions are executed can sometimes be changed without changing the ultimate result, as when two processes are independent and either can run first, the order of the instructions in a virus may be changed and thereby invalidate the antiviral software. Or NULOPS (null operations), instructions to the computer to do nothing for a clock cycle, might be inserted at random points, mutating the sequence of instructions for which the antiviral software seeks. Such changes result in viruses that are called *polymorphic,* because they constantly change the structural characteristics that would have facilitated their detection. Lately, we have begun to see foxy viruses that recognize antiviral software, watch as sectors of the storage device are cleared, and copy themselves over to previously cleared sectors, in effect, leaping over the antiviral bloodhound.

While antiviral packages are a valuable, even essential, part of a sound information security program, they are not in and of themselves sufficient. Good backup procedures and sound policies designed to reduce the likelihood of a virus attack are also necessary.

Directed Threats—Hackers, Criminals, Competitors, and Infoterrorists

Viruses represent a dangerous threat to information assets and systems, but they are mindless and undirected, released as unguided logic missiles into cyberspace by amoral and sociopathic miscreants. Sound security policies, practices, and procedures like those discussed in this book can reduce the risk they represent to a manageable level. Much more dangerous are the risks posed by directed threats, capable and willing adversaries who target the confidentiality, integrity, and availability of our information assets and systems.

Some of these directed threats are outside threats: hackers, criminals, competitors, infoterrorists, and even foreign governments. Such threats use high-tech attacks like password cracking attacks or TEMPEST attacks or perhaps low-technology attacks like social engineering attacks, in their attempts to penetrate our systems and networks and exploit, corrupt, or destroy information. The nature of these attacks and defenses against them are described later. But are such threats pervasive?

Hackers have received a great deal of attention in the press and in the entertainment media. They comprise an interesting subculture, technically astute and talented even if socially and morally depraved. They have been pictured as nerdy teenagers who stay up all night eating pizza, drinking sodas as they crouch over their computers, monitors reflecting off of their bottle-thick eyeglasses, and try command after command until they get through their school's computer security so they can improve their grade point average. If this representation was ever accurate, it certainly is not so today. Today's cyberpunks may be yesterday's juvenile cyber-delinquents grown older, but they tend to be in their twenties and even thirties, although the occasional teenager is still arrested for hacking. To the extent that hackers have a coherent philosophy, it centers around the quaint notion that, "Information wants to be free." The hacker philosophy is libertarian and technocentric. Access to computers and information, they believe, should be unlimited, and hackers should be judged solely by their computer and network skills, not by archaic laws and ethics, the evolution of which has not kept pace with the revolution in technology.

The fantasy of an information Robin Hood whose technical skills and fearless, if illegal, travels through other people's information systems and networks made him (very few hackers are women, for some reason) a maverick folk hero has now succumbed to the same economic reality that changed spies from ideologues to traitors for hire. Hackers today are more likely to try and sell their art as a service than to practice it for its own sake. Data mining of cyberspace has become a viable business, and many hackers try to make a living, or at least supplement their incomes, by finding information for others less technically astute or persistent.

When their activities stray over the line between legitimate research and invasion of privacy or commercial espionage, they become computer criminals and a greater threat to information assets and systems than were the curious or those merely in search of fun, challenge, or peer recognition.

Hackers as computer criminals even advertise their services. One group calling itself "BlackNet" offers to find anything for their clients for a price. Using PGP (Pretty Good Privacy, a popular encryption scheme) and anonymous remailers, BlackNet says it buys, sells, trades, and otherwise deals in information. BlackNet claims to be attempting to create a market in "trade secrets, processes, production methods (especially in semiconductors)...nanotechnology...chemical manufacturing...new product plans..." and so forth.[3]

Once inside a company's systems and networks, the hacker as computer criminal may seek to exploit the intellectual capital of the company, or the hacker may go directly for the gold. Hackers may have the company deliver unpaid-for goods to drop addresses or process checks made out to the hacker through accounts payable. Returning to the Citibank example, the hacker created illicit wire transfers, moving millions of dollars from legitimate accounts in Indonesia and Argentina to other accounts in San Francisco, Tel Aviv, Amsterdam, Germany, and Finland, from which the hacker's accomplices could withdraw the cash. Citibank claims that all but about $400,000 was recovered from the hack. The loss of customers to competitors was much more damaging. Banks across the street (using the same type of security systems) were aggressive in implying that they had never had a security breach. The hacker was identified as a Russian from St. Petersburg. Since we know that Russian organized crime is daring and ruthless, some security professionals speculate that this case is the first of many that will see the Russian gangs exploit the thousands of computer programmers idled by the collapse of the Soviet Union.

Some companies, upon finding a hacker inside their systems and networks, have hired the hacker rather than prosecuting him. Their reasoning was, "Better working for us than against us, and if he's so good at penetrating our security, he can help us be more secure." In practice, such arrangements rarely work out. The amorality and sociopathy that made the hacker a sociopath in the first place doesn't disappear when placed on the payroll. The hacker has merely been converted from an outsider to an insider hacker, now with some level of legitimate access to the company's systems and networks. Abuse of the legitimate access that has been granted is almost predictable.

Social Engineering

It is ironic that one of the most insidious techniques for attacking the security of a system or network is not technological at all, but psychological. Brute-force password guessing can often gain the attacker illicit access to information assets, especially if password management permits the use of weak or easily guessed passwords, but it is infinitely easier to gain access if someone gives it to you.

Social engineering is the art of obtaining the information necessary to achieve access by subterfuge, by talking to lawful users or operators of systems and networks and asking for advice, assistance, or other information that reduces the difficulty of penetration. It is difficult to explain to one who has not seen social engineering in action just how powerful a tool it can be. In one experiment, a team of young hackers was given the main switchboard number for a large organization and asked to see if they could get information to help them penetrate the organization's worldwide computer network. They were not to actually access the network; instead, they were merely to see what they could learn that might aid an attempted penetration. By calling the company and requesting to speak to the network help desk they managed, within 24 hours, they planned to have the organization create a new account for them, give them the user ID and password over the phone, describe the login protocols, and ship by overnight courier—at the target organization's expense and to an unidentifiable address—the software needed to gain access.

Unfortunately, this experiment did not have unexpected results. People whose job it is to help other members of the organization use their computers and networks for the benefit of the organization readily provide assistance and take pride in doing so. Nor are the help desk personnel the only targets. Everyone likes to help others when they can, especially if by helping we can show that we have mastered a complex set of technologies and protocols.

The attacker may play the role of neophyte. By playing dumb, the attacker elicits the respondent's natural desire to help. Posing a problem evokes most technically trained people's love of solving problems. The attacker may subtly challenge the ability of the respondent to handle the system or network, causing the respondent to rise to the challenge. Having the respondent walk through the login protocols and procedures engages the respondent in a procedure accomplished routinely daily or more often, which soothes the respondent's suspicious inclinations. Using the wrong words for computer processes or asking the respondent to define technical terms he or she uses ("What does 'boot the system' mean?") demonstrates helplessness and reinforces the desire to assist. Profuse thanks at the end of the conversation assuage any residual suspicion.

The converse of attacker as neophyte is attacker as expert. The attacker may call an unsuspecting member of the organization and pretend to be from the computer center, or even the security department, and explain that the computer system is malfunctioning and offer to assist with correcting the problem over the phone. The attacker then directs the respondent to go through the login procedure while describing each step, including telling the attacker the user ID and password being entered. Such a ploy is especially effective with lower-status members of the organization.

The most successful social engineering attacks follow a period of intense research about the organization and its systems to be attacked. Knowing the organizational structure, names of individuals that work for the organization, and other facts that are easily obtained by research in the public domain lends verisimilitude when interjected into the conversation. For instance, "I work for Don Jones in accounting" is more believable than "I work in accounting," especially if Don Jones is the head of accounting.

Nor is it necessary to obtain the information targeted on the first call or the first day. One case is on record where the attacker spent more than three years talking to an employee of a major company. An intense personal relationship developed, with exchanges of family information and personal information, all made up on the attacker's side, of course. Eventually the attacker was able to obtain a great deal of information by exploiting that relationship.

Social engineering attacks may involve physical visits to the target organization, as well as telephone calls. An attacker may go "Dumpster diving" to sort through the target organization's trash, knowing full well that a great deal of enormously valuable information ends up there, from passwords to system and network operating instructions. In one case, an attacker stole a uniform from a nearby dry cleaners and used it to pose as part of the janitorial team. During a visit to the organization's computer facility, the attacker was able to steal over 100 floppy disks and put them in a briefcase. The guards on duty routinely searched the briefcase as the attacker left the facility but let the attacker leave with the disks when no suspicious papers or electronic equipment that might belong to the organization was found during the search. The attacker may pose as a potential client, vendor or consultant, or seek an interview as a reporter or writer, or even as a student doing a project for class.

A common form of social engineering attack involves applying for a job. Questions like, "What systems do you use?" or "I'm interested in computer security; how does yours work?" appear more natural in a job interview setting. The attacker may actually take a job if one is offered, even a low-level job, if access will be granted that can be exploited from inside the organization. In one such attack, a sniffer was placed on the organization's network by a newly employed social engineer, and thousands of credit card numbers were collected as they passed through the network from the organization's customers as they purchased services online.

The defense against such attacks is an awareness and training program that informs employees of the nature of such attacks. Every employee of an organization, from the senior executives to the clerical and administrative staff to the janitors and guards, must be informed that such attacks take place, how to recognize them, and what to do if such an attack is suspected. Training and awareness programs are discussed at length later in this book.

Tempest

At the other extreme from the low-technology attacks we call social engineering are high-technology attacks that intercept the electromagnetic signals generated as a by-product of computer operations. All electronic equipment, such as computers, electronic typewriters, printers, and facsimile machines, radiate electromagnetic energy, and computers emit signals that, if intercepted at distances of less than a few hundred meters, can be exploited to reproduce the information being processed by the computer. The name for attacks that collect and exploit such signals is TEMPEST, which stands for Transient Electromagnetic Pulse

Emanation Standard. The term signifies both a specification for equipment and a process for preventing compromising emanations.

In a TEMPEST operation, the attacker needs a radio receiver that can be tuned to the frequencies at which the target signals occur. Such receivers are readily available today on the commercial market for as little as a few hundred dollars. The monitors of modern computers use cathode-ray tubes, much like television tubes, which have electromagnets that control a beam of electrons that is directed at phosphor dots on the monitor's screen. When illuminated, those dots combine to produce the letters and pictures we view on the screen. Unfortunately for security, as they operate, these electromagnets radiate signals, which an attacker can collect and feed into a monitor attached to the receiver, and then that attacker can see what the user of the computer is seeing. These signals readily penetrate walls and windows, so the attacker can be in a nearby room or even in a van parked at the curb outside the organization's facility.

There are three technical defenses against TEMPEST attacks. In the first, special transmitters can be purchased that emit at frequencies designed to mask the escaping radiation of the computers. However, such devices cannot radiate at exactly the frequency of the computers without interfering with those same computers, and that difference provides the attacker room to tune the receiver to receive the computer's signal rather than the interference signal. Such devices don't work well in practice.

Alternatively, special computers can be bought that are designed and built to reduce or eliminate the unintentional radiation. Unfortunately, such computers cost far more—two to five times as much in some cases—than those commercially available computers, which do not have such protection. They may be one or more generations of technology behind the state of the art in commercial, off-the-shelf equipment, with consequently less capability and performance. Finally, the rooms in which the computers and other electronic equipment operate, or even the whole building, may have grounded wires or metal plates incorporated into the walls that abate the signals produced by the equipment. Such shielded rooms obviously cost more to construct than do nonshielded facilities.

Before spending large sums on technology to protect against TEMPEST attacks, managers should consider two things. First, while these types of attacks are certainly technologically feasible, they are difficult to mount. The attacker must control an area near the target computer facility where the receiving equipment and either recorders, exploitation equipment, or both can be located. Pulling a van up outside the target facility and parking for long periods while receivers are tuned and signals are recorded or exploited is often impractical. Simply by being aware of activity in the vicinity, the security force can detect and counter most attacks. Second, because such attacks are difficult, they are rare. As long as such attacks remain low probability, sound risk management practices dictate that it makes little sense to spend a lot on TEMPEST countermeasures.

Attacks on Information Integrity

TEMPEST attacks are directed against the confidentiality of information assets. In such attacks, the object is to access and expropriate the information for the use of the attacker, whether to satisfy some ego need or to result in economic gain for the attacker. Other attacks are directed against the integrity of the information and seek to obliterate the information or change it in some way that reduces or completely destroys its value to its owner.

Consider, for example, the case, discussed earlier, where an employee placed a program on the system of the company that employed him. The program checked the database of employees daily to see if he was still employed, and the day after he was fired and his name was removed from the database, all of the personnel records of the company that were on the computer were erased. Even with a sound backup system, the time and expense of restoring the databases destroyed in such attacks can be significant.

Attacks that completely destroy information assets are not the most dangerous attacks on the integrity of information assets. An attack that compromises only 1 percent of a database, but in which exactly where that 1 percent exists, is not known, renders the entire database at least suspect, if not useless. In one case, mentioned earlier, a senior manager was changing the spreadsheet used by the chief executive officer to manage the company. The database was not destroyed. The values of some, but not all, of the entries were changed a little—not so much as to be obvious, but enough so that the CEO would make bad decisions. The poor decision making would result in, the senior manager hoped, his usurping of the CEO's position. The manager was caught and fired rather than the CEO, but his attack on the integrity of the CEO's spreadsheet was clever in that it was hard to detect and yet could have had significant effects. If such attacks take place over a sufficiently long period of time, they may affect the backups as well as the online data and be very difficult and expensive to correct.

Attacks on Information and Information Systems Availability

Attacks on the availability of information assets and systems are different from those against either confidentiality or integrity, and are generally called denial of service attacks (DoS). The most famous such attack was the Internet worm of November 2, 1988. A worm is a self-replicating program, like a computer virus without stealth features. The term comes from a science-fiction story called *The Shockwave Rider*, written by John Brunner in 1975, in which the idea of such a program was first described. The Internet worm was created by a young graduate student and was released into the Internet, where it began to make copies of itself and send them along to other computers that were attached to the Internet. Those copies made more copies and sent them along, and those copies made still more copies. The result was a sort of chain reaction that clogged up the Internet. In 1988, a few thousand computers were affected for a period of several days while the program was analyzed and countermeasures developed to stop its spread. No one knows exactly how much damage was done, but estimates are in the millions of dollars. The Internet then was much smaller than it is today, and so a successful attack today, would cause much more extensive damage, delivering a staggering blow to the nation's economy, which is highly dependent on the Internet, and perhaps rising to the level of a national security issue. We will expand our knowledge of digital warfare and infowar in later chapters.

The Internet worm exploited a weakness in an e-mail program called Sendmail. The correction for this weakness has been widely distributed, but we have been shocked on occasion to find that older versions of Sendmail are still in use in some organizations. Partly in response to the Internet worm, an organization called the Computer Emergency Response Team, or CERT, was created at Carnegie-Mellon University in Pittsburgh, to serve as a focal point for reporting of computer security problems and vulnerabilities, and for distributing information about how to correct weaknesses being exploited by malicious code or other threats. The information security officers of every organization that depends upon computers should be familiar with CERT and should be on distribution lists for, and implement, the corrections it disseminates.

Another type of denial of service attack is a flooding attack. This type of attack was illustrated when a law firm in California sent out an e-mail advertisement to thousands of newsgroups. This was considered by many to be a serious breach of etiquette, and they responded by flooding the firm's e-mail account with protests. So many protests were received that the Internet service provider that the law firm used was unable to do anything but process the protests. Ironically, it was not the law firm that was most damaged, but the unwitting Internet service provider, which could no longer function.

The law firm sued the ISP based on its contract, which required the ISP to provide e-mail service in return for the fees it charged the law firm, and the law firm won.

The Information Protection Architecture—A Layered Defense

Faced with threats by those willing to misuse, corrupt, or destroy information assets and systems, many people reach almost instinctively for the phone to call an insurance broker. Unfortunately, while some forms of insurance protect organizations against embezzlement or economic losses due to malfeasance of directors and officers, insurance companies are writing policies for the most part that protect against the loss of the hardware incorporated into computer systems and networks, rather than less tangible, but often far more valuable software and databases stored, processed, and communicated on systems and networks. It is little comfort to have a floppy disk that costs about a dollar insured for that single dollar when the disk contains a database or file of intellectual capital worth millions of dollars.

When Mrs. O'Leary's cow allegedly kicked over her lantern and burned Chicago to the ground, fire insurance was born. Insurance companies began to offer policies that protected their clients from financial losses due to fires, but only after the clients had taken reasonable steps to protect themselves using available technology. The insurance companies required the installation of fire-retarding walls and paints, the use of fireproof safes for storage of valuable assets, and the installation of sprinklers and fire extinguishers. In short, the insurance company offered to pick up the residual risk only after reasonable steps had been taken by their clients to abate the risk through applications of available technology. The same pattern can be expected to emerge in the information protection field, but it is only slowly appearing.

Today, the risks associated with possession and use of valuable information assets and systems are, for the most part, borne directly by the organization that must use information security technology and practices to supplement such insurance as is available and affordable in abating the risks. Thus, the protection of confidentiality, integrity, and availability of information assets and systems is founded upon and begins with analysis of the threat and the choice, based on risk management principles, of a balanced mix of technology, procedures, and insurance. See Figure 3-1

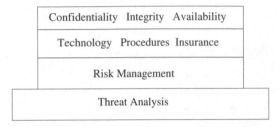

Figure 3-1
Primary Model for
INFOSEC.

| Confidentiality Integrity Availability |
| Technology Procedures Insurance |
| Risk Management |
| Threat Analysis |

The use of technologies and procedures in securing information assets and systems proceeds in three steps. First, protect systems, networks, and information using cryptology, computer science, and countermeasures. We will explore the ways in which such an approach can help secure information later in this book, but be assured that it is not possible to completely secure any system in such a manner, nor would it be cost-effective to do so even if it were possible.

Said another way, it is not possible to reduce residual risk to zero. There is always room, therefore, for threats to exploit remaining vulnerabilities and attack information assets. Consequently, a second step is necessary: auditing and monitoring of the information transactions taking place on the system or network to detect intrusions or attempted intrusions by outsiders and abuses or attempted abuses of privilege by insiders. Finally, it is necessary to react to security-relevant incidents when they occur and to correct shortfalls in system design that leave vulnerabilities to be exploited or failures of security operations or countermeasures to abate residual risk. The details of these steps—protect, detect, and correct—form much of the substance of the later chapters of this book.

Protection is a primary issue when we design or acquire information systems and their operational environments, or when we redesign them after a security-relevant event. Security is best designed into the system from the start, since it is prohibitively expensive to retrofit if it is possible to add later. Consequently, the protect step of our process is focused on research and development of security products and features to be incorporated into our systems and networks. It is a critical aspect of the architecture chosen and a fundamental part of design, development, fabrication, and implementation. It pervades our choice of products and components and evaluation of their contributions to security. It guides integration of the completed system or network, and it is intrinsic to evaluation and testing, to verification and validation, and eventually to certification and accreditation (see Figure 3-2).

Figure 3-2
Protect, detect, and correct layer.

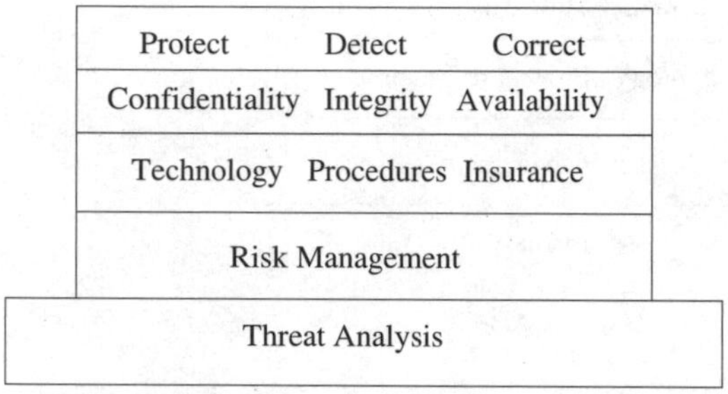

Protect	Detect	Correct
Confidentiality	Integrity	Availability
Technology	Procedures	Insurance
Risk Management		
Threat Analysis		

Detection and correction, on the other hand, are more-latent issues for operation and maintenance of our systems and networks (see Figure 3-3). The detection step of our process is composed of continuing attempts to characterize and understand residual vulnerabilities, to catch and eradicate malicious code before it can compromise or damage information

Figure 3-3
Acquisition, operations, and maintenance.

R&D Architectures Design and development Component evaluation Integration and test Certification and accreditation	Vulnerability analysis Malicious code detection Intrusion detection Auditing and monitoring	Security emergency response Triage Redesign Recertification and reaccreditation
Acquisition	Operations and Maintenance	
Protect	Detect	Correct
Confidentiality	Integrity	Availability
Technology	Procedures	Insurance
Risk Management		
Threat Analysis		

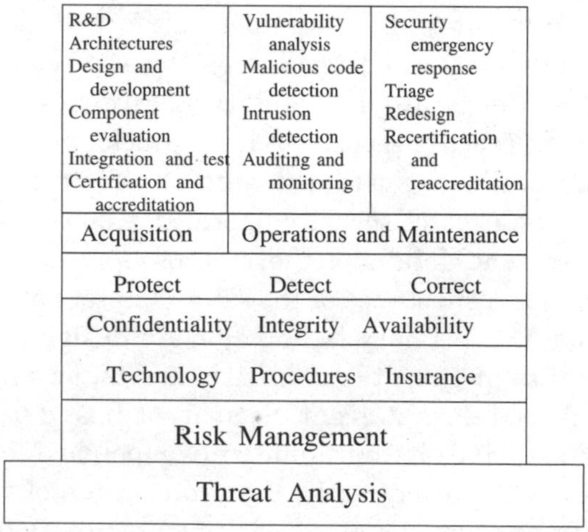

assets, to recognize and, if possible, interdict intrusions, and to identify abuses by those to whom we have given access to our information assets and privileges on our systems.

Correction implies the ability to react to security-relevant events. An emergency response may be appropriate, executed by a qualified, experienced, and practiced team of security experts—an "infoSWAT" team, if you will. Triage may be required to enable isolation of infected portions of systems and networks. Ultimately, problems must be investigated and characterized so that corrective modifications or additional countermeasures can be brought to bear and secure operations restored.

At every step, the decisions that must be made if we are to achieve affordable, cost-effective systems and networks that protect our valuable information assets must be guided and informed by well-considered information security policy. And ultimately, the entire structure depends upon properly trained and alert employees at every level of the organization, from the executives on mahogany row to the clerks in their cubicles and the facilities maintenance personnel in the basement.

This, then, is the architecture within which solutions to the problems of disclosure, misuse, illicit modification, or destruction of valuable information assets and systems must be created and applied (see Figure 3-4).

Figure 3-4
Security policy.

Security Policy			Training and Awareness
R&D Architectures Design and development Component evaluation Integration and test Certification and accreditation	Vulnerability analysis Malicious code detection Intrusion detection Auditing and monitoring	Security emergency response Triage Redesign Recertification and reaccreditation	
Acquisition	Operations and Maintenance		
Protect	Detect	Correct	
Confidentiality	Integrity	Availability	
Technology	Procedures	Insurance	
Risk Management			
Threat Analysis			

Wrap-Up

We have presented INFOSEC in terms of an information protection architecture, which is a cost-balancing act to:

- Minimize vulnerabilities to our information assets and computer systems
- Choose appropriate countermeasures to prevent digital espionage
- Reduce the likelihood of successful attacks

These goals are realized through a group of technologies discussed in Part 3, "Practical Countermeasures." We next look at the importance of an effectively enacted security policy. No countermeasure is effective within an organization unless it has in effect an understood security policy in which employees are given specific circumscribed authority and assume responsibility for the security of the assets they deal with.

Notes

1. Ira Winkler, *Corporate Espionage* (Rocklin, Calif.: Prima Publishing, 1997), 13.
2. *5th Annual ICSA Labs Computer Virus Prevalance Survey.* August 1999, www.ICSA.net.
3. Anonymous, *Wired*, November 1993, 32.

CHAPTER 4

Information Security Policy

Introduction

We have to make decisions to act effectively in the real world. Knowing which decision is the right one depends upon having some sense of "right" and "wrong" or some metric we can use to judge "better" or "worse." Some decisions, of course, are neither—it matters little whether we drive on the right side of the road or the left, so long as we all agree as to which side we will use. The most broadly stated guidance that we use to make decisions is called *policy*. Because policies are such broad principles for guiding decisions, they must be backed up by more-detailed guidance for implementation and application in specific situations. This more-detailed guidance is called by a variety of names: standards, objectives, goals, directions, and so forth.

Information security policy provides the basic guidance we use to decide the *value* of our information assets; the *impact* of their exploitation, corruption, or destruction; and the *level of risk* we are willing to accept in providing for their protection. At the highest level, information security policy is a set of rules we can use when we have to decide where and how to spend scarce resources protecting valuable information. Information security policy, then, *addresses the fundamental issues of what must be protected, how much protection is needed, and for how long*.

Protection applies to confidentiality, integrity, and availability, and the answers to the fundamental questions may, and usually do, differ, depending on which of these foci are being addressed. It is also true that the need to secure information assets varies over time. The date, time, and place for the invasion of Normandy needed to be kept confidential only until June 6, 1944. Information that can be obtained from the government with a Freedom of Information Act request and that has, therefore, no confidentiality requirements may nevertheless require strict protection of integrity and availability to ensure that it cannot be illicitly changed or destroyed.

An Information Security Policy for the Nation

At the highest level, information security policies need not be complex. A few paragraphs suffice to outline the required guidance, even for the entire federal government. The following few rules might serve as the information protection policy for the nation:

1. Information in the possession of the United States government or its departments and agencies is held in trust for, or on behalf of, the citizens of the United States and will be made available on request in accordance with the Freedom of Information Act, except when laws or regulations require that its dissemination be limited.

2. Information is a *strategic asset* vital to the provision of services by the United States government or its departments and agencies. As an asset, information must be protected to an extent and for a period commensurate with its value and the degree of danger posed by its unauthorized disclosure, misuse, or loss.

   a. The confidentiality of information *classified* in accordance with an Executive Order, information deemed to be *unclassified but sensitive*, and information subject to Privacy Act, privilege, proprietary, or other legislative or regulatory protections must be maintained.

   b. Information must be protected from illicit destruction or modification, so that the integrity of the information is assured. Implicit in the concept of information integrity is the notion that, upon receipt of information, the recipient must be able to be sure from whom the information came and that it has not been modified in transit. The sender, in turn, must be able to know that the information was received and by whom.

   c. Information must be available when and where needed to support analytic and decision-making processes.

3. Protection of information and the computers, systems, networks, equipment, personnel, and facilities involved in creating, storing, processing, and communicating information by the United States government or its departments and agencies requires a risk management approach based on a balanced, cost-effective application of security disciplines and technologies, including information systems security, operational and administrative security, personnel security, physical security, and other types of security.

4. Information security requirements are an integral part of program management for all computer and telecommunications systems and shall be addressed throughout the life cycle of programs through which the United States government or its departments and agencies acquire information technology from concept definition through design, development, implementation, operation, maintenance, and disposal.

Information Security Policy for a Corporation or Organization

Such a set of policies is easily adapted to the use of a corporation or other organization:

1. Information in the possession of [Organization], whether belonging to [Organization] or held in trust for, or on behalf of, its customers, clients, subcontractors, or personnel, is an important asset that must be protected to an extent and for a period commensurate with its value and the degree of damage that could result from its unauthorized disclosure or modification, misuse, destruction, or nonavailability. Subject to independent verification:

   a. The confidentiality of sensitive information, including intellectual capital or proprietary data, classified and unclassified but sensitive information belonging to the [Organization], *information concerning the private lives of individuals*, information subject to attorney-client or physician-patient privileges, or information subject to other legislative or regulatory protections, shall be maintained.

   b. Information must be protected from illicit destruction or modification so that the integrity of the information is assured. Implicit in the concept of information integrity is the notion that, upon receipt of information, the recipient must be able to be certain from whom the information came, the sender that it has been received, and both that it has not been modified in transit.

   c. Information must be available when and where needed to support the analytic and decision-making processes that enable [Organization] to function efficiently and to ensure that [Organization] can serve its customers and clients effectively.

2. Each employee will be granted such access as is needed to perform his or her assigned function, but employees will not be given access to information otherwise requiring protection unless and until such access is needed and is formally authorized in accordance with [Organization] conventions and standards.

3. Responsibility for the protection of our information assets rests with all employees and managers of [Organization]. A security compliance organization will be designated and will have the right to access and review, in the course of business, any and all information stored, processed, or communicated on computers, systems,

or networks belonging to [Organization], and no one using [Organization] systems has a right to personal privacy of any information thereon, whatever its source.

4. Protection of information assets calls for risk management using a balanced, cost-effective mix of security disciplines and technologies and may include requirements for information systems security, procedural and administrative security, personnel security, physical security, and other types of security.

5. In protecting its information assets, [Organization] will obey all applicable laws and regulations and charges its employees to meet the highest ethical standards in dealing with clients, customers, vendors, the public, and other [Organization] personnel.

Neither the concepts nor the goals incorporated into such policy statements are difficult to understand. Most people would find little in such broad statements with which to take exception. Taking the next steps toward refining and implementing these policies takes us, however, into realms less subject to agreement.

Classification Management

The process of establishing which information assets are to be protected is called *classification management*. Items of information, which have been identified by the process as requiring protection of confidentiality, integrity, or availability, are said to have been *classified*. In military and diplomatic circles, information is said to be *classified* when it meets certain *criteria set out by Executive Order* specifying that *confidentiality requirements apply for national security reasons*. The term *classified* as applied here has a more general meaning and is used to describe information identified by the classification management process as *requiring any level of protection* of any of the three characteristics we protect.

Level of Application

Before we can apply this process, we have to decide at what *level* the process will have effect. It makes little sense to decide if individual bits or bytes are to be protected. Implementing the number of individual decisions that such policy would require is not feasible. Nor does it make sense to apply the process to individual words, although at times individual words may be particularly sensitive, as in the identities of agents or words descriptive of sources or methods of intelligence collection. The smallest aggregate of words to which the classification management process might apply is a phrase or sentence. Or we might elect as a matter of policy to apply the process only to larger aggregates like paragraphs or even entire documents. Since each individual classification management decision requires time and therefore expends scarce resources, choosing to apply the process to larger aggregates suggests that classification management applied at the paragraph or document level will cost less than if it were applied at the phrase or sentence level.

Ideally, the process of classifying an item of information includes a decision as to what events or elapse of time would permit us to *declassify* the information; otherwise, we will incur additional expense when it becomes necessary to decide if we can ease or stop protecting the information. *Since security costs time and money, it is clearly not desirable to continue classification of an item of information beyond the period during which the protection is required.* Moreover, the ability to analyze information for historical purposes or to establish trends is impeded by its protection from disclosure. Reviewing each item of information to determine if it is now safe to discontinue protection will require one or more decisions, depending upon which characteristics have required protection. Obviously, applying the classification management process to larger aggregates of information means that fewer decisions will be required during declassification, requiring less expenditure of scarce resources.

The United States Government Scheme

The U.S. government recognizes three levels of confidentiality specified in very broad and subjective terms:

(1) *Top Secret* shall be applied to information, the unauthorized disclosure of which reasonably could be expected to cause *exceptionally grave damage* to the national security that the original classification authority is able to identify or describe.

(2) *Secret* shall be applied to information, the unauthorized disclosure of which reasonably could be expected to *cause serious damage* to the national security that the original classification authority is able to identify or describe.

(3) *Confidential* shall be applied to information, the unauthorized disclosure of which reasonably could be expected to *cause damage* to the national

security that the original classification authority is able to identify or describe.[1]

The United States government typically classifies information at the *paragraph level* for the purpose of protecting confidentiality. Paragraphs are preceded by a (TS), (S), or (C) to specify that information in the following paragraph require protection at the Top Secret, Secret, or Confidential levels, respectively. There are no markings specifying the degree to which integrity or availability is to be protected. When declassifying information in response to Freedom of Information Act requests or other requirements to make a declassification decision, the declassification process is applied throughout a document at the individual sentence level and sometimes on a word-by-word basis. Thus, for the government, the declassification process is extremely time-consuming and expensive. The government's classification management policies define information as "any knowledge that can be communicated or documentary material, regardless of its physical form or characteristics...."[2] Information is to be protected from disclosure if it is national security information, the disclosure of which could lead to damage to "national defense or foreign relations of the United States,"[3] or when foreign governments that have provided the information to the United States government have requested that the information be protected.[4] A variety of types of information are recognized as possibly needing protection, including:

(a) Military plans, weapons systems, or operations

(b) Foreign government information

(c) Intelligence activities (including special activities), intelligence sources or methods, or cryptology

(d) Foreign relations or foreign activities of the United States, including confidential sources

(e) Scientific, technological, or economic matters relating to the national security

(f) United States government programs for safeguarding nuclear materials or facilities

(g) Vulnerabilities or capabilities of systems, installations, projects or plans relating to the national security.[5]

Because it is difficult to define precisely the levels of damage that might occur as a result of untimely disclosure and misuse, reasonable people could disagree as to which category should be applied to any particular item on information. Accordingly, classification guides must be

Figure 4-1

The Current
Classification System.

TOP SECRET	TS - BIGOT LIST	TS - SCI	TS - DoD SAP
SECRET	S - BIGOT LIST	S - SCI	S - DoD SAP
CONFIDENTIAL	C - BIGOT LIST	C - SCI	C - DoD SAP
UNCLASSIFIED			

written providing specific directions for determining which category applies to various types of information (refer to Figure 4-1).

Within each of the three basic categories, the government's classification scheme provides for a number of subdivisions and subcategories. The Department of Defense, for instance, has acquisition, intelligence, and operations and support programs that are designated *special access programs*. The DoD is permitted to restrict access to information about such programs by marking program information with codewords indicating that only people who have been granted access to the programs, as discussed later in the section on staff integrity assurance, are permitted access to the information. These programs are further subcategorized as *acknowledged* or *unacknowledged*, with some of the most sensitive programs having certain reporting and oversight requirements "waived." The Director of Central Intelligence has the authority to designate similarly certain programs as *Special Compartmented Information* (*SCI*) programs, which also use *codewords* to designate information that is to be kept in restricted channels. Other access control lists (originally called *bigot* lists) are used to designate access privileges to war plans and information concerning intelligence operations and sources. Still other restrictive markings include *NOFORN* for information that is not releasable to foreign nationals, and *EYES ONLY* meaning to be seen only or to not be said aloud or recorded in sound form by the addressee (Figure 4-2).

The Executive Order provides that other terms may be specified in legislation as requiring protection under the classification management process. For example, the Atomic Energy Act at 42 U.S.C. 2011 et. seq. defines the category of "Restricted Information" and describes the process to be used for its classification and declassification.

Similarly, the Computer Security Act defines a category of information called "sensitive information"—which the defense and intelligence communities denote "sensitive but unclassified" and mark with (*SBU*)—by which is meant:

Any information, the loss, misuse, or unauthorized access to or modification of which could adversely affect the national interest or the conduct of Federal programs, or the privacy to which individuals are entitled under

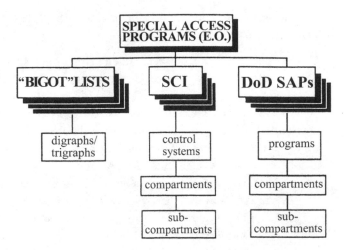

Figure 4-2

Special Access
Programs Structure.

section 552a of title 5, United States Code (the Privacy Act), but which has not been specifically authorized under criteria established by an Executive Order or an Act of Congress to be kept secret in the interest of national defense or foreign policy.

Such a broad definition is so general as to be not very helpful when its application to specific items of information is required. Perhaps a better way to look at the category of sensitive but unclassified information is to view it as that information which is described in exemptions (B)(2) through (9) of the Freedom of Information Act. Since the United States government is a government by, for, and of the people, it is really the people who own any information in the possession of the government other than that which has been given to the government by other governments or by private citizens, corporations, or other organizations, and which is held in trust for the owner(s) while being used by the government for governmental purposes.

Under the Freedom of Information Act, information in the possession of the government *must be disclosed to anyone who asks for it, unless it has been classified in accordance with an Executive Order*—exemption B(1)—or falls into one of eight other categories that the people, through their representatives, have decided are best not disclosed. Since exception B(1) covers classified information, exceptions B(2) through B(9) must be congruent with "sensitive but unclassified" information, since otherwise the information would have to be released on demand.

Sensitive but unclassified information (SBU), then, are those items of information that are:

(1) (A) Specifically authorized under criteria established by an Executive Order to be kept secret in the interest of national defense or foreign policy

(B) In fact properly classified pursuant to such Executive Order

(2) Related solely to the internal personnel rules and practices of an agency

(3) Specifically exempted from disclosure by statute (other than section 552b of this title), provided that such statute:

(A) Requires that the matters be withheld from the public in such a manner as to leave no discretion on the issue, or

(B) Establishes particular criteria for withholding or refers to particular types of matters to be withheld

(4) Trade secrets, commercial or financial information and privileged or confidential materials

(5) Inter-agency or intra-agency memorandums or letters which would not be available by law to a party other than one in litigation with the agency

(6) Personnel and medical files and similar files the disclosure of which would constitute a clearly unwarranted invasion of personal privacy

(7) Records or information compiled for law enforcement purposes, but only to the extent that the production of such law enforcement records or information:

(A) Could reasonably be expected to interfere with enforcement proceedings

(B) Would deprive a person of a right to a fair trial or an impartial adjudication

(C) Could reasonably be expected to constitute an unwarranted invasion of personal privacy

(D) Could reasonably be expected to disclose the identity of a confidential source, including a State, local, or foreign agency or authority or any private institution which furnished information on a confidential basis, and, in the case of a record or information compiled by criminal law enforcement authority in the course of a criminal investigation or by an agency conducting a lawful national security intelligence investigation, information furnished by a confidential source

(E) Would disclose techniques and procedures for law enforcement investigations or prosecutions, or would disclose guidelines for law enforcement investigations or prosecutions if such disclosure could reasonably be expected to risk circumvention of the law, or could reasonably be expected to endanger the life or physical safety of any individual

(8) Contained in or related to examination, operating, or condition reports pre-

pared by, on behalf of, or for the use of an agency responsible for the regulation or supervision of financial institutions; or

(9) Geological and geophysical information and data, including maps concerning wells. Any reasonably segregable portion of a record shall be provided to any person requesting such record after deletion of the portions which are exempt under this subsection (c)(1). Whenever a request is made which involves access to records described in subsection (b)(7)(A) and

(A) The investigation or proceeding involves a possible violation of criminal law,

(B) There is reason to believe that

(i) the subject of the investigation or proceeding is not aware of its pendency, and

(ii) Disclosure of the existence of the records could reasonably be expected to interfere with enforcement proceedings, the agency may, during only such time as that circumstance continues, treat the records as not subject to the requirements of this section.

The effect of this complex classification management system is to divide and subdivide the information universe (Figure 4-3). Individuals may be

Figure 4-3

Compartmentation Scheme to Subdivide Information Universe.

Classification Management

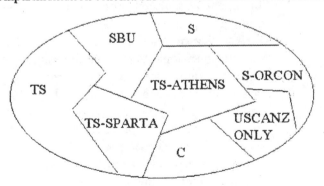

Compartmentation schema subdivide the information universe

Compartmentation is easier to apply (cheaper) than need to know.
In general, greater granularity provides greater protection, but costs more

5 October 1999   COMSEC Solutions,LLC

granted access to certain categories of information but not to other categories. An individual may, for example, have been granted access to material designated TOP SECRET (SPARTA) but not to material designated TOP SECRET (ATHENS), even though both categories of information fall within the overall classification as TOP SECRET. Each individual may be given access to those compartments to which he or she needs in order to accomplish the task or tasks he or she has been assigned.

In the logical extreme, the information universe could be so subdivided that individuals would be given access to exactly that body of information needed to accomplish their job, but not to any information they did not need. Such a classification management scheme would implement the *principle of least privilege*, which many organizations, including the government, claim as their policy.

If the principle of least privilege is the wish of policy organization to implement, why not just do so from the start? In fact, implementing such a policy in its purest form would be difficult, if not impossible, and would certainly cost much more than a compartmentation system. Imagine having to mark and control each document, or each paragraph or sentence, to permit access to those who need them and deny access to those who do not. The continually expanding role of computers in creating, storing, processing, and communicating information makes it barely possible to begin to visualize how such a decision might be made to work mechanically. What about all of the classification management and declassification decisions that would have to be made to apply such a system, even if one could be built?

Much easier and much more economical would be to implement a system that approximates the desired policy by compartmenting information and giving individuals access to compartments, rather than by tailoring each document, photograph, or sound file to every individual that might need access to some portion of it. Such an approach comports well with a risk management, as opposed to a risk avoidance approach to security decisions. Some individuals may receive more access than they need, but significant savings are realized. If the risk of any compartmentation scheme is deemed to be too high, the overall risk can be lowered by creating additional compartments. This would more closely approximate the principle of least privilege but increase the cost due to the additional security that would be required to enforce the more complex system.

Non-government organizations usually have much less complex classification management systems. Many organizations separate information into only two categories: public information, which requires no protection and usually is not marked or labeled, and sensitive information, which requires some degree of protection of integrity, availability, or confidentiality. Sensitive information may be designated as such by any of a variety of markings or labels: COMPANY PRIVATE, PROPRIETARY or COMPANY PROPRIETARY, INTERNAL USE ONLY, and so forth. More complex systems may differentiate privileged information with labels like LEGAL DEPARTMENT ONLY, or information that, if known to competitors, could cost a company business, may be marked COMPETITION-SENSITIVE. In any event, only the largest companies can afford the security policies, practices, and procedures as complex as those used by government to protect information assets.

Thus far, we have considered primarily the dimension of confidentiality. The Computer Security Act includes integrity and availability in its definition of sensitive information. In a complete classification management process, the aggregate to be classified should be labeled as to the degree to which confidentiality, integrity, or availability are to be protected. Additional categories are needed for each of these characteristics. Integrity protection categories might be designated as CRITICAL if severe consequences would be expected to result from unauthorized modification, as in the case of an organization's financial, personnel, or inventory records or its records of orders received and filled. Items not deemed to require integrity protection would not be marked or would be labeled NONCRITICAL. A more complex system would differentiate between the most critical items and less critical items with different markings.

Specifying how soon an item must be delivered upon request often designates availability requirements. Items where lives or highly valuable property are at stake, or where the national security is threatened, might be needed in seconds, or at most, minutes, when requested.

Policy Must Be Reasonable—CIA Case for Invisible Ink

Deciding whether a classified document should remain classified involves a balancing of many of the same factors that were taken into consideration during the initial classification determination. Often those challenging classification determinations attempt to insert a sense of reasonableness into the process, and for good reason. Consider just a few of the millions of classification decisions issued by officials within the federal government over the last few decades:

- The U.S. Army classifying a study on archery under the heading "silent, flashless weapons."[6]

- The U.S. Navy classifying a report on sharks that was derived entirely from publicly available sources, purportedly to keep the documents from falling into the possession of the Soviet Navy, but more likely to keep the information from discouraging recruitment.[7]

- The Joint Chiefs' classifying as "TOP SECRET" a report that criticized the gross abuses of secrecy classification at all levels in the military.[8]

- The Pentagon adamantly refusing to publish information that acknowledged that NASA had sent monkeys into space, despite the fact that the Washington Zoo had already identified its monkeys with a plaque praising their participation in rocket experiments in the U.S. space program. The *Washington Post* reported that the Pentagon explained it was trying to preserve the U.S. relationship with India, where certain obscure sects still practiced "monkey worship."[9]

- The classifying of White House menus as "Top Secret."[10]

- Weather reports produced by an aid to General Eisenhower during World War II still being classified even 30 years after the fact.[11]

- Journalist and former hostage Terry Anderson being denied access to files on his capture and release. After months of waiting for a response to his requests, he did finally receive copies of his own press clips, which had been kept in classified government files.[12]

A notion of reasonableness, however, may extend beyond a specific document. One particular area where reasonableness may, or at least some may argue should always, arise is regarding the effect, if any, the passage of time should have on the classification of a document. Section 3.4 of the current Executive Order in place, E.O. 12958, provides for the automatic declassification of all "classified information contained in records that (1) are more than 25 years old, and (2) have been determined to have permanent historical value under title 44, United States Code...whether or not the records have been reviewed." Of course, even that mandate has exemptions for a federal agency to assert in order to maintain classification on historic documents. But how far should the process extend? Should documents dating back 50, 75, or even 100 years still be classified, regardless of the subject matter? Does reasonableness play a factor in classification determinations, at least with respect to historic documents of over 25 years? It is a question that is still being debated within the legal system.

As of this writing, The James Madison Project, a Washington, D.C. nonprofit organization dedicated to reducing secrecy, was locked in a legal battle with the National Archives & Records Administration and the Central Intelligence Agency (CIA) over whether classified records nearly one century old should be publicly released. The dispute in The James Madison Project v. National Archives & Research Administration surrounds the six oldest classified documents, all of which date back to 1917 to 1918, in the possession of the National Archives. Shortly into the litigation, the CIA informed the U.S. District for the District of Columbia that it was asserting classification authority over the documents.[13]

Exactly what interest could the CIA, an organization created in 1947, have in documents written 30 years before it existed? The subject matter of the documents was revealed to pertain to formulas for the use and detection of invisible ink, an ancient writing technique that dates back nearly 2000 years and that saw use in the Revolutionary War, and World Wars I and II. The CIA asserted "because the information in these documents is instrumental to the CIA's statutory obligation to collect intelligence through appropriate means, which includes the use of covert communication through secret writing methods and detection...classification determinations regarding these documents fall within the purview of the CIA as the agency having the most interest in the subject matter of the information, since the information pertains to intelligence methods currently employed by the CIA."[14]

But more than just an issue of classification authority exists in this case. A much broader and important question arises: Does the passage of time, here more than eight decades, eliminate or lessen the need for secrecy? Is there an overzealous penchant for government agencies to classify information and keep it as such? The case of the invisible ink documents seeks to address a fundamental problem with the classification system currently in use. "Excessive secrecy has significant consequences for the national interest when, as a result, policymakers are not fully informed, government is not held accountable for its actions, and the public cannot engage in informed debate. This remains a dangerous world; some secrecy is vital to save lives, bring miscreants to justice, protect national security, and engage in effective diplomacy. Yet, as Justice Potter Stewart noted in his opinion in the Pentagon Papers case, *when everything is secret, nothing is secret.*"[15]

According to court papers filed by the government, it believes that release of the information would make the "CIA's covert communications systems more vulnerable to detection and compromise by hostile intelligence services or terrorist organizations; facilitate an adversary's development of more sophisticated secret writing techniques; and reveal the CIA's current detection methods of secret writing techniques or other forms of covert communications, prompting our adversaries to undertake countermeasures and/or denial programs to undermine U.S. intelligence-collection efforts." The James Madison Project, however, introduced evidence that the information in question, which primarily encompassed invisible ink formulas in use at the time by the German government but which had been broken by the United States' World War I allies, was not only outdated but had been revealed in various books and articles and through Internet Web sites over the years.

The CIA, however, argued that "[t]his information, along with similar information from the pre-World War II era, constitutes the basis of the CIA's and by extension, the U.S. government's knowledge of secret writing inks and techniques of secret writing detection."[16] The logical extension of this reasoning is that rudimentary information concerning gunpowder must remain classified, since gunpowder use is an essential element of modern military field equipment.

In trying to convince the federal court that reasonableness required disclosure of the six historic documents, The James Madison Project additionally argued that the government's position stood on a dangerous precipice for which the policy implications were frightening. Under such a regime, any technique, even the most innocuous and childlike, could be classified as vital to national security at the whim of an intelligence agency. By way of example, a document on which correction fluid was utilized could be labeled as demonstrative of a method of "secret writing" and stamped as "TOP SECRET." CIA officials could classify a Morse code chart as "CONFIDENTIAL" merely because a planned CIA outdoor retreat intended to demonstrate its use in the field. Native American tribes could be warned not to use smoke signals as a means of communication because the CIA has classified the technique.

Whether the passage of time will become a factor in declassification decisions, either by application of a reasonableness standard or by requirement of law, is still a matter left to be decided.

Policy Must be Balanced and Security-Aware—"Uncle Sam Has All the Numbers"

In 1996, Congress passed the Welfare Law,[17] which overhauled the welfare system. It called for all employers to immediately file reports on every person they hire and then file quarterly reports of the wages of each worker. States must regularly report all people seeking unemployment benefits and all child-support cases. One of the systems put in place by this law was a vast computerized data-monitoring system that includes names, addresses, Social Security numbers, and wages of nearly every working adult in the United States.

The federal government has long gathered personal information for specific reasons, such as collecting taxes. The database, housed at the Social Security Administration, is scheduled to be expanded in an aggressive effort to track down parents who owe child support.

Since July 1999, large banks and other financial institutions have been required to search for data about delinquent parents by name on behalf of the government. Details about bank accounts, money market mutual funds, and other holdings of parents must be disclosed. The magic number, the Social Security number, comes into play when licenses—driver, hunting and fishing, professional, and so on—are issued. Delinquents are identified and licenses are revoked.

What is disturbing about this database is: 1). Never before have federal officials had such legal authority and technological ability to locate so many Americans found to be delinquent parents—or so much potential to keep tabs on Americans accused of nothing (privacy concern) and 2). What an extraordinarily juicy target for hackers (security policy concern). Not since the three major credit reporting agencies intermingled their databases has the target been so interesting to the bad guys.

Lawmakers, federal agencies, and the White House have made moves to expand this "central file on every American" to include identification of fraud by government contractors, improving the efficiency of government and pinpointing debtors, such as students who default on government loans.

The authors address the security concern. Government officials have declared that the system is safe, accurate, and discrete; they also say it is secure.[18] Among reported safeguards is verification of the Social Security number, yet in 1998, the Social Security Administration (SSA) opened up its own Web site only to shut it down three weeks later for security issues relating to Social Security numbers and identification of persons requesting information.

An examination of the program by the General Accounting Office (GAO) shows that officials have downplayed and overlooked a variety of security concerns in working to meet congressional deadlines. The GAO report also revealed that the computer system that houses most of the data has known weaknesses in the security of its automated information systems.[19]

A spokesman for the Americans for Children and Families (ACF) stated, "We're setting aside some of the courtesies in order to accomplish what we're trying to do," and described the network as an "unprecedented, vast amount of information that is updated constantly."[20]

Officials have not publicized their ability to freeze or seize financial assets based on the implementation. The system is a giant electronic information scoop containing names, Social Security numbers, wages, unemployment insurance (UI) recipients, and bank accounts, just to name a few of the data fields. Congress explicitly restricted access to the database to: 1). Social Security Administration (SSA) to verify unemployment reports, 2). U.S. Treasury Department to cross-reference tax deduction claims, and 3). Researchers, who *supposedly* gain access only to anonymous data.

Civil liberties activists are rightfully concerned about the new standard for data surveillance, which uses computers to cross-reference millions of personal records about Americans. In addition to the GAO issues raised about security, the *systems in a dozen states have not been certified by federal officials as meeting security guidelines*. In the authors' opinion, there are at least a dozen holes that a prepared and funded hacker can enter. It could be considered to be a Y2K present.

Wade Horn, a former official in the ACF, agrees with the need to improve the enforcement of child-support requirements. But he is most concerned about the right balance between government action, technical security, and privacy.[21]

OPSEC—Information Security Policy in Practice

The previous sections discussed information security policy and classification management from a broad perspective. Numerous lessons can be learned from the invisible ink case—lest we become too entrenched or paranoid in our thinking. But there is more. The manager of security knows that behind the scenes is a practical side (perhaps a darker side) to implementing information security policy.

Operations security (OPSEC) is the process of protecting critical business information by concealing or changing the indicators that disclose that information. It evolves from risk assessment. Its scope depends on each element of the risk assessment. In our opinion, OPSEC is a cost-effective way to protect sensitive information or government.

Reference to the Economic Act of 1996 reveals that sensitive information can take on many forms:

> All forms and types of financial, business, scientific, technical, economic, or engineering information, including data, plans, tools, mechanisms, compounds, formulas, designs, prototypes, processes, procedures, programs, codes, or commercial strategies, whether tangible or intangible, and however stored, compiled, or memorialized, if the owner has taken reasonable measures to keep such information confidential; and the information derives independent economic value, actual or potential, from not being generally known to, and not being readily ascertainable, acquired, or developed by legal means by the public."

Sensitive information means proprietary economic information, critical business or government information, trade secrets, or sensitive information. The terms are essentially interchangeable.

Risk assessment was discussed in Chapter 3. From a practical standpoint, it is the process of evaluating assets, identifying threat, vulnerability, and consequences of failure to protect those assets, and recommending improvements to prevent loss. The following list sets forth the process in five stages.[22]

Risk Assessment Process

1. Identification and valuation of assets

2. Identification of the threat

3. Evaluation of vulnerabilities

4. Analysis of impact (cost-benefit analysis)

5. Improvement options

The essence of implementing an effective security policy is the ability to associate a value with each information asset. This way, cost becomes a metric for comparing Steps 4 and 5. The manager will need to compare the impact of losing the asset with the impact of spending money to protect it. Ideally, you buy only the protection you need. To protect your assets, you need a program of loss prevention consisting of counterespionage, OPSEC, and security.

Counterespionage (CE) and *counterintelligence (CI)* are activities designed to identify threats to specific information assets. CE or CI report and place those threats in context with vulnerability. Peter Pitorri, an expert in CE, presents five factors of vulnerability to be considered in Step 3 of the previous list.[23]

The Five Factors of Vulnerability In Order of Priority

1. Visibility (or detectability)
   a. What is the probability that espionage agents or competitor intelligence agents will become aware of this information?
   b. What is the probability that those agents could access the information?

2. Utility
   a. What is the probability that the information will be perceived by agents as useful to their employers?
   b. Would the information satisfy published requirements of a foreign intelligence service?
   c. Would it satisfy a competitor's requirements?

3. Perishability
   a. Is there a date beyond which the information will no longer be useful to the competitor?
   b. Can an espionage agent verify and transmit the information before that date?

4. Exploitability
   a. Can the competitor respond to the information in time, and in a manner detrimental to the owner of the information?
   b. Would additional information be necessary for the competitor to exploit the original information to his or her advantage and to the detriment of the owner?

5. Protectability
   a. Do you have a written policy for protecting trade secrets and proprietary information?
   b. Do you limit dissemination of the information (per the security policy) to a few persons who need to know?
   c. Have those persons signed noncompetitive or nondisclosure agreements?

In private industry there are predictable indicators that spell hostility to a company's management and that can lead to acts of revenge, theft, violence, or industrial espionage. Some of these factors are forced relocation, reduction in force, reorganization, and being passed over for promotion. Feuding within managers, sexual harassment, and sexual and racial discrimination in job assignments can incite hostility among the workforce. OPSEC deals with risk by minimizing exposure to harm. Risk management, then, is a balancing act between risk and objectives or, in not-so-popular lingo, "mission." The profitability of any mission is directly related to protecting its assets. It is not possible to protect everything all the time from every threat. It *is* possible and prudent to strike a balance suggested by the risk assessment process.

The line between industrial espionage and normal competitor intelligence is not easy to delineate. Every savvy firm performs a search for publicly available competitor intelligence. Matrices based on open sources show products, prices, markets, and customer base. The research is conducted (mostly) in public documents. Every espionage agent, counterespionage agent, investigator, academe, and researcher begins with a review of public documents for information in the public domain. The World Wide Web is a particularly good source of information on vendors and suppliers, copyrights and patents, licenses, taxes, brokerage reports, investment and public relations reports, addresses of people and company personnel, joint venture proposals and agreements, annual reports, prospectuses and brochures, conferences, trade shows, symposia, banking relationships, countermeasures software, trends in technology, public information databases, Moody's and Dun and Bradstreet reports, and so forth.

Not all firms would be targets for an infocrime; therefore, quality espionage operations are focused operations. They are managed as a business: well organized, staffed, directed, and controlled. This all costs dollars. Spying (collection) efforts, like any other investment, must show a positive return on investment (ROI).

Firms that compete for government defense contracts and high-tech firms in particular represent potentially lucrative targets. Firms that are global or compete in Asia, the Middle East, or France need to be mindful of paid efforts by foreign intelligence agents. Examples of high-tech and non-high-tech targets taken, in part, from *Counterespionage for American Business* by Peter Pitorri, are given in Table 4-1.[24]

Consider for a moment that the above targets are economic ones. Military commanders know that a country can be brought to its knees by seizing control of its communications and broadcast systems and taking away its radar eyes/sonar ears (especially air defense/naval defense). Any attack on a nuclear or chemical weapons compound could be disastrous. What about our nuclear power stations? Some of us remember the blackout of the eastern seaboard caused by a shutdown of electricity at a nuclear power station near the Canadian border. A similar serious situation could occur if an infocriminal were able to disrupt the public switch networks, air traffic control, a routing bank, or city water supply controls (two prankster teenagers recently did this in a low-tech fashion, compromising the water supply to 100,000 people in a Midwestern city.)[25]

Table 4-1

*High-Tech and
Non-Tech Targets.*

Examples of High-Tech Targets
Aviation control and navigation systems
Motherboard or computer processing chips
Radiation hardening for radio frequency equipment
Ultra low frequency telecommunications
Cryptographic based inventions
Space-based reconnaissance systems
High-energy laser technology and applications
Waste disposal technology—especially chemical or nuclear

Examples of Non-Tech Targets
Bidding data
Bond and stock issue plans
Negotiation strategies
Customer lists
Merger/acquisition plans
City development plans
Personal worth statements
Automobile designs
Cosmetics formulas
Marketing/packaging strategy
Wendy's or McDonald's toy designs
Lingerie/perfume marketing and design plans
Recruiting—sports or key executives
Medical data—especially HIV or mental illness information

Automated information systems and networks are juicy targets. In Table 4-2, Pitorri presents us with some common sense principles policy guidelines for automated information systems (AIS) and, in Table 4-3), and a challenge list of dos and don'ts for the new-millennium problem.[26]

The Pitorri lists give us a feel for what kind of quick-and-dirty lists we

TABLE 4-2

AIS Security
Principles.

1. Information must have a dollar value assigned to it.

2. Information with a high dollar value is a valuable asset and must be protected as such.

3. You have the right and the obligation to protect your valuable information.

4. Information is protected by controlling access to it; this requires physical and logical controls.

5. Automated information must be protected by hardened means of recording all attempts at access.

6. AIS must be resistant to attack.

7. All magnetic media must be kept under control, whether it is in storage or in use.

8. There must be a continuing AIS security education program—mandatory for all employees.

9. Each user of the AIS must have access only to that information to which he or she is specifically entitled, and no more.

10. An AIS connected to a communication link is definitely more vulnerable to compromise than one not so connected.

11. An AIS connected to a communications link must be protected at the link and inside the system. [A firewall may be used to protect the outside of the link.]

12. Each person accessing your information must be held accountable for his or her behavior.

need to generate when we consider an OPSEC plan. Information security has had more than 30 years to mature and provide experience. Information security specialists are concerned with generally accepted controls for protecting information from well-known threats. They have developed and documented *best-practice controls* that contribute to meeting *standards of due care and due diligence*.

Standards of Due Diligence

Standards of due care and due diligence are legal terms that arise in liability and negligence civil and criminal litigation.[27] The T. J. Hooper case was the precedent-setting case in the United States to define due care. T. J. Hooper Tugboat Company lost a liability action for failure to have radio receivers aboard to receive weather reports, a failure that resulted in the foundering of two coal barges off the New Jersey coast in March 1928. The operators of the two tugs were found negligent for failure to anticipate the storm, which was reported by radio. At that time it was a not requirement or duty, statutory or otherwise, to carry radios. The

TABLE 4-3

*Protections for the
New Millennium.*

DO
1. Have a risk analysis conducted.
2. Protect unattended terminals; insist on logouts.
3. Protect your media; lock up all removable media.
4. Backup data on a daily basis.
5. Use an audit and access control.
6. Use physical, information, and personnel security to control access to AIS
7. Protect passwords.
8. Install virus protection. [There have been 53,000 viruses logged since 1983.]
9. Practice security from the perimeter of the AIS and at the entrance to the building—not just the keyboard.
10. Initiate and practice a disaster recovery plan.

DO NOT
11. Share passwords.
12. Permit unattended operation on a local area network or wide area network
13. Allow unescorted visitors into any area where data is keyed or displayed.
14. Send computers out for repair with data files on their hard disks.
15. Assume that your information is protected because it is out of sight.
16. Allow employees to work at the keyboards during non-business hours without supervision and accounting for what they are doing.
17. Allow keyboard access to new hires until a background check is completed.

court found that it was common practice for tugboats and barges to do so. The court stated:

> The standard of seaworthiness is not, however, depending on statutory enactment, or condemned to inertia or rigidity, but changes with advancing knowledge, experience, and the changed appliances of navigation. It is particularly affected by new devices of demonstrated worth, which have become recognized as regular equipment by common usage...The general principle is well established that the standard of due care is predicated on two factors: that a practice has become common among prudent persons,

and that the practice is particularly affected by new devices of demonstrable cost-effectiveness which have become recognized as regular equipment by common usage."[28]

Donn B. Parker, an expert in information security, presents a viable definition for standard of due care for AIS:[29]

The standard of due care principle in information security is achieved when a security control or practice is used, or acknowledged as preferred for use, when it is readily available at reasonable cost or is in regular use by many organizations that take prudent care to protect their information under similar circumstances. In addition, the organizations adopting a security control or practice should seek to verify that it meets these criteria. The justification for having such due care controls and practices should stem from common use and availability and prudent management rather than from the desire for explicit reduction of risk.

The existence of a security policy and mandatory standards in an organization is a due care practice. However, if your organization has not adopted a security policy and standards and does not have a good reason not to do so (before a judge), then you are not meeting a standard of due care and you are potentially liable for damages arising out of actions predicated on your AIS and absence of due care.

A *security control* is the policy, practice, device, or programmed mechanism to avoid or deter, prevent or detect, mitigate, investigate and sanction, transfer, recover, or correct information losses. Controls have the objectives of preserving the availability and utility, integrity and authentication, confidentiality and possession of information.[30] Best-practice controls are well-implemented "baseline" safeguards that meet the due care requirement among representative organizations that are advanced in the protection of their information. A *baseline* is a collection of control objectives selected by expert opinions about common use. Organizations use a baseline to measure security status in meeting a standard of due care. For the interested reader, Parker writes extensively on this subject.[31]

A security review may be used to bring an organization to a level of due care controls and practices. It should include a complete, comprehensive analysis of threats and vulnerabilities or a targeted analysis of specific security issues. To identify current standards of due care controls, selected sources are presented in Table 4-4.

Also refer to the Glossary at the back of this book for definitions of acronyms. The reader is cautioned that there is built-in bias of vendors' product specifications, manuals, advice, and standards.

TABLE 4-4

Selected Sources
for Standards of
Due Care.

ANSI
ISO
FIPS 140-1 Cryptographic Module Standards (all FIPS standards are valuable)
British Standards Institute Code of Practice
CRAMM Database Controls
CobiT: Control objectives for information and related technologies
GASSP
U.S. NIST Common Criteria
U.S. NIST *Computer Security Handbook*
ICSA Guide To Cryptography by Randall K. Nichols (New York: McGraw-Hill, 1998, ISBN: 047166-5).
Computer Security Techniques by Donn B. Parker (U.S. Department of Justice, Bureau of Justice Statistics, 1982).
Information Security Policies Made Easy by Charles Cresson Wood (Sausalito: Baseline Software, Inc. 1995).
CSI *Alert*
MSI Training Institute publications
Vendors' product specifications, manuals, and advice
Trade journals, conferences, exhibitions, and books
ITSEC in Europe and TCSEC (The Orange Book) in the United States
RFCs
IPSEC
Vendor firewall, antivirus, cryptographic, network, and biometric standards. (Available at resource and information pages at www.comsec-solutions.com)
Encyclopedia of Security Management: Techniques and Technology by John J. Fay (Oxford, Great Britain: Butterworth-Heinemann, 1993).
Networking Standards: A Guide to OSI, ISDN, LAN and MAN Standards by William Stallings (Reading, Mass: Addison-Wesley, 1993).
Cryptography and Network Security: Principles and Practice 2d ed. by William Stallings (Upper Saddle River, N.J.: Prentice-Hall, 1999).
Fighting Computer Crime: A New Framework for Protecting Information by Donn B. Parker (New York: Wiley, 1998).
Computer Security Handbook, 3d ed., by Arthur E. Hutt, Seymour Bosworth, and Douglas B. Hoyt (New York: Wiley, 1995).
Secure Electronic Commerce by Warwick Ford and Michael S. Baum (Upper Saddle River, N.J.: Prentice-Hall, 1999).
Applied Cryptography, 2d ed., by Bruce Schneier (New York: Wiley, 1996).
CDMA, Cellular Mobile Communications and Network Security by Man Young Rhee (Upper Saddle River, N.J.: Prentice-Hall, 1998).
Biometrics: Personal Identification in Networked Society by Anil Jain, Ruud Bolle, and Sharath Pankanti, eds. (Norwell, Mass: Kluwer Academic Publishers, 1999).
I-4 and ESF benchmark databases of controls and practices (requires membership)

Wrap-Up

Information security policy is the first and most important step in deterring infocrimes. Policy is the broad guideline that we set in place to organize our security controls. The U.S. government uses classification management to identify and segregate information assets for secure treatment. AIS security policy must be balanced and cost-effective. Two cases were presented that appear to be out of balance with respect to classification management and vulnerability assessments. Security controls implemented within a framework of due diligence and due care standards reduce potential for loss. Sources for standards of due diligence and due care were presented for future study.

Notes

1. Executive Order 12958.
2. Ibid.
3. Ibid.
4. Ibid.
5. Ibid.
6. David Wise, *The Politics of Lying 67* (New York: Random House, 1973).
7. Ibid., 67-68.
8. Sanford J. Ungar, *The Papers & The Papers 219* (New York: Columbia Univ. Press/Morningside Ed., 1989).
9. Wise, 67-68.
10. Ibid., 70.
11. Report of The Commission on Protection on Protecting and Reducing Government Secrecy 52 (GPO, 1997; "Commission").
12. Ibid.
13. Civil Action No. 98-2737 (D.D.C. November 9, 1998; TPJ).
14. Declaration of Teresa Wilcox, the Information Review Officer for the CIA's Directorate of Science and Technology (filed 29 March 1999; "Wilcox Decl.").
15. Commission, at xxi.
16. Wilcox Decl. at ¶14.
17. The Personal Responsibility and Work Opportunity Reconciliation Act of 1996.
18. Robert O'Harrow Jr., "Uncle Sam Has All the Numbers," *Washington Post*, 27 June 1999, http:/www.washingtonpost.com/wp-srv/business/daily/june99/privacy27.htm.
19. Michael Kharfen, Administration for Children and Families quote, O'Harrow, op. cit.
20. O'Harrow.
21. Ibid.
22. Pitorri, Peter, *Counterespionage for American Business* (Oxford, Great Britain: Butterworth-Heinemann, 1998), 36.

23. Ibid, 48.

24. Ibid.

25. Greenbay, Wisconsin; AP story titled "Two Teens Dump 2 Million Gallons," 23 June 1999.

26. Pitorri, op. cit., 79-80.

27. District Court SD New York, 15 October 1931, 53 f(2d) 107.

28. Ibid.

29. Parker, Donn B., *Fighting Computer Crime: A New Framework for Protecting Information* (New York: Wiley, 1998) 284.

30. Ibid.

31. Ibid.

CHAPTER 5

Privacy in a Knowledge-Based Economy

Introduction

The tension between the technology of communications—writing, record keeping, databases, and more—and privacy has fostered a myriad of customs, laws, and technologies. The trade-offs to be considered include not only trust and civil society, but also the future of law, commerce, international competitive structures, and the evolution of the expectation of privacy.

The path from memory to written record[1] is fundamentally the history of communications technology. Around 8000 B.C. simple tokens were in use for keeping numerical records.[2] By 4000 B.C. people were identifying personal property with seals.[3] > By 2500 B.C. both numbers and writing systems were in use, and clay tablets were being used to record property transfers, primarily in trade.[4] From that point, the development of maps and other reference material multiplied, followed closely by generic alphabets.[5] By 450 B.C. the Greeks were communicating over long distances using a combination of five torches to depict each letter of the Greek alphabet.[6] And, in 307 B.C. the library at Alexandria would eventually contain almost 750,000 books.[7]

During these early phases of communications technology development, the information recorded tended to be relatively important—histories of great victories in battle, records of the wealth of kings, histories of the ruling lineage. With the proliferation of the knowledge of the technology involved—alphabets, writing tools, and so on—the ability to record events and items became more widespread. As the information recorded progressed to include records of more-pedestrian events, privacy afforded by the vagaries of memory eroded. This was not without benefit. With records, for example, proving ownership became a process of producing a record rather than producing a series of elders to vouch for ownership legitimacy. The process was neither instantaneous nor without controversy:

> Through the spread of record making the practice of using writing for ordinary business, as distinct from using it solely for solemn religious or royal purposes, became first familiar and then established as a habit. Among the laity, or more specifically among knights and country gentry in the first instance, confidence in written records was neither immediate nor automatic. Trust in writing and understanding of what it could—and could not—achieve developed from growing familiarity with documents."[8]

By the mid-1200s of the current era, record keeping had progressed to the point that the record of milk yields on individual farms became commonplace[9] and "vagrants were expected to carry certificates of good behavior."[10] Clearly the notion of privacy was already being eroded by the requirements of society for records and identity proofs.

Supreme Court Justices Louis Brandeis and Samuel Warren, arguing in favor of a constitutional right to privacy, warned us, "Numerous mechanical devices threaten to make good the prediction that what is whispered in the faucet shall be proclaimed from the housetops."[11] We supply a plethora of personal information when we submit tax returns, see a doctor or lawyer, apply for insurance or a credit card, or do any kind of business. Until the advent of computer systems and networks, the information was relatively secure because it was widely separated on an unwieldy medium—paper. Today the ability of computer systems to gather and store vast amounts of data, and make it readily accessible, threatens everyone's privacy.[12]

Two forces are focusing public attention on privacy and the threat to privacy posed by computer systems and networks: technological advances and the increasing value of information. Improvements in computing price: performance ratios in recent years have led to decentralized open systems with consequent diffusion of control and responsibilities for data collection and management. Simultaneously, the value of information, especially in targeting the marketing of goods and services, has greatly increased. Micromarketing improves the efficiency of marketing distribution channels, and marketing focused tightly on individuals requires, of course, that companies store and share personal information about specific individuals. Technological constraints prior to the spread of computers made micromarketing physically and fiscally infeasible. With today's technology, micromarketing is perfectly viable.[13]

As our culture enters the twenty-first century, both individuals and institutions will have to create rules defining appropriate and inappropriate behavior with regard to collection, use, and dissemination of personal information. This is a daunting challenge and an unenviable task, but one that executives, legislators, and all of us must face.

With the invention of the electronic computer and the subsequent advent of computerized database management systems, the ability to both create and keep records has increased explosively. By the late 1960s, the U.S. government—most notably the IRS and the FBI—had discovered the efficiencies in electronic and cross-linked databases.[14] Concomitantly, the availability of information technology increased exponentially. In 1984, several generations of personal computers were already on the market and the Macintosh made its debut. By the beginning of 1999 personal computers featured between 4 and 10 gigabytes

(GB) of hard disk storage. To provide context, one gigabyte of memory can store about 350,000 pages of information.[15] Terabytes of storage capacity is not uncommon for commercial applications.

The invasion of privacy and public unease followed hand in glove with these developments. The federal government was particularly aggressive in collecting information to make its job easier, to prevent fraud, and to increase the efficiency of government services. As Steven Lubar writes:

> The use of computers by the IRS and the FBI became a hot issue in the 1960s, when it became clear that by using computers, the government could keep track of everyone in the country. To some extent, this had been true since the 1930s, since the Social Security bureaucracy had used thousands of file cabinets and millions of punch cards to keep track of payments and accounts. But with more-advanced computers it became much easier. The debate heated up when the Bureau of the Budget proposed a National Data Center to centralize all of the government's databases. Critics hated the idea, raising objections about privacy, and the proposal was defeated. But government agencies continued to collect information, and more and more of it. People's uneasiness about the power of computers prompted the Privacy Act of 1974, which set safeguards against misuse of federal records and some private sector records.[16]

The private sector was not blind to the possibilities, either, and in short order began trading information as both income-generating sources and as a sort of currency in itself. Steve Lubar writes:

> Mail-order firms, which had always built lists of customers, were quick to adopt the computer to expand their lists. By 1970 there were over 500 million names on mail-order lists, available for rent to anyone who wanted them. Combined with information on income—the IRS began to sell aggregate income statistics in the late 1960s—the lists made it easy to target potential customers. The possibilities for using the computer to make money seemed endless.[17]

The marriage of a variety of new technologies, such as bar codes, optical character recognition, and lasers, assisted in the mass computerization of information—such as item pricing—and in the collection of transaction-specific data. Those trends gave birth to a capability called *data mining*, a technique by which disparate information tidbits are exploited in order to derive knowledge.

Data mining (also known as Knowledge Discovery in Databases—KDD) has been defined as "The nontrivial extraction of implicit, previously unknown, and potentially useful information from data." It uses machine learning, statistical, and visualization techniques to discover and present knowledge in a form that is easily comprehensible to humans.[18]

Information exploitation puts privacy on a whole new track. Instead of being a commodity that was exchanged expressly, in limited ways, for specific good—such as a Social Security check—private information is now extracted from piles and piles of data ore. Information regarding grocery store transactions, credit card transactions, governmental transactions (such as getting a driver's license), and more are gathered together and systematically sifted for patterns and other knowledge. The crumbs of data from a consumer's life are gathered together to re-create the cookie of that life, both in positive knowledge and in negative knowledge. (A "cookie" is an insidious block of ASCII text that a Web server can pass on to user to their Web browser memory. It can be used to track users' movements as they explore Web sites.) In other words, not only can what happened be discerned, but also what did not happen. Soon it will be possible for direct marketers to determine that it has been four years since that consumer purchased underwear. In some consumers' minds, being reminded about such requirements and being offered special deals is a positive aspect of life in the information society. For others it is an ominous threat of a Big Brother society reminiscent of George Orwell's novel *1984*. Thus it is that the question of privacy becomes a technological issue worthy of analysis.

Privacy: Challenging Expectations

In order to understand the privacy issues, it is important to understand how the information that feeds the processes is transmitted from person to collector. There are two means of information collection. First, there is the express transmission of personal information from someone to a collector. This expressly transmitted information can be volunteered and/or compelled. Second, there is the collection and aggregation of information not expressly conveyed from a person to a collector.[19]

Volunteering information can have benefits. A growing program is that of grocery store "club cards," which track purchases and provide selected discounts based on buying frequency, volume, and patterns. As Michael Sippey writes:

> The checkout clerk finishes bagging my Oreos, my Fresca, my two containers of Dannon yogurt, and my two boxes of Honey Nut Cheerios. I pay cash,

and let her scan my Safeway Club Card. She makes change, rips the receipt from the register, and scans her eyes down its length for a split second. "Thank you, Mr. Sippey." The Club Card enables Safeway to gather billions of lines of purchase history on their millions of customers in their 1059 stores in the U.S. and Canada. In return, they give away a few dollars here, a few dollars there...just enough to keep people using it. My second box of Cheerios was free, and the Oreos were $1.50 off.[20]

Information can be expressly conveyed somewhat reluctantly, such as in filling out warranty cards for newly purchased products. While legally the warranty is in effect whether or not the card is filled out and mailed back, some consumer perceptions are that the purchaser is at risk if the information is not provided.[21] This is an example of compelled express transmission.

An example of collecting and aggregating data not expressly conveyed is using cookies to collect information on Web browsing patterns. As Christina Sarris writes:

> Cookies allow advertisers to track a user's activities at Web sites and trace the information directly back to the user's computer. Another aspect of cookies enables customers to order from individual Web sites and to store information at each site for repeated use without reentry.[22]

When you are considering privacy concerns, there are three problem areas. First is the collection of information itself. Information has intrinsic value, so more of it is being collected. Improved storage and retrieval technologies enable that trend locally and globally. Furthermore, data collection can sneak in as a consequence of other technology applications, such as bar code scanners in grocery stores.

A second problem area is databases of databases. Automated interpolative capabilities enable diverse databases to share information—drivers license records, grocery store records, marriage records, and credit records can all be combined, with the synergistic result being much more insight into any one person's life than that person may have thought possible. Michael Sippey writes:

> Aggregate level statistics could be sold to neighboring (but non-competing) retailers, so that they too can accurately predict their customers' purchase patterns. Individual level statistics (what food you bought last week) could be sold to direct marketers, couponers, publishers...or even health insurance companies. In the one to one future, your insurance premiums could be adjusted on a near-real-time basis based on your recent food purchase patterns. Buy a steak and sour cream, your premium goes up. Buy bran

cereal and nonfat milk, and your premium goes down. And given the appropriate networked calendar software, they could even schedule you for an appointment with your managed care specialist should your purchases of foods with high levels of saturated fats reach a critical level.[23]

Combining data into data warehouses and data marts results in supercollections of data. Data mining techniques, the third problem area, make that data useable. The use of statistical measures to look for patterns and relationships in diverse data contributes to an unprecedented invasion of privacy that is persistent and lasting beyond not only the specific transaction but also persistent and lasting beyond lifetimes and relationships. As David Cole writes:

> ...though Safeway officials don't sell lists of consumers to manufacturers, they do charge them 5.5 cents per consumer to place coupons of special promotions that reach the kinds of people most likely to respond. For example, a purchaser of generic tomato soup may be handed or mailed a coupon for brand-name tomato soup. As coupon use becomes part of customers' records, Safeway can verify whether the coupon was used or not.[24]

The Good, the Bad, the Ugly

Who uses data mining and data warehouses? And what are they used for? As David Cole writes:

> The USAA insurance company keeps a data warehouse of customer information and uses data mining to predict what kinds of products people will need at specific times in their lives. Southern California Gas merges billing data with credit information and U.S. Census Bureau data in a warehouse, where mining techniques determine how customers would respond to various billing plans. Direct mail now receives response rates of 7 to 11 percent. First USA, MBNA, Advanta, and Capital One banks use data mining techniques to build predictive models showing how people will use credit cards. They send direct mail to those most likely to respond to balance-transfer promotions.[25]

Using all this derived information is good business. It augments revenue streams, it makes selling more efficient and effective, and it reduces waste. All of that contributes to increased productivity and profitability. When one company starts exploiting these capabilities, other competing companies that compete are forced to do so as well to remain competitive. The result is an avalanche of privacy invasion.

Sometimes this information is used for less than honorable purposes. In *Salon* magazine, Jennifer Vogel writes:

> A recent magazine article tells how detailed shopping records were used against a shopper. When Robert Rivera signed up for a Von's supermarket card, he had no idea that detailed records of his shopping habits would one day be used against him. But that's exactly what happened. Rivera was shopping at a Los Angeles Von's store two years ago when he slipped on a slick of spilled yogurt, causing him to fall and shatter his kneecap. Unable to drive, let alone work, he sued the store for damages. 59-year-old Rivera recalls that during the negotiations a mediator played hardball in encouraging him to settle. As Rivera tells it, the mediator indicated that the store had accessed his shopping records, found evidence that he bought a lot of liquor, and advised him that they would use this information against him in court.[26]

Other times, information assumed to be protected is transferred with neither knowledge nor consent of the customer:

> ...Maryland-based Giant Food Inc. was caught earlier this year providing its customers' prescription purchasing information—medical records—to marketers.[27]

Further, all this aggregation of data is primarily tied to two classes of people: those who are dependent upon government aid, such as food stamp recipients, and those who spend money in the consumer society. Those who are able to disappear through the cracks are those who an information society would most want information tracked on—criminals. In the *Washington Post*, Cheryl Thompson writes:

> Sixty percent of the 376 District inmates recorded as walkaways from halfway houses during a recent three-month period were awaiting trial, assigned there by judges or hearing commissioners. And at least 83 of those 226 pretrial inmates who absconded—some more than once—were re-arrested on new charges, including manslaughter and armed robbery.[28]

The Department of Justice has provided testimony to the Federal Trade Commission on the risks involved:

> In the absence of incentives to the contrary, collection, compilation, sale, and use of computerized data bases that provide sensitive consumer identifying information will likely proliferate with the rise of electronic commerce and other cyberspace activity. This increase would be driven both on the supply side and on the demand side of the market. Because electronic

commerce is conducted on computers, the supply of consumer identifying information stored on computers in an easily accessible format will increase as use of electronic commerce increases.[29]

The demand for this information is likely to be potent because of its marketing value for those companies who collect it, both for evaluation of the preferences of particular customers and for estimating the appeal of particular products and services. Other companies who would use it for similar purposes will also seek this information. In fact, as face-to-face interactions decrease, companies will increasingly rely on such information to "profile" market segments. Again, from the Department of Justice:

> The proliferation of these computerized databases will simplify the perpetration of many kinds of fraud, including identity fraud. The [U.S.] Department [of Justice] is concerned about this potential."[30]

Furthermore, as Joseph Reidenberg and Paul Schwartz write in *Data Privacy Law*:

> These issues are complicated by the fact that the concept of privacy and expectations of privacy transcend national borders. On October 24, 1995, the European Union's "Directive on the Protection of Individuals with Regard to the Processing of Personal Data and on the Free Movement of Such Data" was enacted. Because the Directive prohibits international transmission of personal data to countries which do not adequately protect such personal information, and because data privacy law in the United States is spotty at best, the flow of important information from Europe to the United States may be affected. For example, transfer of employee data within multinational corporations or transmission of personal data for marketing purposes may be prohibited. Since intensive trade relationships and economic connections between Europe and the United States have led to growing transfers of personal information, and because of widely debated concerns about misuse of personal data in the United States, "adequacy" is a crucial test. Article 25 of the Directive does not require equivalent levels of protection but asks for adequate regulation as judged by criteria as varied as statutes, court decisions and professional rules. Article 26 contains a long list of exceptions including "unambiguous consent" of the individual concerned or the fact that the data are "necessary for the performance of the contract."[31]

The United States has approached the issue in a fashion very different from the European Union. American laws usually focus on controlling governmental invasions of privacy and often ignore the private sector. In Europe, "data protection" comprises a system of legal rules concerning collection and use of personal information, while in the United States "data protection" refers to intellectual property protection or computer and network security. Under American regulatory philosophy, comprehensive laws are rare. Policies concerning personal privacy are common, but legal rights to privacy are few.[32] Within the legal framework, fair information practice regulations are targeted narrowly, usually protecting only a single activity like video rentals. Issues of collection, storage, use, and disclosure may not be addressed. In the private sector, some trade associations have developed fair information practice guidelines, and a few companies have established policies and practices that offer supplementary protection. However, the history of self-regulation in the area of privacy protection has been disappointing. Most companies in the United States do not have internal data protection policies, and those that do often experience implementation difficulties.[33]

Identity theft, invasion of personal privacy, the ability to track citizen activity at ever-increasing levels of detail, and the creation of virtual twins for marketing and behavior control purposes are all specters raised by the ever-increasing technology of communications. Societal elements from the Department of Justice to a grass roots movement in New Mexico called "No Cards" are weighing in on the debate. Clearly it is a matter of some import.

Goal

The following analysis will examine the various points of view of the stakeholders, identify the critical issues, propose alternatives, and derive conclusions.

Framing the Analysis

There are several competing viewpoints with regard to privacy issues. First, there is the viewpoint of business, which augments its service offerings and increases productivity through use of personal information. Second, there is the viewpoint of government, which is bifurcated between being compelled to protect citizen interests through such legislation as the Privacy Act of 1974 and desiring to increase efficiency and effectiveness of government services through aggregation of personal information. Third, there is the viewpoint of political activists who see in the privacy question a range of possibilities, depending on their particular belief system, from the benefit of being able to identify subversives to the specter of having Big Brother dictate behavior patterns. Finally, there is the viewpoint of the private citizen who is torn between wanting the economic benefits that flow from increased business and governmental efficiencies and wanting to live a private life free from prying eyes. All in all, it is a very tough issue to consider.

Assumptions

The assumptions underlying this analysis include the following:

- Information will retain its value.
- Trading, renting, and selling information will continue.
- Computer systems and data storage devices will continue to grow in capacity.
- Data mining techniques will continue to be refined and grow more powerful.
- People will continue to value privacy.

Critical Issues

While government, corporations, and computer scientists have been going gangbusters at figuring out how to make increasing use of the information at their disposal, other groups have been raising critical issues for discussion.

Benefits of Data Aggregation

There are nontrivial benefits associated with aggregating data and mining it for knowledge. This is a critical issue in terms of the competitiveness of corporations in the information age. The benefits accrue to the corporation, in terms of increased revenue and/or productivity, and to the consumer, in terms of savings on products.

Data Ownership

One of the most important issues raised is: Who owns your descriptive data? From your DNA to your consumption profile, the aggregated data describes who you are. There are those who say that this information should belong to the individual, not to those who have philosophically ripped that descriptive data from the individual in bits and bytes. There are others who say "nonsense" to that claim, arguing that ownership of information belongs to the person who develops or aggregates it. There are two aspects to the data ownership issue: first, who owns the primary data that is collected from or about the individual, and second, who owns the analyzed data that describes an individual but is developed from multiple sources?

A "Right" to Privacy

Another critical issue is: How much privacy is a basic human right? Note that the issue is not worded as to whether privacy is a basic human right, but how much privacy. This issue is colored by cultural and societal concerns as well, and can be characterized at a high level as being absolute, moderate, or nonexistent.

Enforcement

A fourth critical issue is: Assuming a standard of privacy can be agreed upon, how can it be enforced? In order to enforce any standard, proof of violation of the standard is necessary. When the violation is committed through data aggregation, a primary way to determine the fact of violation would be to aggregate supporting data in order to create a profile of abuse. The only other way that comes to mind is mandatory review of data holdings, which would require a whole new bureaucracy—hardly a popular alternative. It seems ludicrous to pass legislation mandating protection of privacy, with the only means of enforcing such laws an invasion of privacy from enforcement authorities. The range of options for this issue can be summarized as no enforcement, self-enforcement, violation reporting, and aggressive enforcement.

Summary of Factors

The factors that devolve from these issues are as follows:

- *Benefits* Increased revenue for the corporation, increased productivity, economic benefits to the consumer
- *Ownership* Primary data ownership, secondary data ownership
- *Rights* Absolute, moderate, or nonexistent
- *Enforcement* No enforcement, self-enforcement, violation reporting, and aggressive enforcement

Alternatives and Stakeholders

When considering the future of privacy and personal information, there are many different alternatives that may be considered. However, a risk exists of overly complicating the analysis so that it becomes impossible to draw conclusions. Because of that, the alternatives considered in this analysis are simplistic in nature. Despite that characteristic, they serve the purpose of broadening the analysis so that the finding can reflect the various constituencies and impacts.

Alternatives

There are three basic alternatives that are available for consideration. These are as follows:

1. *Laissez-faire* and let the buyer beware. This alternative is essentially what exists in the U.S. today.
2. Legislate *protection* from privacy intrusions and some sort of enforcement mechanism.
3. Legislate individual *ownership rights* of people to information that describes their person, personality, or other attributes.

Stakeholders

The stakeholders can be characterized as consumers, corporations, criminals, and government.

■ Consumers are faced with trading information for lower prices and higher efficiencies.

■ Corporations use information to make processes more productive and to increase revenue streams.

■ Government also uses information to make processes more productive and to increase revenue streams, but must also protect citizens from crimes, such as identity theft and fraud.

■ Criminals use information to perpetrate crimes, primarily economic in nature.

Analysis

To perform the analysis, the factors derived from the issues were considered in regard to both the alternatives available and with regard to the stakeholders.

Alternatives Analysis

In the following charts, the three alternatives are identified as A1, A2, and A3. A1 represents *Laissez-faire and let the buyer beware*, A2 represents *legislate protection*, and A3 represents *legislate individual ownership rights*. These charts show the authors' best judgments about how much each alternative supports the factors listed. For each chart, the value 10 reflects the best score—showing either full support or best alignment. The value 1 reflects the other side of the scale—showing least support.

Table 5-1 apportions the factors associated with benefits. The first alternative, A1, supports the three factors more than the other alterna-

TABLE 5-1

Benefits Factors.

	Benefits		
	Revenue	Productivity	Economic
Laissez-faire	10	10	8
Legislate protection	5	5	7
Legislate individual ownership rights	1	1	6

tives, although the support cannot be said to be absolute with regard to economic benefits to the consumer. This is because there are economic benefits to the consumer to be realized from the other alternatives, particularly in terms of gain reflected in renting personal information, such as genetic code to researchers. Because of the restrictions implied in A2 and A3, they are scored lower in terms of revenue and productivity.

Table 5-2 assigns the factors associated with ownership. The third alternative is designed to support ownership interests, so it clearly scores higher with this factor. A2 includes protections, so it is graded higher than A1 for this factor.

TABLE 5-2

Ownership Factors.

	Ownership	
	Primary	Secondary
Laissez-faire	1	1
Legislate protection	5	3
Legislate individual ownership rights	10	10

Table 5-3 assembles the factors associated with rights. For the case of no rights, any alternative will do, so each of them scored high in that factor. However, both A2 and A3 support the concept of rights much more than A1, although that support is subject to enforceability.

TABLE 5-3

Rights Factors.

	Rights		
	Absolute	Moderate	None
Laissez-faire	1	1	10
Legislate protection	8	8	10
Legislate individual ownership rights	8	8	10

Table 5-4 gives the factors associated with enforcement. Even with no enforcement per se, the alternatives A2 and A3 support the concept of enforcement more than A1. Similarly, with increasing levels of enforcement, up to aggressive, all alternatives become supportive, although for different reasons: A1 because it includes the capabilities, technologies, and data required to make aggressive enforcement work; A2 and A3 support it due to legislative frameworks.

TABLE 5-4

Enforcement Factors.

	Enforcement			
	None	Self	Violation	Aggressive
Laissez-faire	1	4	6	9
Legislate protection	5	5	8	9
Legislate individual ownership rights	5	5	8	9

The unweighted data (Table 5-5), when combined, reveals this information. Clearly, the third alternative scores highest in aggregate. However, that is due to the fact that each of the elements is looked at on an equal footing. In the next section, based on the authors experience and research, a sensitivity analysis is performed to give context to the fact that factors are almost never equally weighted in real life.

TABLE 5-5

	Unweighted Data				
	Benefits	Ownership	Rights	Enforcement	Roll-up
Laissez-faire	9.3	1.0	4.0	5.0	4.8
Legislate protection	5.7	4.0	8.7	6.8	6.3
Legislate individual ownership rights	2.7	10.0	8.7	6.8	7.0

Factors Sensitivity Analysis

Given that there is a potential for some of the issues to be more important than others, the next step in performing the analysis was to look at sensitivities in weighting. What would the results look like if benefits were the only issue that mattered? What if some combination of benefits and ownership mattered? These are the questions that are addressed by a sensitivity analysis. In this analysis, weights were assigned to the elements before rolling them into a combined score for each of the alternatives (see Table 5-6).

The different weights were used to calculate roll-up scores for each of the alternatives (see Table 5-7) and then the results graphed, as shown in Figure 5-1. The graph follows the table. As can be seen clearly on the chart, it really does matter what weighting scheme is used.

As can be seen by these plots, the alternatives are indeed sensitive to weightings, particularly in terms of benefits and rights. These two factors (benefits and rights) seem to be the driving concerns in understanding the trade space. Enforcement does not appear to be as sensitive to the weightings.

TABLE 5-6

Alternatives.

	Benefits	Ownership	Rights	Enforcement
All Enforcement	0%	0%	0%	100%
All Rights	0%		100%	
All Own	0%	100%		
All Benefits	100%			
75% Benefits, 25% Own	75%	25%		
75% Benefits, 25% Rights	75%		25%	
75% Benefits, 25% Enforcement	75%			25%
50% Benefits, 50% Own	50%	50%		
50% Benefits, 50% Rights	50%		50%	
50% Benefits, 50% Enforcement	50%			50%
50% Benefits, 25% Own, Rights	50%	25%	25%	
50% Benefits, 25% Rights, Enforcement	50%		25%	25%
50% Own, 50% Rights		50%	50%	
50% Own, 50% Enforcement		50%		50%
50% Own, 25% Benefits, Rights	25%	50%	25%	
50% Own, 25% Rights, Enforcement		50%	25%	25%
50% Rights, 50% Enforcement			50%	50%
50% Rights, 25% Own, Enforcement		25%	50%	25%
50% Rights, 25% Benefits, Enforcement	25%		50%	25%
50% Enforcement, 25% Benefits, Own	25%	25%		50%
50% Enforcement, 25% Own, Rights		25%	25%	50%

TABLE 5-7

Roll-Up Scores.

	Laissez-faire	Legislate protection	Legislate individual ownership rights
All Enforcement	5.00	6.75	6.75
All Rights	4.00	8.67	8.67
All Own	1.00	4.00	10.00
All Benefits	9.33	5.67	2.67
75% Benefits, 25% Own	7.25	5.25	4.50
75% Benefits, 25% Rights	8.00	6.42	4.17
75% Benefits, 25% Enforcement	8.25	5.94	3.69
50% Benefits, 50% Own	5.17	4.83	6.33
50% Benefits, 50% Rights	6.67	7.17	5.67
50% Benefits, 50% Enforcement	7.17	6.21	4.71
50% Benefits, 25% Own, Rights	5.92	6.00	6.00
50% Benefits, 25% Rights, Enforcement	6.92	6.69	5.19
50% Own, 50% Rights	2.50	6.33	9.33
50% Own, 50% Enforcement	3.00	5.38	8.38
50% Own, 25% Benefits, Rights	3.83	5.58	7.83
50% Own, 25% Rights, Enforcement	2.75	5.58	8.85
50% Rights, 50% Enforcement	4.50	7.71	7.71
50% Rights, 25% Own, Enforcement	3.50	7.02	8.52
50% Rights, 25% Benefits, Enforcement	5.58	7.44	6.69
50% Enforcement, 25% Benefits, Own	5.08	5.79	6.54
50% Enforcement, 25% Own, Rights	3.75	6.54	8.04

Stakeholders Analysis

Having performed an analysis of the issues and element factors against each alternative, the next step is to look at each stakeholder and how the issues affect each of them. This will allow extrapolations to be made regarding the attractiveness of each alternative. The stakeholders considered in this analysis are the following:

- Consumers
- Corporations

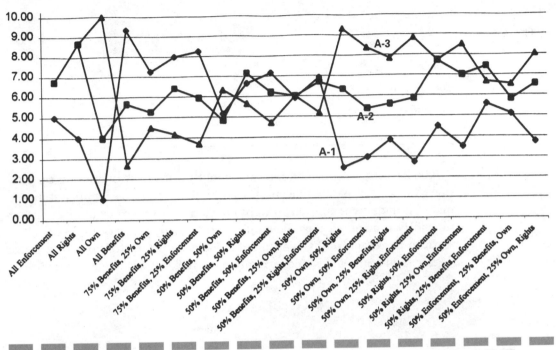

Figure 5-1 The results have been plotted on a graph to show the trends and relative positions more clearly.

- Governments
- Criminals

The following charts show the data regarding how strongly each stakeholder feels about each factor. In this series of charts (and in Figure 5-1), the value 10 represents very strong feelings or very high interest, while 1 reflects the converse of negligible interest or few, if any, feelings about the factor.

In terms of benefits, it is clear from Table 5-8 that corporations are by far the most interested in this factor. Corporations are keenly interested in competitive factors, including productivity, and governments are as well, to a somewhat lesser degree. Productivity and economic strength are critical aspects to the health of a nation. Consumers are more interested in economic benefits to themselves. Criminals are interested in being able to exploit some aspect, such as pervasive data availability, to their own benefit. As such, they are less interested in corporate advantages and more interested in consumer advantages.

TABLE 5-8

Benefits Factors.

| | Benefits | | |
	Revenue	Productivity	Economic
Consumers	3	3	9
Corporations	10	10	6
Governments	8	10	7
Criminals	1	1	9

The concern with ownership falls equally with consumers and corporations, but for competing reasons. Corporations would lose significant investments if data ownership laws were enacted; consumers would benefit significantly if ownership of their information, both primary and secondary, were to be recognized. Governments would be interested, but to a lesser degree, and criminals wouldn't really pay much attention (see Table 5-9).

TABLE 5-9

Ownership Factors.

| | Ownership | |
	Primary	Secondary
Consumers	10	10
Corporations	10	10
Governments	7	5
Criminals	1	1

Rights affect consumers the most, whether they have absolute rights or no rights at all. Governments are concerned with this issue as well, particularly in terms of the government's philosophy of governing. Criminals would be most interested in the situation of nonexistent rights, since enforced rights would greatly encumber any activities they might undertake (see Table 5-10).

TABLE 5-10

Rights Factors.

| | Rights | | |
	Absolute	Moderate	None
Consumers	10	10	10
Corporations	6	5	8
Governments	10	7	10
Criminals	1	1	10

Corporations and criminals are equally interested in the specters of no enforcement and aggressive enforcement, since either could affect their activities dramatically—positively or negatively. Governments have interests in all four scenarios, but are most concerned with self-enforcement, particularly with regulating it (Table 5-11).

TABLE 5-11

Enforcement Factors.

| | Enforcement | | | |
	None	Self	Violation	Aggressive
Consumers	5	5	3	3
Corporations	10	8	8	10
Governments	5	8	6	6
Criminals	10	1	5	10

The combination of the foregoing data into unweighted roll-up data reveals the results in Table 5-12. It shows that corporations have the most interest in the factors, followed by an almost equal interest by consumers and government.

TABLE 5-12

Unweighted Data.

| | Unweighted Data | | | | |
	Benefits	Ownership	Rights	Enforcement	Roll-up
Consumers	5.0	10.0	10.0	4.0	7.3
Corporations	8.7	10.0	6.3	9.0	8.5
Governments	8.3	6.0	9.0	6.3	7.4
Criminals	3.7	1.0	4.0	6.5	3.8

Again, a sensitivity analysis is presented in the following section to give context to this calculation.

Stakeholder Sensitivity Analysis

Figure 5-2 presents a sensitivity analysis using the same weights as before.

Again, the issues of rights and benefits are the driving issues of concern.

Figure 5-2
Sensitivity analysis.

	A1	A2	A3
All Enforcement	5.00	6.75	6.75
All Rights	4.00	8.67	8.67
All Own	1.00	4.00	10.00
All Benefits	9.33	5.67	2.67
75% Benefits, 25% Own	7.25	5.25	4.50
75% Benefits, 25% Rights	8.00	6.42	4.17
75% Benefits, 25% Enforcement	8.25	5.94	3.69
50% Benefits, 50% Own	5.17	4.83	6.33
50% Benefits, 50% Rights	6.67	7.17	5.67
50% Benefits, 50% Enforcement	7.17	6.21	4.71
50% Benefits, 25% Own,Rights	5.92	6.00	6.00
50% Benefits, 25% Rights,Enforcement	6.92	6.69	5.19
50% Own, 50% Rights	2.50	6.33	9.33
50% Own, 50% Enforcement	3.00	5.38	8.38
50% Own, 25% Benefits,Rights	3.83	5.58	7.83
50% Own, 25% Rights,Enforcement	2.75	5.85	8.85
50% Rights, 50% Enforcement	4.50	7.71	7.71
50% Rights, 25% Own,Enforcement	3.50	7.02	8.52
50% Rights, 25% Benefits,Enforcement	5.58	7.44	6.69
50% Enforcement, 25% Benefits, Own	5.08	5.79	6.54
50% Enforcement, 25% Own, Rights	3.75	6.54	8.04

Wrap-Up: Logic, Results, and Conclusions

The results of the analysis show that, across a broad set of alternatives and for a disparate set of stakeholders, the two factors that surface as being drivers in the debate are data rights and benefits derived from increased interpolation of a wide variety of data into knowledge.

The conclusion to be reached having undertaken a broad analysis of interests and alternatives is that there are strong competing interests that need to be brokered gently so that a workable situation is reached for all interested parties. That different societies and cultures approach this issue uniquely is no surprise, but should serve as a guidepost when developing local solutions. Local solutions must play in the global economy, and global solutions must be acceptable at all localities.

Notes

1. The phrase is the title of a book by M. T. Clanchy examining the impact of literacy on society in England during the period of 1066 to 1307: Clanchy, M. T., *From Memory to Written Record* (Oxford, England: Blackwell Publishers, 1993).

2. Bunch, Brian, and Alexander Hellemans, *The Timetables of Technology: A Chronology of the Most Important People and Events in the History of Technology* (New York: Simon & Schuster), 23.

3. Ibid., 23.

4. Ibid., 32-36.

5. Ibid., 38-50.

6. Ibid., 52.

7. Ibid., 54.

8. Ibid., 2.

9. Ibid., 47.

10. Ibid., 48.

11. Alderman, Ellen, and Caroline Kennedy, *The Right to Privacy* (New York: Alfred Knopf, 1995), 323.

12. Ibid., 323-325.

13. Smith, N. Jeff, *Managing Privacy* (Chapel Hill: The University of North Carolina Press, 1994), 7-9.

14. Lubar, Steven, *Infoculture: The Smithsonian Book of Information Age Inventions* (Boston: Houghton Mifflin), 320.

15. Leach, Harold H., "Storage," published electronically March 1998 at http://lcsweb.com/News/storage.htm.

16. Lubar, 321.

17. Ibid.

18. "Introduction to Data Mining," published electronically August 1997, http://www.cs.bham.ac.uk/anp/dm_docs/dm_intro.html, accessed 9 March 1999.

19. Sarris, Christina, Summary of the FTC Public Workshop, "Consumer Privacy on the Global Information Infrastructure" on June 4-5, 1996, http://www.webcom.com/lewrose/article/privacy2.html.

20. Sippey, Michael, "The One to One Future, Part II," *Stating the Obvious*, February 2, 1998, http://stating.theobvious.com/archives/020298.html.

21. Fact Sheet #4: Reducing Junk Mail," http://www.privacyrights.org/fs/fs4-junk.htm.

22. Sarris.

23. Sippey.

24. Cole, David M., "The Data Rush: New Tools Integrate and Exploit the Wealth of Information Publishers Already Possess," January 1998, http://www.naa.org/presstime/9801/data.html.

25. Ibid.

26. Vogel, Jennifer, "Getting to Know All About You: Attention Shoppers—What You Tell Supermarket Clubs May Be Used Against You," *Salon* Magazine, 14 October 1998, http://www.salonmagazine.com/21ST/FEATURE/1998/10/14FEA-TUREB.HTML.

27. Ibid.

28. Thompson, Cheryl W., "Arrested, Charged, and AWOL," *The Washington Post*, 10 March 1999, B1.

29. Charney, Scott, Testimony to the Secretary, Federal Trade Commission, published electronically 21 October 1997, http://www.usdoj.gov/criminal/cybercrime/comment1ftc.html.

30. Ibid.

31. Reidenberg, Joel R., and Paul M. Schwartz, *Data Privacy Law* (Charlottesville, Virginia: Michie, 1996).

32. Ibid., 5-6.

33. Ibid., 6-12.

CHAPTER 6

Security Verification of Systems and Networks

Introduction

The United States government has been very active in protecting its computers, networks, and automated information systems (AIS) since 1988. The process of security verification for a computer system or network is rather complex. This is reflected in the business world in that management of security for commercial computer systems has not kept abreast of that applied to government and defense computers. There are solid lessons to be learned from the government approach to secure computer systems. This chapter investigates two major areas of concern: (1) security verification of computer systems and networks and (2) how to achieve multilevel secure systems. The terms *evaluation*, *certification*, and *accreditation* are used loosely in the security community to describe what should be considered separate and distinct processes. In the following discussion, the authors use these terms broadly:

- *Evaluation* is determining the extent to which a product or system matches an objective *a priori* standard for the degree of trust that can be placed in the product or system, and is independent of the specific operational environment.

- *Certification* is establishment of the *extent* to which a particular design and implementation meets a set of specified security requirements *developed expressly for* the product or system with knowledge of the intended operational environment.

- *Accreditation* is the management decision that a system or network is approved to operate in a particular operational environment using a prescribed configuration.

The processes to which these terms refer are intended to rely on the results of earlier certification on evaluation, and accreditation on certification. This does not mean that evaluation has to be completed before certification begins, nor certification before accreditation begins. We will describe the computer security verification process and options applied to automated information systems and multilevel secure computer systems. An expanded definition of terms used in this chapter has been provided.

Automated Computer Systems— A Formal Accreditation Process

An *accreditation* is a formal declaration that an automated information system (AIS) is authorized to operate in one of four modes (dedicated, system-high, compartmented, or multilevel) using a given set of protective measures and controls that are prescribed to meet specified security requirements for a system. Those safeguards may include, but are not necessarily limited to, hardware and software security features, operating procedures, accountability procedures, access and distribution controls, management constraints, personnel security, and physical structures, areas, and devices. The decision to accredit AIS is based on the certification of the system, as well as other management considerations.

Certification of AIS is the end result of a successful evaluation. That is, the AIS is examined and tested to determine the extent to which a given design and its particular implementation meet a specified set of security requirements. If the AIS satisfies the requirements, it will be certified. Otherwise, it will not be.

Certification is, accordingly, *a priori* to accreditation and depends in turn upon having a *specified set of security requirements against which to evaluate the system*. The entire certification and accreditation process is as follows:

1. Define the *security requirements* for the system.
2. Determine the *set of protective measures and controls* that are needed to meet the security requirements specified for the system.
3. *Evaluate* the system relative to the security requirements.
4. If the evaluation is successful, *certify* the system.
5. Establish *management considerations* for accreditation of the system.
6. Evaluate the system with regard to the management considerations specified in Step 5.
7. If the results of the evaluation in Step 6 are that the system is acceptable, declare that the system is accredited for use in a *specified mode* as long as the safeguards determined in Step 2 are used.

Ultimately, security requirements are determined by the organization that will use the system. This follows from the fact that security requirements[1] are based upon a security policy that is organization-dependent.

Organizations may, however, have many of their security requirements in common with other organizations, and so certain security requirements may be considered to be generic. Evaluation relative to these requirements may be accomplished independently of the organization that will use a system and indeed could be evaluated prior to the organization developing its complete set of requirements.

One attempt to define a generic set of security requirements was the DoD Trusted Computer System Evaluation Criteria (TCSEC),[2] or "Orange Book," and its companion Trusted Products Evaluation Program (TPEP). Security doctrine was updated to mandate usage of TCSEC technology (DoD, March 21, 1988). Equipment, hardware, software, and/or firmware that have been evaluated and found to be technically compliant at a particular level of trust by the National Computer Security Center are placed on an Evaluated Products List, or EPL. Products on the EPL may or may not be satisfactory when evaluated against the complete set of requirements determined by the user organization in Step 1 of the certification and accreditation process. TCSEC has been modernized, renamed, and streamlined for various reasons, but the fundamentals of the process are still valid.

Common Policies and the NSA

Just as the organization may have technical requirements in common with other organizations, it will also almost certainly be subject to laws, rules, and practices established based upon policies generated outside the organization itself. Some aspects of the security policy are not specific to the organization but are imposed by the legal, regulatory, and political environment in which the organization exists.

Policies may also define, influence, or control the evaluation process. The *National Policy for the Security of National Security Telecommunications and Information Systems*[3] designates the Secretary of Defense as the Executive Agent of the government for National Security Telecommunications and Information Systems Security[4] and makes the Secretary responsible for implementing policies and procedures relating to computer and network security.[5] The Director, National Security Agency, is designated the National Manager for National Security Telecommunications and Information Systems Security and is responsible to the Secretary for carrying out the Executive Agent's responsibilities.[6] In particular, the National Manager is to "operate a central technical center to evaluate and certify the security of national security telecommunication and information systems."[7] Clearly, the National Security Agency has a key role to play in evaluation and certification, and, in fact, is directed by National Security Directive (NSD 42) to "Act as the U.S. government focal point for cryptography, telecommunications systems security, and information systems security for national security systems.[8]

It is not mandated that NSA serve as the single, or only, center for evaluation and certification and, indeed, it could be argued that the very definition of "certification," relying as it does ultimately on organization-dependent security policies, contains inherently the notion that centralized certification may not always be possible, feasible, or practical. Nevertheless, a considerable body of expertise has been created and now exists at NSA to perform evaluation and certification of systems and networks. Cost and technical considerations dictate that NSA be used whenever possible. They should act in accordance with policies concerning both security requirements and evaluation and certification procedures in accordance with the transfer of INFOSEC responsibilities effected December 2, 1991, by the Assistant Secretary of Defense for Command, Control, Communications and Intelligence—ASD (C3I).

Difficulties

The processes that we are using for evaluation, certification, and accreditation of our computers, systems, and networks are not working well. When vendors come forward with products, they may be turned away based on lack of resources to conduct an assessment. Those that have products accepted for evaluation can expect years to pass before their products are examined and placed on the Evaluated Products List. The timeline was shortened in the late 1990s, but the turnaround time is still unacceptable in terms of new products and technologies arriving in the marketplace.

Frequently, products are *technologically obsolete* before these processes reach completion. And when these products are finally evaluated, too often the decreased demand that results while the evaluation takes place does not justify the cost of attaining the goal. Certifiers and accreditors may (or may not) take into account that some of the components of the systems and networks they must decide whether to use are evaluated. Even so, each change to a system or network, its operating security mode, or its prescribed safeguards requires additional resources for recertification and reaccreditation.

Certainly the existing processes can be improved, but even significant improvements may not prove sufficient given the declining defense budget expected and the continuous increase in enhanced and new secure products and systems to be evaluated, certified, and accredited. Wholly new processes need to be considered if we are to effectively and efficiently achieve the secure computers, systems, and networks that both government and industry require.

Designated Approving Authority

Deciding to use a system requires us to weigh the configuration and vulnerabilities of the system, the environment in which it will be operated and how it will be operated, the value of the system or the information it contains, and the threat to each. Knowing the vulnerabilities, we can determine the residual risk inherent in using the system. Knowledge of the operational environment allows us to determine how much of the residual risk is abated by other security functions complementary to those of information systems security, such as physical security, personnel security, and operational security, and by the use of information systems security countermeasures. Understanding the threat permits us to assess the dangers of compromise, destruction or loss of integrity, and loss of availability that remains after all of the security features of the system and the complementary ones in its environment are applied. The remaining danger to the system and the data it creates, stores, processes, and communicates is rarely completely eliminated. Instead, the Designated Approving Authority (DAA) must decide if the level of risk remaining is acceptable in the circumstances. If so, the system is accredited for operation in the given situation.

The circumstances in which we operate our computers, systems, and networks are, however, highly dynamic. The threat changes, both from within our organizations and from without, or our understanding of it does. The operational environment is not stable. Our capabilities evolve in complementary security areas. And, of course, our systems themselves are constantly being improved, either to eliminate residual bugs or to enhance their capabilities. These changes force the DAA to reassess the original decision to accredit. Significant changes—a system upgrade, for example—may require a new certification of the system's security capabilities and limitations. More often, changes are small, subtle, and accrete slowly, requiring some care on the part of the DAA in recognizing when the accumulation of changes warrants a recertification. In short, the decision to continue operations is one that must be made frequently—perhaps daily—if security is to be maintained. *The notion that complex systems operating in real-world environments can be certified and then used for long periods without reaccreditation is simply not realistic.* Risk management must take place continuously over the life cycle of the system.

The complexity of the systems we use today also makes it difficult to decide how and by whom the accreditation decision is to be made. Consider as examples message processing computers or guards or gateways connecting different networks. Is the DAA the security manager of the facility in which the computer is to be operated? Or is the DAA the owner/operator of the network(s) to which the computer is attached and over which the messages it processes are sent and received? Or is the DAA the owner of the messages being processed? Each of these parties has a claim to the role of DAA, since each may be damaged by compromise, destruction, or degradation of data caused by the computer. In fact, the DAA may be none of them, as when a system belonging to the intelligence community must be accredited and either the Defense Intelligence Agency (DIA) or National Security Agency (NSA) acts as the DAA.

These choices allow the accreditation process to take advantage of centralized expertise that is simply too expensive to replicate for every site and every system or network. Similarly, an embedded computer system may be centrally accredited at a depot and strict configuration management used to ensure its accreditation is maintained. Although no system should be placed into operation until all of the concerns of the relevant accreditation authorities are resolved, it is nevertheless important to identify a final accreditation authority rather than leave the decision to a committee.

Accreditation is best viewed as a continuous process based on a partnership between:

- A centralized team of experts who are on top of the technologies of systems and networks, security implementation, and security validation

- A site-resident security officer in close touch with the day-to-day changes in the operational situation, the availability of complementary security disciplines and their technologies, and the immediate threat, as well as the exact configuration of the system

Such a partnership is the logical choice for exercising a total quality management approach to continuously accrediting all of the systems at a site. Both auditing by the site-resident staff and "red-teaming" by a centralized team are important parts of the accreditation process. The centralized team is also ideally suited to prepare standards for accreditation, to perform auditing and other quality control functions, and to train both its own staff and the site security officers.

The authorities who have responsibility for information passing through or stored on the system, or who are responsible for networks to which the system is connected, must rely on this partnership to protect their interests as the situation evolves. This is not to say that the reliance is all one way. The partnership also depends on those who own the networks and information upon which the systems act to provide timely information concerning changes that may affect the security of onsite operations.

Evaluation and Certification

In making the complex decision to accredit a computer, system, or network for operations, the DAA is assisted by knowledge of the design, including the overall architecture of the system and the security features that have been incorporated into the system and its components. It is also important to be cognizant of the rigor of the programming practices, documentation, testing, and configuration management employed by the developer. Knowing that the implementation was carefully managed, that the architecture is sound, and that the security features perform in accordance with the security policy for the system, the DAA can concentrate on the other factors influencing the accreditation decision.

Fortunately, the system's architecture and design can be evaluated throughout the development and implementation cycle to ensure that it can operate securely. Management practices can be monitored. Code can be analyzed, line-by-line if necessary, to make sure that little possibility for compromise exists. And testing can be accomplished at the unit level, during integration and under operational conditions, to ascertain the level of assurance provided by the system in maintaining secure operations and communications. Given a standard against which assurance can be measured, a carefully evaluated system can be assigned a security rating that reflects our confidence that the vulnerabilities of the system have been discovered and that we know the level of residual risk inherent in operating the system independently of the operating environment and the threat.

Analytically, the process of evaluation is different from and antecedent to the process of certification. It is possible to undertake the evaluation process starting as late as when the computer, system, or network is available for delivery. At this point in time, all of the design changes have been incorporated into the system and the documentation describing it is complete. The security evaluation may be considered, in such a case, to be an extension of the usual testing process that ensures that the system satisfies the requirements leading to its implementation. Indeed, that part of evaluation that comprises testing of the validity of the security features may be considered simply to be part of the overall testing of the various design features and capabilities of the system. Testing of security features may, in fact, be performed as part of the final acceptance tests, and penetration testing may be undertaken as part of operational readiness testing, to avoid duplication and undue delay in delivery.

Other parts of the evaluation process, including security analysis of the architecture and auditing of the code, are not normally part of the routine testing of a new system and may add greatly to the delivery schedule if they are not begun early in the development cycle. Evaluation of even relatively simple products may take several months, and the average length of time required is on the order of years. Recent experience at NSA places the average time for evaluation at 36 months. The time required is, of course, highly dependent on the nature and complexity of the product being evaluated. Average evaluation times for complex networks are much higher than those for simple standalone devices.

Since the preobsolescence lifetime of high-technology products is sometimes measured in months, an evaluation process that averages years is simply not acceptable. The figure of 18 months is often heard for high-technology products. However, this figure is also somewhat correlated to the complexity of the system or network. Even complex supercomputers may be quickly overtaken by competing brands, but wide area communications networks may have life spans measured in years. Any significant delay in product availability under highly volatile market conditions negatively impacts the product's life cycle value.

Ideally, evaluation and certification should begin at the inception of product or system development and should be completed very soon after completion of functional and operational testing. The efforts of security analysts to determine the soundness of the architecture and design can serve as valuable input to the system developers, avoiding costly and time-consuming corrections downstream in the implementation cycle. Such efforts can be completed as the design is completed, so that no time is added to the delivery schedule by these activities. It may sometimes also be possible to review some portions of the code earlier in the implementation. Not all of the code keeps changing right up to the start of acceptance testing, certainly in the case of well-designed, highly modular systems. As already noted, testing of security features can be incorporated into routine unit, integration, and operational testing to minimize its impact on scheduling.

By overlaying the schedule for accomplishing the activities that comprise evaluation, it should be possible to complete the evaluation process nearly concurrently with completion of the other testing of the system without adding materially to the delivery schedule. Nor does additional risk have to be accepted. While for some lower-assurance products and applications it might be reasonable to accept some additional risk in trade for accelerated evaluation and certification, the overlapping of schedules described here does not presuppose such trade-offs.

Certification, while analytically distinct from evaluation, can be accomplished quickly based upon knowledge gained during the evaluation process and need not further extend the delivery schedule. Today, of course, certification is not accomplished quickly. This is in part due to the separation between the organizations that evaluate and those that certify, impeding the free exchange of information among the authorities responsible for each of these processes.

Resources for Evaluation and Certification

Concurrency of schedules for the evaluation and certification processes with system design and implementation has, of course, implications for efficient allocation of scarcely qualified and competent evaluator and certifier resources. Only for the largest systems and networks would we expect evaluation to occupy a full-time cadre of evaluators and certifiers. In most cases, evaluators and certifiers would be available to work more than one effort at a time, moving from system to system when their efforts are needed as the implementation progresses. This is, in fact, the way that evaluations are managed today. Nevertheless, evaluation and certification are time-consuming processes. Today, systems and networks that handle sensitive but unclassified information or other unclassified information are not formally evaluated. The government requires (by presidential directive) that evaluations of computers, systems, and networks that create, process, store, and communicate classified information be evaluated by government personnel.

The government does not have the internal resources needed to stay ahead of the growing backlog. NSA's Project OUTREACH proposes helping military service personnel and perhaps other government civilians—appropriately trained and qualified, of course—perform evaluations. For example, certification of the Global Decision Support System is being performed by the Air Force Cryptologic Support Center at Kelly Air Force Base, San Antonio, Texas. Unfortunately, the military services and other agency budgets are also under downward pressure, so relying on them to provide evaluation and certification resources will not solve the problem of long delays.

It is interesting to note that, at the current time, applications for evaluation may actually be decreasing and some products that have been submitted are being withdrawn. This appears to be the result of vendors concluding that there will be insufficient return on the required investment for getting evaluated and certified and their belief that demand is not increased thereby. In other words, the current processes themselves are self-limiting. Since government and industry need secure products and systems, this is not desirable and would probably not be the case were the processes performing adequately.

NSA personnel do evaluations exceedingly well, with great competence and dedication. But there are not enough of them. Vendors are sometimes turned away, either because there are not enough resources to evaluate their products or because a preliminary survey indicates that the products may not be ready for evaluation. Of course, since evaluation is best accomplished beginning at the inception of product development, sending the vendor home on this latter basis is only expedient, not ideal.

Changing Role of Government— "Certifying the Certifier"

Based on the perceived and stated need for secure products and systems by both the federal government and industry, the number of products to be evaluated can be expected to grow geometrically, if not exponentially, during the coming years. Forecasts of government budgets indicate that resources to accomplish evaluations and certifications using government civilians or service personnel will face increasing backlogs. The solution lies, at least in part, with private industry. The role of government must shift from that of evaluator/certifier to that of "certifier of certifiers." Such an approach is already in use for TEMPEST evaluations.

Analytically, it would be possible to have the government retain the role of certifier even if the technical acts of evaluation and gathering of evidence in support of the certification decision are performed by private industry. The argument in favor of such retention views certification as a management decision based on the findings of the evaluator. This is not in accordance with the formal definition of "certification" contained in the Rainbow Series published by NSA. Practically, if the evaluation and certification analyses are done by private industry, for the government to retain the role of certifier would either require the government to maintain a cadre of analysts to "evaluate the evaluation"—an unnecessary expense—or, conversely, place the government in the role of rubber stamper of industry findings. The latter is undesirable on philosophic grounds, in that it might place legal liability on the government that should more rightly lie with private industry evaluating and certifying teams.

Harnessing the power of private industry for the evaluation and certification process offers a variety of advantages. Chief among them is that by adopting the role of certifier of certifiers, the government achieves a force-multiplier effect for its scarce resources. Said another way, this will allow us to better allocate our resources to meet the growing demand. Government experts in evaluation and certification would train private industry to perform these functions in accordance with government-developed standards. A company that has earned the right to perform evaluations and certifications by having trained and certified personnel would offer its services to developers who would pay to have their products reviewed. While this cost would eventually appear in the price the developer charges for its products, the cost would be spread across the vendor's entire business base, not borne solely by the government, thus reducing the overall tax burden of evaluation and certification.

Since information systems security features and assurance are desirable characteristics of computers, systems, and networks—always provided that they do not significantly increase cost or impose undue operational burdens on users—being able to market a product with an approved certification should be a discriminant in the marketplace. That is, if two or more similar products are available and only one is evaluated and certified, users will prefer to buy the one that is certified. This will ensure the demand for evaluator/certifier services.

In some cases, it may even be acceptable to dispense with an independent evaluation and certification. Vendors of computers, systems, and networks might be allowed to *self-certify* their own products. Such a self-certification would, of course, be useless without some form of protection for the buyer who elects to buy the product. This protection might take the form of a warranty in which the vendor agrees to correct at no cost to the buyer any problems that arise during some warranty period. From the vendor viewpoint, such a course would be attractive, since it would lock the buyer to the vendor for the warranty period—the buyer would seldom seek another vendor to correct problems that he or she could have fixed for free by the original vendor. Since actual damages would be very difficult to predict and in some government applications might be impossible to calculate, it is unlikely that vendors would be willing to accept such a form of liability. However, it might be possible to include a liquidated damages clause in the purchase contract. Delaying final acceptance until some "burn-in" period of successful operations had elapsed could serve as an alternative.

Government Retains Responsibilities in Evaluation and Certification of Computer Systems

The government's role in evaluation and certification, while it must change in response to the evolving situation, will remain extensive and important. Evaluation and certification are not particularly difficult processes for physically protected systems operating in dedicated mode and using nonrated components. Evaluation, certification, and accreditation are more difficult for multilevel secure systems because they involve inherently greater risk. Thus, for some of our most critical computers, systems, and networks (nuclear command and control, for example) and for some especially important functions (e.g., cryptology), we may always choose to use our best government evaluators and certifiers.

Government personnel will also need to stay abreast of the state of the art in systems development and implementation to continue to perform and specify effective and efficient evaluations and certifications. Where those functions can be delegated, the government will have to provide the standards for their application, and for the training and certification of those who will be allowed to perform them, whether in private industry or in government agencies or military services. Training courses will have to be developed by, and may be taught by, government personnel experienced in these disciplines.

Quality control will be an important issue. Recertification at periodic intervals will be necessary for individuals, organizations, and companies who wish to be able to provide these services. Legal standards and protective clauses will be needed where self-certification is permitted. Spot inspections will be appropriate to provide intermediate checks and balances. And databases of security failures will have to be maintained in order to permit analysis of failure rates attributable to individuals and organizations performing evaluations and certifications.

Conclusions

Today, when the government evaluates, certifies, and accredits computers and networks for operations involving sensitive or classified information, they do a thorough and effective job. However, these processes take much too long, and the level of resources that can be applied to these important processes is dwindling. The number of systems that should be evaluated and certified can be expected to grow at an increasing rate. To avoid the inevitable overwhelming backlog that lies down our current path, the government must seek more efficient and effective processes to accomplish our security assurance functions.

A spectrum of possible processes is available for evaluation and certification. At one end, self-certification may be acceptable if backed up by appropriate warranties or liquidated damages clauses. At the other end, government personnel will continue to evaluate and certify our most critical systems. In between, private industry, acting in accordance with government standards, may be able to take up the slack, which will also spread the cost of the functions across the entire business base for secure systems instead of paying for these services entirely with tax dollars. The government will have to develop training courses and establish procedures and databases for quality control of individuals and organizations certified to perform these functions.

Accreditation is a continuing process based on knowledge of the vulnerabilities of a system, its operating environment, the value of the system and the information it contains, and the threat. While more than one person and organization may have a stake in the security effectiveness of a system, the process must be based upon a partnership between a centralized team of experts that support and train site security officers and the onsite security authority who is best positioned to recognize security-relevant changes in the system, the operating environment, or the threat. Total quality management by this partnership of accreditation of all of the computers, systems and networks operating at the site will ensure that security interests are continuously protected.

Multilevel Secure Systems (MLS)

Multilevel secure, or MLS, systems and networks do two things:

- They create, process, store, analyze, and communicate two or more levels of classified or sensitive unclassified data.

- They offer some level of assurance that only people with the right clearances and need-to-know will have access to data at appropriate classification levels.

MLS is an enabling technology for *interoperable* systems. Without MLS, systems cannot be both interoperable and simultaneously ensure that strategic and tactical information will not be compromised so that all relevant information can be placed at the disposal of appropriately cleared analysts and decision makers. (The alternative to multilevel security is either for the analyst or decision maker to do without some data that might contribute to mission performance, or to have multiple separate systems that run "system high" in order to get data of all of the various security levels to the analyst or the decision maker.)

MLS Perspectives

The need for MLS technology became clear in the late 1970s, when it was realized that the complexity of computers made them highly vulnerable to penetration and that it was not feasible to find and fix all of the security flaws in a typical commercial system. The first MLS prototypes were built during the early 1980s.

These early attempts proved that MLS had to be included as an integral part of computer systems, preferably as part of commercial off-the-shelf systems. This in turn required guidance to industry on what was required for MLS; it also required a quality control process to evaluate industry products. The result (previously discussed) was the development, in 1983, of the DoD Trusted Computer System Evaluation Criteria (TCSEC), better known as the "Orange Book," and its companion Trusted

Products Evaluation Program (TPEP). Also, DoD security doctrine was updated to mandate usage of TCSEC technology (DoD, March 21, 1988).

The TCSEC pioneered technical requirements for MLS and has been used worldwide as a basis for computer security criteria. It has also been the basis for development of a generation of MLS products. However, the TCSEC focused on operating system security, to the exclusion of all else. Interpretations of the TCSEC for networks and database management systems were written. But in the twentieth century, few network products or systems have been developed to these criteria, and their use in operational environments is almost nonexistent.

Cost/Benefits

MLS products are expensive and do not always provide functionality comparable to state-of-the-art nonsecure applications. MLS systems are much less expensive than having to have several systems arrayed around the analyst or decision maker. By allowing replacement of several systems with one, significant savings are realized. These savings are compounded as they extend across the life cycle of the systems.

MLS technology is also in consonance with our overall strategy to reduce costs by consolidating functions and systems. As industry creates the various pieces of technology—secure operating systems, compartmented mode workstations, secure data base management systems, and so forth—we can incorporate them as commercial off-the-shelf (COTS) and non-development items (NDI) into our systems designs. In addition to economic reasons for creating MLS systems and networks, MLS is vital as an enabling technology for interoperability. From Grenada to the Persian Gulf, the importance of interoperable communications has been proven time and again. But interoperability is not sufficient—our systems must also be secure. This is not possible without MLS.

As of September of this year, 56 products have made it through the NSA TPEP evaluation process and been put onto the Evaluated Products List. Of these the predominant level is *low-assurance* products in the C2/B1 range. Though development of high-assurance platforms continues, most attention remains on developing lower-assurance platforms— with particular emphasis on class B1—and most of these have been done by commercial vendors, at their own risk.

The TPEP process has undergone a number of changes in order to speed up the evaluation, which historically took many years to complete.

A significant number of improved or new MLS products are becoming available that appear to overcome many of the shortcomings of past products. A window of opportunity is opening. The next few years will be crucial in determining whether TCSEC-targeted MLS is achievable for more than a tiny subset of DoD systems.

In actuality, multilevel security is still in its infancy and our most valuable secrets are still protected by isolating our highly classified systems. We know the warfighters cannot perform their missions effectively or efficiently without timely, accurate, and complete information. Today we cannot even send multilevel secure e-mail within the Pentagon or between NSA and CIA, much less solve the larger communitywide MLS problems. In summary, despite recent progress, many problems remain. There are too few MLS products, and few of those that we do have are not being used—either because they are too expensive, lack the desired functionality, or are out-of-date. And finally, products that have been evaluated to the TCSEC—in and of themselves—are not a panacea. They do not solve all MLS needs. There are requirements for many types of MLS applications.

Wrap-Up

The U.S government led the way in establishing methods and policy to evaluate its own computer systems. New security technology and new products are coming to the market faster than previous certification methods can effectively handle for either government or commercial organizations that require the technology. We suggest that government might accept new roles of certifying and training the certifier and augmenting self-certification efforts to develop cooperation with commercial organizations. Also, the next few years may tell whether the government TCSEC-targeted MLS is achievable for more than a tiny subset of DoD systems.

Notes

1. National Security Directive 42.
2. National Security Directive 42.
3. Department of Defense Directive 5200.28-STD, "Trusted Computer System Evaluation Criteria."

4. Included in the *National Security Agency Information Systems Security Products and Services Catalog.*
5. National Security Directive 42.
6. NSD 42, Paragraph 6a.
7. NSD 42, Paragraph 6a.
8. NSD 42, Paragraph 7.
9. NSD 42, Paragraph 7h.
10. NSD 42, Paragraph 7b.

Practical Countermeasures

Part 3 is the core group of chapters devoted to practical counter-measures available to the IT organization.

The most powerful technology that we use to ensure our confidentiality of communications and authentication of the communicators is cryptography. Chapter 7 tackles the key cryptographic issues with special focus on current problems. It is a minisource of information on processes.

Chapter 8 details two uses of access controls: 1) controlling enterprise access from a systems perspective and 2) auditing people and physical access to computer systems.

Chapter 9 discusses the science of authentication methods. It presents the digital signatures from three views: technological, political and legal. A model for an effective Public Key Infrastructure (PKI) is presented.

Chapter 10 focuses on the need for permissions management—especially on the Internet. It discusses the various security trade-offs that organizations must consider when attempting to control identification, authentication and authorization on their Web site or computer system.

Chapter 11 defines Virtual Private Network solutions for secure point to point or remote to host communications enacted at the transport layer. VPNs represent secure and cost-effective computer security solutions. They use encryption, certificate authorities, access control and firewalls to ensure integrity of enterprise systems.

Chapter 12 identifies biometric countermeasures, compares them, and reports on some future directions.

CHAPTER 7

Cryptography

Classical Cryptography and Steganography

Among the earliest technological answers to the need for confidentiality and integrity of information was cryptography, or secret writing. Many a child has written messages in lemon juice or milk to be recovered only by intended recipients who knew both that there was a hidden message and that it could be revealed through the use of a warm iron. Many a "secret decoder ring" was carefully guarded in the aftermath of cereal sprees. David Kahn, in his monumental history of cryptography, *The Codebreakers*, traces the history of secret writing to an inscription carved about 1900 B.C. in the tomb of the nobleman Khnumhotep II. The earliest applications were merely transformations of hieroglyphs probably used to indicate emphasis or, occasionally, for calligraphic, decorative, or other reasons. The use of such transformations for secrecy reasons—possibly originally as sort of a game or puzzle—by the Egyptians may have been the true birth of cryptography.[1]

One of the surest ways to preserve the secrecy of information is to hide it so effectively that those who seek to obtain it do not recognize its presence. This way of hiding a message is called a *concealment cipher* or sometimes a *null cipher*. Generals of antiquity are said to have shaved the heads of slaves and tattooed information on the skin, where it would be covered by their hair when the hair grew back. The slaves were then dispatched with the hidden messages that could be recovered by the recipient by reshaving their heads. In other cases, messages were written on wooden tablets that were then covered with a wax coating. A second, innocuous message was inscribed into the wax, effectively hiding the fact that the first, important message existed below.

Spartan officers were each provided with a wooden staff, called a *skytale*, of uniform length and diameter. The skytale was wrapped with a strip of cloth upon which messages were written along the length of the staff. When unwound, the message was readable only when the cloth was rewound by another officer on a duplicate staff.

Edgar Allen Poe, in his short story "The Purloined Letter," described hiding a letter by altering its overall appearance by tearing and dirtying the letter and then turning it over and writing on the back some innocuous and unrelated scribblings. A diligent search failed to recover the document even though it was in plain sight of the searchers, because they believed the immediate appearance without checking for the deeper reality. A modern version of such hiding-in-plain-sight is the use of microdots in which the image of a page is reduced to the size of a dot and replaces a period somewhere in the body of an innocuous document. The hidden message can be easily recovered with a light microscope, but it passes superficial inspection by those who are unaware of the dot's hidden purpose.

Messages may also be hidden within other messages. The true message, "Attack at dawn," is recovered by reading the initial letters of the apparent message, "All the totaled accounts certainly kept at the downtown auditor's with Nancy." By reading the final letters, third letters, last words of sentences, or any other prearranged patterns of characters or words, messages can be hidden within other innocuous writings. Cardinal Richelieu used a template, or *grille*, (Figure 7-1) that, when placed by the recipient over an apparently unrelated letter from the cardinal, revealed the words of the actual message.

Grilles can be made of paper, cardboard, cloth, metal or any other handy material and can have any number of openings of any convenient size or shape. The only requirement is that all communicators have duplicate grilles.

Messages can be hidden handily within other innocuous writings by puncturing a small pinhole under each letter of the hidden message. The true message is easily recovered by holding the innocuous writing up to a light to reveal the pinholes. Such a null cipher was said to have been in common use in London at one time when it was expensive to send letters but cost nothing to send newspapers. If the sender controls preparation of the covering document, the letters of the hidden message can be specified by changes in type fonts, spacing of characters or words, misspellings, or any of a variety of other pointers. The hidden message in Figure 7-2 is painfully obvious, but it could be made much more subtle if fonts differing only slightly were used instead of capital and small letters.

Most word processors today facilitate the change of fonts and even of spacing between characters, words and lines of the text, and so make hiding a message within another message very easy. It has been pro-

Figure 7-1
Grille.

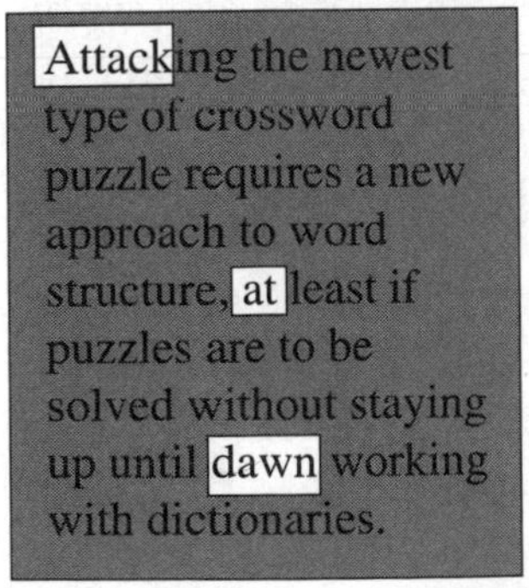

Attacking the newest type of crossword puzzle requires a new approach to word structure, at least if puzzles are to be solved without staying up until dawn working with dictionaries.

Figure 7-2
Message disguised in casing of letters.

THesE TRUTHs We HOLD TO BE SELF-EVIDEnt, THAT ALL MEN ARE CRE-ATED EQUAL, THAT THEY ARE ENDOWED BY THEiR CREaTOR WITH CER-TAIN INAlIENABLE RIGHTS, THAT AMONG THESE ARE LIFE, LIBERTy AND THE PURSUIT oF HAPPINESS, THAT TO SECuRE THESE RIGHTS, GOVERN-MENTS ARE INSTITUTEd AMONG MeN, DERIVING THEIR JUST pOWERS FROM THE CONSENT OF THE GOVERNED, THaT WHENEVEr ANY FORM OF GOVERNMENt BECOMES DESTRUCTIVE OF THESE ENDS, IT IS THE RIGHT OF THE PEOPLE TO aLtER oR ABOLISH IT AnD TO INSTITUTE NEW GOV-ERNMENT, LAYING ITS FOUNDATION ON SUcH PRINCIPLeS AND ORGA-NIZING ITS POWERS IN SUCH FORM, AS TO THEM SHALL SEEM MOST LIKELY TO EFFECT THEIR SAFETY AND HAPPINESS.

posed in certain cases where it is important to be able to identify specific copies of documents—often to detect which copy of a sensitive document has been "leaked" to the press or the public or turned over to enemy (or even friendly) governments—that changes in font or spacing be used to make each copy unique.

Since messages can be reduced to a sequence of ones and zeros, any patterned situation in which two different values are present will do for hiding information. Different-colored bricks or rocks in a wall or tiles in a mosaic could represent ones and zeros. Broken or whole pickets in a fence or large/fat/tall versus small/thin/short books on a shelf would do.

The general term for the art and science of concealment ciphers is *steganography*. Steganography is really an ancient and secret communication form revisited in modern terms. Computer programs implementing steganographic algorithms have begun to appear. One type of such routines replaces the least-significant bit of the bit strings defining the pixels of a graphic image with a sequence of ones and zeros that compose the hidden message to be sent. Since most graphics encodings provide more gradations of color than the human eye can see, the picture will not be noticeably changed by co-opting the least-significant bits for use in hiding a message. A 64-kilobyte message can easily be concealed within a 1024 by 1024 pixel graphic in this fashion, using software available for free or downloadable as shareware in many locations across cyberspace. Figure 7-3, for instance, in its representation as a string of ones and zeros, conceals the entire text of the Gettysburg Address.

Were the image to be intercepted, it is extremely unlikely that the intercepting party would realize that there was a hidden message at all, absent inside information that steganography was being used. This is a defining characteristic of concealment or null ciphers: The message is there to be more or less easily read once the trick of its concealment is known. Other methods of cryptography are available that do not rely on

Figure 7-3
Steganography.

concealment to protect privacy and integrity, although they may be and often are used in concert with methods of concealment. For example, Figure 7-4 conceals a message using a 3DES (triple DES) cryptographic system combined with steganography. Even if the picture is intercepted and determined to have a message within it, the *cracking* would represent a reasonable effort. Such a method represents a threat to law enforcement. Literally hundreds of thousands of pictures are transferred across the Internet in any day and what percentage of this traffic is for illegal purposes is unknown. We turn our attention now to those methods.

Figure 7-4
Message enciphered in 3DES and hidden using steganography.

Basic Terms

Cryptology is the study of codes and ciphers for use in secret transmission of messages from a sender to a recipient, either or both of which may be people, processes on a computer system or network, or a file stored on a computer disc or other storage device. *Ciphers* are methods or systems of secreting messages and may be concealment ciphers as discussed above or may be the transposition and substitution ciphers we explore next. *Codes* are special forms of ciphers in which symbols or groups of symbols replace groups of bits or characters in the original message according to a table or codebook. Creating the codebook requires identifying words, phrases, sentences, or even entire messages and assigning for each a specific symbol or group of symbols. Thus, "Meet me at dawn" might be represented as "QQRST" in the codebook (Figure 7-5).

In either ciphers or codes, the original message to be sent and received is called the *plaintext* or *cleartext*, and the scrambled or hidden message that is actually transmitted is called the *ciphertext*. The process or algorithm used in converting the plaintext to the ciphertext is called variously *encryption* or *encipherment*. Recovering the original message is accomplished by using a decryption or decipherment algorithm.

Cryptology is composed of *cryptography*—the art and science of keeping messages secure—and *cryptanalysis*—the art and science of breaking messages, that is, recovering the messages without foreknowledge of all the details of the system used to secure the message. Successful cryptography that is not readily susceptible to cryptanalysis provides privacy. It may also provide authentication and nonrepudiation, and ensures the integrity of the information comprising the plaintext.

It must be noted, however, that cryptography alone cannot solve all the problems of protecting information assets and systems. It does not ensure availability, so denial of service attacks are still a danger. Nor will

Figure 7-5

Simple encryption system.

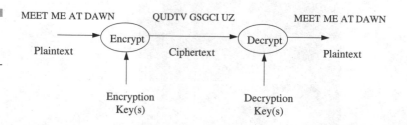

it, in general, protect against viruses, although it can help do so if used as part of a well-developed operation.

Transposition Ciphers

Despite nearly 4000 years of use, cryptography today still relies basically on only two methodologies beyond concealment, both familiar to most schoolchildren. In *transposition* ciphers, the letters of the message to be secretly transmitted are scrambled or repositioned—that is, rewritten in a patterned way—and then sent in a different order from their original form. Thus, the message "meet me at dawn" can be written in zigzag form:

```
M       e       m       a       d       w
  \   /   \   /   \   /   \   /   \   /   \
    e       t       e       t       a       n
```

The transposed message is sent as "Memadw etetan." The recipient, knowing the zigzag method of transposition used, can easily recover the original message.

Other transpositions write messages horizontally into rectangular arrays, reading out the transposed text vertically. The recipient reverses the process to recover the original text:

```
N O W - I S - T H E - T I M E
F O R - A L L - G O O D - M E
N - T O - C O M E - T O - T H
E - A I D - O F - T H E I R -
P A R T I E S - S T O P Z Z Z
```

would be transmitted as:

NFNEP OO––A WRTAR ––OIT IA-DI SLC-E -LOOS T-MF- HGE-S

EO-TT -OTHO TDOEP I––IZ MMTRZ EEH-Z

The square or rectangular (or other shaped) patterns to be used, characters to demark words, sentences, or paragraphs or to be used as fillers, and so forth have to be agreed upon in advance, composing what modern cryptologists call encryption and decryption algorithms. Obviously, very complex algorithms are possible.

For example, a magic square (Figure 7-6) is any square made up of a series of numbers, such as 1 to 25, so arranged that the sum of the numbers in any row, column, or diagonal is the same. The numbers, being a series, serve as an ordering for writing in or reading out a sequence of 25 letters—the first letter of the plaintext replaces the number "1," the second letter the number "2," and so forth. By breaking up the plaintext into groups of 25 letters, transposition of the entire message is easily accomplished.

A knight's tour is a puzzle that uses a chessboard of 64 squares (Figure 7-7). Knights in chess move one space in any direction (except diagonal), followed by one space perpendicular to the direction of the first part of the move. The puzzle is to find a sequence of moves in which the knight traverses the board landing on each square once and only once. Such a pattern, to which sender and recipient have pre-agreed, is obviously well suited to transposing 64 character subsequences of a plaintext message.

Figure 7-6
A magic square.

20	11	2	49	40	31	22
12	3	43	41	32	23	21
4	44	42	33	24	15	13
45	36	34	25	16	14	5
37	35	26	17	8	6	46
29	27	18	9	7	47	38
28	19	10	1	48	39	30

Figure 7-7
A knight's tour of the chessboard.

1	4	53	18	55	6	43	20
52	17	2	5	38	19	56	7
3	64	15	54	31	42	21	44
16	51	28	39	34	37	8	57
63	14	35	32	41	30	45	22
50	27	40	29	36	33	58	9
13	62	25	48	11	60	23	46
23	49	12	61	24	47	10	59

Key words may also play a role in transposition ciphers. For example, if the eight-letter key word "computer" is agreed upon, the plaintext message is written horizontally into an array of eight-by-eight squares. The natural order of the letters of the key word as they occur in the alphabet specifies the order in which the columns of the array are removed to compose the transposition:

Key word	C	O	M	P	U	T	E	R
Letter order	1	4	3	5	8	7	2	6

M	E	E	T	M	E	A	T
T	H	E	F	R	O	N	T
D	O	O	R	O	F	T	H
H	I	L	T	O	N	H	O
T	E	L	A	T	9	P	M

Thus the plaintext "Meet me at the front door of the Hilton Hotel at 9 PM" becomes:

MTDHT ANTHP EEOLL EHOIE TFRTA TTHOM EOFN9 MROOT

The use of two key words further complicates the transposition algorithm. One is used for reading out, just as above, but a second key word is used for placing the message into the square or rectangular block from which the transposed ciphertext is read. For example, the read-in key word "codes" dictates that the message will be placed into the array starting with the first row, followed by the third, fourth, second, and fifth rows. The read-out key word "computer" specifies the reading sequence of the columns of the array as in our earlier example.

Read-out Key Word		C	O	M	P	U	T	E	R
Letter Order		1	4	3	5	8	7	2	6
Read-in Key Word									
C	1	M	E	E	T	M	E	A	T
O	4	H	I	L	T	O	N	H	O
D	2	T	H	E	F	R	O	N	T
E	3	D	O	O	R	O	F	T	H
S	5	T	E	L	A	T	9	P	M

The use of key words in such a cipher vastly simplifies the operational use of the cipher. All of the methodology is pre-agreed upon by the senders and recipients, so only the key words need to be exchanged to permit secure communication using the cipher. Of course, it is vital that the exchange of key words be conducted securely, since anyone having the key can decipher the message. The problem of secure exchange of keys—that is, *of key management*—will be dealt with later.

Substitution Ciphers

In the second methodology, *substitution ciphers* are created by replacing one symbol—say, a letter of a message—with another symbol or letter in some patterned way. Edgar Allen Poe in his short story "The Gold Bug" has pirates using such a substitution of symbols for letters to remind them where they had buried their ill-gotten treasure. In "The Adventure of the Dancing Men," Sir Arthur Conan Doyle has Sherlock Holmes solve the mystery by deciphering the meaning of stick figures that had been substituted for letters in a message.

In a simple case, letters may be substituted for other letters in some patterned way. We might, for example, take the alphabet and place it side by side with another alphabet that has been displaced by a few letters to the right:

A	B	C	D	E	F	G	H	I	J	K	L	M
D	E	F	G	H	I	J	K	L	M	N	O	P

N	O	P	Q	R	S	T	U	V	W	X	Y	Z
Q	R	S	T	U	V	W	X	Y	Z	A	B	C

Then we replace the first letter of the message "Meet me at dawn"— the letter "M"—with its counterpart "P" and so forth to obtain the enciphered message "PHHW PH DW GDZQ." The recipient, knowing the key (in this case, how many places to displace the second alphabet) can use the scheme in reverse to easily re-create the original message. Again, using a displacement of three letters to the left, we obtain the following substitution:

Plaintext: NOW IS THE TIME FOR ALL GOOD PEOPLE TO COME TO THE

Ciphertext: KLTFP QEBQF JBCLO XIIDL LAMBL MIBQL ZLJBQ LQEB

Obviously, any number from 1 to 25 can be used as a displacement, becoming the key for this type of substitution, which, by the way, is called "Caesar's cipher" after Julius Caesar, who was reported to have first used it. The Caesar shift was actually only 3 letters to the right. Roman legion commanders received battle messages so enciphered.

More-complex algorithms use a preselected word, or "key," to determine the scheme. For example, if "magnetic" was chosen as the key, the paired alphabets becomes:

```
A B C D E F G H I J K L M
M A G N E T I C B D F H J


N O P Q R S T U V W X Y Z
K L O P Q R S U V W X Y Z
```

Since each letter can occur only once in each alphabet, repetitions are ignored, so "SECURE" used as a key becomes "SECUR." Two key words may be used to further complicate the substitution:

```
S E C U R A B D F G H I J
M A G N E T I C B D F H J


K L M N O P Q T V W X Y Z
K L O P Q R S U V W X Y Z
```

Displacements may also be used to prevent same-letter combinations from occurring:

```
S E C U R A B D F G H I J
B D F M A G N E T I C H J


K L M N O P Q T V W X Y Z
K L O P Q R S U V W X Y Z
```

The combination of one or more words and one or more displacements constitutes the keys. As was true for transposition ciphers, the use of keys simplifies the operational application of substitution ciphers but requires secure key management.

Neither transposition nor substitution ciphers in the simple forms presented here represent much of a challenge to an unintended recipient who desires to recover the original message, especially if a computer is handy to aid in trying to break the codes used. However, as we shall see, more-complex variations of these two schemes can be used, often in combination with each other, to achieve impressive levels of security.

Block vs. Stream Ciphers

Transposition ciphers act, by their very nature, on blocks of characters or bits, scrambling the natural order in which the characters or bits occur in some patterned way to produce the ciphertext. Substitution ciphers, at least in the simple form presented here, seem, on the other hand, to act on the plaintext one character or bit at a time.

When enciphering or deciphering messages was essentially a pen-and-paper drill, the distinction was not very important. However, the ability to encipher character by character turned out to be extremely useful for encipherment of communications when Teletype machines automated telegraphy. To make such machines work, the Morse code, which had served so well when telegraph operators provided long-distance communications, was replaced by a coding scheme that used a fixed sequence of bits to represent each letter or number, because machines handled bits with ease. Using a stream cipher, the characters could be enciphered as they were typed into the Teletype and transmitted immediately. At the receiving end, the arriving ciphertext could be deciphered character by character as they came in without waiting for a block or all of the message to arrive.

With the advent of computer-based communications systems, the advantage of stream ciphers largely disappeared. Computers work easily with blocks of bits, especially if the blocks are multiples of the byte size or word length used by the computer. Hence, today most widely used ciphers are block ciphers.

Cryptanalysis

An attempted cryptanalysis of a cryptosystem is called an *attack*. Cryptographers always assume that enemies know the encipherment and decipherment algorithms, so security resides entirely in the key or keys used by the cipher. This is, of course, a conservative assumption—the enemy won't always have all the details of the algorithm and its implementation, but it is wise to assume that he or she does and to design ciphers that cannot be broken even if he or she does.

In "The Gold Bug" and *The Dancing Men*, the ciphers are broken by analysis relying on certain underlying regularities in the English language. All languages have such regularities, and so statistics can be used to determine which language is being used, even if the source of a message is not known (Figure 7-8).

By knowing the frequencies with which letters in the English occur, it is possible to almost determine immediately if a cipher is a transposition or a substitution. For example, if "E" is not the most frequent letter in an English ciphertext, the cipher almost certainly involves substitution. By successively replacing letters according to the frequencies of their occurrence in the ciphertext, simple substitutions can often be broken by trial and error (Figure 7-9).

Breaking simple ciphers is a hobby enjoyed today by many enthusiasts. Newspapers regularly print a variety of different cryptograms, created according to a variety of pre-agreed protocols. For a thorough treatment of classical cryptography applicable to such puzzles, we recommend Randall K. Nichols' *Classical Cryptography Course* in two volumes.[2]

Figure 7-8
Statistical regularities in European languages.

	English	German	French	Italian	Spanish	Portugese
Vowels:	40%	40%	45%	48%	47%	48%
L N R S T:	33%	34%	34%	30%	31%	29%

Figure 7-9
Frequencies of occurrence of letters in English.

E	1231	L	403	B	162
T	959	D	365	G	161
A	805	C	320	V	93
O	794	U	310	K	52
N	719	P	229	Q	20
I	718	F	228	X	20
S	659	M	225	J	10
R	603	W	203	Z	9
H	514	Y	188		

Complex modern ciphers that are combinations of transpositions and substitutions, like the Data Encryption Standard (DES), which we discuss later in this chapter, or that use powerful numerical mathematics, like Pretty Good Privacy (PGP), do not succumb easily to statistical cryptanalysis. They are designed to make such cryptanalysis fail. If, as is true with DES, the keys are fixed in length, attacks may take the form of a brute-force attack that simply tries all possible keys, one after another. The time that such an attack will take to recover a plaintext depends directly on the number of bits in the keys. Consider, for example, keys of 2-bit length. Only four keys are possible: 00, 01, 10, and 11. Trying all four will not take very long, and, on average, we will only have to try half of them to find the key being used. But if three bits are used, there are eight keys: 000,001,010,011,100,101,110, and 111. Trying them all will take twice as long, even if only half, on average, must be tested. Four bits yields 16 keys, again doubling the length of time required to recover a key, by brute force, that was used to encipher a specific plaintext. And in general, each additional bit doubles the length of time required for a brute-force attack.

If 40-bit keys are used, there are 109,951,162,776 keys to be tested. For 56-bit keys, as used by DES, there are 72,057,594,037,927,936 keys in the key space. For 100-bit keys, there are 1,267,650,600,228,229, 401,496,703,205,376 keys, one-half of which will have, on average, to be tried. Obviously, for cryptographic algorithms not susceptible to other cryptanalytic attacks, longer keys are safer than shorter keys. But how long is long enough? Hackers, attacking an enciphered message, usually have tiny budgets and must use one or a small number of computers, often scavenging time for their cracking programs. Such an approach could exhaust a 40-bit key space in a few days or perhaps a week, but would be more difficult for a 56-bit key such as is used by the Data Encryption Standard.

Anyone with the technological competence of many undergraduate computer scientists or electrical engineers could use field-programmable gate arrays, a commercially readily available technology, to construct a special-purpose computer that could exhaust a 40-bit key space in a few minutes, but that would require more than a year of continuous operation to exhaust a 56-bit key space. The cost of such a special-purpose computer in 1996 was on the order of $10,000, an amount that might be available to many small businesses.

A larger corporation or a government that could budget a few hundred thousand dollars to build a larger field-programmable gate array device, or even design and build or have built a special-purpose integrated cir-

TABLE 7-1

Key Strength vs.
Attack Technology.

Threat	Budget	Technology	Time to Break	
			40 Bits	56 Bits
Hacker	Tiny	Scavenged time	1 week	Infeasible
Small business	$10 K	FPGA	12 min.	556 days
Corporation	$300 K	FPGA or ASIC	24 sec.	19 days
Big corporation	$10 M	FPGA or ASIC	7 sec.	13 hours
Government	$300 M	ASIC	.0002 sec.	12 sec.

FPGA = Field Programmable Gate Array
ASIC = Application-Specific Integrated Circuits

cuit, might be able to exhaust a 40-bit key space in a few seconds and a 56-bit key space in a few days. For a $10 million investment, the 40-bit key space could be exhausted in less than a second, and the 56-bit key space in a few minutes. A large government-sized investment of a few hundred million dollars in special-purpose integrated circuits would permit development of a device that could exhaust a 56-bit key space in a few seconds and wouldn't even notice a 40-bit key space (see Table 7-1).

Moore's Law states that computer power doubles approximately every 18 months, so the cost to mount a brute-force attack on a key space will decrease by a factor of 10 every five years or so. Consequently, while today a key size of 80 bits could not be exhausted in less than several years even with an investment of hundreds of millions of dollars, 80-bit keys cannot be expected to protect information assets for more than a few years. Using computers, longer keys can be stored and used nearly as cheaply and easily as short keys, so wise managers will opt for *key lengths of well over 128 bits.*

Modern Cryptography

Modern cryptography is almost exclusively concerned with protecting information that is in digital form, a set or sequence of ones and zeros. One or a combination of the two distinct processes—transposition and substitution—may be combined into a complex algorithm and applied with a key, which is also a sequence of ones and zeros, to the plaintexts to create the enciphered message.

Consider a situation in which a text message is to be protected. The message "Meet me at dawn" may be encoded as characters using Table A-2 in Appendix A, producing:

M	E	E	T	NUL	M
01010101	01001101	01001101	01011100	00000000	01010101

E	NUL	A	T	NUL	D
01001101	00000000	01001001	01011100	00000000	01001100

A	W	N	.		
01001001	01011111	01010110	00110110		

Read in the usual way, this becomes the bit stream:

01010101010011010100110101011100000000000010101010100110100000 00010010010101110000000000010011000100100101011110101011000 110110.

But if we rearrange or "transpose" the bits—say, by reading each byte from right to left instead of from left to right so that 01010101 becomes 10101010—we obtain the stream:

10101010101100100100110101011100000000000101011011001000000 00100100100011101000000000001100101001001011110100110101001101 100

If we know the starting point of the bit stream and the length of the byte used to encode a character, it is easy to reverse each byte in order to reconstruct the original stream.

Still another transposition could be obtained by starting with the last bit and creating the transposed bit stream by taking the last bit of each byte and working backwards to the first byte, then the next-to-last bit of each byte, and so forth, producing:

00110001011001111100000000000001110101011011110011101101 00111 01110001000101001100000000000000011110110110111100000000000 000

This stream is also easy to convert to the original stream if we know that there are 16 bytes of 8 bits each.

A wraparound transposition can be obtained by starting at a pre-agreed spot in the sequence—usually not the beginning of any byte—and reading out the bits in the usual manner. For example, if the third bit is chosen as the starting point, we obtain:

010101010011010100110101011100000000000101010101001101000000000
010010010101110000000000010011000100100101011111010101010001101
1001

where the first two bits of the original sequence have been placed at the end of the derived sequence. Computer circuits that produce such transpositions are easy to construct (Figure 7-10).

Substitution ciphers use a key and an algorithm to replace the characters of the message with other characters that appear meaningless to the recipient. In modern communication systems, circuits to accomplish substitution rely on devices called "gates," which take in 2 or more bits and output a bit that depends on the type of gate.

AND gates implement the following scheme. The output is a 1 if both inputs are the same (both "1" or both "0"); otherwise, the output is a 0.

	First input	0	1
Second input			
0		1	0
1		0	1

Inclusive OR gates implement the following scheme. The output is a 1 if either of the inputs is a 1; otherwise, the output is a 0.

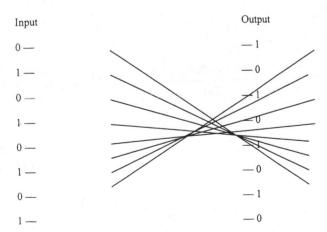

Figure 7-10
A transposition circuit.

Input

0 —
1 —
0 —
1 —
0 —
1 —
0 —
1 —

Output

— 1
— 0
— 1
— 0
— 1
— 0
— 1
— 0

	First input	0	1
Second input			
0		0	0
1		1	1

Exclusive OR gates implement the following scheme. The output is a 1 if either of the inputs, but not both of the inputs, is a 1; otherwise, the output is a 0.

	First input	0	1
Second input			
0		0	1
1		1	0

The Exclusive OR, often denoted XOR, operation is especially useful for cryptographic purposes. If 01101001 is the byte to be encrypted and 11001100 is our key, we can use the XOR operation on each pair of bits to obtain the encrypted byte 10100101:

Original byte	01101001
Key	11001100
Encrypted byte	10100101

This operation is equivalent to binary addition without carrying. That is, $0 + 0 = 0$, $0 + 1 = 1$, $1 + 0 = 1$, and $1 + 1 = 0$ (not 10, since we are not carrying forward). The XOR operation is very useful, since computers are highly efficient at binary addition and so perform the XOR function easily.

To recover the original byte, we simply use the same key and the same XOR operation:

Encrypted byte	11001100
Key	10100101
Original byte	01101001

Thus, the operation is completely reversible using a common key. Pictorially, the encryption and decryption processes are shown in Figure 7-11.

Taking the plaintext as a stream of bits and the key as a stream of bits, the encryption key and the decryption key are identical, and the

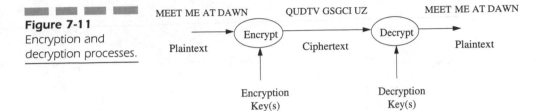

Figure 7-11
Encryption and
decryption processes.

Figure 7-12
Pseudorandom num-
ber generator.

encryption and decryption algorithms are also identical—they are, in fact, merely the XOR operation, which is easily implemented in circuits.

To create the key bit stream, we can use any sufficiently robust pseudorandom number generator. *Pseudorandom number generators* are mathematical functions that produce a sequence of numbers that are apparently random numbers even though they are deterministically produced (Figure 7-12). That is, the sequence of numbers produced by the pseudorandom number generator passes some tests designed to detect the presence of patterns that could be used, in turn, to duplicate the stream of numbers and thus crack the encryption system.

A pseudorandom number generator is like a little machine that cranks out an apparently random, but in fact deterministic, sequence of numbers that is combined by the encryption algorithm with the sequence of ones and zeros composing the plaintext one bit at a time to create the ciphertext. If the encryption algorithm is XOR, the process is simply that of binary addition (Figure 7-13).

Because it is truly deterministic, if we know the seed key, we can duplicate at the receiver the bit stream being created and used at the transmitter to encrypt the stream of bits that make up the plaintext. This same stream, if the decryption algorithm is XOR, is simply added to the ciphertext to re-create the plaintext (Figure 7-14).

Because, as noted earlier, most modern ciphers use a combination of transpositions and substitutions, and because computers deal with

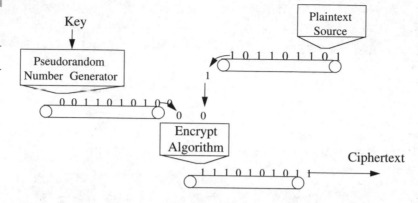

Figure 7-13
Using a pseudorandom number generator to encrypt.

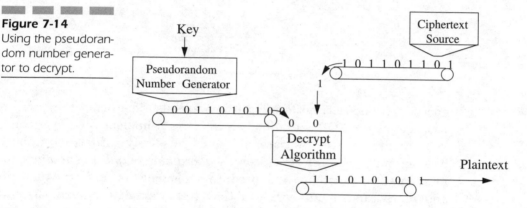

Figure 7-14
Using the pseudorandom number generator to decrypt.

blocks of bits easily, modern ciphers are usually block ciphers. The sequence of bits produced by the pseudorandom number generator is taken in blocks equivalent in length to the blocks of plaintext being processed (Figure 7-15).

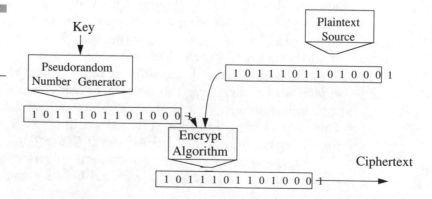

Figure 7-15
Block encryption using a pseudorandom generator.

The decryption process is again just the reverse of the encryption process.

In practice, pseudorandom number generators eventually repeat themselves, so we have, as a practical matter, to choose a function that does not repeat itself after only a short sequence of apparently random numbers is produced. To complete the picture of a practical encryption/decryption system, we need only point out that the pseudorandom number generator we use needs to be primed with a "seed key" for each random number sequence to ensure that the sequence it produces is not always the same. Seed keys may be short relative to the length of the nonrepeating pseudorandom number stream—a few dozen rather than hundreds of thousands to millions of numbers. This greatly simplifies the key management problem we discuss later. With this basis for understanding encryption and decryption keys, seed keys, and encryption and decryption algorithms, we are ready to look at a real, widely used cryptographic system, the Data Encryption Standard.

The Data Encryption Standard

The Data Encryption Standard (DES) is an encryption and decryption algorithm based on a routine called Lucifer that had been developed by IBM during the early 1970s. DES was adopted as a federal standard on November 23, 1976. Its official description was published as FIPS PUB 46 on January 15, 1977, and became effective six months later. DES is a block cipher that encrypts and decrypts blocks of 64 bits. The encryption and decryption algorithms are identical (Figure 7-16). A key of 56 bits is used for encryption and decryption of a plaintext. An additional 8 bits are used for parity checking. Any 56-bit number can be used as a key, but a few keys are weak and must be avoided. The security of the cipher rests, of course, entirely with the key, since the algorithm is known to all.

Figure 7-16
Using the data
encryption standard.

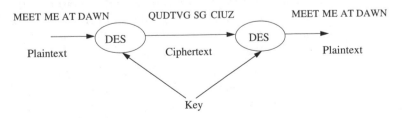

Upon being given a plaintext block of 64 bits, DES performs an initial transposition, scrambling the 64 bits in a patterned way. The resulting 64-bit block is then split into two 32-bit halves. Sixteen rounds each consisting of a substitution and a transposition follow, based upon the key. After the 16 rounds are completed, the resulting two halves are rejoined, and a final transposition, which is the inverse of the initial transposition, completes the enciphering operation (Figure 7-17).

Figure 7-17
Flow details of the data encryption standard.

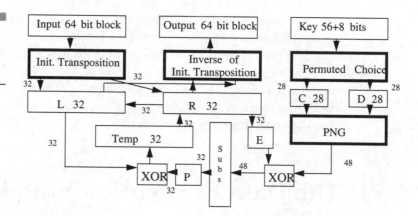

In each round, the bits of the key are shifted, and 48 of the 56 bits of the shifted key are selected. The right 32-bit half of the transposed plaintext resulting from the initial transposition is expanded in a patterned way to 48 bits and is then combined using an XOR function with the 48 bits selected from the shifted key. The next eight simultaneous substitutions convert each 6-bit subblock to a 4-bit output. The resulting eight 4-bit blocks are recombined to a single 32-bit block, which is then transposed in a patterned way and combined with the left half using the XOR function. The resulting 32 bits becomes the new right half, while the old right half becomes the new left half, completing the round. The transpositions in the round are linear and would succumb to cryptanalysis were it not for the nonlinearity introduced by the substitutions.

The initial key value is split by the algorithm into two halves, which are then shifted independently. Consequently, if all of the bits in each half are either 0 or 1, the same key insert will be used for every round. The four weak keys that must be avoided are 0000000 0000000, 0000000 FFFFFFF, FFFFFFF 0000000, and FFFFFFF FFFFFFF. These weak keys are given in hexadecimal format. Remember that every eighth bit is a parity bit in the format that must be supplied to initialize the algorithm.

A few pairs of keys deliver a ciphertext that is identical to the plaintext, so that one of the keys can decrypt messages encrypted with the other. There are six such key pairs:

01FE01FE01FE01FE and FE01FE01FE01FE01, 1FE01FE00EF10EF1 and

E01FE01FF10EF10E, 01E001E001F101F1 and E001E001F101F101,

1FFE1FFE0EFE0EFE and FE1FFE1FFE0EFE0E, 011F011F010E010E and

1F011F010E010E01, E0FEE0FEF1FEF1FE and FEE0FEE0FEF1FEF1.

Another 48 keys produce only four subkeys, which are each used four times. This means that 64 of the 72, 057, 594, 037, 927, 936 possible keys should be avoided; not an overwhelming problem.

There are several good reasons for choosing the Data Encryption Standard for encrypting messages requiring privacy and authentication. DES is widely available in both hardware and software versions, so it is easy to obtain and is often already used by an intended recipient. Moreover, it has been in use for years by many users and is not known to be susceptible to a cryptanalytic attack that significantly threatens its utility. Because it is the federal standard, its choice means that its users have *prima facie* used *due diligence* in selecting it and will not have to prove its efficacy in a negligence suit, as they will almost certainly have to do if another, less well-known cipher is chosen.

On the other hand, there are reasons not to use DES. As we have seen, 56-bit keys are not considered to be long enough by many cryptographers today and they have now been "cracked". (See paragraph below). As a consequence, triple DES, in which a message is enciphered three times using two or three different keys, is widely used in the financial community. Even more important, however, are the difficulties in using DES caused by the need for an expensive and cumbersome key management system.

A Standard under Fire

In July 1998 the roof caved in on the financial and other industries using DES-based cryptography products. The Electronic Frontier Foundation (EFF) announced their DES Cracker project. EFF organized and funded a project to build a specialized DES cracker for less than $250,000. Lead by the brilliant cryptographer Paul Kocher, President of Cryptography Research, the DES cracker broke a DES-cracking speed contest sponsored by RSA laboratories, beating out the combined efforts of massively parallel software from www.distributed.net. It found a 56-bit key in 56 hours by searching about 24.8 percent of the key space, or 88 billion keys tested per second! This is impressive evidence that developers of cryptographic products should not design anything else that depends on single DES. The exciting story of the DES cracker can be found in the EFF's book: *Cracking DES: Secrets of Encryption Research, Wiretap Politics and Chip Design*.[3]

Advanced Encryption Standard

The successor to DES is the Advanced Encryption Standard, or AES. In 1998, researchers from 12 different countries submitted 15 candidates for the AES—the new encoding method that eventually will be adopted by the federal government. Since that time, cryptographers have tried to find ways to attack the different encoding methods, looking for weaknesses that would compromise the encrypted information. On August 9, 1999, NIST narrowed the field of contenders from 15 candidates to five.

The AES will be a public algorithm designed to protect sensitive government information well into the next century. It will replace the aging Data Encryption Standard, which NIST adopted in 1977 as a Federal Information Processing Standard used by federal agencies to encrypt information. DES is used widely in the private sector as well, especially in the financial services industry.

NIST's Information Technology Laboratory chose the following five contenders as finalists for the AES:

- *MARS*—Developed by International Business Machines Corp. of Armonk, New York.
- *RC6*—Developed by RSA Laboratories of Bedford, Massachusetts.
- *Rijndael*—Developed by Joan Daemen and Vincent Rijmen of Belgium.
- *Serpent*—Developed by Ross Anderson, Eli Biham, and Lars Knudsen of the United Kingdom, Israel, and Norway, respectively.
- *Twofish*—Developed by Bruce Schneier, John Kelsey, Doug Whiting, David Wagner, Chris Hall, and Niels Ferguson. (Many members of this group are associated with Counterpane Systems of Minneapolis.)

No significant security vulnerabilities were found for the five finalists during the initial analysis of the algorithms, and each candidate offers technology that is potentially superior for the protection of sensitive information well into the twenty-first century.

NIST requested proposals for the AES on September 12, 1997. Each of the candidate algorithms supports cryptographic key sizes of 128, 192, and 256 bits. At a 128-bit key size, there are approximately 340,000,000,000,000,000,000,000,000,000,000,000,000 (340 followed by 36 zeroes) possible keys.

The global cryptographic community has been helping NIST in the AES development process by studying the candidates. NIST used feedback from these analyses and its own assessments to select the finalists. The studies evaluated security and how fast the algorithms could encrypt and decrypt information. The algorithms were tested on everything from large computers to smart cards.

During the evaluation process, NIST considered all comments, papers, verbal comments at conferences, reports and proposed modifications, and its own test data. Each candidate algorithm was discussed relative to the announced evaluation criteria and other pertinent criteria suggested during the public analysis. A detailed report on the process, "Status Report on the First Round of the Development of the Advanced Encryption Standard," is available on the AES Web site at www.nist.gov/aes.

NIST is making the five finalists available for intensified study and analysis by cryptographers, the public, industry, and academia. Analysis of the finalists will be presented at a conference in April 2000. NIST is accepting comments on the candidates through May 15, 2000. Then it will review the comments and draft the proposed AES (incorporating one or more of the algorithms) for public comment. If all goes as planned, the AES standard should be completed by the summer of 2001.

Key Management

The Data Encryption Standard is an example of a *symmetric* cipher. That is, both the sender and the recipient of enciphered messages must have the same key to make the cipher work. Since the security of the cipher depends entirely, as we have seen, on the key, it is vital that the key to be used is known only to the two parties using the cipher. If a third party can discover the key, either by stealing it or by cryptanalysis, the cipher can no longer guarantee privacy and authenticity.

The processes used to generate symmetric keys in such a way that they cannot be stolen at their source, to transmit them securely to all intended users of the cipher, and to store them securely until they are needed to encipher or decipher messages are together called *key management*. Such a schema may be as simple as using the telephone to exchange keys for e-mail messages that have been encrypted using a symmetric cipher and transmitted via the Internet or as complex as highly secure key-generation facilities coupled with trusted couriers to distribute the keys to secure storage facilities available to the users.

Various steps in the key management processes may be automated. If large numbers of keys are needed, as will certainly be the case when there are large numbers of users, computers may be used to generate the keys. Obviously, the security of the keys depends upon the security of the facility and computer system being used for key generation. Transfer of the keys to secure storage facilities available to the users may be by specially designed portable computers carried by trusted couriers. And, of course, the computer systems used to encrypt and decrypt messages and the facilities in which they are operated must be secure.

Key distribution and management can be significantly simplified by requiring all users to communicate via a central node. Then, instead of each potential pair of users needing a common key, requiring each of n users to have access to and securely retain n-1 keys, each user needs only the key for communicating securely with the central node. Bob, desiring to send a message securely to Alice, sends the message securely to the central node using their pre-agreed key. The central node deciphers the message and reenciphers it using the key it shares securely with Alice, sending the message safely then to Alice. Of course, the central node still must know n-1 keys, but each user is only responsible for the security of its own key and cannot compromise the keys that belong to other users.

It may be possible in some cases to use a key server to distribute keys to pairs of users for their use during specified periods or for specific exchanges of one or a few related messages (called *sessions*). In such systems, all users of the cipher are provided with keys, properly protected, with which they can communicate securely with the key server online. When Alice needs to communicate securely with Bob, she requests a session key from the key server. The key server uses its secure communications paths with Alice and Bob to provide each of them with the same session key, which is used only for that exchange of messages between Alice and Bob and then is (securely) discarded. This approach has the advantage that the central server does not get involved in the decipherment and reencipherment of messages between users.

In any case, the keys for communication with the central node or key server must be created securely and distributed and stored using trusted processes. Such processes are at best expensive and may be slow and inflexible as well. Symmetric cryptography cannot, however, be used without them.

Public Key Systems

In the late 1970s, a breakthrough in cryptography was announced that offered privacy and authentication without the need for cumbersome and expensive key management processes. In this new scheme, two keys were produced that were mathematically related in such a way that each could be used to encipher messages that the other could be used to decipher, a situation reminiscent of some of the weak keys for DES described above. Unlike the situation for weak DES keys, however, knowing one of the key pairs for this new scheme provided no advantage in discovering the other member of the pair.

This meant that if the key pair were generated securely and one of the keys was kept private, the other could be safely published for all to know. Then, anyone desiring to send the holder of the private member of the key pair could use the public member of the key pair to encipher a message that could only be deciphered by the holder of the private key. If Bob and Alice want to communicate privately, Bob uses Alice's public key to encipher messages to her, which Alice reads with her private key. Then Alice enciphers her replies using Bob's public key, which he deciphers with his own private key. For obvious reasons, such schema are called public key encryption systems.

Algorithms

When we peruse the literature of cryptography, we find many pages devoted to the practical and theoretical algorithms that are part and parcel of this science. Most of the public key ciphers available today depend upon a special class of mathematical problems that are theoretically possible to solve, but the solution of which would take so long, even using computers, that finding the solution for any given message is impractical. The security of such ciphers rests on the fact that even

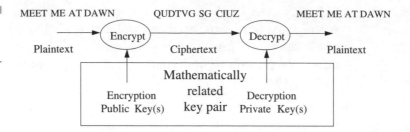

Figure 7-18
Using public key
cryptography.

given the public key, it is infeasible to determine the private key, and given the ciphertext, it is infeasible to determine the plaintext. (See Figure 7-18.)

Among some good texts on cryptography, cryptographic mathematics are explained thoroughly in Bruce Schneier's book *Applied Cryptography*.[4] Elliptic curve cryptography is covered expertly in Alfred J. Menezes, Paul C. van Oorschot, and Scott A. Vanstone's *Handbook of Applied Cryptography*.[5] Cryptographic security and implementation issues are fully covered in Randall K. Nichols' *The ICSA Guide to Cryptography*.[6] The reader is directed to the Reference section at the end of this book for other fine texts on the subject. Our coverage in this chapter will be limited to classification and difficulty of cryptographic systems.

Algorithms are the *raison d'etre* for cryptography. What is needed is a scheme to put the mathematics into simple focus. The author suggests that there are two practical ways to classify cryptographic algorithms. First, we can classify algorithms by their underlying difficulty of mathematical system, and second, we can classify them by their cryptographic purpose. In this chapter we will look at the mathematical systems. Cryptography algorithms span the mathematical gambit of number theory, complexity theory, elliptic curves, vector calculus, tensors, and set theory.

Difficulty of Mathematical Systems

In the first classification scheme, there are three types of mathematical problems considered both secure and efficient—in other words, not *crackable,* found easier than postulated, or impractical to calculate. The three mathematical problems on which practical cryptosystem security are based are as follows:[7]

- *Integer Factorization Problem (IFP)* RSA is the principal and best-known cryptosystem in this category.

- *Discrete Logarithm Problem (DLP)* Examples include the U.S. government's Digital Signature Algorithm (DSA), the Diffie-Hellman key agreement scheme, the ElGamal encryption and signature schemes, and the Schnorr signature scheme.

- *Elliptic Curve Discrete Logarithm Problem (ECDLP)* Examples of this type include the elliptic curve analog of the DSA (ECDSA), the elliptic curve analogs of the Diffie-Hellman key agreement scheme (ECDH), the ElGamal encryption and signature schemes (ECEG), and the Schnorr signature scheme (ECSS).

A second classification method separates cryptographic algorithms by cryptographic purpose or functionality: (1) symmetric, (2) asymmetric, (3) authentication systems, and (4) digital signatures. Obviously, there is overlap among the proposed schemes of classification.

Integer Factorization Systems

Diffie and Hellman discovered the concept of public key cryptography in 1976. Ron Rivest, Adi Shamir, and Len Adleman developed the first practical public key cryptographic system at MIT. The system was named RSA in honor of its inventors.

Security

RSA is the best known of a family of systems whose security relies on the difficulty of the *integer factorization problem (IFP)*. The integer factorization problem is defined as follows.

Given an integer, a whole number, p, is prime if it is divisible only by 1 and p itself. Now, given an integer n, which is the product of two large primes, determine those factors, i.e., find primes p and q such that:

$$p \times q = n. \hspace{2cm} [7\text{-}1]$$

An RSA public key consists of a pair (n, e), where e is a number between 1 and n-1, and n is the product of two *large* primes p and q. It is widely believed that to break RSA in general, the integer factorization problem must be solved (hence, factored) for the integer n. The factorization problem has been studied for over 300 years and no superefficient method of computation has been discovered. Since there is no efficient algorithm for the integer factorization problem, n can be chosen to be large enough to ensure that the system is secure. To provide even short-term security, given today's computing power, n should be at least 150 decimal digits long (150 decimal digits is approximately 500 bits). Hardware implementations in 1999 have become so effective that approximately 300 decimal digits, or 1028 bits, may be a better alternative.

Implementation

RSA, and other members of the integer factorization family, can be used both for encryption and for digital signatures (the digital equivalent of real signatures). To describe the operations used to perform these processes, modular arithmetic must first be defined. Modular addition and modular multiplication modulo n work just like ordinary addition and multiplication, except that the answer to the calculation is reduced to its remainder on division by n, so that the result always lies between 0 and n-1. The phrase "mod n" is written after each calculation to denote modular arithmetic. Modular arithmetic plays a central role in the implementation of all three types of public key cryptosystems.

When RSA is used either as an encryption scheme or as a digital signature scheme, exponentiation modulo n must be performed. Suppose m, a number between 0 and n-1, represents a message. Then the modular exponentiation

$$m^x \ (mod \ n) \qquad\qquad [7\text{-}2]$$

must be calculated for some number x when m is transformed. This modular exponentiation dominates the time taken to perform the transformations involved in the RSA system, so that the time required to calculate modular exponentiation modulo n essentially determines the time required to perform RSA.[8]

In short, the security of RSA, and the other members of the integer factorization family, *rests on the difficulty of the integer factorization problem*, and its efficiency rests on the speed of performing exponentiation modulo n.

Discrete Logarithm Systems

Security

Another mathematical problem defined in terms of modular arithmetic is the *discrete logarithm problem* modulo *a* prime p. Fix a prime number p. Then given an integer g between 0 and p-1, and y which is the result of exponentiating g, we define the following relation between g and y:

$$y = g^x \pmod{p} \qquad [7\text{-}3]$$

for some x. The discrete logarithm problem modulo p is to determine the integer x for a given pair g and y. The prime p used in discrete logarithm systems should also be at least 150 decimal digits (500 bits) in length to provide short-term security.

Like the integer factorization problem, no efficient algorithm is generally known to solve the discrete logarithm problem modulo p. Taher ElGamal was the first to propose a public key cryptosystem based on this problem. In fact, ElGamal proposed two distinct systems: one to provide encryption and one to perform digital signatures. In 1991, Claus Schnorr discovered a variant of the ElGamal digital signature system, which offers added efficiency compared to the original system. The U.S. government's Digital Signature Algorithm (DSA) is also based on ElGamal's work. The aforementioned systems are the best known of a large number of systems whose security is based on the discrete logarithm problem modulo p.

Implementation

As was the case with RSA, modular exponentiation must be performed to operate discrete logarithm systems. In every case, the dominant calculation in each of the transformations is as follows:

$$g^x \pmod{p} \qquad [7\text{-}4]$$

for some integer x, and a fixed number g between 0 and p-1.

Therefore, discrete logarithm systems can be described as a member of the DLP family, which relies on the discrete logarithm problem modulo p, and the *efficiency of the speed of performing modular exponentiation modulo p.*

The Elliptic Curve Cryptosystem (ECC)

The discrete logarithm problem modulo p was described in terms of modular arithmetic on the remainders of division by p. This is not the only mathematical structure that forms the basis for discrete logarithm problems. In 1985, Neil Koblitz and Victor Miller independently proposed the *Elliptic Curve Cryptosystem* (ECC). ECC security rests on the discrete logarithm problem applied to the points on an elliptic curve and has some powerful and unique features available for use in cryptographic systems. ECC can be used to provide both a digital signature scheme and an encryption scheme.

Security

An *elliptic curve*, defined modulo a prime p, is the set of solutions (x, y) to an equation of the form:

$$y^2 = x^3 + ax + b \;(\text{mod } p) \qquad\qquad [7\text{-}5]$$

for two numbers a and b. If (x, y) satisfies the above equation then $P = (x, y)$ is a *point* on the elliptic curve. An elliptic curve can also be defined over the *finite field* consisting of 2^m elements. Such a representation offers extra efficiency in the operation of the ECC. It is possible to define the "addition" of two points on the elliptic curve. Suppose P and Q are both points on the curve, then $P + Q$ will always be another point on the curve. Proof of this statement is beyond the scope of this book; however, it can be found in any of Scott Vanstone's or Neal Koblitz's books in the Annotated References and References section at the end of the book.

The elliptic curve discrete logarithm problem can be stated as follows. Fix a prime p and an elliptic curve. xP represents the point P *added* to itself x times. Suppose Q is a multiple of P, so that

$$Q = xP \qquad\qquad [7\text{-}6]$$

for some x. Then the *elliptic curve discrete logarithm problem* is to determine x given P and Q.

The security of the ECC rests on the difficulty of the elliptic curve discrete logarithm problem. As was the case with the integer factorization problem and the discrete logarithm problem modulo p, no efficient algorithm is known at this time to solve the elliptic curve discrete logarithm problem.[9]

One of the advantages of ECC is that the elliptic curve discrete logarithm problem *is believed to be harder to solve* than both the integer factorization problem and the discrete logarithm problem modulo p. This extra difficulty *implies* that ECC is one of the strongest public key cryptographic systems known today. Moderate security can be achieved with ECC using an elliptic curve defined modulo a prime p that is several times shorter than 150 decimal digits. This is a real advantage from a computer hardware and software implementation viewpoint. Confirming research is still in progress with such brain trusts as the University of Waterloo's Center for Cryptographic Research, with Doug Stinson leading the research. Such noted researchers as Neal Koblitz, Alfred Menezes, Simon Blake-Wilson, Scott Vanstone, and Hugo Krawczyk have joined to discover the secrets of ECC. ECC research is very exciting. As a side note, in 1998 RSA Laboratories agreed to include a version of ECC in its BSAFE toolkit.

Implementation

Just as modular exponentiation determined the efficiency of integer factorization and discrete logarithm systems, so the calculation of:

$$Q = xP \qquad [7\text{-}7]$$

for a point P on the elliptic curve and some integer x dominates the calculations involved in the operation of an ECC cryptosystem. The process of adding elliptic curve points requires a few modular calculations, so in the case of integer factorization, discrete logarithm systems, and elliptical curve cryptosystems, the operation of a public key cryptographic system is dependent upon efficient modular arithmetic. What is very interesting is that the prime p used in an ECC system can be *smaller* than the numbers required in the other types of systems, so another advantage of ECC is that the modular calculations required in its operation are carried out over a smaller modulus. This may lead to a significant improvement in efficiency in the operation of ECC over both integer factorization and discrete logarithm systems. ECC security rests on the elliptic curve discrete logarithm problem, while efficiency is dependent on the fast calculation of xP for some number x and a point P on the curve.

Comparison of Public Key Cryptographic Systems

Security and efficiency are two important issues for comparing IFP, DLP, and ECDLP public key cryptographic systems.[10]

Security

When examining the theoretical security of a public key cryptographic system, the prime consideration is *solving the underlying mathematical problem*. The concepts of complexity, Turing machines, polynomial time algorithms, and exponential time algorithms were introduced (refer to the appendices) to show how the difficulty of solving a mathematical problem is relative to the fastest algorithm available and the problem input size. According to Arto Salomaa, author of *Public-Key Cryptography*, in order to form the basis for a public key cryptographic system, it is emphasized that the fastest algorithm takes exponential time. *The longer it takes to compute the best algorithm for the problem, the more secure a public key cryptosystem based on that problem will be.*

It is also noted that none of the aforementioned problems—IFP, DLP, or ECDLP—have been *proven* to be intractable (i.e., difficult to solve in an efficient manner). Rather, they are *believed* to be intractable because years of intensive study by leading mathematicians and computer scientists have failed to yield efficient algorithms for solving them.

We might ask which is the hardest problem—the integer factorization problem (IFP), the discrete logarithm problem modulo p (*DLP*), or the elliptic curve discrete logarithm problem (ECDLP)? Unfortunately, there are no mathematical problems for which it can be proven that the best algorithm takes fully exponential time. Therefore, this discussion must focus on the best algorithms known today to solve these problems.

There are two types of algorithms: special-purpose and general-purpose. Special-purpose algorithms attempt to exploit special features of the system under consideration, such as the number n being factoring. A general-purpose algorithm solves *all* cases of the problem under consideration. The running time of a general-purpose algorithm is dependent on the *size* of the problem, for example, the size of n to be factored.

Special-Purpose Algorithms

With each of the three problems, there are good special-purpose algorithms that solve the problem quickly in certain special (meaning reduced or easy) instances.

IFP For integer factorization, there is a fast algorithm for $n = p \times q$ provided p-1 or q-1 only has small prime factors.

One of the most powerful special-purpose factoring algorithms is the elliptic curve factoring method (ECM) that was invented in 1985 by Hendrik Lenstra Jr. The running time of this method depends on the size of the prime factors of n, and hence the algorithm tends to find small factors first.

DLP For the discrete logarithm problem modulo p, there is a fast algorithm provided p-1 only has small prime factors. As with the integer factorization problem (IFP), there are two types of algorithms for solving the discrete logarithm problem. Special-purpose algorithms attempt to exploit special features of the prime p. In contrast, the running times of general-purpose algorithms depend only on the *size* of p.

ECDLP The elliptic curve discrete logarithm problem is relatively easy for a small class of elliptic curves, known as *supersingular elliptic curves*, and also for certain *anomalous elliptic curves*. In both cases, the "weak" instances of the problem are easily identified, and implementation merely checks that the specific instance selected is not one of the class of easy problems.

General-Purpose Algorithms

General-purpose algorithms are those that *always* succeed in solving the problem. The integer factorization problem and the discrete logarithm problem modulo p, both admit general algorithms that run in *subexponential time*. These subexponential time algorithms mean that the problem should still be considered hard, but not as hard as those problems that admit only fully exponential time algorithms. Formally, the running time for the best general algorithm (subexponential running time) for both of these problems is of the form of algorithm A, whose inputs are elements of a finite field Fn or an integer n; the form of A is as follows:

$$L_q \{\alpha, c\} = \theta \left(\exp((c + o(1)))(\ln n)^\alpha (\ln \ln n)^{1-\alpha} \right) \qquad 7\text{-}8$$

for a positive constant c, $0 \leq \alpha \leq 1$. α is usually of the order of 1/3, so (1-α) is 2/3. When α satisfies the constraint $0 \leq \alpha \leq 1$, then A is a subexponential time algorithm. When $\alpha = 0$, $L_q \{0,c\}$ is a polynomial in ln n, while for $\alpha = 1$, $L_q \{1,c\}$ is a polynomial in n, and thus fully exponential in ln n.

IFP   Prior to the development of the RSA cryptosystem, the best general-purpose factoring algorithm was the *continued fraction algorithm*, which could factor numbers up to 40 decimal digits (133 bits). This algorithm was based on the idea of using a *factor base* of primes and generating an associated set of linear equations whose solution ultimately led to a factorization. This is the same idea underlying the best general-purpose algorithms used today: the *quadratic sieve (QS)* and the *number field sieve (NFS)*. Both these algorithms can be easily paralleled with many computers working together to *permit factoring on distributed networks of workstations*. Large mainframe computers or supercomputers are therefore not essential to factor large numbers. Table 7-2 contains historical data on the progress of integer factorization.[11] (MIPS stands for millions of instructions executed per second.)

Table 7-2 results indicate that a 512-bit modulus n, in 1999, provides only marginal security when used in the RSA cryptosystem. For long-term security, 1024-bit or larger moduli should be used. Computers took several technical jumps forward during 1994 to 1999. The effect was a reduction in work factor for solving the IFP problem.

DLP   The fastest general-purpose algorithms known for solving the DLP are based on a method referred to as the *index-calculus*. In this method, a database of small primes and their corresponding logarithms is con-

TABLE 7-2

Historical Data on the Integer Factorization Problem.

Year	Number of Decimal Digits	Number of Bits	MIPS Years
1984	71	236	0.1
1988	106	352	140
1993	120	399	825
1994	129	429	5000
1995	119	395	250
1996	130	432	750
1999	155	512	10500

structed, subsequent to which logarithms of arbitrary field elements can be easily obtained. This is similar to factor base methods for integer factorization. For this reason, if an improvement in the algorithms for either the IFP or DLP is found, then shortly after, a similar improved algorithm can be expected to be found for the other problem. As with the factoring methods, the index-calculus algorithms can be easily *paralleled*.

As in the case with factoring, the best current algorithm known for the DLP is the number field sieve. It has precisely the same asymptotic running time as the corresponding algorithm for integer factorization. This can be loosely interpreted as saying that finding logarithms in the case of a k-bit prime modulus p is roughly as difficult as factoring a k-bit composite number n.

The implementation of discrete logarithm algorithms has lagged behind the analogous efforts for factoring integers. It is likely safe to say that taking logarithms modulo a 512-bit prime p will remain intractable for the next three or four years. In comparison, a 512-bit RSA modulus (or more) will likely be factored before the end of the twentieth century. We believe that for long-term security, 1024-bit or larger moduli, p should be used in discrete logarithm cryptosystems.

ECDLP The best general algorithm for the elliptic curve discrete logarithm problem is fully exponential time—its running time is as follows:

$$\theta(\sqrt{p}) \hspace{3cm} [7\text{-}9]$$

In simple terms, this means that the elliptic curve discrete logarithm problem (ECDLP) *may be considered harder to solve with respect to time than either the integer factorization problem or the discrete logarithm problem modulo p*. θ represents the order of magnitude of the problem.

Since 1985, the ECDLP has received considerable attention from leading mathematicians around the world. An algorithm developed by Pohlig and Hellman reduced the determination of l to the determination of l modulo for each of the prime factors of n. Hence, in order to achieve the maximum possible security level, n should be prime.

The best algorithm known to date for the ECDLP in general is the *Pollard rho method*, which takes about $\sqrt{(\pi n/2)}$ steps, where a step is an elliptic curve point addition. In 1993, Paul van Oorschot and Michael Wiener showed how the Pollard rho method can be paralleled so that if r processors are used, then the expected number of steps by each processor before a single discrete logarithm is obtained is $[\sqrt{(\pi n/2)}]/r$. Most significantly, no index-calculus-type algorithms are known for the ECDLP as for the DLP. This is the reason why the ECDLP is believed to be much harder than either the IFP or the DLP. No subexponential-time general-purpose algorithm is known for the ECDLP problem.

Table 7-3 shows the computing power required to compute a single discrete logarithm using the Pollard rho method for various values of n.[12]

As an example, if 10,000 computers, each rated at 1000 MIPS, are available and $n \approx 160$, then an elliptic curve discrete logarithm can be computed in 96,000 years.

Table 7-4 shows the estimated computing power required to factor integers with current versions of the number field sieve.[13] This is also roughly equal to the time it takes to compute discrete logarithms modulo a prime p of the same bit length as n.

Menezes and Jurisic compared the time required to break the ECC with the time required to break RSA or DSA for various modulus sizes

TABLE 7-3

Computing Power Required to Compute Elliptic Curve Logarithms with the Pollard Rho Method.

Field Size (in bits)	Size of n (in bits)	$\sqrt{\pi n/2}$	MIPS years
163	160	2^{80}	9.6×10^{11}
191	186	2^{93}	7.9×10^{15}
239	234	2^{117}	1.6×10^{23}
359	354	2^{177}	1.5×10^{41}
431	426	2^{213}	1.0×10^{52}

TABLE 7-4

Computing Power Required to Factor Integers Using the General Number Field Sieve.

Size of Integer to be Factored (in bits)	MIPS years
512	3×10^4
768	2×10^8
1024	3×10^{11}
1280	1×10^{14}
1536	3×10^{16}
2048	3×10^{20}

using the best general algorithm known. Values were computed in MIPS years, which represents a computing time of one year on a machine capable of performing one million instructions per second. As a benchmark, it is generally accepted that 10^{12} MIPS years represents reasonable security at this time, since this would require most of the computing power on the planet to work for a considerable amount of time.

Menezes found that, to achieve reasonable security, RSA and DSA would need to employ a 1024-bit modulus, while a 160-bit modulus should be sufficient for the ECC. He found that ECC required a smaller modulus than RSA or DSA and that the security gap between the systems grew as the key size increased. For example, 300-bit ECC is significantly more secure than 2000-bit RSA or DSA. Recall that the problem is judged to be the harder problem.

Another way to look at this security issue is to compare the equivalent strength of RSA/DSA keys and ECC keys for smart-card applications. Table 7-5 shows that, in smart-card applications requiring higher levels of security, ECC is able to offer security without a great deal of additional system resources.[14]

TABLE 7-5

Key Size: Equivalent Strength Comparison.

Time to Break MIPS/Years	RSA/DSA Key Size	ECC Key Size	RSA/ECC Key Size Ratio
10^4	512	106	5:1
10^8	768	132	6:1
10^{11}	1,024	160	7:1
10^{20}	2,048	210	10:1
10^{78}	21,000	600	35:1

Efficiency

When talking about the efficiency of a public key cryptographic system, there are three distinct factors to take into account:

1. *Computational overheads*   How much computation is required to perform the public key and private key transformations

2. *Key size*   How many bits are required to store the key pairs and associated system parameters

3. *Bandwidth*   How many bits must be communicated to transfer an encrypted message or a signature

Clearly, the comparisons should be made between systems offering similar levels of security, so in order to make the comparisons as concrete as possible, 160-bit ECC is compared with 1024-bit RSA and DSA. These parameter sizes are believed to offer comparable levels of security.

Computational Overheads   In each of the three systems, considerable computational savings can be made. In RSA, a short public exponent can be employed (although this represents a trade-off and does incur some security risks) to speed up signature verification and encryption. In both DSA and ECC, a large proportion of the signature generation and encrypting transformations can be precomputed. Also, various special bases for the finite field $F_2{}^m$ can be employed to perform more quickly the modular arithmetic involved in ECC operation. State-of-the-art implementations of the systems show that with all of these efficiencies in place, ECC is an order of magnitude (roughly 10 times) faster than either RSA or DSA. The use of a short public exponent in RSA can make RSA encryption and signature verification timings (but not RSA decryption and signature generation timings) comparable with timings for these processes using the ECC.

Key Size   Table 7-6 compares the size of the system parameters and selected key pairs for the different systems.[15] The table presents evidence that the system parameters and key pairs are shorter for the ECC than for either RSA or DSA.

TABLE 7-6

Size of System Parameters and Key Pairs (approx.).

	System Parameters (bits)	Public Key (bits)	Private Key (bits)
RSA	N/A	1088	2048
DSA	2208	1024	160
ECC	481	161	160

Bandwidth   All three types of systems have similar bandwidth requirements when they are used to encrypt or sign long messages. However, the case when short messages are being transformed deserves particular attention because public key cryptographic systems are often employed to transmit short messages, for example, to transport session

TABLE 7-7

Signature Sizes on
Long Messages
(e.g., 2000-bits).

	Signature Size (bits)
RSA	1024
DSA	320
ECC	320

TABLE 7-8

Size of Encrypted
100-bit Messages.

	Encrypted Message (bits)
RSA	1024
ElGamal	2048
ECC	321

keys for use in a symmetric key cryptographic system. For comparison, suppose that each is being used to sign a 2000-bit message, or to encrypt a 100-bit message. Tables 7-7 and 7-8 compare the lengths of the signatures and encrypted messages respectively.[16]

Tables 7-7 and 7-8 suggest that ECC offers bandwidth savings over the other types of public key cryptographic systems when being used to transform short messages.

Comparison Summary

In summary, ECC provides greater efficiency than either integer factorization systems or discrete logarithm systems, in terms of computational overheads, key sizes, and bandwidth. In implementations, these savings mean higher speeds, lower power consumption, and code size reductions. However, as of this writing, the RSA system (based on the IFP) is globally accepted in vendor offerings and may dominate the field until more research information about ECC becomes available. Times are changing. Recently, in 1998, RSA, Inc., announced the inclusion of ECC technology in its basic cryptographic tool kit.

Digital Signatures

In some implementations of public key cryptography, when the private key is used to encipher a message, the public key can then be used to decipher the message. Obviously, such a scheme does not protect privacy, since everyone has access to the public key and can therefore read the message. But only the holder of the private key could have written the message, provided that the private key has been securely kept.

This strong form of authentication that the message received could only have been sent by the holder of the private key corresponding to the public key used to decipher the message is sufficient to prove—in court if necessary, at least in states that have recognized such authentication as valid—that the message did indeed come from the purported sender. The sender cannot repudiate the message. This makes this scheme of encryption as valid as an inked signature on a paper document and is accordingly called a *digital signature*.

Note that this is not a digital representation or image of a pen-and-ink signature, but a message that has been encrypted using a private key and decrypted using a corresponding public key. It authenticates the document because the document could only have been so enciphered using the private key, which is deemed to have been held securely by its owner, because it assures everyone that the message could only have come from the holder of the private key. Digital signatures are exactly the type of authentication needed to facilitate electronic commerce, as will be discussed in detail in Chapter 9.

Certificate Authorities

This by no means implies that public key cryptosystems are without problems in either implementation or use. Since a cryptanalyst will have, like everyone else, access to the public key used to encipher a message, if the message is small, it might be possible to use a brute-force attack and try all possible messages until that one is found that produces the ciphertext observed. Of course, this disadvantage can be easily avoided by padding the message with random bits or characters unrelated to the basic message to be conveyed. Even so, public key ciphers are particularly susceptible to attack when the cryptanalyst can choose different ciphertexts for decipherment and knows what the plaintext is for each such ciphertext. If a digital signature produced by such a cipher, as will be discussed shortly, is the result of the inverse application of the encipherment algorithm, it is vital that different keys be used for encipherment and digital signing if such an attack is to be avoided.

A more fundamental problem lies in the method used to authenticate the public key. If you retrieve a public key from someone's Web page or receive it in an e-mail, how do you know that it really belongs to the person to whom you think it belongs? What has prevented Bob from sending you a public key using Alice's name so that you think it is hers? When you think you are sending a message that can only be read by Alice, you will then actually be sending a message that can only be read by Bob. You should never use a public key unless you are positive that it belongs to the person with whom you are trying to communicate.

To avoid such a problem, you must be very sure that the public key you are using truly belongs to the recipient you intend to receive and read your messages. If you get the key directly from the person, you can be sure it is his or hers. If you get it from a third party, that third party must be one whom you can trust not to deceive you and to not be negligent in forwarding a public key that has not been validated as belonging to the party to whom it purports to belong. For widespread use of public keys among strangers, as will be necessary in electronic commerce, we will need online access to trusted third parties who will maintain databases of public keys in a form called *certificates*, which have been placed into the database only after carefully authenticating their owners. Such trusted third parties are called *certificate authorities*. Of course, it will be vital that the certificate authority store the databases securely and that the certificates, along with their private keys, be communicated securely to those who need to use them.

To see how the scheme works, say Alice wants to send Bob, her stockbroker, an order. She composes her message: "Buy 100 shares of Trigraph, Inc. at $5.00 per share." She uses her private key to encipher the message so that Bob can be assured that it comes, in fact, from her. She then asks her certificate authority to send her Bob's public key certificate. If Bob uses the same certificate authority, his public key certificate is taken from the database, digitally signed with the private key of the certificate authority, and returned to Alice. Alice knows it came from the certificate authority because it is digitally signed and she can decipher it using the public key of the certificate authority. Moreover, she trusts the certificate authority to have authenticated the key when Bob delivered it to the certificate authority, so she knows it truly belongs to Bob. Alice uses Bob's public key to encipher the buy message she has digitally signed with her private key and sends the ciphertext to Bob. If Bob uses a different CA, then cross-certification between CAs would be a requirement.

Bob deciphers the message with his private key. Then Bob asks the certificate authority for Alice's public key certificate and uses it to decipher her digitally signed plaintext, which he now knows only she could have sent. He knows he can rely on the message and make the buy for her. If he sends her a receipt for her message, digitally signed with his own private key, she knows—and can prove—that he got the message. Dates and times can be included on both messages, if desired, or the messages can be passed through the certificate authority, who can add a time stamp digitally signed by the certificate authority using its own private key. Digital signatures and certificate authorities are discussed in more detailed in Chapter 9.

Using Public Key Cryptography for Key Management

Public key cryptography seems to solve the key management problem. Keys must still be created using secure processes because the private keys must be kept private. However, there is no need for expensive and cumbersome processes for distributing and storing keys, since the public keys do not have to be kept private for the scheme to ensure confidentiality and authentication. So why doesn't everyone just use public key cryptography when they need cryptography?

One answer lies in the relative efficiency of the algorithms. Symmetric encryption is generally much faster than public key encryption. The speed difference doesn't amount to much if only small messages are involved, but it can be significant when messages are large. Thus, if bulk encryption is needed to securely send large amounts of information, symmetric encryption is much to be preferred.

But the keys for symmetric encryption are relatively small. Even when the keys are chosen conservatively to prevent cryptanalytic attacks by exhausting the entire key space, they are only a few hundred or thousand bits long. They can be easily and quickly enciphered, then, using at least some forms of public key cryptography and having been exchanged safely with those parties who need them, they can be used for bulk encryption using the faster symmetric routines. Technologically, this solves the problem of key management. Politically, the problem is not so tractable.

Cryptopolitics and Privacy Concerns

Privacy is certainly a matter of great concern in today's densely populated and increasingly connected world, for reasons we have discussed at length elsewhere in this book. But as valuable as it is, privacy is not the only value that must be protected. Privacy is a two-edged sword and as surely as it protects law-abiding members of our community, it can also protect criminals, saboteurs, terrorists, and spies. The first duty of government is to provide for the security of its citizens. The law enforcement and national security communities have found, in the ability to intercept the communications used in planning and executing criminal activities and espionage, a powerful weapon for protecting public safety. Recognizing that cryptography can deny them that weapon by making wiretaps and other forms of communications intercepts useless, these communities have moved strongly to suppress the widespread use of cryptography.

In order to deny the use of powerful cryptography to actual or potential enemies of the United States and to drug traffickers and organized criminals who operate internationally, the United States has made it illegal to export cryptographic hardware or software. The law enforcement and national security communities also seek to assure access to telephonic and data communications within the United States, subject, of course, to requirements for demonstration to an unbiased court that probable cause exists to believe that the communications to be intercepted might reveal a criminal scheme in progress or espionage activities by foreign governments. Since widespread easy-to-use encryption would make their jobs of protecting the public's safety and the nation's security more difficult, these communities undoubtedly have a valid interest in these issues.

Still, others find that the restrictions imposed, or desired to be imposed, by the law enforcement and national security communities are unduly restrictive. Generally applicable laws aimed at denying the right to criminals and spies to use cryptography may also have the effect of denying the right to law-abiding citizens to protect their own privacy using cryptography. Large additional costs may be borne by the nation's information infrastructure, particularly by the public switched network, in meeting the demands for assured access, costs that will have to be passed on to consumers or paid out of tax revenues.

Other opponents point out that cryptographic systems, including DES and public key cryptography, are widely available outside the United States despite export controls, so export controls burden U.S. companies' ability to compete abroad without providing any of the promised enhanced security and safety. If offshore companies can produce software and hardware that include powerful, easy-to-use encryption, the U.S.-produced versions that have severely weakened or no encryption will not be bought in overseas markets. One of the few areas where, as a nation, we have a positive balance of trade may be significantly damaged or lost because of ill-considered and ineffectual export controls. The genie cannot, they assert, be returned to the lamp. One of the most important cases in courts affecting cryptographic export policy is *Daniel J. Bernstein v. U.S. Department of Commerce,* et al. The interesting details and the implications of this case are provided in Appendix O.

Nor is it clear, claim the critics, that the losses do not or will not outweigh the gains at home. Even at home, if cryptography is already widely available and easy to use, what is to stop criminals and domestic terrorists from using it here to protect themselves? Moreover, if billions of dollars are being lost to our economy because of poor information security on our systems and networks, and if cryptography is an important and integral part of improved information security, by suppressing cryptography the law enforcement community may prevent the use of some of the most valuable self-protection technology available to American industry. Their restrictive policies, laws, and regulations may actually be making the problem worse instead of better. The added safety promised by the law enforcement community is chimerical; it cannot and will not occur, and personal freedom of privacy and positive balance of trade will be lost.

Perhaps a middle ground is possible. Permit the widespread use of cryptography needed by electronic commerce and required to safeguard our information assets, systems, and our personal privacy but require that the keys used for licit cryptographic applications be escrowed, or at least recoverable. They would then be available, under proper court order, of course, to the law enforcement and national security communities if needed. And as a by-product, lost or purloined keys will never again be a problem for companies and individuals with the attendant loss of valuable data. Everybody, proponents urge, wins. But questions remain. Who do we trust to hold the keys? It is part of our culture, proven all too often in history, to be suspicious of governmental intent when our privacy is at stake. Are we to empower trusted third parties, not the government, to hold the keys, just as we trust them to authenticate and secure private key certificates? How will the prices for their services be determined and who will pay? And, more seriously, what will force the criminals, terrorists and spies to submit their keys to escrow or ensure their recovery on demand?

These are serious public policy questions for which, to date, there are no answers. Court cases have been filed, legislation sponsored, and regulations proposed. There is much room for reasonable people to disagree as to what should be done and what the consequences are likely to be. Few debates will be more important. Poor choice of policies, laws, and regulations can cripple positive balance of trade, undermine our ability to protect information assets and systems, and deny us the advantages of electronic commerce.

Key Recovery—An Analysis of the Issues and Alternatives Associated with Recoverable Keys

The tension between communications and privacy has fostered a myriad of customs, laws, and technologies. Eavesdropping on others' conversations is considered a breach of etiquette; wiretapping someone's telephone can be a breach of law. Since time immemorial, techniques have been used to hide the content of communications from persons who were not intended to be party to the communication. These methodologies included the use of secret languages, the manipulation of physical characteristics, and the development of the science of cryptology.

The art of hiding information has continued to be used by both good guys and bad guys, by spies and by law enforcement, by merchants and by thieves. The desire to hide information has given birth to microdots and invisible ink, one-time pads and watermarks. It seems as if there is no limit to the imagination of how communications can be hidden.

This trend has become more automated as our world becomes electronically internetted with sophisticated computing machines available for every desktop. The complexity of executing and managing the hiding of information has been simplified to a few keystrokes on a computer. Challenges still remain, but the capabilities supported by the technology are available to the ordinary person on a scale previously unthinkable. Now, instead of requiring special training or complicated mechanisms, all that is required is a piece of software that is small, runs on a desktop computer, and may even be free.

The reaction to the widespread availability of cryptologic capabilities has been an unleashing of a war of words—some innuendo, some plain-spoken—all over the balance between threat and promise inherent in promiscuous privacy. After all, it is not just law-abiding citizens who can use these products for privacy—so can criminals.

How should a free society respond to what, on one hand, appears to be a technological windfall for criminal elements but what, on the other hand, appears to be the normal course of technological progress providing augmented capabilities for ordinary citizens in all aspects of their lives, even as their lives expand into and through cyberspace? The trade-offs to be considered include not only trust and civil society but also the future of commerce, international competitive structures, and the fundamental rights of privacy. Because of the widely available nature of cryptography today within the pervasive telecommunications environment, it has become a key enabling technology for many uses.

Contemporary Uses of Cryptography

One of the premiere applications that cryptography enables is electronic commerce. The ability to conduct market transactions over telecommunications networks has long been a dream. It would reduce the amount of inventory any market would have to keep on hand, it would allow customers to go directly to manufacturers, and it would speed up the overall pace of transactions. However, the implementation details of online transactions have been a stumbling block. How do you, the consumer, know that some nefarious hacker is not stealing your credit card number? How do you, the service provider, know that the credit card belongs, in fact, to the person who is offering it? These are among the issues that concern those hoping to implement electronic commerce on a wide scale. The use of cryptography can alleviate those concerns, particularly with a mixture of symmetric and asymmetric cryptography.

Another critical application for cryptography is in political activism. In repressed areas or in highly sensitive or emotional issues, persons associated with a cause may have very good reasons for not having their identity easily discovered. Fear of reprisals ranging from ostracism to arrest or death can dampen the fervor of even the most courageous activist. Being able to use cryptography over the public switched network to hide identities and communications gives enormous power to those who are laboring against brutal regimes.

One person's brutal regime is another person's benevolent dictatorship, however. What is seen as political activity on one side can easily be viewed as criminal activity from the other side. The use of cryptography to hide criminal activity from a legal government protecting its citizens can cause a government enormous concern, particularly if the political activists are given to blowing up school buses or massacring people at will. The slide into other areas of criminal activity, such as kidnapping, thievery, bank robbery, blackmail, smuggling, and narcotics trafficking rightfully has law enforcement organizations everywhere worried about their ability to deter crime and prosecute criminals.

Problems with Cryptography

Clearly, there are both good uses and bad uses to which cryptography can be put. A fundamental aspect of cryptography is that information is hidden. There are only two ways to discover the information: One is if you have the key to decrypt it, the other is if you are able to crack the code.

Tales of breaking ciphers have long been a favorite of historians and novelists. Stories such as *The Key to Rebecca* by Ken Follett[17] and "The Adventure of the Dancing Men" by Arthur Conan Doyle[18] stimulate the imagination with tales of extraordinary bravery and intellect in discovering and cracking encryption schemes. In *The Key to Rebecca*, the secrets hidden by the cipher pertain to enemy actions during World War II—the ability of the allies to penetrate the code and decipher the contents became a critical linchpin in the success of the war operations in Northern Africa in the campaign against Rommel. In "The Adventure of the Dancing Men," Sherlock Holmes deciphers a cryptogram and thus is able to save a lady's life, catching the criminal in the process. These two stories illustrate the national security and public safety reasons for wanting an assured methodology to decipher hidden messages at will.

One can imagine that the reason that these stories so excite both the authors and the readers is that the information hidden in the cipher stands on the brink between being known and unknown. Between the state of being hidden and being discovered lies a universe of opportunity. In some cases, the fate of political course of events far removed from the immediate situation has been altered by the outcome. As David Kahn writes:

> Military history between the Gallic wars and the World Wars cites thousands of examples of the use of cryptography and many, many cases that illustrate the power of cryptanalysis in resolving battles, crises and even the course of wars. Consider the fall of Réalmont to Henry II of Bourbon, Prince of Condé. When, during his siege, Condé had a secret message from

the town intercepted and decrypted that reported the town's desperate need for munitions, he simply returned the deciphered message and the town surrendered. The incident captured the attention of Cardinal Richelieu, who found cryptology to be admirably suited to the political and diplomatic games in which he engaged on behalf of the French Court. This led to the hiring of Rossignol by the King and the renaissance of modern cryptography as an enabling technology for geopolitical intrigues as well as military victories.[19]

The ability of unauthorized people to crack the codes that hid critical information has long spurred the development of more-sophisticated and secure encryption algorithms. Today's algorithms are so secure that it takes supercomputers to crack encrypted messages that use keys of any reasonable length.

While data is hidden from unintended recipients, it is also hidden from intended recipients who don't have the correct keys to decrypt the message. Keys have been known to be lost—people simply forget what the key is. Keys have also been known to have gotten lost when the sole repository of the key was lost. Say, for example, Fred is working on a highly sensitive piece of work for the company. Just before he leaves work for the day, he encrypts his work, stores it on a disk, locks the disk in a safe, clears his operating buffers and cache space using a special-purpose utility program, and then goes home. That night, tragically, Fred has a heart attack and dies. The only person who knew the key to decrypt the file is now unable to tell anyone (except a medium).

That highlights a real problem using cryptography: death, memory loss, and even maliciousness can sabotage the efforts of keeping private information private. There are policy solutions that can alleviate the problems with lost keys. Fred could have, for example, stored his key in a sealed envelope in a separate safe. That would have allowed his work to be recoverable in case of accident or misfortune.

Key Recovery: A Technology Solution to a Policy Problem

Policy solutions, however, require active management and education of all personnel in an operational environment in order for them to be effective. If there had been a policy requiring Fred to maintain a recoverable copy of his key, it would have been necessary for Fred to abide by the policy. If he simply ignored it or forgot to follow it in the rush of going home at night, the result would have been the same: a lost key.

The concept of a technological solution for the key recovery problem gets around relying on humans to abide by policy. This technological solution is known as *key recovery* or *key escrow*. The purpose of key recovery or key escrow schemes is very straightforward: It is to allow the recovery of encrypted information without the keys.

There are a variety of implementations that have been proposed for key recovery. One of the best known is the Clipper Chip solution. As described by the White House announcement on April 16, 1993:

> A state-of-the-art microcircuit called the "Clipper Chip" has been developed by government engineers. The chip represents a new approach to encryption technology. It can be used in new, relatively inexpensive encryption devices that can be attached to an ordinary telephone. It scrambles telephone communications using an encryption algorithm that is more powerful than many in commercial use today.
>
> This new technology will help companies protect proprietary information, protect the privacy of personal phone conversations and prevent unauthorized release of data transmitted electronically. At the same time this technology preserves the ability of federal, state and local law enforcement agencies to intercept lawfully the phone conversations of criminals.
>
> A "key-escrow" system will be established to ensure that the "Clipper Chip" is used to protect the privacy of law-abiding Americans. Each device containing the chip will have two unique "keys," numbers that will be needed by authorized government agencies to decode messages encoded by the device. When the device is manufactured, the two keys will be deposited separately in two "key-escrow" databases that will be established by the Attorney General. Access to these keys will be limited to government officials with legal authorization to conduct a wiretap.[20]

The two parts of the Law Enforcement Access Field (LEAF) associated with the Clipper Chip were to have been escrowed with National Institute of Standards and Technology (NIST) and the Department of the Treasury.

The Clipper Chip scheme employed a hardware element with associated identification backdoors that allowed an authorized person to get access to the encrypted information. The controls of having two separate parts of the master key escrowed at two different agencies was an essential part of the design that would limit accidental exposure or misuse. Other schemes could be developed that would only have one master key.

The furor that erupted over the Clipper Chip served to bring a robust debate of the issues to the foreground. The most vociferous complainants invoked the image of Big Brother and a lack of privacy anywhere. It was repeatedly pointed out that the stated goals of law enforcement were misleading in the extreme—why would a criminal use an encryption tool that the government could break into at will? The acrimonious debate highlighted these concerns at the same time it identified real reasons for a key recovery system.

On one hand, the elements of government, from federal to state to local, have an interest in being able to archive all communications associated with the business of governance. These elements could, therefore, mandate that all communications with them be done either in the clear or using a recoverable key system.

Similarly, business and industry have an interest in making sure that company proprietary information is not accidentally or maliciously lost. They are not, however, interested in having that data recoverable by an outside agency either now or 50 years from now. The time independence of the recoverable aspect of the proposed key escrow scheme served to make some elements of society very nervous, particularly in reference to changing standards, potential hostilities, or other unpleasant possibilities. While business acknowledges a theoretical need for key recovery, they are adamantly opposed to a mandated key recovery system controlled by the government.

It is likely that other organizations, such as professional groups or social clubs, might at some point in time decide that a key recovery system would be useful for their membership and business transactions. Each of these organizations has a different perspective, different equities to protect, and different implementation requirements.

The reasons for such groups to implement a key recovery system include wanting to:

- Maintain recoverable audits of communications and transactions
- Enable verifiable collection of revenues
- Protect interests
- Provide resiliency in system against errors and mistakes
- Provide recovery capability against problems or accidents

It is clear, therefore, that there are both reasons for and against use of a key recovery system and separable issues on the questions of how one is implemented.

Public and Private Reaction to Clipper

Selected quotes from the Clipper Chip debate highlight the reaction and the response to this issue. The complaints ranged from market-oriented concerns to privacy issues. The persons weighing in on the issue ranged from administration officials to senators and representatives of the United States to private citizens. The result of the uproar was that the Clipper Chip scheme was relegated to government-only use, although commercial sales were still nominally attempted, and the administration went back to the drawing board for a policy regarding encrypted communications.

From a group of senators and representatives concerned over industrial competition:

> Unfortunately, the Administration's most recent encryption initiative shortchanges both U.S. business and law enforcement interests. The proposal is flawed for four reasons: it fails to recognize that top-down, government-imposed policies are doomed to defeat; export policies must be directly linked, or indexed, to advances in technology; export controls must be fully multilateral in order to be effective; and export control decisions will be further delayed by granting the FBI new veto authority over U. S. exports.[21]

From a news article reporting on comments from the Director of the FBI:

> "It is a matter of life or death in years to come that law enforcement have some access to this technology," Federal Bureau of Investigation Director Louis Freeh testified...during a fractious Capitol Hill hearing. The widespread use of robust encryption, he added, "is one of the most difficult problems confronting law enforcement as the next century approaches."[22]

From the same article reporting on comments from Senator Hatch:

> "There appears to be little dispute that the development of some form of key recovery is inevitable," Sen. Orrin Hatch, R-Utah, testified in a hearing before the Senate Judiciary Committee. "What is not at all clear...is whether our national encryption policy should be based upon a government-mandated or controlled key recovery scheme, whether the government should remove itself from this debate...or whether there exists a middle ground."[23]

From a paper published online reflecting on who would actually use escrowed encryption:

No terrorist worth his C-4 will be using encryption software with a backdoor for anything more important than ordering a T-shirt via Netscape like any other American.

It will be the other Americans, the LAW-ABIDING Americans, who can now have their encrypted data broken at governmental whim. No one with anything to hide and half a grain of sense would use key-recoverable encryption.[24]

From the same paper, reflecting on the fairness aspects of the issue:

Widespread encryption is a good thing. It keeps you safe. It means you don't have to live in a glass house if you don't want to. The problem is, it keeps you just as safe from the government as it does everyone else. The government doesn't think that's fair. They like glass houses, so they can see inside.[25]

From a letter by the Software Publishers Association, an industry consortium, to members of the Committee on Commerce:

In its December 1995 study, SPA demonstrated that there were then 497 foreign products containing strong encryption available in at least 67 countries. As these foreign products increase in number and improve in quality, as they have over the last year, U.S. companies will forever lose a foothold in this growing market. What this means for American companies is lower revenues, lost market share, higher production costs and fewer jobs.[26]

From a group of the most distinguished cryptologists in the nation, commenting on feasibility aspects:

Key recovery systems are inherently less secure, more costly, and more difficult to use than similar systems without a recovery feature. The massive deployment of a key recovery infrastructure to meet law enforcement's stated requirements will require significant sacrifices in security and convenience and substantially increased costs to all users of encryption. Furthermore, building the secure infrastructure of the breathtaking scale and complexity that would be required for such a scheme is beyond the experience and current competency of the field, and may well introduce ultimately unacceptable risks and costs.[27]

Post-Clipper Policy Initiatives

The U.S. government did not abandon the idea of key escrow with the massive failure of the Clipper Chip in the eyes of the public. On the contrary, convinced that national security as well as private safety was at stake, the administration went back to the drawing board and attempted to negotiate some intermediary position that would address not only the public's concern over privacy but also the growing outrage from the U.S. computer industry over export controls on encryption products, while maintaining the government's interests.

The various parts of the administration have been very active in drumming up support, as documented by the following extracts. The first is a statement from the Administration on Commercial Encryption Policy given on July 12, 1996:

> The Clinton Administration is proposing a framework that will encourage the use of strong encryption in commerce and private communications while protecting the public safety and national security. It would be developed by industry and will be available for both domestic and international use....The framework is based on a global key management infrastructure that supports digital signatures and confidentiality.
>
> Trusted private sector parties will verify digital signatures and also will hold spare keys to confidential data. Those keys could be obtained only by persons or entities that have lost the key to their own encrypted data, or by law enforcement officials acting under proper authority. It represents a flexible approach to expanding the use of strong encryption in the private sector....
>
> In the expectation of industry action to develop this framework internationally, and recognizing that this development will take time, the Administration intends to take action in the near term to facilitate the transition to the key management infrastructure.
>
> The measures the Administration is considering include:
>
> 1. Liberalizing export controls for certain commercial encryption products.
> 2. Developing, in cooperation with industry, performance standards for key recovery systems and products that will be eligible for general export licenses, and technical standards for products the government will purchase.
> 3. Launching several key recovery pilot projects in cooperation with industry and involving international participation.
> 4. Transferring export control jurisdiction over encryption products for

commercial use from the Department of State to the Department of Commerce.[28]

The second is a news item appearing eight months later in March 1997 on domestic encryption controls that reported on the continuing administration attempts to set up a large infrastructure to manage the introduction and administration of a key recovery system:

> The Clinton Administration has drafted legislation to control the domestic use of encryption technologies and compel participation in key recovery systems open to the government. The bill would:
>
> ■ Create a vast new government-dominated "key management infrastructure" designed to be a prerequisite for participation in electronic commerce.
>
> ■ Compel people to use key recovery as a condition of participating in the key management infrastructure.
>
> ■ Require the disclosure of all private keys held by third parties, without a court order and upon mere written request of any law enforcement or national security agency.[29]

While this legislation was wending its way through the legislative process (unsuccessfully), members of Congress were probing into the extent of FBI activities under previously passed legislation:

> On Thursday, October 23, 1997, the Subcommittee on Crime of the House Judiciary Committee held a hearing to examine concerns about FBI over-reaching in the implementation of the digital telephony law. CDT [Center for Democracy and Technology] senior staff counsel Jim Dempsey testified, along with industry and FBI representatives. CDT and industry had called for a hearing on CALEA [Communications Assistance for Law Enforcement Act] earlier in the year. CDT's testimony stressed that the FBI is trying, contrary to Congress' intent, to use the legislation to expand rather than merely preserve its surveillance capabilities. CDT explained that the proposed industry standard for implementing CALEA goes too far in mandating a location tracking capability in wireless systems and in allowing telephone companies using packet switching protocols to deliver call content to law enforcement when the government is not entitled to receive it. In addition, the FBI is seeking a number of further enhancements. The statutory deadline for compliance with CALEA is October 25, 1998. Most members of the Subcommittee seemed to agree that the deadline would have to be extended.[30]

Finally, in November 1997, a commission studying critical issues relating to the protection of the infrastructure reported out, endorsing the need for a national key recovery system:

> The President's Commission on Critical Infrastructure Protection (PCCIP)…released its comprehensive report on the important issue of protecting America's vulnerable infrastructures. At the same time, however, the report recommends creation of an entirely new infrastructure for storage and recovery of encryption keys—an infrastructure that leading experts in the field believe would itself be vulnerable to the very threats the PCCIP describes. The PCCIP report recommends that the government expedite pilot projects to build "public confidence and trust with the KMI [key management infrastructure] key recovery approach," and calls on the Administration to promote "the implementation of a KMI that supports lawful key recovery on an international basis." (See PCCIP Report, Part 2, Recommendations.) While the report recognizes that encryption is "an essential element for the security of information," the key recovery systems it recommends would actually create new vulnerabilities in the information infrastructure.[31]

Clearly, neither side of the debate has given in or surrendered any ground to the other side.

As of this writing (1999), Congress has before it H.R. 850 "Protection of National Security and Public Safety Act," reported by the Committee on Armed Services and 58-133 Part 5 "Encryption for the National Interest Act" reported out of the Permanent Select Committee on Intelligence. Both bills have key recovery provisions restrictive of public encryption and both are in direct opposition to the more commercially supported SAFE Bill (see Appendix O) that was moving toward passage. Key recovery is an important topic and the balance of this chapter tries to develop some understanding of the dynamics of this issue.

Framing the Analysis

The debate tends to be limited to those who have a near term-specific interest in the outcomes of the argument. The individuals to date who have been most vocal have included administration and law enforcement community officials, cryptologists, computer industry executives, and nonprofit policy think tank representatives. The arguments have tended to invoke emotional concerns on one side and highly technical concerns on the other side.

The point remains, though: The U.S. government is currently debating whether to mandate key recovery for cryptography used in the United States and for dealings with all elements of the United States, including private citizens. The law enforcement and national security communities, who claim that it is necessary to protect the safety of citizens and to ensure a robust national defense, support this proposal. The proposal is hotly criticized by industry and privacy advocates, who claim that it won't work, will cripple the U.S. software industry, and will enable Big Brother.

Goal

This analysis will attempt to clearly identify the driving issues related to the administration's proposal to mandate a recoverable key system, in order to enable judgments among them.

Assumptions

The assumptions underlying this analysis include the following:

1. Current trends will continue as predicted:
    - Electronic commerce will continue to be pushed for its obvious efficiencies and ability to expand existing markets, as well as for its adaptability to the modern way of life.
    - Internetted communications will continue to expand exponentially, and the value of each network will rise exponentially with the addition of every node, thereby increasing the impetus to connect.
    - More customers for cryptography will arise out of the desire for security in communications, reliability in information, and assuredness in transactions.
2. More cryptographic products will be developed and marketed, here and abroad:
    - Cryptography will become a distinguishing characteristic for electronic products and services due to the demand created by the elements of the first assumption.
    - Cryptographic products will be increasingly integrated into software applications for ease of use as well as for product security issues, such as interoperability and correctness.

- As cryptography becomes ubiquitous it will become just one more option to check, essentially becoming invisible to the casual user while becoming a fundamental part of computer systems manufacturers' inventories.

3. And finally, that the use of cryptography will become a normal part of life:
   - For secure electronic transactions
   - For digital signatures
   - For private communications

Issues of Concern

There are a variety of issues that are of concern in considering the federal government's proposal for key-recoverable cryptography. Obviously, there is the issue of cost: How much will it cost to implement and operate such a system, and how does that cost compare to either benefits or detriments of the proposed system? But beyond that issue there are other issues. First, there are the issues related to implementation. Second, there are the issues associated with competitiveness and enforcement. A brief discussion of these issues follows.

Implementation Issues

A critical issue relating to the overall issue of key-recoverable cryptography is the implementation details. As with any piece of equipment or tool, how the tool is used fundamentally affects its usefulness. With computer equipment, how the software and hardware are implemented and managed have fundamental implications to the overall utility and security of the system. The difficulties relating to implementing a recoverable key system on the order of magnitude envisioned by the U.S. government are neatly summarized by a distinguished group of cryptologists who spent several years studying and analyzing the issue. They reported to the world in a document finalized in May 1997. The following is an extract from that document, pointing out the costs, both in terms of money and in terms of security, of such a system:

> The deployment of key-recovery-based encryption infrastructures to meet law enforcement's stated specifications will result in substantial sacrifices in security and greatly increased costs to the end-user. Building the secure

computer-communication infrastructures necessary to provide adequate technological underpinnings demanded by these requirements would be enormously complex and is far beyond the experience and current competency of the field. Even if such infrastructures could be built, the risks and costs of such an operating environment may ultimately prove unacceptable. In addition, these infrastructures would generally require extraordinary levels of human trustworthiness.

These difficulties are a function of the basic government access requirements proposed for key-recovery encryption systems.

They exist regardless of the design of the recovery systems—whether the systems use private-key cryptography or public-key cryptography; whether the databases are split with secret-sharing techniques or maintained in a single hardened secure facility; whether the recovery services provide private keys, session keys, or merely decrypt specific data as needed; and whether there is a single centralized infrastructure, many decentralized infrastructures, or a collection of different approaches.

All key-recovery systems require the existence of a highly sensitive and highly available secret key or collection of keys that must be maintained in a secure manner over an extended time period. These systems must make decryption information quickly accessible to law enforcement agencies without notice to the key owners. These basic requirements make the problem of general key recovery difficult and expensive—and potentially too insecure and too costly for many applications and many users.

Attempts to force the widespread adoption of key-recovery encryption through export controls, import or domestic use regulations, or international standards should be considered in light of these factors. The public must carefully consider the costs and benefits of embracing government-access key recovery before imposing the new security risks and spending the huge investment required (potentially many billions of dollars, in direct and indirect costs) to deploy a global key recovery infrastructure.[32]

Implicit in this critique are the assumptions of methodology and processes that have been developed over the course of time in the practice of cryptography. First and foremost of these practices is the ability to inspect the implementing algorithms. The algorithm implemented in the Clipper Chip was not made publicly available and thus was not available for inspection. Cryptologic mathematicians consider the algorithm to be separable from the actions of the algorithm; in other words, the security of the end product must not be subvertible by weaknesses in the algorithm. Therefore, they like to really scrub down algorithms to make sure they are robust and not exploitable through inherent flaws.

Further, the existence of the master key in a recoverable key system must not weaken the security of the system. This is almost oxymoronic in that the existence of master keys, by definition, introduces additional risk into the overall system. Thus, proving that the security of a system is not weakened by the existence of master keys or the ability to recover keys is a very high hurdle to get over.

Quite obviously the master keys, or other mechanisms enabling key recovery, must themselves not be easily recoverable or exploitable and the algorithm itself must not be exploitable by virtue of the recoverable aspect.

Another issue relating to implementation is identifying who gets to hold the master key. There are several choices here, including a neutral third party whose integrity is unimpeachable. Finding such an entity would be a tremendous feat indeed, particularly in the international arena.

Following on this issue is the question of how protections are ensured once an implementation scheme has been decided on and an escrow agent has been agreed to. There must be controls in the key recovery scheme that provide checks and balances for protections, and there must be legal structures to ensure due process and redress. Furthermore, liability and negligence issues must be defined and legislated. A highly controversial issue that must be addressed is what the recovered keys could be used for. The arguments to date have essentially focused in on public safety, specifically, the law enforcement agency ability to "wiretap" in case of criminal activity. However, it is not infeasible that key recovery could be used by other agencies of the government, such as the IRS, who could use it to audit financial transactions, or Customs, who could use it to audit compliance with treaties and tariffs. Once the cat is out of the bag with key recovery for law enforcement purposes, the extent to which laws can be enforced using key recovery should be specifically addressed.

The converse of this point of view is the issue of citizen self-protection and privacy. Having the ability to protect oneself could be incurably damaged by virtue of negligence or incompetence in the management of the key management infrastructure.

Competitiveness and Enforcement Issues

Orthogonal to these policy issues are the issues relating to practical aspects of everyday life, such as computer industry competitiveness and how to enforce a mandated key management infrastructure.

In terms of market share and industry dominance, there are issues relating to the legality of export controls on encryption products, which are currently controlled as munitions, and the increasing offshore development and lead in encryption products. The stock market consternations of 1999 have underscored the interconnectedness of the economies of the world and the fact that one economy cannot act unilaterally without affecting other economies. As electronic commerce continues to grow and the transparencies of borders continues to become more apparent by the ease of connectedness over the Internet, the wisdom of limiting competitiveness in an area of traditional American strength may come into question.

The accessibility of strong cryptography for illicit purposes is undeniably an issue. The elements of this issue include how bad guys can get strong encryption products and what limits can be enforced upon them. The assumption is that these same bad guys will use the encryption products to further their illegal activities. This issue is complicated by the fact that the fundamental math supporting cryptology is well documented and available at any bookstore, including Amazon.com, the online bookstore. Further, the overseas development of encryption products referred to before gives these elements ready access to strong encryption products right now. Additionally, if someone were to attempt to take strong encryption to the bad guys, such smuggling activities could be undetectable (particularly if the software were encrypted). It should not be ignored that weak encryption, passing the export controls, can be used in ways that makes it stronger when applied appropriately. And finally, hidden encryption, such as steganography, can bypass controls easily.

Factors Derived from the Issues

When considered logically, the issues derive to four basic categories: cost, performance, risk, and impact, which include relevant factors. These principal issues will be used in the process of the analysis.

- *Cost factors*   Implementation, operations, lost opportunities
- *Performance*   Public safety, privacy, other uses (such as tax collection)
- *Risk*   Security, cost, performance, negligence
- *Impact*   Economic growth, international relations, crime, intelligence collection, politics, market share

Alternatives and Stakeholders

Within the concept of key recovery, there are three alternatives that may be considered. The list of stakeholders and factors is extraordinary. This issue touches everyone's life, whether they realize it or not.

Alternatives

There are three basic alternatives that are available to be considered. These are as follows:

A1. *No mandated key recovery system.* Any recoverable key system manufactured would be a niche product (specialized market) and used in a manner dictated by the user.

A2. *Key recovery system coexists with other encryption.* Certain transactions would be required to be conducted using a recoverable key system, such as government transactions, financial data transactions, international funds transfer, and some forms of electronic commerce, while the rest would be unregulated.

A3. *Key recovery system; all other encryption illegal.* All transactions would be required to be conducted using a recoverable key system.

Stakeholders

From the preceding discussion, it is clear that everyone is a stakeholder, whether we understand this or not. Within the U.S. government, all the departments and agencies from Commerce to Treasury to Defense are stakeholders.

State and local governments, as well as foreign governments, are also stakeholders. Each of these entities has to address what it will mean to their operations if the U.S. government mandates an international key management infrastructure.

Nongovernmental organizations, ranging from human rights advocacy groups to environmental groups to democratic activist organizations, are stakeholders as well. Many of these do business with the United Nations, which is physically located in the New York City. While the United Nations is not U.S. territory, the city most certainly is.

All electronic commerce participants are stakeholders, particularly given the nature of the Internet. With dynamic routing, knowing where your packets are going when you send them from your computer to a recipient computer is impossible. Given the hegemony of the U.S. economy at this point in time, it is also highly probable that many dealings will take place with U.S. entities.

Privacy advocates are clearly stakeholders, as are cryptologic mathematicians and other academics. In addition, system manufacturers, who will be expected to implement the individual components of such a scheme are stakeholders, including both U.S. and foreign companies. Individuals are stakeholders, given that all communications are subject to monitoring to determine processes and constraints.

Both organized crime and unorganized crime are also stakeholders, wishing to not be further encumbered from accomplishing their goals.

Analysis

To perform the analysis, the factors derived from the issues were considered with regard to both the alternatives available and the stakeholders. In the following charts, the three alternatives (*No mandated key recovery system, Key recovery system coexists with other encryption, Key recovery system; all other encryption illegal*) are identified as A1, A2, and A3. These charts show the judgments as to what impact each alternative would face in terms of the factors listed. For each chart, the value 10 reflects the best score—showing either no impact, or best impact. The value 1 reflects the other side of the scale—showing most or worst impact.

Alternative Analysis

Table 7-9 shows the factors associated with cost. Clearly, there would be no implementation, operations, or opportunity costs associated with A1, so

TABLE 7-9

Cost Elements.

Alternatives	Implementation	Operations	Opportunity
A1	10	10	10
A2	5	5	7
A3	1	1	1

that alternative was given 10s across the board. A3 would have substantial implementation and operations costs and would also incur opportunity costs as a fundamental repercussion of economics. When a solution is forced, an unknown number of alternative solutions and cascading events go unseen. Additionally, the opportunity to market alternative products is lost both domestically and overseas. Therefore, A3 was given 1s across the board. A2 was found to be in a middle position. Clearly, there would be costs associated with implementing and operating this alternative, but they would not be as heavy as A3. This led to the choice of 5 for each of these two factors. The opportunity costs were judged to be somewhat more than A1, since a proportion of corporate and governmental assets would be diverted from other activities into this one, but not so severe as a moratorium on all other alternatives. Therefore, a 7 was given for that score.

Clearly, if cost alone is an issue, the best alternative would be A1 and the worst alternative would be A3.

For the factors associated with performance, the analysis is shown in Table 7-10. The argument that public safety was a principle reason for pushing for key recovery seemed not to pan out here. When considered in all of its elements, the ability of a key recovery system to ensure public safety seemed less than obvious. For one thing, the ability of private citizens to take precautionary measures (analogous to not walking downtown on a dark night at 2 A.M.) is somewhat lost. The requirement to use a single kind of encryption with a recoverable known key would seem to be a very tempting lure for organized crime: The ability for a citizen to take steps to ameliorate that concern is evaporated under A3. Further, the stated goal of being able to wiretap criminals seems to be of limited use. For one thing, before a judge can grant the authorization to wiretap, the law enforcement community must already have enough evidence to convince the judge that it is not a fishing expedition. This means that there would already be significant evidence in place before the wiretap could occur. Given that less than one-tenth of 1 percent of the wiretapping cases pursued in 1996 featured encryption, this seems to offer, at best, a limited benefit to public safety at a large cost to private deterrence of crime.

TABLE 7-10

Performance Elements.

Alternatives	Public Safety	Privacy	Other Uses
A1	8	10	1
A2	6	8	5
A3	3	2	8

Privacy as a performance element was judged to be best in A1 and worst in A3, primarily for the reasons stated above: that the known ability to recover keys would be an irresistible attractant for criminal elements, including hackers, and that the ability of an individual to take steps to maintain his or her privacy would be greatly eroded. Further, the use of a mandated recoverable key system in an international key management system would provide a great deal of global exposure to the ability to recover the keys as a necessary aspect of global cooperation. These elements tend to limit privacy rather than enhance it, including not only the communications and the transactions but also the configuration information and detailed analytical data on data usage patterns that become available as a direct result of being able to tie a specific packet to a specific user. The threat to privacy was not seen as so draconian with A2, which allows for other systems to coexist, and was seen to be most protected by A1.

The potential for other uses, such as auditing transactions for tax collection or labor standards compliance, is clearly highest with the third alternative. This would take some additional effort, so it was not rated as a 10 but was given the score of 8. The potential for other uses was non-existent with A1—thus the score of 1—and moderate with A2, which would be able to use the system to monitor governmental transactions and perhaps derive some usage out of that information.

So the wrap-up for performance is a mixed bag, with A1 leading for public safety and privacy, and A3 leading for other usage potential.

With regard to risk, there seemed to be an extraordinary amount of risk associated with A3 across the board. No one has ever implemented such a large system with so many users, so many points of entry, so many threats to the security of the system, and with no ability to predict performance. Further, the risk of negligence in any aspect of the system is very high by virtue of the number of humans involved, the complexity of the interconnectivity of systems, the heterogeneity of systems that must coexist within the same infrastructure, and the international nature of the scheme. A2 incurred much of the same risk elements, but on a smaller scale and with backup potential from other systems that seemed to ameliorate some of the risk potential. A1 seemed to have the best risk profile, using the elements of the competitive marketplace and existing legal structure to regulate cost and performance as well as negligence.

An interesting notion related to risk is in the performance arena. This relates not only to the risk associated with the appropriate performance of each alternative but also to the risk of enforcing compliance with the mandates, if necessary. Clearly, there is an extraordinary amount of risk in getting criminals to actually use key-recoverable encryption, particularly since the more successful the criminal is, the more sophisticated and aware he or she is bound to be. Further, there is the nontrivial risk that criminal elements could pretend to use the recoverable-key system while hiding the real information using concealment methodologies, such as steganography. This would fully neutralize the utility of the recoverable-key system.

With regard to risk, it is very clear that A3 carries with it enormous risk, while A1 carries with it little or no risk.

TABLE 7-11

Risk Elements.

Alternatives	Security	Cost	Performance	Negligence
A1	10	10	8	10
A2	4	3	3	4
A3	1	1	1	1

The elements of impact covered the most ground as shown in Table 7-12. Here we see the second instance of A3 receiving a high score, in the area of intelligence collection. Clearly, the impact of having a recoverable-key system in place internationally would aid and abet the collection of intelligence—unfortunately, not to the sole benefit of our government or national defense community. As the system would inevitably attract criminal elements, the system would be a gold mine for foreign intelligence activities, particularly those that already have strong cryptanalysis capabilities.

With regard to economic growth, a robust and competitive industry naturally produces the best elements for economic growth in a sector. Conversely, government-mandated limits on the activities of a sector of the economy not only limits the energy and activity in that sector, it also opens the door for offshore competition, which moves into any neglected area. With the growing number of offshore encryption devices available, adopting A3 would be like handing the rest of the global marketplace to these competitors on a cake platter. There would, of course, be cascading effects in related industries, such as software and hardware manufacturers, because of the assumption that encryption will become ubiquitous and integrated into systems for security and ease-of-use purposes. As U.S. manufacturers are limited in their ability to do that, the global demand for their product will fall off incrementally. This is reflected in the market share factor, with the associated scores showing this impact.

TABLE 7-12

Impact Elements.

Alternative	Economic Growth	International Relations	Crime	Intelligence Collection	Politics	Market Share
A1	10	10	5	3	10	10
A2	7	7	5	5	7	7
A3	3	4	3	8	3	3

The impact on crime is somewhat neutral. With A1, crime will continue as before, with private citizens able to purchase appropriate products for protecting themselves and criminals attempting to get around those products. With A2, there is little additional exposure, given the limited nature of the key recovery implementation and the ability to augment it with other choices of products and services. With A3 there is a slightly worse impact on crime, with the limited ability to wiretap those criminals that meet the criteria of both using the key-recoverable encryption product and having committed a crime with enough other evidence to convince a judge to issue a wiretap approval. This limited ability was, of course, contraposed with the attraction of the criminal element to the key recovery system and a predictable rise in crimes associated with abuse of that capability.

With regard to international relations, there would seem to be need for some serious diplomatic activity to get other nations to sign up to cooperate with the U.S. government on the key recovery system as envisioned in A3. This would impact international relations, most probably adversely, particularly if it were viewed that the United States was attempting to seed the world with easily breakable encryption devices. This would be true to a limited extent with A2 as well, but the availability of other capabilities could make the negotiations more palatable. There seems to be little if any impact associated with A1.

With regard to politics, there could be a very large dampening effect on political speech with A3, particularly if it is viewed that the alternative uses for key recovery are in fact being used. This is true not only domestically but also internationally, particularly since many nongovernmental organizations are based in the United States and actively support activities that are considered illegal, immoral, or unethical in other countries. The protection provided to such activities by products such as PGP would be totally lost with A3. This effect is present but limited in A2 and totally absent in A1.

The summary of the impact analysis is that A3 would have the worst overall impact and A1 would have the best impact overall.

Alternatives	Cost	Performance	Risk	Impact	Roll-up
A1	10.0	6.3	9.5	8.0	8.5
A2	5.7	6.3	3.5	6.3	5.5
A3	1.0	4.3	1.0	4.0	2.6

TABLE 7-13

Unweighted Data.

A roll-up (presentation) of the data combined together without any weighting is shown in Table 7-13. As noted, A1 consistently seems to be the best choice. The only issue where either of the other two alternatives scored closely was in performance, where A2 came close. Recalling the factor analysis for this case, the element that brought the two close was the potential for other uses.

The summary of the data is shown in the Roll-up column. Here, A1 is clearly the leader and A3 is clearly the least desirable choice.

Factors Sensitivity Analysis

Given that there is a potential for some of the issues to be more important than others, the next step in performing the analysis is to look at sensitivities in weighting. What would the results look like if cost were the only issue that mattered? What if some combination of cost and performance mattered? These are the questions that are addressed by a *sensitivity analysis*.

In this analysis, the weights shown in Table 7-14 were assigned to the elements before rolling them up into a combined score for each of the alternatives. The different weights were used to calculate roll-up scores for each of the alternatives, and then the results were graphed. As can be seen clearly in Figure 7-19, it doesn't matter what weighting scheme is used: A1 is clearly the best alternative when considered against the issues.

Stakeholder Analysis

Having performed an analysis of the issues and element factors against each alternative, the next step is to look at each stakeholder and how the issues affect them. This will allow extrapolations to be made regarding the attractiveness of each alternative. The stakeholders considered in

Figure 7-19

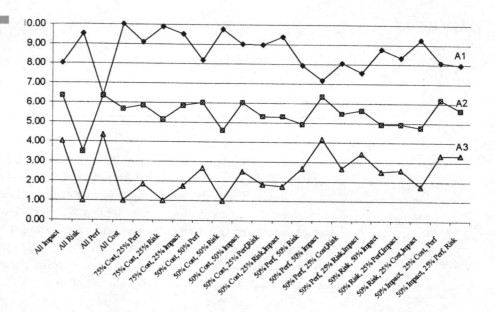

this analysis are the following:

- U.S. government
- Foreign governments
- Nongovernmental organizations
- Electronic commerce participants
- Privacy advocates
- Cryptologic mathematicians
- Academicians
- System manufacturers
- Individuals
- Criminal elements

The following tables show the data regarding how strongly each stakeholder feels about each factor. In this series of charts, the value 10 represents very strong feelings or very high interest, while 1 reflects negligible interest or few if any feelings about the factor.

Table 7-15 presents the data regarding cost. The stakeholders who are perceived to care most about cost elements include electronic commerce participants, privacy advocates, and individuals. Following at a close sec-

TABLE 7-14

Sensitivity Analysis Factors.

	Cost	Performance	Risk	Impact
All Impact	0	0	0	1
All Risk	0		1	
All Perf	0	1		
All Cost	1			
75% Cost, 25% Perf.	0.75	0.25		
75% Cost, 25% Risk	0.75		0.25	
75% Cost, 25% Impact	0.75			0.25
50% Cost, 50% Perf.	0.5	0.5		
50% Cost, 50% Risk	0.5		0.5	
50% Cost, 50% Impact	0.5			0.5
50% Cost, 25% Perf., Risk	0.5	0.25	0.25	
50% Cost, 25% Risk, Impact	0.5		0.25	0.25
50% Perf, 50% Risk		0.5	0.5	
50% Perf, 50% Impact		0.5		0.5
50% Perf, 25% Cost, Risk	0.25	0.5	0.25	
50% Perf, 25% Risk, Impact		0.5	0.25	0.25
50% Risk, 50% Impact			0.5	0.5
50% Risk, 25% Perf., Impact		0.25	0.5	0.25
50% Risk, 25% Cost, Impact	0.25		0.5	0.25
50% Impact, 25% Cost, Perf.	0.25	0.25		0.5
50% Impact, 25% Perf., Risk		0.25	0.25	0.5

ond come stakeholders such as academicians, system manufacturers, and cryptologic mathematicians. The driving concerns here were perceived as those who are most interested in the subject would care most about the costs associated with it, with the exception of individuals who, as "taxpayers," would be forced to finance the entire implementation and operation of any scheme. Any increased costs for groups that operate on fixed or declining budgets, such as academicians, will be significant concerns. For groups who are strongly in favor of privacy issues and economic competitiveness, increased costs, no matter how small, can be expected to irritate. For groups who do not expect to have to contribute

TABLE 7-15

Cost Elements.

	Implementation	Operations	Opportunity	Roll-Up
U.S. Government	7	7	4	6.0
Foreign Governments	2	3	1	2.0
Nongovernmental Organizations	5	5	5	5.0
Electronic Commerce Participants	10	7	10	9.0
Privacy Advocates	10	10	10	10.0
Cryptologic Mathematicians	7	7	10	8.0
Academicians	10	2	10	7.3
System Manufacturers	6	6	10	7.3
Individuals	10	10	5	8.3
Criminal Elements	1	1	1	1.0

significantly to the costs of implementation and operations, costs are of limited concern.

For the elements of performance, each stakeholder rated on strength of interest shown in Table 7-16. As such, this does not become a distinguishing issue in the analysis.

TABLE 7-16

Performance Elements.

	Public Safety	Privacy	Other Uses	Roll-Up
U.S. Government	10	3	10	7.7
Foreign Governments	10	4	10	8.0
Nongovernmental Organizations	10	10	10	10.0
Electronic Commerce Participants	10	10	10	10.0
Privacy Advocates	10	10	10	10.0
Cryptologic Mathematicians	10	10	5	8.3
Academicians	10	10	8	9.3
System Manufacturers	10	10	8	9.3
Individuals	10	10	10	10.0
Criminal Elements	1	10	10	7.0

With regard to the elements of risk, shown in Table 7-17, only two stakeholders are rated as not having a strong interest. These two stakeholders, foreign governments and criminal elements, share the same characteristic as not having to own the results of the alternatives and thus care less about the specific risk elements, such as cost risk or performance risk. The other stakeholders all measured fairly high in this issue category.

The factors associated with impact, shown in Table 7-18, seem to be a strong differentiator. The U.S. and foreign governments, as well as system manufacturers, rated as having high interest in these elements, with every other stakeholder measuring medium-high levels of interest. The lowest interest level, at 5.3, was generated by privacy advocates, who can be characterized as caring less about market share and economic competitiveness as the issues relating to privacy.

Rolling all the data together produces the data shown in Table 7-19. In each column, the high scores are bolded, including the roll-up column. Only one stakeholder does not have any boldfaced numbers—the criminal element. The rest of the stakeholders all rate two or three bold numbers across the columns. The stakeholders who show the most sustained interest across the issue elements are electronic commerce participants, privacy advocates, system manufacturers, and individuals.

TABLE 7-17

Risk Elements.

	Security	Cost	Performance	Negligence	Roll-Up
U.S. Government	7	7	10	10	*8.5*
Foreign Governments	6	3	5	1	*3.8*
Nongovernmental Organizations	10	7	10	10	*9.3*
Electronic Commerce Participants	10	10	10	10	*10.0*
Privacy Advocates	10	10	10	10	*10.0*
Cryptologic Mathematicians	10	5	10	5	*7.5*
Academicians	10	10	10	10	*10.0*
System Manufacturers	10	10	10	10	*10.0*
Individuals	10	10	10	10	*10.0*
Criminal Elements	10	1	10	1	*5.5*

TABLE 7-18

Impact Elements.

	Economic Growth	International Relations	Crime	Intelligence Collection	Politics	Market Share	Roll-Up
U.S. Government	10	8	10	10	8	10	**9.3**
Foreign Governments	6	8	10	10	8	10	**8.7**
Nongovernmental Organizations	3	8	5	10	10	3	6.5
Electronic Commerce Participants	10	6	10	6	5	10	7.8
Privacy Advocates	2	3	6	10	8	3	5.3
Cryptologic Mathematicians	6	5	5	5	5	8	5.7
Academicians	7	7	8	5	9	6	7.0
System Manufacturers	10	10	8	9	7	10	**9.0**
Individuals	9	5	10	3	6	7	6.7
Criminal Elements	3	5	10	10	5	1	5.7

TABLE 7-19

Roll-Up.

	Cost	Performance	Risk	Impact	Roll-Up
U.S. Government	6.0	7.7	**8.5**	**9.3**	7.9
Foreign Governments	2.0	**8.0**	3.8	**8.7**	5.6
Nongovernmental Organizations	5.0	**10.0**	9.3	6.5	7.7
Electronic Commerce Participants	**9.0**	**10.0**	10.0	7.8	**9.2**
Privacy Advocates	**10.0**	**10.0**	10.0	5.3	**8.8**
Cryptologic Mathematicians	**8.0**	8.3	7.5	5.7	7.4
Academicians	7.3	**9.3**	10.0	7.0	**8.4**
System Manufacturers	7.3	**9.3**	10.0	9.0	**8.9**
Individuals	**8.3**	**10.0**	10.0	6.7	**8.8**
Criminal Elements	1.0	7.0	5.5	5.7	4.8

Stakeholder Sensitivity Analysis

Reapplying the weighting figures previously used to perform sensitivity analysis for the factors/alternatives analysis presents the chart and graph shown in Table 7-20 and Figure 7-20.

TABLE 7-20   Sensitivity Analysis Data.

	U.S. Govt.	Foreign Govt.	NGOs	Elec. Com	Privacy Adv.	Crypt. Math.	Acad.	System Man.	Indiv.	Crim. Elem
All Impact	9.3	8.7	6.5	7.8	5.3	5.7	7.0	9.0	6.7	5.7
All Risk	8.5	3.8	9.3	10.0	10.0	7.5	10.0	10.0	10.0	5.5
All Perf	7.7	8.0	10.0	10.0	10.0	8.3	9.3	9.3	10.0	7.0
All Cost	6.0	2.0	5.0	9.0	10.0	8.0	7.3	7.3	8.3	1.0
75% Cost, 25% Perf.	6.4	3.5	6.3	9.3	10.0	8.1	7.8	7.8	8.8	2.5
75% Cost, 25% Risk	6.6	2.4	6.1	9.3	10.0	7.9	8.0	8.0	8.8	2.1
75% Cost, 25% Impact	6.8	3.7	5.4	8.7	8.8	7.4	7.3	7.8	7.9	2.2
50% Cost, 50% Perf.	6.8	5.0	7.5	9.5	10.0	8.2	8.3	8.3	9.2	4.0
50% Cost, 50% Risk	7.3	2.9	7.1	9.5	10.0	7.8	8.7	8.7	9.2	3.3
50% Cost, 50% Impact	7.7	5.3	5.8	8.4	7.7	6.8	7.2	8.2	7.5	3.3
50% Cost, 25% Perf. Risk	7.0	3.9	7.3	9.5	10.0	8.0	8.5	8.5	9.2	3.6
50% Cost, 25% Risk, Impact	7.5	4.1	6.4	9.0	8.8	7.3	7.9	8.4	8.3	3.3
50% Perf, 50% Risk	8.1	5.9	9.6	10.0	10.0	7.9	9.7	9.7	10.0	6.3
50% Perf, 50% Impact	8.5	8.3	8.3	8.9	7.7	7.0	8.2	9.2	8.3	6.3
50% Perf, 25% Cost, Risk	7.5	5.4	8.6	9.8	10.0	8.0	9.0	9.0	9.6	5.1
50% Perf, 25% Risk, Impact	8.3	7.1	8.9	9.5	8.8	7.5	8.9	9.4	9.2	6.3
50% Risk, 50% Impact	8.9	6.2	7.9	8.9	7.7	6.6	8.5	9.5	8.3	5.6
50% Risk, 25% Perf. Impact	8.5	6.0	8.8	9.5	8.8	7.3	9.1	9.6	9.2	5.9
50% Risk, 25% Cost, Impact	8.1	4.5	7.5	9.2	8.8	7.2	8.6	9.1	8.8	4.4
50% Impact, 25% Cost. Perf.	8.1	6.8	7.0	8.7	7.7	6.9	7.7	8.7	7.9	4.8
50% Impact, 25% Perf. Risk	8.7	7.3	8.1	8.9	7.7	6.8	8.3	9.3	8.3	6.0

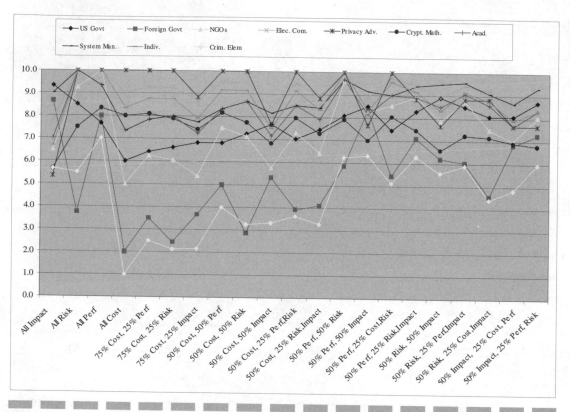

Figure 7-20

Wrap Up—Logic Results and Conclusion

The results of the analysis show that electronic commerce participants, privacy advocates, system manufacturers, and individuals are the stakeholders who care most about the issues associated with the concept of recoverable key systems. Their concerns are primarily associated with the factors of performance and risk. The single alternative that ranks high on both performance and risk is A1. A2 provides equivalent results on the performance issue but falls far short on the risk issue. Additionally, when weights are used to perform sensitivity analysis on the alternatives, A1 consistently outscores both A2 and A3. Relevant scores are shown in Table 7-21.

TABLE 7-21

Relevant Scores.

Alternative	A1	A2	A3
All Risk	**9.50**	3.50	1.00
All Perf.	**6.33**	**6.33**	4.33
50% Perf., 50% Risk	**7.92**	4.92	2.67
50% Perf., 25% Cost, Risk	**8.04**	5.46	2.67
50% Perf., 25% Risk, Impact	**7.54**	5.63	3.42
50% Risk, 50% Impact	**8.75**	4.92	2.50
50% Risk, 25% Perf., Impact	**8.33**	4.92	2.58
50% Risk, 25% Cost, Impact	**9.25**	4.75	1.75

This is not to say that the other stakeholders are negligible to the debate, or that the other issues need not be considered carefully. Clearly, at least the element of cost must be considered carefully, in terms of not only direct cost but also indirect costs. The clear results of this analysis are that A1 is the best choice given the set of assumptions and scoring parameters. Further, the sensitivity analysis shows that A1 is the best choice independent of what the primary concern is.

Candidate next steps in this analysis would be to quantify the cost elements more precisely and to get more concrete data to back up the scores. A comprehensive treatment of this issue could include surveys of each of the stakeholders to get a statistical view of their opinions and levels of tolerance in each of the issue areas.

Notes

1. Kahn, David, *The Codebreakers: The Story of Secret Writing* (London: Weidenfield and Nicholson, 1967), 157ff.

2. Nichols, Randall K., *Classical Cryptography Course*, Vols. I and II (Laguna Hills, Calif.: Aegean Park Press, 1996 and 1997, respectively).

3. Electronic Frontier Foundation, *Cracking DES: Secrets of Research, Wiretap Politics, and Chip Design* (Cambridge, Mass.: O'Reilly, 1998).

4. Schneier, Bruce, *Applied Cryptography*, 2nd ed. (New York: Wiley, 1996).

5. Menezes, Alfred J., Paul C. van Oorschot, and Scott A. Vanstone, *Handbook of Applied Cryptography* (Boca Raton, Fla.: CRC Press, 1996).

6. Nichols, Randall K., *ICSA Guide to Cryptography* (New York: McGraw-Hill, 1998).

7. "Current Public-Key Cryptographic Systems," Certicom white paper, April 1997, http://www.certicom.com.

8. Ibid.

9. Ibid.

10. "Remarks on the Security of the Elliptic Curve Cryptosystem," Certicom white paper, September 1997.

11. Ibid.

12. Ibid.

13. Ibid.

14. "The Elliptic Curve Cryptosystem for Smart Cards," Certicom white paper, May 1998.

15. "Current Public-Key Cryptographic Systems," op. cit.

16. Ibid.

17. Follet, Ken, *The Key To Rebecca* (New York: Signet, 1980).

18. Doyle, Arthur Conan, "The Adventure of the Dancing Men," *The Strand Magazine*, London, December 1903, Vol. 26, No. 156, available at http://etext.lib.virginia.edu/cgibin/browse-mixed?id=DoyDanc&tag=public&images=images/modeng&data=/lv1/Archive/eng-parsed.

19. Kahn, op. cit.

20. Available at http://www.epic.org/crypto/clipper/white_house_statement_4_93.htm, April 16, 1993.

21. Letter of October 15, 1996, to Michael Kantor, Secretary of Commerce from Senators and Representatives Conrad Burns, Ron Wyden, Trent Lott, Lauch Faircloth, Larry Pressler, Larry Craig, Barbara Boxer, Al Simpson, Craig Thomas, Pete Domenici, Patty Murray, Kay Bailey Hutchison, John Ashcroft, Don Nickles, Bob Goodlatte, Zoe Lofgren, Howard Cable, Bill Barr, Sonny Bono, Steve Chabot, and Tom Campbell.

22. Seminerio, Maria, "Is Government-Mandated Key Recovery Inevitable?" ZDNN, 10 July 1997.

23. Ibid.

24. http://shadow.res.cmu.edu/users/mhunter/Politics/encrypt1.html, accessed November 21, 1997.

25. Ibid.

26. Letter of 25 April 1997, to Tom Bliley and Rick White, Committee on Commerce, House of Representatives, from the Software Publishers Association, http://www.house.gov/white/press/105/19970425waschresponse.html, accessed November 21, 1997.

27. Abelson, Hal et al., "The Risks of Key Recovery, Key Escrow, and Trusted Third-Party Encryption," http://www.info-sec.com/crypto/report.html-ssi, 21 May 1997.

28. http://csrc.ncsl.nist.gov/keyrecovery/admin.txt, 12 July 1996.

29. http://www.cdt.org/crypto/admin_397_draft.html, 26 March 1997.

30. http://www.cdt.org/digi_tele/.

31. http://www.cdt.org/crypto/pccip.html, 5 November 1997.

32. Abelson, op. cit.

CHAPTER 8

Access Controls— Two Views

Access controls may be viewed in two different ways. We may look at controlling enterprise access from a systems perspective and consider threats, targets, risk, memory, and so forth. We may also look at it from a contemporary view as a problem in auditing people and physical access to computer systems. We will start with the managing of access to enterprise information, and then move into issues involving employee integrity.

Access Controls—A Systems View for Managing Enterprise Information

The concept of controlling access to information is a twofold issue: First, access to information can and should be controlled, and second, what someone can do with information once access has been achieved can in some cases be controlled. Thus, access control as a topic should be discussed in two sections: first, limit access, and second, manage access.

Introduction

When most security professionals think of access controls, they think mainly of the management of access: the creation and administration of access control lists (ACLs) and the formality of access control procedures. ACLs are indeed a way of managing and controlling access to information, but only if the information is in a computer and stored in files. If the information is being displayed or communicated, ACLs are of little help. Other concepts that spring to mind are discretionary access control (DAC), mandatory access control (MAC), and role-based access control (RBAC), relative to management of access. With DAC, the owner or administrator of the information assumes discretion to set the access permissions for the information, while with MAC and RBAC, access to information is mediated by a formal set of rules. Access control concepts are appropriate when considering access to computerized files or processes, rather than data in other modes such as display or communications.

Access control must be applied from the perspective of control in every state that information is found in the enterprise operation, including not only computerized data files but also photographs, hard-copy files, projected displays, and packets in communication. Further, the information is not always protected within the confines of the enterprise home base. People travel, carrying information with them. Information can be revealed in diagrams scribbled on bar napkins, in casual conversations, through eavesdropping on cell phone conversation, or through shoulder surfing—peering over the shoulder of someone working on a laptop computer to see what is on the screen. Knowing what is not protected is as important as knowing what and how things are protectable.

A critical aspect of any threat is access to the target. As stated previously, for a threat to be a threat, there must be both capability and intent. Having the capability without the intent results in inaction. Having the intent without the capability results in frustration. Therefore, the following relationship exists:

$$Threat = Capability + Intent$$

Assuming the capability to act, the threat needs to have both skill and access. Having access without the skill to act minimizes the threat capability, while having the skill without the access results in unrealizable actions. Therefore, the following relation exists:

$$Capability = Access + Skill$$

Clearly, a major part of defending information assets from every kind of threat is controlling access. This is true for not only malicious threats, such as hostile enemies, but also for natural threats, such as hurricanes and fires. If access to the information asset is limited or controlled or otherwise protected, then the amount of harm that can be done is limited proportionately.

Controlling access is never a wholly sufficient defensive mechanism. It does, however, contribute to an overall protective environment and can provide assistance in the detection phase as well. The benefits that derive from controlling access include the following:

- Denying malicious actors the ability to act
- Deterring potentially malicious actors from acting against your enterprise
- Limiting the number of individuals under suspicion if malicious activity does take place
- Limiting the amount of damage if an access attempt is successful

Limiting Access

Controlling access while information is being displayed is a very different problem from controlling access while information is being communicated over long distances. There are access controls that are specific to information states and access controls that are general in nature. These latter support overall operational policies and include such things as providing badges for personnel and installing locks on doors and windows. These common-sense actions are in fact access control activities performed in support of a larger goal. Distinctive badges on personnel provide an easy way to determine whether someone is supposed to be in a particular area and can assist in preventing such crimes as theft or kidnapping.

Locks on windows are protective, but in emergencies those windows need to be opened, which implies a weakness in the locking mechanism. Fixing that weakness for the sake of information security could endanger lives. This is the kind of operational environment reality that must be taken into account when considering the use of general-purpose controls for information-security-specific purposes.

Managing Access

When the limitations of access are understood, then management activities can occur. Chaos and anarchy cannot be managed—they can at best be survived.

Managing access controls implies specifying what kind of access is allowed to each user and then enforcing those limitations. The kind of access can range from none at all to full unfettered access with full privileges.

There are three schemas that provide a framework for managing access: *discretionary access controls*, *mandatory access controls*, and *role-based access controls*. Each of these stems from a different philosophy in the management of access limitations but can complement each other in complex situations. Access control lists (ACLs) are a key tool in executing the management aspects of each.

The philosophy underlying discretionary access control (DAC) is that the owner or administrator of the information has the knowledge, skill, and ability to limit access appropriately, to control who can see or work with the information. A person running a working group could provide working group members with access to shared files but deny access to anyone else. Alternatively, and more frequently, global access is provided by default.

In mandatory access control (MAC) and role-based access control (RBAC), management of access is much more structured. Both assume a set of formal rules about who can have access to what kind of information and what can be done with that information. Although similar from a philosophical point of view, they point to a different management approach.

In MAC, information is categorized according to sensitivity rather than subject matter. Data in the same general subject matter area can exist in files with different sensitivity ratings. The desire to limit access is derived from those sensitivity concerns. People and processes within a MAC-managed environment are adjudicated as to what kinds of sensitivity levels they are allowed access. The MAC processes enforce these access limitations. For example, information classified secret is accessible only by people or processes adjudicated for access to secret or more highly information. People or processes not adjudicated for secret-level information would be barred from accessing it.

In RBAC, information is categorized according to subject matter, which may reflect some sensitivity criteria inherent in the environment. Persons and processes are adjudicated for access to the information by the role they play within the enterprise. For example, people in the budget department could access and use sensitive budget data, while people in other parts of the enterprise would be denied access to such information.

The three management schemes can exist together. When they do, one must take priority over the others. Generally speaking, MAC rules take priority over both RBAC and DAC rules, and RBAC rules take priority over DAC. For example, a budget person not adjudicated for secret information would not be able to access secret information but would be able to access budget information. Clearly there is potential danger in having more than one access management philosophy in play. The rules must be defined clearly and unambiguously. For example, what if there were secret budget data? It would be very important that the information be first labeled as "secret" and, second, labeled as "budget" to enforce the access limits in correct sequence.

Access control lists provide a methodology of managing the access privileges within systems. An ACL defines information groupings and users (or groups of users) and specifies what kind of access privileges, such as read-only, are allowed. They specify the rules of the access philosophy. Since they are the resident list of access rights and privileges,

ACLs themselves must be protected. Allowing anyone to modify ACLs can undermine the entire access control process.

Managing the access rules in a system requires that access limitations and limitability be understood by all concerned. Access controls are, again, only one method for protecting information. Not all access can be absolutely denied, and in some information states, access control can be problematic.

Specific Access Controls

The following sections identify the different information states and methods that can be used to control access during each state:

- Input
- Processing
- Display
- Temporary memory
- Permanent memory
- Internal transfer
- Communications

There are technological and manual challenges of protecting information. For example, hand-copying a document can be considered to be processing the information. Similarly, a copy of a document in a filing cabinet is in a permanent memory state.

Access controls addresses a high level of control. It is not necessarily what is needed by every enterprise, as risk management analysis will reveal. However, being aware of all the possibilities can assist in designing and managing systems toward the most cost-effective security achievable.

Input

Data is in a particularly vulnerable state while being input. It is subject to accidental and malicious changes and deletions. It is important to identify how the data is being input. Is it coming from an electronic source? Is it being scanned from hard copy? Is it being collected from a bar code reader? Is it being collected through automated measurement techniques, such as a laser range finder? Is a clerk being paid minimum wage typing it into a typewriter? Is the customer providing the data? All these situation-specific details influence how access control can be performed, and to what benefit.

Techniques that can assist in determining appropriate access in this state are generally limited to:

- Data segregation or partitioning of data areas so that access is allowed only to the data being input for the immediate task
- Applying the least-privilege rule to limit actions of those with access to the data
- Specifying who or what process is able to write data into a system
- Constraining data manipulations by those persons or processes writing to a system
- Limiting access to the physical locations where data input is performed
- Limiting access to the computational area where data input is performed, perhaps by segregating it to a physically separate machine

If these access controls are used as part of a comprehensive security program, they can provide a critical element in preventing or limiting malicious activities.

Processing

During processing, manipulations are performed on the data that cause it to be read in and out of temporary and permanent storage in clear form, and a variety of subjects can both access the information and potentially change it. Therefore, controlling access during processing is a function of limiting what processes can access and change the data in question.

During processing, application of the least-privilege rule can greatly assist in controlling access. This rule states that any process or person must be *given* access to data rather than *denied* access. The default situation is that a process or person does not have access; it must be affirmatively granted.

While the least-privilege rule will limit access of known users and processes, access control must also take into account unknown users and processes. How can one control something that is unknown? The answer to this conundrum is, in general, access control procedures. By constraining the ability to spawn or create new processes, access by maliciously generated processes are controlled. By constraining the communications of the system, access by eavesdroppers is controlled.

Methodologies that can be of use in controlling access during the processing state include:

- Partitioning data areas so that processing occurs in virtual isolation
- Applying the least-privilege rule to limit access to the data
- Specifying who or what process is able to write and read data in a system
- Constraining other data manipulations by those persons or processes writing to a system
- Deleting ___ALL___ accepted cookies regularly
- Protecting system from remote access by electromagnetic pulses
- Limiting access to the physical locations where data processing is performed
- Limiting access to the computational area where data processing is performed, perhaps by segregating it on a physically separate machine

While the list of methodologies for controlling access during processing is similar to that for input, the technical aspects can be quite different. The temptation to lump it all together should be assiduously avoided.

Display

Access control during display equates to controlling who can see the data being displayed. This is not merely a function of preventing unauthorized persons from seeing data on a workstation screen. Remote "seeing" via such technologies as radio frequency emanation interception (commonly referred to as TEMPEST attacks) can be possible and undetectable if your facility is not protected against such access. Additionally, the viewing mechanisms themselves must be protected so that unsanctioned viewing is limited.

Accessing data while it is being displayed can be done by peering over the shoulder of someone who is viewing information, by accessing copies of printed material, by using a telescope to spy through windows, or by collecting the signals emanating from display mechanisms.

Methodologies useful in controlling access during the display states include:

- Displaying data in controlled environments where there is little chance that unauthorized viewers are present
- Controlling printings of data so that extra copies are not accessible either in hard copy or in memory
- Controlling copying of data, preventing access through either illicit copying or by subversion of the copying process
- Shielding cables and other emanating media to limit access by technological means
- Using reflective coatings on windows to prevent visual spying
- Using directional coatings on workstation screens to prevent over-the-shoulder viewing

Temporary Memory

The line between temporary and permanent memory is being blurred by the advance of technologies used to store information and the amount of memory incorporated into information processing devices. However, the way in which temporary memory is managed is sufficiently different from the way in which permanent memory is managed that it warrants separate discussion. Temporary memory is generally managed as a scratch pad—useful but not protected, and treated as a common utility within systems. Permanent memory is managed much more proprietarily, with data owners concerned about data integrity and availability, as well as confidentiality, in a structured environment. This difference in management approaches leads to differences in access control.

Temporary memory is used to store information while it is being used, communicated, or displayed. The resident temporary memory in personal computer systems now ranges in the hundreds of megabytes and temporary memory is being integrated into a large variety of machines such as printers. Incorporation of memory has become useful in speeding up processes, since large amounts of data can be moved and then ignored by the central processor.

Controlling access to the data in all this temporary memory can be complex at best. The most effective way to ensure that temporary memory is not used to access data surreptitiously is to make sure that all memory buffers are purged after use. Some equipment may not allow memory purges or cannot be trusted to perform a purge correctly or completely. In these cases, access to the appliance itself, whether physically or virtually, should be constrained.

Methodologies that can assist in controlling access to data in temporary memory include:

- Performing memory purges after each process.
- Filling the temporary memory with random data after each use.
- Turning the equipment off long enough to clear temporary memory (*Note*: This will not work with certain types of temporary memory, such as electrically erasable programmable read-only memory, or EEPROM).
- Controlling physical access to the temporary memory elements.
- Controlling processing access to the temporary memory elements.

Permanent Memory

Permanent memory is used to provide a long-term record of information. It can take the form of printed documents, photographic negatives, or magnetic pulses on a disk (to name a few of its forms). Access controls for information in permanent memory are those that are most widely understood—keeping data in encrypted form to prevent access, creating ACLs, or simply locking the information in a safe, for example. Access to the information can be controlled through physical constraints, such as locks and safes, or through electronic means, such as encryption.

Methodologies that can assist in controlling access to data in permanent memory include:

- Segregating information in physically separate systems, such as separate computers, filing cabinets, access-controlled rooms, or removable drives
- Locking information or documents in a safe
- Creating a set of use privileges for information access, thereby limiting the ability of users to read, write, or perform other actions on information files
- Requiring document sign-out from a protected library

- Use of badging to show employee access privileges to different parts of a facility or different kinds of information
- Use of access control mechanisms in computerized systems to constrain the ability to process or manipulate information
- Encryption

Internal Transfer

Information used in computer systems is constantly in transit. This takes place using data buses and memory caches. Controlling access is as difficult an issue as gaining illicit access. Internal transfer issues are not limited to computer systems, however. Within enterprises, there are also internal transfers taking place. A clerk walking down the hall with some information can also expose information to access that is otherwise protected.

Methodologies that can assist in controlling access while data is being transferred internally include the following:

- Limit the access to the physical medium, including maintenance and repair personnel.
- Maintain strict configuration management of the elements of systems to prevent the incorporation of illicit devices.
- Provide radiation control measures to prevent collection of radiated emanations during transfer.
- Purge memory buffers after information transfer is complete.
- Send packets of nonsense data through the bus following legitimate use.

Communications

Communicating information exposes it to potential access by unauthorized persons. Since it is known that the information will be outside of the direct control of the enterprise, controlling access to the information itself is something that most people intuitively understand. Encrypting the information, however, limits the ability of an authorized person to read the contents. A malicious approach could destroy information in transit as well, so that is another kind of access that must be guarded.

Methodologies that can assist in controlling access while information is communicated include:

- Encrypting or otherwise hiding the contents of the material
- Sending more than one copy by different routes to ensure delivery
- Employing a trusted courier to carry the data

Checking Controls

Access controls are primarily a way of protecting assets. When controls are in place, it is important to check to see if they are working properly—to make sure, for example, that the window is locked and that the fence has not been cut. Verifying operational integrity is a vital part of both the controls themselves as well as detecting any problems.

Access Control—The Contemporary View

Information security is concerned with restricting the ability of threats to corrupt, destroy, or exploit information assets and information systems. Restraint is most easily accomplished by controlling access to the information or the information systems used to create, store, process, or communicate the information. Control of physical and electronic access will ensure the integrity of those to whom we grant authority to read, modify, or delete information.

Physical Access to Systems and Networks

When information is stored, processed, or communicated using computer systems or computer-based networks, gaining access requires gaining physical or electronic access to the system or network. Control of physical access is called "physical security." In theory, if the security of our systems and networks is sufficient, we could allow physical access without danger. In practice, however, physical security is an important component of our security mix. The strengths and weaknesses of physical security are well understood, and physical security can be cost-effective if properly implemented and managed.

Staff Integrity

There are a variety of functions that authorized individuals may need to perform. Some may need to read the information but not need to be able to change or destroy it. Others may need to append information without necessarily changing what is already there. The ability to change and ultimately to destroy information is given only to those persons in whom we have great faith.

Thus, corresponding to the level and duration of protection desired for each item of information, every person who is given authorized access to the information must be assigned a level of trustworthiness. In military and intelligence communities such an assignment is called a "clearance." The level of trustworthiness, or clearance, assigned to an individual depends, roughly, upon his or her need for access to the various levels of classified information and compartments, and upon the degree to which the person has been "vetted" (adjudicated as safe to have access based upon analysis of personal history as discovered through independent, objective background investigations and self-disclosure).

Background Investigations

It is common to ask applicants for employment or increased privileges to provide references and to contact those references to seek assurance that the applicant is trustworthy. Prior employers may be contacted for similar assurances. Schools may be asked for transcripts to verify the applicant's claims of academic qualifications. Such steps seeking more or less objective validations of trustworthiness are part of what security practitioners call "background investigations."

In deciding to grant access privileges to national security information, extensive background investigations are pursued. Not only are the above steps taken, but also visits are made to the neighborhoods of each residence occupied by the applicant for many years prior to the investigation. Neighbors are interviewed, any derogatory information collected is recorded, and reviewed, and a search for corroboration is attempted. Not only are personal references contacted, but since it is assumed that applicant-supplied references will be favorable, secondary references are solicited from each of the primary references and are contacted as well. In addition, birth records are verified. Associations with professional and social organizations are confirmed. Personal finances are also reviewed, based on information provided by the applicant and on independently obtained credit reports. Medical records are reviewed to detect substance abuse, and information concerning known or suspected criminal activities by the applicant is sought from local, state, and federal law enforcement agencies.

Such investigations may take months and cost thousands or even tens of thousands of dollars, but they are justified based on the sensitivity of the information to which the applicant will be exposed. If exposure to less-sensitive information or less-extensive exposure is contemplated, the extent and depth of the background investigation can, in accordance with risk management principles, be at a lower level. The courts have ruled that background investigations for selection/employment in positions of trust to the United States are constitutional. Privacy is not at issue when the applicant gives express permission to be subject to an investigation for purposes of gaining employment in a sensitive position. The courts have linked the *nexus of information* sought on a prospective employee to the required trustworthiness in a position.

Interviews, Tests, and Polygraph Examinations

In addition to a background investigation of a depth and extent consonant with the sensitivity of the information to which the applicant is to be exposed, security authorities may use direct interviews with the applicant, various psychological and medical tests, and polygraph examinations.

Suitability

One of the more pernicious occurrences in personnel security that occasionally arises is the mixing into the evaluation process of elements and criteria that have little to do with trustworthiness, but much to do with prejudice. Under the rubric of "suitability," people who would otherwise be adjudicated as trustworthy are rejected for employment or access privileges because they are too eccentric or have personal characteristics that "don't fit into the organization." Child molesters, so the argument runs, "may not sell their organization's secrets, but we don't want them as part of the work force anyway."

Upon closer examination, such arguments have little to commend them. Certainly, those who commit crimes or violate ethical codes have demonstrated that they held the trust that society placed in them in little regard. Any reasonable adjudicator would deem them poor candidates for further trust and would refuse to grant them privileges to access, modify, or destroy valuable information assets.

Unfortunately, personnel security policies infected with "suitability" criteria go much farther than rejecting proven criminals and known abusers of trust and use the personnel security process to attempt to "homogenize" the workplace. Candidates who look, sound, or act different are rejected not because of objective evidence of untrustworthiness, but because they are different from those who are making and enforcing the personnel security policies. Such reason plagued the famous English mathematician Alan Turing, who couldn't find work after his valuable WWII cracking efforts on the German Enigma cipher machine because of his homosexuality.

The demarcation between valid trustworthiness criteria and suitability criteria is not always clear. Many people who use illicit drugs do not sell their organization's or their country's secrets. Nevertheless, candidates who use illicit drugs do so in defiance of the law and at risk of becoming addicted. Addiction can lead, in turn, to both productivity problems at work and to economic distress as money for yet more drugs is sought. So although illicit drug use does not necessarily lead to security breaches, it can be argued that it does increase the probability of accruing security problems.

Authentication

The essence of communication integrity lies in the recipient of a message knowing from whom the message comes and that it has not been modified *en route*, that is, that the message is authentic. The need for authentication applies not only to messages between individuals but to messages between a user and the computer when computers are being used to create, store, or process information. Thus, there are two related issues: how to determine with some degree of certainty the identity of the information-sending party, and how to be sure that the contents of the information have not been changed.

Identity Verification

In single-user situations where physical access to a system is carefully controlled, the identity of the user may not be ascertained directly. In the more common situation in which many users have access to a system or network, it is important to unambiguously identify specific users. There are three ways this can be accomplished: passwords, tokens, and biometrics.

Passwords: Things You Know

Passwords are commonly used to identify users and control access to computer systems and networks. In a typical situation, each user authorized access to a system or network is provided with a "user ID" and a password. The user ID may be the user's name, but it can be any identifying string of characters uniquely assigned to that individual. Often, the user is allowed to select his or her own password, to make it easier to remember. The user ID-password pair must be provided when the user initiates an exchange of information with the system. The computer checks the user ID and password to make sure that an authorized user has been assigned the pair, and if so, access is granted. While password security clearly provides a greater degree of protection than results from allowing anyone to use the system or network without identification, there are nevertheless serious problems with passwords as they are typically used.

When system users are allowed to select their own passwords, they naturally opt for easily remembered constructions. This leads to two related problems: easily guessed passwords and the use of dictionary words. Allowed complete freedom in choosing passwords, an astonishing number of people choose some variation of their own name. John Smith will choose *smith* or *jsmith* or perhaps *htims* or *htimsj*. Some choose a single letter or a pair of letters. Many users fail to include a change of case (capital letters versus small letters) in their passwords, and very few mix numbers and punctuation marks. A quick tour through the organization's parking lot will usually yield a few vanity license plates, and these often turn up as passwords. On one network, security analysts found that two users merely pressed the Enter key of their computers when prompted to enter their passwords.

Sophisticated intruders, recognizing these proclivities, try them first when trying to break into a system. They will also try the default passwords placed on the systems by the manufacturers, realizing that a few system operators are sufficiently uninformed or lazy that the default passwords will not have been replaced. If all else fails, determined hackers will try every word in a standard dictionary. This is not as difficult as it might sound, since computers are easily programmed to perform the trials. If the passwords are encrypted, the hackers will simply encrypt every word in the dictionary, spelled forward and backwards for good measure, and try them all. When a match is obtained, the hacker can easily recover the word he or she had to encrypt to get the match, and another password has been captured.

Experience shows that where personnel are allowed to choose their own passwords, two-thirds or more of the passwords can be recovered by running a program that tries out obvious choices and dictionary words. Such programs are readily available on many bulletin boards known to the hacker community—and the programs are free!

Sophisticated systems managers do not permit users to choose their own passwords without some restrictions. Knowing how easily self-chosen passwords can be recovered, they either provide passwords to systems users, making sure they are neither easily guessed nor dictionary words, or establish policies that are designed to avoid such traps. For example, a policy that requires that passwords be no less than six characters in length and include at least two numerals might suffice. For example:

- *hab24it* or *run62way* or j41smith (but not if John Smith is 41 years old).

- Changes in case might also be required: *Soft33BaLL*.

- Numerals can be substituted for similar letters; the number one for the small letter "l" and the number "0" for the letter "o," for example, in *100ph01e*.

- The first letters of a saying or phrase can be used. For instance, *wiw1&20*, from "When I was one and twenty" (but not, please *2Bornot2B* or *WYSIWYG*, which are too easily guessed.

- Two or more words can be run together, even if each is a dictionary word, provided that the combination is not also a dictionary word, as in *nounplay* or *softword* or *headspin* (but not *tailspin*). And those become even better if some of the letters are represented as numerals, such as *n0unw1th* or *s0ftw0rd*.

Unfortunately, there is a reciprocal relationship between the difficulty of remembering a password and the likelihood of its being written down and, therefore, recoverable by inspection of the employee's work area or wallet. This is especially true if the user has more than one password granting different sets of privileges or access to different systems or networks. Most security officers have at one time or another found a password stuck to the front of a workstation on a Post-It note or written down on a nearby surface. Ironically, this means that passwords created by a formula like those described above may be more secure than truly random strings of characters such as *beG2B59dwV*.

Yet another requirement that users find onerous is that passwords be changed periodically. Nevertheless, the longer a password is used, the more likely it is that it will be compromised. Policies requiring replacement of passwords should specify the acceptable duration of use, which should, of course, be shorter for information needing a greater degree of protection. The policy should also deny password cycling—that is, changing passwords at the required interval but using two or a few passwords over and over in turn, and minor changes to such changing passwords by simply appending a number to the base password (i.e., *password* becomes *password1*, then *password2*, and so on). In the ideal case, passwords protecting sensitive information are used only once.

Using passwords only once prevents two very clever types of attack. In one, a Trojan horse is placed by an intruder on the system or network and mimics the login procedure. When the user tries to gain access, the Trojan horse prompts for user ID and password, collecting them for later use by the intruder. The Trojan horse then sends the message "invalid logon" to the user and turns the system back over to the legitimate security process, which then prompts for user ID and password, this time allowing access. The user assumes that he or she mistyped part of the logon exchange while, in fact, the password is now compromised. Of course, the ability to place the Trojan horse into the system in the first place depended on access, but such access is not difficult, as we have seen, when users are allowed to choose their own passwords. In other cases, insiders who are exceeding the limits on otherwise authorized access may place the Trojan horse into the system.

The second attack is a network attack using a "sniffer" or packet analyzer to collect the packets of information being transferred over the network from the user's workstation to the security server. As the packets are passed through a store-and-forward switch, they are intercepted and saved for later use by an intruder masquerading as the authorized user. The viability of this attack depends on the interloper having access to a switch located along the virtual circuit connecting the user and the security server. This is possible even on wide area networks but is easily achieved on local area networks by intruders with ready access or insiders exceeding their authorization.

Defeating such attacks is accomplished by requiring that each password be used only once. Implementation of such single-use schema is not, however, so easy. Requiring that a user change his or her password after each session satisfies the requirement, even with simple password systems, but places an extraordinary burden on the user—a burden not easily accepted. Better systems use some algorithm in conjunction with the logon protocol to change passwords after each use. One type of system uses a pseudorandom number generator to change the password, either after each use or based on a clock (changing perhaps once a minute). The user enters the user ID and then enters the pseudorandom number as his or her password. The server mediating the logon protocol knows either the next pseudorandom number in the sequence if a new number is generated at the end of each session, or the current number if the sequence is time-dependent and the clocks of the user and server have been synchronized.

Another type of system uses a challenge and response. The user attempting to log on enters his or her user ID, and the server returns a challenge, which may be in the form of a question to be answered, a word that by prearrangement is paired with another word known to both user and server, or a number that, entered into an agreed upon algorithm, produces a mathematically related but difficult-to-guess number to be supplied in response. Provided that the proper response is given by the user within some reasonable period of time, access will be granted.

Such systems are not foolproof. If multiple simultaneous logons are permitted, the wily hacker can watch the logon with a sniffer and log on behind the authentic user before the time for which the password is valid expires. Policy should deny multiple simultaneous logons for this reason.

Even if multiple simultaneous logons are denied, programs exist that track the logon attempt of an authentic user and mimic the user until the last keystroke(s) of the logon procedure, at which point the program preempts the authentic user with a guess. For example, suppose the system uses a time-synchronized pseudorandom generator. When the user enters his or her user ID, the system expects a certain number, known to both user and server because both know the time-dependent algorithm and the time. Suppose the number is always six digits in length. The hacker watches the authentic user log on and sends duplicate packets to the server immediately after the authentic user sends his or her packets. After the authentic use has entered five digits, the hacker preempts by entering a random digit as the sixth digit before the authentic user can enter the last digit. On one try in 10 the hacker will get in before the authentic user and the authentic user will be locked out.

A similar attack can work where a challenge must be answered with a correct response. If the challenge is a seven-digit number to be answered, say, with another seven-digit number, the hacker preempts after the authentic user has sent the sixth digit. If word pairs or question and response are used, the hacker can use a program that either patiently collects responses until enough are available to permit a preemptive guess, or a dictionary is used to determine a preemptive choice based on the entry of the first few letters by the authentic user.

True one-time passwords are available using protocols that depend on public key cryptography. To use such a system, the user and the server must each have public keys that are known to the other or that are readily available. When the user begins the logon protocol, he or she enters his or her ID. The server responds with a random number that is generated for the session and that will not be used again. The random number is encrypted using the user's public key and sent to the user. Of course, only the user can decrypt the random number (provided always that the user has kept his or her private key secure). The user can then reencrypt the random number using the server's public key and use it as the password. When the server decrypts the random number and it matches the original, the server is sure that the user is authentic.

Passwords provide a range of protection, from slight to significant depending upon their implementation. User-selected, infrequently changed passwords provide only minimal protection—marginally better than no passwords at all. Complex passwords are better but are still open to clever guesses and dictionary attacks. One-time passwords are best, but even they must be carefully implemented to prevent sophisticated hackers from overpowering the protection they offer.

Tokens: Things You Have

Tokens are things you possess that help another person or process verify that you are who you purport to be. Examples include business cards, drivers licenses, picture ID cards, company or organizational badges, automated teller machine cards, dog tags worn by soldiers, signet rings, corporate seals, smart cards containing embedded computer chips, and a host of other devices. Obviously, some tokens provide more reassurance than others—picture IDs are better than business cards, for authentication purposes at least. Some tokens may be used together with a password, such as a PIN for an ATM or credit card, to increase the assurance provided.

Biometrics: Things You Are

Biometric technology measures some characteristic of the user and compares it with a stored representation of that characteristic to ascertain that the user is actually who he or she purports to be. Perhaps the best-known biometric is the fingerprint, but other examples include retina scans, voiceprints, measurements of physical characteristics such as finger length, chemical analyses, and a host of other possible measurements of characteristics more or less unique to the individual. Biometric countermeasures are discussed in Chapter 12.

Wrap-Up

Access controls may be thought of as: 1) controlling enterprise access from a systems perspective and considering threats, targets, risk, memory, etc.; and 2) auditing people and physical access to computer systems. Both are used to manage access to enterprise information.

CHAPTER 9

Digital Signatures and Certification Authorities— Technology, Policy, and Legal Issues

Trust

The science behind authentication methods is sophisticated, and there are different authentication methods as well as different ways to use these methods. *Digital signatures* are a result of the computer and its influence in our daily lives. Digital signatures are perhaps the best known of the various scientific methods for authentication; however, they are mostly misunderstood instruments of *trust*. Trust is the central issue in the use of digital signatures.

Digital signatures become more important each day as we slowly change the way business is conducted. Contracts that were once signed by both parties in person with a witness have transited to agreements being signed and then faxed with a hard copy placed in the postal mail. Not only is the current method time-consuming, slow, and inefficient, it is a somewhat costly way to conduct business in today's frenetic world. Secure digital signatures sent over the Internet can be a quick and inexpensive way to conduct global commerce—with the correct security measures in place.

Digital signatures can be generated very quickly and facilitate binding a document to its owner to help authenticate the message. Since digital signatures require effective-binding processes for a public key infrastructure (PKI) to be practical, a review of the requirements for certificate authorities (CAs) yields some interesting results. Chapter 19 covers the use of public key infrastructure in building trust online—especially for the DoD. The ideal CA is authoritative for the *name space* it represents, thus avoiding issues of "trust." Complex PKI topologies are difficult for CAs to manage and complex for users to understand or effect. Proprietary CAs, serving specialized (chosen) user communities, are favored to issue certificates to clients or customers. These CAs avoid problems with name spaces, third-party assurance, liability, revocation, and PKI management, yet they do not meet the global requirements for e-mail or travel credentials.

Utah's Digital Signature Act is the most influential of the states' enactments concerning digital signatures. A variety of alternative approaches can be observed in other state's laws. This variety results from the many policy choices that must be made in enacting digital or electronic legislation and hinders certificate authorities seeking to offer services on a national or global scale.

The regulation and promotion of certain digital signature-based authentication methods have created many policy issues. Between 1996 and 1998, a flurry of legislation and political initiatives in 37 of the United States and 28 countries has been observed.

Authentication Methods

Authentication methods, including both handwritten and digital signatures, have several functions. They are used to authenticate identity by convincing the recipient of a document that the person to whom the signature belongs actually signed it. Both handwritten and digital signatures serve to validate contractual requirements of assent to terms, along with nonrepudiation. Signatures are not reusable. Digital signatures are mathematically tied to the document they are intended to authenticate.

Authentication in the digital environment is important due to the potential for fraud in open, international computer networks. Three distinct categories of authentication methods are used. The first category relies on shared knowledge such as passwords. The second, biometrics, is based on unique personal characteristics. The third is a hybrid form that can be implemented in hardware or software and relies on an individual's possession of information (e.g., encryption key) or device (smart card).

Either of two approaches will assure the recipient of a valid digital signature that he or she can trust. The first approach is to create a trusted directory of individuals and public keys. When a person receives the digitally signed document, that person verifies the public key of the signer by looking it up in a trusted directory. The drawbacks to this method are the requirements for an available directory: an online search and a check of each signature so signed.

A better method relies on the concept of *digital public key certificates*. The purpose of digital certificates is to associate a public key with the individual's identity. These certificates are electronic documents, digitally signed by some trusted entity, that contain information about the individual, including the individual's public key. Digital certificates are easy to use. When an individual digitally signs a document, that person attaches a copy of his or her digital certificate issued by a trusted entity. The receiver of the message and accompanying digital certificate relies on the public key of the trusted third party that issued the digital certificate to authenticate the message. The receiver can link the message to a person, not simply to a public key. In this model, trust is the central feature of the digital certificate. However, who are the trusted entities and why should we trust them? We can start with the DSS.

NIST and DSS

The National Institute of Standards and Technology (NIST) defined the Digital Signature Standard (DSS) as a cryptographic method for authenticating the identity of the sender of an electronic communication and for authenticating the integrity of the data contained in that communication. The public key system was intended for all federal departments and agencies in the protection of unclassified information. NIST had intended to use the de facto international standard RSA algorithm as their standard for digital signatures. The RSA algorithm is a public key algorithm that supports a variable key length and variable block size of the text to be encrypted. Public-Key Cryptography Standards (PKCS) #1 through 12 were an attempt to provide a standard interface for public key cryptography. PKCS #1 may be the most important of these standards because it defines the method of encrypting and signing data using RSA's public key cryptosystem. PKCS #1 describes syntax identical to that of Privacy Enhanced Mail and X.509 Certificates for RSA public/private keys and three signature algorithms for signing certificates.

The ability to "crack" an encrypted message is a function of the *key length* and *random nature* of the key. The National Security Agency (NSA), insisting on a weaker algorithm, opposed NIST on their RSA choice and, along with the FBI, put NIST under intense pressure to accept the NSA proposal. The NSA-proposed algorithm did not meet the NIST request for secure key exchange in confidential unclassified communications. When all was said and done, NIST publicly proposed the DSS developed by the NSA in August 1991 for unclassified information. DSS approval was announced by the Department of Commerce (DOC) on May 19, 1994, as Federal Information Processing Standard (FIPS) 186, effective December 1, 1994.

Defining Trust

Stewart Baker, former chief counsel for NSA, writes that governments regulate the confidentiality aspects of cryptography because they simply do not trust all users of cryptography.[1] Users of cryptography for confidentiality are also motivated by mistrust. They do not want their communications intercepted or trusted to middlemen. Recent government efforts at TTP, or *trusted third party*, aimed at forcing users to share their encryption keys, has met with serious public opposition. Finding the third party in the equation that all users are willing to trust has proved to be a difficult aspect of the policy.

Cryptography can be used to *calibrate* and *automate* trust, as well as *authenticate* identities, companies, computers, routers, software programs and, of course, digital signatures.[2] The ability to calibrate trust is more important to commerce than the ability to keep data confidential.

Since trust is the nub of authentication technologies, a role for government is assured. Laws and regulations underlie almost all of the private institutions—from banks to telephone companies. These dominate the nation's trust infrastructure. On the federal level, the IRS has agreed to use VeriSign for a test of digital certificates, which if successful, will affect Americans through year 2000 and beyond.

Whereas TTP received a thumbs down, digital signature technology is just the opposite. This is because industry is behind (and actively supports) the government role in cryptographic authentication.

There are two fundamental implementations of digital certificates: the X.509 hierarchy of trusted entities model and the informal Pretty Good Privacy (PGP) web of trust model. The former is used by the credit card industry because it reflects the business model of the industry. Merchants are willing to accept credit cards that have been issued by a bank whose name is on the card. The bank has been authenticated by the credit card company, typically, Visa or MasterCard. It is clear that a chain of trusted third parties is required to permit the consumers and vendors to do business globally. Each entity in the chain is called a certificate authority. The CA's function is to certify that a particular key belongs to a particular individual or entity. The root CA is the original certificate authority. It, along with all the subsidiary CA-issued certificates, is transferred along the X.509 trusted hierarchy path when an individual signs a document using the X.509 approach.

The PGP web of trust model does not have CA's or root authority. It relies on a small community of users who have regular contact and who "introduce" other users based on some level of trust. The model is difficult to incorporate in large-scale operations and has not been fully accepted in more than local user communities. Many like to add their PGP public key to business cards, stationery, and e-mail. As a status symbol it fails to deliver as a usable alternative to X.509 standard.

Digital certificates serve as a source of trust. However, digital certificates can also be used to authenticate an individual's rights or relationships without making any statement about the individual's identity. There are times when knowledge of an individual's identity is unnecessary and maybe undesirable. In this case, a user may rely on special-purpose certificates that can only be used for specific functions, not including authentication of identity. The Secure Electronic Transaction (SET) protocol uses digital signatures and digital certificates to fulfill the data integrity and party authentication functions. SET certificates are issued to cardholders and merchants. They, like credit cards, do not identify the bearer, but rather the bearer's credit line and history. SET uses digital-signature technology to provide extra security to the transaction by authenticating the relationship of a public key to an account number, not by identifying an individual.

Technology—What Is a Digital Signature?

A *digital signature is an electronic method of signing an electronic document that is reliable, convenient, and secure.* An electronic document includes any instrument created or stored on a computer. These include e-mail, letters, contracts, and images. Many states have enacting legislation concerning the use of digital signatures, which is discussed later in detail (also refer to Appendices G and H). The most widely used type of electronic signature relies on public/private key encryption. This asymmetric cryptosystem key-pair technology has been available for nearly 20 years. A public/private key encryption system involves two mathematically related keys that are like large passwords for each user. The *private key*, known only by the "signer," can encrypt a message that only their *public key* can decrypt. Once the private/public-keys are generated using a valid certificate authority, they remain associated with the person who generates the two keys. The certificate authority is a trusted entity that issues certificates to end entities and other CAs. CAs also issue *certificate revocation lists (CRLs)* periodically and post certificates and CRLs to a database or repository.

Lawyers, not users, have distinguished electronic signatures from digital signatures. In an emerging usage, an electronic signature is any electronic analogue to a written signature. It can use any of the three authentication methods. Appendix G demonstrates the lack of uniformity in definitions. However, the formal definition for *electronic signature* is any signature in electronic form, attached to, or logically associated with, an electronic record, executed or adopted by a person or electronic agent with intent to sign the electronic record. Electronic signatures do not have to rely on cryptographic methods. Digital signatures rely on public key cryptographic methods to authenticate information and are discussed subsequently.

Figure 9-1 details the components of *ordinary digital signature schemes*. In Figure 9-1, components in the strict sense are the algorithms *gen*, *sign*, and *test*. *Gen* and *sign* are probabilistic. The main security requirement on an ordinary digital signature scheme is that one cannot forge signatures although one knows the public key. A necessary but not sufficient condition for this is that one cannot compute the secret key from the public key. Such a scheme can never be theoretically secure. For practicality, there must be an upper boundary on the length of the signatures produced with signing keys and messages of a certain length. *The security of such digital signature schemes is computational*. A consequence of computational security is that signature schemes usually depend on a so-called *security parameter*, which determines the length of the problem instances that are supposed to be mathematically infeasible. Choosing a larger security parameter usually makes keys and signatures longer, and signing and testing more time-consuming. One hopes that it also makes forging signatures significantly more difficult, so that the gap widens between the complexities of the legal algorithms (*gen*, *sign*, and *test*) and of forging.

Figure 9-1

Components of ordenary Digital Segnatures. (Reprinted with permission. Source: Pfitzmann, Birgit, *Digital Signature Schemer*, 1996, p. 14.)

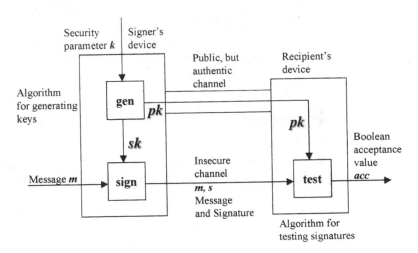

The public key can be distributed freely to anyone the public key owner wishes to communicate with securely. The public key cannot derive the attributes of the private key, although they are related. The private key is derived using the asymmetric encryption algorithm providing message origination authentication and nonrepudiation. One of the not commonly known features of the private and public key is that data encrypted by one key can be decrypted by the other.

Message Digest Function

The *message digest function* is an algorithm that maps the sequence of bits comprising an electronic record into a smaller set of bits without requiring the use of a key or any secret information. Each electronic record yields the exact same message digest every time the algorithm is executed. This method makes it *computationally unfeasible* for any two electronic records to produce identical results unless they are exactly alike. The *digest* is simply a *smaller extrapolated version* of the original message. Digesting a message is a necessary way to speed transmission and assists in verification.

Second, the sender signs the message using his or her *private key*. This digitally signed message is then sent to the recipient. The recipient generates the message hash from the message itself, and then the message is verified using the sender's public key, which was in the recipient's possession before the message transmission. If the two message hashes are the same, the message can be viewed as genuine and authentic. If the hashes do not match, the message is corrupted or a forgery. An important thing to remember is that *the message can still be in cleartext. Digital certificates only validate the message origination and integrity.*

Signing

Signing denotes the *process of applying a digital signature to some message or data.* This works by appending organizational data to the message and optionally transforming the message so that it will pass mail transfer agents unmodified. Any further change to the contents of the message results in corruption of the digital signature. The recipient can detect this using the sender's public key. Although the message data may look unreadable after the transfer encoding, there is actually no protection against eavesdropping at this point. The message is just encoded and *not* encrypted.

When the message is intended for recipients who might not have a compatible system available, any recipient can actually look at the message and read it, although they will not be able to properly verify the signature. The recipient should treat the message with the same caution normally extended to any nonsigned messages.

Encryption renders the message unreadable to anyone but the intended recipients. This means that in order to create an encrypted message, a set of recipients must be chosen. This works by selecting a number of aliases from the user's database. *Based on the alias, the program looks up the corresponding certificate in the database and uses their public key to encrypt the message session key.*

Decryption is the reception of a message and the *removal of security features.* This process is also called the *de-enhancement* of a message. Where a message is not actually encrypted and only signed, the process is usually just called *signature verification.* A message should be considered untrustworthy if any steps fail.

A digital signature should be *time-stamped* to allow the recipient to see when the transaction occurred and to allow the signer the ability to invalidate and terminate the digital signature if it were to be compromised.

The Process of Signing a Document Is Unique

Signing a document is a unique two-step process. First, the message is *hashed* using a message digest function. This is done because the cryptographic algorithms used to encrypt messages are slow. A short representation of the message (message digest) can be created using a cryptographic algorithm known as a one-way hash function to speed the process. The hash function maps strings of bits to fixed-length strings of bits that make it computationally infeasible to find a given input or output that maps to a particular output or input.

Figure 9-2 shows a typical digital signature created using MD5. (Message Digest 5 is a strong algorithm that reduces a document of any size and creates a digest or unique "thumbprint" that is always the same length. An MD5 message digest cannot be reversed.)

Figure 9-2
Digital Signature
with MD5.

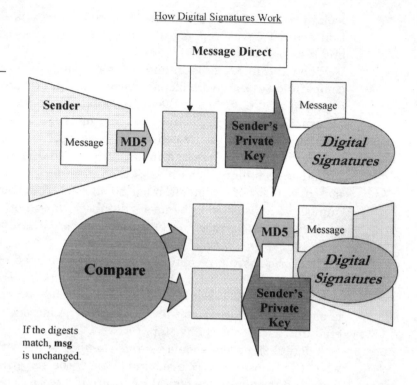

How Digital Signatures Work

If the digests
match, **msg**
is unchanged.

There are three basic assumptions made when we sign a document:

1. Your signature binds you to whatever the document states.
2. The document will not be changed after you sign it.
3. Your signature will not be transferred to another document.

There are laws and conventions that make these assumptions valid, but how is this carried into the networked world? We need assurance that the message hasn't changed (data integrity) and that no one can move our signature to another document we never intended to sign.

Provably Secure Digital Signature Schemes

Research on proving the security of signature schemes centers on two steps in the process. The first step is to recognize that redundancy and hash functions are not some protocol around a real signature scheme.

Instead, the signature scheme comprises everything that happens within a message, and security must be proved for the complete scheme. A second step was to formalize not only the unfeasibility of computing the inverse of a function but also that the scheme must include an active attack and excludes *existential forgery*. Goldwasser accomplished this in his research in 1988. The result was known as the GMR definition.[3] Basically, a signature scheme such as that portrayed in Figure 9-1 is defined as a collection of algorithms *gen*, *sign*, and *test*, such that when the keys are correctly generated with *gen*, two properties hold:

1. Signatures correctly generated with *sign* pass the corresponding test.
2. If any polynomial-time attacker first communicates with a signer for awhile, and then tries to compute a paired new message and a signature, the success probability is very small. During the key generation, the maximum number of messages to be signed must be fixed, and *sign* takes the number of messages as input.

Both properties portend cryptographically strong schemes. GMR is discussed in the literature and reference to it can be found in the resources section.

X.509 Certificates

A *certificate* is a digitally signed data structure defined in the X.509 standard [CCITT] that binds the identity of a certificate holder to his/her public key. X.509 is the X.500 directory service standard relevant to public-key infrastructures describing two authentication methods: simple authentication based on password usage and strong authentication based on public key cryptography. Version 3 added certificate extensions to the X.509 standard and CRL (data structure) formats (Figure 9-3).

There are over 20 standard extensions defined for version 3 certificates and version 2 CRLs. Here are a few important ones. Certification policies can be represented explicitly via object identifier syntax in the certificates. There is a provision for policy qualifier data to allow customization. Cross-certificates can map between (equivalent but distinctly named) policies of different administrative domains and can prohibit such mapping further along a certification path. There is an explicit syntax for imposing name subordination relative to a CA's name, without imposing any constraints on the structure of the certification graph as in

Figure 9-3

Sample X.500
Directory Structure
with Cross
Certification.

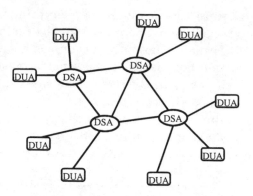

Figure 9-4

Typical fields in
Version 1 X.509
Certification.

Version
Serial Number
Issuer's Signature Algorithm
Issuer Distinguished Name
Validity Period
Subject Distinguished Name
Subject Public Key Information
Issuer's Signature

PEM (Privacy Enhanced Mail, discussed later in the chapter), a competing CA model.

User and CA certificates are explicitly marked as such, and usage restrictions for the public key contained in a certificate can be specified (e.g., a key can be designated as a signature key or a key encryption key).[4]

A major enhancement of X.509 is the introduction of alternative name formats, so that e-mail addresses, DNS (Domain Name Service) names, and IP (Internet Protocol) addresses can appear as identifiers in certificates (Figure 9-4). CRLs have been enhanced to advise the reason for revocation, to allow splitting CRLs into multiple or incremental parts. This feature is a control on the size of a CRL. Dr. Stephen Kent, in his seminal paper on the subject, states that there is little experience with CRL management and much concern that CRLs will be too large, especially for smart card or token applications.[5]

The X.509 standard is relevant to public key cryptographic infrastructures defining two methods of authentication. Standard authentication relies on password usage and strong authentication is based on public key cryptography. The operational period of a certificate should be directly linked to the confidentiality and security required. We can look at the use and rules applied to passwords to draw a comparison. The life expectancy of a password is defined in the organization's security policy. As a simple rule of thumb, the more security that is required, the more often it will need to be changed. This will probably be the same for a digital signature certificate. Administrators have learned to expect the worst case when it comes to their users. They will expect that the users may compromise their private key, and as a precaution, use key expiration dates to maintain a tight control on security.

The public key certificate must be obtained to verify a digital signature. A public key has no identifier with a private key or person. It is only a string of numbers. This adds to the complexity of the transaction. Each recipient must obtain the signer's public key in order to verify the message. To ensure that each recipient is identified with a particular key pair, a third party that is trusted by both recipients must associate a person to a key pair. This trusted third party is called the *certification authority*.

Before users can actually sign documents or encrypt messages, the user must create his or her key database. When creating this database, an asymmetric key pair is created, the public key is put in a self-signed certificate, and the certificate and certificate revocation list are initialized.

From a *cryptographic point of view, the key pair generation is the most important step in this process.* Once the database has been created, the user name cannot be changed. If a new database is required, it must be done with a new key.

The public key component of the user's key pair is stored as a special certificate in the database. Messages are usually encrypted in a way that the sender can read them. The status and values of the current user's certificate should include a distinguishing user name, an actual public key, an algorithm used to compute the digital signature inside the certificate, and a certificate validity period.

The user's certificate will become a properly signed certificate after the import of the certification reply message. Before this stage, it is a nontrusted self-signed certificate.

Symmetric algorithms include the Data Encryption Standard (DES) and triple DES, which processes the data three times with DES, thereby using a session key of double the length of a single DES key. Triple DES is stronger than single DES, but it takes proportionally longer to process data with triple DES than with single DES.

To generate a digital signature, an asymmetric signature algorithm is needed. Currently, the PEM and MailTrusT standards only support the RSA algorithm. *Privacy Enhanced Mail (PEM)* is an enhanced electronic mail system that includes privacy for use on the Internet defined by four RFCs (Request For Comments Nos. 1421-1424), which specify message encipherment and authentication procedures, a key management infrastructure, relevant algorithms and information, and specific details on the electronic formats for key management.

In a strong cryptosystem, each new message is encrypted with a pseudorandomly generated key, the length of which depends on the selected symmetric encryption algorithm. The *randomness of a session key generation* is the center of a cryptographically strong one-way hash function.

Certification hierarchies, certificate chains, and the certificate revocation list are what make the asymmetric cryptosystems so powerful. In order to participate in such a hierarchy, any user must obtain a certificate for his or her public key. This is achieved by creating and sending a certification request to the user's certification authority, which in turn creates a proper certificate that is embedded in a certification reply message, which is sent back. This reply is then downloaded by the user. The user then becomes a member of the *certification hierarchy* (Figure 9-5). The certification process has to be executed only once after the key pair has been generated.

A certification request is like a message that only bears a digital signature. The difference is that the message is signed with the user's newly created private key, which is not yet certified. To all other users in the system this would be a nontrusted message (since the user's key is not properly yet certified), but the certification authority detects this as

Figure 9-5
Certificate
Hierarchy.

Certificate ID	Signed By
PAA (Root)	Self Signed
PCA	PAA
CA	PCA
RA/User	CA

the intended means to forward certification requests. The contents of the certification request's text data is irrelevant; it can be empty. It is not possible for the user who creates the request to check the signature him- or herself. This check will only be possible after the certification process has been completed.

The protection of the private key can be achieved by using a password-derived symmetric key to encrypt the asymmetric private key. In fact, the password does not need to be a single word. It can be a passphrase. It is desirable to use a longer sequence of words, containing uppercase and lowercase letters, as well as digits, symbols, punctuation marks, and so forth. Simply speaking, the longer the passphrase and the more unique characters it contains, the more difficult it is to break. Good security procedures still require that the password be changed at regular intervals. This limits the chance of an attacker or intruder getting the private key file and the matching passphrase at the same time. The password should not be stored on the hard disk or in the Windows Registry.

For each enrolled user, a separate database is maintained. In this database, the (protected) user's key pair is stored along with the certificates from other users that the user has loaded over time. It lists all certificates stored in the database that have an alias. It is these certificates that are used to send encrypted messages to the respective certificate owners. Certificates can be stored in a database without an alias. These certificates may belong to intermediate certification authorities. These certificates are only used to verify *certificate chains*, but not to encrypt messages intended for the certification authority. A display of the trust status of the certificates may be misleading. Certificates can be stored in the database as "nontrusted," with the trust only established on demand when sending a message to this recipient or when verifying a signature that was done with the appropriate public key. Any certificate in the database that has an alias can be deleted. Certificates should be deleted one by one. There will be certificates in the database that do not have an alias. Generally, these certificates should not be removed from the database.

The input data selected (file or clipboard contents) are *hashed* with the hash algorithm and the result is displayed. A *hash function* is a function, mathematical or otherwise, that takes a variable-length input string (called a *preimage*) and converts it to a fixed-length smaller output strength (called the *hash value*). Hash functions have been used by cryptographers and computer scientists for some time. They have many names: compression functions, one-way functions, message digest, fingerprint, cryptographic checksum, message integrity check, and manipulation detection code.

Since neither access to the private key/public key nor the user's database is required, this hash function can be executed freely. A hash value can be used to check the unmodified transmission of otherwise unprotected data. This is especially suitable to check the correct reception of the certification reply message, to determine that the message has not been tampered with during transit. It is a suitable means to verify that the hash value computed at the sender's side is identical to the one computed on the recipient's side. The reference hash value must be transmitted via a different communication method and should be well protected against manipulation. It does not need to be secret. These values are small and could be read over the telephone or faxed. The exact way the certification reply is protected against manipulation should be defined in the security policy.

A one-way hash function is used to:

1. Specify which hash algorithm is used when signing messages
2. Specify which hash is used inside the certificate when creating the user's self-signed certificate
3. Specify which hash is used inside the certificate when creating a certification reply
4. Specify which hash is used inside the certificate revocation list (CRL)
5. Compute the hash value of data

The CRL is a list of revoked but unexpired certificates issued by a CA. Cryptographic hash functions originally required for e-mail were MD2 and MD5. MD5 is a hashing technique that creates a 128-bit message digest. SHA-1 is the Secure Hash Algorithm designed by NIST and NSA to be used with the DSS to ensure the security of the Digital Signature Algorithm (DSA).

More-advanced hashing methods are SHA-1 and RIPEMD-160. Using one of these two algorithms is recommended. The security of these algorithms is much better than that of MD2 and MD5. Discussions of the security of these algorithms may be found in the literature.[6]

Institutional overhead comprises the costs associated with establishing and maintaining a certificate authority service center whether it is kept in-house or outsourced. This cost includes professional accreditation, government compliance, auditing, and any legal and financial liabilities that may arise from any errors, omissions, or negligence. Distributed key administration is one way to spread the costs, control, and workload of the key distribution and management system back into the organization. Establishing subordinate certificate authorities throughout an organization may be viewed as a weak point in the security policy.

Certificates and Alias Names

Automatic addition of new certificates to the user's database can be a good feature. Whenever a message is received from an unknown sender, the certificate (which must be embedded in the message for this to work) is checked in the context of the user's certification hierarchy. If the check is successful, then the message is considered trustworthy and the new certificate can be automatically added to the database.

An *alias name* can be determined automatically, or it can be specified explicitly before the decryption operation is run. When the alias name is determined automatically, a certain subcomponent of the distinguished name of the owner of the new certificate is taken. Once the sender of the message has been put into the user's database with an alias, messages can be encrypted to this user by selecting the alias. To distribute one's own certificate, it is appropriate to distribute signed (but not encrypted) messages. After a message has been decrypted successfully (i.e., its digital signature has been verified), the so-called certification path is displayed. This certification path, starting with the details of the sender's certificate, up to and including the root self-signed certificate, can be used to further check the trustworthiness of the message by inspection.

Attacks on Digital Signatures

Implicitly, one assumes the following cryptanalytic problem: Given the public key and a message, find the corresponding signature. Is it possible that some schemes that seem infeasible to break are vulnerable if one allows stronger attacks and weaker forms of success?

The most important types of attacks, in order of increasing strength, are as follows:

1. *Key-only attack*   The only information the attacker has to work on is the public key.

2. *Known-message attack or a general passive attack* The attacker is given the public key and some signed messages.

3. *Chosen plaintext or active attack* The attacker can choose some messages that the signer will sign for him or her before the attacker must forge a signature on another message on his or her own. In the general case of this attack, the attacker can choose those messages at any time. In effect, the attacker can adapt or apply an adaptive chosen-message attack.

The most important types of success, in decreasing order, are as follows:

1. *Total break* The attacker has found the secret key, or the equivalent way of constructing signatures on arbitrary messages efficiently.

2. *Selective forgery* The attacker has forged the signature on a message that he or she could select independently of the public key and before a possible active attack.

3. *Existential forgery* The attacker has forged the signature on a message that the signer has not signed, and the attacker can choose the message (or plaintext).

The Rabin and Williams schemes were both examples of weaker forms of breaking. Both are similar to RSA, but constructed so that selective forgery with a passive attack was as hard as the integer factorization problem (IFP). An active attack on these schemes was shown to yield a total break. Rabin devised a signaturelike scheme that allowed an attacker with limited resources to find two messages with the same signature, so that by asking the signer to sign one of them, the attacker also obtained a signature on the other.

These attacks were not really noticed until similar attacks were made on RSA. The first attack used the secret RSA operation as a *homomorphism*. By multiplying the signatures on two messages m1 and m2, one obtains the signature on the product m1 x m2. Thus, if the attacker breaks his or her message into two factors and gets the signer to sign those, the attacker can derive the signature on the chosen message (plaintext). Another researcher used a little trickery and reduced the attacker's requirement for two sets of chosen plaintext for signature. These are *selective forgeries* after chosen plaintext attacks, or alternatively, *existential forgeries* after known plaintext attacks.

Existential forgery is possible with a key-only attack in all signature schemes built from the trap-door one-way permutations. The attacker chooses a value and calls it a signature, computes the permutation with a public key, and calls the result a message. The ElGamal scheme is another approach. Although similar to RSA, it is not directly constructed from trap-door one-way permutations. However, no method for selective forgery with an active attack is known at this time.

Assessment of Attacks and Successes

A known plaintext attack is perfectly realistic. Historically, it has been one of the more successful forms of attack on all types of ciphers. On the other hand, a completely unrestricted adaptive chosen message attack is not. If the signer signed arbitrary (random) messages, there would be no need for forgery. It is reasonable to consider restricted forms of active attacks in practice. Every recipient will have some influence on what messages are signed and perhaps determines the message almost completely. An example is a notary public that signs almost everything rather than selective documents.

As to types of success, a scheme where selective forgery is possible cannot be used in practice. Existential forgery may not always be harmful, because the signed message may have no practical value to the attacker. Many of the PGP signed e-mail messages qualify. One does not know what will be of practical value in all applications of digital signature schemes. This is particularly true if data without inherent redundancy are signed. To be on the safe side, every signed message is assumed valuable.

Countermeasures

There are two ad hoc measures against the aforementioned problems. One is to add *redundancy* to messages before signing. In this case, only messages that fulfill a certain predicate are signed; this makes the chosen plaintext attacks more complicated. Furthermore, a signature is only valid if the message fulfills the predicate; thus, existential forgery in the original scheme seems unlikely (highly improbable) to yield a valid message.

The second measure is to apply a one-way hash function to the messages before they are signed. In this case, it is unlikely that an attacker can find messages for a chosen plaintext attack where the hash values actually signed are useful to him or her. An existential forgery in the original scheme should yield a message whose preimage under the hash function is not known. Applying a hash function has the additional advantage that it makes the complete scheme more efficient, if the hash function is fast.

The choice of good redundancy predicates or hash functions is not easy, especially if one wants to execute a fast hash algorithm. There are significant differences in symmetrical cryptologic schemes like DES and an IFP.

Trusting Digitally Signed Documents

A digital signature is *reliable* when it has been issued by a trusted certificate authority (CA), authenticates the sender, guarantees the message integrity, and ensures nonrepudiation of the message. A weakness and major concern of using digital signatures involves the notion that digital signatures can properly assure a person's identification over the Internet or some other nonpresent situation. Digital signatures alone cannot identify people. Digital signatures can only assure the recipient that a particular identification process was completed.

Likewise, a manual signature not witnessed or notarized cannot assure the recipient that the sender was truly the person who signed the document. In fact, a digital signature may have been stolen, or compromised in some way, without the owner even being aware of its theft. Security experts have been essential in defining and detecting the security system holes that digital signatures have created.

Fraud can take place in many ways. On site, a thief can simply use your computer and send a signed message, with your digital signature, without you even being present. The thief only needs to access your computer, devising an ability to bypass your password, create and send the email, delete the item from the outbox, and power the unit down with no one the wiser. Digital signatures require strong security policies to be used as a viable method of conducting electronic business.

Properties of Generic Public CAs

There are four generic properties that a public CA service should exhibit when issuing a certificate to represent a user in interactions with many different applications or services. According to Dr. Stephen Kent, Chief

Scientist-Information Security at BBN Corporation, they are (1) balancing liability concerns, (2) reducing operating costs, (3) defining acceptable levels of assurance, and (4) establishing definitive authority via name spaces. Formal certification models work on the basis that only a few certificates need to be issued to accommodate these four issues for users in many different interactions.

Kent suggests that another approach to certification may be better. It is based on the fact that individuals have many existing relationships with various organizations. These organizations maintain databases for tracking employees, customers, members, and so on. Certificates issued from these proprietary organizations are not for general use but focus on a specific context and thus avoid problems faced by generic public CAs. This limits liability to the certificate user. The level of assurance for authentication is determined solely by the issuer and the data in the issuer's database. Naming problems are reduced because each subject already is assigned a unique name in the issuer's database.[7]

What Makes a Good CA?

The notion of a CA is often confused by the casual observer. The main security requirement for a CA is that it accurately binds a collection of attributes to a public key. It is this public key that is used for encryption of a message and binding the digital signature on documents. The primary attribute bound to a public key is a form of identity, an identity that may be used as input to an access control or human-interpreted trust decision. Of interest is the CA's basis for authority with regard to the name space from which the identifiers in certificates are chosen. In the X.509 model, this is found in the directory-distinguished names, as the essence of identification. Certificates based on this authority are issued and known as *forward*, *reverse*, *subordinate*, or *cross*, depending on whether the certificate is issued to the user, signed by the user, with a CA as the subject, or issued between CAs.

There are two criteria that are very important for a CA: (1) it is crucial to ensure the accuracy of many, if not all, the security attributes in a certificate and (2) that the list of attributes to be vouched for be reduced to prevent errors and to remain authoritative by the CA.

No one single form of identification is appropriate for user interactions. Most individuals hold credit cards, drivers license, passport, memberships, employee ID badges, and so on. Each identifies an individual in a different context, and most are *not* interchangeable. Only credentials that incorporate a picture of the user and are issued by a government agency (passport or drivers license) have a broad utility. Although name information is thought of as the most important attribute in a certificate, the X.509 certificate extensions give rise to a broad range of security-critical attributes. As the number of attributes increases, two problems occur. First, attributes expire or become invalid, and second, there are increased opportunities for management errors as the number of attributes increases.

Types of CAs

There are five types of CAs. They differ in their basis for authority, the name spaces in which they issue certificates, liability limits, and their scope of applicability. Existing CAs fall into these categories:

- *Organizational empowered*   Examples include DoD, NSA, GM, Automotive Network Exchange (ANX), Reynolds Metals, and MIT. They issue badges to employees, ID cards to students, and credentials to subsidiary organizations and consultants. They have *definitive authority* for attesting to the identity of their affiliates.

- *Geopolitically empowered*   Examples include the State Department for passports, and the federal and state governments for identifying citizens and residents.

- *Universally empowered (does not exist)*   The USPS, UN, and ICC has been suggested as possible. No organization can be authoritative for all forms of identity, organization, and geopolitical concerns.

- *Liability-empowered (third party)*   Companies such as VeriSign, CertCo, and CyberTrust are examples of liability-empowered CAs serving the public. They are authoritative for their own name spaces only. They derive their power to vouch for individuals based on their own assertions in certification practice statements. The assumed liability is very small. Marketing is the key to success of these companies, not the ability to demonstrate competence.

- *Proprietary*   Proprietary CAs are a hybrid form. They own private name spaces and have subjects as clients or customers of the companies issuing the certificates, rather than employees.

The Notion of Trust

The web of trust for Pretty Good Privacy (PGP), in contrast to the X.509 model, is a bottom-up, self-centered approach to certification. It includes the notion of *trusted introducer*, an entity who is trusted to act as an intermediary to extend the scope of the web. PGP marks certificates with different levels of trust and has the ability to evaluate trust on the certification path. (Locating a target on the path can be computationally intensive as the web develops to a moderate size. Revocation and CRL is a problem because any given public key may be signed by multiple introducers.) Why should users accept *trust* for certification of an entity by a CA? It is inappropriate for definitive authority. Certain credentials (drivers licenses or passports) must come from organizational or geopolitical CAs. The users trust level of the CA has nothing to do with it. However, trust works in liability-empowered CAs, since CAs such as VeriSign are not authoritative for the name space in which they issue certificates.

Certification Policies

X.509 v3 certificates allow a CA to embed information about policies. These extensions convey information about the security characteristics associated with certificate management, the quality of authentication applied, and the technology employed by the user to protect the private key associated with the certificate (software versus hardware tokens). They mark equivalence between different policies and the form of cross-certification.

The direct reason for inclusion of this information is to use the policy as input to an access control list and access control decisions. Policy information is included as text or references to URLs. Certificates comprise a convenient way to bind data to a user ID (with integrity). CAs have limited authority and that limits the certificate data. The more data, the more likely that one or more of the extensions will become invalid and require revocation.

Lawyers like the idea of incorporating policy data in a certificate to limit the liability of the CA. The liability-empowered CA runs the fine line of assuming full liability for the issued certificates (the user perspective) versus the CA with limited liability (the lawyer's objective). Users and clients continue to negotiate a middle ground.

A Model for the Effective Public Key Infrastructure (PKI)

The preceding analysis suggests several characteristics for good PKIs. The ideal CA is authoritative for the name space it represents, thus avoiding issues of "trust." Complex PKI topologies are difficult for CAs to manage and complex for users to understand or effect. Including authorization data for access control decisions diminishes the lifetime of a certificate and introduces potential error points. Proprietary CAs, serving specialized (chosen) user communities, are favored to issue certificates to clients or customers. These CAs avoid problems with name spaces, third-party assurance, liability, revocation, and PKI management. However, they do not meet the global requirements for e-mail or travel credentials. Cross-certification issues remain a problem.[8]

Other Methods: Biometric and Two-Factor Authentication

Biometrics includes fingerprints, iris scans, retinal scans, voiceprints, digitally captured handwriting, speech, DNA, or any digital information that can be linked to a specific person's biological information. These characteristics are unique to each individual and are considered the most secure mechanism for authentication.

The next method is two-factor authentication. *Two-factor authentication* involves something *I have* in my possession in conjunction with something *I know*. These can be smart cards with encrypted data on the chip and personal identification numbers (PINs), proximity badges that require PINs, or "tokens" with PINS to unlock them in order to operate. The least secure are the single-factor authentication devices we use today, the most common of which is the everyday credit card used to make purchases from a variety of merchants.

Legal Issues—The Limits of Trust

Digital signature technology allows the transmission of sensitive material on a network and restrictive access to it. It works globally and between strangers. It is clear that a trust infrastructure is required to make the technology work. Governments all over the world have embraced digital signatures (see Appendices I and J) and this is a sword of Damocles. The more governments who embrace the technology, the less the general public and corporate world accepts the technology.

We live in a contentious world where almost everybody sues. The object is to find fault with someone (preferably with deep pockets) rather than accept personal responsibility for actions. Assume for a moment that a customer writes his password (for access to a private key) to a smart card and then loses it. Bad guy finds it and knows that he can use it for proof of identity and credit. Bad guy proceeds to use it maliciously. Certificate revocation lists were designed to deal with this type of problem. To make a digital signature scenario work, the customer must check the CRL before entering into a transaction. Visa used to issue books of invalid cards that the merchant was supposed to check before doing business with customers. Exxon forced its retailers to circle both the expiration date and require drivers license on any card not signed. The point is that customers and merchants rarely use CRLs. Returning to our hypothetical example, our customer is burned on a bad signature. He sues the bank and the merchant who accepted the stolen ID. (There is a role for lawyers after the digital revolution.)

Without clear rules about digital signatures and certificates, no one knows how such a suit fares in court. The bank can write a contract with the customer to lock up his or her private key or to make the customer liable for negligence. Consumer groups will attack such a law with all dispatch. They call this the "Grandma picks a bad password and loses house problem." The contractor does not have a contract with the innocent third party—the guy who lost money—by relying on the word of the bank, or so sayeth the lawyers. Without legal certainty on both legal protection and insurance protection, companies with deep pockets will not take that risk. They will stay out of the business of issuing digital signatures and digital certificates for such transactions. We have seen minimal commercial acceptance of digital signature technology in the last 10 years because of the risk.

Market Solutions

Many companies took the plunge. They needed digital signatures to do business—especially globally. They found two answers to the open-ended liability problem. They offered cheap certificates—that is, certificates with sweeping disclaimers freeing them of any liability. The SSL encryption that everyone uses for secure Web connections relies in part on digital signatures to identify the server and the browser to each other. No one guarantees the server's public key. The second market solution comes in the form of "closed-system certificates." Contract law is essentially created by participating companies. For example, Visa uses the SET protocol, issuing certificates to member banks, which in turn issue certificates to all cardholders and merchants. Liability is covered by existing agreements. (Grandma in the previous example only is liable for $50.) SET has been implemented in dozens of countries on the assumption that existing credit card laws and contracts govern the liabilities—hence, the digital signature technology.[9]

Legislative/Legal Approaches to the Potential Liability Challenges

In 1996, the American Bar Association released its Digital Signature Guidelines, which presented a comprehensive framework to handle the legal issues arising from digital signatures. The State of Utah led the way with the first variant of the ABA guidelines. Thirty-seven states enacted (refer to Appendices H and I) regulations[10] that covered more than the issues of rights and obligations of keyholders, certification authorities, and relying parties.

General-Use vs. Limited-Use Statutes

State laws can be broken down into two categories: general-use statutes that apply to public and private sector communications, and limited-use statutes that apply only to government or a narrow commercial sector. Appendix H confirms that legislative activity in the states is of the limited-use variety. Utah's Digital Signature Act is the most influential of the general-use laws to date.[11]

Technology-Specific vs. Technology-Neutral Statutes

Digital signature statutes tend to run the gambit from not incorporating language for a particular technology (public key cryptography) to specific definitions of digital signature and certificate authority and the attendant rights and obligations. State laws fall into four categories: (1) "hands-off", (2) conditional, (3) deferral to executive agencies, and (4) strict, technology-specific schemes. Delaware's system provides only for electronic approval; Kansas sets general criteria for a digital signature; Connecticut leaves regulation up to executive agencies; Utah and Hawaii have enacted laws that incorporate the asymmetric cryptosystem technology. In Utah, it is risky to conduct transactions outside the law where such exacting definitions have been legislated.

Recipient Agreement?

Must the person who receives a message sent with a digital signature actively agree with its use? Say that Person A offers his property for $5000 on the Net and receives an acceptance from Person B that is "signed and binding." Person A confirms the sale by e-mail and his digital signature. Another bidder, Person C, submits a handwritten offer of $6000. Is A bound by B's offer, since it came first? Can he refuse a digitally signed bid? In Utah, a signature is *presumed valid*, so A cannot reject B's acceptance. In Washington, the presumption is *rebuttable* as to validity, but a recipient is not obligated to rely on any digital signature. Person A can simply ignore Person B's acceptance. In Minnesota, a digital signature is *valid unless the recipient objects promptly* to the use of the technology on any grounds. Person A can object to Person B's acceptance on the basis he does not rely on digital signatures if he does so promptly.

Licensing CAs

Utah provides for the licensing of certificate authorities. They are granted a legal presumption of validity if the certificates are issued by a licensed certificate authority. Nonlicensed CAs are not given the same status. Utah's CA licensing requirements are the strictest in the country. Apparently, the lawmakers in Malaysia thought so too and modeled their 1998 Digital Signatures Act after it. Appendix 17 shows the states that have enacted legislation concerning the licensing of CAs.

CA Liability and Privacy

It is clear that parties to a transaction rely on the accuracy of the CA's word and that some liability scheme must be part of every digital signature. Only Utah sets liability guideline for CAs. Current legislation exempts licensed certificate authorities from (1) punitive or exemplary damages, (2) damages due to pain and suffering, and (3) damages due to loss of business or profit opportunity. State laws vary on their application of damages. A certificate authority doing business in several states may face different liability in different states—especially if they are unlicensed. Certificate authorities accumulate a wealth of personal information on their clients. State laws do not address this privacy concern.

Definitions Cover a Lot of Ground

Appendix G shows that there is a wide variety of definitions used in the state laws. These differences cause a certificate authority to meet different criteria depending upon the state whose law is applicable. The very structure of a certificate can be different in Hawaii than in Utah. In Florida it doesn't matter at all what the CA does.

Policy Initiatives—Federal

The Utah law addresses the rights and obligations of three parties:

1. The keyholder who is identified by the public key and who controls the private key
2. The certificate authority who vouches for the public key and ties it to the identity of the keyholder
3. The relying party who gets the public key and the certificate and who decides to trust the certificate

In 1999, the Utah law does not solve the issue of conflicting obligations or the requirement to be state-licensed. Federal lawmakers have entered the arena, proposing four acts in 1997 to 1998. Appendix I presents some of the political initiatives in progress in the US.

Politicians have added their mark on digital signatures with the Electronic Financial Services Efficiency Act (EFSEA) of 1997 and H.R. 2937. The EFSEA prompts industry to establish a uniform digital signature system and other forms of authentication that will be an alternative to existing paper-based methods.

A popular position is that "the federal government encourage the private-sector development of uniform standards for electronic authentication, while not imposing rigid rules that may stifle innovation." H.R. 2937 establishes a self-regulatory agency and a mandatory registration of all certificate authorities providing that service with the National Association of Certification Authorities (NACA). Registration with the NACA will not automatically connect the trusted roots of each CA.

The Electronic Commerce Enhancement Act of 1997 (H.R. 2991) limits the use of digital signatures by the federal government and recognizes only the submitting of electronic forms to the federal government.

The hotly contested Kerry Bill, the Secure Public Networks Act (S. 909), contains voluntary registration of certificate authorities and limits their liability for doing so. The TTP (the registered *trusted third-party* private key recovery) provisions were removed in early 1998.

The Digital Signature and Electronic Authentication Law (SEAL) of 1998 (S. 1594) applies only to banks and financial institutions.

International Policy Issues Similar to U.S. Concerns

Germany and Malaysia have enacted digital signature laws similar to Utah's. Appendix J demonstrates that other countries and political entities have followed suit. Unfortunately, the same policy issues encountered by U.S. lawmakers have spilled over into the global community. Whereas the many digital signature laws enacted in the United States may be coordinated and limited via federal actions, the global picture is less positive.

It threatens the notion of a global PKI because the regulation of certification authorities continues to proliferate. It will potentially mean the stopping of "cheap" certificates because mandatory licensing will impose burdens on international certificates. Businesses will no longer offer the cheap certificates that marginally enhance the security of transactions. Users of the cheap certificates will not risk the prospect of liability in several countries. They will either use an alternative to the technology or not use them at all. CAs will be forced to track and comply with regulatory requirements in various countries. In addition, licensing requirements threaten the use of digital signatures in "closed systems," where a preexisting contractual relationship exists to provide rules of engagement. SET, arguably the most important use of digital signature technology to date, is threatened by the proliferation of registration requirements.[12]

Mandatory licensing imposes a significant financial burden on international certificate authorities. The more conflicting differences in the laws we examine, the more expensive the tracking requirements. International requirements seem to be conflicting. For example, Germany requires that private keys be stored on a smart card and prohibits a private key from being transmitted over the Internet. More laws are not conducive to private certificate systems. It will create disincentives for credit card companies to use digital signatures.

Malaysia, which modeled its law after the Utah statute, has no such requirement. Global certificate authorities will have to create duplicate procedures and security measures just to comply with the first two digital signature laws passed internationally.

German Digital Signature LAW (Article 3 of the Multimedia Law, August 1, 1997, and Digital Signature Ordinance, November 1, 1997)

Germany has enacted the most sweeping legislation on the use of digital signatures and liabilities associated with their use. It envisions the use of public/private key technology and of government approved procedures. It requires that all certificate authorities must obtain a license from the "root" authority. There is strict liability for not doing so. The law recognizes foreign certificates so long as the certificate authorities are from European Union states and demonstrates an equivalent level of security. U.S. certificates would not be recognized in Germany unless licensed. CAs are required by German law to permit inspection of their books to ensure compliance with the law. The Digital Signature Ordinance, Section 1, requires a certificate authority to apply for their license "in writing." Section 5 requires that both the CA and the user must create private/public key pairs. It provides for storage and privacy protections on these keys. Section 8 provides for CRL via the user or the user's representative. The law provides for nine specific requirements for certificates. The law sets a very high standard for security—it should be applauded, but it has received much criticism because of its broad range.[13]

Malaysian Digital Signature Act, 1997

Part VII of the Malaysian law is new and not included in the Utah Act. The Malaysian Act sets out enforcement provisions and investigative powers. The Malaysian certificate authority must have access to the user's private key and access to computerized data pursuant to a warrant (or without one in certain cases). It does not protect the subscriber's private key from any liability of use.[14]

Wrap-Up

The challenge for the implementation and use of digital signatures in our daily lives boils down to the perceived service it can provide coupled with its ease of use. It is now a number of years after the Department of Commerce's approval announcement of the Digital Signature Standard, and we are just starting to see its implementation becoming a reality. There are still many problems to solve. One of the most important issues is that all public key exchange mechanisms can be subject to cryptanalytic attack. We have commercial certificate authorities providing a service for banks and financial institutions in order to facilitate Internet transactions without having a common trusted root. We are deploying systems worldwide with different types of certificates and algorithms. We have not fully identified transaction relationships and the legal aspects.

Individual states are enacting legislation concerning digital signatures (see Appendix H) that has led to a significant number of different legal standards across the United States. It would seem that the general public may be terrified of "Big Brother" and the ability to track each person by following the digital trails of electronic commerce and the seemingly encrypted contents of e-mail by simply tapping into the Internet. Federal initiatives have been conflicting (Appendix I) or technology neutral. The effect is a slow acceptance of digital signature technologies at political levels below state and federal authorities in the United States.

Proliferation of international regulations on certificate authorities (Appendix J) portends a difficulty for a viable global PKI. Cheap certificates and private closed systems users, like SET, may be threatened. Tracking conflicting regulations and making duplicate procedures is costly for businesses.

Notes

1. Baker, Stewart A. and Paul R. Hurst, *The Limits of Trust: Cryptography, Governments, and Electronic Commerce*, (Washington, D.C.: Kluwer Law International, 1998).

2. Ibid.

3. Goldwasser, Shafi, Silvio Mical, and Ronald L. Rivest, "A Digital Signature Scheme Secure Against Adaptive Chosen-Message Attacks," *SIAM Journal on Computing,* 17 February 1988.

4. Kent, Stephen, "How Many Certification Authorities are Enough?", BBN Technologies, unclassified presentation, Cambridge, Mass., 1997.

5. Ibid.

6. Schneier, Bruce, *Applied Cryptography*, 2nd ed. (New York: Wiley, 1996).

7. Kent, Stephen, "How Many Certification Authorities are Enough?", BBN Technologies, unclassified presentation, Cambridge, Mass., 1997. Presentations at RSA Data Conference, 1996, and DIMACS Workshop on Trust Management, 1996.

8. Ibid.

9. Baker, Stewart A. and Paul R. Hurst, *The Limits of Trust: Cryptography, Governments, and Electronic Commerce*, (Washington, DC: Kluwer Law International, 1998). (Baker's analysis is brilliant and his book is highly recommended to all readers.)

10. American Bar Association, *Digital Signature Guidelines, Information Security Committee, Science and Technology Section*, American Bar Association, Draft, 5 October 1995.

11. Utah Code Ann. Section 46-3-401(2) ff.

12. Baker, op. cit., 285.

13. Ibid., 300.

14. Ibid., 306.

CHAPTER 10

Permissions Management: Identification, Authentication, and Authorization (PMIAA)

Overview

Virtually all businesses, most government agencies, and many individuals have Web sites. The number of individuals and companies with Internet access is expanding rapidly, and all have Web browsers with graphical ability. Businesses continue to establish their facilities (at a lightening pace) on the Web for electronic commerce. The Internet offers the promise of inexpensive mass communication and economies of scale for low-cost distribution. However, the reality is that the Internet and the Web are extremely vulnerable to compromises of various sorts.

It is even quite possible that the growth of the global Internet has outpaced the current technical and economic models. The infrastructure growth is potentially "unsafe at this speed."[1] It is a wild beast where maintenance and quality control are pushed by a nonstable technical platform, economically developing markets, and the drive for market share. Since the Internet and the Web are open, communications are inherently difficult to secure. Business must be based on mutual trust. The guarantee of integrity of information and trusted relationships, which is fundamental to commercial success on the Web, is missing. The Internet's economic potential will not be fully realized until service providers can deliver a guaranteed measure of security for mission-critical or large-scale commercial applications.

In response to security requirements of doing business on the Internet, a comprehensive *permission management* system has evolved that include as robust authorization algorithms, X.509 digital certificates, PKI, real-time enforcement of privileges, and a scalable engine capable of processing millions of access control references. At the heart of the process are three critical trust areas. Research by the Hurwitz Group adequately described the process in a white paper entitled "The Security Market Evolves to Meet the Needs of E-Business Applications, 8/22/99."[2]

Identification, authentication, and *authorization* are recognized as critically important trust factors for the future of e-commerce on the World Wide Web (WWW). The technical purview of these factors is significant and can be complex. Most simply, identification consists of providing a unique identifier for automated systems; authentication consists of mapping this electronic identity to the physical world; and authorization pertains to assigning rights to the authenticated identifier. One practical problem for customers is that buying more than one object or service may require communications with many Web sites, each of which requires separate identification, authentication, and authorization procedures.

This chapter looks at the issue of permissions management and e-commerce trust from the perspective of information security, Internet disruptions and denial of service attacks, Web countermeasures, the enabling technology of encryption and the important role it plays, design factors for the deployment of security products on the Web, and various solution frameworks offered by vendors. Finally it looks at selected products offered for customer protection on the Web.

Encryption (covered in Chapter 7) plays an important role in protecting confidentiality, integrity, and authenticity in cyberspace. Standards for labeling a Web site's compliance with security norms help consumers judge where to do business. Digital certificates and electronic cash of various kinds allow authorization for purchases with varying degrees of assurance for both customers and vendors on the Web.

With the technologies described in this chapter, it should be increasingly acceptable for consumers and businesspeople to do business securely on the Internet. Methods for evaluating each Web site's adherence to different levels of security policy will allow the marketplace to define the importance of protecting consumers' private information.

Introduction

E-commerce observers concur that lack of trust is the essential obstacle to continued growth of business on the World Wide Web. The buying public is afraid of engaging in electronic commerce largely because they worry that their electronic transactions will be insecure.

Both merchants and clients need to be confident of the identity of the people and institutions with which they are doing business. At a technical level, these concerns focus on management of permissions for identification, authentication, and authorization. Once again, *identification* consists of providing a unique identifier for automated systems; *authentication* consists of correlating this electronic identity in a legally binding manner to a real-world identity; and *authorization* consists of assigning rights to the authenticated identifier. These three factors are responses to increased security requirements that are part and parcel of the Web experience.

There are some very large problems that arise when vendors and customers move from security in the physical world to security in the networked world of the Internet. These problems arise because a network is a collection of computers linked together. These problems are (1) no one is physically there, (2) duplication and alteration are easy, (3) tasks are easily automated, and (4) everyone is virtually everywhere.

To maintain overall business integrity, organizations need to consider five areas of security: network integrity, system integrity, user account integrity, application/data integrity, and data confidentiality. Figure 10-1 shows these areas with respect to 12 security market segments. As of this writing, about 600 security vendors are addressing a substantial number of concerns. These vendors have introduced hundreds of products, which have limited overlapping functionality. This is a difficult management issue if you are in the IT organization doing business on the Web. The Hurwitz research suggests that security vendors are addressing the problem by integration and standardization work in the areas of identifying users (authentication), privacy of information (data privacy and integrity), controlling access (authorization), and auditing all user activity.[3] Permissions management is a management infrastructure designed to facilitate mapping of the infinite number of users to the infinite number of objects with numerous domains and to associate specific rights and privileges. This permits an intersection of technologies of those groups and domains, as shown in Figure 10-1.

Because customers are not physically present, many forms of security used in day-to-day life cannot be used in cyberspace. For example, since, in cyberspace, a customer can't physically walk into his or her bank, the customer needs to know that the bank's Web server is really the bank's, and the bank needs to know that the customer is legitimate. Second, duplication and alteration is easy. Unlike a photocopy, a copy of an electronic file is byte-for-byte identical to the original version of that file. In some sys-

Figure 10-1

Permissions management. (Source: Selective portions redrawn from PMI diagram from Hurwitz Group Research Bulletin, with permission of the Hurwitz Group)

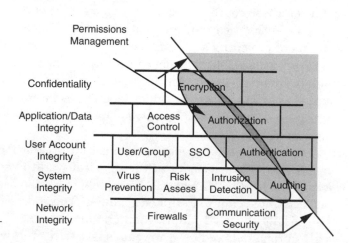

tems, it is not possible to tell when an alteration has been made. Because computer-based information can be easily altered, protection against alteration is critical. The boon of computing power is the bane of computer security. Automated cracking programs flourish on the Net. Because everyone is virtually anywhere, a Net presence may be in a single location, but it can be accessed from anywhere on any other system on the Internet.

Encryption technologies play a crucial role in protecting confidentiality, integrity, and authenticity in cyberspace. Standards for labeling Web sites' compliance with privacy/security policies help consumers judge where to do business. Digital certificates and electronic cash of various kinds allow authorization for purchases with varying degrees of assurance for customer privacy. Single sign-on systems allow clients to establish and prove their identity once and then shop at several electronic locations without further inconvenience. Systems for extending the content and flexibility of digital certificates allow Web sites to tailor their services more closely to the needs and demands of their clientele.

When users communicate securely with an online merchant on the Web, they may establish a session using any of a variety of authentication procedures, such as giving a password, using a physical device (a token), or providing other evidence of their identity (e.g., biometric authentication). During the session that they establish, it is assumed that only the authorized person will transact business with the merchant. One practical problem for customers is that buying more than one object or service may require communications with many Web sites, each of which currently requires a separate identification, authentication, and authorization cycle.

The Heart of the Beast: Identification, Authentication, and Authorization

Concerns about e-commerce security are fundamentally those of *remote access controls*. Remote access technology is a method for providing traveling or homebound users with access to the voice and data networks of the corporation. There are other technologies for handling business while away on travel, such as voice mail, interactive voice response units, and teleconferencing; however, these technologies include wireless security issues not covered in this chapter. We will focus on the Web and on computer access issues.

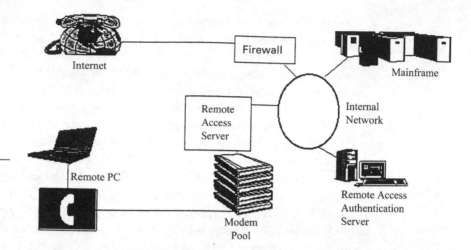

Many organizations use remote access to provide LAN and e-mail access for employees and contractually related users. Remote access is usually designed to support communications from home to mainframes, LANs, e-mail, UNIX systems, and minicomputers. Figure 10-2 shows the most common configuration for remote access use. In this configuration, the remote access system is located inside the firewall and users are directly connected to the internal network after connecting to the remote access system. The remote access system is protected using positive authentication. In most cases, the device is managed by the corporate networking group, and the information security group manages security and user ID activities.[4]

Another view is to think of the World Wide Web as a client/server application running over the Internet and TCP/IP intranets. Any time someone needs to transact business, whether online or face-to-face, the client and the merchant must both provide identification, authentication, and authorization. Users need to be sure that they know exactly who is running the Web server with which they intend to transact business. Merchants need identification of their clients to be sure they get paid for their products and services.

Identification

Identification is "the process that enables recognition of a user described to an automated data processing system. This is generally by the use of unique machine-readable names." In human terms, client and merchant engage in mutual identification when they, for example, tell each other their names over the phone.

Authentication

Authentication is "a positive identification, with a degree of certainty sufficient for permitting certain rights or privileges to the person or thing positively identified." In simpler terms, it is "the act of verifying the claimed identity of an individual, station, or originator." In a human contact by telephone, the client and merchant might recognize (authenticate) each other by their familiar voices. The classic methods for correlating virtual and physical identities in cyberspace are parallel to methods used for authenticating human beings in the physical world.

The four categories of authenticating information are as follows:

- *What you know*   The password or passphrase
- *What you do*   How one signs one's name or speaks
- *What you are*   One's face or other biometric attributes such as fingerprints
- *What you have*   A token such as a key, or a certificate such as a drivers license.

All of these categories of authentication are used in cyberspace. The last example is particularly interesting: Certificates play a crucial role in authenticating people (or programs or machines) in the world of e-commerce. The drivers license, for example, if assumed to be real, tells a merchant that at some time in the past, a certification authority—the issuing Department of Motor Vehicles—has undertaken some measures to ensure that the information on the license is (or was) correct. In cyberspace, verifying the legitimacy of a certificate can be easier than in real space.

Authentication leads to a related concept, that of *nonrepudiation*. A formal definition of nonrepudiation is "the method by which the sender of data is provided with proof of delivery and the recipient is assured of the sender's identity, so that neither can later deny having processed the data." Nonrepudiation, as we shall see in the section below on encryption, depends on asserting that authenticity has not been violated when identifying the source of that transaction or message.

Authorization

Authorization is "the granting to a user, program, or process the right of access." In the real world, authorization is experienced every time a merchant queries a Visa or MasterCard service to see if a customer is authorized to spend a certain amount of money at their establishment. In the mainframe environment, authorization depends on the operating system and the level of security that system administrators have imposed.

Identification and authentication begin when a session is initiated. A *session* is "an activity for a period of time; the activity is access to a computer/network resource by a user; a period of time is bounded by session initiation (a form of logon) and session termination (a form of logoff.)"

However, on the Web, most interactions are sessionless; for example, there is no identification and authentication when an anonymous user accesses a public page on a Web site. There is no logon and no logoff under such circumstances. Web interactions require identification and authorization only when the user and the Web owner agree to establish a secure session. Typically, secure Web site transactions do require some form of logon and logoff even if these steps are not explicitly labeled as such.

Session integrity and authenticity can be violated in a number of ways. *Piggybacking* is the unauthorized use of an existing session by unauthorized personnel. This problem is difficult to imagine in the real world, where it would be unlikely that someone could, say, cut into the middle of a phone conversation to order goods and services using someone else's good name and credit card.

In cyberspace, though, it is quite commonplace for users to initiate a transaction on a terminal or workstation and then to walk away from their unprotected session to go do something else. If a dishonest person sits at the absent person's place, it is possible to misuse his or her session. A common problem of piggybacking is the misuse of someone else's e-mail program to send fraudulent messages in the absent person's name. Another example might have the thief stepping into a session to change an order or to have goods sent to a different address but be paid for by the session initiator's credit card. Such examples of fraud can have disastrous consequences for the victims; in general, every news story about this kind of abuse reduces confidence in the security of e-commerce.

A more technical attack is called *session hijacking*: Hijacking allows an attacker to take over an open terminal or login session from a user who has been authenticated by the system. Hijacking attacks generally take place on a remote computer, although it is sometimes possible to hijack a connection from a computer on the route between the remote computer and a local computer. Hijacking occurs when an intruder uses ill-gotten privileges to tap into a system's software that accesses or controls the behavior of the local TCP (Transmission Control Protocol).

A successful hijack enables an attacker to borrow or steal an open connection (say, a Telnet session) to a remote host for the attacker's own purposes. In the likely event that the genuine user has already been authenticated to the remote host, any keystrokes sent by the attacker are received and processed as if typed by the user.

In summary, identification, authentication, and authorization are normal components of any business transaction and must be guaranteed by the communications systems and software mediating the relationship between supplier and customer. The use of these components is a direct function of the vulnerability of a business's use of the Web.

Web Site Vulnerability

One of the first concerns that a business has when contemplating the Web as a means of generating revenue is the how vulnerable is the business's site? To answer this question, we must differentiate some important security concepts and threats.

Every computer system is vulnerable to attack. Security policies and products may reduce the likelihood that an attack will actually be able to penetrate a systems defense. They may require an intruder to invest so much time and resources that it's just not worth it—but there is no such thing as a completely secure system.

There are four key concepts that appear in much of the literature regarding computer security: threats, vulnerabilities, attacks, and countermeasures. A *threat* to a computer system is defined as any potential occurrence, malicious or otherwise, that affects the computer resources. A *vulnerability* is a point where a system is susceptible to attack. An *attack* is a malicious exploitation of a computer system vulnerability to cause an existing threat to occur. *Countermeasures* are those actions or enactment's of safeguards to prevent threats to a computer system.

Vulnerabilities are classified as physical, natural, hardware, software, media, emanation, communications, and human. The human element is by far the weakest link. The second-weakest link is the modem or telephone. Messages can be intercepted, misrouted, and forged. Communication lines connecting computers to each other, or connecting terminals to a central computer, can be tapped or physically damaged.

Threats are generally classified as unintentional (due to negligence or ignorance) or intentional by an attacker (planned and malicious). Computing horsepower, money, time, personnel, and defined egress usually backs up motivated attackers. There are five major categories of outside attackers: foreign intelligence agents, terrorists, criminals, corporate intelligence teams, hackers or crackers. The newspapers have been full of stories about all five categories.

Outside threats constitute about 20 percent of the security problem, which means, of course, that insiders accomplish 80 percent of all penetrations of computer security. Along with the fired or disgruntled employee and political revenge types, we can add the coerced, greedy, or power players. The most dangerous type of insider is the untrained or lazy. He or she doesn't change passwords, resists security restrictions, doesn't understand data protection, and leaves information in plain view.

The most effective system attack is a combination of a strong outside strategy (for example, breaking into competitors' files to steal their marketing plans) with access by an insider (for example, a marketing assistant who has been bribed with force, money, or sex to give away a password or steal reports).

In order to understand the manner in which potential threats are addressed by computer security specialists, researchers have further generalized computer security system threats by their effects: (1) disclosure, (2) integrity, and (3) denial of service. *Disclosure threats* ("leaks") involve the dissemination of information to an individual by whom that information should not be seen. The vast majority of research and development in computer security since the 1960s has been focused on disclosure threats. One reason for this emphasis has been the importance governments have placed on countering this threat. Much of NSA's initial work in the security area was to protect against this type of threat.

The *integrity threat* involves any unauthorized alteration of information stored on a computer system or in transit between computer systems. A good example of this compromise might be for an ex-spouse (an angry one, obviously) to access the spouse's TRW credit files, to changing the various codes and making the spouse $100,000 behind in everything, with judgments, attachments, and skip trace requirements. If you are the unfortunate victim of such an attack, try to convince a local grocer, whom you have been supporting for five years, that this is all a mistake—a computer mistake, of course. Try to sell a house. Try to buy a new house or rent a room. Try to cash a check with a new vendor. *This is not a what-if scenario*. INFOSEC warriors have used this form of attack very effectively. The Social Security Administration shut down their Web site because they only required name, Social Security number, and one's mother's maiden name as security indicators. Many existing databases have all of this information available. With a little information, anyone can read anyone else's entire financial history.[5]

Until recently, governments were concerned with the disclosure threat, and businesses were concerned with integrity. Both types of environments are vulnerable to both types of threats depending on the application.

The *denial of service (DoS) threat* arises whenever access to computer system resources is intentionally blocked as a result of malicious actions taken by another user. Service may be permanently or strategically delayed. The latter case is referred to as "being stale." DoS has real meaning in the World Wide Web service. AOL recently changed its billing policy to a flat rate. Hackers used the increased customer usage to flood certain e-mail servers with thousands of bogus e-mails. The increased usage on the resources and address confusion caused by attempted delivery of the bogus e-mails caused a DoS for entire sections of the country. Small servers were shut down for 24 hours. DoS threats have not been researched very thoroughly, except for use in DoD and satellite reconnaissance. Think of the consequences in the Gulf War if the Iranians had a serious DoS capability to shut down communications systems controlling U.S. satellites.

Internet/Online Systems

The global Internet represents a two-fold problem: It is a highly unstable portion of the international infrastructure, and it acts as a threat access method. In 1998, e-mail and system outages, coupled with the mad rush to e-commerce and intranets, worked to produce an inevitable dysfunction.

CIWARS (a counterintelligence report) believes that threats will accelerate as large portions of the developing world lose their ability to pay for their Internet access because of devaluated currency and global depression. The Internet community will be forced to make a decision between economics—financial support for economically devastated areas—and the juggernaut of privatization of this once state-controlled facility.[6]

The recent history of the Internet shows the system has suffered disruptions because of DoS attacks (Table 10-1), political intrusions (Table 10-2), severe service failures (Table 10-3), and e-mail outages (Table 10-4). The core principle of a DoS attack is to block access. The tables represent a wide variety of denial of service attacks. A simple category of attack is an e-mail bomb; however, its most complex form could be a sophisticated Internet worm that replicates on each server. Potential vulnerability is extremely high with properly selected targets and the ability to maintain control of the attack situation. Fortunately, most of the DoS attacks to date have only blocked specific sites, or communications points, and have not been directed to system outage.

DoS Attacks

The most basic DoS attack can be accomplished with minimum skill, and the tools to accomplish the DoS attack are openly available. With a limited purpose and select targets, the DoS has high strategic value, especially towards competitive business interruption and as a form of harassment. A DoS is the form of direct hit that would have an even higher strategic value if positioned as an attack scenario within a cascading hit. It may also have value as a referenced approach, since it is a very familiar type of attack and is ideal to drive an expected behavior.

Web page hacks represent most of the incidents in this category (see Table 10-1). It involves the replacement of the front or index page with another page that carries a message designed by the hacker. Generally, the effect is limited to single Web pages or those on the same server. Considering the state of security today, Web pages are highly vulnerable.

We can evaluate the disruption as a limited-effect, direct hit. Though there is limited effect in terms of systemic disruption or ultimate importance, they accomplish a level of publicity and embarrassment for the business entity that was hacked. Further, this attack could be turned into a cascading hit by Web page hacks, perhaps to generate e-mail bombs, or repetitive links in a high-volume environment. Neither approach has surfaced yet.

TABLE 10-1

System Disruption—Denial of Service (DoS) Attack.

18 October 1998	TCP RST Denial of Service
27 August 1998	Hacker Blocks Alaska Internet Access
14 July 1998	Australia Hackers War over ISP Delete 1000 Accounts
10 May 1998	US Points to Tamil Tigers as First Cyberterrorist Attack
29 March 1998	German ISP Hacked
18 March 1998	Smurf Attack Hits Minnesota
02 February 1998	Internet Access in Uruguay Under Attack
30 January 1998	Free-net Shuts Down to Protect Itself from Hacker
22 January 1998	DOS Locks Out Economists Department of Labor Site
13 December 1997	Competitors Attack ISP in Australia
01 December 1997	Password Compromise at ISP
30 October 1997	Yale E-mail Hack Delayed Report
18 October 1997	Virus Used to Delay Bid in Economic Warfare
18 October 1997	Oil Survey Company Gets Virus from Competitor
03 September 1997	Hackers Stop Service at ISP

Political Hacks

Politics is a fertile arena for attack, as shown in Table 10-2. Political hacks get lots of attention but wield little destructive power in terms of the supporting computer network.

TABLE 10-2

Political System Intrusion.

16 October 1998	Hackers Invade India Army Site
15 October 1998	Singapore Says It Must Snuff Out Cybercrime
12 October 1998	Hackers Stay a Step Ahead of China's Cyberpolice
12 October 1998	China Blocks BBC Web Site
01 September 1998	Computer Hackers Raid Australian PM's Web site
18 August 1998	Cyber Vandals Target Indonesia
06 August 1998	Mexican Hackers Declare War on Government
13 July 1998	German Political Party Hacked
17 May 1998	Russians Thwart Hack Attempt During Yeltsin Speech
29 March 1998	Argentine Air Force Site Hacked with Political Message
18 January 1998	Political Hacks in Indonesia

System Disruptions/Outages

The problem is easily described. Entire systems, or individual Web sites, cease operation. Like the telephone outages, many of the problems occur during a software upgrade process, but others occur because of stress placed on the system during high volume. The scope of vulnerability should be considered a significant risk trend for three reasons. First, it reveals an inadequacy in terms of proper software testing and quality assurance. Second, it demonstrates, for capacity outages, a trend to underconfigure systems. Third, it serves as a useful test lab for threats to evaluate the weak point of systems and to calibrate the results from these disruptions.

The vulnerability expressed by Table 10-3 is commercially real. As the problems associated with this situation are inherent to the corporate process, they are organic to exploitation. A significant strategic value could be gained by a threat linking a number of systems in a cascading fault environment.

TABLE 10-3

Internet Failures.

16 October 1998	Hack Puts AOL Off Limits
15 October 1998	Clumsy E-Trader Sends French Market Diving
26 June 1998	WebTV Failure
26 June 1998	Thailand Suffers First Internet Failure
20 April 1998	Schwab Internet Trading System Down
24 March 1998	AOL Outage Due to Electric Failure
10 March 1998	Sprint Corporate Customer Outage
09 February 1998	Nando Times Sportserver: No Update for 13 Hours
24 February 1998	AOL Outage Brief but Dangerous
03 February 1998	Snafu During a Planned Upgrade at MAE-WEST
20 January 1998	Yahoo Stock Service Site Out for Half Day
20 January 1998	Microsoft Travel Web Site Out, High Volume Cited
07 January 1998	Telco Error Causes ISP Outage
07 January 1998	Amazon.com's Web Site Down
07 January 1998	AOL Reports Problems
04 January 1998	Sprint Problems with Hearing-Impaired Service
18 October 1997	MSN Service Problem with Upgrade
18 October 1997	UUNET Problem
02 October 1997	Another AOL Maintenance Outage
02 October 1997	Netcom Hit with Outage
22 September 1997	Social Security Administration Down Three Hours

E-Mail Outages

Millions of people use e-mail daily to communicate on the Net. Table 10-4 shows that many of them had migraines in 1997 to 1998. The results in 1999 are still being evaluated, but it would appear that the outage frequency has significantly increased.

TABLE 10-4

E-mail Outage.

26 March 1998	AOL Email Hit by Another Glitch
12 March 1998	Spam Jams Pacific Bell E-mail Service
26 February 1998	@Home Suffers E-mail Slow Down
26 December 1997	E-mail Meltdowns
7 December 1997	AT&T Worldnet E-mail Outages
2 December 1997	MSN Not Accepting AOL Mail
3 November 1997	AOL E-mail Out Again
28 October 1997	AOL Out Again during Market Crash

Information Security Objectives

Information security manifests itself in many ways. Regardless of who is involved, all parties to a transaction, to one degree or another, must have confidence that certain objectives associated with informational security have been met. This is especially true for business on the Web. Table 10-5 lists some of these information security objectives.

Web Security and Countermeasures

The Web represents a chaotic and exciting technology. It has become the security-balancing act of the 1990s. The Open User Recommended Solutions (OURS) consortium of 60 companies, led by Phillips Petroleum Company, published a tiered approach to commercial security in 1997. The OURS report suggested the following procedure for the commercial user: (1) identify what its Web applications are for, (2) based on this stated use for a company Web site, identify the crucial threats, and then (3) map these threats to the appropriate protection technologies.[7]

The OURS group divided commerce on the Web into three basic application types—advertising, secure Internet/Internet (further subdivided into informational and transactional categories), and electronic commerce. The OURS group suggested that there were nine basic threats to

TABLE 10-5

Information
Security Objectives.

Privacy or confidentiality	Keeping information secret from all but those who are authorized to see it
Data integrity	Ensuring information has not been altered by unauthorized or unknown means
Entity authentication or identification	Corroboration of the identity of an entity (e.g., a person, a computer terminal, a credit card, etc.)
Message authentication	Corroborating the source of the information; also known as *data origin authentication*
Signature	A means to bind information to an entity
Authorization	Conveyance, to another entity, of official sanction to do or be something
Validation	A means to provide timeliness of authorization to use or manipulate information or resources
Access control	Restricting access to resources to privileged entities
Certification	Endorsement of information by a trusted entity
Time-stamping	Recording the time of creation or existence of information
Witnessing	Verifying the creation or existence of information by an entity other than the creator
Receipt	Acknowledgment that information has been received
Confirmation	Acknowledgment that services have been provided
Ownership	A means to provide an entity with the legal right to use or to transfer a resource to others
Anonymity	Concealing identity of an entity involved in some process
Nonrepudiation	Preventing the denial of previous commitments or actions
Revocation	Retraction of certification or authorization

Web security (see Table 10-6) and that these threats could be countered by six safeguards (see Table 10-7).[8]

A rather surprising result from the OURS analysis is that a minority of consortium members felt that encryption was not sufficient to stop Web threats but needed to be combined with protection against data destruction, interference, repudiation, and inadvertent misuse. At the same time, the OURS report suggested that their secure links were under attack (80

TABLE 10-6

Nine Basic Threats
to Web Sites.

1. *Data Destruction* The loss of data on Web site through accident or malice and interception of traffic (encrypted and unencrypted) both going to/from the Web site.

2. *Interference* The intentional rerouting of traffic or the flooding of a local Web server with inappropriate traffic in an attempt to cripple or crash the server.

3. *Modification/Replacement* The altering of data on either the send or receive side of a Web transmission. The changes, whether they are accidental or not, can be difficult to detect in large transmissions.

4. *Misrepresentation/False Use of Data* Offering false credentials, passwords, or other data. Also included is posting of a bogus or counterfeit home page to intercept or attract traffic away from its intended destination.

5. *Repudiation* An after-the-fact denial that an online order or transaction took place (especially for 800- or 900-services).

6. *Inadvertent Misuse* Accidental but inappropriate actions by approved users.

7. *Unauthorized Altering/Downloading* Any writing, updating, copying, and so forth. Performed by a person who has not been granted permission to conduct such activity.

8. *Unauthorized Transactions* Any use by a nonapproved party.

9. *Unauthorized Disclosure* Viewing of Web information by an individual not given explicit permission to have access to this information.

Source: OURS Consortia Report, McCarthy, 1997.

percent of the responses) by data interception and hackers—both of which are countered very effectively by strong encryption algorithms.

Many of the OURS group felt that with the help of passwords and controlled access, encryption was the best security countermeasure. Users on commercial Web servers must be authenticated via encrypted passwords.

Security decisions will only become tougher as companies continue to exploit the power of the Web. Electronic commerce tends to aggravate the difficulties of setting just the right security policy.

Table 10-7 could have a seventh element added, implementation management and security assessment. Practical implementation of security requires the capability to manage and ascertain a site's security. One of the most effective ways to test a Web site is the "tiger team" approach. Commercial firms test their computer systems, and Web systems by attacking them with groups of experienced professionals who work together (*tiger teams*) to ascertain security levels and breach the corporation's computer networks and communications.

TABLE 10-7

Six Best Weapons against Security Threats.

1. *User ID/Authentication*   These range from simple passwords and callback systems to secure one-time passwords and challenge-response tokens (either hardware cards or software-resident).

Usage: All web users.

2. *Authorization*   The network confirms the identity and grants access. Typical approaches include access control lists, authorization certificates, and directory services.

Usage: Secondary-level protection to prevent data modification.

3. *Integrity Control*   This is aimed at the data, not the user. The two key methods are encryption and message authentication, which can ensure that the message has not been altered on the way to the receiver and not read by someone else.

Usage: Excellent for validating secure Internet electronic commerce transactions.

4. *Accountability*   Web managers use various tools to monitor responsibility and ownership. Methods include audit trails, Web server logs, and receipts.

Usage: Accountability is the backbone of enforceable and traceable security policies and practices.

5. *Confidentiality*   This is the keystone of most Web security policies. The technology is aimed at preventing unauthorized disclosure or interception or both. Encryption is the central safeguard. This can mean end-to-end encryption on the network, as well as layered encryption of files, protocols, and secured links. Another option is to use Web proxies.

Usage: Techniques are geared toward data content that must be held strictly off-limits to certain users.

6. *Available Controls*   Protects the integrity of the Web site itself. Technology includes virus protection software and backup/redundancy features.

Usage: Protection of Web and its associated data.

Source: OURS Consortia Report, McCarthy, 1997.

Security Trade-Offs

We should be aware of some natural trade-offs that result when we implement security policies in an attempt to mitigate threats to computer systems from the Internet or Web.[9] These trade-offs can be categorized under usability, retrofitting, assurance, procedures and mechanisms, and security requirements.

Usability   First, there is a negative direct relationship between usability and security. As security increases, the usability of the computer systems is reduced. There is a natural conflict when the goals of information and resource sharing are combined with strict security controls.

Retrofitting Since security is a relatively new concern and since technology is improving in hardware and software at a nonlinear rate, nearly all systems developed register insufficient attention to threats, vulnerabilities, and potential attacks. In order to make an existing system secure, one is faced with the problem of retrofitting security into existing components, mechanisms, and environments. This is especially true when operating systems interface with security kernels and protocols.

Assurance How do we prove that a system is secure? What assurance or body of evidence do we use to prove it? This is a difficult task. The four types of assurance mechanisms that have been used with some success are (1) static test results, (2) dynamic field experiments, (3) formal methods, and (4) tiger team investigation. The fourth method is aggressive and is recommended as the most practical and cost-effective.[10]

Procedures and Mechanisms The mitigation of threats on computer systems requires the integration of suitable procedures and/or mechanisms. These procedures and mechanisms range from management policies on facilities and operations to functional mechanisms designed into the computer system.

Security Requirements Why can't security be designed into computer systems based on suitable security requirements? Two reasons: First, identification of requirements in modern computer systems is nontrivial in terms of effort and complexity of operations; second, the target is ever-changing and potentially technically obsolete in a very short time.

WWW Deployment, Transaction Security, and Technologies
Deployment Issues

There are four specific objectives that must be considered when handling commercial transactions between a large community of vendors and customers using compatible software:[11]

1. *Protect transactions against attack on the Internet.* Transaction should be safe to perform, difficult to replay, modify, or interfere with, and not modified in transit. Transactions involving credit card numbers must be adequately protected from eavesdropping.

2. *Ensure security without prior arrangements between customers and vendors.* Customers and vendors must be able to protect their transactions, even if they have never communicated before.

3. *Apply crypto protections selectively.* Most traffic on the Web consists of visits to unprotected sites. Protection should be applied when needed to protect transaction details, not applied to static Web pages.

4. *The receiving host must be protected from attack by incoming messages.* Both servers and clients on the Web are vulnerable to attack. Vendors' computing systems are targets of Internet attack simply because they are at a fixed address. Client software packages are attractive targets because they store crypto keys, pass codes, or account numbers that validate Internet transactions.

Because of the large community of users that span the range from novice to expert computer user, the Web poses special problems. Three of these are as follows:

1. *The protocol must be widely available and user-friendly.* The forms facility in the Hypertext Transfer Protocol (HTTP) used on the Web has proven sufficient for managing transactions and has been adopted by a broad range of Internet users.

2. *It must be possible to authenticate both the customer and vendor.*

3. *There must be liability for bogus transactions* Typical credit cards in the United States tend to place the liability for bogus transactions on the vendor.

It is clever that the user on the Web can traverse the globe in seconds. The ubiquitous point-and-click interface on a document containing *hypertext links*, which in turn, refer to other documents on the Web that the user sees, allow the user to do this. Click on a document hypertext link and the document is immediately displayed. Practically every important specification document is available via the Internet, as well as the most recent product offerings. The "forms" extensions to the Web provide the essentials needed to perform transactions between users and Web-based vendors.

There are four elements to the Web: browsers, servers, URLs, and pages.

The *Web browser* is the client software that people use to access the Web. The browsers send requests to Web servers, which contain *Web pages* with the information that users can request. Each Web page is identified by a unique *Uniform Resource Locator*, or *URL*. The browser requests a page by sending that page's URL to the server. Pages are written in the popular HTML document markup language.

Traffic between the browser and server follows a protocol called the Hypertext Transport Protocol (HTTP), which uses the TCP transport protocol. The URL tells what protocol to use (usually HTTP), the server host name, an optional port number, and the Web page's file name. Typically, the Web page may have a suffix of "HTML". Responses to a form's GET request typically have the "cgi" suffix to indicate that data is being returned (in a "name = value" format) for processing by the given file. A transaction requires that the client send information to the server.

A Web transaction is actually a pair of connections: one to fetch the Web *form* that collects the transaction data, and another connection to transmit the collected data to the server. This latter connection is called the POST command; it is used to process the request and return a completed Web page to the user. The actual processing of data is done via the *CGI*, or Common Gateway Interface, scripts. CGI scripts can be tailored to run custom programs capable of implementing typical automated transactions.

It might look like this: http://data.host.com:80/spec.html might generate the forms call, http://forms.host.com:80/doform.cgi?clerk = Bob&what = Pay&amt = $100, along with the GET command, GET http://data.host.com:80/spec.html, followed by the POST command, http://forms.host.com:80/doform.cgi?clerk = Bob&what = Pay&amt = $100.

Security

The order of security services that Web forms require is as follows:[12]

1. Transaction integrity

2. Customer authentication

3. Vendor authentication

4. Transaction secrecy

In addition, there are five candidate techniques for providing the security services noted:[13]

1. Protection with passwords

2. Network security via IPSec

3. Connection security via SSL

4. Applications security (secure HTTP [SHTTP])

5. Client authentication alternatives: Reusable passwords, one-time passwords, and SSL client certificates

All of these address some of the security requirements, but not all yield successful solutions. Password protection or PINs alone have no crypto protection and are vulnerable to password sniffing. The best they provide is a weak form of customer authentication. The Web browser embeds the collected password in HTTP requests sent to the server and is vulnerable to attack.

IPSec is a very strong network level protocol. It can block a variety of important threats to Internet traffic like sniffing, spoofing, hijacking, and flooding. It tends to be all or nothing security and has a few shortcomings when used to protect Web traffic. IPSec blocks access to hosts that don't support it or don't have a security association with the initiating host. Although this is the design goal for IPSec,[14] this is inefficient for Web traffic, which carries a lot of data that does not require protection. Crypto protection is inefficient in this case. Key management is not practical between arbitrary Internet customers, especially if validation by a third party is required.

Security applied at the transport level (SSL) provides better control over which security measures are used. The Web browser can identify which connection is going to require security. *SSL*, or *Secure Sockets Layer* by Netscape Communications Corporation, is an ideal protection for Web traffic. SSL can automatically apply encryption and integrity protection to the data it carries. The client and server negotiate to establish a satisfactory set of crypto parameters including acceptably strong encryption ciphers and shared secret keys. Embedded in the browser software is enough public key information to negotiate shared secret keys. Separate protocol identifiers and port numbers are used for SSL traffic. SSL's transport nature means that crypto security measures are applied to data in transit and are lost once the connection is closed.

Secure Hypertext Transfer Protocol (SHTTP) is a set of security functions defined for protecting Web traffic, including forms and transactions. It supports both authentication and encryption of HTTP traffic between a Web client and server. It is an application-specific protocol, which defines specific crypto measures. SHTTP, as marketed by Terisa Systems, has had little market penetration compared to SSL. The latter transport security product seems to have found its niche.

Client authentication can be provided with reusable passwords. This method is not as secure as the SSL authentication with the user's public key. One-time passwords or authentication tokens are an interesting alternative. SecurID card by Security Dynamics is an example of the *challenge-response* approach. It requires the user to generate a one-time password. The password activates the token to give up an access code that the user enters and that the server verifies is correct. Biometric devices can be used. The token essentially contains user-specific secret keys. SSL has the added capability of validating a public key certificate issued to that user. The later technology is still maturing, whereas the token technology is well developed.

Finally, the requirements for deploying a Web application that uses exportable crypto are given here, with the highest-priority requirements appearing first:[15]

1. *Use a capable SSL Web server* It must offer very tight security, implement an up-to-date version of SSL, implement a good RSA key exchange (or ECC equivalent), support a few effective secret key ciphers such triple DES (3DES) or RC5, configure the secret key length to the application, ensure interoperability with SSL browsers, provide server event logging, protect against host subversion, and provide SSL client authentication.

2. *Use a dual-home host for the SSL Web Server* The server host must have two separate network interfaces, one to connect to the Internet and the other to connect to the internal enterprise network. The host must be configured to stop direct traffic flow from one network to the other (i.e., prevent IP forwarding).

3. *Identify the browsers you expect the customers to use* Decide if plaintext transactions as well as SSL-protected transactions will be permitted.

4. *Determine the types of payment you will accept.*

5. *Apply internal server security measures.*

6. *Apply Web server security measures; eliminate unnecessary CGI scripts.* Place read-only protection on Web pages that should not be changing.

7. *Select a widely supported certificate authority* VeriSign adminis-

ters the authority that issued the earliest SSL server certificates and represents a key player in this area, but not the only one.

While the previous discussion focused on SSL, the general concepts apply to all Web browsers that implement transport-level protection, including Microsoft PCT protocol.

When we evaluate Internet offerings from software providers such as Netscape, Microsoft, IBM, Novell, Inc. and others, we see that HTML and perhaps Java work in cross-platform environments, as well as, to a lesser extent, ActiveX (in Microsoft 32-bit environments). These are all technology leaders (Table 10-8).

TABLE 10-8

Technologies on the Web.

_____

(Total References on the Web: 20 Million)

Technology	Tag	References*	% Penetration
HTML	HTML	20,000,000	100%
CGI	CGI	10,000,000	50%
JavaScript	Script	300,000	1.5%
Java	Applet	30,000	0.15%
VB Script	VBScript	1,000	0.005%
ActiveX	Clsid	400	0.002%
Unautomated HTML	—	9,600,000	48%

*Web pages that contain the appropriate HTML tag.
Source: Applications Methods, Inc., 1998.

Technology on the Web

Table 10-8 demonstrates that there is a definite movement toward Web page compatibility using primarily HTML.[16] Corporations want to be able to connect and share information with suppliers, business partners, and customers. Unfortunately, vendors have fielded products with less-than-compatible results. Several security frameworks have surfaced for the Web marketplace.

Frameworks for Secure E-Commerce

E-commerce security is currently under rapid and uncoordinated development. Many manufacturers, industry associations, and standards bod-

TABLE 10-9

Frameworks for
Privacy,
Identification,
Authentication,
Authorization, and
Single Sign-On.

Framework	Privacy	Identification	Authentication	Authorization	Single Sign-on
SSL	Y	Y	Y		
Tokens		Y	Y		
FIPS 196		Y	Y		
Digital certificates		Y	Y		
X.509v3		Y	Y		
SESAME		Y	Y	Y	
Certification authorities		Y	Y	Y	
SET		Y	Y	Y	
OFX		Y	Y	Y	
Kerberos		Y	Y	Y	Y
SSH	Y	Y	Y	Y	
OPS	Y	Y	Y	Y	Y

ies have proposed and implemented different solutions for the problems of ensuring confidentiality, permissions management, identification, authentication, and authorization for e-commerce. This section summarizes key initiatives and provides pointers for further details. The frameworks discussed below emphasize various aspects of e-commerce security. There are several other initiatives that have proposed; however, those listed in Table 10-9 are holding up against the competition. Table 10-9 shows how these frameworks fit together to meet the needs of users and businesses seeking to establish secure business relations through the Internet and the Web.[17]

SSL

As previously mentioned, Netscape Communications created the Secure Sockets Layer (SSL) protocol to protect information being transmitted through the Internet. In addition, the SSL provides for authentication of Web servers and is an ideal protection agent for their traffic.[18]

Tokens

Many identification and authentication methods rely on tokens. These devices are encapsulated microprocessors in a tamper-resistant package usually the size of a thick credit card. One-time password generators have an LCD panel to display an alphanumeric string. It consists of their own serial number combined with the time and date and encrypted appropriately so that only the host software can deduce the serial number of the token that generated that particular string. Such devices currently cost about $30.

Smart cards are similar to the hand-held one-time password generators and can be used for authentication, but they require specialized readers. Some tokens have been created to interact with the common floppy drive. PC Card (formerly PCMCIA) based authentication is available, but these devices are more expensive than smart cards, costing about $60 not counting the readers.[19] Tokens are usually owned by issuing organizations. However, a new approach involves smart cards owned by the user. Such user-owned devices can function as electronic purses and can play a role in anonymous payment schemes designed to protect user privacy.

FIPS 196

The U.S. government's Federal Information Processing Standard (FIPS) 196 defines how public key cryptography (PKC) is used for user authentication with challenge-response systems. Suppliers aiming at government procurement will have to consider FIPS 196 in their system designs.

Digital Certificates

Digital certificates are growing in importance for Internet commerce. To generate digital certificates, users and merchants use secret keys in concert to establish trust. Devices can authenticate each other using digital certificates. Digital certificates are being used to authenticate e-mail and other electronic messages. In addition, corporations can issue digital certificates to employees, obviating the need for user IDs and passwords to gain access to intranets and other corporate networks. However, using certificates outside a single business can be complicated because digital certificates issued under different protocols are, in general, still not interoperable.

CCITT (ITU) X.509v3 Standard for Digital Certificates

Most digital certificates are based on the CCITT (ITU; International Consultative Committee on Telegraphy and Telephony) X.509 version 3 standard.[20] X.509 compliance is believed to enhance interoperability and simplification of security protocols. Groupware vendors are agreed that it is the best way to secure information for Internet transfer. X.509 is currently used by used by VeriSign and GTE Service Corporation. It is supported by Lotus's Domino 4.6, Microsoft's MS Exchange, and Novell's NDS directory service.

SESAME—European Standard for Digital Certificate Authentication

In Europe, Bull, ICL, and Siemens Nixdorf are pushing the SESAME standard for digital certificates. SESAME certificates expire after minutes or days to control access to system privileges. SESAME incorporates X.509 protocols.[21]

Third-Party Certification Authorities

The authenticity of digital certificates can be demonstrated by having each certificate signed by an entity (or person) that is trusted by both parties in the transaction. In one popular model of authentication of certificates, a web of trust among people and organizations ensures that every public key is signed by someone who knows that the public key is authentic. In a more hierarchical model, public keys used to sign certificates are authenticated by certification authorities (CAs) that are themselves authenticated by higher levels of CA. Organizations needing their own certification infrastructure can buy software from vendors. Linking certificates to a directory structure facilitates single-logon systems, where users need to identify and authenticate themselves to a system only once to gain access to all authorized system services.

However, CAs have failed to take into account the importance and history of bilateral trading relations. Today's CA products are "complex, hard to manage and scare the hell out of people."[22] Perhaps as a result of this complexity, a survey in December 1996 by Netcraft and

O'Reilly & Associates that examined 648,613 sites on the Web found that less than 1 percent of Web sites offer both SSL and third-party authentication.

SET—Authorization and Nonrepudiation

The Secure Electronic Transactions (SET) protocol requires digital certificates for each use of a credit card by a user trying to pay a merchant. MasterCard and Visa announced the SET standard in February 1996. SET is also supported by GTE, IBM, Microsoft, Netscape, SAIC, Terisa, and VeriSign.[23]

SET-compliant sites protect merchants from unauthorized payments and repudiation by clients. Banks using SET are protected against unauthorized purchases using their cards. Consumers are protected from merchant imposters and theft of credit card numbers. Supporters say SET will allow consumers to relax about security on the Web.

OFX—Open Financial Exchange

The Open Financial Exchange (OFX) is supported by Microsoft, Intuit, CheckFree, and others. The standard governs digital certificates to be exchanged among financial institutions to authenticate transactions. VeriSign, currently the most important third-party CA, has issued a new type of digital ID called the Financial Service ID that is usable by institutions supporting the OFX specification. The Financial Service ID will secure transactions such as home banking applications.[24]

Authorization and Single Sign-On: Kerberos

Kerberos was developed at MIT in the 1980s as part of an extended scheme for user identification, authentication, and authorization. The system's security depends strongly on protection of a Kerberos server that talks to both users and computer services such as printers and file servers.

Once a user has been securely enrolled in the Kerberos server, the user's passwords never travel to the Kerberos authentication server. Each subsequent request for a bilateral relation with a service by an authenticated user is itself authenticated by the Kerberos server, which issues digital certificates (called "tickets") to allow use of specific services by specific users. Kerberos requires applications and servers to be "Kerberized"—that is, was modified for use with Kerberos. Most off-the-shelf software does not support Kerberos.[25] However, Microsoft defines Kerberos as its Windows NT version 5 default authentication mechanism, and there is considerable interest in extending Kerberos to other applications as part of the Distributed Computing Environment (DCE) supported by a consortium of computer manufacturers.

SSH—Data Fellows Cryptographic Package

The SSH protocol is an application-level protocol used by Data Fellows F-Secure products. SSH guarantees simultaneous authentication of both ends of the connection, secrecy of transmitted information, and integrity of transmitted data. It features 1024-bit RSA host authentication, 768-bit RSA transport key for session keys changed once per hour, and 128-bit session encryption key generated by the user. Strong encryption methods supported include triple DES, IDEA, and Blowfish. SSH has a fully distributed key management. Data integration by strong hash calculation is performed with MD5, MAC, and CRC32. Several user authentication methods are supported, including smart cards, SecurID cards, and pure RSA authentication on traditional, UNIX rhost or hosts.equiv commands. SSH is a popular protocol marketed in Data Fellows F-Secure product lines, available on Macintosh, Windows, and UNIX platforms.[26]

OPS—Open Profiling Standard for Authorization and Single Sign-On

The Open Profiling Standard, backed by Netscape, Firefly, and VeriSign, removes the need for users to reenter their identifying information more than once on Web sites. It is also designed to allow Web sites to tailor their presentation to a user by reading personal information that has been authorized by that user and is transmitted to the server via virtual cards ("vCards") and digital certificates. The OPS is supported by privacy activists such as the Electronic Frontier Foundation, EPIC, and eTRUST/CommerceNet (now TRUSTe).

The Role of Encryption

All of the technologies being proposed by competing companies and consortia, including tokens, secure protocols for data transmission, digital certificates, and standards for trusting Web sites, involve some form of encryption (Chapter 7). With respect to cryptography for e-commerce, the asymmetrical class has helped e-commerce the most in recent years.

Asymmetric encryption algorithms use different *keys* for encryption and decryption. Instead of creating a single key that handles both encryption and decryption, as in symmetrical encryption algorithms, the key-generation function creates two different keys at once that are peculiarly complementary.

One key is used to encrypt the cleartext, and a different key is used to decrypt the ciphertext. Whatever is encrypted by one of the asymmetric keys can be decrypted only by the other key—and vice versa, since one can encrypt with either key and then decrypt successfully with the other key. Public key cryptosystems (PKCs) uses the fact that complementary keys can decrypt only what each key's complement encrypted.

To prove the authenticity and integrity of a message, the sender can encrypt the cleartext using the sender's private key. Any recipient can verify both the integrity and authenticity of the cleartext by decrypting the ciphertext using the sender's public key. If the ciphertext can successfully be decrypted using the sender's public key, then only the user of the corresponding private key could have created the ciphertext.

Typically, the asymmetric algorithms used in PKC take a long time for encryption and decryption. In addition, longer messages naturally take longer to encrypt than short ones. To reduce the time required for tedious asymmetric encryption and decryption, one creates a digital signature under the PKC by generating a mathematical *hash* of the cleartext.

As mentioned previously, a *hash function* is any method that creates a short sequence of data to be used in verifying the integrity of its source; a checksum is an example of a hash total. For instance, the last four digits of most credit cards are a checksum. The algorithms for generating a hash are selected to generate a very different value for the cleartext modified by even so little as a single character.

For example, if someone makes a mistake in reading his credit card number out over the telephone so that one of the digits is wrong, it is very unlikely that the original four-digit checksum will be correct. When the incorrect card number is checked by the credit card company, the erroneous checksum instantly identifies that the mistake has been made.

To shorten the time required for systems to check message integrity,

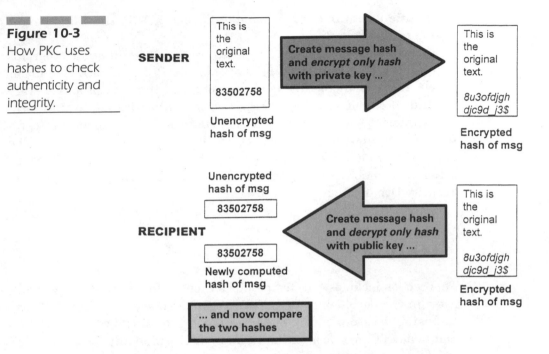

Figure 10-3
How PKC uses hashes to check authenticity and integrity.

the PKC usually does not encrypt the entire message. Instead, the PKC implementations create a hash total, and it is the hash that is encrypted using the sender's private key. The recipient can decrypt the hash using the sender's public key and then independently calculate the hash value. If the recalculated hash matches the decrypted hash, then the message is unchanged and it has been authenticated to have originated with the holder of the corresponding private key.

Figure 10-3 illustrates how PKC uses hashes to check for authenticity and integrity. PKC does not usually encrypt the entire message. It normally creates an encrypted hash total which authenticates the origin. The hash itself is based on the complete encrypted form of the message and when the hash has been authenticated the message would then be decrypted.

Interoperability

Competing standards make it difficult for users and corporations to communicate effectively. Many observers hope that the field will develop standards for interoperability of the different certificates and protocols. Most of the directory/certificate linkage schemes that relate certificates to specific users and servers generally use LDAP, the Lightweight Directory Access Protocol.

Application programming interfaces (APIs) allow different programs to interoperate. It is frustrating that several API frameworks are under development by competing vendor groups and that the proposed standards do not spell out how to progress from authentication to authorization. Gradient Technologies, a Kerberizing specialist, supports integration of the public key infrastructure (PKI) with Kerberos/DCE. The SecureOne framework integrates APIs for antivirus programs, authentication, encryption, and digital certificates. RSA, VeriSign, McAfee, and Security Dynamics support SecureOne.

Products

This section includes selected products thought to be particularly significant in the developing field of Web commerce security (Table 10-10). Inclusion does not imply endorsement by the authors or COMSEC Solutions LLC, nor does exclusion imply criticism in any form.

TABLE 10-10

Functionality of Some E-Commerce Security Products.

Products	Privacy	Identity	Authenticity	Authorization	Single Sign-On	Extended Information
VeriSign Digital IDS		Y	Y			
DigiCash	Y			Y		
CyberCash	Y			Y		
Security Dynamics SecurID		Y	Y	Y		
Bellcore S/KEY		Y	Y	Y	Y	
VeriSign Private Label Digital ID Services		Y	Y	Y	Y	Y
NCR SmartEC TrustedPASS		Y	Y	Y	Y	Y

VeriSign Digital IDs

VeriSign has established itself as the supplier of digital certificates with the largest base of commercial and individual customers among the third-party CAs. The Digital IDs use RSA cryptography with 1024-bit key length and are being used by more than 16,000 Web servers and over 500,000 individuals. VeriSign's Server Digital IDs enable organizations to establish secure sessions with visitors. The Server Digital IDs authenticate the Web site and ensure that customers will not be fooled by unauthenticated Web sites of unscrupulous con artists who make their sites look as convincing as those of real businesses.

Digital IDs dispense with the need for users to memorize individual user IDs and passwords for different Web sites. Digital IDs are issued by CAs and securely exchanged using SSL. VeriSign verifies a server operator's identity using Dun & Bradstreet, InterNIC, and other authenticating information such as articles of incorporation, partnership papers, and tax records. VeriSign (or other CA) signs a Digital ID only after verifying the site's authenticity in these ways.[27]

AOL offers VeriSign Digital IDs to let customers and merchants authenticate each other. The server generates a random session key that is encrypted by the secret key from the server's Digital ID. This session key expires in 24 hours, and each session uses a different session key, making it impossible for a captured certificate to be misused. From the user perspective, Digital IDs are easy to use. The Web user clicks on a credit card icon on the Web site. The user then fills out a form that automatically provides the merchant's Web server with the user's public key, a list of desired purchases, and the user's digital certificate. The merchant's software decodes the user authentication and corresponding bank identification to process the order.

Generally, Digital IDs are implemented for automatic use by Web browsers and e-mail software. However, currently, the VeriSign smartcard system requires a card reader on the client system.

VeriSign has been working on new digital certificates, including new attributes to extend personalization of Web sites. The current version of Digital IDs has limited fields for user information that can be used to personalize Web site responses. One of the limitations of the VeriSign scheme is that each Web site visited by a user must request the client Digital ID for reauthentication. If access control lists (ACLs) are to be linked to Digital IDs, every authorized user for a specific site must be entered into a database for ACL implementation.

DigiCash

DigiCash provides smart-card payments and software *ecash* using the PKC.[28] This system is designed to enhance user privacy; for example, a user can use a different digital pseudonym (account identifier) for every organization.

Traditional security measures trace individual identity, but the DigiCash approach ensures anonymity of each user while simultaneously ensuring data integrity and nonrepudiation of transactions. Certificates of receipt are digitally signed to prevent repudiation of the transaction. The DigiCash system allows purchases to be subject to "cooling-off periods" during which they can be reversed. DigiCash protocols require a secret authorizing personal identification number (PIN) that would make use of a stolen or lost smart card difficult.

DigiCash is open to implementation on any device. It is hoped that this open system can allow merchants to take advantage of the best solutions available rather than to be tied to a single supplier. Merchants can lock out individuals who abuse their relationship. This locking function would allow the new system to be extended to polling and voting with security and anonymity.

DigiCash's ecash is a software-based payment system for use on any computer and network. The ecash system requires DigiCash software to be installed on each user's workstation. Such a system makes micropayments for services and products delivered via the Web economically feasible.

CyberCash

CyberCash customer information is sent encrypted to a merchant Web server, which signs and forwards it to CyberCash as a secure intermediary. The merchant never sees the customer's credit card number because it remains encrypted while on the merchant's server. CyberCash securely decrypts and reformats the transaction and sends the information securely to the merchant's bank. The merchant's bank securely forwards a request for authorization of the purchase to the customer's bank. The customer's bank sends a digitally signed authorization back to CyberCash, which then securely returns the authorization (or denial) to the merchant. The merchant in turn notifies the customer of the acceptance or rejection of the purchase.[29]

The secure exchange depends on non-Internet communications between CyberCash and the financial institutions. CyberCash is integrating its electronic cash system with the SET protocol. AOL is an example of a large vendor that offers CyberCash authentication for its Web-hosting services.

Security Dynamics SecurID and ACE/Server

Security Dynamics is the leading provider of token-based authentication using the SecurID and ACE/Server.[30] These systems are widely used for identification and authentication within corporations. However, penetration of the wider commercial market is problematic because of the capital cost of the hardware. It remains to be seen how the public will accept having to pay for and carry such tokens.

Bellcore's S/KEY

The S/KEY version 2.6 from Bellcore is a system for one-time password authentication via software only. S/KEY uses a challenge-response system. The one-time password is never stored on the client or on the server, and it never crosses the network. S/KEY complies with the Internet Engineering Task Force (IETF) standard RFC 1938 on one-time passwords.[31]

Wrap-Up

Identification, authentication, and authorization are normal components of any business transaction and must be guaranteed by the communications systems and software mediating the relationship between supplier and customer. The Web (the entire global Internet) is subject to a variety of computer-related, denial of service, and virtual attacks. The growth of e-commerce will be hindered until vendors supply security solutions that are trustworthy as well as interoperable in terms of systems design. Encryption technology plays a significant technological role in protecting both the merchant and the customer on the Web. Encryption technology provides the glue for electronic transactions, trust, customers, security products, and merchants doing business on the Web.

Notes

1. CIWARS Intelligence Report, Volume 2, Issue 23, 13 September 1998, p. 4, http://www.Iwar.org.

2. Hurwitz Research Bulletin, "The Security Market Evolves to Meet the Needs of E-Business Applications," 22 August 1999, http://www.gradient.com/news/analysts/hurwitz_pmi.htm.

3. Ibid.

4. *Remote Access Best Practices*, Financial Information Security Consortium, 22 September 1997, http://www.icsa.net/library/research/bp.shtml.

5. Nichols, Randall K., *ICSA Guide to Cryptography* (New York: McGraw-Hill 1998).

6. CIWARS, op. cit.

7. McCarthy, Vance, "Web Security: How Much is Enough?" *Datamation*, Volume 43, No. 1, January 1997 (Report on OURS Consortia).

8. Ibid.

9. Amoroso, Edward G., *Fundamentals of Computer Security Technology* (Upper Saddle River, N.J.: Prentice-Hall, 1994).

10. Nichols, op. cit.

11. Smith, Richard, *Internet Cryptography* (Reading, Mass.: Addison-Wesley, 1997).

12. Ibid.

13. Ibid.

14. Nichols, op. cit.

15. Smith, op. cit.

16. *Web Technologies* (1998): http://www.appmethods.com/index.htm.

17. Kabay, M. E., ICSA white paper, March 1997.

18. SSL: http://search.netscape.com/newsref/std/SSL_old.html.

19. Tokens: http://www.zdnet.com/pcmag/features/inetsecurity/authentication.htm. (Anonymous, "Internet Security: Authentication," *PC Magazine Online*, 1997).

20. CCITT: http://www.zdnet.com/pcweek/news/0526/26apro.html. (Reported by Michael Miller, "Standard For Exchanging Personal Info Moves Forward," *PCWeek Online*, 27 May 1997).

21. Digital CA: http://www.zdnet.com/pcweek/reviews/0428/28cert.html> [Reported by Dave Kosiur, "Role of Digital Certificates Looks Secure, PCWeek Online, 4/30/97.]

22. <http://www.news.com/News/Item/0,4,15222,00.html>. [Tim Clark, "Locking up Home Banking, C/Net, 10/14/97.]

23. SET: <http://www.zdnet.com/pcmag/news/trends/t960201d.htm. (Anonymous, "MasterCard and Visa Join Forces for Electronic Commerce," *PC Magazine Online*, 1 February 1996).

24 OFX: http://www.news.com/News/Item/0,4,15222,00.html. (Tim Clark, "Locking up Home Banking," C/Net, 14 October 1997).

25. Kerberos: http://alycia.dementia.org/kerberos.htm.

26. Data Fellows F-Secure SSH Technical Description from Client, August 1999

27. VeriSign: http://digitalid.verisign.com/id_intro.htm

28. DigiCash, Ibid.

29. Cybercash: http://www.cybercash.com/cybercash/shoppers/shopsteps.html

30. http://www.xcert.com

31. Bellcore: http://bellcore.com/BC.dynjava?SkeyPDGeneralProductDescription

CHAPTER 11

Virtual Private Networks

Overview

Watching the Internet grow is like tracking a wild animal. It has no boundaries and few rules to cage it. It has linked people and organizations otherwise physically separated and has proven to be an inexpensive, reliable means for interorganizational communications and data sharing. Millions of users are connected to the Internet. It has become an ideal means for information retrieval and exchange. Corporations have found the Internet to be a fertile area to make money and an easy place to advertise goods and services. The Internet is also an efficient and opportune medium for illegal activities such as data tampering, eavesdropping, and theft.

Because of the inherent wildness of the beast, companies and organizations around the world have concluded that data security is a fundamental requirement. Secure *VPN* (virtual private network) solutions, using encryption, certification, firewalls, and access control, present an attractive option for data security needs and represent a growing sector of the network security market. Managers who recommend a move to a VPN solution do so because of increased need for data security and reduced networking costs. On the security side, a VPN keeps unwanted users out of private computer networks and encrypts all information going out of a local network. It builds a wall between a company's private network and the outside world, via the Internet or nonsecure backbone, and hides information leaving the network so that unwanted users are unable to read or modify it.

From a savings standpoint, VPNs represent a cost-effective means of communicating over the Internet for geographically separated employees and business partners. Using the Internet is far less expensive than private leased lines, Frame Relay, or ISDN networks. VPNs allow network managers to increase in a cost-efficient manner the span of corporate networks, remote network users to securely and easily access their corporate enterprise, corporations to securely communicate with their business partners and customers, and service providers to grow their business by providing substantial incremental bandwidth and value-added services.

With the arrival of IPSec (IP Security Protocol), managers have a standardized means of implementing security for VPNs. IPSec is a protocol suite—a set of Internet Protocol (IP) extensions that provide security services at the network level. IPSec technology is based on modern cryptographic technologies, making possible very strong data authentication and privacy guarantees. Furthermore, all of the encryption and authentication algorithms and security protocols used in IPSec are well studied and have survived years of scrutiny. Consequently, the user can be confident that the IPSec facility indeed provides strong security.

IPSec can be implemented in routers or firewalls owned and operated by the organization. This gives the network manager complete control over security aspects of the VPN, which is much to be desired. The alternative is to seek a solution from a service provider. A service provider can simplify the job of planning, implementing, and maintaining Internet-based VPNs for secure access to network resources and secure communication among sites.

Public vs. Private Networks

A *public network*, like the public telephone system and the Internet, is a large collection of unrelated peers who exchange information almost freely with each other. The people who access the public network do not need to have any commonality and generally communicate with only a small fraction of potential users.

A *private network* is composed of computers owned by a single corporation that share information specifically and solely with each other. The owners are assured that those are the only computers using the network, and others will only see that information that is among the using group members. The typical corporate local area network (LAN) or wide area network (WAN) are examples of a private networks.

The line between private and public is usually thought to be a *gateway router*, where a company will erect a *firewall* to keep intruders from the public network out of their private network, or keep internal users from perusing the public network. Firewalls are computer hardware, software, or both used to restrict and monitor usage of a computer or network. A gateway router is a special-purpose device or dedicated computer that attaches to two or more networks and routes *packets* from one network to the other. Gateways route packets to other gateways until they can be delivered to the final destination directly across one physical network. *The packet is the smallest unit of data transmitted over a network or the Internet.* Packets are *numbered by the sender* and routed independently through the Internet to the recipient. *The route of each packet is determined by the load and availability of any given segment of the network, thereby relieving traffic overloads on busy networks.* The packets are then reassembled in order by the receiving computer. Each packet contains from 40 to 32,000 bytes of information.

Mobility

Mobility of personnel has changed the way that companies have organized their LANs. From separate, isolated branch offices, with their own e-mail, naming schemes, and favorite network protocols (generally incompatible with other office setups), companies found that it was profitable to interconnect. Traditionally, this was done with 800- numbers and leased lines. Both are billed flat rate plus mileage and represent significant costs. The cost is prohibitive when a company has multiple offices across the country or overseas.

Private networks typically have difficulty supporting traveling executives, salespeople, and other personnel. Distributed and remote computing is now a well-established practice. Traveling employees and telecommuters access their corporate network by dialing into remote access servers to download e-mail, share files with other employees, and use the network resources (printer, fax, and file servers) as if they were directly on the LAN. Remote computing technology has existed for some time and has proven reliable from most locations. Again, the problem is rising telecommunications costs.

Virtual Private Network Technology

Virtual private network technology represents a crossover from public to private networks. VPNs allow creation of a secure, private network over a public network such as the Internet. This is done through IPSec, *encryption, packet tunneling,* and *firewalls*. VPN dramatically reduces annual telecommunications expenses by advantageous use of the relatively low-cost Internet connectivity. The leased-line costs are skirted by using the Internet as a WAN. VPN technology appears to be cost-effective for both large and small companies. The government is employing VPN technology in many DoD sites throughout the country.

A VPN is a way to *simulate* a private network over a public network (Internet). It is *virtual* because it depends on the use of *virtual connections*—that is, *temporary connections* that have no real physical presence but consist of packets routed over various machines on the Internet on an ad hoc basis. Secure virtual connections are created between two machines, a machine and a network, or two networks. Tunneling is one example of a VPN. A *tunnel* is established between the user's machine and a server at the corporate site. Tunnels have the additional advantage over a LAN connection of easier filtering, since it is done at a single point and the boxes actually route the packets such that each packet takes the optimal route to the intended LAN.

Clear Advantages

Beside lower costs, VPN technology offers other clear advantages:

1. Home office employees can securely connect to the home network by dialing into a local ISP/national network such as AOL or CompuServe.

2. Employees seconded at customer sites may connect to their corporate network via the customer's Internet connections and tunnel through the customer's private network to the Internet and into their corporate LAN.

3. Customers and channel partners can be granted *extranet* access to certain restricted areas of the company private network. The extranet is an extension of the private network bounds. It is accomplished by equipping the partner or customer with VPN client software and creating the appropriate account in the database. This works with the de facto standard of TCP/IP traffic, and the partner is able to build a secure link into a selected area of the company's network, with user-specific privileges.

4. Intranet access to sensitive corporate data can be granted to restricted employees or departments by establishing a subnetwork area in the company LAN.

5. VPN savings grow with the network. The more branch offices added, the more cost-effective the technology. In addition, the intranet brings a degree of flexibility just by adding access. There is an ease of management because it is no longer necessary to manage PVC lines between offices. Global expansion is ideal for international connectivity.

6. VPNs are platform-independent. The Internet Protocol can run over any communications infrastructure. Any computer system

that is configured to run on an IP network can be incorporated into a VPN with no modifications required except the installation of remote software.

7. VPNs can be implemented between corporations. VPNs that connect multiple corporation networks are known as extranets. Intracompany VPNs (intranets) and intercompany VPNs (extranets) differ only by their management. The company solely manages resources of the former; the latter is a shared resource solution—especially for the management of authentication and encryption keys.

Internet Security Concerns

Despite the positive revolution produced by the Internet, it is still a wild animal. The following problems still exist:

1. Reliability

2. System maintenance

3. Access

4. Security

5. Information warriors

The Internet was not designed with security in mind. The credo of the Net is "Everything should be free-flowing." For corporations or governments to trust their sensitive data to the Internet, technology is required to ensure that the right people are accessing the corporation's networks and that outsiders cannot read transient data. Consider just three of the many threats to corporate data flowing on the Net:

1. *Network intrusion*   This is every administrator's nightmare. With an intrusion attack, someone outside is able to access machines on your network as if that person were the owner or administrator of that machine. This type of attack is very common on the Internet.

2. *IP address spoofing*   This involves someone on the Internet pretending to have an IP address on the inside of your network. This is done to circumvent a packet filtration firewall, which can block traffic based on source or destination. Spoofing is also used to launch denial of service (DoS) attacks, which can either completely overwhelm a machine or prevent it from completing a job.

3. *Packet sniffing*   In the electronic commerce world, packet sniffing is a serious risk. It occurs when a machine connected to the network is used to spy on traffic as it streams on by. The sniffer can dissect the data streams for passwords or other sensitive data. The ultimate vantage point for a packet sniffer is directly connected to your network. On the Internet, it is more complicated; packet sniffing is accomplished at the Internet service provider or at one of the network access points (NAPs), where backbone providers come together.

Standards and Traffic

There are three emerging VPN standards: PPTP (Point-to-Point Tunneling Protocol), L2TP (Layer 2 Tunneling Protocol), and IPSec (IP Security). The PPTP, L2TP, and IPSec specifications are sets of requests for comment (RFCs) to the IETF (Internet Engineering Task Force) that describe protocols to be used for tunneling. All are suggested for inclusion in the IP protocol, IPv6. IPSec is already implemented in IPv4. PPTP was supported by Microsoft and Ascend to support packet tunneling in Ascend's remote access server hardware and Microsoft's NT software. The backers of the PPTP protocol combined efforts with Cisco Systems and its L2F protocol to produce a hybrid called L2TP.

IPSec is an initiative to add security services to the IP protocol. IPSec is the preferred solution for IP environments because it has security built in. PPTP and L2TP are most appropriate for multiprotocol environments, but both require additional support to deliver data privacy, integrity, and authentication. Unless augmented with IPSec, PPTP and L2TP *cannot support extranets effectively because extranets require keys and key management.* Furthermore, PPTP was developed originally, by Microsoft and others, as an extension of the PPP (Point-to-Point) protocol used for TCP/IP of serial lines (dial-up modem connections). PPTP "tunnels" or encapsulates IP, IPX, or NetBEUI protocols with IP packets.

Conceptually, there is no difference between using PPTP for client-to-firewall communications and using IPSec-enabled IP stack on the client to talk to the firewall and establish a VPN. PPTP does support tunneling of non-IP protocols. Non-IP traffic includes protocols such as IPX, DECNet, SNA, and AppleTalk. By definition, non-IP traffic cannot be part of a VPN because it is not IP-based. Thus, non-IP traffic should always be treated as nonmember traffic and handled by access control components such as router filters or firewalls. *Member traffic* is defined as IP traffic where the source and the destination workstations are within a VPN. *Nonmember traffic* is defined as all other IP traffic to network resources that are not in a VPN.

The Internet is a natural filter because it handles IP traffic and non-IP traffic, must be encapsulated for it to be transported. If the Internet is used to connect trusted networks via VPNs, the Internet will filter non-IP traffic. Trusted networks are composed of workstations in which users are given open access to other systems with little concern about sabotage or abuse. Untrusted networks are composed of workstations in which unknown and untrusted users could abuse or sabotage the organizations' network resources.

The Internet is an untrusted network for most corporate traffic. Security issues and potential abuse have prevented many corporations from using the Internet to connect to offices without using the cryptographic security inherent in VPNs. Even the public WANs provided by the major telecommunications carriers (Public Switched Telephone Network, or PSTN, Frame Relay, and X.25) are accessed by hundreds of thousands of users and must be considered untrusted. It is the twofold ability to design trusted and untrusted portions of a corporate network and the ability to connect trusted networks via an untrusted network that makes VPN technology so inviting.

Finally, a serious problem with PPTP is that it is only supported on NT servers. In order to support this, a site must be running an NT-based firewall or must provide a hole through the firewall to allow PPTP traffic through. The latter means foregoing any firewall control over what is permitted over the PPTP session, resulting in VPNs with complete access and no VPNs with controlled access.

PPTP has not yet been widely adopted, and L2TP suffers from similar limitations. It has been contended that PPTP adds tunneling to the PPP protocol, allowing address conflict resolution in a similar fashion to IPSec's tunneling services. PPTP would, in theory, be used on top of the IP (as opposed to PPP, which is used below it and only in certain links) to produce a virtual point-to-point line through the IP network, thus providing tunneling services similar to IPSec's. From a scale standpoint, PPTP merely provides a virtual dial-up line through the IP network. It does not provide a secure VPN at any scale.

The IETF draft PPTP standard is not the same as the Windows NT 4.0 implementation. The standard does not provide for any encryption, and this is a serious flaw. It actually references the IPSEC protocol suite as a sensible way to provide these services in PPTP implementations. The

Windows NT implementation provides built-in software encryption through Windows NT RAS security function. This means that even if this were good encryption (it is not), then an NT RAS server would be needed in the network for translation. Either way, PPTP does not provide a key management system of any type.

Driving Force

A growing number of VPN, security, and major network companies have joined in their support of the IPSec protocol. Of the three standards, IPSec is the only protocol being driven by major network users. At least six companies—AXENT Technologies, Check Point Software, Network Associates, RADGUARD Ltd., TimeStep Corporation, and VPNet Technologies—have passed independent certification requirements for both encryption and product interoperability using the IPSec protocol for VPNs.

Automotive Network eXchange (ANX)

Perhaps the single most important VPN is that of the Automotive Network eXchange. Developed jointly by the Automotive Industry Action Group (AIAG) and Bell Communications Research, the ANX will link automotive trading partners into a single, secure network for electronic commerce and data sharing. It will bring thousands of companies involved with the auto and trucking business sectors, with annual earnings in excess of hundreds of billions of dollars, into one single communications environment. It will clearly change the way business is conducted. Other industries are watching the ANX project. Aviation, health care, defense, home building, and other industries are keeping an eye on this development, because it will determine the rules for communications between and within corporations involved in multiple-component products and services.

Interoperability

The IPSec standard, based on the ISAKMP/Oakley key management protocol is becoming a dominant force internationally for communications. Adherence to the IPSec standard is the proper tool for interoperability. It guarantees that encrypted information is secure on its path from one network to another, and it allows the encrypted data to be deciphered only by relevant people, in the appropriate networks, with encryption systems manufactured by different vendors. VPN solutions that are not interoperable limit the growth of the VPN communications and are very expensive to run. The ANX embracing of the IPSec standard as its management protocol speaks loudly to the case.

VPN Technologies

A VPN is a conglomerate of useful technologies. These include encryption, authentication, tunneling, and IPSec, which may or may not be combined with firewalls to design a secure VPN system. We will first discuss the IPSec crypto-based VPN solution and then cover the firewall-based VPN solution.

IP Security, Secure Virtual Private Networks, and Encryption

Encryption is the starting point of any VPN solution, and the key differentiation between good and bad VPN solutions is the use of well-established encryption algorithms and strong encryption keys. Additionally, establishing VPNs requires agreement in four different areas: the mechanism for encryption, the algorithm for encryption (and the key size and padding to use), the mechanism for key exchange negotiation, and the algorithm to use for key exchange. The IPSec standard covers all four areas. All of these need to be coordinated and communicated. The technologies exist today and are implemented in both firewall-based and crypto-based VPNs.

The responsible manager may choose from a variety of encryption and authentication packages and products. Proprietary solutions raise a number of problems. First, how secure is the solution? If proprietary encryption or authentication schemes are used, there may be little reassurance in the technical literature as to the level of security provided. Second is the question of compatibility. No manager wants to be limited in the choice of workstations, servers, routers, firewalls, and so on by a need for compatibility with the security facility. Enter the Internet Protocol Security (IPSec) set of Internet standards.

The principal feature of IPSec that enables it to support these varied applications is that it can encrypt and/or authenticate all traffic at the IP level. Thus, all distributed applications, including remote logon, client/server, e-mail, file transfer, Web access, and so on, can be secured.

Figure 11-1 is a typical scenario of IPSec usage. An organization maintains LANs at dispersed locations. Nonsecure IP traffic is conducted on each LAN. For traffic off-site, through some sort of private or public WAN, IPSec protocols are used. These protocols operate in networking devices, such as a router or firewall that connects each LAN to the outside world. The IPSec networking device will typically encrypt and compress all traffic going into the WAN, and decrypt and decompress traffic coming from the WAN; these operations are transparent to workstations and servers on the LAN. Secure transmission is also possible with individual users who dial into the WAN. Such user workstations must implement the IPSec protocols to provide security.

Benefits of IPSec

Some of the benefits of IPSec are as follows:

■ When IPSec is implemented in a firewall or router, it provides strong security that can be applied to all traffic crossing the perimeter. Traffic within a company or workgroup does not incur the overhead of security-related processing.

■ IPSec is below the transport layer (TCP, LTDP), so it is transparent to applications. There is no need to change software on a user or server system when IPSec is implemented in the firewall or router. Even if IPSec is implemented in end systems, upper-layer software, including applications, is not affected.

■ IPSec is usually transparent to end users. There is no need to train users on security mechanisms, issue keying material on a per-user basis, or revoke keying material when users leave the organization.

■ IPSec can provide security for individual users if needed. This implementation would be of particular usefulness for off-site employees and for setting up a secure virtual subnetwork within an organization for any sensitive application.

342

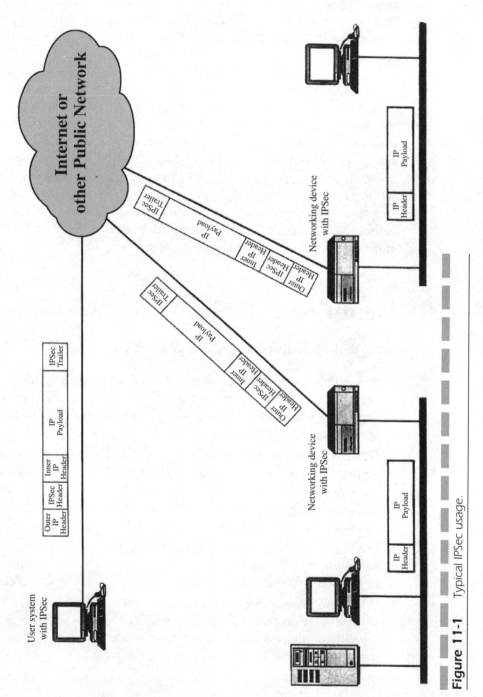

Figure 11-1 Typical IPSec usage.

IP-Level Security

One issue has to do with whether security is being provided at the right protocol layer. To provide security at the IP level, it is necessary for IPSec to be a part of the network code deployed on all participating platforms, including Windows NT, UNIX, and Macintosh systems. Unless a desired feature is available on all of the deployed platforms, a given application may not be able to use that feature. On the other hand, if the application, such as a Web browser/server combination, incorporates the function, the developer can guarantee that the features are available on all platforms for which the application is available. A related point is that many Internet applications are now being released with embedded security features. For example, Netscape and Internet Explorer support Secure Sockets Layer (SSL), which protects Web traffic. In addition, a number of vendors are planning to support Secure Electronic Transaction (SET), which protects credit card transactions over the Internet. However, for a virtual private network, a network-level facility is needed, and this is what IPSec provides.

IPSec Functions: Authentication, Encryption, and Key Exchange

IPSec provides three main facilities: an authentication-only function referred to as *authentication header (AH)*, a combined authentication/encryption function called *encapsulating security payload (ESP)*, and a *key exchange function*. For VPNs, both authentication and encryption are generally desired, because it is important both to (1) ensure that unauthorized users do not penetrate the virtual private network and (2) ensure that eavesdroppers on the Internet cannot read messages sent over the virtual private network. Because both features are generally desirable, most implementations are likely to use ESP rather than AH. The key exchange function allows for manual exchange of keys, as well as an automated scheme.

The current IPSec specification requires that IPSec support the Data Encryption Standard (DES) for encryption, but a variety of other encryption algorithms may also be used. Because of concern about the strength of DES (and the recent IFF DES cracker announcement), it is likely that other algorithms, such as triple DES (3DES), will be widely used, possibly as early as this year and certainly by some time in 1999. For authentication, a relatively new scheme, known as HMAC, (*H* stands for "embedded hash algorithm" and *MAC* stands for "message authentication code") is required. 3DES is a recommendation for future product certification by COMSEC Solutions.

Transport and Tunnel Modes

ESP supports two modes of use: transport and tunnel mode. *Transport mode* provides protection primarily for upper-layer protocols. That is, transport mode protection extends to the payload of an IP packet. Typically, transport mode is used for end-to-end communication between two hosts (e.g., a client and a server, or two workstations). ESP in transport mode encrypts and optionally authenticates the IP payload but not the IP header (see Figure 11-2).

Figure 11-2
Scope of ESP
encryption and
authentication.

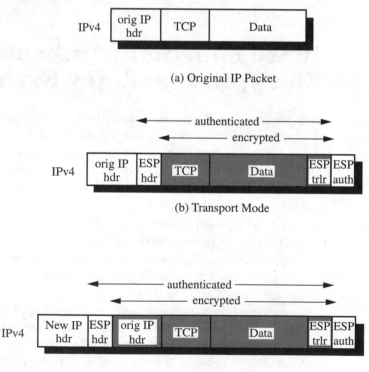

(a) Original IP Packet

(b) Transport Mode

(c) Tunnel Mode

This configuration is useful for relatively small networks in which each host and server is equipped with IPSec. However, for a full-blown VPN, tunnel mode is far more efficient. *Tunnel mode* provides protection to the entire IP packet. To achieve this, after the ESP fields are added to the IP packet, the entire packet plus security fields is treated as the payload of new "outer" IP packet with a new outer IP header. The entire original or inner packet travels through a "tunnel" from one point of an IP network to another; no routers along the way are able to examine the inner IP header. *Because the original packet is encapsulated, the new, larger packet may have totally different sources and destination addresses, adding to the security.* Tunnel mode is used when one or both ends are a security gateway, such as a firewall or router that implements IPSec. With tunnel mode, a number of hosts on networks behind firewalls may engage in secure communications without implementing IPSec. The unprotected packets generated by such hosts are tunneled through external networks by tunnel mode SAs (security associations) set up by the IPSec software in the firewall or secure router at the boundary of the local network.

Here is an example of how tunnel mode IPSec operates. Host A on a network generates an IP packet with the destination address of host B on another network. This packet is routed from the originating host to a firewall or secure router at the boundary of A's network. The firewall filters all outgoing packets to determine the need for IPSec processing. If this packet from A to B requires IPSec, the firewall performs IPSec processing and encapsulates the packet in an outer IP header. The source IP address of this outer IP packet is this firewall, and the destination address may be a firewall that forms the boundary to B's local network. This packet is now routed to B's firewall, with intermediate routers examining only the outer IP header. At B's firewall, the outer IP header is stripped off and the inner packet is delivered to B. ESP in tunnel mode encrypts and optionally authenticates the entire inner IP packet, including the inner IP header.

Key Management

The key management portion of IPSec involves the determination and distribution of secret keys. The IPSec architecture document mandates support for two types of key management:

- *Manual* A system administrator manually configures each system with its own keys and with the keys of other communicating systems. This is practical for small, relatively static environments.

■ *Automated*   An automated system enables the on-demand creation of keys for SAs and facilitates the use of keys in a large distributed system with an evolving configuration. An automated system is the most flexible but requires more effort to configure and requires more software. Therefore, smaller installations are likely to opt for manual key management.

The default automated key management protocol for IPSec is referred to as ISAKMP/Oakley and consists of the following elements:

■ *Internet Security Association and Key Management Protocol (ISAKMP)*   ISAKMP provides a framework for Internet key management and provides the specific protocol support, including formats for negotiation of security attributes.

■ *Oakley Key Determination Protocol*   Oakley is a key exchange protocol based on the Diffie-Hellman algorithm but providing added security. In particular, Diffie-Hellman alone does not authenticate the two users that are exchanging keys, making the protocol vulnerable to impersonation. Oakley includes mechanisms to authenticate users.

ISAKMP by itself does not dictate a specific key exchange algorithm; rather, ISAKMP consists of a set of message types that enable the use of a variety of key exchange algorithms. Oakley is the specific key exchange algorithm mandated for use with the initial version of ISAKMP.

Key Generation

Since encryption systems are known, the strength of the encryption process comes down to the key used in encrypting and deciphering transmitted data by the component machines of the VPN and the protocol used in the key management process. A key's strength is a combination of the three factors:

1. *Key length*   In general, the longer the better and the tougher to break. Today, 56-bit keys are insecure. Key lengths of 90 to 168 bits are better.

2. *Key exchange mechanism*   Keys are the common secret upon which the whole encryption process is based. Key exchange needs to be secret, automatic, and frequent, and not just at the end of a key generation session.

3. *Key generation* The use of truly random keys ensures the highest level of security. With true random numbers as bases for encryption keys, it is impossible to know or predict the structure of past or future keys. Software random-number generation systems have been cracked. Hardware-based systems are more difficult to crack.

Security Associations

A central concept that appears for IPSec is the security association. *The SA is a one-way relationship between a sender and a receiver.* If a peer relationship is needed for two-way secure exchange, then two security associations are required.

An Internet destination address and a security parameter index (SPI) uniquely identify a security association. Hence, in any IP datagram, the destination address in the IP header and the SPI in the enclosed ESP header uniquely identify the security association. The SA defines the parameters for IP exchange, including the encryption and authentication algorithms, the encryption and authentication keys, and filters that determine which IP traffic will be subject to IPSec processing. Thus, the SA gives the VPN manager great flexibility in how the VPN is configured.

Authentication Header

The authentication header provides support for data integrity and authentication of IP packets. The data integrity feature ensures that undetected modification to a packet's content in transit is not possible. The authentication feature enables an end system or network device to authenticate the user or application and filter traffic accordingly; it also prevents the address spoofing attacks observed in today's Internet. The AH also guards against the replay attack described subsequently.

Authentication is based on the use of a message authentication code, known as HMAC, which requires that the two parties share a secret key. The message authentication algorithm is used to calculate a message authentication code known as a MAC, using an algorithm known as HMAC. HMAC takes as input a portion of the message and a secret key and produces a MAC as output. This MAC value is stored in the Authentication Data field of the AH header.

Figure 11-3
IPSec authentication header.

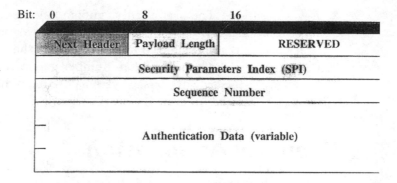

The authentication header consists of the following fields (Figure 11-3):

- *Next Header (8 bits)* Identifies the type of header immediately following this header.

- *Payload Length (8 bits)* Length of authentication header in 32-bit words, minus 2. For example, the default length of the Authentication Data field is 96 bits, or three 32-bit words. With a three-word fixed header, there are a total of six words in the authentication header, and the Payload Length field has a value of 4.

- *Reserved (16 bits)* Saved for future use.

- *Security Parameters Index (32 bits)* Identifies a security association.

- *Sequence Number (32 bits)* A monotonically increasing counter value, used in replay protection.

- *Authentication Data (variable)* A variable-length field (must be an integral number of 32-bit words) that contains the MAC for this packet.

Antireplay Service

A *replay attack* is one in which an attacker obtains a copy of an authenticated packet and later transmits it to the intended destination. The receipt of duplicate, authenticated EP packets may disrupt service in some way or may have some other undesired consequence. The Sequence Number field is designed to thwart such attacks.

When a new SA is established, the sender initializes a sequence number counter to 0. Each time that a packet is sent on this SA, the sender increments the counter and places the value in the Sequence Number field. Thus, the first value to be used is 1. If antireplay is enabled (the default), the sender must not allow the sequence number to cycle past 232-1 back to zero. Otherwise, there would be multiple valid packets with the same sequence number. If the limit of 232-1 is reached, the sender should terminate this SA and negotiate a new SA with a new key.

Because IP is a connectionless, unreliable service, the protocol does not guarantee that packets will be delivered in order and does not guarantee that all packets will be delivered. Therefore, the IPSec authentication document dictates that the receiver should implement a window of size W, with a default of W = 64. The right edge of the window represents the highest sequence number, N, so far received for a valid packet. For any packet with a sequence number in the range from $N - W + 1$ to N that has been correctly received (i.e., properly authenticated), the corresponding slot in the window is marked.

Inbound processing proceeds as follows when a packet is received:

1. If the received packet falls within the window and is new, the MAC is checked. If the packet is authenticated, the corresponding slot in the window is marked.

2. If the received packet is to the right of the window and is new, the MAC is checked. If the packet is authenticated, the window is advanced so that this sequence number is the right edge of the window, and the corresponding slot in the window is marked.

3. If the received packet is to the left of the window or if authentication fails, the packet is discarded; this is an easily audited event.

Message Authentication Code

The MAC calculation takes place over the entire enclosed TPC segment plus the authentication header. When this IP packet is received at the destination, the same calculation is performed using the same key. If the calculated MAC equals the value of the received MAC, then the packet is assumed authentic.

Privacy and Authentication

The encapsulating security payload (ESP) provides confidentiality services, including confidentiality of message content and limited traffic flow confidentiality. As an optional feature, ESP can also provide the same

Figure 11-4
IPSec ESP format.

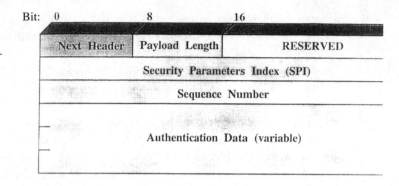

authentication services as AH. Figure 11-4 illustrates the format of an ESP packet. It contains the following fields:

- *Security Parameters Index (32 bits)*   This field identifies a security association.

- *Sequence Number (32 bits)*   A monotonically increasing counter value, this provides an antireplay function, as discussed for AH.

- *Payload Data (variable)*   This is a transport-level segment (transport mode) or IP packet (tunnel mode) that is protected by encryption.

- *Padding (0 to 255 bytes)*   The purpose of this field is discussed later.

- *Pad Length (8 bits)*   This field indicates the number of pad bytes immediately preceding it.

- *Next Header (8 bits)*   This field identifies the type of data contained in the Payload Data field by identifying the first header in that payload (for example, an extension header in IM or an upper-layer protocol such as TCP).

- *Authentication Data (variable)*   This is a variable-length field (must be an integral number of 32-bit words) that contains the integrity check value computed over the ESP packet minus the Authentication Data field.

Encryption and Authentication Algorithms

The Payload Data, Padding, Pad Length, and Next Header fields are encrypted by the ESP service. If the algorithm used to encrypt the payload requires cryptographic synchronization data, such as an initialization vector (IV), then this data may be carried explicitly at the beginning of the Payload Data field. If included, an IV is usually not encrypted, although it is often referred to as being part of the ciphertext.

The current specification dictates that a compliant implementation must support DES. A number of other algorithms have been assigned identifiers and could therefore be used for encryption. These include:

- Three-key triple DES
- RC5
- IDEA
- Three-key triple IDEA
- CAST
- Blowfish

As with AH, ESP supports the use of a MAC, using HMAC.

Padding

The Padding field serves several purposes:

1. If an encryption algorithm requires the plaintext to be a multiple of some number of bytes (e.g., the multiple of a single block for a block cipher), the Padding field is used to expand the plaintext (consisting of the Payload Data, Padding, Pad Length, and Next Header fields) to the required length.

2. The ESP format requires that the Pad Length and Next Header fields be right-aligned within a 32-bit word. Equivalently, the ciphertext must be an integer multiple of 32 bits. The Padding field is used to ensure this alignment.

3. Additional padding may be added to provide partial traffic flow confidentiality by concealing the actual length of the payload.

Certificate Authorities—Verifying Third-Party Identities

IPSec has another component that is not generally interoperable among vendors but is important to the overall security solution. The final component of the IPSec-compliant secure VPN is called a *certificate authority,* or better known as the *CA.* The CA is a trusted third party—someone whose identity you can already prove and who can vouch for the identity of people with whom you are trying to communicate. Think of the CA as a bank or your priest or minister, one who knows you well and can vouch for you and other people.

In the world of online verification, the CA's software issues certificates tying three things together:

1. Identity verification; anything that uniquely identifies that server to you in a meaningful way—like Social Security number or name and address,

2. The public key that a person uses to sign his or her identity to online documents

3. The CA's public key that is used to sign and authenticate the entire package

The CA is the defense against "man-in-the-middle" spoofing attacks against key exchanges. Whenever an exchange is initiated with someone, the CA must sign it with its digital signature. It is possible to check the signature against the one on record with the CA (just like a bank). They have to match. The CA's signature is highly public and useful, thwarting attempts at forgery. The CA's signature is normally protected by very strong encryption, again thwarting counterfeit signatures.

ISAKMP/Oakley provides for third-party verification using the established industry standard X.509 format certificates. Other formats exist and are supported—hence the disagreement amongst vendors about CAs. When someone initiates the ISAKMP/Oakley exchange with you, or responds to one you have initiated, that person has to sign the data first sent with his or her digital signature. You then connect with the CA through a specialized X.500 server designed for this task and request a certificate belonging to that person. You first check the certificate signature against your copy of the CA's signature to make sure the CA really issued it. If it checks out, you then look up the signature attached to the certificate for the person you have initiated the exchange with, and check the data that was just signed. It is really a chain of trust that begins with the trust in your CA's signature, which is then used to verify someone else's. The whole process is done in the background and automatically.

Equipment Registration (aka Initial Certification)

Certification is the registration and identification of VPN components. It requires establishing well-defined secrets between a centrally controlled certification authority and any VPN gateway unit protecting a site. A VPN should not be "easy to join" to unwanted entities that may want to connect as members. Easy-to-guess passwords are to be avoided. Adding new gateways, sans encryption, requires hardware tokens, because they can be used to load secure information, offline, to the gateway. After the initial secret information is transferred, the rest of the certification process should be automated and secure (encrypted and signed).

IPSEC Tunneling vs. Network Address Translation (NAT)

Firewalls provide control or prohibit access to the internal, private network. Controlled access is useful for clients, customers, and partners needing access to a particular system on the inside of the security perimeter at particular hours during the day.

Many firewall products provide a network address translation (NAT) service, which is similar to the IPSec's tunneling feature. There are some commonalties but they are also critically different. Private networks use NAT exclusively to allow using nodes with illegal addresses to communicate with an external network, whereas IPSec tunneling is used to allow nodes in private networks on either side of a public network to communicate with each other. NAT does hide source addresses by replacing them with that of the firewall device itself. It only excludes nodes on the public network from initiating communications with them, and it prevents nodes on any network outside the firewall from being able to initiate communications with the hidden node. With IPSec tunneling, the addresses are hidden from the bulk of the public network, but a node on another part of the secure VPN can still initiate communications right through the public network. NAT, therefore, is a single-point process at the firewall itself, while IPSec tunneling takes place at two tunnel endpoints. NAT can hide addresses but excludes external nodes from communication. Tunneling still allows external nodes to initiate communications.

The technologies are not competitive. NAT services in a network that also provides a secure VPN will allow users to surf external Web sites. Only when the need is for secure communications end-to-end, between two private networks and right through an insecure public network, does IPSec tunneling work.

Joint Technology

The need for firewalls does not go away with the advent of IPSec, even if IPSec is on every computer in an organization. Internet firewalls enforce an enterprise network security policy and are part of a perimeter defense. IPSec on every desktop provides for privacy and authentication, but it does not ensure that the corporate network security policy is enforced (what services are allowed, when to use virus scanning, etc.). Firewalls to enforce a policy that requires private links between networks (sites) even if desktop users cannot or do not use encrypted connections.

Access Control

Encryption without effective and efficient access control (firewall devices) may be a poor VPN solution. Two issues of importance in evaluating the strength of access control features are the operating system and its methodology:

- *Operating system*   Software solutions are based on well-known operating systems, such as UNIX or NT. Hacking methods are also based on the same principles. Bugs and holes are well known on the Internet, and hackers use them regularly to attack the system. Hardware operating systems are less well known to the average hacker. They employ real-time operating systems and therefore are immune to the security holes of their software counterparts.

- *Methodology*   The effectiveness of a firewall is linked to the scope of its inspection technique. Access control systems must be able to analyze all levels of incoming and outgoing data, including the content payload itself.

VPN solutions should provide both of the above capabilities to be sufficiently secure.

Performance

Networking environments have developed with increasing rapidity. As such, the speed of communications represents one of the most significant areas of development. Effective VPN solutions must operate at true wire speeds. Those that do not become a bottleneck. The performance issue becomes more critical when complex encryption algorithms are used, such as 3DES or RC5. Hardware-based solutions, which are dedicated to the task of generating and processing encryption algorithms, may be better suited to coping with the longer encryption algorithms and may provide a communications infrastructure better adapted to future growth.

Basic requirements of a VPN solution may include two other criteria:

1. *No single point of failure* This characteristic is achieved through incorporation of automatic gateways (redundancy) into a VPN. A VPN should distribute security functions throughout the network. There should be no centralized session or key distribution authority, and each gateway should initiate its sessions and generate its own keys.

2. *Flexible management* A VPN management structure should allow for centralized and regional control and auditing. Network managers need to determine the control matrix appropriate for their network. In this way, all management traffic will be secure. Appendix P provides a comparison of management features for various VPNs on the market, as well as deployment options.

Wrap-Up

The driving force for the acceptance and deployment of secure IP is the need for business and government users to connect their private WAN/LAN infrastructure to the Internet for (1) access to Internet services and (2) use of the Internet as a component of the WAN transport system. Users need to isolate their networks and at the same time send and receive traffic over the Internet. The authentication and privacy mechanisms of secure IP provide the basis for a security strategy.

Because IP security mechanisms have been defined, independent of their use with either the current IP or IM, deployment of these mechanisms does not depend on deployment of IPv6. Indeed, it is likely that we will see widespread use of secure IP features long before IPv6 becomes popular, because the need for IP-level security is greater than the need for the added functions that IPv6 provides compared to the current IP.

IPSec provides managers with a standardized means of implementing security for VPNs. Furthermore, all of the encryption and authentication algorithms, and security protocols, used in IPSec are well studied and have been time-tested. Therefore, the user can be confident that the IPSec facility indeed provides strong security.

IPSec can be implemented in routers or firewalls owned and operated by the organization. This gives the network manager complete control over security aspects of the VPN, which is much desired. The alternative is to seek a solution from a service provider. A service provider can simplify the job of planning, implementing, and maintaining Internet-based VPNs for secure access to network resources and secure communication between sites.

CHAPTER 12

Biometric Countermeasures

Introduction

Biometric countermeasures have at their heart a biometric system. They have been forwarded by both commercial and government groups as an answer to complete enterprise security. At the very least, biometric countermeasures can be viewed as effective secondary measures. At the worst, they can be viewed as intrusions on the privacy of individuals. In the United States, in general, biometric technologies have not enjoyed commercial success. They have, however, enjoyed serious use by law enforcement and DoD agencies. Biometrics has been accepted more comfortably in Europe, especially when integrated with smart-card technologies. In Chapter 12, we identify biometric methodologies, compare them qualitatively, and report on future directions.

Biometrics has a supporting language of its own. The Glossary has a special section devoted to biometric definitions, sourced from public documents available from the Biometric Consortium (www.biometric.org) and the International Computer Associations Biometric Consortium Library (www.icsa.net). Gary Roethenbaugh, the ICSA Biometrics Editor and Industry Analyst, was another important source of information. His *Biometrics Explained* focuses on users of biometric technology and is highly recommended reading.[1] Perhaps the best text on this subject is *Biometrics: Personal Identification in Network Society*, edited by Anil Jain, Ruud Bolle, and Sharath Pankanti. Joseph P. Campbell, Chair of the Biometric Consortium, and Jim L. Wayman, Director of the National Biometric Test Center at San Jose State University, are among the many world-class contributors to this work.[2] It is highly recommended.

A Little History

Commercial advancements began for biometrics in the 1970s. During this period, a system called "Identimat" was installed in a number of top secret sites to control access. This measured the shape of the hand and looked particularly at finger length. Production of Identimat ceased in the late 1980s. Yet its use pioneered the application of hand geometry and set a path for biometric technologies as a whole.

Running parallel to the development of hand technology, fingerprint biometrics was making progress in the 1960s and 1970s. During this time a number of companies were involved in automatic identification of fingerprints as an assist to law enforcement. The manual process of matching prints against criminal records was laborious and used far too much manpower. In the late 1960s the FBI began to check fingerprints automatically, and by mid-1970s, it had installed a number of automatic fingerprint systems. The role of biometrics in law enforcement has mushroomed since then, and Automated Fingerprint Identification Systems (AFIS) are used by a significant number of police forces throughout the globe. Fingerprinting is now exploring a range of civilian markets, with limited success.

The first system to analyze the unique pattern of the retina was introduced in the mid-1980s. Dr. John Daughman at Cambridge University paved the way for iris technology. Today's speaker verification biometrics has roots in technological achievements of the 1970s, while biometrics such as signature verification and facial recognition are relative newcomers to the industry.[3]

Bringing a biometric product to market and proving its operational performance is an expensive and time-consuming process that is necessary before a system can become fully operational. However, such systems are now in place and are beginning to prove themselves across a range of diverse applications.

Opportunities

A number of situations require an identification of a person in our society. Have I seen this applicant before? Is this person an employee of this company? Is this individual a citizen of this country? Many situations will even warrant identification of a person at the far end of a communication channel. The Internet has made this latter type of identification a difficult problem.

Accurate identification of a person can deter crime and fraud, streamline business processes, and save critical resources. MasterCard estimates of credit card fraud reach $450 million per annum, which includes charges made on lost and stolen credit cards. Unobtrusive positive personal identification of the legitimate ownership of a credit card at the point of sale would greatly reduce credit card fraud, as about $1 billion worth of cellular telephone calls are made by cellular bandwidth thieves, many of which are made from stolen personal identification numbers (PINs) and/or cellular telephones. An identification of the legitimate ownership of the cellular telephones would prevent many thieves from stealing bandwidth. A reliable method of authenticating legitimate ownership of an ATM card would greatly reduce ATM related fraud of approximately $3 billion annually.[4]

A positive method of identifying the rightful check payee would also reduce the billions of dollars misappropriated through fraudulent encashment of checks each year. A method of positive authentication of each system login would eliminate illegal break-ins into traditionally secure computers. The United States Immigration and Naturalization Service stipulates that it could each day detect and deter about 3000 illegal immigrants crossing the Mexican border without delaying legitimate entry into the United States if there were a quick way of establishing positive personal identification.

First Principles

Biometrics is a group of high-level security technologies, representing niche security systems. The key element of this technology is its ability to establish identity and reinforce security—an ideal secondary countermeasure for computer systems.

The term *biometrics*, strictly speaking, refers to a science involving the statistical analysis of biological characteristics. Biometric countermeasures are concerned with technologies that *analyze human characteristics for security purposes*. The statistical science of biometrics continues in the background and should be treated separately from biometric countermeasures. A biometric is a *unique,* measurable characteristic or trait for *automatically recognizing* or verifying the identity of a human being.

Biometric technologies are concerned with the physical parts of the human body or the personal traits of human beings. It is important to note the term *automatic* in the above definition. This essentially means that a biometric technology must recognize or verify a human characteristic quickly and *automatically, in real time*. The most common *physical biometrics* are the eye, face, fingerprints, hand, and voice, while signature and typing rhythm are *behavioral biometrics*.

Associating an identity with an individual is called *personal identification*. Resolving the identity of a person can be categorized into two fundamentally distinct types of problems with differing inherent complexities: (1) *verification* and (2) *recognition* (more popularly known as *identification*). Verification (*authentication*) refers to the confirmation or denial of a person's claimed identity. (Am I who I claim to be?)

Identification (who am I?) refers to the problem of establishing a subject's identity—either from a set of already known identities (called a "closed identification" problem) or otherwise (an "open identification" problem). The term *positive personal identification* typically refers (in both verification as well as identification context) to identification of a person with high certainty. The term *identification* is used either to refer to the general problem of identifying individuals (identification and authentication) or to refer to the specific identification of an individual from a database, which involves a one-to-many search.[5]

Identification Methods

In a broad sense, establishing an identity (either in a verification context or an identification context) is a very challenging and difficult problem. An identity is woven into the fabric of everything that a person represents and believes. Also, an engineering approach to the (abstract) problem of authentication of a personal identity is to reduce it to the authentication of a concrete item related to the person.

Biometric products are often said to have the highest levels of security. There are three stages of security with biometrics at the pinnacle:

- The third and highest level of security is biometric technology—*something that you do* and *something that you are*.

- The second level of security is *something that you know*, such as a password to access a computer or a PIN to access funds at a bank teller machine. ATMs actually use a combination of something that you have (ATM card) and something that you know (PIN) to establish an identity.

- The lowest level of security is *something that you possess*, such as an ID badge including a photograph or a personal key to a house or car.

Traditional approaches of identification using *possession* as a means invites lost, stolen, forgotten, or misplaced items. Further, once in control of the identifying possession, by definition, any other "unauthorized" person can abuse the privileges of the authorized user.

Knowledge as an identity authentication mechanism introduces the frailties of human memory: difficult-to-remember passwords/PINs versus easily recallable passwords/PINs (e.g., pet's name, spouse's birthday). Prevalent methods of identification based on possession and knowledge are keys, employee badge, drivers license, ATM and credit cards, easily guessed by adversaries.

It has been estimated that about 25 percent of the people using ATM cards write their ATM PINs on the ATM card itself,[6] thereby defeating the possession/knowledge combination as a means of identification. As a result, these techniques cannot distinguish between an authorized person and an impostor who acquires the knowledge/possession, falsely enabling the access privileges of the authorized person.

Another approach to positive identification has been to reduce the problem of identification to identification of the physical characteristics of the person. The characteristics could be either a person's physiological traits, for example, fingerprints, hand geometry, or behavioral characteristics, such as voice and signature. This method of identification of a person based on his or her physiological/behavioral characteristics is *biometrics*.

The primary advantage of such an identification method over the methods of identification using something that you possess or something that you know is that a biometric identifier cannot be misplaced or forgotten; it represents a tangible component of "something that you are." While biometric techniques are not an identification panacea, when combined with the other methods of identification, they are beginning to provide very powerful tools for problems requiring positive identification.

Biometric Measurements

Any human physiological or behavioral characteristic could be a biometric provided it has the following desirable properties: (1) *universality,* which means that every person should have the characteristic, (2) *uniqueness,* which indicates that no two persons should be the same in terms of the characteristic, (3) *permanence,* which means that the characteristic should be invariant with time, and (4) *collectability,* which indicates that the characteristic can be measured quantitatively.[7]

In practice, there are some other important requirements: (1) *performance,* referring to the achievable identification accuracy, the resource requirements to achieve an acceptable identification accuracy, and the working or environmental factors that affect the identification accuracy, (2) *acceptability,* which indicates to what extent people are willing to accept the biometric system, and (3) *circumvention,* which refers to how one might fool the system by fraudulent techniques.[8]

TABLE 12-1 Comparison of Biometric Technologies.

Biometrics	Universality	Uniqueness	Permanence	Collectability	Performance	Acceptability	Circumvention
Face	High	Low	Medium	High	Low	High	Low
Fingerprint	Medium	High	High	Medium	High	Medium	High
Hand Geometry	Medium	Medium	Medium	High	Medium	Medium	Medium
Keystrokes	Low	Low	Low	Medium	Low	Medium	Medium
Hand Vein	Medium	Medium	Medium	Medium	Medium	Medium	High
ins	High	High	High	Medium	High	Low	High
Retinal Scan	High	High	Medium	Low	High	Low	High
Signature	Low	Low	Low	High	Low	High	Low
Voice Print	Medium	Low	Low	Medium	Low	High	Low
Facial Thermograms	High	High	Low	High	Medium	High	High
Odor	High	High	High	Low	Low	Medium	Low
DNA	High	High	High	Low	High	Low	Low
Gait	Medium	Low	Low	High	Low	High	Medium
Ear	Medium	Medium	High	Medium	Medium	High	Medium

Table 12-1 compares biometric technologies based Anil Jain, Ruud Bolle, and Sharath Pankanti experience.[9] No single biometric technology is expected to effectively satisfy the needs of all identification (authentication) applications. A number of biometrics have been proposed, researched, and evaluated for identification (authentication) applications. Each biometric has its strengths and limitations; and accordingly, each biometric appeals to a particular identification (authentication) application.

Biometric Procedures

All biometric products essentially operate in a similar way. First, a system captures a sample of the biometric characteristic. Unique features are then extracted by the system and converted into a mathematical code. This sample is then stored as the *biometric template* for that person. The template may reside in the biometric system itself, or in any other form of memory storage, such as a computer database, a smart card, or a bar code.

There may also be a *trigger*, or a means of tying the template to the person. Here a PIN can be given to the end user, which is keyed in to access the template. Or a card holding the template may simply be inserted into a card reader. Whatever happens, the end user interacts with the biometric system for a second time to have his or her identity checked. A new biometric sample is then taken and then compared to the template. If the template and the new sample match, the end user is granted access. This is then the basic premise of biometrics: A *sample of a person's biometric data* is captured, and the biometric system decides if *it matches another sample.*[10]

Biometric systems do not guarantee 100 percent accuracy. Human beings are inconsistent, and both physical and behavioral characteristics can change slightly over time. For example, a fingerprint can be scarred and a signature may acquire irregularities as a person ages. Furthermore, the way a human being interacts with a machine can never be as constant as the machine itself. Stress, general health, working and environmental conditions, and time pressures all effectively conspire to make humans inconsistent. This is especially true in product field trials.

The biometric system must allow for these subtle changes, so a *threshold* is set. This can take the form of an accuracy score. Comparison between the template and new sample must exceed the system's threshold before a match is recorded. If the new biometric sample is sufficiently similar to the previously stored template, the system will determine that the two do in fact match. If not, the system will not record a match and will not identify the end user.

All biometric systems use the four-stage procedure of *capture, extraction, comparison, and matching*—but different methods and techniques to deal with the human factor are introduced. At the heart of the biometric system resides a proprietary element—*the engine*—which extracts and processes the biometric data. This may apply an algorithm or an artificial neural network. It extracts the data, creates a template, and computes whether the data from the template and the new sample match.[11]

In summary, biometrics operates using the following four-stage procedure:

- *Capture* A physical or behavioral sample is captured by the system during enrollment.

- *Extraction*   Unique data is extracted from the sample and a template is created.
- *Comparison*   The template is compared with a new sample.
- *Match/Nonmatch*   The system decides if the features extracted from the new sample are a match or a nonmatch.

Identification, Recognition, and Verification

At this stage a distinction must be made among the terms identification, recognition, and verification that constantly circulate throughout the biometric community. Both *identification* and *recognition* can be grouped together. These terms refer to the one-to-many process. A sample is presented to the biometric system during enrollment. The system then attempts to find out to whom the sample belongs by comparing the sample with a database of samples in the expectation of finding a match. *Verification* is a one-to-one process, in which the biometric system seeks to verify identity. Here, a single biometric sample is matched against another. A person enrolls and a sample is captured; afterwards, a new sample is captured and the biometric system compares the new sample with one previously stored. If the two match, the machine effectively confirms that the person is the valid claimant.

It must be remembered that the same four-stage process of capture, extraction, comparison, and match/nonmatch applies equally to identification, recognition, and verification. The only real difference is that identification and recognition involve matching a sample against a database of many, while verification involves matching a sample against a database of one.

False Rejection and False Acceptance

As a biometric system is put to use, it will either match or not match the extracted biometric data. The biometrics industry has for a number of years used two performance measurements to rank the level of matching accuracy, focusing on the system's ability to allow access to authorized users and deny access to those who are unauthorized. These are known as the *false rejection rate (FRR)* and *false acceptance rate (FAR)*. To mystify the process even further, the FRR is sometimes referred to as the Type I error rate, while the FAR is the Type II error rate.

The *false rejection rate is concerned with the number of instances an authorized individual is falsely rejected by the system.* The *false acceptance rate* refers to the *number of instances a nonauthorized individual is falsely accepted by the system.* Both rates are expressed as a percentage using the following simple calculations:

FRR:

$$\frac{\text{Number of false rejections}}{\text{Number of authorized recognition or verification attempts}} \times 100$$

FAR:

$$\frac{\text{Number of false acceptances}}{\text{Number of impostor recognition or verification attempts}} \times 100$$

Less frequently used is a rate known as the *equal error rate (EER)*, which is the point at which the FRR and FAR meet or cross over. For example, a system with an FRR and FAR of 1 percent will also have an EER of 1 percent. The use of false rejection and false acceptance rates has led to a significant amount of debate within the biometrics industry, particularly concerning the statistical significance of such a simplified calculation. The above formulas are perhaps surprisingly simple given the large number of variables that may be presented to the biometric system. For example, the performance of a biometric system, and therefore the FRR and FAR, may be affected by:

- *Environmental conditions* Such factors as extreme temperature and humidity can affect a system's performance.

- *The age, gender, ethnic background and occupation of the user* For example, callused hands from manual work can affect the performance of fingerprint systems.

- *The beliefs, desires, and intentions of the user* If a user does not wish to interact with the system, then performance will be affected.

- *The physical makeup of the user* A user with no limbs cannot use hand- or finger-based biometrics.

Each of the above factors can influence false acceptance and rejection rates. These rates, when published by biometric vendors to illustrate performance, can be the result of a laboratory test under *controlled conditions*. Performance claims must therefore be treated with care. As the above variables are introduced, the rates will be adversely affected. False rejection and acceptance rates must also be treated with care because they can be calculated using a *one-try* or *three-try* method, depending on the nature of the biometric application and the type of biometric system being put to use. This suggests that a user may either be given a single attempt or three attempts at comparing the new sample with the template. Common sense dictates that if three attempts are used, this will improve the false rejection rate.

The other inherent problem in the objectivity of the FRR and FAR is that the rates can be manually configured. For example, a bank will require a very high level of security at the door of its main vault. The bank may therefore decide that the false acceptance rate must be less than 0. 1 percent. In other words, the system might grant unauthorized access for one in a thousand instances. The bank may be even more insistent and require a false acceptance rate of 0.001 percent (1 in 100,000 instances). A biometric vendor can alter the system's FAR so that these rates can be achieved. However, to do this, the false rejection rate will suffer as a consequence. The end result is that the FRR and FAR are not a statistically significant means of evaluating performance, being far too simplistic. The only real advantage is that they allow a basic understanding about a product's performance. If being used as a guide to performance, it is essential that the false rejection rate and false acceptance rate are considered in unison and that the circumstances of the application are noted.[12]

A Biometric Taxonomy

A useful method of reconciling the various circumstances that affect performance has been put forward by James Wayman of San Jose State University. His biometric taxonomy recognizes that the performance of a biometric system depends on the application for which the system is being used and a host of contributing circumstances. Taxonomy is an invaluable tool in assessing the nature of an application. It helps users and implementers understand that all applications have differences and can affect the performance of the system in entirely different ways. Each of the partitions shown in Table 12-2 helps to classify the role of biometrics within a given application.[13]

TABLE 12-2

San Jose State University Biometric Taxonomy.

Cooperative versus Noncooperative User
Overt versus Covert Biometric System
Habituated versus Nonhabituated User
Supervised versus Unsupervised User
Standard Environment versus Nonstandard Environment Source

Applying additional partitions can extend the taxonomy—when circumstances allow. For example:

Private versus Public—Whether the application is private and self-contained or open to the public

Educated versus Noneducated—Whether the user is fully educated in the workings of the system

In summary, biometrics typically performs better in environments where:

1. The end user is cooperative.
2. The biometric system is overt, and the end user is habituated and familiar with it.
3. The end user is supervised by an expert.
4. The system operates in a standard environment not subject to climatic change.
5. The application is private, and end users are fully educated about the system's operation.

Technologies

Biometric systems now come in many shapes and sizes, ranging from hardware, software, OEMs, software development kits, or complete solutions. Systems may be marketed and sold by vendors directly or through various distribution channels, such as systems integrators, strategic partners, or value-added resellers. All biometric systems have the principles of capture, extraction, comparison, and matching in common. Yet biometric technologies focus on different parts of the human makeup, so the workings of each technology and each vendor's specific system will differ. This section treats the operation of each biometric technology within the four stages of capture, extraction, comparison, and matching.

Eye

Biometrics that analyze the eye are generally thought to offer the highest levels of accuracy. They can be divided into two specific technologies: *iris* and *retina* biometrics.

Iris   The iris is the colored ring of textured tissue that surrounds the pupil of the eye. Each iris is a unique structure featuring a complex pattern. This can be a combination of specific characteristics known as corona, crypts, filaments, freckles, pits, radial furrows, and striations. It is claimed that artificial duplication of the iris is virtually impossible because of its unique properties and that no two irises are alike. The iris is closely connected to the human brain and is said to be one of the first parts of the body to decay after death. It is therefore very unlikely that an artificial iris could be re-created or that a dead iris could be used fraudulently to bypass the biometric system.

The iris recognition process is as follows:[14]

CAPTURE   A black-and-white video camera captures an image of the iris in a well-lit environment. Contact lenses do not interfere with image capture. Sunglasses and glasses, however, do affect the capture process (Figure 12-1).[15]

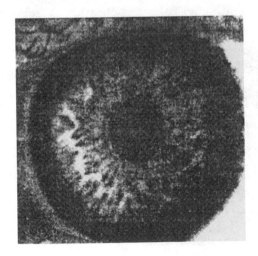

Figure 12-1
Identification based on iris. The visual texture of iris could be used for positive personal identification.

EXTRACTION Unique features of the iris from the captured sample are extracted by the biometric engine. This is then converted into a unique mathematical code and stored as a template.

COMPARISON One-to-one verification or one-to-many identification is then performed, resulting in either a match or nonmatch.

Retina The retina is composed of light receptors and a layer of blood vessels situated at the back of the eye. The layer of blood vessels is the primary focus of biometric interest. As with the iris, the retina forms a unique pattern and begins to decay quickly after death. *Retina biometrics is generally regarded as the most secure biometric method.* Unauthorized access to a retina system is virtually impossible. A precise enrollment procedure is necessary, which involves precise orientation of the eye to achieve an optimum reading. However, with a lack of false acceptance, this may increase the probability of false rejections being made by authorized end users.

The process of retinal eye scanning is as follows:[16]

CAPTURE The eye is positioned in front of the system, approximately 3 inches from an eyepiece. The end user must view a series of markers through the eyepiece and align them. When this is done, the eye is sufficiently oriented for the scanner to capture the retina pattern. An area known as the *fovea*, situated in the center of the retina, is scanned, and the unique pattern of the blood vessels is captured (Figure 12-2).[17]

EXTRACTION The biometric engine maps the position of the blood vessels; a unique mathematical representation is stored as a template.

Figure 12-2
Identification based on retina scan is perceived to be the most secure biometric for authenticating identity.

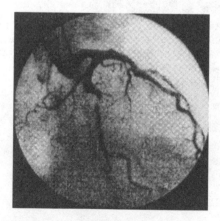

COMPARISON One-to-one verification is performed. The capture process is repeated and the new sample and template are compared, resulting in either a match or nonmatch.

Face

Identifying an individual by analyzing his or her face is a complex process usually requiring sophisticated artificial intelligence and machine learning techniques. A number of biometric vendors are actively involved in marketing systems using either standard video or thermal imaging to capture facial images. The face is a key component in the way human beings remember and recognize each other. Artificial intelligence programming is needed to simulate human interpretation of faces. People change over time. Facial hair, glasses, and the position of the head can affect the way a biometric system can match one face with another. Machine learning is important to adapt to these changes and accurately compare new samples with previously recorded templates. Therefore, face recognition technologies are highly dependent on the extraction and comparison engine. To prevent an individual from circumventing a system, this core element of the biometric system must be capable of accurately extracting unique characteristics.

The process of face recognition is as follows:[18]

CAPTURE Standard video techniques use a facial image, or a collection of images, captured by a video camera. The precise position of the user's face and the surrounding lighting conditions may affect the system's performance. The complete facial image is captured, and a number of points on the face are then mapped. For example, the position of the eyes, mouth, and nostrils may be plotted so that a unique template is built. Alternatively, a three-dimensional map of the face may be created from the captured image. Thermal imaging analyzes heat caused by the flow of blood within the face. A thermal infrared-sensitive camera captures the hidden, heat-generated pattern of blood vessels underlying the skin. Because infrared cameras are used to capture facial images, lighting is not important and systems can capture images in the dark. However, such cameras are significantly more expensive than standard daylight units. (See Figure 12-3.)[19]

EXTRACTION A proprietary algorithm or neural network within the biometric engine converts the facial image sample into a pattern and then a unique mathematical code. This is stored as a template.

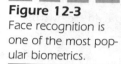

Figure 12-3
Face recognition is one of the most popular biometrics.

COMPARISON One-to-one verification is the most common method of comparison. However, certain systems are capable of one-to-many identification. A new facial image is captured and compared with a previously stored template or templates. This results in either a match or non-match.

Finger

Fingerprinting analyzes the unique patterns on the tips of our fingers, and finger geometry incorporates at the shape of the finger rather than the print itself.

AFIS

Automated Fingerprint Identification Systems (AFIS) match a single fingerprint against a database of fingerprints. This can be applied in law enforcement or civilian applications. For law enforcement, prints are collected from crime scenes, known as latent prints, or are taken from criminal suspects when they are arrested. In civilian applications, such as large-scale national identity schemes, prints may be captured by placing a finger on a scanner or by electronically scanning inked prints on paper. An AFIS can scan and capture fingerprint data from paper-based prints and then match the captured data against a database. A method of capture presenting an inked or latent print to the system obviously differs from that explained above. This is not about verifying identity, where an individual's characteristics are captured and matched by some form of a human/machine interaction. AFIS is concerned with a one-to-many match rather than a one-to-one match, since it checks to see if a sample is held on file as opposed to verifying that one sample matches with another. Yet the principles behind the two methods are similar. The data from a fingerprint sample is captured and extracted; then it is compared against the database of samples to determine if there is a match.[20]

Fingerprints Background

Fingerprint biometrics is largely regarded as an accurate method of biometric identification and verification. Most one-to-many AFIS and one-to-one fingerprint systems analyze small unique marks on the fingerprint—which are known as *minutiae*. These may be defined as fingerprint ridge endings or bifurcations (branches made by fingerprint ridges). Some fingerprint systems also analyze tiny sweat pores on the fingerprint, which, in the same way as minutiae, are uniquely positioned, differentiating one person from another. Other aspects of the fingerprint that can be analyzed are the density or the distance between fingerprint ridges (Figure 12-4.)[21]

Certain conditions may affect the fingerprints of individuals. For example, dirty, dry, or cracked prints will all reduce image capture. Age, gender, and ethnic background are also found to have an impact on the quality of fingerprints. The way a user interacts with a finger scanner is another important consideration. By pressing too hard on the scanner surface, for example, an image can be distorted. Vendors are addressing these problems so that scanners are ergonomically designed to optimize fingerprint capture.

Figure 12-4
Fingerprint patterns.

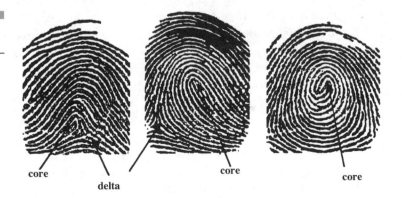

Fingerprint technologies can be divided into one-to-one verification and one-to-many identification technologies, such as AFIS. Both of these techniques share common principles and practices. However, to avoid confusion, certain distinctions must be made. AFIS technology, for example, uses a process known as *binning*, predominantly taking place in law enforcement rather than civilian applications. Here, fingerprints are categorized by characteristics such as arches, loops, and whorls and held in smaller, separate databases according to their category. Binning refines the use of AFIS in law enforcement. Searches can be made against particular bins, thus speeding up the response time and accuracy of the AFIS search. Traditionally, the binning process was cumbersome, with trained staff manually selecting characteristics and binning prints. Over the past few years, however, technology has developed to perform binning automatically by the AFIS itself.

A key difference among the various fingerprint technologies on the market is the means of capturing a print. One-to-one fingerprint verification systems use four main capture techniques: optical, thermal or tactile, capacitance, and ultrasound. One-to-many AFIS products capture prints using the optical technique or by electronically scanning fingerprint images from paper prints.

Fingerprint Verification

The process of one-to-one fingerprint verification is as follows:[22]

CAPTURE The optical image technique typically involves generating a light source, which is refracted through a prism. Users place a finger on a glass surface, known as a platen. Light shines on the fingerprint, and the impression made by the print is captured. Tactile or thermal techniques use sophisticated silicon chip technology to acquire fingerprint data. A user places a finger on the chip sensor, which senses heat or pressure from the finger. Fingerprint data is then captured. Capacitance silicon sensors measure electrical charges and produce an electrical signal when a finger is placed on the sensor surface. The core element of capacitance techniques, as with tactile and thermal methods, is the chip sensor. Using capacitance, the miniature peaks and troughs of fingerprint ridges and valleys are analyzed. An electrical signal occurs when fingerprint ridges contact the sensor. No signal is generated by the valleys. This variance in electrical charge produces an image of the fingerprint. Ultrasound image capture uses sound waves beyond the limit of human hearing. A finger is placed on a scanner, and acoustic waves are used to measure the density of the fingerprint pattern.

Extraction   The biometric engine extracts fingerprint data contained in the print. A unique mathematical representation of the print is then stored as a template.

COMPARISON   Fingerprint systems are usually capable of both one-to-one verification and one-to-many identification. Although performing identification, these are not dedicated AFIS systems. During the comparison process a new sample is compared with a template or templates. This results in either a match or nonmatch.

Fingerprint Identification/AFIS

The process of one-to-many automatic fingerprint identification is as follows:[23]

CAPTURE   When enrolling individuals, the live-scan capture process is the same as the optical technique described above. Law enforcement AFIS systems, also known as booking stations, capture all 10 fingerprints. A civil AFIS, however, need not capture all fingerprints and can operate effectively using one or two. Latent prints, those taken from the scene of a crime, or ink prints on paper can also be captured by the AFIS using a flatbed scanner.

EXTRACTION   The process of binning fingerprints refines the extraction process. Minutiae data is extracted and is stored as a template on a database.

COMPARISON   A new sample, captured by live-scan, latent, or paper scanning techniques, is compared against the database of prints. If binning has taken place, the comparison will be against the bin that holds similar features as the newly presented print. This results in either a match or nonmatch.

Finger Geometry

A handful of biometric vendors use finger geometry, or the measurement of finger shape, to determine identity. The geometry of one or two fingers may be analyzed depending on the biometric system being used. Measurements of unique finger characteristics, such as finger width, length, thickness, and knuckle size, are then taken. Finger geometry systems can perform one-to-one verification or one-to-many identification. The main advantage is that these systems are robust and can accommodate a high throughput of users.

The process of finger geometry is as follows:[24]

CAPTURE As with fingerprint verification, the method of capture depends on the system being used. There are currently two main techniques on the market. The first measures the geometry of two or more fingers. A camera takes a three-dimensional measurement when an end user places the index and middle finger of either the right or left hand onto a reader. The second technique requires a user to insert a finger into a tunnel so that three-dimensional measurements of the finger can be taken.

EXTRACTION The three-dimensional measurements are then extracted by the biometric engine, and a template is created.

COMPARISON The new 3-D sample is compared with the template. This results in either a match or nonmatch.

Hand

There are essentially three biometrics that look at characteristics of the hand. These are hand geometry, vein pattern analysis, and palm identification.

Hand Geometry

Hand geometry, as with finger geometry, takes a three-dimensional image of the hand and measures the shape and length of fingers and knuckles. It is one of the industry's torchbearers and has been in use for many years—predominantly for access control applications. Although hand geometry, like finger geometry, does not achieve the highest levels of accuracy, it is convenient to use. Again, the primary advantage is that large volumes of users can be processed quickly.

The process of hand geometry is as follows:[25]

CAPTURE A user places a hand on the hand reader, aligning fingers with specially positioned guides. A camera positioned above the hand captures an image. Three-dimensional measurements of selected points on the hand are then taken.

EXTRACTION The biometric engine extracts the 3D measurements into a unique mathematical identifier, and a template is created.

COMPARISON Hand geometry is predominantly used for one-to-many identification. A new 3D sample is compared against a database of templates. This results in either a match or nonmatch.

Vein

Development of a biometric that analyzes the distinctive pattern of veins in the back of the hand has been continuing for a number of years. The technique, known as *veincheck*, focuses on the unique pattern of blood vessels that form when a fist shape is made by the hand. The underlying veins structure, or vein tree, is captured using infrared light.

The basic veincheck process is as follows:[26]

CAPTURE The most accurate image is captured when the fist is clenched and skin on the back of the hand is taut. Infrared light is directed at the back of the hand, and the infrared camera is positioned above to capture the image. Any area of the hand where infrared light is reflected produces a light and indistinct image. A darker image is obtained for the vein pattern, as the veins absorb the infrared light. The system therefore acquires the unique vein tree pattern made by the darker veins.

EXTRACTION The vein tree data is extracted by the biometric engine and stored as a template.

COMPARISON New samples are compared with the template. This results in either a match or nonmatch.

Palm

Palm biometrics can be closely aligned with fingerprinting and, in particular, AFIS technology. As with fingerprints, ridges, valleys, and minutiae data are found on the palm. These are usually analyzed using optical capture techniques. This area of the biometrics industry is particularly focused on the law enforcement community, as latent palm prints are equally as useful in crime detection as latent fingerprints.

The basic palm identification process is as follows:[27]

CAPTURE Palm biometrics are predominantly used for one-to-many identification, and the capture process is essentially the same as the optical technique described for fingerprinting. A *palm print* system captures prints when a hand is placed on a scanner. Latent or ink palm prints can also be scanned into the system in the same way as an AFIS.

EXTRACTION Minutiae data is extracted by the biometric engine, and the palm print data is stored as a template on a database.

COMPARISON A newly captured print, by live-scan, latent, or paper scanning techniques, is compared against the database of prints. This results in either a match or nonmatch.

Signature

Signature biometrics is often referred to as *dynamic signature verification (DSV)* and detail the way we sign our names. It is the method of signing rather than the finished signature that is important. Thus DSV can be differentiated from the study of static signatures on paper. A number of characteristics can be extracted and measured by DSV. For example, the angle at which the pen is held, the time taken to sign, the velocity and acceleration of the signature, the pressure exerted when holding the pen, and the number of times the pen is lifted from the paper can all be extracted as unique behavioral characteristics. A signature cannot be re-created using these unique characteristics, making forgery extremely difficult. The other advantage of signature biometrics is that the signature is one of the most accepted means of asserting identity. It is also used in a number of situations to legally bind an individual, such as the signing of a contract. These factors have taken signature biometrics to a number of diverse markets and applications, ranging from checking welfare entitlement to document management and pen-based computing.

The basic DSV process is as follows:[28]

CAPTURE Signature data can be captured via a special sensitive pen or tablet. The pen-based method incorporates sensors inside the pen. The tablet method relies on the tablet to sense the unique signature characteristics. Another variation on these two techniques is *acoustic emission*, which measures the sound that a pen makes against paper. Typically, for all DSV systems, a user will sign a number of times so that the system can build a profile of the signing characteristics (Figure 12-5).[29]

Figure 12-5
Signature for
analysis.

EXTRACTION   The unique signature characteristics are extracted, coded by the biometric engine, and stored as a template.

COMPARISON   Signature biometrics typically use one-to-one verification. The new signature sample and template are compared. This results in either a match or nonmatch.

Voice

Voice biometrics focuses on the sound of the voice, not what is being said. It is therefore important to distinguish this technology from those that recognize words and act on commands. Voice recognition software may recognize words and type a letter or automate instructions given over the telephone. This is not a biometric technology. To avoid any confusion with *voice* recognition, the terms *speaker* recognition, verification, and identification should be used.

The unique sounds of a human voice are caused by resonance. The length of the vocal tract, the shape of the mouth, and the shape of the nasal cavities are all important. Sound is measured as affected by these specific characteristics. The technique of measuring the voice may use either text-independent or text-dependent methods. In other words, the voice may be captured with the user uttering any form of phrase, words, or numbers (text-independent) or by a specifically designated password combining phrases, words, or numbers (text-dependent). Voice biometrics is particularly useful for telephone-based applications. We are all used to speaking on the telephone, and biometric systems can be easily incorporated into private or public telephone networks. However, interference and other background noise over these networks can affect the performance of voice biometrics. Not only is this biometric popular, it is frequently used with mixed encryption technologies for privacy and authentication.

The basic voice biometric process is as follows:[30]

CAPTURE   Users speak into a microphone and utter a previously selected (text-dependent) or random (text-independent) phrase. This process is usually repeated a number of times to build a sufficient profile of the voice (see Figure 12-6).[31]

EXTRACTION   The biometric engine extracts the unique voice signal and a template is created.

Figure 12-6
Voice print. X-axis and Y-axis represent time and signal amplitude, respectively.

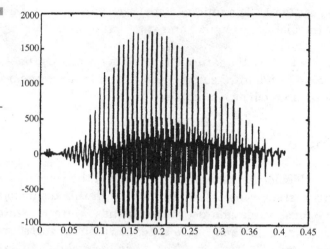

COMPARISON One-to-one verification is the preferred method. The user speaks into a microphone; the new voice sample and template are then compared. This results in either a match or nonmatch.

DNA

Analysis of human DNA, although now possible within 10 minutes, is not sufficiently automatic to rank DNA as a biometric technology. When technology advances so that DNA can be matched automatically, in real time, DNA may emerge as a significant contender against the existing biometric industry. However, DNA sampling is at present extremely intrusive and usually requires some form of tissue, blood, or other body sample. This method of capture will have to be refined. DNA is also very much entrenched in crime detection and will therefore continue to remain within the law enforcement arena.[32]

Keystroke

Keystroke biometrics, more commonly referred to as *keystroke dynamics*, analyzes typing rhythm. Keystroke dynamics are behavioral and evolve over time as users learn to type and develop their own unique typing pattern. The ultimate aim is to be able to continually check the identity of a person from their typing into a keyboard. Another use of this biometric is to crack random-number generation schemes based on mouse or key-stroke movements to generate a session key.[33]

Standards

Interoperability issues have plagued the introduction of effective biometric products into the market, translating to a problem in workable standards. There are two standards that have had significant impact on the biometrics industry. First, the FIPS PUB 190 entitled "Guideline for the Use of Advanced Authentication Technologies," September 1994, leads the way for introducing biometric devices, tokens, smart cards, and other practical devices. More recently, the DoD funded an interface specification, the Human Authentication-Application Program Interface (HA-API), which was aimed at improving operability and ease of implementation of biometric access controls for the U.S. government and DoD computers. Biometric manufacturers develop products within these guidelines and their own proprietary API procedures. Until there is agreement on the API issue, interoperability for large-scale biometric applications will be constrained.[34,35]

Three working consortiums have gathered developers, users, and system integrators to upgrade existing standards to facilitate easy implementation. Spearheaded by Compaq Corporation, the BioAPI consortium started its work April 27, 1998. SAFLINK Corporation, in conjunction with The National Registry, Inc., and funded by DoD, initiated the HA-API product mentioned above. They have produced some impressive work. Biometric API (BAPI) is a working group of more than 30 companies that have developed technical specifications, software developer kit tools, and device module interface specifications. The directions are positive; the coordination is not.[36-38]

One of the best sources of unbiased information on biometrics, standards, legislation, consultants, vendors, associated privacy issues, training, conferences, and much more is the Connecticut Department of Social Services, Biometric Identification Project.[39]

Design Issues—Pattern Recognition

It is not clear whether the use of the features and philosophies underlying the identification systems heavily tuned for human use (e.g., faces and fingerprints) is effective for fully automatic processes.[40] Nor do we know whether identification technologies inspired and used by humans are indeed amenable and effective for completely automatic identification systems. In fact, it is not even clear if the solutions solely relying on biometrics-based identifications are the most desirable engineering solutions in many real-world applications. Both a different set of functional requirements demanded by the emerging market applications and the retrospective wisdom of futility of myopic dependence on human intuition for engineering designs suggest that full automation of biometrics-based identification systems warrants a careful examination of all the underlying components of the positive identifications of the emerging applications.

A biometric-based identification (authentication) system operates in two distinct modes: enrollment and identification (authentication). During enrollment, biometric measurements are captured from a given subject, relevant information from the raw measurement is gleaned by the feature extractor, and feature/person information is stored in a database. Additionally, some form of ID may be generated for the subject (along with the visual/machine representation of the biometrics).

In identification mode of operation, the system senses the biometric measurements from the subject, extracts features from the raw measurements, and searches the database using the features thus extracted. The system may either be able to determine the identity of the subject or decide the person is not represented in the database.

In authentication mode, the subject presents his or her system-assigned ID and the biometric measurements. The system extracts features from the measurements and attempts to match the input features to the features corresponding to subject's ID in the system database (i.e., the template). The system may then either determine that the subject is who he or she claims to be or may reject the claim. In some situations, a single system operates as both an identification and an authentication system with a common database of identity/feature associations.

In Figure 12-7, human vision is fooled by many subtle perceptual tricks, and it is hoped that machine vision may be better equipped in correctly recognizing the deceit in some situations. Although a typical human subject may wrongly believe the faces shown in this picture to belong to Vice President Al Gore and President Bill Clinton, on closer inspection, one could recognize that both the faces in the picture identically show Bill Clinton's facial features and the crown of hair on one of the faces has been digitally manipulated to appear similar to that of Al Gore.[41]

Design of a biometrics-based identification system could essentially be reduced to the design of a pattern recognition system. The conventional pattern recognition system designers have adopted is a sequential phase-

Figure 12-7

Pattern recognition
problems.

by-phase modular architecture. Although it is generally known in the research community that more integrated, parallel, active system architectures involving feedback/feed-forward control have a number of advantages, these concepts have not yet been fully exploited in commercial biometrics-based systems.

Given the speed, accuracy, and cost performance specifications of an end-to-end identification system, the following design issues need to be addressed:

1. How should the input data/measurements (biometrics) be acquired?

2. What internal representation (features) of the input data is invariant and amenable for an automatic feature extraction process?

3. Given the input data, how should the internal representation be extracted from it?

4. Given two input samples in the selected internal representation, how should a matching metric that translates the intuition of "similarity" among the patterns be defined?

5. How should the matching metric be implemented? Additionally, for reasons of efficiency, the designer may also need to address the issues involving:

- Organization of a number of input samples (representations) into a database
- Effective methods of searching a given input sample representation in the database

Applications

Biometric countermeasures have been used in several applications, including law enforcement, access control, computer systems, physical access, and telephone systems.

Law Enforcement

The law enforcement community is perhaps the largest biometric user group. Police forces throughout the world use AFIS technology to process criminal suspects, match fingerprints, and bring guilty criminals to justice. A number of biometric vendors are earning significant revenues in this area. It is primarily geared towards palm print and AFIS technologies.

Access Control

All other biometric applications—that is, those not involving crime detection—utilize some form of access control. Whether it is securing benefit systems from fraud, preventing illegal immigrants from entering a country, or preventing prisoners from leaving a prison, controlling access is the underlying principle. Access control ensures that authorized individuals can gain access to a particular area and that unauthorized individuals cannot. This is a rapidly expanding market. Fraud is an ever-increasing problem, and security is becoming a necessity in many walks of life. Access control, therefore, will not be restricted to the application areas mentioned in this section and will branch out to other market opportunities, as soon as a need is identified.

Computer Systems (aka Logical Access Control)

Fraudulent access to computer systems affects private computer networks and the expansive Internet in the same way. Confidence is lost, and the network is unable to perform at full capacity until the hole in security is patched. Biometric technologies are proving to be more than capable of securing computer networks. This market area has phenomenal potential, especially if the biometrics industry can migrate to large-scale Internet applications. As banking data, business intelligence, credit card numbers, medical information, and other personal data becomes the target of attack, the opportunities for biometric vendors rapidly escalate.

Physical Access

The general application area of physical access can be used to illustrate the deployment of biometrics that cannot be categorized in any other way. There is no limit to the kinds of organizations using biometrics to secure the physical movement of people. Schools, nuclear power stations, military facilities, theme parks, hospitals, offices, and supermarkets around the globe employ biometrics to minimize security threats. As security becomes more and more important for parents, employers, governments, and other groups, biometrics will be seen as a more acceptable and therefore essential tool. The potential applications are infinite. Cars and houses, for example, the sanctuary of the ordinary citizen, are under constant threat of theft, and biometrics, if appropriately priced and marketed, could offer the perfect security solution.

Telephone Systems

Global communication has truly opened up over the past decade. Cellular telephones, dial-inward system access (DISA), and a range of telecommunication services are now available. Yet these are under attack from criminals. Cellular companies are vulnerable to cloning (where a new phone is created using stolen code numbers) and new subscription fraud (where a phone is obtained using a false identity). Meanwhile, dial-inward system access—which allows authorized individuals to contact a central exchange and make free calls—is being targeted by telephone hackers. Once again, biometrics is being called upon to defend this onslaught.

Voice biometrics is obviously well suited to the telephone environment and is making inroads into these opportune markets.

Biometric Encryption—The Merging of Biometrics with Cryptography

With the proliferation of information exchange across the Internet, along with the storage of sensitive data on open networks, cryptography is becoming an increasingly important feature of computer security. Many cryptographic algorithms are available for securing information, and several have been discussed previously in this book. In general, data will be secured using a symmetric cipher system, while public key systems will be used for digital signatures and for secure key exchange between users. However, regardless of whether a user deploys a symmetric or a public key system, the security of his or her communication is dependent on the secrecy of the secret or private key, respectively. Because of the large size of a cryptographically strong key, it would clearly not be feasible to require the user to remember and enter the key each time it is required. Instead, the user is typically required to choose an easily remembered pass code that is used to encrypt the cryptographic key. This encrypted key can then be stored on a computer's hard drive. To retrieve the cryptographic key, the user is prompted to enter the pass code, which will then be used to decrypt the key.

There are two main problems with the method of pass code security. First, the security of the cryptographic key, and hence the cipher system, is now only as good as the pass code. Due to practical problems of remembering various pass codes, some users tend to choose simple words, phrases, or easily remembered personal data, while others resort to writing the pass code down on an accessible document to avoid data loss. Obviously, these methods pose potential security risks. The second problem concerns the lack of direct connection between the pass code and the user. Because a pass code is not tied to a user, the system running the cryptographic algorithm is unable to differentiate between the legitimate user and an attacker who fraudulently acquires the pass code of a legitimate user.

As an alternative to pass code protection, biometric authentication offers a new mechanism for key security by using a biometric to secure the cryptographic key. Instead of entering a pass code to access the cryptographic key, the use of this key is guarded by *biometric authentication*. When a user wishes to access a secured key, he or she will be prompted to allow for the capture of a biometric sample. If this verification sample matches the enrollment template, then the key is released and can be used to encrypt or decrypt the desired data. Thus, biometric authentication can replace the use of pass codes to secure a key. This offers convenience, as the user no longer has to remember a pass code, and secure identity confirmation, since only the valid user can release the key.

There are various methods that can be deployed to secure a key with a biometric. One method involves remote template matching and key storage. The biometric image is captured, and the corresponding template is sent to a secure location for template comparison. If the user is verified, then the key is released from the secure location. This provides a convenient mechanism for the user, as they no longer need to remember a pass code. This method would work well in a physical access application where the templates and keys may be stored in a secure location physically separated from the image capture device. In this scenario, the communication line must also be secured to avoid eavesdropper attacks. However, for personal computer use, the keys would likely be stored in the clear on a user's hard drive, which is not secure.

A second method involves hiding the cryptographic key within the enrollment template itself via a trusted (secret) bit-replacement algorithm. Upon successful authentication by the user, this trusted algorithm would simply extract the key bits from the appropriate locations and release the key into the system. Unfortunately, this implies that the cryptographic key will be retrieved from the same location in a template each time a different user is authenticated by the system. Thus, if an attacker could determine the bit locations that specify the key, then the attacker could reconstruct the embedded key from any of the other users' templates. If an attacker had access to the enrollment program, then he or she could determine the locations of the key by, for example, enrolling several people in the system using identical keys for each enrollment. The attacker then needs only to locate those bit locations with common information across the templates.

A third method is to use data derived directly from a biometric image. Albert Bodo proposed such a method in a German patent.[42] This patent proposed that data derived from the biometric (in essence, the biometric template) be used directly as a cryptographic key. However, there are two main problems with this method. First, as a result of changes in the biometric image due to environmental and physiological factors, the biometric template is generally not consistent enough to be used as a cryptographic key. Second, if the cryptographic key is ever compromised, then the use of that particular biometric is irrevocably lost. In a system where periodic updating of the cryptographic key is required, this is catastrophic.

An innovative technique for securing a key using a biometric has been developed by Mytec Technologies, Inc., based in Toronto, Canada. The solution developed by Mytec does not use an independent, two-stage process to first authenticate the user and then release the key. Instead, the key is linked with the biometric at a more fundamental level during enrollment and is later retrieved using the biometric during verification. Furthermore, the *key is completely independent of the biometric data*, which means that, first, the use of the biometric is not forfeited if the key is ever compromised, and second, the key can be easily modified or updated at a later date. The process developed by Mytec Technologies is called *Biometric Encryption*. During enrollment, the Biometric Encryption process combines the biometric image with a digital key to create a secure block of data, known as a Bioscrypt. The digital key can be used as a cryptographic key. The Bioscrypt is secure in that neither the fingerprint nor the key can be independently obtained from it. During verification, the Biometric Encryption algorithm retrieves the cryptographic key by combining the biometric image with the Bioscrypt. Thus, Biometric Encryption does not simply provide a yes/no response in user authentication to facilitate release of a key, but instead retrieves a key that can only be re-created by combining the biometric image with the Bioscrypt.

Note that Biometric Encryption refers to a process of secure key management. Biometric Encryption does not directly provide a mechanism for the encryption/decryption of data, but rather provides a replacement to typical pass code key protection protocols. Specifically, Biometric Encryption provides a secure method for key management to complement existing cipher systems. Although the process of Biometric Encryption can be applied to any biometric image, the initial implementation was achieved using fingerprint images.

This Biometric Encryption process is fascinating and complex. It is well described in Chapter 22 of *The ICSA Guide To Cryptography*.[43,44] Lessons can be learned from the successes and technical directions that this crossover technology reports. Smart card manufacturers have already developed similar technologies to combine biometric and cryptographic precepts.

Wrap-Up

Biometrics is the science of automatically identifying individuals based on their unique physiological or behavioral characteristics. The market for biometric products has been constrained by standards, interoperability, design requirements, cost, and politics. The technology is interesting and certainly has a place in supporting access control requirements and very sensitive authentication requirements.

Notes

1. Roethenbaugh, Gary, "Biometrics Explained," NCSA, Draft v2.0, 1997. In 1998, NCSA changed to ICSA and a new version of this document was filed at the ICSA library at www.icsa.net.

2. Jain, Anil, Ruud Bolle, and Sharath Pankanti, eds., *Biometrics: Personal Identification in Networked Society*, (Norwell, Mass.: Kluwer Academic Publishers), 1999.

3. Roethenbaugh, op. cit.

4. Jain, op. cit.

5. Lange, L. and G. Leopold, "Digital Identification: It's Now at Our Fingertips," *EEtimes* at http://techweb.cmp.com/eet/823, Vol. 946, 24 March 1997.

6. Parks, J. R., "Personal Identification—Biometrics," *Information Security,* D. T. Lindsay and W. L. Price, eds. North Holland: Elsevier Science, 1991), 181-191.

7. Clarke, R. "Human Identification in Information Systems: Management Challenges and Public Policy Issues," *Information Technology and People*, Vol. 7, No. 4, 1994, 6-37.

8. Newham, E. *The Biometric Report*, SJB Services, New York, 1995. Available at http://www.sjb.com.

9. Jain, op. cit.

10. Roethenbaugh, op. cit.

11. Ibid.

12. Ibid.

13. Wayman, James L., "Technical Testing and Evaluation of Biometric Identification Devices," Chapter 17 in Anil Jain et al., *Biometrics: Personal Identification in Networked Society*, Kluwer Academic Publishers, 1999).

14. Roethenbaugh, op. cit.

15. Picture courtesy of Jain, op. cit.

16. Roethenbaugh, op. cit.

17. Picture courtesy of Jain, op. cit.

18. Roethenbaugh, op. cit.

19. Picture courtesy of Danryan@danryan.com.

20. Roethenbaugh, op. cit.

21. Jain, op. cit.

22. Ibid.

23. Roethenbaugh, op. cit.

24. Ibid.

25. Ibid

26. Ibid.

27. Ibid

28. Ibid.

29. Picture courtesy of Jain, op. cit.

30. Roethenbaugh, op. cit.

31. Picture courtesy of Jain, op. cit.

32. Jain, op. cit.

33. Ibid.

34. Colombi, Major John, Ph.D., USAF, "Human-Authentication API," Interface Specification, U.S. Biometrics Consortium, jmcolom@alpha.ncsc.mil.

35. FIPS PUB 190, "Guideline for the Use of Advanced Authentication Technology Alternatives," September 1994, http://csrc.ncsl.nist.gov/fips/fip190.txt

36. BAPI, www.isosoftware.com/bapi/index.htm

37. BioAPI, www.bioapi.org/BioAPI.htm

38. HA-API, www.saflink.com/haapi.html

39. See www.dss.state.ct.us/digital.htm11

40. Jain, op. cit.

41. Picture courtesy of Jain, op. cit.

42. Bodo, Albert, *Method for Producing a Digital Signature with Aid of a Biometric Feature*, German patent DE 42 43 908 A1, 1994.

43. Nichols, Randall K., "Biometric Encryption," Chapter 22 in *The CISA Guide to Cryptography* (New York: McGraw-Hill, 1998).

44. See www.mytec.com for product information.

PART 4

Enterprise Continuity Planning

The chances are better than average that your corporate network or personal computer systems will be attacked under one of the categories of digital espionage. In previous sections, we have characterized computer crimes and their perpetrators, introduced INFOSEC principles based upon risk analysis, recommended written security policies be in place and enforced, and discussed practical countermeasures supported by cryptographic and biometric technologies.

Part 4 is directed to security managers at their desks. They know that they are a target. They know that their computer systems are at risk as well. What they need is a defensive blueprint for security activities before, during, and after an attack on their computers. Although every enterprise is different, people react differently to crisis, and no blueprint can be 100 percent effective, the exercise is still valuable because it focuses attention on the resources and types of decisions that a corporation or individual needs to make. Like a good disaster plan for a hurricane or a serious plant explosion, many departments are involved, for instance, public relations, communications, transportation, security, management, and technical services.

Chapter 13 addresses security blueprint commonalties that IT managers may use for proper planning. Their plan needs to be flexible for responses and up-to-date for communications. We learn to think in terms of risks and plan accordingly. The bottom line is, with today's technology, the information security manager had better have his or her own "blueprint" in place or a nice-colored résumé in readiness.

Chapter 14 looks at managers in the heat of battle. Their computers are under attack and their customers are showing them a side that they prefer not to see. There are some common-sense actions managers can take to mitigate the attack and make the transition back to normal easier. The chapter discusses the process of completed security incident analysis. It looks at action items that may be used to track down the perpetrators, plug the holes, liaison with law enforcement, and revisit the battlefield.

CHAPTER 13

Before the Attack: Protect and Detect

Warm-Up Exercise

Your computer network is a bull's-eye target. What counteractions are you prepared to take? All the actions that are performed before an attack or an incident occurs are critical to your ability to detect anomalies, initiate countermeasures, and execute corrective actions. The activities associated with risk management (Chapter 3) support and enable those functions. The reason we implement and maintain security features within our computer system are because there *are* threats and there *are* vulnerabilities that may be exploited. Knowing what the threats and vulnerabilities are, however, is not enough. We need to know what we should do in terms of implementing protective measures. To gain that understanding we must first define what we need.

Before we can define solutions to a problem we must know what the problem is. In a practical sense, the following simple matrix is a way to help define the scope of a problem. Having that done, we are then able to postulate solutions.

Table 13-1 initiates the selection process. For the specific operational environment, defining the elements that fit into each square of the matrix assists us in defining what kind of protective measures need to be in place. With regard to confidentiality, integrity, and availability, the three protective attributes are what information should we protect, how much of it should we protect, and how long should we protect it?

For example, in a hospital environment, information such as patient records would clearly need to be protected in terms of all three attributes. But how much confidentiality is needed? How much integrity, or availability? The answers to these questions depend on the specifics of the operating environment. Suppose a hospital is engaged in telemedicine and regularly treats patients at remote locations, which requires that information such as patient records, diagnostic data, and medical staff consultations be communicated between physical operating locations. In this situation, it is possible to define specifically how much pro-

TABLE 13-1

Broad-Based
Protection Matrix.

	Protection Attributes		
	Confidentiality	Integrity	Availability
What needs to be protected?			
How much protection does it need?			
How long must that protection be accorded?			

tection is needed and for how long that protection must be accorded. Patient information must be protected in terms of confidentiality during transit and while at rest (i.e., stored in either electronic or physical form). Integrity of the data must always be ensured, particularly if the data is being used for real-time diagnostics or in support of medical decisions. The availability of the information must be such that it supports the operational construct, which could be defined in terms such as "the diagnostic data must be available to all members of the consulting medical team within 30 seconds of transmission."

In the foregoing example, another dimension surfaces for consideration. At what level should protection be applied? Are all patient records confidential? What about insurance forms or patient bills? Do we apply the protection to individual paragraphs, sentences, reports, or the complete file? How will the policy be enacted across the organization?

Describing these requirements points us to the next step, which is defining the requirements for the information environment supporting the operational environment. We next focus on the vulnerabilities in our environment that subvert our operational requirements and describe threats that we must protect against and be prepared to detect.

Repeatability

A critical aspect of this process is that it must be done over and over and over again. No operational environment remains the same over time. People come and go, and the level of understanding with which they interface with the operational mission changes accordingly. Supporting systems change in terms of capability and interfaces. A major concern that must be addressed continually is the increasing connectivity between elements of information support systems. Each time something changes in the environment, the system attributes and requirements should be reviewed to determine if the risk profile has changed and if any technology or policy changes are required to keep the security solutions relevant.

Defense Blueprint for Managers

When we have a broadly defined idea of what information needs to be protected, it is time to establish a flexible *blueprint* for defense against computer attacks. It consists of nine building blocks: organization, risk analysis repeatability, vulnerability and threat assessment, countermeasures, backup, antivirus measures, training and awareness, auditing and monitoring of transactions, and lastly, staying on top of current information. The corporation blueprint needs to be in clear and simple nonpolitical writing, circulated widely in the organization for comments, signed by the CEO and every management level from supervisor up, issued, posted for all to see, reevaluated regularly, and added to critical training sessions for both salary and hourly labor components in the organization. Rewards should be linked to effective implementation by all departments. It should be as important as posted Equal Opportunity Organization statements, safety bulletins, and antidiscrimination statements, with one important difference. The security blueprint needs to be enforced and equality/fairness has nothing to do with it. Computer attacks are not fair to anyone. They are anything but equal.

Block 1: Information Technology Organization and Security Management

INFOSEC management is the corporate activity that controls systems protecting the information systems of an organization from all external and internal threats. Information systems are found at every level of corporate activity: general, divisional, and local, whether differentiated geographically or functionally. Information systems acquire, process, store, retrieve, and share the information resources and intellectual property of an enterprise. The following discussion is applicable to all organizations—only the depth of personnel deployment is variable.

The organizational model of an information security system should be modular and replicated at each echelon of the organization. An INFOSEC module should be attached to each information system. An integral network of control will link these modules modeling the corporate hierarchy itself.

The chief INFOSEC manager should be an officer on the staff of the organization's chief information officer (CIO). He or she requires a line relationship to INFOSEC managers in staff relationships with managers of systems, central facilities, information systems, applications, terminal areas, networks, and offices. Formal titles include:

- System security officer (SSO)
- Central facility security officer (CFSO)
- Information system security officer (ISSO)
- Terminal area security officer (TSO)
- Network security officer (NSO)
- Office information security officer (OISO)

Information security management exists to safeguard the confidentiality, integrity, and availability of IT assets. Three basic functions are needed by any enterprise desiring to establish and maintain information security management: policymaking, implementation, and compliance monitoring. Policymaking is a function reserved for top management. As shown in Figure 13-1, it flows from considerations of business strategy and information systems strategy.

One of the missions of INFOSEC is to protect information assets by selecting, installing, and maintaining safeguards against threats. INFOSEC risk analysis demands continuous acquisition and cataloging of information about:

- Cost of information assets in terms of replacement, correction, unavailability, fraud, waste and abuse, and liability to third parties
- Assessment of threats in terms of severity, frequency of occurrence, immediacy, and asset endangerment
- Effectiveness of safeguards in terms of threat-asset specificity, and cost in terms of price, installation, maintenance, and personnel requirements

Figure 13-1
IT security policy as a management function.

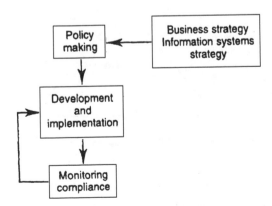

■ Incidents of asset loss, compromise, or endangerment

All of the above elements must be addressed. Implementation and development are functions of the corporate security infrastructure (Figure 13-2), which consists of 14 components in the second layer:[1]

Management	Operating systems
Personnel and organization	Software utilities
Physical assets	Peripheral software
Logical assets	Operations
Data security	Applications development
Hardware	End-user computing
Environment	Communications

Block 2: Risk Analysis Repeatability

Security levels must change to compensate for organization and business changes. In that control process, risk analysis (Chapters 1 and 3) is a decision model (viewed dynamically) to help management plan security. The dynamic "dimension" is important because it forces a continuous cycle of review of IT security.

Risk analysis is a method for planning security. Risk management is carried out at all organizational levels by top management and by operating management.

Figure 13-2
Corporate IT security infrastructure.

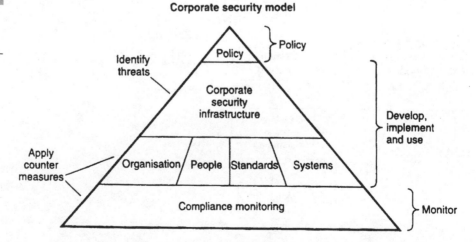

Two types of methods are used: one for analyzing (planning) and the other for controlling (scanning). The method must be able to (1) analyze the current security posture and (2) suggest changes and new safeguards. New safeguards may be selected by either performing a cost-benefit analysis or by a due diligence examination of lists of evaluated safeguards. In either case, the risk analysis procedure must be able to describe the system under analysis and to supply a corporate *knowledge base* with information on threats, safeguards, and other external components.

To cope with change, the *risk-analysis procedure must be able to update* the *knowledge base* with new information. To handle change in the system under analysis, it is important that the risk-analysis tool be able to save a description of a system so it will be necessary only to enter recent changes when doing a new analysis.[2]

Another task of risk analysis is to handle different functional levels within a computerized information system. Each one will require different methods of data acquisition and analysis. The functional levels are as follows:

- Physical environment
- Operating system
- Application system
- Communication system

But there are other reasons to do a new risk analysis. There could have been some change in the environment (inside or outside the organization) that could affect the input mix. Therefore, the environment must be scanned continually for significant events.[3] Examples of external events that could trigger a new risk analysis are as follows:

- New threats (e.g., viruses)
- New technology (e.g., PC, LAN, etc.)
- New laws (e.g., copyright acts)
- New safeguards available, or old ones not allowed (e.g., Halon 1301)

Examples of significant internal events are as follows:

- New application systems
- New or a major change in software, hardware, or communications
- Major change in organization (e.g., new departments, new people)

From a life cycle point of view, a new system risk analysis may be required for any of the following events:

- Requirements review
- Preliminary design review
- Critical design review
- System implementation
- System monitoring
- Periodic ISO 9000 reviews

Block 3: Vulnerability And Threat Assessment (Revisited)

Chapter 3 discussed the management of risk and threats to a computer system. The discussion centered on the architecture required to reduce sources of danger to the information technology systems. We proposed a nonquantitative model for use in thinking about the factors that enter into risk management and in assessing the qualitative level of danger posed in a given situation:

$$\text{Level of risk} = \frac{(\text{Threat} \times \text{Vulnerabilities})}{\text{Countermeasures}} \times \text{Value}$$

Vulnerabilities are characteristics of our situations, systems, or facilities that can be exploited by a *threat* to do us harm. Managers must consider the possible consequences of attacks from a wide variety of different threats, each of which may act on a specific vulnerability different from those attempted to be exploited by other independent threats and any of which may be unrecognized. *Countermeasures* may abate the danger even if there are malevolent and capable threats as well as vulnerabilities, which can be exploited by those threats. Countermeasures reduce the likelihood of a successful attack and so lessen risk.

The impact of a successful attack depends upon the *value* of the target. As the value of the target rises, the impact of a successful attack goes up as well, and so our sense of risk increases. Consequently, *impact* is a *force multiplier* in our algorithm.

It is often not possible to evaluate in any quantitative sense the factors in the risk management algorithm. Even if it were easy to determine the cost of potential countermeasures, the *likelihood* of the threat successfully attacking, the extent of our vulnerabilities, and the impact of a possible loss are at best uncertain. As with most management problems, insufficient information makes security decisions more of an art form and less of a science. Table 13-2 presents examples of likelihood estimates based on progressions of powers of 10 times 3.

This uncertainty is a contributing cause to our tendency to rely on *risk avoidance*. By assuming the threat to be capable, intent, and competent, by valuing our potential targets highly and by conservatively estimating uncertainties, we reduce risk management to "What are our vulnerabilities and how much do countermeasures cost to eliminate them?" The management problem is "How much money can I spend and where can I spend it most wisely?" By careful analysis, we may be able to estimate the value of each factor in our equation and balance the risk of loss or damage against the costs of countermeasures and select a mix that provides adequate protection without excessive cost.

John Carroll describes the properties of threats that may be quantified for risk analysis: likelihood, the number of times a year a particular threat is expected to be presented to the system, and severity, the consequence of realization of a threat.[4] Consequences of the realized threat depend not only on the target but also its impact. Impact includes deprivation of resources, destruction and theft of services or resources, unauthorized modification, and unauthorized disclosure. Table 13-3 categorizes some estimates of severity.

The basic equation for estimating annual cost of loss requires multiplying the likelihood of a threat by the cost of its impact. Navy Studies concerning likelihood estimates are old, unfortunately sparse, and user-

TABLE 13-2

Likelihood
Estimates.

Time	Likelihood	Event
Daily	300	Initial program load
Weekly	30	Complete backup
Annual	3	Upgrade operating system
Every 3 years	.33	New Microsoft Office Suite
30 years	0.033	War in the Gulf
30,000 years	0.000033	Human race returns to surface from hiding

TABLE 13-3

Severity Estimates.

Time	Severity	Event
3 seconds	3	Typing error
30 seconds	30	Revise a sentence
5 minutes	300	Restore a file
50 minutes	3000	Restore an application
24-72 hours	100,000-300,000	Restore a custom database
72 hours	300,000	Restore home PC and portable after Havoc virus attack
60 days	3,000,000	Restore accounts payable system and salary master

specific.[5] However, they are widely published and do provide fundamental information for managers to review for their organizations.

Ultimately, the risk management process is about making decisions. The impact of a successful attack and the level of risk that is acceptable in any given situation are fundamentally policy decisions. The threat is whatever it is, and while it may be abated, controlled, or subdued by appropriate countermeasures, it is beyond the direct control of the security process. The process must focus, accordingly, on vulnerabilities and countermeasures. Vulnerabilities are design issues and must be addressed during the design, development, fabrication, and implementation of our facilities, equipment, systems, and networks. Typically, to make any asset less vulnerable raises its cost, not just in the design and development phase but also due to more-extensive validation and testing to ensure the functionality and utility of security features, as well as in the application of countermeasures during the operation and maintenance phase.

Cost-Effective Risk Management

A fundamental problem of risk management, then, is to link the choice of design characteristics that reduce vulnerabilities and the choice of countermeasures to threat and impact in order to create a cost-effective balance that achieves an acceptable level of risk. The process, condensed from Chapter 3, is as follows:

1. Assess the impact of loss of or damage to the potential target.
2. Specify the level of risk of damage or destruction that is acceptable. This may well be the most difficult part of the process.
3. Identify and characterize the threat.
4. Analyze vulnerabilities.
5. Specify countermeasures.
6. Allow for uncertainties.

In practice, the estimates needed to apply such a risk management process are accomplished in only gross terms. Threat level or uncertainty may be assessed as high or low. Impact may be designated as severe or moderate.

Cost-of-Loss Models

Of the five components of risk analysis (threats, assets, system vulnerabilities, countermeasures, and design constraints), asset valuation has had the most corporate time invested in its discovery. Asset valuation is intimately connected with vulnerabilities, countermeasures, and constraints. Companies know how much their people, software, hardware, communications, environment, and information flow costs. Assets may be valued by cost or by importance to the organization. Whereas the engineer and IT specialists see assets in terms of order of magnitude estimates, which include asset exposure, standalone value, attractiveness, and dependence, the accountant has a clearer view because he or she sees the process of covering loss. The accountant asks the question, how much will it cost to make the organization whole after a loss? The focus is on historical data and the cost to acquire an equivalent service.

There are numerous accounting practices that define the cost of loss to an organization:

1. *Replacement model* An asset costs more for replacement than its original sales price. It wastes, depreciates, or becomes obsolete. The tax code provides for book value reduction by several methods, e.g., straight-line depreciation, sum of the year's digits, fixed percentage on declining balance, and accelerated depreciation. The rules are many, and it requires a certain perseverance to keep up with the thousands of pages of methodology.

2. *Repair model*   A repair model addresses restoration of the system integrity after an unwarranted modification. One of the authors had to restore two PC computers and one portable, with this manuscript on them, after a "Havoc" and "Stealth" combined attack. The cost of repair to restore functionality included three new Zip drives, 56 hours of labor, and nearly $1000 for replacement software.

3. *Compromise model*   The compromise model attempts to quantify the cost of unauthorized disclosure of trade secrets or sensitive information. Patent legal disputes and insurance cases (especially involving death) use this form of model to evaluate assets.

4. *Service model*   Telephone companies, auto repair, plumbing, and HVAC are examples of industries using this model. The value of services delivered is established on a cost per unit time. The cost is made as a basis for revenue lost or that would have been generated before the attack on the asset took place.

5. *Transference model*   The entire world seems to be following this model. The transference model deals the transfer of risk to another party, usually an insurance company. Adverse consequences can be mitigated, but the cost to business can be high. We see extended warranties, fire, theft, flood, third-party risk assumptions, economic deterioration costs, service interruptions, bonding, and so on—and we see many lawsuits.

6. *Catastrophe model*   IT managers have a unique view. They know what the complete disruption of corporate computer systems can do to the viability of the organization. The challenge is to balance the effectiveness of new technology and products with the right level of technology. Models that maximize the worst-case scenario and compare them to expected/probable losses are becoming more popular for budget purposes.

Carroll presents a gross classification of assets by impact and level of investment to the corporation. He defines four responses to adverse events: destruction, improper modification, unauthorized disclosure, and denial of services. Table 13-4 reveals an increasing level of investment and concern based on hardware, software, and support items. The challenge of management is to fine-tune the levels to be meaningful to their organization. This is being done in some large manufacturing concerns with the help of interdisciplinary teams.[6]

TABLE 13-4

Asset Classification.

Impact	Level 1	Level 2	Level 3
DESTRUCTION			
	Hardware		
		Computers	Supercomputers
			Mainframes
			Superminis
			Miniclusters
			Minicomputers
			Workstations
			PCs
		Peripherals	
			Disk drives
			Tape stations
			Mass storage
			Optical storage
			Terminals
			Printers
		Communications	
			Modems
			LANs
			PABXs
			Crypto boxes
	Information		
		System programs	
		Application programs	
		Database applications	
		Data files	
		Documentation	
	Support		
		Test equipment	
		Environmental support	
		Power conditioning	
		Fittings and fixtures	
		Office equipment	
		Furniture	
		Buildings	
DISCLOSURE			
	Hardware		
	Information		
	Support		
MODIFICATION			
	Hardware		
	Information		
	Support		
DELAY/DENIAL			
	Hardware		
	Information		
	Support		

Source: John M. Carroll, *Computer Security*, 3rd edition.

Block 4: Apply Countermeasures— System and Network Security Management

Standalone systems and isolated operational environments and the efficiencies and capabilities afforded by networking are powerful incentives to hook internal systems together, as well as connecting access ports to external systems, such as the Internet. Unfortunately, with that additional access and power comes increased, often exponentially increased, vulnerabilities. Networked systems provide greatly expanded challenges in terms of protection and detection because of the myriad vulnerabilities.

Network Vulnerabilities

Networks have vulnerabilities at:

- The user's workstation
- The server
- The router/gateway
- The communications path

In addition, to make matters even more complex, there are special vulnerabilities that depend on the protocol structure.

Because of this tremendous spread of vulnerabilities, technical solutions cannot provide an entirety of an answer. Instead, a viable and affordable network security capability must incorporate not only technical solutions but also policy and procedural solutions. There are many different ways to conduct attacks on networked systems and on the networks themselves. The easiest, least expensive, and most effective approach is to simply suborn the users. With an insider's assistance, an attack on a network is made much easier to execute and much harder to detect. Another way of attack is interception: intercept traffic at or between nodes of the network, and/or intercept radiation from the hardware (TEMPEST).

Yet another way is to attack the entry points ("hack in") or to attack the protocol. Protocols were designed for reliable communication and, as a result, often have weak points. Some of the attacks that take advantage of protocol design features include sequence number attacks, loose source routing and bogus routing attacks, domain name attacks, and SMTP (Simple Mail Transfer Protocol) attacks.

Sequence number attacks are based on the premise that some systems use sequence numbers as a way of identifying "trusted" machines. The attacker attempts to guess or predict the starting sequence number for the target system. The objective of this attack is to get a legitimate connection through the use of a trusted sequence number. Once that is accomplished, typical monitoring activities would not detect the presence of the attacker in the system because he or she would then be disguised as a legitimate user.

Loose source routing or bogus routing attacks are based on the provision by TCP/IP of dynamic routing algorithms. The loose source routing option allows the initiator to specify the route, and an attacker can actually divert return packets by inserting bogus routing information

The Domain Name System (DNS) is used to map IP addresses to domain names (e.g., ninet.research.att.com = 192.20.225.3). By attacking the DNS and altering the inverse map, the information used by the target machine to resolve addresses becomes incorrect and the subject packets appear to come from a legitimate source. This then becomes a powerful way to break through firewalls that rely on packet source filtering to restrict access through the firewall to packets only from identified sources.

SMTP and Sendmail attacks should have been eradicated by now, due to intense coverage and publicity associated with these attacks and how to deal with them. SMTP is a protocol that defines how mail is sent in a TCP/IP network, while *Sendmail* is a utility supporting mail functions used in standard UNIX. The challenges associated with Sendmail stem from the fact that it runs with root privileges and automatically executes Multipurpose Internet Mail Extensions (MIME) encoded messages.

An attacker can use this feature to insert root-privileged processes in the target machine. At a very high level, the attacker sends an electronic message containing an executable command to the target machine. The target machine, if it is not configured correctly, will automatically execute the command with the inherited privileges of the source of the command, which in this case would be `sendmail`. This allows the attacker to execute a command with root privileges, even though the attacker him- or herself could not execute that command normally. Doing so enables the attacker to remotely open a door into the system, an advantage the attacker can exploit to do other things.

Protecting the networks and the systems connected to the networks begins with competent system administration but does not end there. Systems must be protected by a comprehensive security posture that includes physical, personnel, and operational security features integrated synergistically with technical countermeasures and active detection capabilities.

Encryption in Networks

A common way to protect the confidentiality and integrity of data being transmitted over networks is to encrypt the data. There are two basic methods of applying encryption: link encryption and end-to-end encryption.

Link encryption means that the encryptors are located at each of the nodes (switches and routers) of the network. The information is only protected link by link; it is encrypted when it leaves the node and decrypted when it arrives at the destination node. The switch or router contains cleartext, and while in the node computer, all layers of the protocol have access to the cleartext.

End-to-end encryption ensures that the information is protected until it reaches the peer level. The information is encrypted at the origination and then encapsulated in its encrypted state by lower-level protocol in packets for transmission. The information "above" the encryption level is open—in other words, the protocol levels above the level at which the information is encrypted see the data in its cleartext form, while those protocol levels below the encrypting level see the data in its encrypted form. This is important because of packet addressing. If the encryption is at transport level, then the address fields must remain unencrypted or pseudoaddresses must be generated. The computers need to know where to send the packets—they can't do that if all they can see is encrypted data.

There are, of course, network security issues associated with encrypting and decrypting information over networks over and above the challenges associated with managing the cryptography. For example, it is important that there be a way to determine the sensitivity levels for each node in a network. You would not want a system that is used by members of competing organizations being able to receive and decrypt proprietary information. Typically, a system of labels is generated that identifies what levels of sensitivity each node is capable of handling. With such a scheme, consistency of labels becomes an important issue. If system A has sensitivity levels A1, A2, and A3, and system B has levels B1, B2, B3, and B4, both common sense and secure communications require that a mapping be defined between the A levels and the B levels.

The Internet Protocol Security Option is an extension to the TCP/IP protocol that defines a security level from certain option bits in the IP datagram. Peer entities must agree on the meaning of the levels and must trust each other to implement the levels correctly and securely.

Unless care is taken, each system can be secure itself but a weakness for the other. From a network security perspective, *greater connectivity means greater vulnerability*. Dozens of network-specific attacks are known.[7]

Block 5: Backups

"Back up your data" is a commonsense statement. So why is backing up data ignored in contingency planning for an enterprise? It ranks as the number one audit failure in many corporations.

There are two essential prerequisites that must be included for effective contingency planning. Without these elements, contingency planning is a waste of time. These prerequisites are as follows:

1. *Information backup* It is essential to maintain data files in backup format to permit reconstruction and restoration of vital primary computer files. Backup record protection is necessary whether or not the original computer facility or an alternate facility is used, since primary computer files are always subject to risk of damage or destruction. Vital records must be backed up for every computer system. This implies that there must be a vital records program and contingency plan.

2. *Management commitment* Unless contingency planning is motivated by a firm commitment from management, it will fail. Management must provide both tangible and intangible support. Failure of a contingency plan usually is a management failure.

There is a substantial amount of literature devoted to policy, procedures, and items to back up in enterprise planning. Arthur E. Hutt wrote a particularly good article on the subject, "Contingency Planning and Disaster Recovery," which is Chapter 7 in the *Computer Security Handbook*, cited in the Notes. IT managers will find useful planning tools and questionnaires in his article.

Vital Records

An essential prerequisite to contingency planning is the preservation of vital records. Hutt presents seven elements for an effective vital records program:[8]

1. Determine the specific importance and sensitivity of all records in order to classify information by its impact on business continuity.

2. Assign responsibilities to assure that information that is necessary to reconstruct the vital records of the organization is always up-to-date and readily available.

3. Designate the files to be considered vital to the organization to be protected by:

    a. On-site protection, such as three-generation backup for magnetic media and disks in vaults or special filing cabinets

    b. Duplication of records onto media such as paper, magnetic tapes, disks, or microfilm

    c. Off-site storage of copies of vital records

    d. Archival storage in a secure location to meet long-term legal or regulatory requirements

4. Maintain a current inventory of information needed to re-create data and operate a backup facility (e.g., critical applications, equipment configuration(s), engineering change levels, operating system and version, program library, data files, programs, program documentation, and operating documentation, as well as supplies and other material needed for immediate recovery processing).

5. Whenever new systems are created, or existing systems altered, create new backup for these programs and the associated documentation promptly; store at the off-site and on-site backup locations.

6. Off-site backup is an absolute necessity to ensure the survival of vital information. Locate the off-site backups OFF-SITE!

7. Test recovery programs and procedures every six months. [Our recommendation is monthly—our failure experience has been higher than Hutt's.]

In summary, corporations need management commitment and a plan for vital records backup. The backups need to be scheduled and performed—not ignored.

Schedules

Well-thought-out schedules for backup files is an important part of any effective backup strategy. Managers need to consider:

■ Frequency of backup cycle and depth of retention generations must be determined for each data file. (Also the sensitivity level needs to be established.)

- Backup strategy must anticipate failure at any step of the processing cycle.

- Master files should be retained at convenient intervals.

- Transaction files should be preserved to coincide with master files, so that prior generation of a master file can be brought completely up-to-date to re-create a current master file.

- Real-time files require special backup techniques, such as duplicate logging of transactions, use of before images and/or after images of master records, time-stamping of transactions, and communication simulation.

- Database management systems (DBMS) require specialized backup.

- File descriptions need to be maintained over time to coincide with each version of a file that is retained; for DBMS systems this may entail keeping separate versions of data dictionaries.

- Integrity of backup media so that it can be used when needed. This involves using the appropriate technologies such as electronic vaulting or mirror imaging to automate the process.

Block 6: Antivirus Measures

No attack can be as annoying, disabling, and prone to monetary loss as one resulting from a computer virus. A *computer virus* is a computer program capable of reproducing itself in systems other than the one in which it was created. As it spreads, it "infects" the system. It must be deliberately placed in a computer and always requires a *trigger* or external request for execution.

Computer viruses can be only a line or two of programming code, hidden within a program. They can be benign and limited to sending a greeting to amuse or annoy, or they can be malicious, written specifically to damage other programs and alter data. They are capable of infecting all types of computers regardless of size.

A virus may attach itself to another software program and hide in it, or it may infect a computer's operating system. The majority of known computer viruses are software viruses, but in 1999 there have been instances of physical damage when the computer's system became so stressed by a virus that the computer hardware overloaded.

No system is immune to computer viruses, and there is no 100 percent effective data security method. A system may become infected with a computer virus simply by running a program that contains that virus. While infection through infected disk was originally the primary method of spreading a virus, communications involved in connectivity allow additional points of attack through telephone lines and the communications networks. The Internet is the major launching point for the spread of viruses.[9]

Computer Virus Classification

Different types of computer viruses generally reside on the host as programs whose purpose is to infect files and possibly disrupt the host machine. Viruses vary in length, elaborateness, and speed according to the type of target they attack, the area of the system they infect, and the amount of damage they inflict.

Computer viruses can be classified by disruptive effects or the amount of damage a virus inflicts. Four general classes of viruses are discussed in the literature: innocuous, humorous, altering, and catastrophic. *Innocuous viruses* cause no noticeable disruption or destruction within a computer system. They do not corrupt data or interfere with the normal functioning of the computer system. *Humorous viruses* display a humorous text or graphic message without causing any damage or loss of data. They are not intended to inflict any permanent damage. *Altering viruses* are more severe than the first two classes. These viruses are data diddlers—that is, they alter system data subtlety, without authorization, in ways that make the changes difficult to detect. Among the possible methods of altering data diddling are adding or deleting a digit, moving a decimal to a different place, changing the numeric order sequence of an element, and substituting a different but similar number or letter. Although difficult for the user to detect, the changes can cause disastrous results. *Catastrophic viruses*, true to its name, causes widespread destruction of data, both on the main system and on peripheral devices. These viruses activate suddenly and, generally, without warning. This classification is on the increase as of this writing.[10]

Patterns of Activity for Specific Viruses

Viruses attack computers in a variety of ways:

1. *Boot sector viruses*   The boot sector is defined as being the first logical sector of a hard disk or floppy disk. This usually contains

the loading or "booting" instructions for the computer. Because it executes in advance of all other parts of the system, it normally loads the computer's operating system and initializes the computer's memory to begin processing. A virus in this sector copies the original boot sector program to another location on the disk and then writes a copy of its own code on the boot sector. Every time the computer is booted up, or whenever software is being run, the bogus code is executed instead of the original boot sector code. Infections of the boot sector are among the most complex viruses known and the most difficult to detect, and they can evade detection by retrieving and executing a saved copy of the original boot sector each time the computer is booted from an infected disk.

2. *TSR RAM viruses*   Terminate-and-stay-resident (TSR) viruses hide themselves in the computer's random access memory (RAM). Each time the disk operating system (DOS) is executed, the TSR viruses pass their request to DOS and subsequently take control of the operating system. Typically, these viruses cause system crashes but rarely change the file size. TSR viruses can evade detection by keeping the file size as it was and redirecting the interrupt responsible for determining the amount of conventional memory available.

3. *Application software viruses*   Application software viruses copy their virus code to a program file and modify the program file so that it gets executed first. The application software virus can accomplish this either by overwriting the existing code or by appending itself to the program file. The viruses destroy the program's executable code when they overwrite the program file, making it impossible for the program to run. But this same trait also makes them easily identifiable. The most sophisticated application software viruses make copies of themselves with a .com extension each time the user accesses an executable program file.

4. *Stealth viruses*   Stealth viruses constantly change their patterns in an effort to blend with their environments. Having become widespread during the 1990s, these viruses avoid detection because they do not change the size of infected files. Additional means of avoiding detection include their ability to bypass DOS interrupt calls when installing themselves and removing traces of themselves by removing their code from infected files before the code is presented to the program making the request.

5. *Mutation engine viruses*   Using special language-driven algorithm generators, mutation engine viruses can create an infinite

variety of completely original encryption algorithms. Each time they replicate, these viruses produce an entirely different code. They avoid detection via scanning programs due to their constantly changing "signature" or virus pattern. Since the changing code becomes too variable to predict, even constant virus pattern updating in virus scanning products cannot effectively detect mutation engine viruses.

6. *Network viruses*   File servers have also been attacked. Within the LAN environment we find boot sector/partition table viruses, program infectors, and NetWare-specific viruses. The more networking, the more points of vulnerability and the greater the risk of an increased spread of computer viruses.

Increasing Numbers of Viruses

The list of viruses appears endless. In its survey of over 300 corporations, ICSA reports that in 1999 a third generation of virus development began with the introduction of the "Happy 99," "Melissa," and "Explore.zip" viruses. These are *communications-enabled*, not passive in replicating, and designed to exploit the Internet. Antivirus (AV) products are the best line of defense. However, corporations are not using AV products effectively. The difference between effective and noneffective use translates into a 20-fold virus risk reduction.[11] In the first quarter of 1999, virus encounters for all classes (macro, boot, file, mixed, and other) was 191,932 for the surveyed companies. The corresponding 1998-quarter data was 76,196. This translated to an average downtime of 30 hours with 3 percent of the respondents requiring 1000 hours to recover from the virus attacks. The cost of damage ranged from $2000 to $100,000. In some cases, the number of PCs affected in a corporation was 3500.[12]

The data is clear. IT managers need to have AV countermeasures in place and use them!

Block 7: Training and Awareness— Developing a Security Program

Technical countermeasures such as firewalls, encryption, strong identification and authorization, and other security measures can mitigate many of the problems and can provide a critical element in the protective stance. However, no solution offers complete security. It is crucial that these elements be part of a more comprehensive security program that incorporates not only technical countermeasures but also physical, personnel, and operational security considerations in a structured attempt to protect, detect, and when necessary, correct and recover.

Good security starts with good policies (see Chapter 4). The policies reflect the security and operational requirements of the environment of:

- What needs protection?
- How much protection is needed?
- For how long is protection necessary?

Asking the three critical policy questions assists us in structuring policies that address the vital concerns of the operational environment. Addressing the issues in terms of classical protective attributes (confidentiality, integrity, and availability) enables us to add dimensionality to those policies and gives us the ability to use risk management to make decisions about what to do and about the priority of each step.

Risk management (see Chapter 3) implies that there is a level of risk that is either too expensive to mitigate or not efficiently avoidable. Disasters can, and do, happen. That is why the security program must go beyond merely protecting systems and must address what happens when something goes wrong. The three elements of the security program can be described as follows:

1. *Protect*   Design systems and networks to protect information assets.
2. *Detect*   Monitor to detect intrusions by outsiders and abuses by insiders.
3. *Correct*   Isolate and stop attacks, correct vulnerabilities, and reestablish enhanced secure operations.

When specifying the security program, it is also critical to assign specific responsibilities, so that everyone knows exactly what they are supposed to be doing and what level of performance they will be expected to deliver. The responsibilities assigned should not create conflicts of interest but should create checks and balances. A typical problem arises from how the information technology support personnel relate to security personnel and to the security program.

Information security as part of information management creates a conflict of interest when it dictates that information security is part of traditional security force, subordinating high-technology capabilities to low-technology management. This is an artifact of slowly changing organizational structures. Before computers became integral parts of every organization, it was traditional to separate the information technology functions from the other security functions, such as physical security. The personnel populating the traditional security positions tended to be people with training as guards or police, with emphasis on traditional crime deterrence and detection techniques. When individuals with those types of backgrounds are combined with computer and information technology specialists, there is a tendency for misunderstandings and communications problems. Each group speaks a different language with different assumptions and different backgrounds. Yet it is vital to integrate the efforts of the two groups in order to have a good security program. Understanding the challenges up front can do a lot to alleviate potential problems: Awareness of an issue is the first step to solving it. Cross-discipline training can both sensitize each group to the capabilities and challenges associated with each other's specialties and engender cooperative efforts that span the security continuum.

Cooperative effort requires specific and employee-aware management practices. Senior management defines objectives and develops policies to meet those objectives. Middle management defines procedures to ensure proper policy implementation. And all employees or members of an enterprise are responsible for executing security procedures. Basic methods of protecting against damaging events include the following:

- System verification and validation (certification and accreditation)
- Backups and beta sites, including backup communications
- Physical security; access control and alarm systems
- Staff integrity checks and employee agreements
- Physical and electronic access control
- Proper storage of documentation and software licenses
- Training and awareness programs
- Use of cryptography and key management
- Use of antiviral products

The above methods should be used within a security program that provides for periodic vulnerability analyses of systems, networks, and audits and monitors information transactions. It is a good idea to have a properly trained and equipped computer emergency response team (CERT), although in some cases, it will not be cost-effective to have a dedicated CERT. There are, however, companies emerging into the marketplace that provide outsourcing for CERT capabilities, thereby enabling even the smallest enterprise access to an emergency response capability.

It should go without saying that the security procedures be documented in detail, although a typical finding in security consulting is that security procedures are poorly documented and usually well out-of-date. It is too easy to let security documentation lapse with time only to find, when disaster strikes, that the procedures and policies are inadequate. Hand in hand with the recommendation to revisit security documentation periodically to ensure that it is relevant is the recommendation to practice disaster recovery procedures for all types of disasters. Walking through the processes can highlight areas where they need to be changed or updated or, in some cases, totally revised.

General security information should be part of the security documentation, including at the very least:

- Contact list for all relevant individuals
- Internal; security, IT, management, beta sites
- External; police, fire, medical, utilities, backup service
- Computer emergency response team
- Operations specialists
- Physical security specialists
- Facilities engineers
- Computer and communications security specialists
- Attorneys

In addition to general information, the security documentation should also include the following:

- Policies and procedures related to security (current versions)
- Detailed threat analysis for the organization at each location
- Definition of the relationship between IT support and security personnel
- Documentation of all system components and software
- Facilities' blueprints and evacuation plans
- Documentation of security compliance audits
- Software licenses and contracts for use of external systems.

While some of these items may seem like overkill, consider a situation where a disgruntled employee who was just let go decides to get revenge by both setting fire to the administration offices and by calling the Software Protection Alliance to report anonymously that your organization has been using pirated software on many of your machines. In this situation you are faced with two problems simultaneously: dealing with the fire disaster and dealing with the charges of piracy. In order to recover business operations quickly, having the ability to prove ownership of the software licenses enables you to quickly deal with the one problem and then focus all your energies on the other.

This example may strike some readers as being too far-fetched to be realistic. However, a recent review revealed that problems rarely occur singularly—instead, it is much more likely to have more than one problem occur simultaneously. Some of these situations are causal, some of them coincidental. However, if your business continuity plans depend upon having only one disaster at a time, those plans will come up short when they are needed most. Companies must develop disaster planes and make them public to their employees, as well as provide training.

Block 8: Auditing and Monitoring Information Transactions

A critical part of the activities that must be performed during normal operations are the functions of *auditing* and *monitoring*. In some cases, such as in the financial services industry, certain practices associated with auditing are mandatory. These practices are very well documented and will not be covered here, although the generic concepts share the same basic philosophy. This block in the blueprint requires detailing, as it is the essential glue for the methodology.

Auditing and monitoring activities are simply:

checking to make sure that everything is okay.

It makes no sense to put a lock on a door if you never check to see if it is locked and the lock is unbroken. It makes no sense periodically to put an alarm on a window if you don't check to determine if the alarm works. Auditing and monitoring is little more than keeping an eye on your system—to make sure it is doing what it is supposed to be doing *and* to make sure that it is not doing what it is not supposed to be doing. While simplistic, this construct implies a quite complicated series of events. Deconstructing the statements at the first level produces the following questions, each of which are directly applicable to the auditing process:

Checking...

How do you check?   *How often* do you check?

What do you check?   *Who* does the checking?

...to make sure...

How do you make sure?   *What* is sure?

How much sureness do you need?   *When* is checking completed?

...everything...

What constitutes everything?   *Where* are the borders?

How much detail do you need to go into?

...is okay.

What is okay?   *What is not* okay?

How do you find out if it's okay?   *How* do you find out if it's not okay?

Every organization and every system is unique. While there are fundamental principles associated with the practice of auditing and monitoring information transactions, the specifics will be different in each operational environment. Answering these questions provides the kernel of understanding required to perform auditing. As noted, there are several categories of questions that attempt to get to the issue of what, when, where, how often, and why. A comprehensive approach to addressing these factors provides an integrated and holistic auditing process.

Putting all this knowledge together provides a framework for performing auditing functions. Then there are existing tools, techniques, and procedures that can be applied to the specific challenges associated with auditing in an automated or semiautomated environment. Let's address each of these issues in turn, showing tools, techniques, and procedures that are useful for each issue, and then showing how each is linked together to provide the holistic process that is desired.

For the purposes of this discussion, the following definitions will be used.

Auditing   *Auditing* is a systematic examination of all aspects of an operational environment to check compliance with the stated policies and operational requirements for the environment. An audit may include such varied activities as checking personnel hiring procedures, testing information system processes, or testing the environment as a whole with simulated attacks. The purpose of an audit is to ascertain the *state of performance within an operational environment*, including the automated components as well as the nonautomated components. In some cases, both forward and reverse transaction auditing may be required. In forward transaction auditing, a transaction must be provable from the point of origin to the point of termination. In reverse transaction auditing, a transaction must be provable from the point of termination back through the system to the point of origin.

Auditing activities may take place with any variety of periodicity according to the operational requirements of the environment—from hourly to daily or yearly. Additionally, there may be varying levels of audits that take place. A subset of auditing activities may take place daily, while a full-scale in-depth audit may take place less frequently, such as quarterly or monthly.

Monitoring   *Monitoring* is periodically checking aspects of the operational environment to maintain awareness over the state of the environment, typically with the goal of ensuring that there are no problems. Monitoring activities can include both automated and nonautomated activities, such as profile analysis of computer-generated system usage/audit data, radar detection of movement within sensitive areas, guards checking lock integrity, or atmospheric pressure checking within communications conduits. Monitoring activities are the tactical equivalent of auditing activities—the minute-by-minute, day-by-day activities that ensure the integrity of the operational environment.

Both auditing and monitoring activities should be planned into the operational environment from the very beginning. For example, the capability to check the veracity of system processes is greatly enabled if that capability is designed in as an integral part of the system. The ability for malicious individuals to circumvent detection capabilities can be greatly curtailed by such forward thinking.

Now let's break down the phrase "checking to make sure everything is okay" to examine each element.

Checking...

The core of auditing and monitoring is the act of checking: checking transactions, checking authorizations, checking integrity, and checking the state of the security features. The risk management decisions and the policies in place define the things that are checked and the frequency with which they are checked.

There may be external influences on the requirements for checking. For example, if the system is a financial system, then there are certain rules stipulated by the standards of accounting that dictate what kind of auditing must be performed on the system. For other kinds of systems, the rules may be less clear. For example, what kind and how much checking would be useful in an online service provider system? Would it matter what kind of service is provided—such as electronic commerce versus Web site hosting? Of course it would matter.

The kind of checking the service provider would need to perform in an electronic commerce operational environment would include monitoring the state of system security features, reconciling transaction audit logs, and checking the physical security aspects of the environment. Given the speed with which electronic commerce occurs and the concomitant speed with which electronic fraud or theft may occur, the service provider may well be justified in performing such checks very often. Additionally, depending on the size of the operation, it could be appropriate for the service provider to use some of the tools that the credit card industry uses: artificial intelligence programs that check profiles for suspicious activities and issue alerts when such activities are noticed.

The type and frequency of checks that a Web site hosting service provider would need to perform are likely to be very different, again, depending on the kinds of services provided. Assuming any Web site of sufficient size and activity is more cost-effectively hosted by the owning organization (which may or may not be a good assumption but which serves as the basis for discussion here), the kinds of Web sites to be hosted by the service provider are likely to be fairly stable and small. In this operational environment, the service provider may simply check to see that the power is always on and that the communications linkages always work. If contracts with the clients include other services, such as integrity checking (to ensure that their sites are not hacked), then other checks would be necessary as well (such as checking to make sure none of the Web sites have been replaced or checking to make sure updates are performed by authorized users only).

The bottom line is that the auditing and monitoring must be sufficient to provide support to the protection, detection, and correction goals for the operational environment.

A fundamental standard that must be considered is how much auditing is required in order to manage your risk effectively? How much auditing and monitoring would a reasonable person perform in his or her daily activities? Remember, risk is composed of elements of threat and vulnerability. Regular audits and constant monitoring of your system can provide valuable clues to the state of threat activity against your system, as well as highlight any vulnerabilities that are being exploited.

There are certain sets of things that must be checked in auditing and monitoring. Three that make up the basic set are the functions of the information system, the protection mechanisms of the information system, and the detection mechanisms of the information system. The functions of the information system must be checked to make sure that they are operating according to plan and that they are not operating aberrantly. This is referred to as *positive* and *negative* testing.

Positive Testing   Positive testing establishes that the functions are performed correctly. In this situation, you would test to see that a transaction as performed is done correctly and according to the protective mechanisms in place. For example, you could test to see that a medical record is updated without its confidentiality being compromised.

Negative Testing   Negative testing is making sure that the information system is not doing what it should not be doing. This is much more difficult and much less certain than positive testing for the simple reason that it requires both an exhaustive test of the logic of a system and a great deal of imagination as to how that logic could be manipulated by malicious individuals. With the complexity of modern computer systems, exhaustive negative testing is far too expensive and time-consuming for most risk management decisions. However, a shortcut method that may be used employs a professional security consultant who mimics a potential threat agent mindset in order to test the system. In this way, a system can be stressed reasonably thoroughly and any high-probability attack profiles can be discovered.

The protection mechanisms must be checked to make sure that they are in place, have not been tampered with, and are operating properly. Again, it is futile to have a fence if a hole in the fence goes unnoticed because its integrity is never checked. Designing in features to the protective mechanisms to check their operational status and integrity can make this easier, or at least more automated. Running an electric current through a fence can provide indications that the fence has been cut—by monitoring the electric current. Maintaining negative atmospheric pressure in a sealed communications cable conduit can provide indications that the conduit has been breached—by monitoring the pressure (opening the conduit to the normal atmosphere will raise the pressure, which can be measured). In both of these examples, the protective measure (the fence or the cable conduit) is monitored to ensure that it is working properly and has not been tampered with by any force, malicious or otherwise.

The detection mechanisms must be checked also to ensure that they are in place, operating properly, and unmodified. For example, if the monitoring equipment on the above-mentioned fence or cable conduit were modified to ignore a change in status of the item monitored, then the protective mechanism could be breached without recognition of that fact. Detection mechanisms include a wide range of things in any operational environment and should be recognized as such. Not only the automated monitoring systems, such as those described above, are detection mechanisms but also the processes that support everyday business endeavors and every member of an enterprise can serve as a detection mechanism. Properly educated and trained, employees can be the first to be aware if something is amiss—not quite right—within the operational environment. Even if they are unable to identify immediately what is amiss, the uneasy sense (or sense of unease) that things are not as they should be can be a powerful detection mechanism.

The Testing Process

The frequency with which the system is checked can vary widely according to the risk management decisions made regarding the protection of the system. For example, a thorough audit of a home personal computer system may occur only every year or so, because the threat and vulnerability information indicates that there is low probability of an attack and also because the active countermeasures, such as virus scanning, are adequate to negate what threats are likely to attack. The monitoring aspect may be limited to checking periodically to see that the system is still physically in place (i.e., checking to see that it hasn't been stolen) and running the virus scanner in the background to warn of suspicious activity by software modules.

However, in commercial systems where there are responsibilities and regulations associated with the provable performance of a system (for example, a financial transaction system), both regular and in-depth audits as well as real-time monitoring of system performance, status of protective measures, and system usage would be crucial, and regularly scheduled in-depth audits would be required. In that kind of situation, automated tools that process data collected specifically for the purpose of auditing and monitoring the system are necessary.

There are two elements that make automated tools attractive. The first is that automated tools never have to take a coffee break or go home to nurse sick children; they are always on guard and they operate predictively and repetitively, performing the most mind-numbing tasks with precision. The second is that automated tools can perform complex analyses on enormous volumes of trivial data. The volume of data collected in systems can be too large for a human (or even a team of humans) to process. Comparing what time each user logged in and logged out, what files were accessed, and what was done to each file, then comparing those actions to the roles and responsibilities of each user requires the processing speed and patience of a computer, and reserves the human brain for what it does best—reasoning with incomplete or uncertain information.

What information is checked depends on the system. In a multiuser high-profile system, like a financial transaction system, you would want to audit and monitor every aspect associated with data processing, from compiling new code for the system to processing ordinary transactions. This would necessarily result in a huge amount of data, which would necessarily need to be processed in a protected manner. One of the critical challenges in designing a useful auditing and monitoring system is incorporating a mechanism for writing the audit and monitor data to a secure second system that cannot be corrupted by an intruder or an attacker. One way this can be accomplished is by creating a protected write-only stream of data to a CD-ROM and providing a verifiable log of what happened and in what sequence. There are engineering challenges inherent in this solution, including protecting a buffer space for storing the data before it is written to disk. The different speeds with which the hardware components actually operate create these challenges, which must not be overlooked in engineering a secure solution.

Who Audits?

Deciding who does the checking can be as difficult as engineering the auditing and monitoring processes. There are three separable issues here:

1. How are auditing and monitoring capabilities incorporated into the operational environment?

2. Who performs the everyday functions of monitoring the system and conducting routine audits?

3. Who performs in-depth compliance audits?

The auditing and monitoring capabilities must not be designed and implemented by a single person who could benefit from shortcomings or weaknesses in those systems. Consider this the fox-in-charge-of-the-henhouse rule: To keep the fox from succumbing to temptation, it is best not to tempt him—likewise, when designing and implementing an auditing and monitoring capability. The best solution, obviously, is to have the auditing and monitoring capabilities designed and implemented by a team of individuals, none of whom can benefit individually from flaws in the system or knowledge of internal workings and each of whom only know a portion of the entire system. If the organization is so small that the fox must be involved, then invoke a two-fox rule. Any capability proposed by one fox must be implemented by another fox, thus creating a check and balance on any one fox's knowledge base. The ability to monitor and audit the foxes' activities should be a crucial element in this arrangement.

The auditing and monitoring functions themselves should be performed by individuals who are not in a conflict-of-interest situation both in the day-to-day activities and also in the in-depth compliance audits. The most common mistake is to appoint individuals to audit and monitoring duties who, by virtue of their positions, have such conflicts. Typically, this involves personnel working in the computer support organizations who, as an additional duty, are assigned the responsibility to review the computer-generated audit data. This situation not only shortchanges the auditing and monitoring functions (by limiting the de facto auditing and monitoring activities to only computer system activities, as well as by excluding synergy with other security features, such as physical security), it also puts those individuals in a difficult situation. The difficulty can arise from elements such as resource allocation as well as from blame allocation. For example, if a problem is found, who pays for the fix? Does it come out of the baseline computer system budget? If so, are there competing requirements that may cause the security requirement to get lower priority? When the individuals responsible for identifying the problems are the same ones who must allocate resources across competing requirements, their ability to argue for the security-related fixes could be compromised.

A rule of thumb to consider is this: Ask who would be to blame if something went wrong with the system protections and then to map out who is subordinate to that person. None of those people should be associated with inspecting the system. There is too much danger in conflicting job requirements, in overlooking one problem in favor of another, or in engaging in cover-up activities for the short term. Instead, the inspectors—the audit team—should be composed of those who have no vested interest, one way or the other, in the state of the system, have the requisite skills to conduct a competent audit, and have the ability to report the findings of the audit to a person in sufficient enough authority that the results of the audit do not get lost or suborned.

This means that the audit team typically should not report to the CIO, but to the CEO, depending on the structure and responsibilities of the organization. At the very least, the audit team should not report to the head of the information systems security team. In complex and sensitive systems, the audit team is best composed of outsiders who have no ties to the organization at all. This enables them to do a fair and complete workup of the information system without fear of politics or of repercussions.

...to make sure...

Answering the questions relating to "making sure" involves a detailed understanding of the specific operational environment. How do you make sure? What is meant by "sure"? How much sureness is needed? All of these relate to what kind of system there is, how much computerized operations are being performed versus how much paper-based operations, and who is performing the operations.

In order to know what constitutes "sure," performance criteria must be specified. This provides the ability to establish thresholds and measurement criteria that together define the concept of "sure" for the specific operational environment. For example, in a hospital environment, a policy may be that no unauthorized person may have access to patient records. Performance criteria associated with this policy is fairly straightforward: The number of unauthorized individuals having access to each patient record must be zero. Testing this proposition is trickier. Testing for this performance criteria requires that all vectors through which access could be had must be examined and monitored to ensure that no unauthorized person gets access to one or more patient records. Considering that Doctor X may be authorized for access to the records of Patient A and Patient B but not for the records of Patient C, the tests and monitoring tools must take into account specific individual privileges, supporting updates as required. If a change is made to access privileges, then the definition of "sure" as interpreted by the auditing and monitoring functions must change too. When Doctor X was not authorized access to the records of Patient C, the practical definition of "sure" included a codicil that Doctor X could not and had not accessed the records of that patient. When Doctor X was called in as a consulting physician to Patient C, the practical definition of "sure" should have changed.

The concept of "sure" is, of necessity, modified by practicality as appropriate to the operational environment. In the above case, doctors as a group are likely to be more trusted in a hospital environment than other groups, such as maintenance staff. The practicality of the situation, then, would tend to limit the thoroughness of checking to establish "sureness" with regard to Doctor X to most likely a cursory check on file access. In this specific situation, "sure" would most likely be defined fairly loosely. However, if the hospital was one that handled heads of state or other dignitaries, the definition of "sureness" could well be interpreted much more strictly, with concomitant checking to establish compliance with the desired state of "sure."

...everything...

The concept of "everything" is very similar to that of "sure." It is defined by the performance criteria and the security requirements of the operational environment. For example, the security aspects of a grocery store differ fundamentally from those of an elementary school. In a grocery store, the public is encouraged to enter and to look at the merchandise. Security measures in a store include measures to prevent theft by both employees and the public but do not include positive identification of every person who walks through the door. In an elementary school, security concerns center on the safety of the children. Kidnapping, abduction, molestation, and other harmful actions are the focus of the elementary school security concerns. Members of the public who wish to visit should not be allowed to walk in freely, there should be some measure of positive identification of persons who do visit, and the privacy information of the children should be protected.

Because of these fundamental differences in the security concerns of the two operational environments, the "everything" that needs to be checked and ensured for "okayness" becomes fundamentally different as well. In the grocery store, the "everything" would include such things as the inventory control devices, the personnel hiring practices, the employee performance reports, the register balances, and the transaction reports. In the school, the "everything" would include such things as the privacy protection measures, visitor identification and control measures, personnel hiring procedures, employee performance reports, student accountability processes, and record access controls.

...is okay.

"Okay" is defined by the environment in which you operate or live and is directly related to "sure." For example, in a home environment you may not have the same concerns about authenticating the individuals accessing information that you would in a work environment. There are several reasons for this. One is that in your home environment you may have more physical control over information, whether by dint of limited access to the home itself or by limited number of people living in the home. Additionally, you may have better knowledge and trust in the individuals at home, as well as a comprehensive knowledge of their skill level. Finally, at home there is typically an intertwined interest providing an additional level of assurance that you may not have at work. At work there are a large number of individuals who are less known than in the home environment. You may have known the individuals for only a short period of time, they may have interests that are substantially different from yours, and/or they may not have the correct skill set required to prevent mistakes or omissions. What is "okay," therefore, is heavily influenced by the environment in which you exist.

Another factor that impacts the definition of "okay" is content. Dealing with nuclear secrets is obviously much more critical than dealing with lunch menus at the local high school. However, there is an additional dimension to the information itself that pertains to its criticality or need for protection other than its inherent sensitivity. Laws, regulations, and policies define that additional dimension. You may have no control over these things—and probably won't—but that does not relieve you of the requirement to comply with them. In many cases there are significant penalties for not complying to ensure such compliance. These cases include financial transactions as well as personnel data.

"Okayness" must thus be defined *a priori*. The concept of okayness must be derived from an analysis of the environment, an understanding of the information needs and flows, and an assessment of what "okay" means in that environment. It must also be tied directly to the performance criteria and reflected in the policy statements.

Putting It Together

Combining all the elements together provides the framework for understanding the fundamental requirements for auditing and monitoring in an operational environment. Auditing and monitoring are how you ensure that your protections are in place and operational, as well as a principal method of detecting when protections fail or are inadequate. These critical functions are thus a linchpin of your business continuity planning.

In summary, based on the analysis of your operational environment, planned and specific audits and monitoring activities should be conducted to ensure compliance with performance requirements (which includes security performance requirements) and policy statements. Individuals with no conflicts of interest that could shade their objectivity in either the process itself or the outcome should undertake these activities. The results of the activities should be communicated clearly and fed back into ongoing risk management efforts.

Block 9: Stay on Top

Computer attacks are on the increase, and they are becoming more effective. Enterprise managers need to stay current, and this is a tough job at best. Listed below and in the References are some helpful places to start the process of continuous learning:[13]

Incident Response Centers

Australian Computer Emergency Response Team (AUSCERT)
http://www.auscert.org.au/
E-mail: auscert@auscert.org.au
Phone: +61-7-3365-4417

CERT(sm) Coordination Center
http://www.cert.org/
E-mail: cert@cert.org
Phone: +1-412-268-7090

Computer Incident Advisory Capability (CIAC)
http://ciac.llni.gov/
E-mail: ciac@llnl.gov
Phone: +1-925-422-8193

Defense Information Systems Agency Center for Automated System
  Security Incident Support Team (ASSIST, for DoD sites)
http://www. assist.mil/
E-mail: cert@cert.mil
Phone: +1-800-357-4231

Federal Computer Incident Response Capability (FedCIRC)
http://www.fedcirc.gov/
E-mail: fedcirc@fedcirc.gov
Phone: +1-888-282-0870

Forum of Incident Response and Security Teams (FIRST)
http://www.first.org/
E-mail: first-sec@first.org

The German Research Network Computer Emergency Response Team
  (DFN-CERT)
http://www.cert.dfn.de/eng/dfncert/
E-mail: dfncert@cert.dfn.de
Phone: +49-40-42883-2262

NASA Incident Response Center (NASIRC)
http://www-nasirc.nasa.gov/nasa/index.htm
E-mail: nasirc@nasirc.nasa.gov
Phone: +1-800-762-7472

Federal Bureau of Investigation (FBI)—National Infrastructure
  Protection Center (NIPC)
http://www.fbi.gov/nipe/index.htm
E-mail: nipc@fbi.gov
FBI Field Offices can be found at http://www.fbi.gov/fo/fo.htm
European CERTs
http://www.cert.dfn.de/eng/csir/europe/certs.html

Security Web Sites

Here are some useful Web sites for security information:

- http://www.infosyssec.org/infosyssec/index.html
- http://www.cs.purdue.edu/coast/
- http://www.telstra.com.au/info/security.html
- http://www.ntbugtraq.com/
- http://www.nsi.org/cornpsec.html
- http://www.sans.org

- http://www.securityportal.com
- http://www.icsa.net/

   Following are U.S. government security Web sites:

- http://www.itpolicy.gsa.gov/
- http://www.cit.nih.gov/security.html
- http://cs-www.nist.gov/
- http://www.bc.org/

Vendor-Specific Tracking—Cryptography/INFOSEC/Biometrics

- http://www.comsec-solutions.com
- http://www.certicom.com
- http:/www.counterpane.com
- http://www.RSA.com
- http://www.cs.georgetown.edu/~denning/crypto/index.html
- http://www.danjryan.com
- http://www.julieryan.com

Training

- http://www.rsa.com
- http://www.sans.org
- http://www.certicom.com

Security Books

Check the reference section at the back of this book for a current and varied selection of security books. They are available through Amazon at www.amazon.com or www.fatbrain.com.

Security Mailings

Send your subscription requests to the email address listed.

- Bugtraq Full Disclosure List: listserv@netspace.org

- CERT Advisories: cert-advisory-request@cert.org
- CIAC Advisories (ciac-bulletin): Majordomo@rumpole.llnl.gov
- COAST Security Archive: coast-request@cs.purdue.edu
- Firewalls Digest (firewall-digest): majordomo@greatcircle.com
- FreeBSD Security issues: majordomo@freebsd.org
- Intrusion Detection Systems (ids): majordomo@uow.edu.au
- Linux Security Issues: linux-securfty-request@RedHat.com
- Legal Aspects of Computer Crime (lacc): majordomo@suburbia.net
- NT Bugtraq: listserv@listserv.ntbugtraq.com
- The RISKS Forum (risks): majordomo@csl.sri.com
- WWW Security (ww-security-new): majordomo@nsmx.rutgers.edu
- The Virus Lists (virus-I Ft virus): LISTSERV@lehigh.edu

The above lists are not inclusive and are a starting point for further investigations.

Notes

1. John M. Carroll, Computer Security, 3rd ed. (Oxford, U.K.: Butterworth-Heinemann, 1996). Figures 13-1 and 13-2 reproduced with permission.

2. There are several commercial risk-analysis packages available on the market, including CRAMM: CCTA Risk Analysis Management Methodology by Robin Moses; IST/RAMP and CRITI-CALC: Risk Analysis Package by Robert Jacobson at International Security Technology; LAVA: Los Alamos Vulnerability/Risk Assessment System by Suzanne Smith at Los Alamos National Laboratory; IRAM: Livermore Risk Analysis methodology by Abel Garcia, Sergio Guarro, and Charles Cresson Wood; MARION: Methodology for Computer Risk Management by CLUSIF in France; RISKCALC: tool developed by Lance Hoffman at Hoffman Business Systems, 1986; RISKPAC by New York Bank, Profile Analysis Corp. by Peter Browse and James Laverty. There are others that may be found by searching the Internet.

3. Carroll, op. cit.

4. Ibid, 479.

5. Hutt, Arthur E., Seymour Bosworth, and Douglas B. Hoyt, eds, " Chapter 7: Information Security Risk Management," in Computer Security Handbook, 3rd ed., by John M. Carroll (New York: Wiley, 1995).

6. Carroll, op. cit., 494.

7. Cheswick and Bellovin list 40 weak points in their book Firewalls and Internet Security: Repelling the Wily Hacker, (Reading, Mass.: Addison-Wesley, 1994).

8. Hutt et al., op. cit., Chapter 7.

9. Levine, Diane E., "Viruses and Related Threats to Computer Security," Chap. 19 in *Computer Security Handbook*, 3rd ed., edited by Arthur E. Hutt et al. (New York, Wiley, 1995).

10. "Fifth Annual ICSA Labs Computer Virus Prevalence Survey," August 1999, available from http://www.icsa.net

11. Ibid.

12. Ibid.

13. Parts of these lists courtesy of SANS Institute, *1999 Network Security Roadmap*, from www.sans.org

CHAPTER 14

During and After the Attack Special Consideration— The Web Server

During the Attack: Detect and React

When an event happens, reactions should be swift and sure. Any time lost trying to figure out what to do is time that allows resources to be lost and attackers to gain advantage. Consider the example of a guard discovering a broken lock on a door leading to a secure facility. The time between discovery and when reactive measures are instituted, such as inspections at all ingress and egress points, is time for the perpetrator to escape. Similarly, with a natural disaster such as an earthquake, time is critical. From the moment the earthquake is detected to the time when alternative operations are established is a window of operational vulnerability where data, transactions, and possibly even lives may be lost.

Having good detection capabilities is one part of the effort to ensure operational capability in all situations and having sufficient reaction capabilities is another part. Without the ability to react constructively to a detected problem, the result is knowledge without power. Assuming he or she is not a Dilbert-type manager, he or she may know something is wrong but not what to do, or may lack the ability/authority to do anything. Having the ability to react constructively is knowledge enabling power. The manager knows something is wrong, so he or she immediately reacts to limit the damage, to contain the problem, and to produce a solution.

There are a number of things that a proactive manager can do. These include (1) continually monitor and audit the operational environment, (2) put in place security emergency response teams, (3) perform system and network triage, (4) reconstitute capabilities at a backup location, (5) encourage employees to report any indication of an the attack, (6) analyze the attack, plug the holes, and set future directions, and (7) secure the Web server first—it often represents a company's most critical vulnerability.

Continually Audit and Monitor the Operational Environment

Keeping an eye on the operational environment is critical to detecting problems or attacks. Seeing that the chain-link fence has been cut is an indicator that someone may have penetrated the perimeter. It may also, of course, be a ruse designed to draw your attention away from the actual attack activity. In any event, seeing a hole cut in the fence is an indicator that all is not as it should be. A prudent manager would then launch activities to find out what exactly is going on—where the hole came from and why must be answered with positive knowledge in order to be able to make any kind of assertions about the state of security of the environment.

The requirements for monitoring and auditing should be engineered into the environment. If this is done, the environment benefits from integrated security, but more importantly, there can be less intrusion into other operational activities by the monitoring and auditing activities. The more transparent these actions are to the casual user, the less likely it is that they will be circumvented or sabotaged.

Having a regular surveillance program to monitor the elements of the environment for integrity and compliance is a critical element of proactive security. There are four primary elements in a holistic monitoring program, three of which have to do with the people in the environment. First, personnel in the environment must be continually aware of their surroundings, know who is acting in what capacity, and know whether things are complying with policy. Second, managers must be aware of the activities of subordinates. Managers bear a special responsibility in monitoring activities because of their inherent responsibility for the actions of subordinates. Third, the security forces, such as guards and security staff, must routinely monitor the state of the environment and activities in the public areas. This can and should be augmented by automated monitoring technologies, such as cameras and other sensors. Finally, the information systems must be monitored for attacks or other problems.

There are three stages of auditing that must be attended to in a comprehensive proactive security environment. The lowest level of these auditing activities is the automated transaction auditing. At this level, transactions in the environment are collected and audited routinely. An example of this might be the routine analysis of personnel traffic in a facility as recorded through the use of badge readers. This kind of auditing can reveal potentially suspicious activity or could provide evidence to support allegations of misconduct.

The second level of auditing manifests itself as periodic examinations of the enterprise for compliance to security policies. This includes making sure that the information systems are being used in compliance with security policy, that human resources personnel are following security policies when an employee leaves the company, that security awareness training is being conducted routinely and that no employee is able to skip the training, and that personnel are not able to enter areas where they have no business. In short, every aspect of the security policies must be checked periodically to make sure it is being followed correctly within the environment.

The highest level of auditing is a thorough examination of the environment to ensure that not only are security policies being followed but also that systems are working correctly and that systems are not working incorrectly. In other words, this level is a full-blown, in-depth examination of the environment for compliance to security requirements.

Performing regular and routine monitoring and auditing activities in the enterprise is the first critical step to finding problems or seeing an attack. During nonproblematic times, these actions will provide a baseline of activity that can assist in determining whether an attack is under way or not.

During problematic times, while under attack, having such processes in place provides you with the critical knowledge necessary to know where the attacks are coming from or where the problems are originating. This critical information can be used to isolate attacks and limit their effectiveness.

Monitoring and auditing data can also be used in post attack activities, such as recovery, if properly maintained. The operational structure of the enterprise can be re-created from audit data possibly, or evidence useful in criminal prosecutions can be developed from auditing and monitoring data.

Security Emergency Response Teams

Security emergency response teams (SERTs) are exactly that: teams specifically trained and equipped to respond to security emergencies. When a problem is detected, a SERT will jump into action and execute the plans that have been developed and formalized as policy throughout the organization. Managing a SERT effectively can provide robust and efficient capabilities. SERTs that are composed of modular elements, with each element specializing in a different area, such as physical security or computer security, allows an incident-specific SERT to be compiled. This allows the SERT to respond as needed with the required resources and without interference from extraneous resources trying to be helpful.

SERTs should be exercised regularly with dummy runs—that is, walking the team through each type of situation and updating reaction techniques as needed. Practicing notification and reaction procedures is essential to effective response during an actual crisis. For those enterprises without the resources to have a comprehensive SERT in-house, there are now companies offering these capabilities as an outsourced service. For those with in-house SERTs, training with the company lawyer or legal counsel can provide critical feedback for conducting actions legally and protecting evidence in case of actual operations. The members of the SERTs should be trained in the legal issues associated with SERT activities, particularly regarding information systems.

System and Network Triage

When an attack against a system or network is detected, it may be impossible to stop the attack without fairly drastic measures. An example of this would be an insider who is unidentified at the time the attack is detected and who has managed to create many different accounts to provide cover and concealment for his or her activities. In this case, it may be necessary to perform triage on the system.

The term *triage* is borrowed from warfare emergency medical care focused on saving as many patients as possible in extreme situations, such as on the battlefield, by the assignment of priorities. Casualties were sorted into three groups: those who would die no matter how much care was given, those who would live even if the treatment was delayed, and those who would die without immediate care but who might live if immediate care was received. *Triage* is also used more generically to refer to any system of establishing the order in which acts are to be carried out in an emergency. The application of the term to information security, then, implies the setting of priorities of action. This must be based on the *a priori* analysis of the operational environment and the identification of requirements for the security of the system. If analysis revealed that a certain system was integral to the continued operations of the enterprise, then a valid triage action could be to sever the connection between the mission-critical system and the vector of the attack, thereby protecting the mission-critical component from the attack. Alternatively, severing connections among multiple systems may be a way of limiting the effects of an attack: to stop a cascade of effects before catastrophic failure can occur.

The objective in developing a triage capability is to define the components and operational elements of the alert responses. It should include the following actions:

- Define the stages of heightened alert—this may result from different inputs from your detection capabilities or from environmental considerations, or a combination of the two.
- Develop triggers for your detection and response capabilities.
- Define operational responses within the context of your security poli-

cies and enterprise operational requirements—and, if need be, update your policies in response.

- Develop specific triage tools and methods.
- Test the validity of the comprehensive construct with exercises to make sure your processes work and are responsive to your needs.
- Document the processes, exercises and results.

Fundamental to the consideration of what the enterprise should do to protect itself from attacks through the use of triage is the development of *thresholds* and *graduated response options*. Cutting off an arm in response to an ingrown nail is clearly not an appropriate response. Yet, if the arm were infected and gangrenous, amputation may well be the correct response. Understanding that the different levels of danger and appropriate responses is part of risk management assists in defining the actions associated with triage responses.

Performing *detection* and *warning functions* within a complex and interconnected information environment requires a methodology that recognizes the complexity of the technologies and works within that framework to respond appropriately with both active and passive measures. Implicit in maintaining a comprehensive and responsive defense posture is recognition that systems change with time and context—what is trivial one day may have significant influence the next, depending on how activities are evolving. The various levels of response should additionally reflect simple effects as well as combinatorial effects. For example, it should be possible to go from the lowest level of alert to the highest as required without undue delay.

A prime requirement for defense is the ability to communicate a heightened level of alertness to the elements of a system. There are analogies in warfare—such as the Def Con (defense condition) System—and in humans—adrenaline and the "fight or flight" syndrome. In conventional constructs, as levels of threat intent increase, defensive interests expand accordingly. Security perimeters and pickets are deployed to "furthest" extent to provide "early warning" and support to indications and warning functions. Prophylactic actions are established and taken to provide greater protection to critical systems as the need arises. Defense of the information infrastructure is complicated by interconnectivity and recognition that a heightened state of alert must extend to all connected systems. At a high level of excitement, the response could include disconnecting from parts of the infrastructure. Conceivably, if warranted, there could be emergency protocols that extend across lower levels of system protocols, from physical-layer protocols to transport-layer protocols. A workable alert and response process requires a comprehensive legal, regulatory, and operational infrastructure that garners participation at some level by every element.

A description of a scheme that serves as a starting point for an analysis of how a workable construct could develop is shown in Figure 14-1. This figure is for illustration only—any specific scheme would necessarily be unique to the operational environment it is designed to support. Figure 14-1 provides a starting point for thinking about what would comprise levels of emergency situations and what would be appropriate responses to those situations.

For the Normal level shown in the chart, there is a normal level of threat from crime and incompetence as well as a normal level of activities in all sectors of the enterprise. The goal of the security plan should be to minimize the effects of normal problems. Responses required at this level of alert status would therefore be what should amount to the normal actions and requirements that always exist, such as due diligence in

Figure 14-1
Example: Triage Alert Conditions and Responses

	Situation	Responses
Alert 4	Active attack on system or other disaster activity (such as fire or earthquake).	Disconnect critical elements from public infrastructure. Implement emergency plans.
Alert 3	Detection of multiple intrusions or attempts to breach security features of operational environment.	Implement alternate routing and limit interconnectivity to minimal states. Begin "aggressive" forensics investigations.
Alert 2	Detection of intrusion or other malicious activity.	Disconnect all unnecessary connections. Turn on real-time audit. Begin mandatory reporting to central control. Activate interface with external authorities.
Alert 1	Detection of minor problems in one part of the system. (Ex.: out-of-profile user)	Increase incident monitoring, look for patterns, alert enterprise to increase awareness of activities, begin increased monitoring of critical elements.
Normal	Normal level of threat from crime and users.	Normal actions and requirements.

protecting information systems and assets, performing "reasonable person" levels of maintenance activities, compliance with appropriate financial transaction auditing requirements, and compliance with all applicable rules, regulations, and laws. A valuable by-product of adopting a triage alert response framework could be a wider understanding of what "normal" security requirements are; this can be used as a training tool on applicable laws, regulations, and policies within the enterprise.

For Alert 1, the situation is one in which activity is detected, but it is not clear whether it is accidental, malicious, or incidental to other activities. This is illustrated as a user operating out of profile—perhaps entering the facility at 2 A.M.—but it could be something innocuous as well. The specific triggers and thresholds would have to be established through analysis of the operational environment and the security requirements. In large organizations, it conceivably could be something like a 10 percent increase in help desk calls. Or it could be notification from some external authority, such as the Carnegie-Mellon CERT, of an active threat. Responses at this level could include increased incident monitoring and cooperative analysis, looking for patterns across a wider range of variables including perhaps source, users, time, connections, and equipment; alerting all elements to increase awareness of activities; and beginning selective intensive monitoring of critical elements, turning on expanded audit and tracking capabilities with central reports.

For Alert 2, the situation could be characterized as that of a heightened security posture, such as in response to a large-scale increase in help desk inquiries or to a specific incident of malicious activity. Responses could include a systematic disconnection of all nonvital connections as an attempt to start locking the doors and restricting access to a few well-monitored and recognizably engineered connections. Another type of response could be the broadcast of advisory notices over diverse media to all elements of enterprise, similar to a public emergency broadcast warning. Limiting connections should force a channeling of hostile activity—thereby making it easier to track and collect information on the activity—as well as reducing the number of back doors that are subject to attack. Additionally, it could simplify the audit and monitoring functions of critical systems. A possibility that should be considered is turning on real-time audit for critical systems, although this would certainly require specialized tools and augmentation of audit analysis teams to handle increased workloads. At this point, it may also be desirable to begin interfacing with official agencies, such as the FBI, Secret Service, and police, to support forensics investigations.

For Alert 3, the situation is clearly serious with significant unwarranted activity under way. Responses could include implementing emergency alternate routing, limiting interconnectivity to minimal states, and performing disconnections to protect the main body of the infrastructure. Transferring operations to a backup facility either in whole or in part may be warranted according to the situation.

For Alert 4, the situation is critical and represents widespread problems that undermine an ability to function. Again, these problems could range from natural disasters, such as fire, hurricanes, or tornadoes, to active criminal activity, such as robbery or arson. Responses could include disconnecting critical elements from public infrastructure, deploying temporary systems as required, possibly implementing emergency protocols, and transferring operations to a backup facility.

A triage plan for a specific enterprise should reflect the security requirements, the operational environment, and the policies in place.

Reconstituting Capability at a Backup Location

Having an ability to quickly and efficiently transfer operational capability to a backup location may be an operational requirement for the enterprise. When New York City experienced the bombing of the World Trade Center, those business operations that had considered what to do in case of disaster were best able to survive in the long run. Smaller enterprises, some that had not considered such a situation, had to scramble to find alternate modes of operation, such as travel agencies dependent on phone connections and drop-in customers. The unprepared went out of business at least for a while and some permanently.

A critical question to ask is this: How long can the enterprise exist without operating? If it is five minutes, then a "hot" backup site and real-time switchover capabilities are required. If it is a month, then there is more flexibility in making the arrangements for a backup facility. The question is not as clear-cut as with catastrophic disaster. In the case of catastrophic disaster, insurance may provide some level of cushion for the transition. If a crime is committed in your facilities (for example, a murder), the police may seal off the area for a significant amount of time and insurance may not cover any of the losses incurred. If the area that is sealed off includes your data processing equipment, you may need to switch over operations immediately.

A corollary question is how much information can the enterprise afford to lose permanently? In the case of a catastrophic disaster, such as a bombing, the information may well be destroyed if the only copy of it is in the facility. If this is not acceptable, then there must be real-time backup of information occurring to minimize losses. In the case of the police sealing off spaces in your facility, the data may not be destroyed, but neither is it accessible. If it is the only copy its utility is thereby destroyed. These considerations must be taken into account when developing reaction and correction plans and capabilities.

The bottom line is that to provide business continuity, you should be able to reconstitute both the operational environment and the information within a reasonable amount of time, where "reasonable" is defined by your specific operational needs.

Develop a Nonhostile Environment

Several years ago, New York City was the scene of a brutal stabbing murder. Twenty-six witnesses watched from their apartments and on the street and heard the screams of a young female teacher as she was repeatedly stabbed. None of witnesses called the police or attempted to help. The crime was over and the woman died in the street. People didn't want to get involved. The system at that time was so oppressive to the witness that getting involved had no payoff. The incident led to one of the first Good Samaritan laws, which relieved the passerby from liability if he or she helped another citizen in medical or physical danger.

Similarly, managers can make their working environment so oppressive that employees will not report a security incident and "certainly not an attack"—even though they watch it take place in the computer facility. Managers who punish the employee who reports the problem and assume that the reporter is somehow involved are part of the problem themselves, not the solution. Managers need to set up supporting policies and act in positive ways to ensure that security incidents are reported so that SERT teams can be activated in a timely manner. There is generally too much money and too many employees affected to play silly power games. Continuous employee training ranks as the best answer. It has been estimated that only 15 percent of employees will report a security incident in progress to their supervisor and less than five percent will take the incident to the responsible department manager. This indicates a significant problem that must be addressed if an enterprise expects to harness its most important asset: the people who live and work within the operational environment and who know the systems intimately.

After the Attack—Pick Up the Pieces and Classify the Attack

After your department reloads programs and operating systems, checks for virus infections, runs status and diagnostics on the system, determines damages, and provides a situation report to senior management, it is time to *classify the attack and make preparations in anticipation of a second wave.* Systems administrators need a high-level understanding of the methods attackers use to penetrate computers to prevent attacks in cyberspace. You cannot effectively fight a war without some knowledge of your enemy's weapons. The Information Technology Laboratory, National Institute of Standards and Technology, provides guidance on tricks of intruders and educates the public on how to stop them.

Overview of Attacker Tools

In-depth resources are available on the Internet that enable intruders to penetrate computer networks. Detailed software vulnerability information is publicly discussed in newsgroups. Attacking tutorials are available that describe how to write automated programs that penetrate computers by taking advantage of these vulnerabilities. Thousands of automated software tools have been written that enable anyone so inclined to launch computer attacks. Computer attacks are no longer found on obscure pirate bulletin boards but rather on publicly available commercial Web sites whose sole purpose is to provide this information. In addition to being freely available, these attacks are becoming easier to implement. A few years ago, one had to have UNIX to run an attack and had to know how to compile source code. In 1999, attacks with user-friendly graphical user interfaces (GUIs) that run on Windows hosts are available. Attack scripts are easy to use and dangerous to the victim. It is vital that systems administrators understand the danger these attacks pose and how to protect their networks.

Classification of Computer Attacks

When we say "computer attack," we mean programs run to gain unauthorized control over a computer. It is essential to know what type of attack was used on your enterprise. Knowing the nature of the attack indicates what countermeasures should be imposed to improve security. Attacks take a variety of forms but generally fall into the following categories:[1]

1. *Remote penetration*   Programs that go out on the Internet (or network) and gain unauthorized control of a computer.

2. *Local penetration*   Programs that gain unauthorized access to the computer on which they are run.

3. *Remote denial of service*   Programs that go out on the Internet (or network) and shut down another computer or a service provided by that computer.

4. *Local denial of service*   Programs that shut down the computer on which they are run.

5. *Network scanners*   Programs that map out a network to determine which computers and services are available to be exploited.

6. *Vulnerability scanners*   Programs that search throughout the Internet looking for computers vulnerable to a particular type of attack.

7. *Password crackers*   Programs that discover easy-to-guess passwords in encrypted password files. Computers can now reveal passwords so quickly that many seemingly complex passwords can be classed as plain language.

8. *Sniffers*   Programs that listen to network traffic. Often these programs have features to extract user names, passwords, or credit card information automatically.

Statistical Sampling of Publicly Available Computer Attacks

In 1998, NIST categorized and analyzed 237 computer attacks found on the Internet out of an estimated 400 published attacks. This sample yielded the statistics shown in Table 14-1.[2]

The Most Popular Attacks on the Internet—Which One Disabled Your Company Computers?

There are literally hundreds of attacks that can be launched against your systems. It simply isn't possible to address every single one of them. However, an overview of some of the more common ones can reveal what

TABLE 14-1

NIST Statistics.

Statistic: 29% of attacks can launch from Windows hosts.

Lesson: One does not need to understand UNIX to be dangerous. We are in an era of "point-and-click" attacks.

Statistic: 20% of attacks are able to remotely penetrate network elements (e.g., routers, switches, hosts, printers, and firewalls).

Lesson: Attacks that give remote users access to hosts are not rare.

Statistic: 3% of the analysis enabled Web sites to attack those who visited the site.

Lesson: Surfing the Web is not a risk-free activity.

Statistic: 4% of attacks scan the Internet for vulnerable hosts.

Lesson: Automated scanning attack tools, which find easily compromised hosts, abound. System administrators, with management concurrence or with professional assistance, should scan their own systems regularly.

Statistics: 5% of attacks are effective against routers and firewalls.

Lesson: The Internet infrastructure components themselves are vulnerable to attack. (To the computer industry's credit, most attacks were denial of service and scanning, and only a few were penetration attacks.)

vulnerabilities should be highest on a "fix" list. In March 1999, the most popular attacks (or vulnerable applications) found by NIST were Sendmail, ICQ, Smurf, Teardrop, IMAP, Back Orifice, Netbus, WinNuke, and Nmap.

Here's what to look for:

1. *Sendmail (aka "It's Alive!")*   Sendmail is a utility associated with the UNIX operating system that has been exploited by attackers to bypass security controls. It was one of the elements exploited by the 1987 Internet Worm. One of the most aggravating issues associated with the Sendmail utility is that no matter how often it is patched or updated, old versions with exploitable holes keep cropping up. One of the ways this happens is when the system administrators restore old system tapes for archive information or as a result of system problems. Having an unpatched or outdated version of Sendmail on your system is an invitation for attacks from any location, because the knowledge of how to exploit Sendmail features for devious purposes has been extremely well publicized.

2. *ICQ*   ICQ is a sophisticated chat program that stands for "I-Seek-You." It is currently owned by America Online and used by over 26 million users. In 1999, several ICQ attacks were developed that

allowed one to impersonate other people and decrypt "encrypted" traffic. An attacker would use these attacks by going to a chat room and finding two people who are friends. The attacker then pretends to be someone's friend and sends him or her a Trojan horse (malicious code embedded into a legitimate program) via ICQ.

3. *Smurf*   Smurf uses a network that accepts broadcast ping packets to flood the target with ping reply packets. Think of Smurf as an amplifier allowing an attacker anonymously to flood a target with a huge amount of data.

4. *Teardrop*   Teardrop freezes vulnerable Windows 95 and Linux hosts by exploiting a bug in the fragmented packet reassembly routines.

5. *IMAP*   The Internet Message Access Protocol (IMAP) allows users to download their e-mail from a server. IMAP server software was released in 1998 with a vulnerability that allows a remote attacker to gain complete control over the machine. A large number of mail servers use the vulnerable IMAP software.

6. *Back Orifice*   Back Orifice is a Trojan horse that allows a user to remotely control a Windows 95/98 host with an easy-to-use GUI.

7. *Netbus*   Netbus is similar to Back Orifice, but it works against Windows NT as well as Windows 95/98.

8. *WinNuke*   WinNuke freezes a Windows 95 host by sending it out-of-band TCP data.

9. *Nmap*   Nmap is a sophisticated network-scanning tool. Among other features, Nmap can scan using a variety of protocols, operate in stealth mode, and automatically identify remote operating systems.

Now That We Have ID'd Them, How Do We Prevent the Majority of Computer Attacks?

Managers must know that protecting one's networks from computer attacks is an ongoing and nontrivial task. However, some simple security measures will stop the majority of network penetration attempts. For example, a well-configured firewall that has been correctly installed and is regularly maintained can provide a significant level of protection against outside attacks. It can do nothing, of course, about the insider threat. Antiviral software that is regularly maintained and used can also significantly reduce potential problems on systems. NIST's ITL presents 14 security measures that, if implemented, will help secure a network.[3] Compare their recommendations with the procedures that your department has in place prior to the attack and the procedures that were not followed by your staff. Refer to the Notes for additional sources.[4-9]

1. *Patching*   Companies often release software patches in order to fix coding errors. Unfixed, these errors often allow an attacker to penetrate a computer system. Systems administrators should protect their most important systems by constantly applying the most recent patches. However, it is difficult to patch all hosts in a network because patches are released at a very fast pace. Focus on patching the most important hosts (applying triage methods, as discussed earlier in the chapter), and then implement the other security solutions mentioned below. Patches usually must be obtained from software vendors.

2. *Virus detection*   Virus-checking programs are indispensable to any network security solution. Virus checkers monitor computers and look for malicious code. One problem with virus checkers is that they must be installed on all computers for maximum effectiveness. It is time-consuming to install the software, and weekly updating is required for maximum effectiveness. Users can be trained to perform these updates, but they cannot be relied upon. In addition to the normal virus checking on each computer, we recommend that organizations scan e-mail attachments at the e-mail server. This way, the majority of viruses are stopped before reaching the users.

3. *Firewalls*   NIST reports that firewalls are the single most important security solution for protecting one's network. Firewalls police the network traffic that enter and leave a network. The firewall may disallow some traffic or may perform some sort of verification on other traffic. A well-configured firewall will stop the majority of publicly available computer or Internet-related attacks.

4. *Password crackers*   Hackers often use little-known vulnerabilities in computers to steal encrypted password files. They then use password-cracking programs that can discover weak passwords within encrypted password files. Once a weak password is discovered, the attacker can enter the computer as a normal user and use a variety of tricks to gain complete control of that computer and your network. While used by intruders, such programs are invaluable to systems administrators. Systems administrators

should run password-cracking programs on their own encrypted password files regularly to discover and expose weak passwords.

5. *Encryption*   Attackers often break into networks by listening to network traffic at strategic locations and by parsing cleartext user names and passwords. Thus, remote password-protected connections must be encrypted. This is especially true for remote connections over the Internet and connections to the most critical servers. A variety of commercial and free products are available to encrypt TCP/IP traffic.

6. *Vulnerability scanners*   Vulnerability scanners are programs that scan a network looking for vulnerable computers. The scanners have a large database of vulnerabilities that are used to probe computers to determine the vulnerable ones. Both commercial and free vulnerability scanners exist.

7. *Configuring hosts for security*   Computers with newly installed operating systems are often vulnerable to attack. The reason is that an operating system's installation programs generally enable all available networking features. This allows an attacker to explore the many avenues of attack. All unneeded network services should be turned off while new operating systems are being installed.

8. *War dialing*   Users often bypass a site's network security schemes by allowing their computers to receive incoming telephone calls. The user enables a modem upon leaving work and then is able to dial in from home and use the corporate network. Attackers use war-dialing programs to call a large number of telephone numbers looking for those computers allowed to receive telephone calls. Since users set up these computers themselves, they are often insecure and provide attackers a back door into the network. Systems administrators should use war dialers regularly to discover these back doors. Both commercial and free war dialers are readily available.

9. *Security advisories*   Security advisories are warnings issued by incident response teams (SERT) and vendors about recently discovered computer vulnerabilities. Advisories usually cover only the most important threats and thus are low-volume and high-utility reading. They describe in general terms the threat and give very specific solutions on how to plug the vulnerability. Excellent security advisories are found from a variety of sources, but the most popular come from the Carnegie Mellon Emergency Response Team at http://www.cert.org.

10. *Intrusion detection*   Intrusion detection systems detect computer attacks. They can also be used outside of a network's firewall to see what kinds of attacks are being launched at a network. In addition, they can also be used behind a network's firewall to discover attacks that penetrate the firewall. In addition, they can be used within a network to monitor insider attacks. Intrusion detection tools come with many different capabilities and functionalities. For a paper on the uses and types of intrusion detection systems, see http://www.icsa.net/services/consortia/intrusion/educational_material.shtml.

11. *Network discovery tools and port scanners*   Network discovery tools and port scanners map out networks and identify the services running on each host. Attackers use these tools to find vulnerable hosts and network services. Systems administrators use these tools to monitor what host and network services are connected to their network. Weak or improperly configured services and hosts can be found and patched.

12. *Incident response handling*   Every network, no matter how secure, experiences some security events (even if false alarms). Staff must know beforehand how to handle these events. Important points that must be resolved are when should one call law enforcement, when should one call an emergency response team, when should network connections be severed, and what is the recovery plan if an important server is compromised? CERT provides general incident-handling response capabilities for the United States (http://www.cert.org). FedCIRC is the incident response handling service for the civilian federal government (http://www.fedcirc.gov).

13. *Security policies* (refer to Chapter 4 for more information)   The strength of a network security scheme is only as strong as the weakest entry point. If different sites within an organization have different security policies, one site can be compromised by the insecurity of another. Organizations should write a security policy defining the level of protection that they expect to be uniformly implemented. The most important aspect of a policy is creating a uniform mandate on what traffic is allowed through the organization's firewalls. The policy should also define how and where security tools (e.g., intrusion detection or vulnerability scanners) should be used in the network. To obtain uniform security, the policy should define secure default configurations for different types of hosts.

14. *Denial of service testing* (for firewalls and Web servers)   Denial of service (DoS) attacks are very common on the Internet. Malicious attackers shut down Web sites, reboot computers, or clog up networks with junk packets. DoS attacks can be very serious, especially when the attacker is clever enough to launch an ongoing, untraceable attack. *Info-executives serious about security can launch these same attacks against their own sites to determine how much damage can be done.* This is a very good idea. We suggest that systems administrators or vulnerability analysis consultants perform this type of analysis on the network.

Special Security Consideration— Secure Your Web Server First

The company Web site is a powerful tool that enables businesses, government, and private users to share information and conduct business with your firm on the Internet. It is also a high-risk target for an organization. Organizations—small and large, private and public—devote many resources to creating attractive, attention-getting Web sites, but they may be neglecting basic security controls. Recent attacks on Web sites have shown that the computers that support Web sites are vulnerable to attacks that can range from minor nuisances to significant interruptions of service. After the attack, check your Web server first.

Review Procedures/Plans for Securing the Web Server

While most incidents cause minor embarrassment or inconvenience, many intruders cause real problems and severe losses. Every organization should establish a security program that assesses the risks of attacks and takes steps to reduce the risks to an acceptable level. Each organization has to decide its sensitivity to risk and how open it wants to be to the external world. When resources are limited, the cost of security incidents should be considered and the investment in protective measures should be concentrated on areas of highest sensitivity. However, too often managers take the complete wait-and-see approach (essentially ignoring the proactive methods in Chapter 13) and then find themselves in a reactive, how-do-I-recover mode. In the meantime, angry customers are calling. NIST provides some carefully thought out strategies that are usually effective before and during (preferably not after) the attack.

NIST suggests applying three levels of Web security techniques:[10]

Level 1: Minimum Security

1. Upgrading software/installing patches
2. Using single-purpose servers
3. Removing unnecessary applications

Level 2: Penetration Resistance

1. External firewalls
2. Remote administration security
3. Restricting server scripts
4. Web server shields with packet filtering
5. Education and personnel resource allocation
6. Techniques listed in Level 1

Level 3: Attack Detection and Mitigation

1. Separation of privilege
2. Hardware-based solutions
3. Internal firewalls
4. Network-based intrusion detection
5. Host-based intrusion detection
6. Techniques listed in Level 2

NIST's Techniques to Secure Web Servers

The most common methods for protecting Web servers include:

- Removal of unnecessary software
- Detection of attacks upon a Web server
- Correction of flaws in remaining software

- Restriction of an attacker's actions when a part of a Web server is compromised

- Protection of the rest of the network if a Web server is compromised

Web Servers Require Frequent Upgrading and Patch Installation

One of the simplest and yet most effective techniques for reducing risk is the installation of the latest software updates and patches. Web servers needs to be frequently examined to determine what software should be updated or patched. Any software on a Web server that an attacker could use to penetrate the system must be regularly updated. Software in this category includes the operating system, servers or any software that receives network packets, software running as root or administrator, and security software. NIST recommends the following:[11]

1. Make a list of such software and write down the associated version numbers.

2. Find the Web page for each piece of software and make sure that the latest version is installed.

3. Find and install the available patches for the applicable version of the software. Each software vendor provides unique instructions on how to install its patches, and usually these instructions are very simple. Be careful to follow vendor instructions; patches must often be installed in a set sequence for the process to work.

4. Verify that patched software functions correctly.

Single-Purpose Servers

Organizations should run Web servers on computers dedicated exclusively to that task. A common mistake is to try to save money by running multiple servers on the same host. It is not uncommon to run an e-mail server, Web server, and database server on the same computer. However, each server run on a host provides an attacker with avenues for attack. Each newly installed server then increases the organization's reliance upon that host while simultaneously decreasing its security. Given the decreasing cost of hardware and the increasing importance of having fast Web servers, it is generally effective to buy a dedicated host for each Web server. When a Web server constantly interacts with a database, it is best to use two separate hosts.

Removing Unnecessary Applications

All privileged software not specifically required by the Web server should be removed. For the purposes of this document, privileged software is defined as software that runs with administrator privileges or that receives packets from the network. Operating systems often run a variety of privileged programs by default. Many systems administrators are not even aware of the existence of many of these programs. Each privileged program provides another avenue by which an attacker can compromise a Web server. It is crucial that Web servers be purged of unnecessary programs. For greater security and because it is often difficult to identify what software is privileged, many systems administrators remove all software not needed by a Web server.

External Firewalls

Managers need to verify that the public Web server is installed outside of the organization's firewall. In this configuration, the firewall prevents the Web server from sending packets into an organization's network. If attackers on the Internet penetrate the external Web server, they have no more access to the organization's internal network than they had before. If a Web server is inside the organization's firewall and is penetrated by an attacker on the Internet, the attacker can use the Web server as a launching point for attacks on the internal systems. Thus, these attacks would completely bypass the security provided by the firewall.

Remote Administration Security

Since it is often inconvenient to administer a host from the physical console, system administrators often install software on Web servers to allow remote administration. From a security perspective, this practice is dangerous and should be minimized or eliminated. NIST recommends that remote administration security may be increased by:[12]

■ Encrypting remote administration traffic such that attackers monitoring network traffic cannot obtain passwords or inject malicious commands into conversations.

- Using packet filtering to allow remote administration only from a designated set of hosts.

- Maintaining this designated set of hosts at a higher degree of security than normal hosts.

- Not using packet filtering as a replacement for encryption, since attackers can spoof Internet Protocol addresses. With IP spoofing, an attacker lies about his or her location by sending messages from an IP address other than the attacker's own.

Restrict Server Scripts

Most Web sites contain scripts (small programs) created locally by Web site developers. A Web server runs these scripts when a user requests a particular page. Attackers can use these scripts to penetrate Web sites by finding and exercising flaws in the code. To find such flaws, an attacker does not necessarily need the script source code. Scripts must be carefully written with security in mind, and system administrators should inspect them before placing them on a Web site. Do not allow scripts to run arbitrary commands on a system or to launch insecure (or non-patched) programs. Scripts should restrain users to doing a small set of well-defined tasks. They should carefully restrict the size of input parameters so that an attacker cannot give a script more data than it expects. If an attacker is allowed to do this, a system can often be penetrated using a technique called "buffer overflow." (With a buffer overflow attack, an attacker convinces a Web server to run arbitrary code by giving it more information than it expected to receive.) Run scripts with nonadministrator privileges to prevent an attacker from compromising the entire Web server in the event that a script contains flaws.

Web Server Shields with Packet Filtering

A router can be used as a poor man's firewall. A router set up to separate a Web server from the rest of the network can shield a Web server from many attacks. The router can thwart attacks before they reach the Web server by dropping all packets that do not access valid Web server services. Typically, the router should drop all network packets that do not go either to the Web server (port 80) or to the remote administration server being used. For additional security, only allow a preapproved list of hosts to send traffic to a Web server's remote administration server. By doing so, an attacker can only compromise a Web server using the remote administration server via a restricted set of network paths. The filtering router shield offers similar protection to that of removing all unneeded software from a host, since it prevents an attacker from requesting certain vulnerable services. Be aware that setting up a router with many filtering rules may noticeably slow its ability to forward packets.

Education and Personnel Resource Allocation

Attackers are able to penetrate most Web servers because the systems administrators are either not knowledgeable about Web server security or did not take the time to properly secure the system. Web site administrators must be trained about Web server security techniques and rewarded for spending time securing the site. Several excellent books and training seminars exist to aid administrators in securing Web sites.

Separation of Privilege

Regardless of the security measures established for a Web server, penetration may still occur. If this happens, it is important to *limit the attacker's actions on the penetrated host. Separation of privilege* is a key concept for restricting actions once a part of the host is penetrated. To establish such control, partition the various host resources among a set of user accounts. An attacker who penetrates some software will then be limited to acting within that single user account instead of having control over the entire system. For example, a Web server can run as one user, but the Web pages can be owned by another user and with the Web server given read-only access. Then, if attackers penetrate the Web server, they cannot change the Web pages owned by other users.

Intrusion detection software can run as another user to protect it from being modified by an attacker penetrating the Web server user. For the best security, run the Web server process as a user that has write privilege only in a few privately owned *temporary* directories. This requires storing the Web server software as read-only under one user but running it as a different user.

Hardware-Based Solutions

Hardware can implement separation-of-privilege concepts with a greater degree of security than software because hardware is not as easily modified as software. With software implementations, if the underlying operating system is penetrated, the attacker has complete control of all files on a Web server. Using read-only external hard disks or CD-ROMs, Web pages and even critical software can be stored in a way that an attacker cannot modify the files. The usual configuration is for the Web server to have a read-only port to the external hard disk while another well-protected computer has a read-write port so that the Web pages can be updated. Note that an attacker who penetrates a protected Web server can still copy data, change the copied data, and serve up the changed pages.

Internal Firewalls

Modern Web servers often serve as front ends to complex and possibly distributed applications. In this situation, a Web server often communicates with several other hosts, each of which contains particular data or performs particular computations. It is tempting to locate these computers inside of an organization's firewall for ease of maintenance and to protect these important computers. However, if an attacker can compromise a Web server, these back-end systems may be penetrated using the Web server as a launching point. Instead, it is a good idea to separate the Web server back-end systems from the rest of the organization's networks using an internal firewall. Then, penetration of the Web server and subsequently the Web server's back-end systems does not provide access to the rest of the organization's networks.

Network-Based Intrusion Detection

Despite all attempts to patch a Web server and to securely configure it, vulnerabilities may still exist that are known to the outside world. Also, the Web server may be perfectly secure, but an attacker may cleverly overwhelm the host's services such that it ceases to operate. In this kind of environment, it is important to know when your Web server has been compromised or shut down so that service can be quickly restored. Network-based *intrusion detection systems (IDSs)* monitor network traffic to determine whether a Web server is under attack or has been compromised or disabled. Modern IDSs have the ability to launch a limited response to attacks or notify systems administrators via e-mail, pagers, or messages on a security console. Typical automated responses include severing network connections and blocking sets of IP addresses.

Host-Based Intrusion Detection

Host-based IDSs reside on a Web server. Thus, they are better positioned to determine the state of the Web server than network-based IDS, yet they provide the same benefits and in some circumstances can detect attacks better because they have finer-grained access to the Web server's state. However, some drawbacks exist. An attacker that penetrates a Web server can disable host-based IDS, thereby preventing it from issuing a warning. In addition, remote denial of service attacks often disable host-based IDSs while disabling the Web server. Remote DoS attacks enable an attacker to remotely shut down a Web server without actually penetrating it. Host-based IDSs are useful, and they should be used in conjunction with the typically more secure network-based IDSs.

Limitations of Existing Solutions and Gaining Additional Assurance

Considerable research has addressed issues of proving software secure. In some cases, it is possible to do this, but it is very costly and time-consuming. Usually, by the time software is proven secure, it is obsolete and replaced with an unproven new version. Therefore, today's software is not proven secure and application of standard Web security techniques cannot guarantee that a Web server will be impenetrable.

The Web server can be made quite resistant to attacks by using the stated Web server security techniques in addition to using trustworthy software. By "trustworthy," we mean software that can be demonstrated by some measure to be secure. The security afforded by software can be assessed by studying past vulnerabilities, using software specifically created with security as the principal goal and using software evaluated by trusted third parties.

First, some level of assurance in software can be gained by looking at the past vulnerabilities discovered in different Web server software. The number of past vulnerabilities is an indicator of future vulnerabilities and also reflects how well the software was crafted. Trustworthiness is directly related to the quality of the software product. A poorly crafted product built explicitly to meet security needs remains a poorly crafted product and, therefore, is not trustworthy.

Second, some companies specialize in creating very secure Web server software and some boast that no vulnerabilities have ever been discovered. Users have to balance vendor's security claims against any security-performance trade-offs that have been made.

A third way to gain a level of assurance in software is to use evaluated and validated software. Many private-sector organizations perform third-party evaluations of commercial products in order to verify a particular level of security. COMSEC Solutions, LLC (www.comsec-solutions.com) has established a solid reputation as a consultant in this area.

The National Information Assurance Partnership (NIAP) is a joint venture between NIST and NSA. NIAP has helped create an international standard (ISO/IEC 15408) for specifying security requirements of IT products and evaluating them to that specification. It provides a framework by which commercial companies can have product claims tested by a third party and (if desired) obtain a certificate of validation from NIAP. Various security-enhanced products are currently under evaluation, including the firewalls of three major U.S. vendors. We can expect NIAP-evaluated Web server software in the future.

Wrap-Up

Too many managers wait until their company computers have been attacked to act against intrusions. Whether because of lack of budget or lack of respect for the attacker, the results are expensive and generally unforgettable. SERT teams perform the triage and apply the appropriate tools or policy to mitigate and ultimately protect against another wave of attacks. Triage is usually thought of as a system of alerts based on expected situations and responses. To be effective, SERT teams must practice regularly.

After an attack it is prudent to classify the attack and determine the attack methodology. The company Web site is such a powerful corporate tool and attractive target that special consideration is required for its security. NIST has developed comprehensive security techniques for protecting the Web server, which have been presented with the authors' positive recommendations.

Notes

1. "Computer Attacks: What They Are and How To Defend Against Them," Information Technology Laboratory, National Institute of Standards and Technology, May 1999, available from www.nist.gov/itl/lab/bulletns/may99.htm

2. Ibid., 2.

3. Ibid., 3.

4. Interesting papers that detail computer attacks include "Understanding the Global Attack Toolkit Using a Database of Dependent Classifiers" and "Understanding the World of Your Enemy with I-CAT (Internet Categorization of Attacks Toolkit)" at http://www.itl.nist.gov/div893/staff/mell/pmhome.html

5. General Computer Security Information: NIST Computer Security Clearinghouse at www.csrc.nist.gov

6. Federal Computer Incident Response Capability at www.fedcirc.gov

7. National Information Assurance Partnership (NIAP) at www.niap.nist.gov

8. Center for Education and Research in Information Assurance and Security at www.cerias.purdue.edu

9. Carnegie Mellon Emergency Response Team at www.cert.org

10. Information Technology Laboratory, National Institute of Standards and Technology, September 1999, available from www.nist.gov/itl/lab/bulletns/sept99.htm

11. Ibid., 2.

12. Ibid., 3.

PART 5

Order of Battle

Information Warfare (IW) operations consist of those actions intended to protect, destroy, exploit, corrupt, or deny information or information resources to achieve a significant advantage over an enemy. IW is based on the value of a target and the cost to destroy or disable it. IW involves much more than computers and computer networks. It encompasses information in any form and transmitted over any media. IW includes operations against information, support systems, hardware, software, and people. It is arguably more damaging than conventional warfare. Part 5 covers a whole spectrum of topics within the purview of IW.

Chapter 15 combines the concepts of information security, INFOSEC, countermeasures and policy. It applies them to the more global view of national security. A systems methodology to analyze the effects of various security contributions is presented.

Chapter 16 discusses information warfare in terms of the enemy's decision cycle. It looks at the way value is assigned to information targets and the resulting countermeasures indicated to the defender. Risk assessment may be politically, technologically, or behaviorally based.

Chapter 17 is a fascinating look at the weapons, intelligence, and cyberspace environment for IW. A multidimensional model of the services (telecommunications, radio, cellular communications, personal communications systems, paging, mobile satellite services, very small aperture terminals, and direct TV) is overlaid with the theoretical OSI (open systems interconnection) framework and practical hardware implementations.

Chapter 18 continues the discussion by adding planning, targeting, and deployment issues for effective IW. The focus is on the unique features of IW.

Chapter 19 switches to the government-wide effort to deploy a functional PKI infrastructure by 2001. There is a serious effort to build trust-on-line. However, the challenges of workable standards and interoperable equipment have not been fully solved. This chapter discusses PKI in depth.

Chapter 20 recognizes the contribution that cryptography plays in the scheme of both government and commercial computer countermeasures. Cryptography exists in a particularly active political environment. On September 16, 1999, Clinton relaxed the export controls on cryptography (after 3 years of tightening efforts) or did he? Chapter 20 reviews the laws governing the use of cryptography and its impact on U.S. industry.

CHAPTER 15

The Big Picture

Introduction

Applying security measures within an environment requires an approach that takes into account the specifics of the environment itself, the available resources with which security may be provided, and an understanding of risk trade-offs. The security measures themselves comprise a mixture of technologies, operational practices, and circumstance management.

People living within a home implicitly (some explicitly) assess their security requirements and take appropriate precautions. Strangers are not admitted without some sort of vetting process, usually performed visually and based on past experiences and education (such as reading the newspaper). An elderly female homeowner alone on a Sunday afternoon is far more likely to allow a petite woman into the house than a tall and strong man, whatever the plea for admittance might be and independent of the truth of the matter. Trust is allocated in a way least likely to result in harm. Thus, when a woman is accosted at 2 A.M., the reaction inevitably is "what was she doing out at 2 A.M.?"

Some items in the home are protected for confidentiality reasons—for example, a dieter having a bowl of chocolate ice cream may draw the curtains to prevent the neighbors from knowing about it. Some other items are protected for availability—the doors are locked so that the television is available when the occupants want to watch it. Yet other things are protected for integrity—deeds and liens are kept in fireproof safes or safe deposit boxes at remote locations.

All of these actions are taken in the context of protection, detection, and correction. Door locks and window shades provide protection. Detection is provided by fire alarms and visual inspection of the premises. Correction is supported through insurance policies and true test copies on file at the courthouse.

All of these actions are additionally performed by an implicit application of risk management. If homes are located in primarily rural areas, less attention is paid to locking doors and windows. In dense urban areas, doors and windows are locked religiously. As the value of possessions rises, attention to keeping them safe rises as well. This is done in the context of impact, of course. The impact of having a television stolen is much higher to someone who makes minimum wage than it is to someone who is the CEO of a Fortune 500 company. On the other hand, the television in the CEO's house is likely to benefit from the additional security on the premises that protect more-valuable treasures, such as the original artwork on the walls.

The threats and vulnerabilities for the homes are different as well. The threat to a poor homeowner rises primarily out of petty theft and "normal" crime—the criminal behavior that most of the population is exposed to by virtue of neighborhoods and circumstances. Generally, the poorer the neighborhood, the greater the threat, although that is not always true. The threat to the CEO must get through many barriers imposed by exclusivity and money, resulting in theft on a major scale, kidnapping, or other, rarer crimes—the very environment precludes casual crime. In fact, the choice of specific environment is a countermeasure to the threats that face people who have less choice in the matter. CEOs don't live in run-down urban tenements.

This is, of course, a trivial discussion of home security issues, but it serves to make the point that the concepts of risk management, security concerns, and security phases are germane to every environment. Implicitly or explicitly, every person does some level of security engineering of their home environment. This same analysis is required in every environment. Each environment is unique and must be analyzed for security reasons. Approaching security from a holistic point of view contributes to engineering a better solution. One must consider all the information assets of the corporation not just specific or favored ones. As more and more valuable information resources slip into the realm of cyberspace, the boundary (already artificial) between information security and other kinds of security will continue to fade and security efforts will be integrated. In the meantime, understanding the specific issues associated with information security allows an affordable solution to be engineered that provides sufficient security for the amount of resources available.

Setting Priorities

The first step in any engineering activity is specifying priorities. In engineering information security, setting priorities requires an understanding of the importance of information to your enterprise. It is not sufficient to simply understand the value of each bit of information as it exists independently of each other piece; each piece must also be understood as to how it contributes to your competitive stance. The two elements of the environment are static knowledge and the use of knowledge.

Information and Competition

If information were not valuable, none of this would be worth discussing. However, information is not only valuable, it also is growing steadily in value. The age that we are living in underscores this value: the information age. So it goes without saying, and yet here we say it, to develop an effective security program, you must understand exactly what is of value in terms of your enterprise and specifically in terms of your competition.

Who are the adversaries who would attack your information? Why would they do that? Answering these two questions is a fundamental part of risk analysis. It is also very, very difficult to do. Being able to predict malicious activity requires that well-meaning individuals purposefully contemplate criminal activity and life on the dark side. For those not practiced in these kinds of exercises, it is too easy to ignore potential threats. "Why should XYZ attack our information assets? We (a) haven't done anything to them, (b) don't have anything of value to them, or (c) aren't competitors of theirs." Understanding value requires assessing that value from the other side's point of view. What you may consider to be of limited value may have greater perceived value from someone else's point of view. For example, a Web page may have limited value to an organization in the grand scheme of things, but vandalizing that Web page may have great significance for a casual hacker who can then brag to hacking buddies that he or she achieved a difficult feat. The resulting embarrassment for the organization may cost more than what securing the Web site would have cost had the risk been correctly understood.

Who Is the Threat?

Those who potentially would do you harm exist in several general categories:

1. Accidental antagonists, who clumsily or by negligence cause you harm

2. Vandals, who have attacked you simply because you are there

3. Hackers, who are attempting to gain knowledge about anything that is denied to them or who may be selling their technical expertise to someone with other motives

4. Thieves, who attack you simply to further their own interests

5. Insiders, who compromise or steal information assets for a variety of motivations ranging from disgruntlement to financial gain

6. Competitors, who attack you to gain advantage or to achieve dominance in the competition

7. Terrorists, who are attacking the relationship between the general populace and governing structures or technologies

8. Armed forces, engaging in information warfare activities

9. Incidental antagonists, who harm you or attack you in the course of attacking someone else because you are a link, because you are closely networked, or because you happen to be in the way

This is not a comprehensive list, but it provides a basis for starting to understand where your potential problem areas may lie. Understanding these elements helps identify where you should go to collect information on potentially harmful activities. Gathering information on an ongoing basis is a critical element to successfully defending your enterprise. For example, if it suddenly becomes vogue in certain hacker circles to count coups on Web sites of a certain industry segment and your enterprise is in that segment, knowing that bit of information allows you to ratchet your security higher in areas where the hackers are most likely to attack.

Accidents happen. The tales of cables being ripped apart by backhoes are legion. One of the best tales of accidents was reported in the Metro section of the *Washington Post* on April 1, 1999:

> The manner in which a natural gas leak came about yesterday in Old Town Alexandria, forcing the evacuation of a block of town houses, was something Rube Goldberg might have cooked up.
>
> About noon, according to Renee DeSandies, a Washington Gas spokeswoman, a worker was unloading drywall in the 700 block of South Fairfax Street, when the boom on his truck hit a power line.
>
> The live wire hit the truck, electricity surged through the vehicle, and "the tires blew," DeSandies said. That caused a steel rim on a tire to fall off, sending the current into the ground and through a water pipe to a gas line, which ruptured, she said.
>
> No one was injured, DeSandies said. The gas was turned off, and crews spent much of the day looking for and containing the leak, she said.

[*Authors' note*: This story may have some technical holes, according to one of our senior engineering review team. The tires actually insulate the vehicle from the ground, 50,000 volts are not generally carried in the lines around a residential neighborhood, there is usually not enough power in the lines to rupture a gas line, which is steel pipe, and if it did, then how did a cast-iron pipe line survive? If the gas line was ruptured by a power surge, there should have been an enormous explosion and fire, which was not mentioned in this article. If the tire does blow and the vehicle is stationary, the rim does not fall off. What is more likely is that the truck was overloaded and parked over the gas line without any planking to spread the load. Hitting the power line with the boom was a coincidence. The article did not indicate which tires blew; drywall trucks usually have multiple tires in the rear and single tires in the front, so the cause of the blowout is not known. The object was to illustrate the domino effect, and the story does do that. One should make his or her own mind based on the facts.]

It is impossible to characterize such accidents ahead of time, but the dependence on systems should certainly take into account the possibility of occurrence of bizarre events. If your enterprise requires a high level of availability of communications, for example, depending on a single link is indubitably a very poor planning decision.

The probability or the likelihood of being attacked by one or more of these potential antagonists varies dramatically from enterprise to enterprise, and over time, as circumstances change. Characteristics that influence likelihood of attack include visibility, amount of connectivity, sheer size, amount of influence, type of work performed, and even physical location. Each enterprise must analyze the probabilities from its unique perspective.

Insiders who have motivation to violate enterprise security are the most troublesome security risks, because they are already inside the system operating at some level of trust. Obviously, the higher the level of trust in which they operate, the more serious the potential problem. When an insider decides to violate security, he or she acts with the motivation of one or more of the other categories but from the inside. That is the reason for naming insiders as a separate threat category. The vandal who acts from inside has vastly more capability to do harm than the vandal who attacks from the outside, just as the thief who acts from inside an enterprise has the potential for stealing more than the thief who attacks from the outside. Protecting against the insider threat requires that some level of distrust be maintained at all times against individuals operating at a granted level of trust. While this sounds like an oxymoron, it is best characterized by the Russian saying that Ronald Reagan appropriated during his presidency: "Trust, but verify."

Vandals and hackers operate in a pseudorandom pattern, and information on their activities can be garnered from law enforcement agencies and other elements of the law enforcement community. Some vandals and hackers operate from the motivation of proving they can do something. Protecting your assets from vandals is at once the easiest and the most difficult challenge. Many of these individuals are semiskilled at best, so they go after the targets. Raising the ante by implementing easy and relatively inexpensive protective features, such as strong passwords and encryption, may be enough to persuade the average person to go on to the next target.

Some of the more technically competent individuals are keen for a technical fight, however. These are a small and select group who consider security features a challenge rather than a deterrent. Protecting your assets from this highly skilled subset requires constant vigilance, an ability to recognize an attack when it occurs, and quick corrective capabilities. Limiting an attack's effectiveness through electronic triage can be a potent defense against this class of vandal.

The concept of electronic triage is that of isolating elements of a system that are under attack or compromised from other elements of the system to limit contagion or attack effectiveness. It is analogous to amputating a foot to save a leg. The nice part about electronic systems is that later, when the attack has abated or has been rebuffed, the "foot" can be reattached. A form of triage that is particularly useful in large-scale virus infestations is that of quarantine. By isolating computers from each other, the enterprise can be systematically cleaned and restored while limiting the possibility of reinfection.

The motivations of thieves and competitors are more easily understood. Thieves steal from you or use your enterprise elements to commit illegal actions. These could include not only out and out theft but also actions such as money laundering, in order to further their causes. Competitors want to gain competitive advantage. That could result in theft of trade secrets or industrial espionage. It could also, in extreme cases, result in denial of service attacks or other more direct attacks on information assets. One critical element that competitors could attack could be the enterprise decision cycle, discussed in a following section. Slowing down your decision cycle could allow them to act more quickly than you are able to, which results in competitive advantage to them. In the information age, this could be a critical edge.

Terrorist groups and armed forces could attack your information assets directly or indirectly despite, or maybe even because, you are a commercial enterprise. Consider that the armed forces of Israel attacked a nuclear power plant in Iraq, the armed forces of the United States attacked a chemical factory in Sudan, and terrorists bombed dance halls in Germany. Again, the value in a target is in the eye of the beholder: If an attack supports strategic goals, then it becomes a real possibility. With armed forces, it is likely that advance warning of hostilities will be available. Understanding the likelihood that a terrorist group would launch an attack on your systems or information assets requires an understanding of what terrorists are trying to achieve and how they view your role in the environment they are trying to change. A group of terrorists operating as insurgents in a country trying to overturn a governing group is trying to communicate to the populace that the government is unable or unwilling to protect its citizens. If your enterprise is viewed as an arm of that governing group, then your enterprise is a potential target. Other terrorist groups have other goals and values. Typically, terrorists are geographically focused, although this could change as the information age progresses. Keeping abreast of political issues in all areas where your enterprise is located can help alert you to any potential problems from this category of threat.

A form of terrorist that is not geographically focused and not even particularly politically motivated is that of what may be termed "Luddites." These individuals are concerned about the encroachment of technology on human existence and attack that relationship. One of the most visible of these recently was Theodore Kaczynski, aka the Unabomber. He attacked those whom he viewed as pushing technology—scientists and researchers, amongst others. While he chose to use bombs against people to make his point, he could just as well have chosen to use bombs against systems or logic bombs against systems.

All of these types of attacks are possible from the bank-shot point of view as well. Any of the above could attack or harm your information assets in order to further an attack on a different entity, or achieve some larger purpose (such as cascading failures), or they could simply be the accidental result of an attack on someone else. Just because an attack is accidental doesn't make the results any less painful or real.

What Do They Want?

The attack is almost always as a result of a desire for some end goal; almost always, because sometimes it may be an accident, as noted above. However, barring accidents and acts of God, understanding value from an adversary's point of view can help to clarify security planning decisions.

Things of value include the following:

1. The proverbial mountaintop
2. Negotiable elements, such as money, stocks, or capital equipment
3. Secret information, such as trade secrets or insider knowledge
4. Technology use
5. The destruction of some asset
6. Competitive advantage

The "mountaintop" is a way of describing the "because it's there" behavioral phenomenon. Attacking your assets may provide value to the attacker simply from the ability of being able to brag that he or she did it. An attacker who is motivated by the value of a mountaintop may do one or more things when finally achieving that goal. The attacker could:

- Plant a "flag," showing that he or she was there
- Simply take a picture and leave (i.e., by copying data)
- Take proof that he or she was there
- Use that "pinnacle" as a stepping stone to another elusive target
- Destroy some or all of the elements of the target

Things of extrinsic value, such as negotiable elements and secret information, are perhaps the most recognizable on the list. Attackers who are after these kinds of things are more understandable in their actions because threats are analogous to everyday life. Robbers steal; spies spy. As everyday things of value become more virtual, the venue for committing theft and espionage goes virtual as well. An interesting twist to this is the existence of things that are of intrinsic value that are not trade secrets, which exist solely in the information realm. These include software applications, which software pirates target for theft, databases used as the basis for enterprise operations, and data records of all sorts, including network routing information.

To achieve access to these items of interest, the attackers may attack through electronic means or through physical means. If an attacker wants a database, for example, he or she may well simply steal a hard drive containing the database. If an attacker wants a software application, he or she may simply steal the computer that has it loaded. The attacker who is after an information asset with intrinsic value is not necessarily limited to a cyberspace approach. On the other hand, using a cyberspace approach can be very fruitful indeed. The use of financial transaction networks by a thief in Russia to steal money from Citibank in New York is perhaps the most publicized event of this sort.

The use of technology might be the item of value that the attacker is after. It may be that the attacker wants to make free phone calls or have untraceable voice mail, so he or she attacks a company's public branch exchange system and creates an account for him- or herself on it. The attacker might want to use an enterprise's high-bandwidth networks for Internet access or may want to use data storage space to exchange pirated software or other, less palatable types of information with others. The illicit use could bog down enterprise operations, destroy enterprise capabilities through file overwrites, or bring official intrusion into enterprise operations when law enforcement organizations identify the activities occurring. At the very least, this kind of illicit use could force the enterprise to adopt different operational behaviors. One company we know of was forced to close down an anonymous FTP site that it made available to clients because software pirates came to use it for their purposes. The resulting traffic was so overwhelming that neither the company nor the clients could use the site for legitimate purposes: It had, essentially, been stolen from them.

Alternatively, attackers could seek to destroy the asset being attacked. The motivation for destroying the asset could be because it poses an obstacle to a goal, because it represents a competitive advantage, or simply because it is there. Another reason to destroy an asset would be to force all activity onto a redundant asset that might be less secure, thereby allowing the attacker to violate confidentiality or integrity security requirements.

Knowledge as a Target

Information assets are increasingly the lifeblood of the economy. Before 1940, information was important—often vitally so—but cumbersome to use and therefore limited. Predominately, information was in the form of words, and information storage was in the form of books and files. After the cascade of inventions revolving around the use of electromagnetic pulses in World War II, information changed character dramatically and the entire landscape changed. The invention of radar, the harnessing of electromagnetic radiation in other forms, and especially the invention of the electronic computer have all contributed to an explosion of information available in an extraordinary number of forms. Now, besides books, files, and accountant punch cards, there are databases, palmtop computers, cell phones, and e-mail.

To highlight what is at risk, examining the kinds of information that exist today in myriad forms helps draw the boundaries. Consider the following information applications:

■ Medical records digitized and inserted into a tooth for positive identification

■ Magnetic strips with identifying information on the back of drivers licenses

■ Automatic teller machines that allow you to interact remotely with your bank

■ Wireless Internet connections that allows you to access the Internet and send e-mail from anywhere

■ Communications systems serviced from satellites

■ Data mining techniques that cull subtle patterns out of large amounts of disparate data

■ Just-in-time manufacturing support services

Each one of these applications is a testament to the information age. Harnessing the ability to collect, process, analyze, store, retrieve, and display information in infinite combinatorial forms has given the human intellect an ability to imagine things that were simply not possible before and then do those things.

However, as with any advance comes new responsibilities and problems. With the ability to collect and analyze information comes new responsibilities regarding privacy. With the ability to do banking remotely comes new problems with theft and fraud not easily managed through old security approaches.

Because of this, it is necessary to discuss knowledge as a target for security issues. There are three main areas in which knowledge can be attacked. First, someone who is not entitled to see the information may breach the secrecy or confidentiality of knowledge. Second, the integrity of the information may be compromised. And finally, the availability of the information may be denied or degraded.

When we speak of confidentiality, we are concerned with ensuring that access to the information or knowledge at hand is controlled in keeping with its sensitivity or value. Confidentiality requirements can be determined in many different ways. First, the law may mandate them. For example, certain private information has legislated protection when being handled by specific agencies or organizations. Government agencies are required by law to protect privacy information. Medical and judicial records are accorded some level of protection as well. However, laws vary from jurisdiction to jurisdiction. Data privacy laws are different in the European Union and the United States, for example. Another way confidentiality requirements can be determined is through a contract. A contract between two parties may require that certain information be kept secret. Yet another way that confidentiality expectations can be determined is by enumerating the operational requirements of an enterprise. Trade secrets, for example, may be recognized within an organization as information that must be kept secret.

Integrity is the word used to describe the security attribute of correctness and wholeness. The integrity of data can be a serious problem. If your bank account suddenly is missing several thousand dollars, the integrity of your bank account is called into question. An integrity problem like that is fairly visible. Integrity problems are not always so noticeable; changing a few bits in an extremely large database can be essentially invisible. Integrity requirements also can be determined in a number of ways, including legislation. Auditing requirements associated with tax collection and banking oversight spawn integrity requirements, for example. A competitive business environment also can breed integrity requirements. An example of this would be in the communications arena—high-quality data signals and a low error rate are integrity concerns. Another example can be found in the lucrative arena of name list sales—a list of names that has a high percentage of unreachables would be less valuable than a list of names that has a low percentage of unreachables.

Availability is the term used to describe the quality of being able to access a service whenever needed. Getting a busy signal when you dial into an Internet service provider is an example of an availability problem. If you get a busy signal once in a blue moon, chances are that you will tolerate the inconvenience. However, if you always get a busy signal when you dial in between 6:30 and 8:30 P.M., then that ISP has serious availability problems, and as a result, so do you. You can't get to your e-mail, you can't do research on the Internet, you can't engage in e-commerce transactions, and you can't chat with your geographically distant friends. While on a recreational level, this lack of availability is probably not threatening in any real sense, it will nevertheless drive you to find another ISP. Therefore, for the ISP, providing sufficient availability becomes a business issue. In other applications, availability can be a matter of life and death. The availability of the 911 emergency phone system is a self-evident example. Another example is that of the availability of medical records during an emergency. Knowing that an unconscious patient is allergic to some treatment option can literally save that person's life.

The threats to knowledge are that it can be destroyed, altered, denied, and compromised. The repercussions to the owners or maintainers of the information and systems can range from inconvenience to serious legal issues. Identifying the requirements for security in an environment is a first step in protecting that knowledge from attack. Protection must be accompanied by detection mechanisms that alert you when the protective measures are breached or other problems occur. Correction measures that are in place ahead of time allow knowledge bases to be recovered quickly.

Knowledge in Use as a Target

Most information security discussions focus on the threats to knowledge and the systems that support knowledge. However, there is an emerging reality that makes the process of using knowledge just as much a potential target as the knowledge itself. This emerging reality is termed *knowledge management* by some, *competitive advantage* by others. In short, it is the use of information technology that allows competitors to do things faster, cheaper, and better.

To understand the nature of what is targeted, it is necessary to understand the concept of a decision cycle. The fundamentals of a decision cycle were succinctly described by Col. John R. Boyd in his philosophical examinations of "Patterns of Conflict," a complete description of which can be found at http://www.belisarius.com/. In these works, Col. Boyd described the use of knowledge as a process of four fundamental stages, each of which can be expounded upon to increase the complexity of the discussion. The following sections describe the simplistic decision cycle processes and the effect that emerging knowledge management techniques have upon the processes of the decision cycle.

Decision Cycle, Classic: The OODA Loop

A *decision cycle* is how the process occurs from observation to action. In any competition, from warfare to business, each movement of the players is as a result of observing the environment and acting based on that observation. This is also, of course, true in everyday life. A child sees a piece of candy and takes it. That is a simplification of the course of

Figure 15-1

events, however. The child sees something, characterizes it as candy, decides, based on previous experience, that he likes candy, and then, finally, takes it. In business, a merchant sees that there is a shortage of a good in the area, thinks about what kind of a markup he could make by being the sole purveyor of the good, decides to import the good and sell it in order to make that profit, and finally places the order for the good.

In all these examples, the first step is an observation: "Hey, there's no linseed oil being sold in town!" (See Fig. 15-1)

Once that observation is made, then the observation is put into context. It is characterized through intelligence and experience. This characterization lays the basis for decisions.

In our example, the merchant characterizes the shortage of a good in context of what it means to him: "I run a store and sell things. I could sell linseed oil if I had some. If I had some linseed oil, I would be the only person in town who had it to sell. If I were the only person in town with linseed oil to sell, then I could charge whatever I wanted for it. If I could charge whatever I wanted for it, I could make a lot of money." (See Fig. 15-2)

One or more decisions are developed based on the observation and the characterization of the observation. These decisions represent a range of possible actions, based on a variety of desired outcomes.

The merchant's range of decisions include deciding that importing linseed oil is more trouble than it is worth, deciding to get a cooperative effort together of all the merchants in town to import linseed oil so that everyone can profit, or deciding to import linseed oil for himself and sell it himself. (See Fig. 15-3)

Figure 15-2

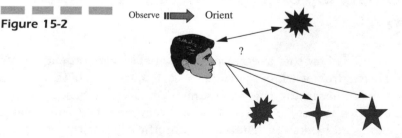

Figure 15-3

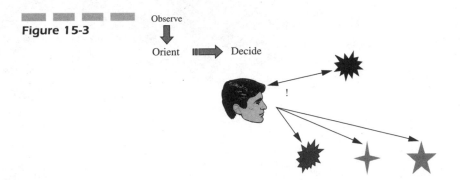

Once a set of decisions has been formulated, then a choice is made among all the possible decisions and a resulting action is taken.

So now our merchant imports linseed oil and makes it for sale in his store. (See Fig. 15-4)

At this point, the merchant must sit back and make a new observation. He may observe that no one is buying the linseed oil, or he may observe that people consider buying the linseed oil but don't complete the purchase. These new observations would then set off a new cycle of observation—orientation—decision—action. This is known as an *OODA loop*.

The process from observation to action is called the "decision cycle." Each trip around the loop constitutes one decision cycle, as shown in Figure 15-5.

A competitive advantage occurs when someone is able to go through the steps of the decision cycle faster than others. This is *knowledge in use*. If the merchant in the preceding example had been slow to notice the shortage of linseed oil, had been slow to characterize the observation, had been slow in making decisions, or had been slow in acting, someone else may well have imported linseed oil before he did, thereby ruining any advantage that might have existed for him.

Figure 15-4

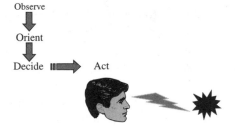

Figure 15-5
A single decision
cycle.

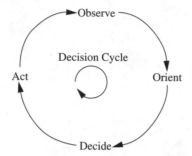

Minimizing the amount of time from observation to action creates a faster decision cycle and conveys competitive advantage by empowering faster actions on observations. This is a desirable condition for competitors in business, *les affaires d'couer*, and warfare, as well as in almost every other aspect of life.

A Revolution in Information Affairs

The explosion of information technologies has enabled a revolution in how the decision cycle is completed. As the ability to harness information technology for every aspect of the decision cycle has increased, the competition to get through the decision cycle faster has increased. Newspapers compete to have the headline stories first, medical researchers compete to have the breakthrough treatments first, and businesses compete to get products to the correct market faster. The problem is this: How can the decision cycle time be minimized?

The answer is both simplistic and complex, as shown in Figure 15-6. For the first step in minimizing decision cycle time, each step in the decision cycle must be performed in the minimum amount of time possible. The time taken to observe must be minimized, the time taken to characterize the observations must be minimized, the time taken to scope out possible decisions and come to a single best decision must be minimized, and the time taken to act must be minimized.

One way of looking at the decision cycle time is as follows: The time to complete a decision cycle (t_{DC}) is the amount of time it takes to observe (t_{Ob}) plus the amount of time it takes to orient (t_{Or}) plus the amount of time it takes to decide (t_D) plus the amount of time it takes to act (t_A). This can be written mathematically as follows:

Figure 15-6

Minimizing the decision cycle.

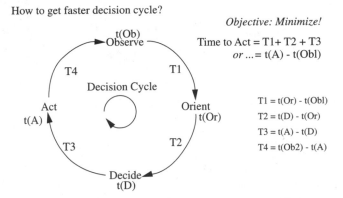

How to get faster decision cycle?

$$t_{DC} = t_{Ob} + t_{Or} + t_D + t_A$$

The problem is that eventually the laws of physics limit the amount that the decision cycle can be increased. Independent of what time-saving measures are incorporated, there are hard limits, in terms of the speed of processing, the speed of communications, the speed of product transport, and others, that are reached. These hard limits dictate the fastest decision cycle time that can be attained.

However, that answer doesn't tend to sit well with the average human being who doesn't react well to hard limits. This attitude is best reflected in the saying, "If you're not cheating, you're not trying."

So how to speed the decision cycle past those hard limits? The answer lies in reformulating the definition of what characterizes time in the decision cycle. Instead of looking at the time to complete a decision cycle as being the sum of its parts, it can be considered to be the difference in time from observation to action. In other terms:

$$t_{DC} = t_A - t_{Ob}$$

This redefinition allows the processes of the decision cycle to be reordered—the "cheating" required to achieve faster decision cycles than would be possible before. Instead of performing the steps in sequence, why not see how many of them can be done ahead of time? If you've already done the orient-and-decide steps ahead of time, then the decision cycle effectively becomes redefined as shown in Figure 15-7.

The question is then how do you redefine the decision cycle? The answer is, by strategic knowledge management.

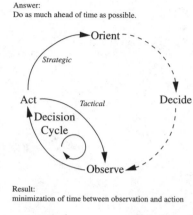

Figure 15-7
Redefining the decision cycle.

Decision Cycle 2: The Next-Generation Decision Cycle

The growing field of knowledge management brings to the table a profusion of tools that can be used to advantage in competition, including databases, models, simulations, studies, and so on. (See Fig. 15-8)

In this reconfigured decision cycle process, the orient step is performed first. Massive amounts of information are collected and combined to do this. The environment is characterized and modeled. Simulations are performed that examine the relationships between stimuli and result according to all the data available and complex mathematical characterizations of behavior patterns. All possible future worlds are predicted, and all possible activities in those future worlds are examined for context and result.

Using the same example as before, the merchant would characterize the demand for linseed oil, compile a comprehensive list of all linseed oil

Figure 15-8

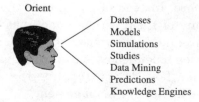

Figure 15-9

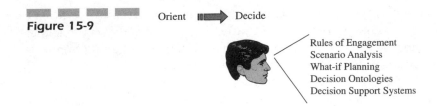

Orient ➡ Decide

Rules of Engagement
Scenario Analysis
What-if Planning
Decision Ontologies
Decision Support Systems

producers, compile a list of all previous purchasers of linseed oil and their demographic information, analyze usage patterns, analyze geographic weather patterns, postulate shortage conditions, and characterize profit possibilities.

Based on those characterizations, a set of decisions can be made and programmed into automated equipment. For example, our merchant could program a "buy" order for linseed oil when certain market and weather conditions were to be met. (See Fig. 15-9)

This *a priori* characterization of all possible desired decisions allows the decision cycle to become simply a matter of observing and acting. However, it becomes necessary to use automated observation capabilities to get the most utility from the construct. It does little good if the observation is done manually, requiring interface with other equipment or manual processes. Instead, an observation agent (such as an infobot) is used to collect stimuli and trigger actions when conditions are met that meet described thresholds. (See Fig. 15-10)

The merchant places his observation agent online, and it sits silently collecting information. When the information collected matches the described thresholds as characterized in the orient and decide steps, the appropriate action is triggered. This action is preprogrammed automatically and very fast. This type of acting can be considered analogous to reaction rather than action, but that really trivializes the capabilities of the process. With enough exposure and training, humans can develop automatic reactions that are quite complex. That philosophy is the cor-

Figure 15-10

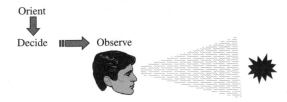

Orient
↓
Decide ➡ Observe

nerstone for many leadership training programs for stressful vocations. Exposing individuals to as many situations as possible allows the leader to react quickly when a situation develops, rather than having to puzzle through all possible courses of action. (See Fig. 15-11)

Because this entire system is based upon the concept of comprehensive knowledge management, the results of the action feed back into the cycle at two nodes, as shown in Figure 15-12. There is an immediate tactical feedback loop back to the observation step, so that the next observation is contextual, and a strategic feedback into the orientation step so that the models and predictions can reflect the new state of reality.

That this modified decision cycle process is being used today can be illustrated by a variety of real-world events. Consider the stock market crash of 1987 in the United States. One of the contributing factors to the crash has been widely held to be the use of automated trading programs. These trading programs were set to buy or sell stock based on predecided thresholds. If a certain stock met certain thresholds described by trading

Figure 15-11

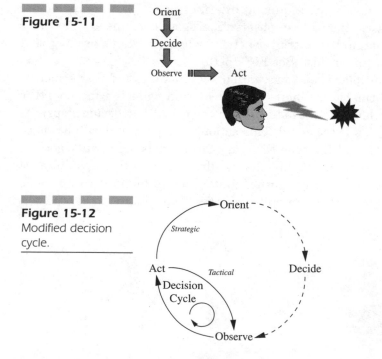

Figure 15-12
Modified decision
cycle.

volume, price trends, and other data, then a buy or a sell order would be automatically placed without human intervention. Unfortunately, these programs were uncontrolled and selfish—when the trend in the stock market started down and the volume of trades was up, the automatic trading programs started placing sell orders. This contributed to the frenzy by placing downward pressure on prices and raising the trading volume even more. These data points were in turn interpreted as emergencylike conditions by the automatic trading programs, which placed even more sell orders. As a result of this experience, firewalls were put in place. These firewalls serve the purpose of controlling feeding frenzies like this, by altering the conditions: When a certain percentage of value has been lost in certain key indicators, trading ceases for the day. This provides a cooling-off period and allows the strategic feedback mechanism to incorporate the conditions fully into the orient step, which reconfigures the decision space for the next trading day. In the decade since these "firewall" conditions have been adopted, the conditions have been met only a few times, but each time the process has worked to stabilize the trading environment.

Another example of the modified decision cycle in action is seen in just-in-time manufacturing processes. The plan of action for the entire manufacturing process is decided ahead of time and then executed. As conditions reach thresholds, parts are brought into the process for incorporation. There is room for minor changes in the schedule of events, according to the whims of real life, but major changes can cause widespread problems throughout the entire chain. When a short-term power outage occurs, the schedule can be modified to reflect the changes. When workers go out on extended strikes, however, effects cascade throughout the entire system.

Another example is just-in-time logistics support for the retail industry. Stores keep track of inventory through the use of integrated databases and know exactly how many of each kind of goods are in stock at any moment—when one is sold the bar code reader at the register sends a data update to the centralized database. When the level of stock reaches a threshold, an order is placed with the manufacturer to replenish the stock. This takes a lot of the guesswork out of running a store, makes it more efficient, and contributes to lower prices. It also contributes to the manufacturer's decision processes on what to manufacture—if something is selling well, more of that item needs to be produced.

This is strategic knowledge management, or knowledge in use.

Repercussions of Attacks on Second-Generation Decision Cycles

Clearly, the ability to make decisions faster and better than a competitor is an enviable ability. This makes it also a potential target for attack. Consider this: If you could force your competitor to doubt or mistrust his or her second-generation decision cycle, the competitor would be forced to go back to the first-generation decision cycle, which is by definition slower and less agile. So it is that the actual processes of the decision cycle become a target for attack. This is the category of attacks on knowledge in use.

The question is how can the decision cycle processes be attacked? This gets into very subtle areas. Conceptually, what can be attacked are the perceptions of the users and the specific elements of the decision cycle process, including the following:

1. Actual models and simulations supporting the decision process
2. Trust in the validity of the orientation step
3. Decision support systems
4. Trust in the decision support systems
5. Observation systems
6. Trust in the observation systems
7. Action systems
8. Trust in the action systems

It is interesting to note that it is not necessary to actually attack the systems themselves to cause the competitor to default back to the first-generation decision cycle. If you are able to cause your competitor to distrust one or more of the process elements, then that competitor will choose not to use it even though it may be perfectly okay to do so.

Seeding information contrary to what is predicted can create distrust in these process elements. If a competitor acts one way based on second-generation decision cycle processes, but the information received back indicates that the outcome was not as predicted, then the competitor will wonder what went wrong. Depending on what stimulus is delivered to the competitor, different elements of the competitor's second-generation decision cycle processes may come under suspicion. Using this kind of operation at carefully selected opportunities can support a sustained advantage in the competition for the perpetrator. If the process works well enough most of the time, the enterprise under attack may not detect they are being attacked.

Carefully synchronized stimuli can serve to create distrust in all of the process elements over time. This has an added advantage of denying the competitor any easy fixes. The competitor can't simply replace a module and get back to an operational status. When distrust grows over the entire systemic process, the competitor must default back to the first-generation decision cycle for an extended period of time. This can provide the attacker with an overwhelming advantage in decision cycle times over a sustained period of time.

The preceding attack descriptions are based upon stimuli. Providing false, misleading, or semi-true information is the critical element of this attack profile. The stimuli must, of course, be delivered in a way that appears trustworthy and credible. It must also be delivered in a way that gets noticed. If the stimuli are missed, the attack fails. However, seeding stimuli in supporting arenas can augment an attack on trust if the attacked party decides to research the circumstances and verify whether the information received is true or not.

Attacking the elements of the decision cycle can involve one or more of the following:

1. Inserting false data into the applications, causing them to skew

2. Inserting software that subverts the goals of the system

3. Disabling parts of the system

Providing false data into models and simulations can cause them to execute predicted behavior patterns that are not exactly right. They might be close to right, but just far enough off to cause the resulting decision processes to make different decisions, which then would prompt different actions. It might also prompt different interpretations of the observations because of the preconceived nature of the environment. The same sort of results could be achieved by inserting false data into the observation processes or the action processes. If the action processes, for example, receive data that was not sent from the observation processes, the actions would be executed just as if they had come from the observation processes.

Inserting software into the applications that support the processes enables the goals of the system to be subverted. For example, a software patch to an observation application could prevent the observation system from "noticing" certain precise conditions, while correctly "noticing" every other set of conditions. This could be very useful if the goal of the attacker is stealth or secrecy. Inserting complex rules into a knowledge engine could achieve the same results with even less chance of detection.

And, of course, parts of the system could simply be disabled or destroyed. If the database feeding the models and simulations is destroyed, the entire system collapses. If the infobot responsible for acting is disabled, no action is possible. If the observation application is disabled or destroyed, the action application waits indefinitely instead of acting.

These examples make it clear that it is not sufficient to protect only the information within the system. Information that feeds the system from outside must be verified and vetted. Each component system should be routinely audited and tested for correctness. The processes should be reverse-engineered routinely and run by a team of humans to ensure that correct actions are being taken.

In other words, the process of knowledge use must be continually audited and verified.

Systems Engineering the Security Solution

Every security solution is unique to the environment and the enterprise specifics. Each enterprise has unique security requirements, some of which are defined by the environment. Systems engineering a security solution must reflect this uniqueness.

The practice of information security is built around the concept of risk management. Risk is typically considered to be a combination of threats and vulnerabilities, where the potential for a threat to act on an information environment is made possible by the vulnerabilities existing in that environment. Countermeasures can mitigate or lessen this potential.

Threats include both natural phenomena, such as fires and floods, and hostile actors. The ability for a threat to cause problems can be characterized as a combination of capability and intent. Without capability, the threat is powerless; without intent, the threat will not act. For natural phenomena, the intent is inherent in its existence. With human actors, intent can be mitigated through a variety of means, such as negative feedback and education. Capability is a combination of access and skill. Without access, skill is useless; without skill, access has limited value. Threat access can be mitigated through access control mechanisms, such as doors and locks. Threat skill can be mitigated through obscurity of technical details and complex operational procedures. It is generally easier to mitigate threat access than threat skill.

Managing risk is an iterative process of determining the threats, vulnerabilities, potential countermeasures, and the impact of information security failure. Countermeasures can include not only technologies but also policies and operational procedures.

Because the information environment is not static, the risk profile is constantly changing. With every change of personnel, hardware, software, and operational procedures, new vulnerabilities are potentially introduced into the environment and must be assessed. With each new vulnerability, threats are accorded new pathways for action that must be mitigated. All of this must be done in considered, managed action, weighing the benefits of additional security measures against the costs of such measures.

Security Attributes

The security attributes of confidentiality, integrity, and availability need to be considered separately for both information and for transactions.

Confidentiality

The security attribute of confidentiality refers to the goal of keeping information from unauthorized disclosure. This also can be known as maintaining secrecy. Maintaining secrecy of information requires that unauthorized subjects be prevented from accessing the information. Maintaining secrecy of transactions requires that the transactions be conducted sans observers.

Information for which confidentiality might be an important attribute includes trade secrets, operating procedures, and personnel data. An example of a transaction for which confidentiality might be an important attribute is information exchange between organizations considering a merger—the fact of communications between the two organizations could attract unwanted attention.

There are four classes of secrets that are not mutually independent (information may belong to more than one class simultaneously). One kind of secret is that which reveals sources or methods information. For example, an item of information may in itself be routine and common but may still require confidentiality protection because the divulgence of that data would reveal a source or a method. Another kind of secret is one that reveals relationship information. A third kind of secret is one that is time-dependent. For example, information may require confidentiality protection for only a short period of time, during which divulgence of that information could jeopardize plans or give someone an unfair advantage. A fourth kind of secret is a true secret—information that requires confidentiality protection in and of its own right.

Each of these represents different challenges from a protection point of view. A time-dependent secret needs to be protected only for its time period, while a true secret may need to be protected in all instantiations for the lifetime of an individual. Clearly, different engineering solutions are required for these different requirements, and yet they all fall under the rubric of "confidentiality."

Integrity

The security attribute of integrity refers to the wholeness and continued unchanged nature of information. The attribute of integrity also should be considered for both information itself and for transactions. Information for which integrity may be a required attribute includes bank account balances, credit reports, and hospital records. Transactions for which integrity may be a required attribute include bank transfers and computer logins. A special-case subset of integrity is nonrepudiation, which refers to a requirement that parties to a transaction be unable to deny the participation.

Availability

As mentioned, availability refers to being able to use and manipulate information, or conduct transactions, when desired. For information environments such as those supporting telemedicine, the attribute of availability is a critical attribute. For other information environments, such as long-term research projects, availability may not be as critical.

Security Phases

Given that it is impossible to guarantee 100 percent perfect security, the information security measures should cover not only the first-level protective actions but also the processes associated with detecting problems and reacting to those problems. These include the protect, detect, and connect phases.

Protect

The "protect" phase is the first line of defense, where security measures are taken to mitigate vulnerabilities and reduce the ability of threats to act. Goals of protection are to deny unauthorized users access to information or systems, to deny attackers knowledge that can be used in support of attacks, and to engineer systems to be resistant to threat actions.

Detect

Given that protect mechanisms may eventually fail, it is important to have detection capabilities that check to see that protections are still in place and working properly. When a violation of protection measures is noted, the detection measures should issue an alarm.

Connect

This phase includes all activities associated with rectifying problems and regaining full operational capabilities. The "correct" phase could include actions as diverse as taking a single system offline or hot-switching entire operations to a backup facility.

Engineering Security

Based on the risk assessment for the operational environment, security solutions should be engineered across the space of the security attributes and the security phases. The elements for each should be integrated to provide synergistic systems behavior. Before solutions can be chosen, however, it is important to understand what elements need security in the information environment. Table 15-1 describes the questions that must be asked to reach this understanding.

Table 15-2 takes the engineering process to the next level, considering the phases of security.

Information States

The engineering of security must also take into consideration the fact that information can be handled by a variety of different technologies depending on what process it is undergoing. Most security schemas

TABLE 15-1

Determining
Security Needs.

	What?	How Much?	How Long?
Confidentiality	▪ What information needs confidentiality protection? ▪ What transactions need confidentiality protection? ▪ What information does not need confidentiality protection? ▪ What transactions do not need confidentiality protection?	▪ How strongly must confidentiality be protected? ▪ What is the minimal level of confidentiality for every asset that requires protection?	▪ How long must confidentiality be ensured? ▪ When will it be allowable to release or degrade the protections?
Integrity	▪ What information needs integrity protection? ▪ What transactions need integrity protection? ▪ What information does not need integrity protection? ▪ What transactions do not need integrity protection?	▪ How strongly must integrity be protected? ▪ What is the minimal level of integrity for every asset that requires protection?	▪ How long must integrity be assured? ▪ When will it be allowable to release or degrade the protections?
Availability	▪ What information needs availability protection? ▪ What transactions need availability protection? ▪ What information does not need availability protection? ▪ What transactions do not need availability protection?	▪ How strongly must availability be protected? ▪ What is the minimal level of availability for every asset that requires protection?	▪ How long must availability be ensured? ▪ When will it be allowable to release or degrade the protections?

TABLE 15-2

Engineering
Security across
Phases.

	Protect	Detect	Correct
Confidentiality	▪ What could cause a problem with confidentiality? ▪ What can be done to protect the confidentiality of information and/or transactions? ▪ How long must that protection be accorded? ▪ How strong must that protection be?	▪ How can breaches of confidentiality be detected in this environment? ▪ What kinds of alarms are needed if problems are detected? ▪ Who should the alarms notify?	▪ How fast do the breaches to confidentiality need to be stopped? ▪ How can the confidentiality be restored? ▪ What must be done to restore protection of confidentiality? ▪ Are there any steps required to restore user confidence in the system?
Integrity	▪ What could cause a problem with integrity? ▪ What can be done to protect the integrity of information and/or transactions? ▪ How long must that protection be accorded? ▪ How strong must that protection be?	▪ How can breaches of integrity be detected in this environment? ▪ What kinds of alarms are needed if problems are ▪ detected? Who should the alarms notify?	▪ How fast do the breaches to integrity need to be stopped? ▪ How can the integrity be restored? ▪ What must be done to restore protection of integrity? ▪ Are there any steps required to restore user confidence in the system?
Availability	▪ What could cause a problem with availability? ▪ What can be done to protect the availability of information and/or transactions? ▪ How long must that protection be accorded? ▪ How strong must that protection be?	▪ How can breaches of availability be detected in this environment? ▪ What kinds of alarms are needed if problems are detected? ▪ Who should the alarms notify?	▪ How fast do the breaches to availability need to be stopped? ▪ How can the availability be restored? ▪ What must be done to restore protection of availability? ▪ Are there any steps required to restore user confidence in the system?

restrict security efforts to protecting only the information while it is being stored or while it is being communicated. Some also consider the security challenges inherent in processing the information. However, significant opportunities to circumvent security requirements exist in the other states, as noted in previous chapters. An example of this can be seen in the use of encryption for security purposes; the data *must* exist at some time prior to encryption and at some time after decryption in cleartext. If an attacker was interested in the information, it would make more sense to get to it while it is in cleartext than while it is encrypted. Comprehensive security must take all information states into account.

There are six general information states in a system:

1. Collected and input into a system
2. Processed
3. Viewed
4. Stored in dynamic memory
5. Stored in permanent memory
6. Communicated between systems

Additionally, the dynamic state of transitioning between states is a potential area of vulnerability that should be considered.

Security Technologies

In a perfect world, enterprises requiring security would be able to use software with no bugs on systems that were fault-free. Then these enterprises would only have to worry about the operational environment challenges, such as malicious insiders and external espionage. However, this is far from a perfect world, and enterprise managers must not only protect against operational environment challenges but also contend with the requirements to use commercial off-the-shelf (COTS) hardware and software. Further, managers are forced to change out these already less-than-trustworthy systems every few years as technology eclipses itself.

This situation results in an operational environment in which it is practically impossible to trust any element in the system. Because of this, a robust market of technologies has emerged offering add-on solutions for the security of systems. These security technologies provide significant assistance to the challenge of providing security.

However, the technologies vary greatly in their utility and cost. Some technologies are very expensive and very specialized in their application to security challenges. Others are very expensive but broader in their application. Others yet are less expensive but with narrow application.

The challenge to the security manager is how to pick the best suite of technologies that provides the capabilities required for the unique security challenges in the enterprise operational environment. To do this, it is critical that the contributions of the technologies to specific security challenges be understood. Cryptography, for example, can assist in confidentiality and integrity challenges but is useless for availability issues. Firewalls assist in denying access to external threats but are useless against internal threats. For security professionals, it is a large challenge to keep up with the state of the art of security technologies. For those with no education in security, the challenge is overwhelming.

In Table 15-3, some technologies are identified that can help achieve security goals. A brief explanation of the security contribution is given in the second column. In the right-hand section of the table, the security attributes of confidentiality, integrity, and availability are abbreviated as C, I, and A, while the security engineering phases of protect, detect, and correct are abbreviated as P, D, and C. If the technology makes a direct contribution to either the security attribute or the phase, an X is placed in the applicable box.

This makes no judgment on *how much* the technology contributes, but merely notes a contribution. It must be noted that the effectiveness of any security measure depends greatly on the integrity of its integration into the environment and usage within the operational context.

The selection of technologies and practices is a matter of matching the security needs of the environment to what is available. Further, operational constraints may preclude the ability to use some security technologies. A large metropolitan hospital emergency room clearly has the need to keep patient information secret and whole. However, this need is contradicted by the need to treat patients extremely quickly and effectively. Clearly, security processes and technologies that create a roadblock to treating the patients would be more counterproductive than productive. In this situation, alternatives must be found.

These kinds of trade-offs are found in every operational environment. Therefore, selecting security tools is not only a matter of deciding what the security requirements are and selecting a set of technologies that support those requirements, it is also a matter of analyzing the operational environment and the systemic needs of the enterprise. Then those systemic needs must be considered against the security needs.

TABLE 15-3

Security
Technologies.

Technology/Processes	Security Contributions	Applicable Attributes and Phases					
		C	I	A	P	D	C
Antipiracy software	Controls valid software in use. Prevents back doors and data corruption.		X		X	X	
Antiviral software	Prevents data corruption and theft.	X	X	X	X	X	
Audit data reduction system	Supports detection of problems.					X	
Auditing/monitoring systems and networks	Supports detection of problems.					X	
Backups	Mitigates data corruption problems.		X	X	X		X
Computer emergency response team	Supports correction and recovery from problems.					X	X
Configuration management system	Supports data integrity and use detection.		X		X	X	
Content scanning system	Scans system for specified content, identifying data transfer or problems.	X	X			X	
Cryptography	Supports secrecy and integrity.	X	X		X		
Disaster recovery/ Business continuity exercises	Supports ability to recover quickly.						X
Disaster recovery/ Business continuity planning	Supports ability to recover quickly.						X
Disk drive lock	Physically locks the disk drive, preventing use except with the key turned.	X	X		X		
Employee activity monitoring system	Supports detection of insider problems.					X	
Employee background investigations	Prevents malicious insider problems.				X		
Employee badging system	Provides identification of personnel inside plants.	X	X		X	X	
External security monitoring service	Prevents outsider access.	X	X	X	X		
Firewalls	Mitigates external attacks.	X	X	X			
Identification authentication system	Verifies the identification of users.	X	X		X	X	

TABLE 15-3

Security
Technologies.
(Continued)

Technology/Processes	Security Contributions	Applicable Attributes and Phases					
		C	I	A	P	D	C
Independent security assessments	Provides vulnerability knowledge.					X	X
Intrusion detection systems	Detects malicious activity.*						X
Network monitoring	Detects malicious activity.*						X
One-time password system	Supports high-confidence communications linkages.	X	X		X		
Password cracking system	Checks passwords for strength.	X	X		X		
Removable disk drives	Protects disks and contents from access.	X	X		X		
Uninterruptible power supply	Provides power backup in case of outage.			X	X		

*Malicious activity is any activity contrary to the goals of the organization, including theft and sabotage.

In some cases, the systemic needs will be found to easily support the security needs. In other cases, they may contradict each other, as in the case of the emergency room environment. In still other cases, systemic needs may be able to be reengineered in a way that both increases security capabilities and streamlines operations within the environment.

Putting It Together

Table 15-3, presented above in alphabetical order, can also be sorted by security contribution. Looking at it in that light provides a different view of what is available to help secure an enterprise's information environment. From this new view, shown in Table 15-4, it becomes apparent that most of the technologies and processes common in the contemporary business environment are focused towards protecting confidentiality and integrity.

The choice of technologies for use in securing a particular environment must be augmented with operational practices and circumstance management. Selecting the best mix of technologies for the environment

TABLE 15-4

Technology/
Process
Contributions.

Technology/Processes	C	I	A	P	D	C
	Applicable Attributes and Phases					
Antiviral software	X	X	X	X	X	
External security monitoring services	X	X	X	X	X	
Firewalls	X	X	X	X		
Content scanning system	X	X			X	
Cryptography	X	X		X		
Disk drive lock	X	X		X		
Employee badging system	X	X		X	X	
Identification authentication system	X	X		X	X	
One-time password system	X	X		X		
Password cracking system	X	X		X		
Removable disk drives	X	X		X		
Backups	[	X	X	X		X
Antipiracy software		X		X	X	
Configuration management system		X		X	X	
Uninterruptible power supply			X	X		
Audit data reduction system					X	
Auditing/monitoring systems and networks					X	
Computer emergency response team					X	X
Disaster recovery/Business continuity exercises						X
Disaster recovery/Business continuity planning						X
Employee activity monitoring system					X	
Employee background/investigations				X		
Independent security assessments				X	X	
Intrusion detection system					X	
Network monitoring					X	

will typically be heavily influenced by the amount of money available to be spent. Each one of these capabilities costs something—from hundreds of dollars to hundreds of thousands of dollars—and contributes to only a part of the security requirements. Further, each technology is potentially subject to subversion. People are a critical component in any enterprise, and a determined foe can find a way around any security technology.

Policies, practices, and common sense must make up the short fall. These must cover the span of protection, detection, and correction. Policies, practices, and common sense must support the protection of confidentiality, integrity, and availability, as well as support the detection of problems in those areas. Being ready to react to any situation and correct it is predominately a policy and practices issue.

Education and training of the personnel within the environment complete the engineering solution of security. Not only do education and training establish the policies and practices as normal operating procedures within the environment, they also serve to continually remind enterprise members of the need for security.

Wrap-Up

There will never be total security within an environment. Time and again, supposedly secure enterprises have been proven to have been compromised. The most amazing incident in recent years has been the revelations of the secrets of the KGB, which were painstakingly smuggled out over years by a determined worker.

Because total security is impossible, it is necessary that a mixture of technologies, operational processes, and circumstance management be selected that fit the security goals of the specific enterprise environment. Further, those security measures must be continually assessed for relevance and effectiveness, and changes made when appropriate.

It's a difficult task. The complexities of the information dimension are enormous, and it is not simply the knowledge base that is at risk—the knowledge in use is at risk as well. Managing security is not for the faint at heart.

CHAPTER 16

Information Warfare

The subject of "information warfare" has gained prominence in the last decade. The concept implies a sort of hostile technology, or one that is out of the control of normal people and one that appeals to the fears that surround all new discoveries or capabilities. The speed with which electronic information technology—computing, networking, telecommuting—has inculcated society leaves a great many gasping for breath as they attempt to keep up with the pace of change. When that same technology is imbued with the characteristic of hostility, as implied by the term *warfare*, it becomes a subject for vast speculation and titillating intrigue. And that is exactly what we have seen. Ordinary, normal, and even ancient forms of conflict have been redesignated as part of "information warfare." And yet, what does that really mean?

What in fact is warfare itself? During the vast majority of our existence as sentient beings, warfare was not strictly defined. Everyone knew what warfare was—it was when a bunch of armed men came and took over your land, cattle, money, water supplies, or other things of value (including women and children sometimes). During these periods in history, it was not particularly necessary or even useful to have a strict delineation between warfare and other sorts of banditry and mayhem. The distinction between a raid by a gypsy band and a group of warriors from a neighboring kingdom simply did not much matter—the result was the same, and there was no United Nations or World Court to which to air grievances. A broader view of warfare would be an armed conflict between opposing forces for nationalistic or economic reasons.

With the globalizing influences brought about, first slowly and then with increasing speed, by the expansions of the European states, Asia, and Africa beginning in the second half of the twentieth century, the need to differentiate between state-sanctioned warfare and criminal behavior began to become pressing. These definitions started to become codified in the 1600s and gained increasing specificity over the past hundred years. Warfare is now so strictly defined that international legal action is possible against perpetrators of unlawful actions, such as crimes against humanity. Who can conduct warfare is defined, what they can do is defined, and how they have to treat opposing forces is defined.

Within this context of strictly defined warfare, a new dimension has emerged. The global interconnectedness of uncontrolled information flows that transcend borders and redefine authority relationships is viewed by some as a threat in and of itself. For those people, information warfare is about spreading ideas. It is viewed by others as a conduit for a threat. For those people, information warfare is about attacking and defending information assets—including physical assets, such as nodes, and virtual assets, such as online communities.

One thing that is constant in the varying discussions of information warfare is the need to protect information assets and the potential for harm in a variety of different elements. Just as a stick lying on the ground is simply a stick until it is used to bludgeon a mugging victim, so are the majority of information techniques and technologies benign until imbued with the hostile intent and will of an adversary. The following discussion attempts to give some context to the subject of information warfare, but the bottom line remains the same: Warfare is not conducted by inanimate objects. It is conducted by sentient beings who use tools, techniques, and technologies in order to achieve some goal. The tools, techniques, and technologies may be perfectly useful for nonmalicious purposes until used by individuals wishing to cause harm.

Information Warfare

The uses of information form the basis for understanding information warfare. From the days of dedicated runners carrying news over the plains of Greece, through the eras of signal fires and carrier pigeons, to today's use of encrypted broadcasts via satellites, information has always been a crucial component of decision making. Where once strategists spoke of the importance of accurate and timely communications for coordinated battle plans, our strategic thinkers now presume that basic communications capability and plot instead of executing operations within the opponent's "decision cycle." The *decision cycle* is defined as the time that it takes the enemy to respond to stimuli and make a decision to react. This evolution is a direct consequence of the technological explosion in the enabling technologies that quickly and accurately convey information—data, pictures, ideas—to diverse components with few physical barriers.

The Decision Cycle

Whereas the decision cycle prior to the wholesale acceptance and implementation of automated information technology was fairly simple, serial in nature, and time-dependent, today's decision cycle is fast paced, at best time-neutral, and somewhat parallel in execution. The old decision cycle could be described fairly elegantly as a process of observing something, giving context to that observation, making a decision on what to do based on the observation and the context, acting on that decision, and then observing the results.

There has always been a level of competition in competitors' decision cycle capabilities. Generals who were able to act faster on observations were able to leverage information to their relative advantage. As a result, many innovations in communications were made. Signal fires allowed early generals to coordinate troops across mountainous terrain and vast distances. Balloons extended the vision of the battlefield and allowed greater perspective and context to observations. Encryption allowed messages to be sent in secrecy.

As the level of competition has increased with the advent of wireless communications, portable computers, and expert systems, as well as other technologies, the process of the decision cycle has been pushed to its physical limits. As these limits were reached, the old process of observe, get context, decide, and act became a bottleneck in otherwise light speed operations.

And so modifications were made. Instead of waiting to observe some action occurring, situations were modeled and observations predicted. With this expanded knowledge base of what might occur in hand, actions could be predecided—if this occurs, do this. Rules of engagement laid out the constraints of these actions and provided a context for the events. The ability to model, simulate, and otherwise characterize possible occurrences is predicated upon having sufficient information about the environment, the actors, and the potential events. This is made possible through large databases, worldwide data collection efforts, and sophisticated data mining techniques. Automating the actions that are based on the predefined decisions is simply a matter of programming them into a system, and then placing the system in a position to receive observations. When the observations reach a triggering level, action is stimulated based on the predefined decisions and rules of engagement. The cycle thus becomes inverted from its original form, with context forming performed first, decisions being formed second, observations collected third, and actions performed as hair-trigger functions based on all of the above. Of course, all of the observations and actions are additionally fed back into the system in real time.

This decision cycle works much faster than the old one, and as such it is subject to problems when the modeling is not performed well, or the rules of engagement don't take into account unprecedented activities, or when too many automated decision systems start feeding on each other's actions in a sort of infinite logical loop. The stock market crash of 1987 was worsened significantly by the use of automated trading programs, and the result of that crash was to implement systemic limits on trades when thresholds are reached. In other words, the people in control recognized the limitations of the automated decision cycles and put automated decision controls in place that act when the first set of automated decision systems start feeding on themselves. (It's a fascinating example of technology and countertechnology. Using the same tools, one controls the other.)

These advances have not been relegated solely to civil life. As information-related technology has evolved, so has its utility to warfare. Technology not only enables modern warfare, it shapes the very way we think about war. The state of that evolution is now at a point where it is possible to conceive of the information infrastructure, content, and technologies as parts of an information dimension to warfare. This is separate and distinct from other dimensions and subject to the same complexities of planning and strategic thought as the more conventional dimensions of air, land, and sea.

This concept, more commonly referred to as *information warfare*, or *infowar*, is being examined, studied, and explored by many of the world's strategic thinkers, much as half a century ago the new dimension of air warfare was being explored. And, much as the great air strategists had significant challenges to overcome in their quest to define air as a separate and independent dimension of warfare, infowar is facing a degree of challenge and skepticism from the professional warrior community. While all elements of the U.S. armed forces have information warfare units and capabilities, and many other nations do as well, the interfaces between the traditional warfighters and the information warriors is not well defined or understood. How can an air attack be coordinated with an information attack? These kinds of issues are being worked through as new ideas and concepts are developed. The new generation of warrior, with an intuitive lifetime experience with information technologies, will push this capability forward tremendously, because for them it will be natural rather than some frighteningly new and bizarre notion force-fit into a traditional armed forces.

This chapter is an initial high-level exploration of the concept of infowar: that is to say, how the information dimension of modern war can be utilized knowingly and proactively in support of national policies, goals, and interests. Understanding the elements of information warfare is only a beginning, however. Understanding how all of them fit together with normal life—economic development, environmental controls, family structures, cultures, and so on—is a critical element of understanding the true challenge of information warfare.

Elements of Infowar

Information warfare is the logical next step in competition. It is simply a reflection of the exponential growth of information-related value, technology, and applications within the more conventional framework of life in general. The elements of infowar can be extrapolated from the elements of conventional warfare as adapted for the dimension of information. When considering what is and what is not within the boundaries of this new discipline, however, ideas can get muddled quickly. It is useful, therefore, to consider simple examples in order to frame the discussion of offensive infowar operations. Here we examine only the actions, not the actors. Who will be performing these actions, and with what degree of legitimacy, is a whole other discussion.

One of the most obvious elements of offensive operations is a *direct attack* on the physical elements of the information infrastructure. For example, shooting the feed horn off of a microwave antenna with long-range sniper fire effectively puts that node of an information conduit out of business. On the other hand, shooting the maintenance personnel who try to replace the feed will keep it down. Both are effective in achieving the desired result, but there may be argument about whether shooting the maintenance personnel is part of infowar or not. That type of concern is not addressed in this discussion. Intermediate positions include attacks on databases, programs, and applications, as well as on logistics systems, acquisition systems, and training support systems.

A less obvious element of offensive operations is the use of Madison Avenue "positioning" techniques. An example of this would be to subtly frame an opponent's perceived decision space to make it appear unfavorable to persist in activities contrary to U.S. national interests. The weapon in this case is information, the target is the opponent's decision process, and the methods of delivery are legion.

It becomes clear after considering just the extreme examples that the realm of offensive infowar operations comprises more than just activities wholly within the dimension of information. Rather than exhaustively defining the boundaries for such concepts in this paper, therefore, the guideline followed is to consider any offensive action that affects the opponent's ability to use, manipulate, or communicate information as a member of the discipline.

The Playing Field

The activities of infowar can be effective within the dimension of information itself and on any element that supports, feeds, or interacts with the dimension of information. This includes a new battlefield known as *cyberspace*, that consensually imagined universe where information reigns supreme; but it also includes computers, modems, printers, fibers and wires of all sorts, antennas, electricity, intelligence, and systems and maintenance personnel. Targets include physical entities, data, decision processes of national leaders, and the popular will of the citizenry. The playing field is practically infinite, delimited for each operation by the weapons chosen, the methods of engagement used, the strategy, and the metric for success. Because of this, defending against information warfare is as simple as defending your computer and as complex as defending your network. It requires cooperation between competing entities, and solitary actors can't do it. Thus the challenge of information warfare is not only a simple offense and defense question within the information dimension but also a management issue for intertwining corporate, personal, and governance capabilities.

Implications for Conventional War Strategies

In his book *Technology and War*, Martin Van Creveld divides the history of war into four periods: the Age of Tools (2000 B.C. to circa 1500 A.D.), the Age of Machines (circa 1500 to 1830), the Age of Systems (1830 to 1945), and the Age of Automation (1945 to present). In this book, he postulates that "technology gave birth to complexity, complexity to an extraordinary requirement for information, and the requirement for information to paperwork. The avalanche of paperwork that is threatening the most advanced modern armies would have overwhelmed them long ago had it not been for the introduction of mechanical data-processing equipment."

The concepts explored here are an attempt to understand the next logical step in this evolution. As the introduction of nuclear weapons has affected both the conduct of war and the relationships between nations (to the point of introducing both a new form of war—the cold war—and new forms of diplomacy—mutual assured destruction and thermonuclear détente), so can it be presumed that the introduction of the information dimension as part of the landscape of war will fundamentally affect the nature of what we now call conventional war. Properly executed, offensive infowar can preclude the need to fire a single round of ammunition, either by preventing the outbreak of hostilities or by the destruction of an enemy's capability to wage modern warfare by the destruction of its command and control and support systems. *The strategies and tactics that make this possible are fundamentally different from those of either conventional or nuclear warfare.* In what other dimension of war is invisibility a possible attribute? In what other dimension is geography a trivial constraint?

Information Revolution

Changes are occurring in the definition of security for both countries and individuals. We are in the midst of a social and economic revolution, akin to the industrial revolution, which has been called the "information revolution." Just as the industrial revolution changed the way people lived, where they lived, how capital was created and how it was distributed, and how governance worked, so too is the information revolution changing all those elements of life. Because the information infrastructure upon which this revolution depends knows no geopolitical boundaries, this revolution extends across the domains of diplomacy and its extension, warfare, engendering a new dimension to warfare—information warfare.

Much has been written about information warfare in the past two years. Landmark studies include the report of the President's Commission on Critical Infrastructure Protection and the Defense Science Board's Report on Information Warfare—Defense.

In policy-level discussions, information warfare is generally described as encompassing those actions designed to gain information superiority and to deny its advantages to an enemy. By information superiority we mean more, better, and faster information—whether obtained by exploiting your own technological capabilities or by attacking your opponent's information and information systems to make them less, worse, and slower than your own. Its desirability is self-evident.

These definitions are so broad that they fail to completely satisfy almost everyone, as evidenced by a pervasive unease permeating the national security community that is responsible for determining what the threats are and how the nation should best prepare to defend itself. Who specifically is threatening our information realm? How are they going to act? What will the results of those actions be? Will we see them coming? Where will they be coming from? Where should we post pickets for warning? Clearly, something is missing—a vital ingredient that will make all the pieces fall into place and allow forward progress in the development of information warfare strategy, tactics, doctrine, and procedures.

This missing link is the *geopolitical context* of the postulated struggle. The world in which information warfare must be waged is characterized as *transnational* in nature, with highly intertwined interests caused and reinforced by the explosive growth of information technologies. While it is recognized conceptually that the global playing field has changed in both form and substance, this recognition is rarely evident in discussions of national security means and ends. And yet it is this fundamental change in form and substance that defines the future of our nation's security and our way of life.

Rather than laboriously assessing the implications of information in all its myriad forms applicable to the national security needs of the United States, what must be assessed is the implication of information technology on the cooperative communal relationship that is currently known as the nation-state. Of course, that's a much harder nut to crack.

Certainly it is not without utility to study the application of the latest technologies to the protection and achievement of national goals and security. The history of warfare is, in one sense, a story of the evolution of technologies and their application to geopolitical struggles. The introductions of the longbow, the crossbow, the machine gun, and the thermonuclear bomb all changed the nature of warfare. The use of horses, tanks, airplanes, and spacecraft each had a fundamental impact not only on the tactics of battles, but on the very nature of the battlefield itself. The advent of telegraphy, radio, radar, and multispectral sensing revolutionized warfare. Now solid-state electronics, computers, networks, and fiber optics will enable new ways to project power. The Joint Security Commission of the DoD and CIA reported: "Networks are already recognized as a battlefield of the future. Information weapons will attack and defend at electronic speeds using strategies and tactics yet to be perfected. This technology is capable of deciding the outcome of geopolitical crises without the firing of a single weapon."[1]

But a more broad-ranging analysis of the impact of technology on the character and discourse of nation-states reveals much deeper issues. Since before the dawn of recorded history, humankind has been enslaved to the reality described by the high school equation speed $\times$ time $=$ distance. *As the speed of our transportation and communications increased, the distance we could cover in a unit of time decreased.* Our attention was taken from the village to the shire to the nation and eventually the world. Our notions of "we" versus "they" have always been based on the realities of speed, time, and distance. But no longer.

In the universe of information systems and networks, speeds are bounded only by the rate pulses of light can move through optical fibers and the speed at which electrons can move between thin layers of silicon. In such a world, distance loses its meaning. The new pluralism is enabled by modern telecommunications systems. Since Saigon is as close to Brooklyn as Chicago is to Gdansk, that is to say, no distance at all in cyberspace, the old geopolitical boundaries that defined—and protected—us no longer work. When our currency and intellectual capital, as well as our philosophies and bigotries, move at the speed of light, those who believe as we do can band together in virtual communities more easily than we used to create cities, counties, and countries. When our weapons move at like speeds and the battlefield is our systems and networks, the targets our information assets and infrastructure, and the goal the crippling of our ability to respond militarily and the destruction of our economy and our way of life, we have to rethink what we mean and intend by "national security."

Just as aviation, and more lately space travel, opened the third dimension to both commerce and warfare, and conquest of the electromagnetic spectrum opened a new and previously invisible domain for exploitation, the creation of world-spanning computer networks opens a new realm for exploration on behalf of both commerce and conflict. Each of these changes required a new vision of our world and a reevaluation of who we are as individuals, families, tribes, and geopolitical entities, and how we can and must relate to one another. Faster transportation and faster communications opens our world to new experiences, new ideas, and new threats. Knowledge *is* power, both in its ability to inform as well as to persuade, a fact well understood from Socrates and Plato to Hitler and Churchill, from Julius Caesar to Vladimir Ilyich Lenin to Ronald Reagan.

Still, the changes causing consternation and retrospection in the current geopolitical climate have less to do with the intrinsic power of information than with the flow of information between and amongst people. The breakthroughs in the last half century in the means and speed of transmitting information have changed the dynamics of information, enabling a new pluralism and wresting control of information transit away from those who have become accustomed to that advantage. The widespread availability of and access to television has become a powerful force for change and a significant channel of influence. The emergence of high-speed and high-capacity interactive networks multiplies that effect with every node added. The ability of tyrants today to meter and control the flow of information from unsanctioned sources is severely diminished. It seems clear to those working with data processing and communications technologies, and experiencing the full force of the information transfer capabilities, that the genie is out of the bottle and has only granted the first wish of the information age. It is yet to be discovered what the second and third wishes will be, when they will be granted, and what the effect of those wishes will be.

This, then, is the challenge: to develop an understanding of the emerging information-based world and to understand the challenges to our socioeconomic and geopolitical entities in that future. Only then can we truly understand what information warfare may be and what it may mean.

Our forecast of that future must encompass all dimensions of human life, including the technological, economic, managerial, political, social, cultural, intellectual, religious and ethical, and ecological dimensions. When President Clinton made the statement, "These things know no national boundaries....", he was talking about global organized crime. The same statement, and the same fear, applies to global disorganized networks. No one owns the Internet—it was invented in the United States, but it has long since passed out of our control.

The "cyberspace" of systems and networks has truly become a global resource, analogous to the seas and the sky. In 1621, international law was invented based upon the necessity to resolve conflicts on the then-boundless mainland. We have yet to fully develop the ethics, morality, etiquette, and laws needed to mediate behavior online and resolve conflicts that arise there.

The challenge that faces us is to determine what the community itself is becoming, what communal security is becoming, and to determine how to preserve our cherished ideals of personal freedom and democracy in this future. Human intellect developed the concept of democracy in an age when information and its transfer were more predictable and controllable, and when leadership was the province of those with the most education and learning. Human intellect must develop the concept further if it is to survive in an era of promiscuous communication and empowerment of all members of society, including the more fanatical, less educated, and least thoughtful of our brethren.

Defining National Security

What is national security? As the recent conflicts in Bosnia and the Persian Gulf have illustrated, this concept is not confined to simply securing the borders. It has much broader implications than that, and in this globalized world, national security is as highly intertwined as economics. So how can one identify and assess the implications for the national security of the United States of the pervasive access to both information and information technology by individuals and groups at all socioeconomic and political levels worldwide?

A critical first challenge is defining national security. Whereas traditionally "national security" has been viewed in terms of military, diplomatic, and economic arenas, it is clear that the emergence of information technologies fundamentally changes the matrix and qualifies information itself to be a separate dimension of the nation's security.

The opportunities and full implications of the information technology revolution are gradually being recognized and acted upon by a broad range of actors that include both governmental and various nonstate organizations that may be legitimate, informal or illicit. For these actors, connectivity has meant increases in access and influence commensurate with their level of network connectivity. Connectivity has also enabled those at all levels to end-run traditional hierarchies, which results in turn in a diffusion of power. The simplicity and ease with which these traditional power structures are bypassed are directly observable by other groups and individuals, who quickly adopt the same techniques for their own purposes. It is the subversion of traditional roles related to the control of information and its flow that most seriously affects the security of the nation-state. The vulnerabilities of the information assets and information infrastructures of states, while of serious concern, can only be fully appreciated within the broader context of information power and information politics.

The vulnerabilities of the existing information infrastructure of the United States have been thoroughly examined and reported on by various commissions and task forces over the last two decades. Critical key findings are that overwhelming changes in the traditional geopolitical structure of the world are occurring, with or without concurrence from traditional power structures, and that our policies for dealing with vulnerabilities of the information age must be informed by those changes and will require innovation in how information assurance is conceived and delivered.

This is not a comprehensive treatment of the subject. It is clear, however, that treating the issues of information assurance and information warfare merely as a matter of technological applications will not be sufficient. The research and theoretical underpinnings of this area are only now in their formative stages. Work by eminent social and political scientists such as David Ronfeldt and John Arquilla must be combined with the work of technologists such as Claude Shannon and Thomas Rona to develop a comprehensive understanding of the forces at work. What should be pursued is nothing less than a unified theory of information that accounts for not only the technology but also for the human perversities.

Key Points

The impact of information technologies on the traditional geopolitical structure of nation-states and their security implies changes to institutions and processes that are unavoidable, irresistible, and unless proper precautions are taken, potentially very destructive. These changes stem from increased use of computers and networks in creating, storing, processing, and communicating information, the application of information technology to efficient and global collaborative work environments, and the vulnerabilities and dependencies introduced by the technologies themselves. The institutions and processes that will be changed, and are in fact already changing, include those that administer governance and those that ensure communal security. The new pluralism that is enabled by information technologies at once adds richness to our lives and discourses and threatens to undermine the social structures that have secured the nation-state.

Central to our understanding of information assurance and information warfare is the role of "information" itself, an abstraction divorced from the technologies that store, manipulate, and transmit it. Information is a valuable asset, independent of the information systems and technologies used to store, process, and exchange it. Because it has value, it is increasingly a target for theft by criminals and destruction by terrorists. The sophistication, and hence seriousness, of these threats is growing even as we continue the transformation of our society and virtually all its institutions into its new technology-enabled pluralistic form. However, there is also the use of information as a means to bring like-minded people together to work together for a common cause, undermining the traditional authority roles. With this force, established powers can be made to change their actions.

Effective information assurance is not possible without compe-

tent information management and the commitment of leaders and policy makers to implement and support them. The challenge to authority doesn't denigrate the contributions that authority can make through education, leadership, and innovation. Coordinated efforts in all three of these dimensions are required if we are to achieve better information assurance and thereby enhance the security of our nation, our society, and our way of life. It may seem to traditional authority figures that this is a dilution of the role of authority, and perhaps it is. But in the intertwined new world, authority activities must be "outsourced" to the lowest level wherever possible in order to establish the greatest resiliency and robustness as a whole.

Growth of Vulnerabilities

The growth of vulnerabilities arising directly from the intertwining of information technologies in society has been documented to an astonishing degree in the last two decades. One of the first publications of the modern era to explore the problem was "America's Hidden Vulnerabilities," a report by the Panel on Crisis Management of the CSIS (Center for Strategic and International Studies, Georgetown University, Washington, D.C.) Science and Technology Committee published in 1984. A short list of some of the most influential publications include:

- *Computers At Risk: Safe Computing in the Information Age*, a publication of the National Academy of Sciences National Research Council in 1990

- *Cyberocracy is Coming* by David Ronfeldt, 1992.

- "Redefining Security"; a report by the Joint Security Commission to the Secretary of Defense and the Director of Central Intelligence; Washington D.C., February 28, 1994

- *Offensive Information Warfare: A Concept Exploration*, published by the Center for Naval Analyses in 1994

- "Critical Foundations Thinking Differently," a report of the President's Commission on Critical Infrastructure Protection (PCCIP), published in 1997.

These and literally hundreds of other publications have examined and reported on the challenges facing our combined security by new threats enabled by information technologies. These challenges stem from the increasing interconnectivities of information systems, as well as the increasing dependence on information systems in all aspects of our daily lives. Complicating the scene is the enormous infrastructure that supports and enables information technology, such as the electrical power grid and the public switched networks, which are in turn dependent themselves upon computers and information processing.

This chapter acknowledges and applauds the fine work that has gone before and attempts to stand on those giants' shoulders in order to see what may lie ahead, specifically in the arena of challenges to our national security.

Traditionally, national power and national security have been viewed in military, diplomatic, and economic terms. Joining those elements are the emerging components of information and information technology (IT). Timely, accurate, and complete information has always been important, even vital, to national power and national security. However, we have reached a stage at which increases in these quantitative characteristics are driving a qualitative change. A fundamental shift in the importance of information is under way—a shift partly because of IT but also because of behaviors that individuals, businesses, and states are exhibiting as a result of IT.

Most analysts agree that the thermonuclear-based superpower confrontation we call the Cold War was not won merely by military hegemony, but largely on the diplomatic and economic fronts with a strong military supporting them. The historic themes of global competition were anchored in territory (distance), population, and resources, and were strongly influenced by huge nuclear weapons arsenals that were the monopoly of the superpowers. Lesser states were dependent on protection by superpowers and joined blocs led by one or the other. Additionally, there was direct economic competition among the superpower blocs, but it was always associated with and modified by the security arrangements that were the centerpiece of global affairs. To a real degree, that calculus has been replaced by the newly emerging power of IT networking that permits and enables a vastly more complex matrix of ethnic, economic, political, and social alliances and enmities—in short, a new pluralism. This pluralism exists not only among nation-states, but pervades them, with individuals and groups with like interests joining online in virtual communities that need not and do not recognize traditional geopolitical boundaries.

In recent years, virtually all major institutions and organizations, from nation-states to religions and from transnational commercial enterprises to military alliances, are exploiting the increased functionality, efficiency, and productivity promised by IT connectivity. Unfortunately, with increased connectivity also comes increased vulnerability. Absent appropriate policies, technologies, practices, and procedures to protect information, connectivity means that anyone with access to these information networks has the power to access, manipulate, misuse, or destroy the information resident on or transiting over the networks. Many public and private sector organizations have yet to take the time to consider either the nature or magnitude of this problem. This is a legitimate cause for concern.

This dilemma was recognized in a CSIS report over a decade ago, as the following extract illustrates:

> The United States relies for its very existence—economically, socially, and politically—on an extraordinarily sophisticated and intricate set of long-distance networks for energy distribution, communication, and transportation. Because these networks also rely upon each other, a truly serious disruption in any one will cascade quickly through the others, rending the vital fabric of our nation at its most crucial points. Under these circumstances the ability to respond to national security crises will at least be severely constrained and may be completely interrupted for some crucial interval.
>
> Communication networks, an essential tool for the management of national crises, of other types of networks, and of commerce, are particularly susceptible to human interference. Electronic funds transfers (EFT) have become the vital arterial network of the U.S. and international banking communities upon which all domestic business and foreign trade depend. Four of the major networks alone transfer the equivalent of the entire federal budget every two to four hours. Yet these systems make heavy use of minimally protected common carrier networks, and the critical data about the U.S. economy that flows over them enjoys not even the simplest encryption to impede eavesdropping. Potentially more serious is the ease with which occasional false data could be injected; the resulting loss of confidence by users could destroy the banking system.[2]

Such warnings did result in some improvements in the technological design, regulation, and management practices of the networks. However, during the decade since the CSIS report was written, the networks and their infrastructure components, their functions, and their uses have greatly proliferated and diversified. Their complexity has increased. The competitive pressures for economic growth and rapid implementation of new technical capabilities have not been balanced by demand for adequate technical, legal, regulatory, and managerial protective measures. The result, in some areas, has been an increased potential for disruptive failure, as well as the overall appearance of a much greater number of inadequately protected, attractive targets for purposeful abuse and unwanted exploitation. Complicating this from a public policy point of view is the fact that little of this critical infrastructure is owned by governmental organizations. The crisis of the commons is emerging to be a crisis of the privately held commons.

The opportunities and full implications of the information technology revolution are gradually being recognized and acted upon by the broad range of state actors, as well as by nongovernmental organizations for whom connectivity on a global scale has meant increases in access and influence. Connectivity also results in the bypassing of traditional governing hierarchies and the diffusion of power. In all cases, these nations and organizations are led to conclude that information has power, in and of itself, independent of the technologies that were used to create, store, process, and communicate the information. This power exists in contrast to classic metrics such as strategic location, raw material resources, population, and so on. In fact, information, even without any substance, may arguably be the most important commodity in assessing the true strength of any group in the coming age.

Our dependency on information and IT gives rise to profound vulnerability. Traditional barriers of time and distance that have permitted us to hold trouble at arm's length have been rendered irrelevant. The information-based infrastructures that we depend upon for our security, and that are omnipresent in our workplaces and daily lives, have become vectors for assaults on our information-rich lifestyle.

A Revolution in Relationships

Today, every aspect of an individual's daily existence is intertwined with information technology. Microprocessor-controlled products such as cars and planes, robotics, expert systems, wired buildings, intelligent transportation systems, and network management systems surround us. From facsimile machines to satellite communications, information technology is enabling humans to communicate faster and farther than ever before. As more individuals become networked to each other, the value of the network increases exponentially. When there were only a few telephones, they were a laboratory curiosity. Millions of telephones become an intrinsic and vital component of our economy. Similar results apply to computer networks. This phenomenon was identified by Dr. Robert Metcalfe, who defined what he calls the Law of the Telecosm. This law links "the power of a network—literally how much it can do—to the square of the number of connected machines: $P(n) = n$ [squared]"[3]

In the global community, this increasing influential power of information technology provides previously ineffective marginalized groups with additional means for both direct challenges to authority as well as indirect media for intragroup communications, planning, and management. Recent cases include the B-92 radio station in Bosnia, the use of the Internet by the Chiapas revolutionaries to marshal global attention to their cause, and the use of tape-recorded messages by Iran's Ayatollah Khomeini while in exile in Paris. These examples illustrate the breakdown of boundaries, both physical and customary. Where the cracks in the wall appear, the ideas of the possibilities become apparent to all observers, thus leading to more cracks. Information workers supported by the technological backbone maintain the flow of information:

> Reporters arrive to cover earthquakes, floods, and political upheavals with satellite antennas packed in suitcases. The links between the financial markets of New York, London, Tokyo, and Hong Kong have created a global stock market....In our homes, we can receive dozens of television channels delivered by satellite to cable systems or directly to our backyards. Rooftop antennas link corporate offices, insurance agencies, manufacturing plants, bank branches, and convenience stores. But perhaps the change has been greatest in those parts of the world that did not have reliable communications before the satellite era. Twenty-five years ago, most developing countries were linked to each other and the outside world only by high-frequency [HF] radio. Today their Intelsat earth stations enable them to communicate reliably with their neighbors as well as with the rest of the world."[4]

The repercussions are felt in all spheres of authority, including formal governance structures as well as in traditional familial, religious, and ethnic authoritative structures. All elements of the authority relationship can be affected, sometimes greatly. The following extract provides an example of the power of information technology in either directly challenging authority or in inciting a challenge to authority:

> Serbia might be one of the last eastern European countries to log on to the Internet, but its pro-democracy movement is using cyberspace with a vengeance.
>
> Leading the charge are Belgrade university students, who wasted no time in going electronic when President Slobodan Milosevic annulled a string of opposition wins in local elections held last November.

"The first thing we did after starting our protest was create home pages on the Internet," said Milos Lukic of the Students' Internet Centre, a high-tech "trench" in the battle for reinstatement of the opposition victories and sweeping democratic reforms...

The Internet has been an important weapon for both the students and the parallel protest movement led by formal opposition parties, because of the government's tight control over the media, mainly television...

The power of the Internet became apparent early in the crisis when the government, rattled by street protests, closed down Belgrade's only two independent radio stations, B-92 and Radio Index. B-92 is hooked up to the Net, and in a matter of minutes reported the shutdown on its home page (at http://www.siicom.com/b92). Responses poured in from inside Serbia and abroad.

"The international support was important, but we were more encouraged by numerous requests for our news to be emailed," said Drazen Pantic, a computer specialist at B-92. In the end the government relented and both stations reopened a few days later...

Opposition parties also have discovered the advantages of the Internet. They started later than the students and independent media organizations, but now give daily coverage of the protests, information about opposition leaders, their political agenda and plans for further demonstrations.[5]

Similarly, a sustained challenge to authority is being waged using information technology in areas of the world that are not war-torn:

Masari's Committee for the Defense of Legitimate Rights in Saudi Arabia fires off as many as 2,000 faxes of two to four pages every week, he said. Many go to students and Islamic centers in Europe and the United States, but 600 to 800 of them go to Saudi Arabia, he added. "Saudi [Arabia] is very fax-oriented. Once it was chic; now it is almost a religious duty," Masari said in an interview. "We send to places where we think we might have sympathizers: government offices, courts, hospitals, the social security administration, military bases and big companies. If one secretary makes a copy..." Faxes scourge repression, corruption and mismanagement that Masari said have undermined the authority and legitimacy of the 6,000-strong Saudi royal family.[6]

Recognizing the effect that information technology has on globalization trends as well as on individual capabilities, it is logical to assume that more information will be shared more widely. As that information is shared, each participant in an authority relationship is able to compare his situation with those of others in the same or other authority relationships. This comparison will affect the perceived value of the services in the authority relationship, and in those cases where defects or derogation are perceived, may cause a loss of equilibrium.

Attempting to close down the channels of communication is a short-sighted and probably futile effort; recognizing the effects and working with them is much more likely to stave off catastrophic challenges to authority.

The growth of the media and network technology permits the generation and dissemination of information much faster than has ever been possible up to this time. These factors, taken together, now pose a significant new consideration for nation-state governments—the velocity at which new and destabilizing ideas can be disseminated. Governments are still composed of people who need a human time scale to consider factors presented and then act. The traditional time available to gather data and to deliberate is now being compressed, and the window available within which authorities can act is expressed in the same near-real-time context as the ceaseless flow of information within the new wide area networks that pervade our countries and continents. Failure of governments to first catch up, and then keep up, with the "refresh rate" of destabilizing information is self-reinforcing as groups challenging the traditional authority structures discern that they now have the ability to affect public awareness and sentiment out of proportion to their size, budgets, and geographical hegemony. The initiative is clearly in the hands of those who are proactively controlling the nature, timing, and mechanisms of information dissemination—in essence, the tempo of crises.

The use of information technologies for direct and indirect challenges is not limited to the Internet and related data networks. Destabilizing information may be spread by the media as well. When contemplating the role of the media in an IT-enabled pluralist world, we must consider several dynamics, as detailed in the following sections.

Manipulation of Media

Manipulation of media can take the form of manipulating or withholding access, or of selective cooperation by traditional authorities or challengers in story generation and transmission. In an environment of heavy dependency on media information sources, political, military, or popular reaction to reported events could be significantly affected. This is true in every aspect of media performance, including the timeliness, precision, and slant of the message. The media may be duped by those seeking to present a deliberately misleading message (a concept known as *disinformation*). The Allied Forces in the Gulf War provided the media with ready access to amphibious forces that appeared to be readying for an attack on Iraq, when in fact no such attack was intended. Information about the forces was duly reported in international news broadcasts known to be reviewed by the Iraqi command.

Alternatively, the media may be used as an agent of influence by those presenting an accurate picture of events, but one that is calculated to foster a specific reaction within an influential sector of the viewing public. The recent case that is perhaps best known to the American public is the portrayal of U.S. Army casualties being dragged through the streets of Somalia. By dutifully beaming these viewpoints to global audiences in real time, the "free and independent media" can be co-opted as an active agent of a belligerent power, who may be working in direct opposition to U.S. national interests at that moment. In so doing, the newsperson's camcorder provides a bully pulpit for bit players who would otherwise find it impossible to directly resist western political or military efforts.

Media organizations known or believed to be "favorable" to the local authority's position may receive special privileges of access to key leadership figures or facilities. In so doing, these privileged groups appear to have a more detailed, timely, or better documented story to tell, thereby gaining viewer support and strengthening the credibility of their news and editorial positions. This particular mechanism of controlling media message output—actively aiding cooperative organizations in their efforts to outshine their competitors—is the bridge to the second, and even more serious area of concern: manipulation by media.

Manipulation by Media

This type of manipulation can be used to deliberately support or oppose a particular viewpoint, based on the news organization's national affiliation, sponsorship, or political stance of the owners. This is an insidious danger, and one that is, on the surface, difficult to confront in a free society. The fact that the media has enormous influence on the masses and their leaders is unarguable. The presumption that those individuals who control large and pervasive media organizations have views and commitments that place them at a particular point on the political and ideological spectrum is similarly unavoidable. Given that, how can we be surprised that these "media barons" might use their considerable influence to build constituency for positions with which they are sympathetic, while denigrating those they oppose?

This is hardly a new phenomenon. William Randolph Hearst was singularly influential in precipitating the Spanish-American War, at least in part as a means to boost circulation for the benefit of his newspaper empire. Within the context of this discussion, it would be completely proper to credit him with manipulating public opinion—and national policy—by substantially controlling the flow of information within the American society of that time.

Any attempt to frame solutions to the problems associated with the media and its role in information warfare gets very sensitive, very quickly. We readily acknowledge the vital importance of freedom of expression and of the press as bedrock principles of our society. In fact, the existence of a free press is usually held up as a leading test of the maturity of democratic institutions and principles in emerging democracies—and very properly so. Notwithstanding that, we feel it is reasonable—even necessary—to note and characterize the dangers that manipulation of the press can bring.

As with many other aspects of the information age, the sword cuts two ways. Instant, global reporting brings us insight, access, and cultural exposure that most of us could never achieve otherwise. On the other hand, a society that digests information and forms opinions largely on the basis of 20-second sound bites is one that is vulnerable to manipulation through the medium of those sound bites. A government whose real-time intelligence fusion and analysis centers prominently display, and routinely rely on, privately owned media reporting to supplement official means of data gathering is one that has an obligation to think carefully about the integrity (i.e., editorial backdrop) of that data stream in various scenarios.

In the end, there is only one sure and reasonable solution to the profound dependency, and thus vulnerability, of Americans and their government on information. Arthur Hays Sulzberger once said, "Along with responsible newspapers, we must have responsible readers." Updated for the times, today one might say that in an information-rich and dependent society, we must have responsible and accountable media, serving the interests of a society that is willing to protect its right to think, decide, and act on the basis of objective and complete information.

The Growing Issue of Nonstate Actors

The term *nonstate actors* refers to those persons or groups who are acting independently of national agendas, as opposed to those who may be apparently independent, but who are in fact significantly engaged in advancing nation-state interests. Seen through this lens, we are once again forced to confront the unpleasant reality that the current and future problem is significantly more complex than the one we faced during the Cold War. The investment needed to acquire significant capability to exploit, disrupt, degrade, or destroy information and information systems or networks does not require large amounts of cash, personnel, space, technology, industrial base, or unique expertise. There are no critical or raw materials or significant industrial precursor processes that may be detected, traced, or regulated (in contrast, say, to the acquisition and refinement of plutonium). The skills, tools, and techniques required for effective use of the relevant equipment are easily obtained in ways that leave no audit trail. The small and inexpensive amount of terminal equipment required to achieve global network access is readily available from commercial sources and is lost within the legitimate development of information infrastructures in support of commercial enterprise.

Rational nation-states can usually be trusted to act in furtherance of interests that can generally be identified and predicted. However, in the new technology-enabled cyberpluralism, nonstate actors will be much less visible and consequently less predictable as to the nature, timing, or location of their actions. When we recognize that nonstate actors can be seen as embracing acts of political, ethnic or religious terrorism, vandalism, wanton destructiveness, and theft through a complex set of motivations, we must acknowledge that responding to the magnitude and unpredictability of this problem will prove challenging. There also will undoubtedly continue to be rogue nation-states that are similarly motivated; however, these states normally can be identified and singled out for especially cautious treatment by the international community.

The conclusions we must draw from this broadened list of motives and actors point to an expanded potential for compromising or destroying our critical systems and processes, including those that provide for the welfare and security of our nation. The result is a great broadening of our vulnerability to destabilization.

Nonstate actors need not be fanatical ethnic or religious factions or terrorist groups. Some of the most powerful and IT-capable nonstate actors are transnational commercial organizations. As consolidation of industries and firms proceeds, independent commercial enterprises reach the size of nation-states in terms of gross revenues, capital resources, personnel, facilities, and production capacity. Moreover, these transnational companies owe allegiance to no nation-state or bloc, but act to maximize revenues and profits while lowering tax liabilities to traditional governments. This allows moderate- to large-scale companies to become global in scope and influence while, at the same time, weakening the traditional nation-state.

In some cases, the interests of nation-states and transnational enterprises converge, while in others nation-states they have been co-opted. In either case, we can see the power, influence, and capabilities of the state, such as national intelligence capabilities, being harnessed to influence the outcome of commercial negotiations in favor of certain transnational commercial enterprises. Where the transnational nonstates are illicit, their interactions with nation-states can impact a wide range of national diplomatic and security concerns. As we examine the question of global organized crime in all its manifestations, it is essential that the United States consider the whole range of actors, even states themselves, as potential perpetrators of industrial espionage, organized crime, and terrorism in the information age.

In conclusion, the responsibility and capability of our government to ensure the welfare and security of the American people is certainly a matter of securing the information infrastructure of the nation. This can only be accomplished within the context of a new technology-enabled pluralism in which both other nation-states and various legitimate and illicit nonstate actors can use the information infrastructure in furtherance of their own goals. Our nation must preserve and advance its place in global economic markets, enjoying the full benefit of enhanced productivity that flows from our strategic advantage in information technology and the economic advantages that are provided by a technology-enriched commercial environment and electronic commerce. We must also be able to identify, measure, and calculate the increased vulnerability and risk to our national security that we face in the new technology-enabled cyberpluralism.

A New Look at Security

Historically, the central role of the military has been to protect the society from which it springs and to project power abroad in pursuit of geopolitical strategies. As threats to the nation-state have evolved, so have the capabilities and responsibilities of the military. The military has been bound by the notions of distance and time with the rest of society, and defense was understood and planned and operated in spatial and temporal terms. Early on, when the perceived threat was to the sanctity of the actual territory of our homeland, our military forces defended at the shoreline and border, the Navy built and operated a near-coastal capability, and there were essentially no U.S. military forces stationed overseas for any purpose. The United States followed a policy of isolationism and a strategy that avoided entanglements in foreign affairs that could draw the country into foreign wars.

Later, we came to see that a more global role for ourselves was unavoidable and perhaps even desirable, and we developed a thin line of "skirmishers" in far-flung locations as a way of calling visible attention to the expanded perception of our national interests. The understanding was that when and as needed, the numbers and types of forces required to fight decisively could be generated here at home, taking advantage of the time and distance bought by the thinly defended outposts. As the speed of our transportation and communications increased, distance and time to react diminished, and we recognized that the nature of conflict had changed as well. We deployed substantial forces to forward areas, fully expecting to conduct a whole conflict in remote theaters. We also recognized the strategic threat posed by long-range bombers, intercontinental ballistic missiles, and missile-capable submarines off our coasts, but because defense against such threats to the homeland was difficult or impossible, we pursued strategies of deterrence.

In a world pervaded by computer systems and networks, the notions of time and space that formed the foundation of prior strategies and tactics have to be reconsidered. The topography of cyberspace is very different from that of the geopolitical units with which our diplomatic and military forces have prepared to deal. Geopolitical boundaries are not reproduced, and cannot be reproduced, in the universe of networks. Information and information weapons move across those networks at electronic speeds. Attacks can occur without warning, and it may not be immediately apparent even that an attack is taking place, much less its source. Electrons wear no uniforms and carry no flags.

Nevertheless, a full-scale strategic attack on the United States could conceivably affect every aspect of our computer-enriched economy. Targets might include our telephone system, the power grid, air traffic control and other transportation systems, the financial community, law enforcement, and our ability to recall reserves and mount a military response. The effects of a successful attack might involve few deaths directly, although many deaths could result indirectly, but it would have profound consequences for our economy and our way of life. Not since the threat of a strategic thermonuclear exchange has our homeland been so directly threatened. Our evolving notions of security must take this new reality into account.

The emergence of the new cyberpolitical pluralities offers additional concerns for communal security. It is important to note that the emergence of cyberpolitical units do not eliminate geopolitical threats but add complexities to the existing litany of potential problems. How the U.S. reacts to the emergence of this new class of problem may determine its success in continued security at home and protection of our interests abroad. Attempting to repress or contain these emergent units is impossible if we are to maintain the freedoms we cherish.

The challenges proffered by these entities are simultaneously internal and external. The security of the nation is threatened both by the evaporation of containing and protecting borders and by the diffusion of power enabled by widespread information networks. To modify the national security infrastructure in a meaningful manner that best relates to the emerging cyberpolitical realities requires an analysis of the authority relationship and how it is being diffused and weakened. With that understanding, a new view of security can be developed and strategies employing that view can be adopted.

There are several elements that need to be revisited:

- *The composition of the authorities*   Who are they? What value do they provide? Why are they empowered to lead? What are the limitations on their power?

- *The composition of the new cyberpluralities*   Who are they? What support do they provide to the authorities, if any? What services do they expect to be provided by the authorities? What limitations do they place on authorities' actions?

- *The composition of the relationship between the two*   How is it negotiated? How are changes made and disputes resolved?

By "authorities" we mean those who have traditionally been empowered to lead, manage, issue commands, and enforce obedience. They obtain that power in a variety of ways: strength of arms, personal charisma or expertise, tradition or organizational position, persuasive rational argument, or by being chosen by an electorate with the power to appoint its leaders. Life-or-death power and its ability to extract absolute obedience is, however, rarely possible for individuals, and purely coercive power cannot exist in complex societies where the exercise of authority can only be accomplished through the organized behavior of groups. Obedience and cooperation are not inevitable, and even in the most repressive and tyrannical governments, there are factions and subgroups where pluralism allows the possibility of dissent, disobedience, rebellion, and revolution. The new information technologies diffuse the power of traditional authorities and enable the activities of these pluralities, the "new cyberpluralities," which, because of the borderless nature of cyberspace, are not completely within the boundaries and hegemony of any single nation-state. Just as authorities must provide services to their subjects in return for their right to rule and command the services of the subjects, or they will not long retain their exalted positions; authorities must learn to deal with the new cyberpluralities with whom they must coexist, be they ethnic, religious, or political in nature or transnational commercial enterprises.

Whether an authority will be able to successfully exercise control in this new arrangement will depend on the perception and judgment as to whether obedience or cooperation will lead to the rewards expected (or lack of the punishment promised), and whether this reward will satisfy a fundamental need for safety and security, social affiliation, esteem or prestige, autonomy or power, or feelings of competence and achievement. The willingness of the new entities to be governed will be great if they need satisfaction, think that the authority's rewards will be instrumental in satisfying those needs, and deem it likely that the services they provide will satisfy the authority's objectives so that the reward will follow. Lacking assurance of any one of these factors undermines the authority's influence and leads to a challenge to the authority.

Influence is always reciprocal. To control, one must allow oneself to be controlled to some extent. The coercive dictator must punish insubordination or suffer the loss of credibility. Tradition-based systems must offer loyal, obedient supporters warmth and security. Even charismatic leaders must give of themselves, allowing followers to see, hear, and touch the authority. Such reciprocal systems tend toward equilibrium if they are to survive for any length of time. Changes to that equilibrium result from either extrinsic or intrinsic changes to the authority, the new cyberpluralities, the services either provides, or the environment in which they relate to each other. Some changes can enhance the rewards both the authority and the nonauthorities receive from their relationship, and both can mutually benefit from the change. Other changes reduce the actual or perceived value of the services provided by the authority, the services provided by the new cyberpluralities, or both. The resulting dissonance challenges the authority and leads to either realignment of the services to reachieve equilibrium or shatters the relationship entirely.

The constriction of time and subsequent decrease in the significance of distance between peoples adds to the ability of ideas, concepts, methods, and technologies used in external situations to creep into the knowledge bases and skills repertoires of both the authority and the new cyberpluralities. The constriction of time and distance leads to increasing contact between different authorities, nation-states, and cyberpluralities, which in turn often leads to increasing tendencies to interfere either purposefully or accidentally in those other authority relationships.

The impact of the increasing interfaces among authority relationships is also significant in the realm of negotiations regarding the authority relationship boundaries. In the new reality, the authority relationship boundaries are not necessarily physical, but lie where the ability of the authority to exert influence over the new cyberpluralities fades into subservience to another authority relationship. This boundary may, in fact, be a fluid and unstable zone, changing with context. A striking example of the fluidity of the boundary of authority relationships is exemplified by the separation of church and state within the United States: In theory, a legislator representing all of his or her constituents should represent their desires and concerns, even though those go against the legislator's personal religious beliefs, in legislative activities. In this case, the authority relationship the legislator participates in as a church member has a fluid boundary with the authority relationship he or she participates in as a legislator.

The impact of information technology and globalization has been to increase the number of authority relationships it is possible to participate in and thereby create more boundaries to be negotiated. Each boundary intersection creates friction. The more often the boundaries come into contact, the more friction is created. This energy must be released in some manner. Traditional means of expending this energy have included warfare, police action, and lawsuits.

Evolutionary advances and revolutionary leaps occurring in technology, trade, and politics are causing a redefinition of identity and relationships. The cause and effect is that national interests are intertwined almost to the point that there are essentially no such things as strictly internal policies anymore. Internal policies affect businesses, which are increasingly international and, in any case, trade internationally. Unfavorable policy brings international pressure for change. Internal policies also affect people, who are increasingly able to communicate with sympathetic supporters in other parts of the world. The political and industrial leadership of the United States is continually pressured by such supporters to change its policies regarding dealings with countries with oppressive internal policies. Similarly, transnational organizations, such as Shell Oil and Pepsi, have encountered pressures by their consumers to change operations (or even eliminate them) in other parts of the world.

The technological advances and social changes seen since the end of World War II have engendered interrelationships and interdependent interests to an extent that the borders between national interests are blurring quickly. The way we do business, as well as the manner in which we settle disputes, is changing. Where 30 years ago businesses used to stockpile raw material for use in manufacturing, now "just-in-time" supply delivery systems have increased the efficiency of manufacturing and simultaneously reduced any strategic reserve capacities. Instantaneous, high-volume data processing and communications have likewise been harnessed in the practice of both war and commercial competition.

The potential for conflict in the information dimension is not limited to countries. Technological breakthroughs in information-processing technologies are driving changes in the international environment. The ability to effortlessly conduct business on a global scale, the proliferating communications interconnectivities, the explosion in computerized support structures, and the redefinition of money as a virtual entity all contribute to a growing irrelevance of physical location.

The nature of how individuals, corporations, and states interact with information is also changing as a result of these technological leaps and has also created a whole new market for the previously esoteric trade in information. Information is a growth industry. The corporation is redefining itself based on international standards and mass customization. A new entity called the *virtual corporation* is evolving, with small, highly flexible operating units tied together by common need and mission through a backbone of information. The personal computer revolution has enabled individuals to not only access massive amounts of information but also to process that information using sophisticated mathematical algorithms. The harnessing of information by corporations has enabled leaps in productivity and redefined the process of international trade. It has also redefined the corporation itself, creating transnational organizations that call many countries home at the same time that they call no country home. The complex interactions of currency exchange rates, national interest rates, and other financial gauges have created a whole new entity called *derivative money*.

The growing rise of multinational and international corporations is creating a strain on the practice of international diplomacy and challenging existing authority structures. An example of that can be seen in the arguments over awarding the status of Most Favored Nation (MFN) to China by the United States. The arguments against MFN were that China is an abusive and repressive nation that has a horrible record of human rights abuses. The arguments for MFN were that cutting off trade with China would unfairly punish the neighboring countries that serve as ports of entry for trade and would negatively affect the ability of U.S. corporations to compete for the vast Chinese market against other corporations headquartered in other nations. The results have been a series of predictable debates featuring moral outrage followed by a reluctant passage of MFN status.

Similarly, it is increasingly difficult to wage war now without convening an international coalition and getting the imprimatur of the United Nations. The last four expeditions that U.S. troops have participated in—Desert Storm, Somalia, Bosnia, and Haiti—were all internationally sanctioned endeavors. The international cloak gives the U.S. political rationale for the military activity, as well as a handy excuse for not being more involved than absolutely necessary (such as in Bosnia), but it also serves as an example of limitations on authority in a globalizing and technology-enriched world.

These challenges to authority are felt inside of organizations as well. As technology affects our day-to-day activities, traditional staff arrangements may be obviated. When it is possible for a VP to talk directly to an engineer or an accountant to send e-mail to the CEO, the traditional lines of communications are broken and the authorities vested in those relationships are challenged. The span of control has been modified too, requiring either a lot of coordination or a redefinition of what an organizational chart should look like. The new organization charts reflect the changes enabled by information technology—changes that allow workers to quickly and effortlessly share information, data, and thoughts with contacts at every level of the organization and in every part of the organization. This emerging organizational structure reflects a structure of overlapping tasks and parallel processing where multiple tasks can go on at once without being dependent on serial processes or traditional authority relationships. More frequently these days, we are seeing innovative organization charts that are attempting to reflect how the organizations of now are actually working. The existing authority relationships that moved out of equilibrium are being disposed of, are readjusting, or are finding a new equilibrium.

Imposing a structure that does not work and/or does not reflect accurately the way individuals operate effectively hamstrings an organization. People who are motivated to get the job done will work outside of the organization chart and, as a result, will cause confusion and challenge authority within the established chain. People who are motivated to play by the rules will become increasingly frustrated and will lose any initiative for finding solutions to problems, becoming moribund in their attempts to fit into the structure. The value of the authority service will decline in the eyes of the non-authority, creating a situation conducive to a challenge to that authority.

The challenges enabled by the information technology revolution pale in comparison to what may come to pass soon. As people become more intensely networked and communications sharing becomes more robust, the challenges may arise from communal will rather than overt actions. In his book *Out of Control*, Kevin Kelly speaks of what he calls "hive mind phenomena"—if everyone knows exactly what is required, they will intuitively do their part in enabling the answer:

In a darkened Las Vegas conference room, a cheering audience waves cardboard wands in the air. Each wand is red on one side, green on the other. Far in the back of the huge auditorium, a camera scans the frantic attendees. The video camera links the color spots of the wands to a nest of computers set up by graphics wizard Loren Carpenter. Carpenter's custom software locates each red and green wand in the auditorium. Tonight there are just shy of 5,000 wandwavers. The computer displays the precise location of each wand (and its color) onto an immense, detailed video map of the auditorium hung on the front stage, which all can see...As the audience waves the wands, the display screen shows a sea of lights dancing crazily in the dark, like a candlelight parade gone punk....

"Let's try something else," Carpenter suggests. A map of seats in the auditorium appears on the screen. He draws a wide circle in the white around the center. "Can you make a green `5' in the circle?" he asks the audience. The audience stares at the rows of red pixels. The game is similar to that of holding a placard up in a stadium to make a picture, but now there are no preset orders, just a virtual mirror. Almost immediately wiggles of green pixels appear and grow haphazardly, as those who think their seat is in the path of the "5" flip their wands to green. A vague figure is materializing. The audience collectively begins to discern a "5" in the noise. Once discerned, the "5" quickly precipitates out into stark clarity. The wandwavers on the fuzzy edge of the figure decide what side they "should" be on, and the emerging "5" sharpens up. The number assembles itself.

"Now make a four," the voice booms. Within moments a "4" emerges. "Three." And in a blink a "3" appears. Then in rapid succession, "Two...One...Zero." The emergent thing is on a roll.[7]

Information technology impacts directly on the elements of the authority relationship because it enables the sharing of ideas and connectivity between those who would otherwise not be connected. With the emergence of cyberpolitical units, the traditional hierarchies—the authority relationships of the industrial age—are diminished in power and ability to exercise hegemony unless positive action is taken to include the members of the virtual community in an active participation in governance and protection of communal security.

Effective Information Assurance

In this emerging cyberpolitical world with complex interconnectivities in information systems and content, ensuring effective information assurance is a nontrivial challenge. In this environment, mutual defenses are truly mutual. When your systems are connected to a network, they are connected to every other system as well as other networks connected to that network. The weaknesses in defenses at any node on that network can endanger your systems and information. Yet disconnecting from the network is not a viable option either.

To summarize, in the emerging cyberpolitical era, economic competition overshadows direct military competition. These economic competitions, as practiced by modern, market-economy organizations, bridge private and governmental interests. Information-based technologies are being eagerly employed by all sectors of society, including business, government, and private sector. Information-based competition, focused on achieving an economic advantage by acquiring confidential and proprietary business information such as design secrets, proprietary technologies, and market plans is a key piece of current international affairs. Such competition, being naturally linked to classic national objectives and interests, including trade, diplomatic, and security-related issues, fosters some degree of active collaboration between commercial and state entities, depending upon the extent to which their interests coincide. In some cases, the cooperation is very visible and extensive.

Detailed understanding of the technology by its users is often limited, and is, in fact, a design goal known colloquially as "user-friendliness." Those who have knowledge, access, and motivation may exploit unknown, undocumented, and even deliberately hidden flaws. In addition to vulnerabilities inherent in information networks and systems, information itself is a powerful weapon made more so by the explosion of paths through which information can be disseminated.

To understand information assurance in this context requires an appreciation for the exposure caused by networking, the practical applications of security technologies and practices, and the mutual dependence for robust security. The ability to assign value to information (as well as the importance of even trying to do so) is a critical outcome of this situation. Identifying a specific dollar value for some piece of information can be difficult with answers ranging from very simple and rigorous dollar amounts to completely emotional and nonreproducible hunches. However difficult to value, it is clear that information has value from a security point of view. The content of the information, its veracity, and its availability all contribute to its value. Concomitantly, its unavailability, doubtful reliability, or limited content all detract from its value. The banking and finance community provide us with clear examples of direct value of information, both in terms of availability and in terms of content, since the products and processes of that industry are assessed in terms of monetary value.

Valuing information content and infrastructure is necessary in order to justify the investment in information assurance. The ability to have information assurance is directly related to expenditure of effort in associated technologies, policies, and methodologies. There are existing technologies, practices, and methodologies that provide significant levels of information assurance to those who invest the time and effort to avail themselves of those resources, but the protection does not come inexpensively. Effective information assurance is a well-balanced mix of technological and nontechnological solutions. Technology alone can't provide robust information assurance. It must be augmented by practices and policies covering every aspect of the operational environment, including personnel hiring practices, physical access constraints, and business continuity planning.

Developing the understanding at each node of the global network for this kind of protective stance is fundamentally a problem of education. A government/civil partnership over a considerable period of time is appropriate leadership for this type of effort. Such an effort must be focused on building a common appreciation for safe computing habits, appropriate etiquette, and acceptable behavior patterns, as well as developing a more thorough understanding of the technical aspects of protection, detection, and correction. Such an effort will be thoroughly unsuccessful if it does not include the society at large. For as long as we wait to commence such an effort, we all remain as exposed and vulnerable as our weakest members.

There are several existing trends that underscore the importance of awareness and education, as well as cooperation. First, information and recipes for both writing malicious software (such as viruses) and exploiting vulnerabilities (such as how to execute a "SYN flood attack" to deny service to an internet service provider) are widely available, published both electronically and in "dead tree" format. This information allows even neophytes with little technical expertise to become threats.

Second, just as scientists stand on the shoulders of giants to see farther, so do social misfits. As the basis of knowledge grows, so does the complexity of the attack capabilities. Thus, it is that automated programs that assist in creating virus programs now offer additional features, such as encryption and polymorphism. It would be naive to believe that there might be any loss in capability or complexity in threat capabilities against information systems; to the contrary, a very sound assumption is that this body of knowledge and capabilities will continue to grow. As threats with significant resources (such as criminal syndicates or national governments) enter this field of research, the body of knowledge will increase commensurately.

Third, maintaining a capable defensive posture against threats requires continuous commitment of resources and energy. This is complicated by the fact that expenditure of effort by one node in a network can be undermined by lack of effort by one or more other nodes in the network. The requirement for cooperative attention to common security practices is fundamental to collective security capabilities. If done correctly, it could enable further efficiencies in the information sphere by enabling economies of scale in technology investment. However, full effort would still be required in the nontechnological aspects of information security and assurance, such as good practices and policies.

A thoughtful mix of capabilities provides robust information assurance. It begins with risk assessment, a process that must be revisited periodically, since no organizational environment ever remains in stasis. The risk assessment takes into consideration every aspect of the environment, examining it for vulnerabilities. These vulnerabilities are not limited to those existing in information systems but also include vulnerabilities in personnel practices, physical security, and other aspects of the environment.

A second aspect of risk assessment is an examination of potential threats. The assessment of threats, again, is not limited to those who would solely act against the information systems but includes all potential threats, such as forces of nature and accidents. Focusing on threat alone can be detracting: Proving the existence of an actual threat can be impossible. A threat consists of both the capability to act and the motivation to act. Malicious acts against information systems can be performed with ordinary capabilities, thus eliminating the capability as a distinguishing feature of a threat. Motivation can change in a nanosecond, thereby changing a nonthreat into a threat almost instantaneously. Advance notification of hostile intent is clearly not a distinguishing characteristic of threat. Since threats cannot be completely identified in advance, postulation of threats is a useful tool. Considering every type of threat that may take action provides a comprehensive assessment of the potential dangers that exist. This understanding can underscore assessment of value and aid decision processes related to assignment of resources.

With an understanding of vulnerabilities and threats comes the opportunity to incorporate safeguards and countermeasures into the operational environment. These countermeasures also contribute to the risk assessment, both for the protections they offer and the new vulnerabilities they may introduce into the environment. An example of vulnerability introduced by a countermeasure is that of the compromised password; the password is a countermeasure to vulnerability, but it contains its own vulnerabilities that must be assessed and understood. Finally, the value of elements within the environment must be assessed to give context to the risk assessment. The impact of a compromise of a school lunch menu is markedly different from the impact of compromise of an electronic payment system, and the measures to mitigate such impact should be commensurate with that value.

Once the risk assessment has provided a comprehensive understanding of the operational environment, decisions can be made on how protective measures will be incorporated into the environment. The protective capabilities include both technological and nontechnological aspects, as mentioned previously. Technologies can include firewalls, cryptography, and automated audit capabilities, while nontechnological capabilities include enforcing practices, setting policies, and operating with due diligence.

The protections must be assumed to be less than 100 percent certain, however. Protection is only the first part of a continuity of capabilities-planning activity. Once protective measures are in place, detective measures must be incorporated. It does no good to lock a door if the lock is never checked for integrity; neither does it do any good to have a fence if the fence is never checked for holes. Similarly, the protective measures in an operational environment must be checked for correctness and continued viability through detection capabilities. This then places the enterprise in a position to respond to correct the situation when a breach of security is detected.

The ability to manage the implementation and ongoing operations of a comprehensive protect-detect-correct capability is obviously much more than computer science. It requires managerial skills, operational security skills, physical security skills, and system engineering skills as well. This leads to the inevitable conclusion that effective information assurance requires more than skillful computer scientists and more than standalone technology solutions.

There are currently less than 10 universities in the United States that offer full-fledged majors in information security; of these, only one is multidisciplinary in nature.[8] The rest are contained within the computer science departments. Similarly, the vast majority of jobs in the information security field are technical in nature, focusing on the application of technological solutions in information technology systems. Little emphasis is given to the study and implementation of policies and management practices that reinforce and support information assurance in the workplace. And yet, the greatest threat to information assurance is undoubtedly the malicious insider. So much effort has been focused on keeping out intruders that the technologies and methodologies to detect an insider acting contrary to the goals of the organization have been left to chance. A fundamental aspect of the insider is the fact that he or she is, in fact, an authorized and trusted member of the enterprise. In other words, the insider has already breached the great majority of the protections. What is necessary in view of this fact is sound management oversight, enforcement of operating policies, and comprehensive detection capabilities.

Combining the emerging cyberpolitical pluralism with the existing limitations in information assurance points out the need for wider ranging education and fertile areas for research and development.

The nature of networks is rapidly changing both in terms of network technologies and architectures and the user focus, especially with the emergence of online commercial and social activity. The nation on the whole is increasingly more dependent on networks for day-to-day and crisis management functions. Unlike Wall Street's rule of thumb that, due to intrinsic market forces, anticipated disasters do not happen, *impending information disasters are not subject to the same level of understanding, risk management, or ownership*. Indeed, much learning on the subject has been from emergency responses rather than total quality management. On today's Information Superhighway:

- Security and privacy is nonexistent in some places.

- Backdoor on-ramps abound.

- Electronic commerce contents are subject to inspection, hijacking, and replay at any time.

Information assurance as it applies to the National Information Infrastructure and our nation's economic security in defensive information warfare may be viewed as a classical quality problem,[9] the inadequacy of which has several characteristics:[10]

- *Lack of constancy of purpose*   What goals exist related to security, privacy, and assurance are currently focused on the immediate time frame and often emphasize short-term, reactive efforts. The key escrow proposal is a prime example of this.

- *Emphasis on short-term results*   Security is currently seen as a state rather than a continuing process. Additionally, the contribution of security to the bottom line of an enterprise is not easy to quantify, nor is it easily demonstrated in traditional quantitative risk assessment models.

- *Audits and self-assessment deficiencies*   Audit reports revealing exploitable vulnerabilities and inadequacy of controls collect dust waiting for follow-on reports and actions. Frequently this results in exacerbated vulnerabilities. Self-assessments tend to be inadequate in scope and depth. Security objectives for industry or government are often not well defined, understood, or actionable.

- *Mobility of management*   Such mobility does not imbue trust in employees or vendors, or offer long-term assurances that the problem is being adequately addressed in emerging technologies, public policy and regulation, and operations best practices.

- *Meaningless measurements*   Of the intrusions detected by systems administrators, only an estimated 5 percent ever get reported to management, law enforcement, or other incident tracking systems. This data covers only those systems with detection capabilities in place and then only external intrusions. No meaningful analysis can be performed with this data.

- *Recovery costs far outweigh prevention*   Numerous studies of software quality and physical design have shown that designing it right the first time is far more cost-effective than piecemeal reinforcements and recovery efforts. Without backups and redundancies, the cost of recovering information itself from destruction or corruption can be infinite.

▪ *Excessive potential liabilities*   The potential for loss of market share, product liability, and negligence charges are alleged to inhibit sharing of information about security vulnerabilities, thereby restricting the growth of the body of knowledge on best practices and methodologies.

Clearly, these characteristics highlight the point that effective information assurance relies on a holistic approach to information security technologies, policy, and management. This requirement will become increasingly important as new technologies emerge and become integrated into the infrastructure.

The June 23, 1997, edition of *Business Week* contains a section entitled "Information Technology Annual Report." The articles appearing in the section describe a future with more potential for marvel than most of us could imagine in our wildest dreams. Even discounting the ever-present hype in any future-vision piece, the potential for new technology in the next decade is staggering. It is interesting to note that virtually nothing in the edition addresses any consideration of the ways the emerging technologies might be abused for political purposes, terrorism, financial gain, or other ill intent. Security is more expensive when it is retrofitted, and security is almost always the last consideration.

There are many reasons for this all-too-typical condition. Product and service developers are under pressure, often extreme, to meet tight deadlines. They are trying to be the first on the market with a new technology, or they are trying to respond to pent-up demands or requirements. The pressures to compete are immense, and development cycles are so short that decisions are made in real time. Frequently, developers are not inclined to think in terms of how the technology might be abused or misused. They are even less likely to examine the implementations of new technologies to look for unintended "features" or vulnerabilities.

Innovative leadership, both formal (government) and informal consumer watchdog groups, and education of the consuming public can contribute to changing the expectations and practices of the industry. Just as public outcry and changing expectations resulted in cars being equipped with safety belts, curtains being made with flame-resistant fabric, and gasoline pumps being checked for accuracy, so too can public outcry and changing expectations affect the standard features and protective mechanisms in software products, communications networks, and online services.

Liability concerns may become a dominant motivating factor for establishing best practices or at least minimum acceptable practices for security in information systems and telecommunications. Any best practices must be international in both scope and acceptance to be successful, although local responsibilities can provide inducement for adoption of safe practices on a larger scope. It may even be conceivable that the adoption of liability standards and assignment of responsibilities in a global interconnected world can be forced from one very large domain with global reach and leverage, such as the European Union or the United States.

An interesting example of this potential for cascading standards is illustrated by Principle 7 of the OECD cryptography guideline, which states: "Whether established by contract or legislation, the liability of individuals and entities that offer cryptographic services or hold access to cryptographic keys should be clearly stated.[11]" Merely by raising the issue, a standard of knowledge is levied. Liability concerns are an extremely important factor for cryptography, as they are, in general, for security, and such concerns have discouraged both companies and government agencies from offering key recovery or key escrow services.

Users face the same obligation to follow best practices. Any company or individual making use of computer or communications systems that they own and operate for their own benefit must consider the risk of attacks on their own systems by their own employees or others who may get physical access to their systems. They also need to protect against the potential liability from an insider using the company's system as a base to attack other systems outside the company. They may even bear "downstream liability" if someone from outside breaks in to their computer and then uses it as a base from which to launch attacks on others.

Having characterized the general problem of information assurance, specific barriers, gaps, and shortfalls can be identified. There are identifiable activities that would greatly improve the existing information assurance posture. These include the following:

1. There is a standard mechanism to track, assess, and share threat and vulnerability information across all sectors of society, both local and global.

2. Information protection and security become routine expectations.

3. The quality assurance process integrates security in the development of information technology products and services.

Leadership that recognizes the power of the individual to make choices and to cooperate or not is necessary to rally support for these efforts. Education is required so that individuals and groups understand how each person's actions contribute to or detract from information assurance activities. Innovation is needed to develop the incentives and technologies that encourage and enable proactive security activities. There are policy, technology, and behavior issues associated with these three elements.

As an example of how these three areas interplay, consider the development of a cooperative indications and warnings function for information attacks. Given the variety of vulnerabilities that underlie our infrastructures, the rate at which we introduce new technology (and hence new vulnerabilities), and the rate at which the skills and organization of potential adversaries are increasing, the ability to get early warning—or even concurrent warning—of an attack can greatly diminish our potential loss. Such a function needs to fulfill two important goals: indications that an attack may be imminent or under way, and warning of specific attacks to enable increased defense responses.

Developing such a capability requires both cooperation and technology. Cooperation among government, commercial, and civilian communities is necessary to share the information, since no one sector owns or controls any portion of the information infrastructure that all three depend upon. This cooperation stems from both policies and behaviors. Technology is needed to improve our ability to detect suspicious activity, to contain its potential consequences, and to trace the path the attack is taking automatically. Much preattack behavior can look similar or identical to authorized system activity, making accurate detection of attacks difficult. Tracing can be done manually today with exceptional cooperation, but not fast enough to stop an attack in real time. Improved detection technology is needed.

Policy-Based Issues

Existing risk assessment processes do not consider the full range of threats and vulnerabilities on a national level, intersecting different infrastructures. Although many different assets are individually effective in evaluating specific niches of risk, most limit their vision to their immediate sector or controllable assets. Existing intelligence collection, law enforcement, and private/corporate processes are not organized to support effective collation of data to assemble a synergistic view of the vulnerabilities, countermeasures, or threats, especially in light of potential infrastructure higher vulnerabilities. No process now in place can pull together, share, and coordinate necessary details to allow accurate and thorough risk assessments across infrastructure elements to determine whether broader assurance actions are required.

The security structure today is analogous to the days of walled cities, where protection and certainty of security ended at the walls. Our "walls" today are firewalls. To evolve an environment more analogous of safe intercity and international travel and trade, the area between firewalls is currently the realm of outlaws and bandits. Cooperation between law enforcement activities and corporate interests should be negotiated in one or more ways to enable synergistic efforts. This could be reflected in regulatory actions, similar to safety standards for automobiles, or by other means. Leadership and innovation are critical to solving these issues.

A critical aspect of policy initiatives should include the application of *confidence building measures* (CBM) to the overall efforts of information assurance. CBM have long been viewed as a logical and valuable approach to restore or improve stability and reduce tensions in international relationships. CBM generally require top-down support from the highest levels. Typical CBM include information exchange, consultation, access, notification, observation, constraint, education exchange, and cooperative exercises. They often start with small efforts at the working level. These small efforts encourage face-to-face discussions and agreements to implement and operate the agreed-upon solutions developed for initially modest goals. Success leads to a higher level of trust that more-complex efforts can be undertaken. The Hot Line and the Incidents at Sea Agreement, which established procedures to avoid the numerous near-misses and occasional collisions that had been occurring between Soviet and U.S. naval ships and planes, are both examples of specific CBM agreements between the former Soviet Union and the United States.

Many of today's regional conflicts and disputes are applying the lessons of CBM to reduce tensions, encourage trust, and build stability. The lessons gained from CBM in international relations can be applied to the challenge of information assurance through creative leadership practices, innovative investment, and education. CBM can encourage industry and government to reduce or eliminate barriers and build trusted relationships to deter and investigate threats or attacks against elements of the critical infrastructures. The basic principles of CBM require leadership support from the top, small initial efforts to develop personal relationships while achieving success, and a continuous building on successes to develop more sophisticated, trusted relationships.

Technology-Based Issues

There is a lesser role that technology can contribute to effective information assurance. Not only can specific technologies provide point protection, such as firewalls, they can also aid the detection of problems or attacks and then assist in implementing the corrective actions. In addition, technology can potentially obviate the need for such measures. For example, the adaptation of public key cryptography to electronic commerce holds the promise of eliminating some of the more-complex and time-consuming protective measures.

Besides the strictly computerized technologies that need additional development, there is an entire range of technologies that have received little attention to date but that could provide enormous benefits to effective information assurance. Chief amongst these technologies is the area of human-computer interaction (HCI), a multidisciplinary technology area that focuses on the interplay between human and computer system. Developing more-sophisticated HCI capabilities requires understanding of the principles of such interaction, which ultimately focuses on human perversities and use patterns. A ripe area for exploration would be security innovations within the HCI. First steps that are being explored are the incorporation of biometric security capabilities, such as fingerprint or keystroke analysis, into the interface.

In order to develop the technology solutions and innovations, emphasis on education and research is required. Here again, leadership can play an important role. Sponsored research projects, specific educational incentives, and targeted tax credits could all provide added incentive to the development of new and innovative technological solutions. Coupling this technology development thrust with efforts to raise the expectation levels of information system users can provide both supply and demand for the innovations.

Behavior-Based Issues

Currently, information protection is not a high priority among many information system users. At the corporate level, when there are budget cuts, information security budgets are often among the first to go. Additionally, users are not typically aware of vulnerabilities, threats, or even appropriate countermeasures such as virus-scanning software.

The reason for this lack of priority and pervasive lack of knowledge is directly attributable to the speed with which information technology has intertwined itself into the basis of common existence and expectations. It is easy to acquire information technology and fairly easy to get it to work. The expectation of security is not yet a driving issue for system developers, and the knowledge that security is an issue is not yet widespread amongst the using public.

To achieve an effective information protection posture, information security must become part of our culture—a standard consideration in how we conduct ourselves on professional and personal levels when using information systems. This clearly is a nontrivial undertaking that requires leadership by example, pervasive education, and awareness efforts, along with the development of innovative technology solutions that encourage secure behavior patterns.

Findings

The complexity of the subject at hand and the limitations of our knowledge base clearly constrain our ability to delineate a specific set of findings and recommendations. However, that constraint is not total. The following three findings conclude our examination of the emerging world and security issues within it.

Finding 1

The impact of information technologies on the traditional geopolitical structure of nation-states and their security implies changes to institutions and processes that are unavoidable, irresistible, and unless proper precautions are taken, potentially very destructive.

These changes stem from increased use of computers and networks in creating, storing, processing, and communicating information, the application of information technology to efficient and global collaborative work environments, and the vulnerabilities and dependencies introduced by the technologies themselves. The institutions and processes that will be changed, and are in fact already changing, include those that administer governance and those that ensure communal security. The new pluralism that is enabled by information technologies at once adds richness to our lives and discourses and yet threatens to undermine the social structures that have secured the nation-state.

There are several critical aspects of this finding:

- Classic individual, organizational, and national values, ideals, and vital interests, while unchanged in concept, are profoundly altered in their forms of expression.

- Through a solid partnership of government, industry, and other collective institutions of an informed society, we may hope to understand and hence achieve lasting security and prosperity in the information age.

- Authority figures must change their focus from providing management to that of providing cooperative leadership. Compliance processes must reflect that emerging sensibility.

- Classic American values of freedom and privacy appear to be in conflict, which is unresolved at this early stage in our understanding of the information age. The resolution of this conflict will resonate into both the conduct of business and into national security.

Finding 2

Central to our understanding of information assurance and information warfare is the role of "information" itself, an abstraction divorced from the technologies that store, manipulate, and transmit it.

Information is a valuable asset, independent of the information systems and technologies used to store, process, and exchange it. Because it has value, it is increasingly a target for theft by criminals and destruction by terrorists. The sophistication, and, hence, seriousness, of these threats is growing even as we continue the transformation of our society and virtually all its institutions into its new technology-enabled pluralistic form.

There are several critical aspects of this finding:

- Within the increasingly interconnected national and global networks that support and mediate our information activities, it is increasingly true that "to be connected anywhere is to be connected everywhere." Threats to national information assurance, therefore, can exist and be effective from anywhere in the world, with virtual impunity and little chance of being detected or contained.

- The range of potential adversaries is extensive, from disgruntled or lunatic individuals to hostile groups, including nation-states. An ability to determine adversarial interest is limited by the ubiquity of the technologies and the speed with which hostile intent can be formed. Capabilities that are benign in the hands of a nonhostile actor can become devastating in the hands of an adversary, with the difference being intent.

- No communal defense mechanisms exist that can detect attacks in progress in the information dimension, thereby limiting reaction and correction activities. Documentation and reporting of incidents is vol-

untary, inadequate, and casual. This necessarily limits our understanding of the breadth of the problem and hampers a coordinated
response. However, it is believed, with some limited supporting evidence, that attacks on data, information processes, and network service functions are frequent and increasing.

■ There are effectively no national boundaries or controlling jurisdic-
tions on the highly internationalized internet, intranet, public wide
area networks, and other fast lanes of the Information
Superhighway. This both complicates defensive actions and increases
exposure to malefactors beyond our immediate ability to punish and
deter. This de facto situation necessitates some other approach than
the classic extradition and criminal prosecution model used in physi-
cal-dimension crimes.

■ Clear definitions of jurisdiction and cooperation are needed at the
federal, state, and local level. Clear understanding of the information
territory and its dependence on the critical physical infrastructures
are highly desired if we are to realize the "safe streets" equivalent of
the information age.

■ Federal, state, and local law enforcement lack properly trained and
equipped personnel to effectively investigate cases involving electronically stored and transmitted data.

Finding 3

Effective information assurance will not be possible without competent
information management and the commitment of leaders and policymakers to implement and support them.

There are three aspects of this issue: education, leadership, and innovation. Coordinated efforts in all three of these dimensions are required
if we are to achieve better information assurance and thereby enhance
the security of our nation, our society, and our way of life. There are several critical aspects of this finding:

■ Response to the effects and realities of information warfare is not the
sole domain or responsibility of any part of society, but of all parts.

■ There is a significant body of knowledge that exists in the practice
and management of information security that is unfortunately limited to a small cadre of aficionados. Within the last two years, the
demand for information security practitioners has grown thanks in

part to the continued emphasis on the subject by parties such as the DoD's Defense Science Board. This role of raising awareness within the community at large is invaluable to the permeation of information security into all elements of society.

- On the other hand, there is a lack of focused and integrated information assurance curricula and research emphasis reflecting multidisciplinary, information value management and policy issues in addition to technical and engineering subjects at our schools and universities. Less than 10 universities and colleges in the United States offer degrees in information security, and the vast majority of that number sequester the programs in the computer science field. While computer science is a necessary part of information security practice and understanding, the management and social science aspects of the field must not be ignored.

- Education of citizenry, all of whom make up the core of modern information users, must include morality and ethics of conduct. The lessons that we teach our youth, by both positive and negative reinforcement, about what is right and wrong in physical space (including the rules of polite society) must be carried through to our instruction in the proper conduct in cyberspace.

- Efforts to engage industry sectors in developing standards for information assurance practices and applications contribute to a more resilient information infrastructure. Recent examples of these types of cooperative efforts include the development of Secure Socket Layer (SSL) protocols and the emergence of organizations offering testing and evaluation services to product vendors.

- Government organizations can play a complementary role to industry efforts by sponsoring research and development efforts and through innovative tax and regulatory incentives for developing and maintaining information assurance in this digital age. An example of the innovation that could spur incentive to initiate such efforts is the proposal developed by the Department of Defense Information Security Director in 1993: developing an analogous structure to fire insurance for information systems. This proposal held that just as fire insurance carries with it the requirement for appropriate safeguards and good practices, so could information system insurance carry with it the requirement for appropriate information security technologies, practices, and policies. And just as fire insurance would cover losses incurred, so would information insurance play a vital role in the continuity of business operations.

Notes

1. The Joint Security Commission, "Redefining Security," a report to the Secretary of Defense and the Director of Central Intelligence, Washington, D.C., 28 February 1994.

2. Center for Strategic and International Studies, "America's Hidden Vulnerabilities: Crisis Management in a Society of Networks," a report of the Panel on Crises Management of the CSIS, SSIS Science and Technology Committee, Washington, D.C.: Georgetown University, 1984.

3. Ramo, Joshua Cooper, "Welcome To The Wired World," *Time Magazine*, 5 December 1997, http://mouth.pathfinder.com/time/magazine/1997/int/970203/special.welcome_to.html

4. Hudson, 1.

5. Niksic, Alexandra, "Serbia's Digital Demos," *The Irish Times*: 10 February 1997, http://www.irish-times.com/irish-times/paper/1997/0210/cmp2.html

6. Montalbano, William D., "For Dissident, Just the Fax Causes British-Saudi Rift," *Los Angeles Times* (originally published Saturday, 27 April 1996, Home Edition Part A, Page 1), http://www.saudhouse.com/news/april/1.htm

7. Kelly, Kevin, *Out of Control: The Rise of Neo-Biological Civilization* (Reading, Mass.: Addison-Wesley: 1994), 8-9.

8. Eastern Michigan University offers a concentration in information security through their multidisciplinary program in technology studies.

9. Deming, W. Edwards, *Seven Deadly Sins of Quality,*

10. Kluepfel, Hank, "Inside Out You Turn Me," *Internet Magazine*, May/June 1996.

11. For complete definition of OECD principles, see: Denning, Dorothy E., *Information Warfare and Security:* Addison Wesley, 1999, pp. 397-98.

CHAPTER 17

Information Warfare Weapons, Intelligence, and the Cyberspace Environment

Historical Interlude: ECM-IFF

Turn the clock back to 1940. Hitler's blitzkriegs had rolled over his sadly unprepared neighbors while Pearl Harbor remained a peacetime area for the U.S. Navy, and nearby Honolulu was as it had been for many years, a serviceman's overnight and weekend dream. Communications security was almost primitive, what with the use of plain-language messaging and encrypted Morse transmissions only a step or two beyond that. War was half a world away for the officers and men and women of the Pacific Fleet, the Marines, and the Army.

In the Atlantic, America was supplying a steady flow of new merchant vessels—Liberty Ships—to our allies under a program called "Lend-Lease." The U-boat fleet was systematically sinking these almost as fast as they were launched. But change was in the wind as the first hints of the Information Revolution appeared. A desperate race was underway to develop Radio Detection and Ranging, RADAR, by British, German, and American laboratories. Although the fact that a "radio echo" could be detected returning from a solid target was known as early as the days of Marconi wireless, it had been little more than a curiosity until its potential as a wartime weapon was realized. Huge, unwieldy antennas sprang up along the British shoreline, and likewise in strategic locations in the German homeland and conquered territories. The primary problem to overcome was the difficulty in generating high-power radio waves at very high frequencies: the shorter the wavelength, the more diminutive the antenna and the more accurate pinpointing of a target would become.

The United States felt relatively secure, the ocean providing a safety zone that would erode as World War II progressed and the role of aircraft and rocketry became paramount. Not so Great Britain. Necessity the mother, a vital invention came into being, simple in hindsight but monumental in its effect upon radar, at Birmingham University: the magnetron. Its significance to the war effort was recognized in the United States, and the development effort was moved to the laboratories of the Massachusetts Institute of Technology. With this device, microwaves of high power could be generated and the physical size of transmitters, antennae, and receivers could be compressed sufficiently to make radar practical on board ships, and shortly thereafter in bomber and fighter aircraft. The electronic war began in earnest.

Concomitantly, the more that could be learned about the enemy, the more conclusive could be the impact of the "endgame," the battle's conclusion. Big guns and aircraft meant that war would be conducted beyond the line of sight, over the horizon. A bomber carrying a load of incendiaries is a vulnerable target for fighter aircraft and antiaircraft artillery. How does the pilot avoid what otherwise would be inevitable? By using *ECM*, or *electronic countermeasures*—for instance, confusing the enemy radar that is guiding its associated aircraft and artillery. In its early forms, upon detecting the enemy's radar signal, the pilot would release bundles of "chaff," aluminum foil cut in half-wavelengths of the radar signal, to float lazily behind his position at that moment while he took evasive action. The chaff—called "window" by the British because a good radar operator could "see through" it with a keen sense derived from experience—would cause shells to explode harmlessly behind their targets. Since Morse code was the radio language of choice, it was equally important to confuse Morse operators by blanketing their signals, injecting false words and messages into the stream of incoming code, and disguising the enemy "fist" (style) to appear as "friendly." In later years ECM would become *EW—electronic warfare*—with greatly extended information gathering, interception, and cryptological capabilities.

With information being of such vital importance, aircraft were soon deployed with their sole purpose being its acquisition. These defenseless planes, sometimes called "ferrets," carried neither offensive nor defensive armor, because their sole purpose was to draw enemy radar-directed fire, then sense, measure, and record every bit of information possible about the enemy's radio and radar systems. Soon it became painfully evident on both sides that a radar signal could be detected at twice the distance that it could produce an effective echo. Also, with a little ingenuity, the enemy could be conned into firing barrages at nonexistent targets, and a sortie of, say, five fighter aircraft could be made to appear as 25, or even a hundred. On this basis, a 10 times larger sortie can become a thousand planes in the radar's eye. Demoralizing an enemy can be even more effective than killing him.

A relatively benign but equally valuable aspect of ECM is to know which seagoing vessels are "friendlies," and which are enemy. Thus, *Identification Friend or Foe* (IFF) was developed and immediately extended to include aircraft. This took the form of a simple electronic transmitter-receiver that sends a series of short pulses (such as in Morse code) on one frequency and receives the echoed information on a different frequency. The transmitted pulse, being encoded, interrogates similar equipment on the unknown ship or plane, triggering a different coded response from the target plane's receiver, which, in wartime, would have to match the "code of the day" or else. As differentiating the enemy from a friend in quick time became more vital with the advent of rocket-boosted missiles, IFF information became itself a matter of life and death for the craft's occupants, as a "wrong" return signal can automatically aim and fire a highly unfriendly rocket.

These developments of wartime have found their place in today's peacetime—and, of course, in the "war" against crime. Today, both defense and civilian aircraft carry IFF equipment.

And the magnetron? It has become ubiquitous: Every microwave oven in the home, office, and restaurant has a magnetron as its heart, operating at the orbital frequency of the hydrogen atom's single electron.

Complexity of Information Warfare

Given the complexity of the concepts of information warfare and the effects of information technology on societal structures, it is somewhat difficult to postulate what weapons are in an information war. This chapter is intended more to stimulate the imagination rather than to be a definitive list of information weapons. The imaginations and technological achievements of humankind may result in the obsolescence of these postulated weapons in the near future, but the debate and discussions about how an information war may be engaged and defended against are a valuable contribution to the collective consciousness.

When defending your information assets, it is useful to understand what you are defending against. This area of knowledge includes not only *weapons* but also *tactics*. A weapon can be more or less effective depending on how it is used—a knife used in trench warfare is fairly limited in utility, while a knife used by a special-forces operative in a covert raid can achieve a whole different level of utility. Therefore, weapons must be discussed in terms of both what they are and how they may be used. This view of a weapon is much the same as the view of threat: A weapon's potential for harm is a function of both capability and access. The capability of a knife is the same, independent of where it exists. The access allows it to be used to greater or lesser effectiveness.

Additionally, a weapon only becomes a weapon when it is used for malicious or hostile purposes. A knife can be a perfectly peaceful tool, useful for cutting carrots in the kitchen, until it is picked up with the intent of stabbing someone. We all know the potential for danger from knives, since we have been educated in that potential by our parents, our teachers, and our media. Other potential weapons can be subtler. Mystery writers have long tantalized readers by using bizarre objects as the weapon in a murder. Examples include frozen meat and icicles. Both of these example mystery novel weapons have the inherent ability to lose the quality that made them dangerous in the hands of a malefactor: they were hard and stiff when frozen but then became nonthreatening when melted or cooked.

Since the technologies that enable information connectivity and automated processing are ubiquitous and legion, it is important to not discard any from consideration at this juncture simply because it appears nonthreatening. Imagination can describe situations where the most innocuous technology can turn deadly when in the proper state and in an enemy's hands. Defense in depth requires that such imaginative explorations be conducted, so that all avenues of danger are identified and defensible. For example, nascent technologies that are commonplace today may give way to integrated applications that currently only exist in science fiction and medical research, such as computer-brain integrated capabilities. The weapons possible in that sort of world are vastly different from the ones that are potential weapons today. Thus, the following discussions of specific weapon types should not be considered to be static, but merely the starting point.

Given that, the weapons that can be utilized in information warfare operations range from the commonplace to the unique. A very large book would be needed to discuss all possibilities in detail; this section discusses the concepts in general. How the weapons are used and the specific targets against which they are used must be tailored to meet the goals of a specific operation.

Weapon Components

All weapons consist of several basic components. These components include at the very least the following elements:

- Infrastructure, or body
- Targeting system
- Payload
- Mobility system

Illustrative examples of this premise are provided in the following two examples:

	Example 1: A Rifle	Example 2: Air-Dropped Bomb
Body	Gunstock	Bomb casing
Targeting System	Rifled barrel with sights	Bomb sights
Payload	Bullet	Explosive material
Mobility System	Gunpowder charge	Airplane

A goal in weapon design is to integrate all components so tightly that efficiency is increased. A smart bomb is more effective than a dumb bomb; a self-propelled missile with integrated targeting is more efficient than one that must be externally controlled or requires conveyance to the target.

Information weapons have the same components as any other weapon. They must have a body, a targeting system, a payload, and a means of conveyance. Some information weapons are contained within an information body—such as a software executable. Others are contained within other types of bodies. With some information weapons, the targeting is analogous to dumb bombs: the person launching the weapon points it in the right direction and hopes it gets close to its mark. With other information weapons, targeting is extremely precise. Some information weapons are self-propelled, such as worms, while others require external conveyance mechanisms.

Understanding these elements of information weapons helps us understand how to protect against them. Clearly, the elements that are of highest interest are the targeting mechanisms, the mobility mechanism, and the payload. However, in some weapons, understanding the nature of the body can assist in protection and detection measures as well.

Hostile Information Technology

When a computer scientist thinks of information warfare weapons, some of the first thoughts that spring to mind are of the activities and logic weapons most commonly associated with hackers, such as the use of password crackers and computer viruses, Trojan horses, logic bombs, time bombs, and malicious worms. These entities are indeed part of a weapons set that can be used specifically in the information dimension. Some weapons are more insidious than others, changing data in subtle ways that affect decision processes or produce distrust of systems rather than simply destroying the system or its data. Some weapons can be used to attack the operations of an information system, some could be used to manipulate data, and some could be used to violate secrecy—in other words, to spy.

The end goals or purpose of the weapon use can vary depending on what is desired by the malicious party. For example, if an enemy wanted to destroy the confidence of a set of citizens in their government, that enemy could use one or more weapons in various ways to send powerful messages to the citizenry about the lack of trustworthiness of the government. But this linkage of weapon and goal implies tactics. Before discussing tactics, it is necessary to identify potential weapons. Some technologies that could be used as weapons in an information war are described in the following sections.

Radiated Field Exploitation: TEMPEST

Electronically powered technologies emanate radiation as a natural by-product of the electrical processes. This has been understood for many years and, in fact, has a rich history in protection technologies. The cover name "TEMPEST" was given to the study and control of unintentional electronic signals emitted from automated data processing equipment by the U.S. government, and requirements still exist for controlling those emanations for sensitive equipment. The chief worry has been the violation of confidentiality, since collected emanations can sometimes be processed so that the content is visible to the collector. This is but one potential, however. Intercepting those emissions can also be used to gain signal clock synchronization for other weapons, for selecting jamming frequencies, or perhaps to enable a terminal screen compromise.

RF Weapons

Of course, just as the digital data that a computer uses is composed of ones and zeroes, so can a computer system be affected by the synchronous pulsing of electromagnetic energy at specified frequency ranges. Also known as *bit flipping*, the use of coherent RF (radio frequency) weapons has a wide range of potential, from the random distortion of data to the remote insertion of directed energy viruses. A major criticism of the utility of RF weapons is that for them to be successful, they must be gentle, and that implies geographic proximity. That geographic proximity can be achieved in a multitude of ways; examples include the insertion of a transmitter into a computer by a repair technician or the introduction of modulation onto the power supply to the computer system.

EMP Bombs

The electromagnetic nature of computers and supporting peripherals makes them susceptible to specific weapons such as electromagnetic pulse bombs. These weapons overwhelm a system with electromagnetic energy that can erase or badly damage stored data within memory and fuse circuits, as well as fry modems. EMP is most well recognized as a by-product of nuclear detonations, but it may be deliberately produced by conventional explosions as well.

With radiated field exploitation weapons, the targeting ranges from extremely crude to extremely precise. The ability to get close to a specific target assists in targeting precision. If the target is not readily available, then cruder targeting is required, which results in more destruction. In this situation, protecting a high-value target too much could be a counterproductive strategy. Allowing it to be more exposed could allow an enemy to target it more precisely, which would then enable them to use a more precise weapon. This would potentially save ancillary targets—targets of opportunity in the area—from destruction. Planning on this leads one to a strategy of controlled destruction rather than absolute protection, which can be additionally used as a means to gain information on enemy intentions.

Viruses

Malicious code is probably the best known of virus weapons, although not usually considered in that context. *Computer viruses* are those programs that stealthily infect other programs, self-replicate, and spread within a computer system or network. Typically small, they are difficult to detect, with some of the more recent versions having active antidetection protection measures. Modern computer viruses may be encrypted, compressed, or made polymorphic to reduce probability of detection.

Malicious or Compromised Software

Malicious code seems particularly appropriate for use in a targeted information warfare capability, and it is probable that in the future, more-precise targeting of payloads will be demonstrated. As they currently exist, it is difficult to use malicious code weapons with any degree of predictability or probability of success. This limits their usefulness and opens the possibility of usage to one's own side of the conflict. So using malicious code is probably very dependent upon what end results are desired. Weapons like viruses are essentially uncontrolled and uncontrollable. A weapon that can be aimed at one or more specific systems and then released through cyberspace to hunt down its target would be very useful.

Trojan Horse

In addition to being externally introduced, malicious code can be inherent in a program. As the image invoked by its name implies, a *Trojan horse* is a computer program with an apparently or actually useful function that contains additional functions that sneakily do things that the user of the program would not necessarily execute willingly. For example, a spreadsheet program could contain additional logic to make surreptitious copies of all of the data files on a system. The user of the spreadsheet program would not be aware of those activities occurring while working with its legitimate functions.

Worms

Similar to viruses, *worms* are self-replicating but not parasitic (i.e., they don't attach to other programs). As demonstrated dramatically by the Internet Worm of 1988, they can deny legitimate users access to systems by overwhelming those systems with their progeny. Worms illustrate attacks against availability, where other weapons may attack integrity of data or compromise confidentiality.

Flaws

Inexpert programming, by accident or misguided purpose, can be the source of problems in a computer system. Defined by the Orange Book as "an error of commission, omission, or oversight in a system that allows protection mechanisms to be bypassed," the use of a *flaw* in information warfare has infinite potential. The insertion of a flaw into a system could be done with other information warfare weapons, such as the use of coherent RF weapons, over networks from remote sites, or it could be designed in by an agent in place, as described later in the chapter.

Trapdoors

Another category of inexpert code with potential in information warfare is that of trapdoors. A *trapdoor* is a hidden software or hardware capability that allows system protection mechanisms to be bypassed. Trapdoors are accessed through some secret technique, such as a convoluted key sequence. Anyone who has ever programmed knows that despite best efforts, no program ever works correctly the first time (or even the first 10 times). A trapdoor is a commonly used device by programmers to make sure there is always a way into the code to fix bugs, no matter what the problem. It is also a gateway to sneak into a system without being noticed. The device is usually removed before the program is compiled to a finished executable file, but it is frequently neglected in the last-minute flurry of completion.

Logic and Time Bombs

Logic and time bombs are a type of malicious code very well suited to hostile activities. A *logic bomb* is a sequence of code buried within a larger computer system that executes when a specific system state is realized. An example could be a program that checks for the presence of a piece of data within a file (say, an employee's name within a payroll list), and when the specified logic state is reached (the existence of the employee's name is false), the bomb "explodes" (the software program commands the memory of the entire system to be erased). A *time bomb* is very similar to the logic bomb; this type of software program waits for a specific time to be realized and then executes. The Y2K expectation might be considered an inadvertent example.

Logic Torpedo

Weapons like viruses are essentially uncontrolled. A weapon that can be aimed at one or more specific systems and then released through cyberspace to hunt down its target would be very useful. In the case of malicious code, the body of the weapon is the software itself. Depending on the type of malicious code, the weapon may be more or less detectable. The targeting of malicious code can be extremely crude, such as with viruses, or very precise, such as with logic bombs. The *payload capability* also ranges from being more of an annoyance than any real destruction to being extremely dangerous.

Manipulation

One of the effects that can be accomplished with malicious code is data manipulation. With the increasing technological capability for processing and integration of data comes an opportunity to use those capabilities for nefarious purposes. The composition and content of pictures as well as databases are vulnerable to advanced techniques of manipulation. This potentially is a highly potent form of hostile activity that may be undetectable unless steps are taken ahead of time to detect hostile data manipulation. Data integrity becomes of paramount concern in this scenario.

Covert Channels

A *covert channel* is a communications channel that allows information to be transferred in a way that the owners of the system did not intend. Variations include *covert storage channels* and *covert timing channels*. Use of a covert channel is an effective way to insert a virus into a computer system.

Timing Weapons

Timing weapons, also known as *insidious clocks*, affect the timing of internal clocks to throw off system synchronization. These are particularly effective in radar installations.

Conventional Weapons on Information Targets

It should not be overlooked that conventional weapons, such as rifles and bombs, in the hands of armies and saboteurs can be remarkably effective in offensive information warfare operations, not only in attacks against the physical infrastructure of the information dimension but also in perception management and positioning operations. Conventional weapons use falls into one of two categories: *normal use* and *extra-normal*. The normal usage case is typified by a physical attack against some element of the information dimension and ranges from the physical destruction of system elements to more oblique activities, such as stealing the hard drive from a computer system. It achieves a goal of information warfare through the conventional use of conventional weapons.

The extra-normal case is the special use of weaponry to achieve specific Information warfare goals. Examples could include forcing a user group off of one communications link (such as fiber-optic conduits) onto a more exploitable link (such as microwave radio) by bombing the fiber switching station, swaying public opinion by bombing an airliner and blaming it on an opponent group, modifying some elements of enemy databases to undermine trust in their own systems, or assassinating randomly chosen enemy programmers.

Imaginative Weapons against Information

Psychological Operations

This category of special weapons encompasses the rest of available tools to prosecute elements of offensive infowar. *Psychological operations* (PsyOps) techniques and tools have a special place in the world of infowar and are included in this category, but they do not encompass the whole set of special weapons. PsyOps implies that in order to conduct "armed propaganda" in an effective manner, it is necessary to destroy police installations and authority, cut outside lines of communications, including telephone, switching, cable, radio, and computers, discredit proper authority, hinder medical assistance, and do what is necessary to create havoc and civil disorder.

Following are examples of other special or imaginative information weapons.

Agents in Place

Agents in place in system development organizations, standards committees, and as network managers can be very useful in terms of acquiring knowledge of system vulnerabilities and planting (prepositioning) weapons.

Noncooperating Weapons

A weapon used for information warfare purposes does not necessarily have to know that it is being used or understand the real results of its activities. This situation is common in espionage, where the use of false flag covers in recruiting can turn an otherwise unachievable objective into a success. Use of CNN and other news media to manipulate perception of events in Desert Shield/Desert Storm is a prime example of the use of a noncooperating weapon.

Positioning

The Madison Avenue advertising community has been using what they call *positioning* techniques for years to make people buy certain brands or products. These techniques are used to encourage or discourage certain behaviors. An example would be to highly publicize instances of computer systems locking up with no way to fix or diagnose the problem. Such scare tactics would encourage development programmers to hide trapdoors in their work to ensure that all the work they put into the system would not be wasted in the event of a malfunction.

Public Relations

The art of public relations is well understood in politics, marketing, and publicity as a way to get persons to think in favorable terms about the subject of the PR pitch. It could be extrapolated to information warfare as part of the deterrence process to keep opponents thinking favorably about us or our interests, and/or to instill a perception that going against our national interests is tantamount to going against their own interests.

Stimuli

The use of stimuli to overstress a target system can have desirable effects on that system without necessarily destroying it. For example, an intelligence system designed automatically to produce situation reports could be overloaded by supplying too many inputs (i.e., situations to report), thereby causing a reaction or degradation in the system. The reaction caused would be system-specific, but it could range from triggering the system's automatic data-thinning algorithms, thereby causing the system to dump data, to slowing the system down dramatically as it tries to process all the data being received. In the later case, the slow-down could result in the user receiving grossly time-late products, which could cause them to miss important data or ignore the data they did get.

The weapons that can be utilized in offensive infowar operations range from the commonplace to the unique. It would be the subject of a very large book to discuss all possibilities in detail. This section discusses the concepts in general: how the weapons are used and how the specific targets against which they are used are tailored to meet the goals of the operation.

Information Warfare and the Intelligence Machine

The realities of IW operations run very close to the process of intelligence. Some appear as less of a process and more as an intelligence machine. As warfare has evolved from hand-to-hand combat through the various stages of mass and attrition warfare to maneuver warfare and coordinated precision strikes, the level of information required to fight those wars has increased proportionately with the level of technology used (see Figure 17-1).[1]

The military intelligence machine is a very expensive business, which in the more developed countries is active every hour of every day of the

What is intelligence?

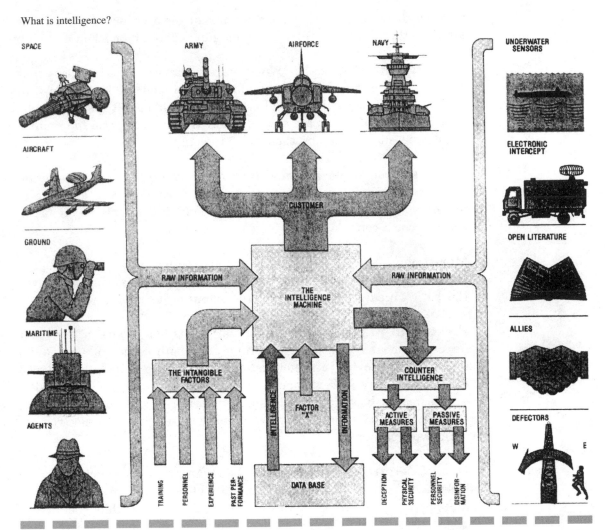

Figure 17-1 The intelligence machine.

year. The fuel of these mighty machines is raw information, which is sucked in from many sources, some of which are illustrated in Figure 17-1 and described in the following sections.

Space Space is currently the intelligence person's dream. With sensors able to roam at will over every country, unfettered by fences or frontiers, there are no "no-go" areas for satellites. Known in political circles as "national technical means," satellites bring/send back information as

detailed as the first flight of a new aircraft or the accuracy of a missile or
even whether the caliber of a new tank gun is 123mm or 125mm.

Aircraft Aircraft like the AWACS have radar and other sensors that
can see far into hostile territory and that can feed the "take" down to
their bases as it is received (i.e., in real time). Although at first sight they
appear vulnerable, they are able to detect threats early and to organize
countermeasures to ensure their own protection.

Ground Ground sensors range from radars and remote sensors to the
soldier with binoculars. The major problem is range limitations due to
terrain and weather, which is why so much emphasis is placed on air- or
space-borne reconnaissance.

Maritime Maritime surveillance includes both surface ships and submarines. Mounting a multiplicity of sensors, these ships can range over
the world's oceans, limited only by the extent of "territorial waters."

Electronic Warfare Electronic warfare is today one of the most
important means of gathering information in both peace and war. Radio
intercept can provide raw information from insecure radio links and also
build up pictures of deployments, tactical dispositions, individual idio-
syncrasies (of both commanders and operators), and equipment use.
Intercept activities cover radio, radar, microwave, and other electromagnetic transmissions.

Open Literature Open literature is a source that is sometimes overlooked. All nations produce vast amounts of paper on military subjects
(newspapers, magazines, pamphlets, books), as well as films and videos.
These are valuable not only for the factual information they give away
but also for the insight they afford into thought processes and moral
influences on commanders and staffs.

Allies Allies are frequently a valuable source of information and also
help to spread the load in this very expensive undertaking.
Unfortunately, the traffic on such "two-way streets" does not always flow
with equal freedom in both directions.

Agents Agents are the traditional source of the most vital information,
because they are able to penetrate right into the heart of the hostile system. This frequently enables them to gather not only cold facts (how

many tanks, what type of ships, etc.) but also the feel and methods inside the heart of the enemy camp.

Underwater Sensors   Underwater sensors now cover large areas of the ocean floor, particularly in the "choke points." They are designed to give information not only on ship and submarine movements but also on the ocean itself.

Counterintelligence   Counterintelligence is the protection for this vast machine. This includes active measures such as deceiving the enemy and the use of disinformation. Passive measures are mainly a matter of security: physical and personnel. The former is becoming an increasingly expensive and technology-oriented task as the threat becomes more and more sophisticated. The latter is an endeavor to protect against leaks, but this will never be totally foolproof.

Defectors   Defectors are invaluable prizes to intelligence services, because, like the better agents, they can give information in depth about their specialized areas.

Databases   Databases form a pool of knowledge built up by the intelligence machine over the years, which enables every new bit of information to be analyzed properly. It is rather like a jigsaw puzzle where each piece is fitted in using a combination of the fragment of a picture and the shape of the sides, with each new piece making completion slightly easier and slightly more inevitable.

Intangible Factors   Intangible factors also contribute to the effectiveness of the machine. These include the standard of training, the quality of the people in the organization, the collective experience of the machine, and its past performance.

Factor X   Factor X is an important aspect possessed by some organizations. It is the ability to be in the best place at the right time, to know who has a certain piece of knowledge, and sometimes just to be lucky.

All these disparate elements have to be welded together and processed, leading finally to an output—intelligence. This is then handed over to the operator, military or political, who must then decide what to do with it. *The goal of information warfare is to attack all of these areas and strangle, intercept, or change the information flow to the ultimate customers.*

Strike the Eyes

It is surprising that there are so many attacks on Web sites and so few on more important targets. In Tae Kwon Do, one of the first moves is to take out the target's eyes, or if this is not feasible, take out his solar plexus so that he cannot breathe. When he can't breathe, his head will follow. In the Gulf War, one of the first targets the alliance forces attacked was the enemies' radar.

The concept of using overhead platforms to observe events on the earth can be traced back to the *aerostiers*, or balloonists, during the French Revolution, in 1794. The United States used balloons during the Civil War. During World War II extensive use of airplane photography was made. The 1950s and the Cold War saw the development, production, and deployment of a variety of aircraft and spacecraft to monitor events in the Soviet Union. The capability of these systems has improved in numerous ways over the ensuing years. Satellites now have longer lifetimes, produce more detailed images, and transmit their imagery in real time.

Some aircraft and spacecraft are capable of producing high-quality imagery in situations where standard visible-light photography is not feasible. These alternative means of obtaining imagery rely on equipment sensitive to wavelengths outside of the visible-light portion of the spectrum, which ranges from 0.0004 to 0.00075 mm.

Photographic equipment can be either film-based or the television type. A conventional camera captures a scene on film by recording the varying light levels reflected from all the separate objects in that scene. An electro-optical camera converts the varying light levels into electrical signals. (These are also called pixels or picture elements.) Each signal has a numerical value, and the process transforms a picture (analog) image to a digital image that can be transmitted electronically to distance points. The analog signal can be displayed on a video screen or printed as a photograph.

Imagery can be obtained using visible-light, near-infrared portions of the electromagnetic spectrum, thermal from the mid and far infrared portions of the spectrum, or imaging radar [aka radio detection and ranging] . Thermal infrared imagery can detect buried structures, such as missile silos or underground construction, by measuring the temperature differences between the target and the earth's surface. Radar imagery is produced by bouncing radio waves off an area or object. The returning waves allow formation of a picture of an object. Since radio waves are not attenuated at certain frequencies by water vapor in the atmosphere, they are able to penetrate cloud cover. Meteorologists tracked 1999's Hurricane Floyd, as it roared up the East Coast, using this technology.

Collection

The most important means of producing imagery (and one of the more sensitive research areas) is via the use of satellite systems. The United States has relied heavily on a variety of systems since the first satellite was launched in 1960. Satellites are the most productive of U.S. image collection systems because they are able to overfly without hindrance and can provide imagery almost instantaneously. They have some limitations. Even if already in orbit, they cannot be dispatched to cover events on short notice. They fly a well-known path—a predictable path—providing time for terrorist groups to hide their activities from view as the "eye in the sky" flies overhead. In addition, they are very expensive, forcing priorities to be set for the intelligence required. Aircraft reconnaissance is used to supplement the satellite coverage because of their quick response time.

Other means of information collection have been used less frequently. For example, during the Persian Gulf War the United States relied on Unmanned Aerial Vehicles (UAVs)/Remote Piloted Vehicles (RPVs) in addition to manned reconnaissance aircraft. Equipped with television and forward-looking infrared sensors, these pioneers operated day and night, making a total of 307 flights in Operation Desert Storm to support military operations.

Processing and Interpretation

Imagery can be obtained from the visible-light portion of the electromagnetic spectrum using either film-based or television-type photographic equipment. Even imagery obtained via a conventional camera instead of a digital imaging system can be converted into digital signals. The signals can then be computer-processed to improve the quantity and quality of information being extracted. Specifically, computers disassemble a picture into millions of electronic bits and then use mathematical formulas to manipulate the color contrast and intensity of each spot. Each image can be reassembled in various ways to highlight special features and objects that were hidden in the original image. Such processing allows:

- Building multicolored single images from several pictures taken in different bands of the spectrum, making existence of the patterns more obvious to the human eye

- Restoring the shapes of objects by adjusting for the angle of view and lens distortion

- Changing the amount of contrast between objects and backgrounds

- Sharpening out-of-focus images

- Restoring ground details largely obscured by clouds

- Conducting electronic optical subtraction, in which earlier pictures are subtracted from later ones—making unchanged buildings in a scene disappear while new objects, such as missile silos under construction, remain

- Enhancing shadows

- Suppressing glint, and glare

Processing plays a crucial role in easing the burden on photogrammetrists and photo interpreters. *Photogrammetrists* are responsible for determining the size of objects from overhead photographs using, along with other data, the shadows cast by objects. *Photo interpreters* are trained to provide information about the nature of the objects in photographs, based on information as to what type of crates carry MiG-21s, for instance, or what an IRBM (intermediate-range ballistic missile) site or fiber-optics factory looks like from 150 miles in space. Information is provided using interpretation keys such as those listed in Table 17-1.[2]

An interpreter might see a picture with excavations, mine-head frames, derricks, piles of waste, conveyor belts, bulldozers, and power shovels, but with just a few buildings. The interpreter's *key* would suggest that this is a mine. Special kinds of equipment, the tone or color of the waste piles and the ore piles, as well as knowledge of local geology, might further indicate that what the interpreter sees is a uranium mine.

The utility of any imaging system is a function of several factors—the most prominent being *resolution*. Photo analysts can define resolution as the minimum size that an object must be to make it measurable and identifiable. The higher the resolution, the greater the detail that can be extracted from a photo. It should be noted that resolution is a product of

TABLE 17-1

Joint Imagery
Interpretation Keys.

World Tanks and Self-Propelled Artillery	Major Surface Combatants
World Towed Artillery	Minor Surface Combatants
General Transportation Equipment	Mine Warfare Types
World Tactical Vehicles	Amphibious Warfare Types
Combat Engineer Equipment	Naval Auxiliaries
World Mobile Gap and River Crossing Equipment	Intelligence Research Vessels
Coke, Iron, and Steel Industries	Shipborne Electronics
Chemical Industries	Shipborne Weapons
World Electronics	Airfield Installation
World Missiles and Rockets	Petroleum Industries
Military Aircraft of the World	Atomic Energy Facilities
Submarines	

Source: Defense Intelligence Agency Regulation 0-2, "Index of DIA Administrative Publications,"
December 10, 1982, pp. 35-36.

several factors: the optical or imaging system, atmospheric conditions, and orbital parameters. The degree of resolution required depends on the specificity of the intelligence desired. Five different interpretation tasks have been differentiated. *Detection* involves locating a class of units or objects or an activity of military interest. *Generic identification* involves determining general target type, and *precise identification* involves discrimination within target type of known types. *Description* involves specifying the size-dimension, configuration-layout, components-construction, and number of units. *Technical intelligence* involves determining the specific characteristics and performance capabilities of weapons and equipment. Table 17-2 provides examples of the resolution required for interpretation tasks.

Factors other than resolution that are considered significant in evaluating the utility of an imaging system include coverage speed, readout speed, analysis speed, reliability, and enhancement capability. *Coverage speed* is the area that can be surveyed in a given amount of time, *readout speed* the speed with which the information is processed into a form that is meaningful to photo interpreters, and *reliability* the fraction of time in which the system produces useful data. *Enhancement capability* refers to whether the initial images can be enhanced to draw out more useful data.[3]

TABLE 17-2

Resolution
Required for
Different Levels of
Interpretation.

Target	Detection	General Identification	Precise Identification	Description	Technical Intelligence
Bridge	20 ft.	15 ft.	5 ft.	3 ft.	1 ft.
Communications radar/radio	10 ft./10 ft.	3 ft./5 ft.	1 ft./1 ft.	6 in./6 in.	1.5 in./6 in.
Supply dump	5 ft.	2 ft.	1 ft.	1 in.	1 in.
Troop units (bivouac, road)	20 ft.	7 ft.	4 ft.	1 ft.	3 in.
Airfield facilities	20 ft.	15 ft.	10 ft.	1 ft.	6 in.
Rockets and artillery	3 ft.	2 ft.	6 in.	2 in.	.4 in.
Aircraft	15 ft.	5 ft.	3 ft.	6 in.	1 in.
Command and control hq.	10 ft.	5 ft.	3 ft.	6 in.	1 in.
Missile sites (SSM/SAM)	10 ft.	5 ft.	2 ft.	1 ft.	3 in.
Surface ships	25 ft.	15 ft.	2 ft.	1 ft.	3 in.
Nuclear weapons components	8 ft.	5 ft.	1 ft.	1 in.	.4 in.
Vehicles	5 ft.	2 ft.	1 ft.	2 in.	1 in.
Land minefields	30 ft.	20 ft.	3 ft.	1 in.	—
Ports and harbors	100 ft.	50 ft.	20 ft.	10 ft.	1 ft.
Coasts and landing beaches	100 ft.	15 ft.	10 ft.	5 ft.	3 in.
Railroad yards and shops	100 ft.	50 ft.	20 ft.	5 ft.	2 ft.
Roads	30 ft.	20 ft.	6 ft.	2 ft.	6 in.
Urban area	200 ft.	100 ft.	10 ft.	10 ft.	1 ft.
Terrain	—	300 ft.	15 ft.	5 ft.	6 in.
Surfaced submarines	100 ft.	20 ft.	5 ft.	3 ft.	1 in.

Sources: Adapted from U.S. Congress, Senate Committee on Commerce, Science, and Transportation, *NASA Authorization for Fiscal Year 1978, Part 3* (Washington, D.C.: U.S. Government Printing Office, 1977), pp. 1642-43; and Bhupendra Jasani, ed., *Outer Space—A New Dimension in the Arms Race* (Cambridge, Mass.: Oelgeschlager, Gunn & Hain, 1982), p. 47.

All the above functions are computer-controlled, computer-guided, computer-related, computer-stored, and computer-connected. These "eyes" would be the ideal targets that information warfare weapons could attack. The effect would be quite a bit more than the destruction of some government or commercial Web site. It is no wonder that the DoD is concerned with the 100 or so reported attacks per day on its computers and why it puts so much emphasis on protecting its computer-based eyes.

The Cyberspace Environment

We mention *cyberspace* throughout this book. But what is the environment and hence, the information battlefield in which we can apply our information weapons for cyberspace? There are some common points, some common equipment, some common processes, and a gaggle of protocols—with but few common handshakes.

Since we are dealing with computer-related, -controlled, -influenced, -converted, and -connected functions, we differentiate cyberspace environment as overlapping models: (1) open systems interconnection model (OSI), (2) practical/physical model, and (3) protocol model. We can view these as a three-dimensional space where each model represents an axis. Our primary interests are the inputs, outputs, and processes relating these three models to any one of eight services. These services support intelligence processes (our machine in Figure 17-1) and information warfare processes trying to strangle this machine.

Services

There are eight services, representing eight technologies on pillars in the cyberspace environment. There are many authoritative books on each one of these technologies; our purpose is to enumerate some of the dynamics of the cyberspace model.[4] These are as follows:

1. Telecommunications
2. Radio
3. Cellular communications
4. Personal communication systems (PCS)
5. Paging
6. Mobile satellite services (MSS)
7. Very small aperture terminals (VSAT)
8. DirecTV

Cyberspace customers do business in one or more of the above services. This is true for commercial, intelligence, government, military, and other organizations. Services can be related to three-dimensional paths though our cyberspace model.

OSI

The Y-axis for our model may be represented as the standard OSI seven layers. From lowest level to top they are as follows:

1. Physical layer
2. Data-link layer
3. Network layer
4. Transport layer
5. Session layer
6. Presentation layer
7. Application layer

Outputs are the easiest to understand and the most constrained. They correspond to the application layer of the standard OSI model. People have relatively few senses to work with. We basically hear or see outputs. Outputs can be in the form of voice, video, or plain data. For the services mentioned, telecommunications outputs are all three; radio is generally voice or data, cellular systems are voice or data, PCS is a combination voice/data, paging is data, MSS is voice and data, VSAT is a special voice/data/video output and direct TV is voice/video.

Practical/Physical Model

The practical model or implementation may be thought of as the X-axis of the construct. Here we are concerned with how we connect things and how fast we can push data through the connections. There are at least six layers of this axis. From most general to most detailed they are as follows:

1. Transmission media
2. Physical media interface
3. Front-end processing
4. Digital channel rate
5. Number of channels (and the EE's favorite bandwidth)
6. Channel processing protocols; the various handshakes that control the flow of data from input to output for each service

The first five elements on the X-axis or practical model correspond to the OSI physical layer. They deal with connections and conversions required to move information from the *input* to the *output* side for each service. The sixth element is the most complicated, as it deals with transferring data from layer to layer. It overlaps the physical layer at the "connectors" and then transfers data from the data layer to the network layer, to the transport layer, to session layer, to the presentation layer, and, finally, to the applications layer. The *channels* are responsible for movement, transfer, and storage between inputs from the service to the output to the customer. The customer sees only the output results: voice, video, or data. Channel processing is one of the most exciting fields of study today. Considerable current research is aimed at improving the signal progress through channels. As an example, modems have moved from 2400 bps to 110,000 bps, and cable TV modems are capable of millions of bits of data transfer.

Transmission Media

There are commonalities among the economical transmission media for the eight services[4]:

1. Copper wire/coaxial cable
2. Fiber/fiber optics
3. Microwave
4. Satellite
5. Radio

In terms of services, telecommunications systems rely on copper wire/coaxial cable, fiber, microwave and satellite. Radio relies on radio both HF (IEEE high-frequency range 3-30 MHz) and VHF/UHF (IEEE very high and ultra high frequencies ranging from 30-300 MHz to 300 MHz to 1 GHz). Cellular uses copper wire and coaxial cable, fiber optics, microwave radio, and UHF radio. PCS relies on UHF/microwave radio, paging is primarily UHF radio, and Mobile Satellite Services (MSS) use L/S (IEEE 1 and S bands are frequency ranges from 1-2 GHz and 2-4 GHz, respectively). VSAT uses C band, Ku band, and Ka band radio (IEEE frequency ranges of 4-8 GHz, 12-18 GHz, and 27-40 GHz). Finally, DirecTV shares the Ku band radio media.

Physical Media Interface

Data moving between, though, or on the transmission media enter the physical interfaces in only two basic ways. Data is either *converted* or *received*. In terms of services, for telecommunications, wire/cable is converted in an analog converter, or analog-to-digital converter, fiber is converted in a fiber-to-digital converter, microwave is received in a microwave receiver, and satellite data goes through a satellite receiver. Depending on the frequency level, radio is received by either a HF or VHF/UHF receiver. Cellular is similar to telecommunications in that cell links will be converted from digital or analog or fiber sources and mobile cell links will be received because they are UHF radio. PCS uses UHF/ microwave receiving, paging only UHF receiving. MSS uses a special L/S band receiver. VSAT uses a C, Ku, or Ka band receiver. Finally, DirecTV relies on a C/Ku band receiver.

Front-End Processing

As we continue our trip down the X-axis, going from input to output devices, we encounter several roads with the interface endpoint at the data-link layer being *channels*. After conversion or reception of the signals, the next step for all services is to *demultiplex*. Demultiplexers split signals and transfer them for processing at the appropriate rates. Rate is not only consideration, the number of channels or subchannels is a factor because it determines the maximum amount of information that can be transferred for a particular service. We can think of a channel as a tube through which data is forced to flow at maximum rates. We can see it as a potential *choke point* to deliver an IW weapon against. Conceivably, this attack would be more effective than an intrusion against the IP at the network layer, where many commercial countermeasures are applied.

Telecommunications

Data from the analog-to-digital converters may be fed to any one of T-n (North American T-carrier level 1-4, DS-n, digital signal level n) lines and demultiplexed into 56/64 Kbps digital channels. Microwave inputs are demultiplexed by SONET (synchronous optical network) and separated into channels that permit 52 Mbps to 2.56 Gbps information flow. Satellite communications may be transferred through high-speed ISDN (integrated services digital network) connections providing for 64 Kbps (kilobits/sec).

Radio, Cellular, PCS, and MSS

These services use one or more of the following front-end processing protocols:

1. *FDMA*   Frequency-division multiple access
2. *TDMA*   Time-division multiple access
3. *DAMA*   Demand assignment multiple access
4. *CDMA*   Code division multiple access

VSAT and DirecTV

These two services use a variety of demultiplexing processes:

1. DAMA/TDMA/FDMA
2. SCPC—Single channel per carrier
3. S-ALOHA—Slotted, random time-division multiple access protocol
4. Wideband FM video

Paging

Paging uses one channel and directly moves 20 to 80 characters/message.

Channels

Midway on the X-axis are the channels that can be generated or controlled by multiplexing prior to its becoming a function of service. The number of channels is dependent upon the input service. Telecommunications inputs can be as low as 1 for analog, a T-4 line can provide 4032 channels, and the number of channels from a satellite input is upwards into the hundreds of thousands. Radio links range from 8 to 128 channels, which can flow from 2400 to 110,000 bps or 16 to 32 Kbps TDMA multiplexed. Cellular service provides a wide range of channels available to the user, ranging from 3— 1999 and rates from 8 to 19.2 Kbps. PCS, paging, and DirecTV usually flow through one channel. VSAT works on 24 channels at 64 Kbps. This is but a sampling of the flows and channel breakdowns.

Data-Link Layer

There are also some commonalities in equipment used for channel processing. There is very little commonality between processing protocols at the network through applications layers on the Y-axis or OSI model. Common data equipment are as follows:

1. Analog interface
2. Modem
3. Digital interface
4. Codec
5. Code converter
6. Descrambler /decompression (video/audio)

From a services standpoint, telecommunications, radio, and cellular all use analog, modems, digital interfaces, or codec units at the data-link level for channel processing. PCS and MSS use codec and digital interface equipment. Paging requires only a code conversion. DirecTV requires special descrambling units with video/audio decompression capability.

Cyberspace Quagmire

Cyberspace becomes cloudy when we look at the number of different and noncompatible protocols that carry data from the data-link device (i.e., modem or digital interface devices) to the application and the user waiting for the data, voice, or video at his or her user terminal. Some of the names they go by are TCP/IP (Transmission Control Protocol/Internet Protocol), SNA (systems network architecture), X.25 (ITSS recommendation, layers 1 to 3 of user network interface for a packet-switched public data network), Frame Relay, ISDN (Integrated Services Digital Network), CDPD (cellular digital packet data), SDLC (synchronous data-link control), and SNDCP (subnetwork-dependent convergence protocol). There are at least 100 more protocols in the mix.

Perhaps the best known protocol is TCP/IP, which is used in telecommunications, radio, and VSAT. The TCP/IP model uses a LAN or ISDN/X.25 for high-level data-link control at the data-link layer, the IP protocol at the network layer (where much countermeasure protection is applied), the TCP protocol at the transport layer, and higher-level applications layer protocols such as FTP (File Transfer Protocol), Telnet (standard Internet terminal emulation protocol), and SMTP (Simple Mail Transfer Protocol). A good reference relative to the TCP/IP protocol is *IPng and TCP/IP Protocols* by Stephen A. Thomas.[5]

Wrap-Up—Chokepoints

Cyberspace represents a fertile ground for deployment of information weapons. Information weapons have the same characteristics as their conventional counterparts, and they can have a devastating effect on the

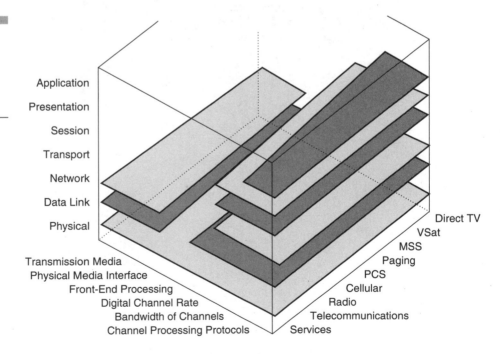

Figure 17-2
Intersecting Technologies in Cyberspace. (Nichols-Ryan cyberspace model).

target with concomitant personnel losses. Developing intelligence is integrally linked with the process of information weaponry.

We have presented a gross model of the cyberspace battlefield that overlays the OSI and practical models with the various services and customers involved. There are commonalities of equipment for processing data, voice, and video-based systems. These commonalities (such as the demultiplexing functions) represent potential *chokepoints* that make possible-to-likely targets against which to launch an information warfare weapon. Shutting down a system via a chokepoint could knock out several services across the board (all the services that are supported by the computer or computer switching system). Channel-processing produces the most stardust in cyberspace. An IW attack against the channel-processing protocol could effect a limited denial of service.

Notes

1. Kennedy, Colonel William, *Intelligence Warfare: Penetrating the Secret World of Today's Advanced Technology Conflict* (New York: Crescent Books, 1983).
2. Richelson, Jeffery T. *The U.S. Intelligence Community*, 3rd ed. Westview, 1995.
3. Ibid.
4. *Information Warfare*, Questech, Inc., 1996.
5. Thomas, Stephen A., IPng and the TCP/IP Protocols: Implementing the Next Generation Internet (New York: Wiley, 1996).

CHAPTER 18

Methods of Employment

Weapons may be deployed either positively or negatively. Specific planning for a scenario should be a reflection of the target, the method in which the weapon is to be used to ensure the highest probability of success, and the goal to be accomplished (Figure 18-1).

The possible outcomes that can be achieved in infowar include the following:

- *Denial*   The manipulation of a target to prevent it from being used reliably by its primary users.

- *Destruction*   The physical destruction of a target so that it cannot be used. Examples of destruction techniques include (1) inserting a virus that sends read/write commands to a disk head so often that the head fails, (2) blowing up a switching center or a power station, (3) delivering a strong electromagnetic pulse to a system to fry its circuits, or (4) shooting a bullet through the tracking/pointing mechanisms of a satellite dish.

- *Exploitation*   The manipulation of a target to exploit it for some purpose. This can include use of the target as a conduit for other weapons, intelligence gathering, insertion of false or misleading information, or manipulation of the system to slow it down, create distrust, or degrade availability.

Figure 18-1
Weapons.

BASIC DATA REQUIREMENTS
Weapons

- **Anti-TEMPEST**
- **Malicious Code**
    - Computer Virii, Worms, Trojan Horses, Logic Torpedos, Time Bombs, etc
- **Covert Channels, Flaws, and Trapdoors**
- **Data Manipulation**
- **EMP Bombs (non-nuclear)**
- **RF Weapons (bit flipping)**
- **Conventional**
- **Agents in Place**
- **Non-Cooperating Weapons, Stimuli**
    - Media, perception, false flag operations
- **Positioning, Public Relations**

Note that the targets may be hardware, software, firmware, netware, information, or any combinations thereof. Methods of delivery of the weapons to achieve the possible goals are interesting and important. Delivery of the conventional weapons is widely understood, so the following list of delivery methods is limited to infoweapons:

- *Direct launch*   Sending a worm, logic torpedo, virus, or other form of attack directly into a system is the most direct way to deliver an infoweapon. A caution in doing this is that friendly systems should be vaccinated or isolated to minimize the possibility of fratricide or collateral damage.

- Forward-basing   Using a variety of means, placing weapons in areas (systems, networks) where they might lie dormant until required could be attractive if their security can be ensured. Alternatively, forward-basing weapons and allowing them to be discovered may have desired outcomes also, perhaps in terms of deterrence.

- *Hacking*   Utilizing flaws, trapdoors, or faulty security, technologically sneaking into a system allows an agent or process access to exploit, deny, or destroy that system.

- *Remote insertion*   Using coherent RF (radio frequency) signals, directed-energy viruses may be inserted into systems by any unprotected port (e.g., the modem or power supply). One of the more interesting scenarios to consider is that in which a directed-energy virus is used to activate a trapdoor, allowing more direct and expeditious access to the target system.

Targeting

The science of targeting is the intelligent combination of the location, utility, and priority of potential targets with a choice of weapon and an assessment of the weapon's probable effect on a given target. (See Figures 18-2 to 18-4 for types of targets.) With a large variety of weapons and methods of using those weapons, it is important for a prioritized set of targets to be developed in advance of any potential engagement, to facilitate the coordination of an offensive attack and to assist in the wise utilization of resources.

Additionally, there are equities issues. If communication channels are destroyed by infowar operations, *communications intelligence* (COMINT) will suffer. If databases are destroyed or their integrity is

Figure 18-2
Connectivity targets.

BASIC DATA REQUIREMENTS
Connectivity

Where are the critical nodes?
Where are the weak links and vulnerabilities?

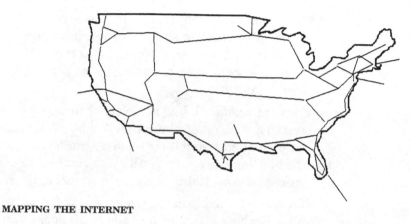

MAPPING THE INTERNET

Figure 18-2
Connectivity targets.

BASIC DATA REQUIREMENTS
Equipment
Hardware, Software, Firmware

- **What characteristics are exploitable?**
  - What kind of operating system is being used?
  - What version?
  - What communications protocol is used?

  - How are logins accomplished?
  - What level of audits are taken?

Figure 18-3
Exploitable equipment.

Figure 18-4
Topology.

BASIC DATA REQUIREMENTS

Topography

What is the topography of computer usage?
Where does information reside?
Who accesses that information?

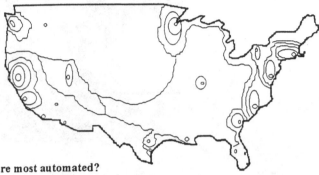

What industries are most automated?
What backup procedures do they use?
What is their level of exposure?

Figure 18-4
Topology.

attacked, *computer intelligence* (COMPUINT) will not be able to exploit covert access to those systems (unless, of course, the weapons of destruction are used in such a way that we know what has been changed and how, but the enemy does not). Denial of availability of systems and networks to the enemy may make these unavailable to us as nodes of cyberspace leading to other targets—similar to neither friend nor foe being able to use a bombed-out bridge. The analog of a pontoon bridge that is unknown and/or unavailable to anyone, except the chosen targets, may be created.

Cyberwar Integrated Operations Plan (CIOP)

Similar to the Single Integrated Battle Operations Plan (SIOP), an integrated operations plan for war in cyberspace would prove useful in coordinating the efforts of many disparate resources all contributing to the

Figure 18-5
Sample Elements of
CIOP.

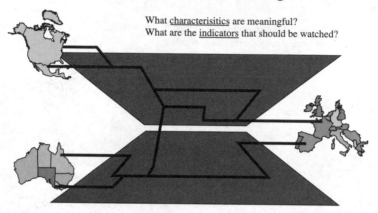

BASIC DATA REQUIREMENTS
Surveillance & Warning

What <u>characterisitics</u> are meaningful?
What are the <u>indicators</u> that should be watched?

end goal. Integrating operations plans allows for coordination of operations, best use of resources, and higher probability of success in an operation. For any given scenario, a list of targets and their relative priority of engagement should be developed to guide the process. As an example, a CIOP would develop a complete plan for target surveillance and advance warning (Figure 18-5).

Candidate Targets

The functional and physical entities that would serve as targets for information warfare (IW) enable and support information processes at differing levels of abstraction. They include the public switched network (PSN), the automated teller machine networks (such as Most and Cirrus), the financial transaction network; electronic money; credit; the Global Command and Control System (GCCS); tactical Command, Control, and Communications (C3); medical nets; corporate nets; weather; cars; petroleum and gas transport; logistics; process controls; interfaces; transportation; the air traffic control system; the nascent intelligent vehicle highway system; and others.

These functional entities hide an incredibly complex set of physical entities that continually evolve and change, usually completely transparently to everyone except for the person applying the change. To complicate matters, the functional entities represent interests that may additionally share physical infrastructure elements with other functional entities. This introduces the phenomenon of *nonlinear cascading effects*, where an attack on one functional entity may impact other functional entities or where an attack on a physical infrastructure element may impact multiple functional entities. The challenge of confining damage and impact is thus magnified, but so is the ability to target systems with predictable effects. Intuitively, it would seem that there should be linkages between functional entities and attack probabilities. Because of the intertwined state of international finance, a non-self-destructive nation attacking the U.S. financial system appears to be unlikely. The repercussions on their own economy would be unpredictable and probably unfortunate.

The targets that exist for infowar are widely varied. While the following listing examines many potential targets, there are ethical questions that arise over the prosecution of some of these targets. For example, currently it is agreed within the international community that the members of the health profession, whether or not in uniform, and health-related facilities will not knowingly be targeted during warfare. In fact, this notion is so widely subscribed that it becomes both a propaganda tool (accusing the enemy of bombing the hospital) and a protective measure (hiding military forces in a hospital to prevent them from being shelled). Extrapolating from this, it would be understandable if there were an adjunct at the Geneva Conventions negotiated proscribing direct attack on a medical support computer system. But what about utilizing the medical support system as a conduit for a weapon into enemy cyberspace? Would that be considered analogous to smuggling rifles in an ambulance?

The following are potential infowar targets:

- *Autonomous sensor systems* Sensors that are designed to operate autonomously (without human intervention) can be exploited to send false data back to the controlling system but can also be used as conduits for other infoweapons such as viruses, logic torpedoes, and worms.

- *C2 infrastructure* This includes the civilian and strategic leadership, the decision process, societal support structures such as the police, other governmental entities like the Bureau of Land

Management, and the strategic oil reserves. Attacking these targets can sow discord in an opponent's society, thereby fracturing the decision-making process or any consensus, denying an opponent the ability to marshal needed resources to rebuff an attack, or diverting attention from other activities.

- *Communications infrastructure*   The physical part of a communications infrastructure includes microwave antenna towers, switching stations, telephones, radios, computers, and modems. Nonphysical portions include the data, electrical systems, and management support systems.

- *Economy*   The economy of an entity is vulnerable to a variety of potential threats. These include control mechanisms (such as exchange rates, tariffs, and price controls), an electronic version of money (meta-money), financial support infrastructure (including money transfer systems and automated stock trading systems), and management systems that monitor the economy. Less directly, the mechanisms controlling a country's debt could be exploited.

- *Industrial Base*   Production lines, research and development efforts, and employment associated with the industrial base are attractive targets. Keeping a country from fielding an advanced system by creating or inducing errors in the system's development cycle not only can keep the country from having that capability, it can also create self-doubt in its ability to handle advanced technologies, thereby keeping it from trying new or innovative things. Planting agents in production lines and R and D centers can provide access to forward-base infoweapons. Providing employment by hosting industry on foreign soil can create predisposed favorable attitudes within that populace while providing access for propaganda and perception management activities.

- *Information infrastructure*   Computers, networks, and media are self-evident targets in infowar, for physical destruction, denial of service, soft kill, and exploitation. Additional targets include overnight mail delivery companies, fax machines, and the public telephone system.

- *Logistics*   The modern logistics system is dependent to a high degree on the computer backbone that identifies supply requirements, positions materials, tracks deliveries, and schedules resources. Attacks on that backbone can severely impact the ability of the dependent forces to establish or maintain a deployment.

■ *Medical support systems* Medical technology, such as laser surgery, anesthesia, and gamma ray imaging, is controlled by computer systems (and dependent on electricity). In the drive to increase the productivity of the medical profession and to decrease the cost of medical services, an increasing percentage of patient support services are also relying on computer from billing to medicine dispensing to life-support systems.

■ *Power grid* Physical support structures such as power stations and transformer nodes are vulnerable to physical destruction and denial of service. Degrading control system reliability can lead to voluntary shutdown of systems, particularly if there is a perceived threat of physical harm. An example would be compromising the reliability of a nuclear power station control system. Another vulnerability would be creating a power sink in the system that drains power out, creating brownouts and blackouts. A secondary effect would occur on systems depending on the power grid for electricity, such as civilian infrastructure computer systems. The public memory and continuing apprehension regarding the Northeast Power Blackout of 1965 serves to illustrate the possible effect on public order.

■ *Public infrastructure* Elements of the public infrastructure such as libraries, local databases (e.g., Department of Motor Vehicles), and tax records are prime targets for exploitation and data manipulation. Holding such elements hostage could be effective strategies in infowar.

■ *Public transit* The classical lines of communication are the sea, air, and rail lines, all of which are computer-dependent in modern societies. Cutting these lines dilutes or denies the opponent the ability to move mass quantities of anything—information (e.g., newspapers), people, food, medical supplies, or weapons. Additionally, there are psychological consequences that result in creating holes in the supply system. Interfering with the control of these systems (for example, rail schedules) would create cascading chaos.

■ *Smart systems* Microprocessor-controlled products, such as cars and planes, robotics and other expert systems, wired buildings, intelligent transportation systems, and network management systems (such as traffic sniffers) are potential targets.

■ *Training* If the enemy fights as they train, by subverting the training system, one can degrade their ability to fight. Subversion is possible by subtly changing the rules of the game, by altering the data, or by feeding false stimuli into the system (such as leaking doctored portions of military training manuals).

Intelligence Preparation

Conceptually, an IW attack consists of applying a weapon to a physical part of an information system in order to induce an effect with military or national impact. At some point, all attack plans must identify which specific components of the system—ranging from the 0s and 1s that represent the data through to and including the persons in the system—will be attacked with what weapon or weapons in order to have an operable plan. A complicating factor is that many of the physical entities that underlie the intricately interconnected information infrastructure support not a single function but many functions. An attack, therefore, must be designed to take this into account, perhaps even exploiting this feature (Figure 18-6).

The extent to which this information is acquired will play a large role in determining the objectives of an offensive program. For example, a foreign entity with little access to data on a particular information system probably will have difficulty designing an effective weapon to accomplish a specific task, planning and implementing an attack, and determining the effectiveness of the attack. As a result, the foreign entity, in this case, may choose only to use the weapon to harass and would accept as positive any degradation of performance that they are lucky enough to pro-

Figure 18-6
Intelligence.

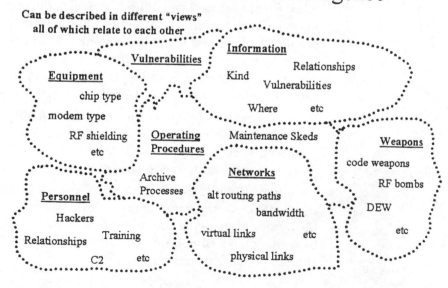

Essential Elements of Intelligence

duce. On the other hand, if the objectives of the foreign entity are to produce a specific response within a certain time frame, they could not confidently use the weapon. Thus, a lack of information would likely preclude employing the information weapon.

As with all other forms of warfare, intelligence information is the key to developing and employing effective information warfare plans and operations. Whether developing a system to degrade foreign fighting capabilities or protecting military information systems, detailed technical information on the target's hardware, software, and operations is essential. The degree to which the attackers are able to acquire information on the targeted system will determine the degree to which analysis of exploitable vulnerabilities may be used. This includes access to the targeted system and weapon employment opportunities. This is the means to design efficient and effective delivery vehicles and weapons, and to develop useful measures of effectiveness.

Correlative to the classic *Intelligence Preparation of the Battlefield* (IPB) in conventional warfare, intelligence preparation for infowar is even more important to success in any potential conflict.

Comprehensive Strategic Information

Comprehensive intelligence data is required for the identification of targets. It is also required in order to identify potential opponents, to know or be able to guess the intentions of those opponents, and to predict what actions those opponents will be predisposed to take. Cybersensors need to be developed to collect intelligence in cyberspace, and full use should be made of *open source intelligence* (OSINT), *electronics intelligence* (ELINT), *communications intelligence* (COMINT), *computer intelligence* (COMPUINT), and other sources of data. Data-gathering techniques will need to be refined, to collect important information while not overloading the intelligence evaluating community with meaningless or useless information. Intelligent targeting of systems, such as Advanced Intelligent Network control systems, can produce rich results.

Mapping of the cyberspace topography could be done in artificial or imaginary terms, as opposed to physical terms such as geographic, but it is key to understanding paths and vulnerabilities. In the conduct of any campaign, it is necessary to know where the opponent is located. Identifying network nodes gives a framework for operations planning. Using data-gathering tools, such as those of network management, this information can be gathered automatically. To do so is, of course, a double-edged sword, since open source methodologies are subject to other-side infowar initiatives and provide rich opportunities for disinformation.

An *Information Order of Battle* (IOB) needs to be created and maintained, identifying systems, networks, and facilities in terms that are useful for targeting (Figure 18-7). As a result of understanding what the IOB consists of and what are normal operations, triggering incidents that indicate activities can be linked to infowar *Defense Conditions* (Def Cons), which in turn can provide real-time guidance to planning and executing operations.

Infoweapons Damage Assessment (IDA) can be calculated for destruction or denial on this capabilities baseline, using the same techniques as the data-gathering process to determine if a system is still operational.

Information Order of Battle

- ## IOB Could Be Comprised Of Various Pieces:
  - ### Data Base
    - Combine elements of already existing databases with new elements
    - Automated data collection over Internet
  - ### Automated Analyses Tools
    - Time is an attribute humans can't process fast enough
    - Too much information for humans to deal with
    - "Maps" continuously change
  - ### Innovative Display
    - While in physical space things don't change very often, in Cyberspace they change continually. In order to understand what Cyberspace looks like, time must be an inherent feature of the display.

Figure 18-7   Information Order of Battle.

Weapons Capabilities

Part of the intelligence effort must be *Scientific and Technical Intelligence* (S&TI) to be used in determining what the vulnerabilities of the enemy IOB are and what effect our infoweapons have on their systems as well as what infowar capabilities they have. This type of intelligence data can be used for targeting and for developing countermeasures against the opponent's infowar capabilities.

Metric for Success

The metric used to identify success is of primary importance in waging any campaign. The method for measuring success and progress must be defined succinctly and in measurable terms, with a definite end goal.

It is not sufficient to define what success means in terms of the conflict being considered. The metric for success must additionally take into account what the opponent's metric may be. Specifically, the measure of success used must be in direct opposition to the opponent's measure of success, for the very simple reason that otherwise there can be no resolution of the conflict. If the opponent measures success in terms of occupying and controlling territory (whether physical or in cyberspace), then a goal of simply containing the enemy is probably not going to be sufficient.

Additionally, the metric must be achievable. A goal of converting every Christian into a devout Muslim is clearly not achievable; neither is the converse.

Possible Enemies

The traditional opponents faced across the negotiating tables that comprise the prospective antagonists in a conventional warfare situation may not comprise the total set of possible antagonists in an information war, particularly one fought in the dimension of cyberspace. Enemies used to be ideological enemies; today there may be economic enemies who are also political friends. The competing interests of other geopolitical units (e.g., countries) are most easily identified and understood. There are established diplomatic protocols that serve as a conduit for information and the intelligence-gathering process is in tune with activities that may constitute a threat to national interests.

Our world is evolving towards a pluralistic society fostered by communications. This implies that cyberspace topography is gaining in importance with respect to the more classical geopolitical units based on geographic location. Corporations, economic partners, ideological groups—all possibly unlocatable in the classical sense—may present direct or indirect threats in the future. The global information networks are allowing the development of a new class of antagonist as well: demographic groups held together with a bond of common interest but not physically collocated.

Identification of these entities and the threats they represent will be a task for the intelligence gatherers. The challenge presented by this changing world is only partially one of collecting pertinent information in enough time to protect and defend against any attack, however. Another equally formidable piece to this challenge is the protection of individual rights and freedoms while pursuing that goal of national defense.

Phases of Conflict

Infowar can, like more conventional types of warfare, exist in various forms such as terrorist, guerrilla, limited, theater, or strategic. It may exist independently or be an adjunct to other warfare operations. Its phases, like those of its counterparts, are peace, crisis, and hostilities. At each phase the dimension of infowar may be fully, partially, or not at all engaged, depending on the situation. Additionally the dimension of infowar may engage in phase escalation far in advance of other dimensions of a conflict according to the specific contribution it may make. These phases may be characterized at a high level in the following terms:

- *Peace* Monitor and collect strategic intelligence; "position" opponents; influence decision-making process; implement Theodore Roosevelt's Big Stick Policy; prevent conventional/nuclear conflict; succeed economically, politically, and ideologically.
- *Crisis* Control evolution of the crisis.
- *Conflict or hostilities* Minimize own losses; prevent or enhance collateral damage; successfully conclude engagement.

The objective at each phase is to achieve specific goals in support of national interests. The goal may be to prevent escalation of a conflict or perhaps to deter conflict altogether. Conversely, the goal may be to prosecute a campaign to its ultimate conclusion. The goals must be defined in terms of the metric for success, and this will help define the strategies and tactics utilized in any given phase.

Questions abound, including: What is national security? What should the role of the defense community be? What is the relationship of infowar to intelligence? How can IW threats be treated appropriately without eviscerating the Constitution? What is IW in a practical sense? How much money should be spent on *defensive IW* (DIW), and who should manage that expenditure? What exactly is DIW and how can it be implemented in a practical sense? It is a measure of the complexity of this challenge, in terms of both technical details and paradigmatic change, that these questions are not easily answered.

Intuitively, IW seems like a good thing. It is potentially less than lethal and conceptually has the promise of delivering a knockout punch at the weigh-in (to paraphrase Vice Admiral (retired) Jerry O. Tuttle). Both the defense community and society as a whole are using information processing technologies to leverage existing resources and the very ubiquity of those technologies make them seem like a pervasive commodity waiting to be exploited for competitive purposes.

However, the concept of IW grows less tractable the more thought given to it. Our vulnerabilities are obvious—and seemingly endless. Our level of understanding of what exactly those vulnerabilities are is low, as is our understanding of how the exploitation of vulnerability would affect diverse information-rich logical functions such as the financial infrastructure.

To further terrify us, it is clear that we as a nation do not have a lock on the technologies involved. This is not like nuclear physics—information processing technologies are taught and used worldwide. Further, because of the increasing interconnectivity of the global information infrastructure, international standards are in some cases spontaneous, thereby creating uncontrollable vulnerabilities that could be exploited by causing cascading effects to ripple through the global Net.

This new state of affairs comes close on the heels of the end of the Cold War. It is an interesting exercise to consider the strategy with which we ended the Cold War and then to consider its application in an information rich world. That strategy was, of course, the high-technology arms race. Whether the United States could have actually fielded the technologies at stake or not is still a matter of debate, but it is fairly clear that we were much more prepared to up the ante monetarily and our opponent simply could not keep spending at that rate. The technologies in question were esoteric, with limited application in other venues.

What would happen in an IW arms race? Consider the technologies involved: computer science, network engineering, software engineering, electrical engineering, ergonomics, psychology, and information engineering, to name merely a few. These are not esoteric but the lifeblood of contemporary community. These technologies are widely available in a "third-wave country" (as described by the Tofflers) such as Germany or Japan, but would require some (small) investment for a first or second wave nation. If such a nation decided that they had to develop a robust IW capability, they would first and foremost increase their knowledge base in those areas. Emphasis would be placed on sending students to universities and training programs with the end goal of being able to recruit some of them into the nascent IW program. Not all of the students would be either good enough or with the appropriate level of trustworthiness, so some percentage of those students would be allowed to use their skills in society at large. These students would bring with them the expectation of using information tools in their lives and would be prone to adapting environments to fit their particular skill sets.

After only a few years of following such a strategy, the nation could conceivably have a stronger economy regardless of whatever IW capability might ensue. Additionally, the nation would have developed a much more robust understanding of information system vulnerabilities and have implemented steps to protect their own systems, with obvious implications to the U.S. intelligence community as well as any potential aggressor.

IW is based on some fairly precise and common technologies, but it is difficult to explain to those not intimately familiar with information technologies why IW is dangerous. Trying to discuss the implications of covert channels or timing attacks is challenging. It comes as no surprise, therefore, that the emphasis to date in the public debate about IW has focused on hacking. This is dangerous because it dilutes the appreciation of the real problem: an organized attack against the information infrastructure of the United States. When would an attack be of strategic significance? Is it one that takes down Wall Street for a day? Probably not. Is it one that takes down 90 percent of the functionality of the New York Stock Exchange, the American Stock Exchange, the Port of New York and New Jersey, the Port of Long Beach, and the air traffic control system for a week? Maybe. Such an attack would certainly ripple through the American economic community, but would it be of sufficient magnitude to be more than a blip analogous to Hurricane Andrew, the

Northeast Power Blackout of 1965, or the Blizzard of 1996? The answer is debatable because we lack the context and understanding with which to answer such a question.

Understanding conceptually how an attack of strategic significance could be mounted is a first step in developing the needed context. The marshaling of resources and knowledge to attack one target implies a baseline of complexity, but the addition of each new target makes the proposition exponentially more difficult. Further, if the targeting has the intention of preventing reconstitution of capability, then secondary targets must also be attacked. In addition to the direct resources involved, conducting such an operation requires a very large amount of intelligence information. Where are the critical vulnerabilities, how can they be attacked, and how will the attacks be coordinated are merely the most obvious questions. Additional information required for the attackers includes understanding the timing required for successful attacks and what actions would be required to prevent immediate reconstitution of the target, as well as being able to predict effects with some degree of certainty. These are nontrivial requirements.

Intelligence activities must precede actual operations in all cases—for more-conventional warfare, the intelligence collected and analyzed provides targeting information, including location and characterization, as well as indicators of the importance of the target. In information warfare, these qualities are still in place. The question arises when the mode of operation is considered. In conventional warfare, the military commander decides upon the application of a weapon to a target after reviewing the situation and making a strategic or tactical decision. The order to put "iron on the target" is carried out by warfighters either directly or from weapons systems platforms. In information warfare, the order to attack a target will come from the military commander as well, but who will put the *virtual* iron on the target?

This has always been a tricky question in that the intelligence practitioners in our society have been strictly segregated from the operators. This is due to our culture, history, and values, and is strictly reflected in our legal and administrative structures. However, the burgeoning field of information warfare, which is often an insidious application of electronic computing technologies to conflict between parties, is beginning to blur those lines to a point where we are now having to face the question of whether our intelligence apparatus can and should be used in offensive operations.

The nature of some *information warfare* operations is that you either use the person or team most familiar with the system to be attacked, which can be an intelligence community professional, or you must train someone to perform the operation. This could be analogous to having a choice between a certified automobile mechanic and an engineer working on a broken car: The engineer certainly has the capability to figure out what is wrong with the car and eventually fix it, but the mechanic will be able to do it correctly the first time, in less time, with the right parts and tools, and with all the tricks of the trade that day-to-day hands-on experience brings.

Is it right or proper to order individuals from the intelligence community to insert malicious software into opposing systems, manipulate or destroy data in enemy databases, or disrupt enemy decision processes? This question spans our concept of governance to include separation of powers and our moral values, as well as our concept of just warfare. We can look at why it might be desirable to use intelligence professionals for IW operations and what dangers would be engendered by their usage.

Potential Contributions

To frame the discussion, it is first worthwhile to question whether in fact there are contributions that intelligence professionals can bring to the conduct of information operations that are demonstrably unique—different or better than could be harnessed without that contribution. What intelligence operators can contribute that is worthwhile include the following:

1. Knowledge of the information targets at an amazing level of detail
2. Knowledge of how the targets are used and how they can best be manipulated, destroyed, and altered to accomplish the most meaningful results
3. Understanding of trade-offs between exploiting a target for classic intelligence purposes and performing operations on that target— the classic equity problem

The intelligence community has long been collecting very detailed information on enemy communications, command and control systems, and leadership relationships. The professionals who collect and analyze that information have an in-depth knowledge of the physical structures, but also the logical structures, the inherent weaknesses, and the vulnerabilities. The reflexive knowledge these individuals would bring to an information operation would far eclipse someone with more generic skills, however smart and intuitive. Familiarity with the systems in question would allow real-time operation changes with higher probabilities of success.

The characteristics of having spent time looking at lots of information, having developed an intuitive feel for the data and the relationships between the types of data, having experienced operational cycles in the targeted system, and having a holistic vision of the system beyond the individual components are invaluable. This knowledge, tempered by the ingrained appreciation of the intrinsic value of the intelligence data placed at risk, compromised, or destroyed by the operation, adds dimension to the experience. This combination of attributes can be characterized as a kind of wisdom or knowledge maturity. It is not that someone else could not develop the intuitive feel for the information, systems, and targets that the intelligence professionals have, but it is in fact the case that it would take a significant amount of time for a second party to replicate that understanding.

Dangers Lurking

There can be considered to be two kinds of intelligence for the purposes of this discussion: that which is military in nature, such as the location and intentions of an opposing tank battalion, and that which is civil in nature, such as the organization of an adversary's leadership. This is by no means a clean division, but it serves as a framework within which to consider the role of intelligence professionals in a warfare scenario. As the physical distance from the battlefield increases, the role of the intelligence professional in the actual conduct of the war has tended to decrease. The intelligence analyst with the army battalion is intimately engaged in the execution of hostile acts. The intelligence analyst at the Pentagon is remotely engaged if at all. The intelligence analyst at the FBI is not at all engaged.

What dangers are there in allowing intelligence professionals to participate in operations? The conventional argument is that there are currently divisions between the collectors and analyzers of intelligence data, and the practitioners of warfare and national policy that protect each side. The practitioners of national policy and the warfighters are able to go into conflict scenarios without the danger of endangering national security. Additionally, it is one thing to have NSA employees perform operations (they can be considered to be part of the military arm of the United States government even though the Agency itself is an independent agency of the U.S. government for whom the Department of Defense acts as executive agent); it is another thing altogether to have intelligence professionals from other parts of the intelligence community perform operations. The candidate organizations potentially affected include not only the CIA but also the Departments of Energy, Treasury, and Justice.

On the other side of that coin, intelligence professionals who are tasked solely with collecting and analyzing intelligence without being responsible for the use to which that data is put are intellectually freed from having to worry about whether the data they are collecting is useful or not, what the data will be used for, or the morality of their activities—issues that the operators must always confront. In short, there is a globality of responsibility that we have judged to be desirable in protecting.

An additional and very important argument is that to give the people who have detailed privileged information the ability to act on that information is to effectively create a monster of untenable proportions that would soon be uncontrollable. Absolute power corrupts absolutely; who would guard the guards?

This is probably the most controversial and important of all the arguments. Once the power to act has been given to those who know, strong controls must be levied on those who do act to protect those values that we as a society hold dear.

Uniqueness of IW

The problem, as discussed previously, is that when one is considering the realm of information warfare, the realities of IW operations run very close to what military intelligence is. As warfare has evolved from hand-to-hand combat through the various stages of mass and attrition warfare to maneuver warfare and coordinated precision strikes, the level of information required to fight those wars has increased proportionately with the level of technology utilized, thereby engendering a professional class of information gatherers.

As information becomes more useful and increasingly necessary to the conduct of warfare, the class of individuals closest to that information become increasingly of value. Their normal and everyday activities range from that of analyzing the enemy's ability to conduct warfare to discerning exploitable weaknesses in an enemy's information systems (physical and logical). This translates directly into a vital skill for successful information warfare operations.

IW is the information dimension to warfare. It follows that the individuals most knowledgeable about information would be most useful to the conduct of operations in that dimension. For example, the intelligence professional whose job it is to surreptitiously enter into a database and remove copies of the data stored there is best suited for the job of intruding into that database to change or destroy the data. He or she knows where the weaknesses are, where the traps are, and where the potential for exploitation lies. If the professional didn't, he or she would not be successful in his or her duties as intelligence gatherer. Developing the detailed knowledge required to support an operation to deny, degrade, or destroy an opponents air defense system requires that the organization charged with devising the plan and executing the operation would need to collect and analyze intelligence data from many different sources to understand exactly what the operational procedures are for the system, what the operating components are, where the known vulnerabilities are, and where the unknown vulnerabilities are. This, of course, is the classic quadrant of knowledge as depicted here. It is a valuable asset to the person who knows not only what is known, but also what is unknown and what is unknowable. An effective attack would avoid doors that are known by the system owners to be open; these doors may be part of a trap or at least watched. Additionally, the operational schedule needs to be known so that the attack is made at the most auspicious time—the cyberspace analogy to attacking at dawn.

The sensitivity of sources and methods is hinted at by the above discussion but is a nontrivial part of this problem. An additional value accrued to the professional class of gatherers comes from those sources and methodologies used to get the information. The intelligence required to support the above-described type of operation is of necessity far ranging and in depth. The sources and methods to collect this type of data are highly sensitive and if compromised would reveal much about the way that we can and do collect information, on our adversaries as well as our friends. Before the concept of information warfare became a viable reality, it was expedient to relegate the collectors and analyzers of this information to a tightly controlled and shielded enclave. The more people who are exposed to the information thus protected incrementally decreases the totality of security. This in and of itself is a strong argument for using the individuals who already have the access to conduct the operation, rather than clearing in more people. As time periods leading to conflict or war shorten, this argument becomes more compelling. The time required to vet (perform a thorough background investigation) an individual's trustworthiness may be eclipsed by the requirement to act decisively and quickly.

The logical next question is whether that level of knowledge is really required. This in-depth knowledge is required for the operator because when dealing with complex systems, such as computer systems, alternatives are needed in case the original plan is untenable. The person carrying out the operation has to know what to do if something goes wrong or the configuration is changed or some aspect of the plan needs to be changed or modified. This type of knowledge is currently restricted to the intelligence community, but as IW operations become more viable, there will be more arguments over who will do it. The infantry does not currently have the expertise. The only people who do are the classic INFOSEC community and the more unique intelligence collectors. To share this knowledge with operators is to expose some very sensitive national secrets, as well as require operators to gain some very highly specialized expertise.

Potentials

Surely a compromise exists, and it is imperative that the compromise be engineered with full comprehension of the potential problems, traps, and pitfalls that surround the advantages of any particular solution. An idea that may stimulate the discussion is the concept first published by Martin Libicki and Jim Hazlett in the Summer 1997 *Joint Forces Quarterly*: "Do We Need an Information Corps?" The question may not in fact be whether we need an information corps, but how to harness the one that already exists without endangering liberty, freedom, and privacy.

The range of solution space includes:

1. Use the best talent for IW operations wherever it is found

2. Use only military personnel for IW operations

3. Develop some solution in between

Concepts that must be considered in this exercise include the separation of powers, governance, oversight, safeguards, and operating procedures. Given that, some notions that might be considered baseline concepts are as follows:

■ The individual giving the order to attack cannot be someone with a conflict of interest. An individual with an outstanding loan in a foreign country cannot be allowed to be the person ordering an attack on the banking system of that country.

- Safeguards must be established to prevent unjust gain from the operation. Just as we do not allow our military members to plunder conquered troops or villages, neither should the operator or the team be allowed to plunder conquered systems.

- Human rights must be safeguarded. When a conflict arises and the decision to attack an adversary is made, reasonable steps must be taken to prevent protected entities, such as hospitals, from being attacked.

- If systems are taken prisoner, those systems may be considered to be eligible for reasonable protection in accordance with the values reflected by the Geneva Conventions. While at first blush this may seem laughable, consider that these systems have the potential for containing data of extreme value to the human race, including parts of the human gene mapping or control of tissue.

Wrap-Up

IW is unique. Weapons deployment requires specific planning based on knowledge of the target, the method in which the weapon is to be used to insure the highest probability of success, and the goal to be accomplished. Comprehensive strategic intelligence is required for target identification, coordination of attack methodologies and to gain a sense of the opponent's intentions. Critical to IW is the IOB or Information Order of Battle, which is composed of automated databases, automated analysis tools, and innovative displays. Critical to an IW deployment is the metric used to measure success of the attack.

CHAPTER 19

Public Key Infrastructure: Building Trust Online

Building Trust Online with PKI

Information technology (IT) tools are essential to a company's ability to maintain profitability in today's economy. However, the central principle of "doing business" remains the same: Find a need (modern translation: "niche") for a product or service in the marketplace and fill it. Today the easiest way to fill a niche better, faster, and cheaper than the competition is to employ IT to automate tasks and allow easier flow of business information. However, firms who increase their connectivity with customers, suppliers, and business partners must address the increased risk such interfaces bring.

As always, firms must document the "who, what, where, when, and how" of their transactions to demonstrate their ability to be profitable. Computers do this very well. Automated logs rapidly record transactions. However, they do this blindly, as they only record information presented to them. To ensure firms are recording valid and accurate information, they must employ information technology tools that ensure the confidentiality, integrity, and availability of their transactions. Firms must ensure they are talking to their customers and business partners to preclude the loss of reasonable control of vital business information. Deploying *Public Key Infrastructure* (PKI) with other carefully planned *information security* (IS) policies and practices provides firms with a cost-effective means to capture, store, and protect vital business information.

In its most basic form, PKI is an attempt to employ proven mathematical relationships implemented through hardware and software, to establish trusted relationships among users, computers, and applications within a network. Therefore, the physical and logical details of the PKI implementation must be trustworthy. *An error in the trustworthiness of the implementation casts reasonable doubt on all trust relationships built upon that implementation.* For this reason, firms must design, document, build, and periodically test the entire PKI implementation to ensure the trustworthiness of its operation. In today's system engineering shops, it is all too common to hide a lack of good engineering practices behind concepts such as rapid application development (RAD). When considering PKI, firms should not circumvent sound engineering processes and discipline.

Although industry has yet to widely implement PKI, there appears to be general acceptance of its principles. PKI is an attempt to bring to cyberspace the feeling of trust that develops from traditional, face-to-face transactions. Though many consider PKI premature and often cite costly, failed attempts at its deployment, there have been success stories that signify a growing trend towards its widespread use[1]. In fact, the Department of Defense has directed the deployment of PKI throughout its Defense Information Infrastructure by October 2001.[2]

DoD has a history of requiring business partners to operate at the same or greater levels of IT capability. DoD and its prime contractors conduct business in nearly every sector of private industry on some level.

The decision to develop PKI is shifting from "whether to" to "when to" deploy it. PKI is an emerging, but viable *means of building trust* into electronic commerce relationships. However, PKI changes the business process by altering the way users interact with their systems. Therefore, deciding to deploy PKI is a *business decision* rather than a *technology decision only*. Therefore, firms who require or desire to build trust into their automated processes should involve all functions in the planning, design, implementation, and deployment of PKI.

PKI Overview

Although some young IT professionals might find this hard to believe, fast food restaurants used to fill your soda for you. Simply put, there were no free refills. Distributing soda was a customer service function, which was why they located the machine behind the counter. Today, customers are performing this function themselves (literally at the same and/or higher prices). Modern fast food business models have obviously found that it is cheaper to transfer the control (i.e., "trust") of soda consumption to their customers than pay employees to perform this service. Thus, they have moved the soda machine to the customer's side of the counter.

Mentally transposing this visual example of blurred boundaries between firms and their customers onto information-intensive businesses emphasizes their need to control internal and external interfaces. Information security is the practice of gaining said control. Reaching into recent history again, recall the late-night public service announcement that stated: "It's 10 o'clock. Do you know where your children are?" Perhaps a more modern example for IT firms is, "It's anytime day or night. Do you know where your vital business information is?" Firms must implement IS so their customers have confidence that they know the answer to this question.

Although public key encryption has been available for more than two decades, it is now the latest technology that organizations are pushing to deploy. Three factors driving interest in public key encryption are as follows:

1. Growth of intranets and extranets

2. The exploding e-commerce market

3. An increasingly mobile and remote workforce

In these open network environments, public key cryptography provides identification, authentication, confidentiality, message/transaction integrity, and nonrepudiation. Thus, with public key cryptography, any organization can control access to its network and guarantee the validity of its electronic transactions.

As Harry DeMaio writes in the article "Getting Started in PKI":

...PKI is a system for publishing the public-key values used in public-key cryptography. There are two basic operations common to all PKIs:

1. Certification is the process that binds a public-key value to an individual, organization, other entity, or even some other piece of information, such as a permission or credential.

2. Validation is the process that verifies that a certificate is still valid.

How these two operations are implemented is the basic defining characteristic of all PKIs."[3]

PKI allows users to interact with other users and applications, obtain and verify identities and keys, and register with trusted third parties. It sounds simple, but pulling together the infrastructure to support public key cryptography is a complex process, as shown in Figure 19-1.

In general, PKI includes the following components to support the use of public key cryptography:

■ *Certificate authority (CA)* Entity that issues and revokes certificates for a set of subjects and is ultimately responsible for their authenticity. Someone with a high level of trust must manage it.

■ *Registration authority (RA)* Performs functions related to verification of identity and registration information. This allows the separation of the functions of certificate issuance and signing (by the CA) and verification of identity and registration.

■ *Public key certificate directory* Stores public key certificate information in a central location. Directories are usually based on the X.509 ISO telecommunications standard.

Figure 19-1
PKI supports users of
trust relationships.

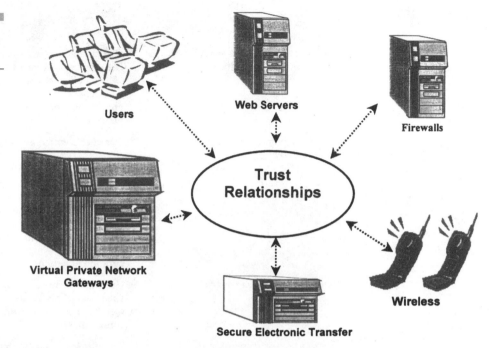

■ *Certificate revocation list (CRL)*   This is a directory structure or data structure for publishing certificates that have been revoked. If a certificate is compromised, if the holder's authorization expires, or if there is a fault in the binding of the certificate to the holder, it is revoked and placed on the CRL. The CRL is created by the CA and is a list of serial numbers that have been revoked during their validity period and which should not be trusted. The CRL v2 protocol defines several reasons which might be included as an extension, such as lost but not compromised. This list is then signed by the CA's private key, thus ensuring the integrity of the data and its authenticity. This list is generally available first from the CA and alternatively from a directory. The directory may be set up as an entry for the CA and could have a certificate attribute such as "certificate-revocation-list:binary" in which current values of the list would be stored for download.

In addition to these components, PKI must describe the management protocols firms will use for certificate management functions such as registration, validation, issuance, and revocation. Examples of these protocols include PKIX Certificate Management Protocol (CMP) and message formats such as Certificate Management Message Format (CMMF) and Public-Key Cryptography Standards (PKCS). The Public-Key

TABLE 19-1

Basic Concepts to Consider Prior to Investing in PKI.

Question	Concerns/Issues
What are the risks associated with relying on digital certificates?	■ PKI changes business processes by altering the way users interact with systems. ■ Nonrepudiation may preclude misbehavior by some users, while strong encryption may encourage others to use systems for criminal activity.
Can the current infrastructure support PKI?	■ Use of encryption impacts system performance. ■ PKI-enabling applications incurs development costs, and some legacy applications cannot be made PKI-enabled. ■ Users need real-time access to public key directories. ■ Cost/benefit analysis should compare functionality of PKI against required infrastructure modifications.
How are certificates used?	■ Certificates can authenticate (trust) users and their transactions, etc. ■ Certificates can be used with encrypted communications.
Where are certificates stored?	■ Certificates can be stored in tokens or workstations. ■ Management of certificate authorities can be done in-house or outsourced, or some form of hybrid system can be developed. Whatever the system, the method of implementing the CA is critical to ensuring that users can trust the CA and all subsequent trust relationships.

Cryptography Standards are a set of standards for public key cryptography developed in cooperation with an informal consortium (Apple, DEC, Lotus, Microsoft, MIT, RSA and Sun) that includes algorithm specific and algorithm independent implementation standards.

Other protocols allow users to easily verify certificates and CRLs from directories, repositories, and other users. These are typically designed to work within the framework of existing protocols such as FTP, HTTP, Lightweight Directory Access Protocol (LDAP), and e-mail.

PKI also includes policies and guidelines, such as certificate policy and rules governing their usage, certificate practices statements, technical and administrative security controls, CA contractual requirements and documents, and subscriber enrollment and termination processes.

Firms that are investing in building the infrastructure for public key cryptography must address a number of questions, as outlined in Table 19-1.

A Basic PKI Architecture

After defining the functional requirements for PKI deployment, a firm must carefully consider the basic PKI architecture. It is important to note that there are many PKI components to assemble to provide the required functionality. The main building blocks are a CA and a network and application framework that can make use of the CA's certificates. Building PKI architecture requires careful consideration of the selected policies and procedures, hardware, software, organizational structure, and security measures. Firms should not underestimate the complexity of integrating the PKI building blocks based on the simplicity of the PKI model.

Policies and Procedures

The requirement for a disciplined approach to the design, implementation, and operation of PKI deployment starts with sound policies and procedures. While there are dozens of policies and procedures required for building and maintaining a trustworthy network, there are several policies unique to PKI that increase its functionality. The first of these is the *Certification Practice Statement*. This is a combination policy and practices document that states the details of design and maintenance of the CA. The management practices recorded in this document allow organizations to decide whether they are willing to trust certificates the CA publishes. It also lists the format and implementation details of the digital certificates that the CA creates.

Another document unique to a CA is the *certificate policy*. This policy documents how and under what circumstances a certificate is valid. The rules within this policy sets limits and conditions on the level of trust associated with the use of certificates. A certificate policy allows the users to decide how much trust to place in the certificate for a given use in a given environment. An example would be a certificate policy that states that a certificate was good only for verifying a purchasing agent's authority up to a maximum of $10,000 on a single purchase order.

An X.509-compliant digital certificate uses three extension fields in support of the applicable certificate policies:[4]

- *Certificate policies*   If flagged noncritical, this field lists certificate policies the CA declares are applicable uses but without excluding other uses for the certificate. If critical, this field lists the policies that outline the only allowable uses. This field may also convey qualifier values for each identified policy.

- *Policy mappings* "This extension may only be used in CA-certificates, i.e., certificates for certification authorities issued by other certification authorities. This field allows a certification authority to indicate that certain policies in its own domain can be considered equivalent to certain other policies in the subject certification authority's domain."[5]

- *Policy constraints* The first option for this field gives a CA the ability to require explicit certificate policies to be present in all subsequent certificates in a certification path. The second option allows a CA to disable policy mapping by subsequent certification authorities in a certification path. This keeps CAs from propagating inherited and transitive trust relationships among certificates issued at lower levels in a certification path.

One other policy document unique to a CA is the *cross-certification policy*. This document states how and under what conditions a CA will trust a certificate from a CA beyond its own certification path. In most real-world PKI implementations, cross-certification policies are necessary to implement working with outside organizations.

Hardware/Software Requirements

In any PKI architecture, the minimum hardware necessary is to have a dedicated server functioning as the CA, another one hosting the public directory, application servers that have been "PKI enabled," and workstations servicing user applications. The software needed to provide full PKI functionality comes in several specialized pieces that more or less parallel CA hardware. Table 19-2 lists the hardware and software required for implementing PKI functionality.

Security considerations require dedicated CA software. In fact, security of the CA server is so important to the trust level associated with its certificates that all firms using certificates to enable transactions requiring a high level of trust should design a technically and physically secure building around the CA server.

CA software is capable of generating digital certificates either directly or through interaction with end user software. Certificate generation involves creating two public and private key pairs: one is for encryption and the other for authentication or digital signature. Most CA implementations store private encryption keys in a secure, proprietary database. Many also store the information needed to recover a certificate upon the loss of the electronic copy. Such storage features are useful in

TABLE 19-2

Hardware/Software
Requirements for a
Basic PKI
Implementation.

Hardware Platform	Specifications	Software	Comments
CA Server	Server or high-end workstation	CA Application Secure OS	Dedicated, secure backups are essential.
Public Key Directory	Varies according to certificate population.	Normally an X.500- or LDAP-compliant directory.	Often replicated across an organization for easy, local access. Must be accessible to all certificate users and applications.
Certificate Revocation List	Varies according to number of certificates revoked.	CRL directory application.	Often replicated across an organization for easy, local access. Grows larger over time. Must be accessible to all certificate users and applications.
PKI-Enabled Application Server	Varies according to application.	Developer toolkits are available to help PKI-enable applications	Cost, technology, or system/network design may prohibit enabling some legacy applications.
User Workstation	Varies according to application	CA Workstation Client	Enables certificates storage, retrieval, and use.

most real-world implementations, as they compensate for personnel changes, and the loss or failure of storage tokens. Some CA implementations store only private encryption keys and only generate new certificates, if one is inadvertently destroyed. Another major feature of a CA is the ability to revoke certificates and add them to the CRL.

The next server needed is a host for the public key directory. This server must be made readable to all users and application servers intended to use the digital certificates that the CA issues. Because of this need for visibility, these directories are often replicated throughout an organization. Replication provides redundancy, assists performance, and allows the local environments to be maintained in a more secure fashion.

A directory may not be necessary in all PKIs. An architecture concerned only with identification and authentication will not necessarily require a directory. A directory is only concerned with distribution of certificates to non-owners of the certificate for encrypting documents to the owner. Application servers may not require directory assets at all. They may query the directory for purposes of downloading a copy of the CPRL to check validation of a certificate. Some processes are designed to be effective without a directory.

A CRL is usually created, signed and stored by the CA. Access to the CRL is generally separated from the CA for system loading in larger PKIs. This ensures the CA will be available to process revocation requests. The directory is used to certify additional users and process CRL requests. The CRL is a data structure stored on the directory as an attribute of the CA directory. The CRL data structure is downloaded on demand by applications requiring it. Of course, the size will vary greatly depending upon how a firm uses certificates. For example, a firm requiring new certificates for every tenth transaction might revoke thousands of certificates a day. It would be more productive for this firm to define a policy of short-lived certificates so expiration will occur and CRL lengthening would not become an issue. One firm, Security Dynamics, is creating a server that can issue session certificates good for only that session and then expire.

Another piece of the PKI hardware is the servers that host PKI-enabled applications. While these servers do not require more processing speed or power than ordinary application servers do, they must communicate with the public key directory and CRL to properly process digital certificates. In some designs, public keys are presented to web servers in the client authorization process and do not need to access the directory. Of course, firms must PKI-enable applications too. Before an application can automate the acceptance and use of digital certificates as a basis for creating a trusted relationship, it must be able to process them. PKI-enabled applications have the functionality to check digital signatures using the public keys associated with certificates and validate them using the public key of the issuing CA. There are several firms that offer developer toolkits that contain code libraries to help automate the task of enabling an application to use digital certificates.

Other hardware and software needed to support a PKI deployment are user workstations and the CA client. This software automates the generation, usage, storage, and validation of digital certificates on behalf of the user. It is essential to store digital certificates on user hardware (hard drive or token) in a manner that the user's workstation can read. This type of software also automates the tasks of destroying or invalidating a certificate whenever it is on the CRL.

The security of the generation, storage and use of private keys on the user workstation is a major consirn in the assurance level of a particular PKI. The CRL is also a public directory structure listing information on all certificates that the CA has revoked. Each time a certificate is validated using the public key of the issuing CA, the CRL should also be checked to ensure the issuing CA has not canceled or revoked it.

Organizational Structure

After completing the basic policies and specifications of hardware and software, firms must modify their organizational structure to support the management and operation of the CA. Each PKI will have different organizational and implementation specific needs that affect the management of the CA. However, the management structure required to support a CA comes from a couple of critical layers regardless of the implementation details.

In hierarchical order, the first layer is the *CA manager*. This management position is responsible for day-to-day security and operation of the CA in accordance with the set policies and procedures in the certification practice statement. The CA manager is also responsible for coordinating with a firm's management on the development of certificate and cross-certification policies.

The second management layer is the *registration authority* (RA). In most firms there are multiple RAs with each one responsible for its functional area organization. The RA is responsible for managing the creation, distribution, use, and revocation of certificates for its organizational element. The RA would provide input into the development of PKI policies and procedures consistent with the needs of its organization, such as the development of organizational procedures outlining the process for authenticating users and issuing certificates. Other RA roles would include identifying organizationally specific needs for certificate policies and cross-certification policies to the CA manager and senior organizational management.

The third management layer in the operation of a CA serves as a *local registration authority* (LRA). This position is similar in function to the RA. LRAs actually oversee the day-to-day approval, distribution, and revocation of certificates at the line level within a firm. This position is critical to most large firms with remote offices. The LRA makes PKI useful to the average user. Depending on the size of a firm, LRAs may be responsible for user training, CA client software installation, and handling of certificate issuance and revocation requests.

Security Measures

Security measures combine the policies and practices, hardware and software, and organizational elements required to implement a basic PKI infrastructure. Without the application of pertinent security measures, the CA would lack the stability and traceability necessary to gain user trust and acceptance. If potential users do not trust PKI, they will not use it.

A firm must develop policies, plans, and procedures that govern the design, implementation, and use of PKI within its organizational and physical environment. To ensure trust, a firm must implement security policies, plans, and procedures at the operational, physical, or technical layers of its organizational environment.

Operational policies, plans, and procedures address issues such as threat analysis, vulnerability analysis, personnel security, data security, computer security, and user training. Firms should consider this layer as the "people" layer. Its goal is to implement sound security policy, train users on their responsibilities, and hold them accountable for meeting those responsibilities.

Another layer of security management is the physical security layer. The goal of this layer is to prevent physical access to equipment or communications signals. If firms cannot secure CA hardware, software, data, and physical premises, there is no basis for trusting the CA. Physical access to computer equipment by unauthorized personnel always equates to the compromise of any trust in its implementation.

The final layer is the technical layer. This layer supplements the other two layers and often automates tasks associated with establishing and maintaining the security of a given CA. Examples of technical security measures include using intrusion detection technology, and virtual private networking technology and implementing best practices when installing and configuring computer and communications equipment.

PKI Deployment

Public key encryption is a promising technology that addresses many of the security issues arising as organizations expand their internal networks and provide access to their information systems for customers, suppliers, business partners, and other third parties. It is an enabling technology for electronic commerce, since public key encryption provides a means for user authentication, data integrity, confidentiality, and nonrepudiation. Thus, the interest in public key cryptography continues to grow. Despite the high demand for basic security services, <u>the IT industry has not deployed public key systems widely, because doing so requires the existence of developed PKI</u>.

PKI is in the early-adopter phase; therefore, the industry does not have extensive experience in building this infrastructure. Deploying PKI components requires planning and preparation. Specifically, firms need to realize that, although the goal of PKI is to build trust into the online business environment, in its effort to do so, PKI changes existing business processes. PKI deployment results in significant changes for users, application developers, network and system administrators, and security managers. Effectively managing these changes is key to successful implementation. Still, the potential benefits of public key systems result in most organizations considering "when" and not "if" they will deploy PKI.

Application Integration

PKI is a utility infrastructure, not an end in itself. It is useful and cost-effective only if firms apply it to many applications. Therefore, an important consideration is whether the applications are PKI-enabled. Applications must have the functionality to check digital signatures using the public keys associated with the certificates and to validate the certificates against the CRL by using the public key of the issuing CA. If the applications requiring PKI security are not PKI-ready, then modification or replacement is necessary. Also, firms must familiarize application developers with PKI and implement procedures for its use in application development efforts. This can significantly impact the PKI cost/benefit equation. Firms may find that application modification is very expensive and/or there are not enough PKI-ready replacement applications to justify the overhead of PKI.

Certificate Authority

The CA acts as a trusted third party, vouching for the certificate it issues. Establishing and maintaining trust in the CA is critical to acceptance of its certificates. Error in the trustworthiness of the implementation of the CA will cause suspicion in all trust relationships built upon that implementation. The trust level of the CA stems from the strength of the policies and procedures that establish it, so firms must carefully consider them before deployment.

Another policy that needs careful consideration from the onset of PKI deployment is cross-certification. Sooner or later users will need to connect with outside organizations, which means there will be a need to trust certificates that another CA validates. Therefore, firms must clearly define the policies and practices under which the CA will accept a certificate from another CA to build and maintain trust in the system.

Scalability

Deploying PKI in a corporate environment for internal purposes is the simplest implementation. Generally, the corporation already has a name space in which it identifies each employee by assigning a unique employee number. Firms can simply build on their existing structure by providing certificates that bind public keys to these unique employee numbers. In this manner, the corporation has control over the process and the computing environment, and therefore, infrastructure development for the CA is minimal.

The impact of extending PKI from supporting a few hundred corporate users to hundreds of thousands of users can be significant. Certificate management and maintaining CRLs becomes very complex when the user community is large and/or geographically dispersed. In such cases, it is necessary to establish multiple CAs, so system performance may also become an issue. The major effort and cost in developing and deploying a PKI is building the infrastructure. Registration is a function of certificate management and has a major cost impact for larger PKIs.

Scalability becomes even more complex when firms extend PKI to users outside the corporate environment. This is a realistic issue for e-commerce applications. Generally, multiple CAs are necessary, so firms must assess the impact PKI and its associated trust issues will have on systems performance. Perhaps the best approach of deploying PKI is to start with a carefully staged pilot project that gradually expands outward by adding applications and associated user communities. This methodology can limit the scope of a given implementation to support a manageable learning curve while also allowing for the incorporation of user feedback and lessons learned in future expansions.

Management and Administration

Figure 19-2 illustrates three options of CA management. The choice of the correct option depends on the user community and/or application. For example, a given company may choose to maintain its own CA for its corporate intranet applications and outsource the CA for customer-based applications. Proper decision making involves carefully considering the economics of multiple CAs, as well as the complexity of establishing trust relationships. Another consideration is the availability of experienced personnel. Because PKI is in the early-adopter phase, there are not many people who know how to deploy and administer it.

Regardless of the option chosen for administering the CA, PKI deployments must maintain a process administering CRLs. This may not be difficult for internal users with a single CA. However, it becomes extremely complex for electronic commerce applications with heterogeneous CAs that require real-time revocation. One company, ValiCert, reports that its product can process multiple CAs on a Validation server. In this way, all applications can request validation from a single source.

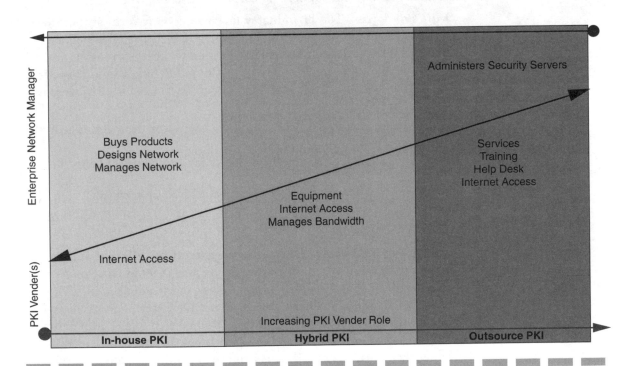

Figure 19-2   CA Implementation options.

Interoperability and Standards

PKI standards are still emerging. There is a risk associated with an investment in PKI components as these standards evolve. Because there are different standards for different types of certificates, certificates will require a high degree of interoperability. This issue becomes particularly significant once firms extend PKI beyond supporting corporate users on the intranet. Therefore, firms deploying PKI must carefully consider standards when planning their deployments to ensure continued interoperability in the future. Such planning should include decisions on:

■ *Legacy standards*   Perhaps the easiest method of avoiding the risk of interoperability is for a firm to deploy PKI based on its own standards. Firms know their own hardware, software and people, so developing standards on a system of limited scope should be relatively easy. However, it is likely that users will eventually need to connect with the outside world. If legacy standards are not broad enough, interoperability will become significant when the firm extends PKI beyond supporting corporate users on the intranet.

■ *Draft standards*   The IT industry is working on several standards that the IT community will likely adopt in the future. The bodies developing these standards usually promote wide distribution and review of draft standards before officially publishing them. However, a firm that selects a draft standard on which to base its PKI deployment faces risk in that:

1. Interpretation of the draft standard may vary from community to community.
2. The published, final standard may vary significantly from the draft.
3. The IT community may not adopt the selected draft standard. This is analogous to the choice between Beta or VHS standards for VCR systems.

■ *Evolution of technology*   There will very likely be different standards involving different types of certificates as new technologies emerge. Such certificates will require a high degree of interoperability. The concept of timing a business process is not new. However, rapid evolution of technology raises the question of when to implement a given solution set versus waiting for the next breakthrough to come onto the market. Firms facing the decision to expend time and energy now to deploy PKI must carefully consider the trade-off between entering the e-commerce market earlier than their competitors and, hopefully, capturing more business, or waiting until technological evolution makes it easier to deploy PKI.

Protecting Private Keys

PKI needs a means for protecting private keys. Various methodologies are available with differing security and cost trade-offs. For example, a PKI deployment might store private keys on a user's hard drive with password protection. Such systems use passwords to encrypt private keys. If the hard drive (or computer) is stolen, the problem of cracking the key is one of guessing the password. PIN-protected smart cards are another option for storing private keys. The chip in a smart card has the ability to perform signature and decryption operations, so the key never has to leave the smart card, significantly reducing the likelihood of compromise. However, using smart cards means deploying card readers and drivers, as well as the cards themselves.

Firms must also consider key recovery, shown in Figure 19-3. In a deployment of any size, it is likely that users will lose or forget keys regardless of how they are stored. If there is no provision for key recovery, the system is more secure but faces risk of a significant loss of productivity, if the users cannot access the system. Furthermore, if a firm opts for

Figure 19-3   Key recovery process.

key recovery, it must establish a secure process that has minimal impact on user productivity, while allowing for continued user confidence.

Regardless of the method chosen for protecting and/or recovering private keys, the mere existence of keys changes existing business processes. For example, if users routinely place their car keys and wallets in their desks upon arriving at the office, they are likely to continue this practice after a firm implements PKI. Therefore, firms might consider the use of biometrics to control system access. If a firm chooses to employ tokens (that go onto key rings) or smart cards (that go into wallets), then its change-management effort needs to focus on reshaping the users' behavior, which may compromise the security and trustworthiness intended to be inherent in the "new" system.

User Acceptance

Currently, the number of passwords users have to use is a source of frustration for them. Remote access authentication devices require users to carry, care for, and protect tokens. New technology such as public key systems will further confuse the user and complicate usage of the system. Users will probably have multiple keys to manage. For instance, the user may have two keys on one system, one for encryption and one for digital signatures, and two more for another system due to incompatible system formats. Therefore, a firm must incorporate change management in parallel with PKI deployment. Firms must plan for and institute training and awareness programs to promote and support user acceptance of PKI.

Business Case

PKI is a technology that solves the business problem of how to control access to the network and guarantee the validity of electronic transactions. It is a very exciting technology and has tremendous potential for enabling e-commerce. However, PKI is a utility that forces change into existing business processes. Firms must give careful consideration to the high cost of a PKI implementation, particularly if it does not accomplish the necessary planning, design, and preparation prior to deployment. As firms implement PKI in new applications and user communities, they should continue to carefully compare it with other technologies that might provide better solutions in their industries.

As mentioned, PKI is in the early-adopter stage. Nevertheless, a number of organizations, particularly in the financial community, are implementing it. Often, the first deployments are for specific applications or user communities. Once these are successful, the organization expands PKI to include other users and systems. Two examples of successful deployments follow.

Bank of Ireland

Public subscription established the Bank of Ireland by Royal Charter in 1783. In recent decades the bank has embarked on a strategy of becoming a broadly based financial services group by serving its home market while geographically diversifying its earnings by serving select markets abroad.

To exploit the era of Internet banking, the Bank of Ireland is deploying PKI for its Business On-Line service. Central requirements of the technology behind its Business On-Line service are ease of use and administration, flexibility in terms of integration with new and legacy systems, and the implementation of full-strength security.

Public key cryptography meets these requirements, and therefore, the bank has selected Baltimore's UniCert CA technology. Baltimore provided toolkits to allow the bank to security-enable both its browser-based Java applications and legacy systems. The system also allows for the complete management of digital certificates. Using Business On-Line, the bank's business customers will be able to use Web browsers to conveniently access a wide range of account services. The security that the underlying PKI provides will ensure the confidentiality of critical financial information, while maintaining an accurate, reliable record of transactions.

ABN AMRO Bank

The ABN AMRO Bank ranks among the top 10 largest banks in the world. Headquartered in the Netherlands, ABN AMRO has a presence in 74 countries and over 90,000 staff worldwide, and it provides universal banking services consisting of commercial and investment banking products to national and international corporate operating clients, as well as retail banking services for both personal and private banking customers. As a global bank, ABN AMRO needs a cryptographic infrastructure for use by internal, bank-to-bank, and customer-to-bank transactions worldwide.

Corporate Cryptographic Infrastructure (CCI) is the bank's initiative to deliver cryptographic services across their international infrastructure, in a consistent manner, to any user or application, on any computer platform, anywhere in the world. The main security components of CCI are cryptographic services for authentication, data integrity, confidentiality, and nonrepudiation, along with PKI for creating and revoking digital certificates and security management services. The bank's requirements were for a flexible system capable of easily integrating with a range of third-party products. The fundamental principle of CCI is that the utilization of cryptographic services should be both platform- and application-independent if it is to achieve its real potential. Furthermore, there is a clear trend toward adding security end-to-end and making it independent of the transport networks to achieve improved agility with security.

The Department of Defense Chooses PKI

Currently, the DoD plans to incorporate PKI into its Defense Information Infrastructure (DII) by October 2001.[6] DoD plans to have the initial operating capability for the PKI portion of its overall secure communications system in place with the full operating capability to be in place by March 2002. Although this is an ambitious effort when considering its scope, it is a clear example of the widening acceptance of PKI.

DoD PKI will serve as a cornerstone of the DoD Key Management Infrastructure (KMI), which is part of the layered information assurance specifications supporting the DoD Defense in Depth strategy for its massive array of information systems. The strategic design is to provide roadblocks at critical entry points and throughout the enterprise networks, as well as systems to thwart internal and external threats. Critical focus areas for the DoD strategy of protect, detect, and respond is to be layered throughout its IT environment. These focus areas include:

- Wide area networks connecting DoD systems, vendors/trading partners, other federal/state agencies, and allies
- DoD local area networks connection points to WANs
- Host servers, applications, operating systems, and communications hardware/software used on DoD LANs
- Introducing systems to detect and respond to intrusions at all levels,

analyze the intrusion signature, and provide timely, correlated data on the intrusion to entities throughout the enterprise

■ Provision of KMI services

The DoD definition of PKI includes the whole framework and all the services providing the generation, production, distribution, control, and accounting of public key certificates. Basically, the PKI will provide the support services necessary for the infrastructure to achieve secure encryption and authentication of network transactions, along with data integrity and nonrepudiation.

The overall plan for implementation of the PKI is extremely ambitious and will require extensive effort and coordination not only within the DoD framework but also with other federal agencies, commercial providers, industry standard groups, allied militaries, and governments. The Defense Information Systems Agency (DISA) and the National Security Agency are trying to ensure the DoD architecture achieves standard implementations and specifications by working with vendors and standards groups. They are trying to make sure this implementation meets DoD interoperability requirements through the tracking of emerging commercial standards from groups like the Internet Engineering Task Force (IETF) and working closely with the National Institute of Science and Technology (NIST) on federal standards.

In the DoD plan "Public Key Infrastructure Roadmap for the Department of Defense," DoD planners seem to have learned a valuable lesson from past mistakes with evolving technology.[7] There is apparently recognition that government-developed implementations will not be able to keep pace with the open-standards approach and the dynamics of the commercial IT environment, which constantly work to improve systems and applications. Unlike previous government-developed systems, this DoD system should be capable of keeping pace with and incorporating improvements made to the technology and interfacing with vendors and federal or foreign counterparts while maintaining appropriate levels of security.

Much of this "wisdom" on behalf of planners likely stems from the development and deployment of two other DoD PKI systems: the initial operational FORTEZZA PKI that supports the Defense Mail System (DMS) and a pilot medium-assurance-level PKI. Government off-the-shelf technology formed the basis of the FORTEZZA PKI effort. Most likely, this project contributed significantly to a better understanding of the dynamics of the technology development, resulting in the decision to work with and leverage the commercial marketplace.

This strategy will require the DoD to initially leverage the current capabilities available and to constantly monitor changes, improvements, and innovations in the marketplace to "grow" the PKI implementation into the complete system that it envisions. In other words, the design is to be flexible enough to evolve with the technology. The DoD is to use open commercial interfaces, cryptographic standards, and protocols, which it will ultimately define in the information architecture technical specifications. The DoD will also prohibit the use of nonconforming applications in this DoD PKI architecture. The objective of the DoD PKI is to provide certification services with the following characteristics:

- Is commercially based (to allow outsourcing to the extent practical)
- Is standards-compliant
- Supports many applications and products
- Provides secure interface/interoperability throughout DoD (to include its vendors, allies, and pertinent federal agencies)
- Supports key exchange with digital signature capability
- Supports key and data recovery
- Complies with Federal Information Processing Standard 140-1

Current government planning for DoD PKI requires two levels of security, with one protecting unclassified/sensitive information and one protecting classified information. The system will use Class 3 and 4 levels for protecting nonclassified mission-critical, mission-support, administrative-sensitive information on open, unencrypted networks. Class 5 will protect classified information on open networks or in any other risk environments. There is no current DoD-wide application protecting Class 3 and 4 levels, while the Electronic Key Management System (EKMS) currently supports Class 5 applications. EKMS and DoD PKI will become part of the overall DoD KMI.

Like any public key system, DoD PKI will have to incorporate and ensure the compatibility of certificate management, registration, and PKI-enabled applications. DoD PKI certificate management will require the assignment of CAs and directory services on an unprecedented scale. Plans are for DoD PKI to issue both identity certificates and encryption certificates. The system is also to provide for private key recovery for encryption certificates to support data recovery as well.

CAs will be part of a layered hierarchy starting with DoD root CAs who will be responsible for managing subordinate DoD CAs, DoD CA servers, and external CAs (ECAs). The DoD will provide and operate all root CA and server activities, as well as any subordinate DoD CA activity associated with classified, mission-critical, or command-and-control applications. To minimize overhead and hardware costs, the DoD may employ commercial service providers as ECAs for systems providing unclassified mission- and administrative/format-sensitive data support. The DoD will continue to outsource ECAs as long as the commercial solutions are cost-effective (less expensive than DoD managed/operated systems) and meet all of the assurance requirements of the higher classes of the DoD PKI. If outsourcing cannot meet the cost objectives or lacks proper security parameters, the DoD will also develop, procure, and operate this activity in-house.

There will be a common set of attributes for DoD Class 3 identity and encryption certificates. The minimum attributes will include items such as citizenship, government or government contractor affiliation, and service or agency affiliation. The certificate will include items such as a version number, issuer's name, serial number, entity identification or user's name, public key, period of use, and other privileges, as needed. Other DoD programs, such as DMS, may require additional attributes for the certificate. The DoD anticipates that privilege levels for Class 4 and 5 will be progressively more stringent but capable of being downward-compatible as necessary for the less secure network/applications. The DoD certificate management program is to accomplish the following:

- Certify the user's identity by providing digital signature for each certificate.
- Provide directory services to distribute the user/entity certificates and appropriate revocations (see next bullet), plus other information as desired (i.e., e-mail and postal addresses, and phone numbers).
- Manage certificate revocation by:
  1. Posting CRLs to the certification directory.
  2. Providing a method for real-time checks of revocation status.
- Archive certificates and CRLs to include those revoked or expired. This activity serves to support nonrepudiation of digital signatures and to provide proof for at least the period of any pertinent statutes of limitation.
- Set up the tools and procedures for implementation.

The Local Registration Authorities (LRA) will accomplish registration for DoD PKI by using a special DoD PKI software tool suite. LRAs are to be responsible for verifying the information on the certificate to include the user's identity and any other applicable attributes. A preregistration concept will directly deliver the certificate and key information to the end user in the following process:

1. The LRA authenticates to the CA server and then registers the user via the common Web-based registration application using SSL.

2. The LRA identifies the user and then provides appropriate information to the user for authentication to the server in accordance with the requirements and processes of the certificate policy for the appropriate assurance level(s).

3. The user employs the authentication information (token or software application) and a secure connection to the CA server to submit a common registration application and then requests a certificate. The system generates a digital signature key pair, and sends the public key to the CA server.

4. The CA processes the user's request and then generates a certificate, posts it to the directory system, and sends the certificate to the user.

5. The user then loads the certificate onto the selected token.

Figure 19-4 illustrates the DoD PKI architecture and the envisioned interrelationships of the CAs and LRAs.

After completing this single registration process, multiple applications can use a given user's token throughout the DoD architecture. With a digital signature certificate, the user can request additional certificates at the same assurance level (i.e., key exchange certificates).

In the DoD plan, responsibility for implementation of the DoD PKI program belongs to the DoD PKI Program Management Office (PMO). The responsibility for overall program management of the DoD PKI belongs to the NSA. NSA is providing the Program Manager (PM), and Defense Information System Agency (DISA) is providing a Deputy PM. The DoD PKI PMO is responsible for ensuring DoD PKI interoperability within DoD and with other federal entities, allies, and appropriate vendors. NSA is in charge of the research and development efforts for all of the centralized components supporting root CAs/CA servers and for the specifications to be provided industry for commercial PKI products and applications. The DoD PKI PMO will procure the central operational

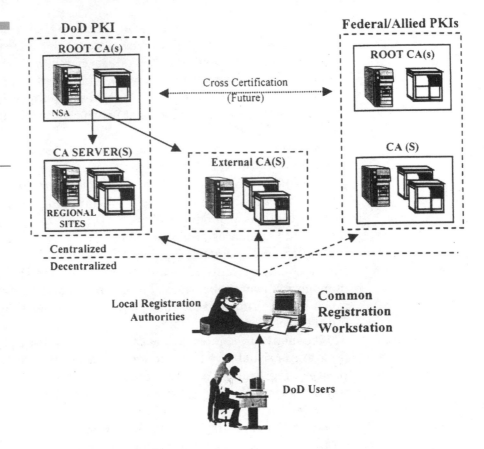

Figure 19-4
DOD PKI architecture. Source: From Version 2 of the "Public Key Infrastructure Roadmap for the Department of Defense."

infrastructure components (such as the CA servers and central directories). The armed services, DoD, and federal agencies, and the various warfighting commanders-in-chief (CINCs) are responsible for the development of any service, agency, or command-specific applications and the procurement of the local infrastructure items (such as LRA workstations, local directory servers, and PK-enabled applications). Beginning in FY01, the DoD PKI PMO will coordinate with and assist the CINCs and services in identifying procurement resources. [This is an interesting division of power. We wonder if there is duplication of effort similar to the 1940-1941 MAGIC where the Army and Navy wouldn't share intercepts. Who's going to be responsible for coordinating downward compatibility?]

The implementation of a project of this scope is contingent on an extensive coordination effort and many technological entities and applications working together. Since some of these technologies and applications are not yet operational or even developed, there are significant technical and implementation risks associated with the DoD PKI program. These risks exist in areas such as application processing, revocation architecture, identities and attributes, interoperability, directories, and scalability—the same risks that private firms face in deploying their own PKI systems.

Commercially available PKI applications (1999) currently only partially support the DoD PKI-targeted security requirements. An agreement on PKI standards should overcome much of this problem, but the DoD does not control the acceptance of standards or the implementation into applications or products. Thus, DoD plans to coordinate its requirements with standards groups and hopes that its interaction with industry leaders will ultimately produce the required PKI-compliant applications. If not, the only alternative would be for DoD to develop and manage its own applications, an expensive alternative. Again, this is much like the timing issue that private businesses face, when considering the evolution of technology.

Like many large, international firms, the biggest risk to the DoD PKI program is scalability for functions such as compromise recovery, key recovery, registration, directory access, and key management. Since PKI technology is still evolving, there is no data on the scalability of the overall system or for most of these functions. Pilot programs and modeling based on the early deployments will be a key part of the development strategy and critical to discovering and overcoming or mitigating scalability problems. DISA and NSA are developing a model that should aid in the planning, engineering development, and early deployments of the PKI. This model will also measure the impact of the system on telecommunication and network systems.

The DoD PKI PMO will face many decisions over the next few years. Its decisions will have a greater impact in that they will affect an organization of over four million employees, whose activities impact national security and therefore may result in life-and-death decisions. Additionally, there will have to be a resolution on how the DoD PKI infrastructure will support tactical requirements. Users on tactical deployments will likely not have easy access to the static infrastructure elements available at their home bases (i.e., LAN/WAN infrastructures, CA servers, directory services, and CRLs). The DoD PKI PMO will have to assess the need and feasibility of providing a rapid mobilization capability if tactical units require it.

Wrap-Up—Predictions

E-commerce will continue to change the way we do business, but it has not yet changed business. Firms must continue to find niches in the market and fill them in timely and cost-effective means. Although employing IT tools to automate tasks and business processes improves efficiency and reduces overhead, firms will eventually have to open their systems to customers, suppliers, and business partners to continually outpace the competition. At such time, firms will need the ability to automate trust to exert control over these interfaces.

PKI builds functionality into the trust that strong public key cryptography provides to open systems. However, as PKI is in the early stages of development, firms must carefully consider how best to apply this technology. The lack of formal PKI standards on which to build applications that will continue to be interoperable as technologies evolve brings risk to PKI deployments. Also, as implementing PKI changes the business process, parallel management-change efforts are necessary to support user acceptance.

The need to bring a measure of trustworthiness online will overcome the resistance to change. Despite its lack of maturity, PKI is a viable methodology for ensuring the confidentiality, integrity, and availability of vital business information. Furthermore, as early adopters share success and failure stories, the incorporation of lessons learned will serve to strengthen PKI. Finally, firms can expect government to exert its influence. If DoD is willing to take on large-scale initiatives such as the ambitious DoD PKI program, it is likely that it will require its business partners to implement PKI, as well.

PKI is a solid technology tool for building and maintaining trust into online transactions. However, PKI changes current business processes, and therefore, deciding whether to deploy PKI is a business decision. Carefully consider it, plan it, manage it, and do it.

Notes

1. Bhimani, Anish, "All Eyes on PKI," *Information Security Magazine*, October 1998, http://www.infosecuritymag.com
2. "Public Key Infrastructure Road Map for the Department of Defense," Version 2.0, Revision C, 1999.
3. DeMaio, Harry, "Getting Started with PKI," *Information Systems Security*, Summer 1999, 27-36.

4. PKIX Working Group, Internet Draft, "Certificate Policy and Certification Practice Statement Framework," November 1996, 5-9.

5. Ibid.

6. "Public Key Infrastructure Roadmap for the Department of Defense,".

7. Ibid.

CHAPTER 20

Cryptography Politics: Encryption Export Law and Its Impact on U.S. Industry

President Clinton Relaxes Crypto Export Rules

As our book moved toward its final edits, some fascinating news was reported by Declan McCullagh in *Wired News*:

> 8:10 a.m. 16.Sep.99.PDT Washington, D.C.—Clinton Relaxes Crypto Exports
>
> "The Clinton administration is expected to announce greater freedom for U.S. firms to export privacy-protecting encryption products Thursday afternoon.
>
> ...
>
> The decision is part of what a source calls "three pillars" of a new White House policy that also includes efforts to protect U.S. critical infrastructure and additional powers granted to federal law enforcement.
>
> ...
>
> White House officials hope the compromise will satisfy tech firms, who have long argued that President Clinton's executive order restricting overseas shipments hurts U.S. competitiveness.
>
> ...
>
> U.S. law enforcement officials have opposed the wide distribution of encryption products, and the FBI has even sought to make it a crime for Americans to distribute them domestically.
>
> ...
>
> The regulations, the details of which will eventually be fully released by the Commerce Department, will likely include continued government review of products to be exported, and restrictions on keeping undesirable end users, such as terrorists, from having access to crypto software and hardware."[1]

Attorney General Reno, Defense Secretary William Cohen, and Commerce Secretary William Daley made the announcement at the White House jointly at 6:44 P.M. EST on 9/16/99.

Later that night, Ted Bridis with the Associated Press released another update:

Clinton-Encryption
APf 9-16-99 11:26 PM

> WASHINGTON (AP) — The White House agreed Thursday to allow U.S. companies to sell the most powerful data-scrambling technology overseas

with virtually no restrictions, a concession to America's high-tech industry over law enforcement and national security objections.

The move was a defeat for the Justice Department, which had forcefully argued that criminals and terrorists might use the technology to scramble messages about crimes or deadly plots.

Even as the new policy was announced, Attorney General Janet Reno said at the White House, "In stopping a terrorist attack or seeking to recover a kidnapped child, encountering encryption might mean the difference between success and catastrophic failure." She said the policy "will mean that more terrorists and criminals will use encryption."

To help law enforcement, the White House will urge Congress to give the FBI $80 million over four years to develop techniques to break messages scrambled by terrorists.

...

The administration will allow high-tech companies to sell even the most powerful encryption technology overseas to private and commercial customers after a one-time technical review of their products.

...

The export limits never directly affected Americans, who are legally free to use encryption technology of any strength. But U.S. companies have been reluctant to develop one version of their technology for domestic use and a weaker overseas version, so they typically sell only the most powerful type that's legal for export, even to Americans.[2]

With much fanfare came the late night U.S. Newswire story about the Cyberspace Electronic Security Act of 1999 (CESA) proposal transmitted to Congress by President Clinton.

Text of Clinton Transmittal Letter on Cyberspace... OTC 9-16-99 10:22 PM

WASHINGTON, Sept. 16/U.S. Newswire/ — Following is the text of a letter from President Clinton, released today by the White House:

TO THE CONGRESS OF THE UNITED STATES:

I am very pleased to trasmit for your early consideration and speedy enactment a legislative proposal entitled the "Cyberspace Electronic Security Act of 1999" (CESA). Also transmitted herewith is a section-by-section analysis.

There is little question that continuing advances in technology are changing forever the way in which people live, the way they communicate with each other, and the manner in which they work and conduct commerce. In just a few years, the Internet has shown the world a glimpse of what is attainable in the information age. As a result, the demand for more and better access to information and electronic commerce continues to grow—among not just individuals and consumers, but also among financial, medical, and educational institutions, manufacturers and merchants, and State and local governments. This increased reliance on information and communications raises important privacy issues because Americans want assurance that their sensitive personal and business information is protected from unauthorized access as it resides on and traverses national and international communications networks. For Americans to trust this new electronic environment, and for the promise of electronic commerce and the global information infrastructure to be fully realized, information systems must provide methods to protect the data and communications of legitimate users. Encryption can address this need because encryption can be used to protect the confidentiality of both stored data and communications. Therefore, my Administration continues to support the development, adoption, and use of robust encryption by legitimate users.

At the same time, however, the same encryption products that help facilitate confidential communications between law-abiding citizens also pose a significant and undeniable public safety risk when used to facilitate and mask illegal and criminal activity. Although cryptography has many legitimate and important uses, it is also increasingly used as a means to promote criminal activity, such as drug trafficking, terrorism, white collar crime, and the distribution of child pornography.

The advent and eventual widespread use of encryption poses significant and heretofore unseen challenges to law enforcement and public safety. Under existing statutory and constitutional law, law enforcement is provided with different means to collect evidence of illegal activity in such forms as communications or stored data on computers. These means are rendered wholly insufficient when encryption is utilized to scramble the information in such a manner that law enforcement, acting pursuant to lawful authority, cannot decipher the evidence in a timely manner, if at all. In the context of law enforcement operations, time is of the essence and may mean the difference between success and catastrophic failure.

A sound and effective public policy must support the development and use of encryption for legitimate purposes but allow access to plaintext by law enforcement when encryption is utilized by criminals. This requires an approach that properly balances critical privacy interests with the need to preserve public safety. As is explained more fully in the sectional analysis that accompanies this proposed legislation, the CESA provides such a balance by simultaneously creating significant new privacy protections for lawful users of encryption, while assisting law enforcement's efforts to preserve existing and constitutionally supported means of responding to criminal activity.

The CESA establishes limitations on government use and disclosure of decryption keys obtained by court process and provides special protections for decryption keys stored with third party "recovery agents," CESA authorizes a recovery agent to disclose stored recovery information to the government, or to use stored recovery information on behalf of the government, in a narrow range of circumstances (e.g., pursuant to a search warrant or in accordance with a court order under the Act). In addition, CESA would authorize appropriations for the Technical Support Center in the Federal Bureau of Investigation, which will serve as a centralized technical resource for Federal, State, and local law enforcement in responding to the increasing use of encryption by criminals.

I look forward to working with the Congress on this important national issue.[3]

WILLIAM J. CLINTON
THE WHITE HOUSE
September 16, 1999.

Executive Summary

The exportation of strong encryption technologies is a topic in which two diametrically opposed sides are waging a battle over an issue that has ramifications for both national security and the technology industry within the United States. The U.S. government is seeking ways to protect its critical information infrastructure and to prevent foreign governments, criminals, and terrorists from engaging in activities deemed harmful to the interests of the United States. Law enforcement, intelligence, and military authorities within the United States oppose easing restrictions against the export of strong encryption products because of their concerns that the technology will be utilized by entities whose interests are inimical to those of the U.S. On the other hand, there are several groups in favor of easing or totally lifting any bans on the export of encryption technologies by individuals and companies from the United States.

As many companies within the U.S. move into the global marketplace, they have developed a need to protect their informational assets from the prying eyes of foreign governments and companies. Often the only secure methods of protection involve the use of strong encryption. By restricting the export of certain encryption technologies from the United States, we are placing our companies at risk. Also, as a world leader in the development and sale of software products, many companies from the U.S. are realizing that they must have strong encryption capabilities as a feature of their products to be competitive among the products of foreign nations. By limiting their ability to export products that are comparable to their foreign counterparts, the United States has adversely affected its ability to compete on a global scale. Many within the academic arena also consider the restrictions on the export of encryption information to be a violation of their First Amendment rights, which directly affects their ability to teach and engage in academic pursuits across international borders.

Herein lies the crux of the debate: How do we protect our national interests while limiting the impact on U.S. businesses? Efforts by U.S. law enforcement agencies to implement key escrow and key recovery programs have met with stiff resistance from many members of the public and private sector alike. President Clinton's position appears to be one of restriction, which is consistent with former stances taken by the U.S. government. However, efforts by members of Congress to ease restrictions have also surfaced in the form of proposed bills. Challenges to the legality of the current (and past) regulations governing the export of encryption technologies have been few and for the most part unsuccessful in federal court to date, with decisions going in both directions. Any clear legal direction in this matter will eventually have to come from the U.S. Supreme Court. Efforts within the international community to restrict the spread of strong encryption technologies have also proven to be ineffective, allowing our foreign competitors to gain an unfair advantage by compromising our information and by gaining further market shares for products that require strong encryption as a feature.

In short, we believe that current export restriction may do more to harm U.S. interests than good. These restrictions have inhibited the operations of U.S. companies while failing to prove that they can adequately protect U.S. interests. Efforts to prevent the export of strong encryption products are somewhat ethnocentric in that they labor under the assumption that the United States is the only place that can create such technologies. In reality, many foreign competitors will just fill the void left by U.S. restrictions with products of equal and better quality, all to the detriment of U.S. companies.

Introduction

The explosive growth of the commercial use of cryptography systems applied to information technologies is proving to be a valuable, yet contentious, issue. Many are against restricting the advancement, public availability, and application of cryptography. There are those who believe restraints are necessary to ensure that technology does not impose unintended consequences for societies, governments, and individuals. This chapter addresses United States' policies concerning cryptography and current law and its impact on United States' information technology.

U.S. Cryptography Export Policy/Export Controls

Current law and policy places no formal restriction whatever on products with encryption capabilities that may be sold or used in the United States. In principle, the domestic market can obtain any type of cryptography it wants.

Brief Description of Past and Current U.S. Export/Import Controls

For centuries, military forces have used cryptography to decipher enemy messages, resulting in the encryption technology of today being categorized as a weapon. The export of encryption technology from the United States is heavily regulated, thus preventing vendors from shipping strong encryption in their products. Currently, the United States controls the export of cryptographic technologies, products, and related technical information as "munitions." However, as enterprises turn to encryption technology to make new electronic commerce initiatives possible with partners and customers worldwide, the full brunt of these restrictions will be felt. Export controls also have had the effect of reducing the domestic availability of products with strong encryption capabilities.

Export controls on cryptography and related technology data have been a pillar of national cryptography policy for many years. In the

United States, cryptography policy and information about cryptography was largely the province of the National Security Agency (NSA) until the 1970s. Although a small market existed for unclassified commercial cryptography, the most advanced cryptographic techniques were classified and were limited to military, diplomatic, and intelligence use.[4] However, these policies have caused controversy because they set in opposition the needs of NSA cryptanalysts and law enforcement officials against public researchers and corporate investors.

In the past, the governing authority regulating import and export of products with cryptographic capabilities to and from the United States was derived from the following two items of legislation:

■ The Arms Export Control Act (AECA) of 1949, intended to regulate munitions

■ The Export Administration Act (EAA), which was intended to regulate dual-use products (products that have both military and civilian applications)

The AECA is the legislative basis for the International Traffic in Arms Regulation (ITAR), administered by the Department of State, in which the U.S. Munitions List (USML) is defined and specified. Items in the USML are regarded as munitions for purposes of import and export. The EAA is the legislative basis for the Export Administration Regulation (EAR), administered by the Department of Commerce, which defines dual-use items on a list known as the Commerce Control List (CCL). The EAA expired in 1994 but has been continued under presidential executive order. A revised AECA of 1976 and ITAR of 1992 severely restrict U.S. companies from exporting any and all military and intelligence-related technologies.[5] During the Cold War, most aspects of encryption technology, including the hardware, software, and mathematical algorithms upon which cryptography is based, were classified as military technologies and placed on AECA's "Munitions List." This same list is used to prohibit the export of tanks, fighter jets, and aircraft carriers.

As noted previously, cryptography export was formerly controlled by the ITAR. At the end of 1996, oversight for cryptography export was transferred to the Department of Commerce. The export policy was relaxed to favor export of data-recovery cryptography. This initiative was announced in a statement by Vice President Gore on October 1, 1996, and further elaborated in a November 15, 1996, executive order and memorandum. The Commerce Department drafted the Export Administration Regulations of December 30, 1996. In Executive Order 13206,

Administration of Export Controls on Encryption Products, President Clinton removed cryptography hardware, software, and technologies from the AECA Munitions List and placed them under the statutory responsibility of the U.S. Department of Commerce. Specifically, management of encryption fell under the regulations addressing dual-use commodities outlined in the EAA of 1979.[6] This move greatly eased the government controls on public use and the export of strong cryptography. The only major requirement for exportation was a key escrow system.

Key Recovery System

Key recovery is a process that enables third-party access to encrypted messages. Unlike key escrow, which involves storing keys or key parts with an escrow agent, key recovery can also include creating a "backup" (considered by some as a "back door"). Creating a backup of the user's private key information would enable third-party access to keys or the plaintext of encrypted messages. Concerns have been raised about the complexity, scalability, and legality of such a technology.

This major shift in policy was met with increased enthusiasm from the public sector as well as the government. Vice President Gore stated in an 1996 interview with Gary H. Anthes that "this initiative will make it easier for Americans to use stronger encryption products—whether at home or abroad."[7] While some public researchers and corporate investors were wary of the key recovery mandate, most involved in the ensuing debate accepted this prerequisite, which was one of President Clinton's major requirements for easing encryption regulation. The U.S. government has given industry a two-year grace period at the end of which there will need to be a viable key recovery system in place and operating.

William Reinsch, the Undersecretary for Export Administration at the U.S. Department of Commerce, wanted the policy to move beyond U.S. borders to create a worldwide standard for key escrow. He theorized that if escrow became pervasive and institutionalized in international commerce, terrorists and criminals would be forced to use cryptography technologies with key recovery systems.[8] This also would help prevent U.S. companies from relocating overseas to avoid current U.S. escrow requirements.

It has been noted that sophisticated criminals and terrorists will not use the encryption systems that require key escrow registration. However, if an international referendum requires all encryption systems and users to register their keys, it is believed, that criminals and terrorists will be forced into the escrow system. A worldwide key escrow system will not be put into place quickly but, with serious effort, it might be attainable, or so thinks the administration.

The Reinsch plan, in practice, is a failure.

Brief Description of Future U.S. Export Controls

To date, administration officials have succeeded in maintaining strict export controls, while cryptography advocates have blocked government-mandated back doors. The Federal Bureau of Investigation and the Department of Justice have long argued that domestic encryption products should be required to include key recovery systems. Cryptography advocates assert that government restrictions cannot control strong encryption that is already globally available. Many cryptographers agree that the key recovery features weaken, complicate, and raise the costs of cryptographic systems without meeting law enforcement needs. The world's leading cryptographers have concluded that escrowed encryption (third party maintains keys) by design introduces a system weakness. If the procedures that protect against improper use of the keys somehow fail, information is left unprotected.

The Security and Freedom Through Encryption Act

A bipartisan coalition in the U.S. House of Representatives has cosponsored a bill (The Security and Freedom Through Encryption, or SAFE, Act, H.R. 850) to protect the freedom Americans currently enjoy when it comes to computer privacy and to lift restrictions on the sale of U.S. encryption products overseas. SAFE can be summarized as follows:

- First introduced by Rep. Bob Goodlatte (R-VA) in February 1997 as a bill that would relax export controls on selected strong encryption products.

- Includes a provision that allows U.S. citizens to use encryption of any strength (currently, anything stronger than 64-bit key encryption is considered munitions and is illegal to export).

- Gives Americans the freedom to use any type of encryption, anywhere in the world, and allow the sale of any type of encryption domestically.

- Prohibits the government from creating a back door into citizen's computer systems (i.e., mandatory key escrow).

- Relaxes U.S. export controls to permit the export of generally available software. This includes mass market or public domain software, such as PGP, and other types of software and hardware under a license—that is, if a product with comparable security is commercially available from foreign suppliers.

- Creates criminal penalties for the unlawful use of encryption in furtherance of a crime; currently, up to five years' imprisonment for a first offense and up to 10 years for each subsequent offense.

- If approved, would prohibit the federal government from mandating access to codes used to decipher encrypted data.

Law enforcement officials oppose this bill because criminals will be able to hide their activities with stronger encryption. The FBI wants back doors to allow agents to decipher encrypted files easily with a court order.

Recent Developments

House Commerce Subcommittee Rejects Domestic Controls on Cryptography

As of June 16, 1999, the House Subcommittee on Telecommunications voted against an amendment to the SAFE bill, which would have guaranteed the government access to the plaintext of any encrypted communications or computer file. The amendment would have, for the first time ever, imposed domestic controls on encryption in the United States. However, the Committee voted to adopt amendments similar to those approved by Congress, including a provision for a Net Center to provide high-technology support to law enforcement.

Armed Services Committee Amends Proposed Export of Encryption Technology Legislation

On July 21, 1999, the Armed Services Committee recommended an amended version of legislation governing the export of encryption technology. Known as the Weldon-Sisisky-Andrews Amendment, this proposed law:

- Reaffirms authority of the President to control export of encryption production products for national security purposes.
- Establishes statutory framework for export control of high-performance encryption products.
- Requires the President to establish a performance threshold for encryption. Encryption products that fall below the threshold would be permitted to be exported without a license. Encryption products above the threshold would require an export license.
- Requires a one-time technical review for all encryption products proposed for export.
- Allows the President to establish certain sectors that would be subject to license free treatment of encryption products above the threshold, consistent with current U.S. policy.
- Requires the President to review the adequacy of the performance threshold every six months.
- Establishes an advisory board to review and advise the President on the foreign availability of encryption products.

Safe Act Awaiting Full House Consideration

As of July 23, 1999, five committees in the House of Representatives completed consideration of the SAFE Act, which would lift most export controls on strong encryption. Each of the five committees approved a different version of the bill; three left it essentially intact, while two adopted modifying amendments. When the full House takes up the bill and amendments per Union Calendar, 149 members will be presented with a choice between very different approaches to privacy and security.

U.S. Allies Reject Key Recovery

As of June 9, 1999, while the Clinton administration continues to support export controls and some in Congress push domestic controls, the United Kingdom, Germany, and France have rejected key recovery solutions. This demonstrates that the global trend is running against the U.S. policy approach to export controls.

In 1999, George Washington University's Cyberspace Policy Institute performed a study on encryption technology export restrictions by the U.S. government and its impact on industry growth outside the United States. The Americans for Computer Privacy (ACP), a privacy rights organization funded the study titled "Growing Development of Foreign Encryption Products in the Face of U.S. Export Restrictions." This study reported that, globally, an increased number of encryption-related products are being developed, while the United States continues its restrictions on their export. According to the report, since 1997 there has been a 22 percent increase in the number of encryption products developed outside the United States. There are a total of 184 foreign cryptographic products that use high-level encryption technology. The majority of these products come from companies in industrialized countries such as the United Kingdom, Germany, Canada, Australia, Sweden, and Israel.

The legislative counsel for the group, Bruce Heiman, said the study shows that encryption products made outside the United States provide about the same level of functionality and adherence to standards as those made by U.S. companies. The study mentioned that foreign companies are using U.S. encryption export restrictions as a tool in their marketing efforts to imply that U.S. encryption products may be weaker because they cannot stand up against their products. "Foreign companies are using U.S. export restrictions to market their own products," said ACP Executive Director Ed Gillespie.

Competing in the International Market

By limiting the export of strong encryption products, the U.S. government is only limiting the ability of U.S. companies and businesses in the international market. The U.S. government has put restriction on exports of encryption technology to prevent it from falling into the hands of terrorists or criminals. The U.S. companies that make encryption products have argued that such products are available worldwide, so export restrictions limit only their ability to compete in the international market. "Other countries are taking advantage of our administration's shortsighted encryption policy," said Gillespie. "While they (*foreign countries*) continue producing strong encryption products, the U.S. will lag behind and eventually lose high-tech leadership in the world economy."

Information technologies, which must be international in scope to address common encryption algorithms, encryption applications, key management, and distribution methods irrespective of national boundaries, need cryptography for vitality and growth. Foreign governments have policies to restrict public access to encryption services in telecommunications. U.S. export controls constrain domestic and internal growth of encryption services. Other key players in this industry have less severe export restrictions. Competition generated by the growth of encryption technology will not only advance development of encryption technology but also improve ease of use, key management, and application innovation.

Encryption Technology Standards and National Security

The U.S. government is faced with a two-pronged problem. Prohibiting cryptographic applications will harm economic growth and competitiveness in the expanding world of online products and services. Permitting such cryptographic exports will potentially weaken military security by providing new encryption capabilities to its adversaries. In both cases, U.S. national security is at issue, as noted in Nuclear Regulatory Commission (NRC) studies of 1988, "Global Trends in Computer Technology and Their Impact on Export Control," and 1991, "Finding Common Ground: U.S. Export Controls in a Changed Global Environment." These documents point out the following:

> The U.S. risks diminution in the advancing world market for telecommunications, and lost opportunity to lead the international encryption technology industry in establishing standards, quality, and privacy telecommunication services worldwide.
>
> The U.S. gains more by strengthening commercial competitiveness and

products—upon which the military is increasingly dependent—than what is lost by permitting international exposure of cryptographic systems.[9]

Electronic Commerce Industry

Traditionally, cryptography has been exclusively military technology controlled by the NSA, but this scenario is changing rapidly. The availability of cryptography will soon be extremely important to the future of electronic commerce, as well as the future of the American economy. This importance will rise less from the direct sale of cryptography services and products than from the enabling effect the existence of cryptography will have on the services that will form the foundation of the future information economy. Cryptography will eventually be embedded in most communications products and services; it will not be a "standalone" or "add-on" feature as it is today. It is in the direct interest of any industry that hopes to benefit from electronic commerce to encourage wide availably of high-quality, inexpensive cryptographic products that enable secure communications and commerce. Encryption products are increasingly being used to secure communications and electronic commerce over the Internet.

Electronic commerce is taking off globally. However, consumers and businesses need to have confidence that any transaction they make online is safe. Only the widespread availability of strong encryption and a digital signature system on a global level will provide that confidence.

Political Implications: Who Wins, Who Loses

The fervent desire of the Presidential Administration, Congress, DOJ, FBI, and NSA to restrict strong encryption export has hurt American companies and citizens. In the information age, the most important business asset of many companies is information. The current U.S. export controls represent a significant hindrance in protecting sensitive and vital information that may be exchanged with overseas customers.

While this example clearly illustrates the politics in the United States, especially in the 1990s, that have played a crucial role in defining America's development of encryption for commercial applications, it is only part of a bigger story. From telecommunications to e-commerce, some form of encryption technology is used to protect the information sent over online mediums. Current U.S. export restrictions in many ways have propelled American businesses toward finding ways around the export restrictions. The cryptography export ban has been a major driving force behind telecommunications expansion into foreign markets by means of mergers and acquisitions. Companies such as AT&T and MCI have formed strategic alliances and acquired controlling stakes in foreign telecommunications companies to bypass U.S. restrictions and take advantage of less stringent and more realistic European and Asian encryption regulations.

The political implications of continuing the current ban on encryption technology exportation is closely tied to commercial and national security interests of the United States. The current ban on encryption threatens to:

- Compromise privacy for U.S. citizens at home and abroad
- Provide unfair commercial and economic advantages to foreign corporations who are able to use strong encryption technology to protect their information assets
- Impede the spread of vital encryption technologies to online media, which has become a vital link in America's critical information infrastructure

The passage of an unaltered SAFE Act, H.R. 850, would definitively redefine the use of encryption technology for the worse. It will allow U.S. companies to sell the same products at home and abroad, and help the U.S. sustain its economic viability in the global economy. It will also actively encourage the use of international standards in cryptography, such as the Advanced Encryption Standard (AES), by businesses and private citizens. The SAFE Act will, at the same time, make communications and transactions between people in the United States and overseas more secure by providing stronger encryption that will limit intentional intrusion into private communications. The unaltered SAFE Act will still allow the Secretary of Commerce, with "possible guidance" from the White House and/or Congress, to restrict the export of all:

> ...computer hardware, software, computing devices, customer premises equipment, communications network equipment, and technology for information security (including encryption), except that which is specifically designed or modified for military use, including command, control, and intelligence applications.[10]

Without the strongest-possible encryption technology in information systems for private citizens and businesses, much of our personal or sensitive information can be readily compromised. Weak 56-bit encryption makes it easy for industrial spies to glean information that may be critical to the operations of a company. It also allows unauthorized individuals to gain access to information that is sensitive but not classified, from e-mail communications between government contractors and government employees corresponding with colleagues overseas. The "metric of trust" in cryptography is encryption.[11] By allowing strong encryption, we can guarantee the authenticity and integrity of the information being sent and received. The United States' current export ban on encryption hinders our economic future in international commerce and robs everyone of that metric of trust needed to sustain business over online media.

However, the SAFE Act would, in some respects, hinder law enforcement in carrying out its duty effectively and in a cost-efficient manner. For example, say that an employee in a bank or other financial institution embezzles several millions dollars and uses an encryption scheme to transfer the money overseas. Law enforcement may be pressed to do the impossible to try to decipher information from an encryption algorithm that is possibly uncrackable in a reasonable time, even with sophisticated equipment to conduct the cryptanalysis.

In short, our current export ban on encryption is also counterproductive to the national security of the United States in that it fails to address the restriction of encryption in a viable way.

Source Code vs. Object Code

Legal challenges to export encryption "code" in the U.S. involve source code and object code. The following definitions are from Alan Freedman's *The Computer Desktop Encyclopedia*:

> **source code**   Programming statements and instructions that are written by a programmer. Source code is what a programmer writes, but it is not directly executable by a computer. It must be converted into machine language by compilers, assemblers, or interpreters.[12]
>
> **object code**   The native language of the computer...it must be presented to the computer as binary-coded machine instructions that are specific to that CPU model or family. Although programmers are sometimes able to modify [object code] in order to fix a running program, they do not create it. [Object code] is created by programs called *assemblers*, *compilers*, and *interpreters*, which convert the lines of programming code a human writes into the machine language the computer understands."[13] [Also called *machine language*.]

The Three Relevant Cases Since 1996

There are three main cases to date that have challenged the legality of U.S. government export restrictions on certain types of encryption. In all three cases, individual citizens have brought suit against the U.S. government in an effort to overturn previous decisions by either the U.S. Department of State or the U.S. Department of Commerce concerning denials for export licenses of their (plaintiffs') encryption source code. The majority of claims have arisen over allegations that the U.S. government was violating the First Amendment rights of the plaintiffs by restricting their ability to distribute their source code in various electronic formats. It is interesting to note that major corporations with a tremendous stake in the issue of exportable encryption technologies have not been responsible for any of the lawsuits filed to date. The majority of support for the plaintiffs in all three cases appears to be coming from free speech and civil liberties advocates. To further cloud the issue, both the regulations and the enforcement agencies governing encryption export have changed in the last several years as a result of Presidential Executive Orders (i.e., from the Department of State to the Department of Commerce). This last factor has resulted in several of the plaintiffs being placed in the position of having to address their claims under both the new and the old regulations governing export restrictions (due in part to their appeals of district court rulings).

Karn Case

Mr. Philip Karn's case originated after he attempted to obtain a license to export source code for cryptographic algorithms contained in Bruce Schneier's book *Applied Cryptography: Protocols, Algorithms, and Source Code in C*. Karn submitted a request to the State Department to determine whether the book was subject to the provisions of the ITAR. The State Department ruled that the written format was not subject to the jurisdiction of the ITAR. However, several computer disks containing encryption source code that were mentioned in the book were not considered in the State Department decision at the time. Subsequently, Karn submitted another request to the State Department concerning the computer disks in question and was informed that the disks were covered by the provisions of the ITAR as defense articles under the United States Munitions List. After making several unsuccessful appeals concerning the State Department's decision, Karn filed suit.

In Karn v. U.S. Dept. of State, 925 F. Supp. 1 (D.D.C. 1996):

Karn alleged "that the State Department's designation of a diskette containing source codes for cryptographic algorithms as a defense article subject to the export controls set forth in the ITAR, when the State Department deemed the book containing the same source codes not subject to said export controls, is arbitrary and capricious and an abuse of discretion in violation of *the Administrative Procedures Act (APA), 5 USC 706 (2)(A)*. Karn also raised a number of constitutional claims."

Specifically, Karn alleged "that the State Department's regulation of the diskette violated his First Amendment right to freedom of speech and arbitrarily treated the diskette differently than the book in violation of his Fifth Amendment right to substantive due process."[14]

The district court judge in this matter was clearly not persuaded by Karn's argument, as it was his opinion that this was not a matter for the court system but rather a "political question." The judge felt that Karn "in an effort to export a computer diskette for profit, raised administrative law and meritless constitutional claims because he and others have not been able to persuade Congress and the Executive Branch that the technology issues do not endanger U.S. national security."[15] The judge ruled that under the ITAR, Karn was not entitled to a judicial review of the designation of his diskette as a defense article.

Also, the judge sided with the State Department by regulating the export of the diskette not because of the expressive content of the comments and or source code, but because of the belief that the combination of encryption source code on machine-readable media will make it easier for foreign intelligence sources to encode their communications:

The government considers the cryptographic source code contained on machine-readable media as cryptographic software and has chosen to regulate it accordingly.[16]

Professor Karn appealed his case in Karn v. U.S. Dep't of State, 107 F.3d 923 (D.C.Cir. 1997). However, because of the subsequent transfer of jurisdiction over encryption exports to the U.S. Department of Commerce, the appellate court sent the case back down to the district court for a review of Karn's administrative law claim under the new regulations.

Bernstein Case

Dr. Daniel Bernstein, the plaintiff in this case, was a college professor who wanted to distribute encryption software in source code form to both foreign and domestic entities. Bernstein had developed a mathematical algorithm for encrypting information, which he titled "Snuffle." Bernstein documented his algorithm as both an academic paper and as source code using the programming language C. He intended to publish his source code within the scientific community for academic reasons. At the time, the U.S. Department of State was responsible for decisions concerning what encryption technologies could be shared on an international scale. Bernstein claimed that he had submitted a request to the U.S. Department of State for a determination as to whether his academic paper and source code fell within the purview of the ITAR. The reply from the State Department indicated that all of the items were in fact considered "defense articles" and, therefore, subject to export restrictions. About one year later, Bernstein divided each portion of his work into separate entities and submitted another request to the State Department for a determination of each item separately. Bernstein was subsequently informed that all of the items were considered defense articles (a decision that was later changed to cover only his source code after he initiated legal action against the State Department).

Bernstein initially filed suit against the U.S. Department of State (Bernstein I) in the District Court for the Northern District of California seeking "declaratory and injunctive relief from their enforcement of the *Arms Export Control Act (AECA), 22 U.S.C. 2778*, and the *International Traffic in Arms Regulations (ITAR), 22 C.F.R. 120-30 (1994)*; on the grounds that they are unconstitutional on their face as applied to plaintiff (Bernstein)."[17] In his suit Bernstein alleged that the AECA and ITAR violated his First Amendment rights and were too broad as they were written. Bernstein claimed that the source code in which he wrote his encryption program was a class of speech protected by the First Amendment. The State Department argued that the source code was "functional rather than communicative." The court found the source code to be a form of speech (even if it was functional). The court also found that the source code was protected under copyright law as a "literary work." As a result of the ruling, the court declined the State Department's motion for dismissal and ruled, "cryptographic source code is speech protected by the First Amendment and that Bernstein's claims could be decided in a court of law."[18]

In a subsequent ruling in Bernstein v. United States Dep't of State, 945 F. Supp. 1279 (N.D. Cal. 1996) (Bernstein II), the court concluded that the ITAR licensing procedures for cryptographic software failed "to provide for a time limit on the licensing decision, for prompt judicial review and for a duty on the part of the State Department to go to court and defend a denial of a license, thus making the ITAR licensing system as it applies to cryptographic software an unconstitutional prior restraint in violation of the First Amendment.[19]

In Bernstein v. United States Dep't of State, 974 F.Supp. 1288 (N.D. Cal. 1997) (Bernstein III), the playing field changed somewhat after President Clinton issued an executive order changing control of nonmilitary encryption products and related technology from the State Department to the U.S. Department of Commerce. Under the *Export Administration Regulations (EAR), 15 C.F.R. Parts 730-774*, most encryption hardware and software may not be exported without a license from the Bureau of Export Administration (BXA), which is part of the U.S. Department of Commerce. Under the EAR, printed materials containing encryption-related source code were not subject to the EAR. However, that same material in electronic or storage media form was still subject to the EAR. The court found "that the encryption regulations issued by the BXA appeared to be even less friendly to speech interests than the ITAR."[20] The court ultimately ruled, as with Bernstein II, that the encryption regulations were an unconstitutional prior restraint in violation of the First Amendment. However, the court declined to impose a national remedy and instead insisted that its rulings be applied as narrowly as possible to address Bernstein's case.

In Bernstein v. United States Department of Justice, the U.S. Court of Appeals for the Ninth Circuit issued a decision on May 6, 1999, affirming the district court's previous decisions. While the panel was divided, majority members ruled, " export controls on encryption source code are an unconstitutional prior restraint on speech." The court held that the "export controls lack procedural provisions." As with the district court before, the members of the circuit court felt this issue to be worthy of possible consideration for review by the United States Supreme Court at a later date. The government, moreover, has reserved the right to restrict source code in printed form that may be easily "scanned," thus creating some ambiguity of whether printed publications are necessarily exempt from licensing.[21]

It should be noted that, immediately following the circuit court's decision, the BXA and the DOJ released statements that said "the decision does not affect the applicability of the EAR to exports and reexports of encryption hardware and software products or encryption technology. This includes controls on the export of encryption software in source code."[22]

The Bernstein Case is a landmark case. Appendix O presents additional materials surrounding this case.

Junger Case

In July 1998, the case of Junger v. Daley, United States Secretary of Commerce was heard in the United States District Court (N.D. Ohio, Eastern Division). Junger claimed that the EAR violated rights protected by the First Amendment and made essentially the same claims as Bernstein. Junger was a law professor at Case Western Reserve University Law School in Cleveland, Ohio, where he maintained a Web site to provide information about courses he taught. Junger wished to post on his Web site various encryption programs that he has written to show how computers work. Junger submitted applications to the Commerce Department in order to determine whether they restricted the materials from export that he intended to post.[23] Junger was informed that the majority of the information that he wished to place on his Web site would require a license (with the exception of a printed book chapter containing encryption code).[24] "The court found that the although encryption source code may occasionally be expressive, its export is not protected under the First Amendment."[25] The judge in this case ruled that the overwhelming majority of encryption source code was more functional than expressive. The judge disagreed with the ruling in the Bernstein I case in that words were not protected under the First Amendment just because they were capable of being written down in a language.[26] Also, the judge felt that EAR did not overly restrict the export of encryption products in that it did allow exports of products that were not "inconsistent with American national security and foreign policy interests."[27]

In March 1999, an appeal was submitted to the United States Court of Appeals for the Sixth Circuit on behalf of Junger. The appeal addressed the same arguments presented before in Bernstein and Junger that source code was, in fact, protected speech under the First Amendment and that EAR failed to provide the procedural safeguards required to handle issues arising from dealings with the BXA.

Summation of Legal Issues

A review of the legal decisions made in this area indicates that even the judges are awaiting further guidance from the U.S. Supreme Court concerning the constitutionality of the U.S. government export restrictions in place. The courts appear to be reluctant to rule on this matter, which they consider to be more of an executive and legislative issue rather than a judicial one. However, the courts have addressed some of the relative issues. Plaintiffs in the above-mentioned cases have addressed several aspects of the export debate concerning First Amendment protections for the distribution of source code, whether decisions by the U.S. government agencies regulating such exports are subject to judicial review, and whether the regulations in place are overbroad and vague. It is interesting to note, that the *U.S. government appears to be less inclined to dispute instances in which encryption related source code is distributed in printed format.* In reality, distribution of the same material in an electronic format is about the same considering the minimal effort required to transform most printed materials into an electronic format with today's readily available technology. Also, while the court ruled in favor of Bernstein during his appeal, it should be noted that the opinion rendered was not unanimous. The dissenting judge even referred to the Junger case for his interpretation of the appropriateness of declaring source code as a form of protected speech. In short, this matter has not been decided by the above three cases, and it is clear that it will take a review by our highest court to set a clear precedent.

International Policy

Internationally, many countries have relaxed controls on the exportation of cryptographic tools. In 1999 the Electronic Privacy Information Center conducted "Cryptography and Liberty 1999: An International Survey of Encryption Policy," which focused on four major areas of cryptography policy:

1. Controls maintained by each government regarding the domestic use of cryptography in their country

2. Controls maintained by each government regarding the importation of computer programs or equipment that permit cryptography

3. Controls maintained by each government regarding the exportation of domestically developed computer programs or equipment that permits cryptography

4. Identification of the agency or department of each government responsible for setting policy on the use, importation, or exportation of cryptographic technology[28]

About 230 countries and territories were asked to participate in this survey. Of the countries that did respond, most acknowledged that domestic controls are sparse and rarely enforced. That same course is generally taken toward key escrow and recovery. Some countries are encountering pressure from their intelligence and law enforcement agencies that insist on establishing sufficient financing to conduct effective surveillance. In summary, the survey concluded that export control is an effective method for controlling the use of encryption products. Due to the lack of international consensus, this effort will continue to develop and enforcing export controls will continue to arise out of each country's national security effort. The inception and continued growth of online services only compounds the lack of controls:

> The Internet has significantly changed the effectiveness of export controls. Strong, unbreakable encryption programs can now be delivered in seconds to anywhere in the world from anywhere with a network connection. It has been increasingly difficult for countries to limit dissemination, and once a program is released, it is nearly impossible to stop its redissemination, especially if it is in one of the many countries around the world with no export controls. In the United States, export controls are used as a justification to limit the availability of encryption on domestic Internet sites and thus serve as indirect domestic controls on encryption.[29]

The dialog for international consensus is prefaced in the following international agreements:

- Organization for Economic Cooperation and Development
- Coordinating Committee for Multilateral Export Controls
- The Wassenaar Arrangement

Organization for Economic Cooperation and Development

In November 1992 the Organization for Economic Cooperation and Development (OECD) set guidelines for an information security policy for its member countries. Its security objective was to "protect the interests of those relying on information systems from harm resulting from failures of availability, confidentiality, and integrity."[30] The OECD guidelines were further defined by the following principles: accountability, awareness, ethics, multidisciplinary, proportionality, integration, timeliness, reassessment, and democracy. In March 1997, the OECD expanded the general information security policy and adopted an international cryptography policy. The spirit of the OECD's efforts are cast from this statement:

> Governments want to encourage the use of cryptography for its data protection benefits and commercial applications, but they are challenged to draft cryptography policies that balance the various interests at stake, including privacy, law enforcement, national security, technology development, and commerce. International consultation and cooperation must drive cryptography policy because of the inherently international nature of information and communications networks and the difficulties of defining and enforcing jurisdictional boundaries in the new global environment.[31]

Recognizing that the OCED's recommendations are nonbinding, each member has no real incentive to follow any particular set of rules, but rather to take under consideration the following guidelines for developing cryptography policy:

- Cryptographic methods should be trustworthy in order to generate confidence in the use of information and communications systems.

- Users should have a right to choose any cryptographic method, subject to applicable law.

- Cryptographic methods should be developed in response to the needs, demands, and responsibilities of individuals, businesses, and governments.

- Technical standards, criteria, and protocols for cryptographic methods should be developed and promulgated at the national and international level.

- The fundamental rights of individuals to privacy, including secrecy of communications and protection of personal data, should be respected in national cryptography policies and in the implementation and use of cryptographic methods.

- National cryptography policies may allow lawful access to plaintext or cryptographic keys of encrypted data. These policies must respect the other principles contained in the guidelines to the greatest extent possible.

- The liability of individuals and entities that offer cryptographic services or hold or access cryptographic keys should be clearly stated, whether established by contract or legislation.

■ Governments should coordinate cryptography policies. As part of this effort, governments should remove, or avoid creating in the name of cryptography policy, unjustified obstacles to trade.[32]

The OCED is playing an active role in maintaining ongoing dialog in the public and private sector on the importance of secure electronic communications. In June of 1999, they held a joint OCED and private sector workshop on electronic authentication at Stanford Law School. In March 1998, a forum was held in Paris to discuss self-regulation of Internet content. In 1997, a workshop on cryptography policy was held in Paris focusing on the emerging market economy.

Coordinating Committee for Multilateral Export Controls

Dissolved in March 1994, the Coordinating Committee for Multilateral Export Controls (COCOM) was designed to discourage import/export of cryptography without a granted license. The main goal of the COCOM regulations was to prevent cryptography from being exported to "dangerous" countries (i.e., countries thought to maintain friendly ties with terrorist organizations, such as Libya, Iraq, Iran, and North Korea).[33]

Wassenaar Arrangement

Signed by 33 nations in 1996, the Wassenaar Arrangement, a follow-up to COCOM, was designed to control the export of strategic military weapons, dual-use goods, and emerging technology. In 1998 the *Wassenaar Arrangement on Export Controls for Conventional Arms and Dual-Use Goods and Technologies* was updated to include the export of mass-market encryption tools. The changes that focused on cryptography are as follows:

■ The General Software Note waiver has been changed to exclude the previous general exemption for mass-market cryptography software.

■ Mass-market software using symmetric key lengths greater than 64 bits is now controlled.

■ Non-mass-market software using symmetric key lengths greater than 56 bits is controlled.

■ Non-mass-market software using asymmetric keys based on integer factorization and lengths greater than 512 bits is controlled.[34]

The inconclusive nature of these international agreements demonstrates little support for global restriction on cryptography export. These agreements will continue to serve as a dialog for policy development.

Wrap-Up

In this chapter, we have reviewed U.S. cryptography export policy and export controls. We have examined the core issues regarding U.S. encryption export policy, political implications, the business community, legal challenges, and international policy.

In our opinion, there is no unified position on encryption export controls that benefits all concerned parties. Several bills have been shelved restricting the technology, along with several shifts in policy on behalf of from lax to no restrictions concerning encryption export. The SAFE Act has been marked up by five committees in the House of Representatives and has been submitted to the floor of the House for a vote. The executive branch of the United States has, via the SAFE Act as presented, authority to impose controls on certain encryption products. Even if all the parties shifted to one side of this debate, that would not guarantee a global acceptance or effective implementation of encryption technology.

We believe the U.S. gains more by strengthening commercial competitiveness than we lose by permitting international exposure of cryptographic systems. As an example, the cryptography export ban has been a major driving force behind telecommunications expansion into foreign markets by means of mergers and acquisitions. Companies such as AT&T and MCI have formed strategic alliances and acquired controlling stakes in foreign telecommunication companies to bypass U.S. restrictions and take advantage of less stringent and more realistic European and Asian encryption regulations.

The international community will continue to debate the best method to effectively implement encryption export controls. While this debate continues, the United States must be sensitive to the role it plays in the world market. However, many officials against relaxation of present encryption export policy believe that there is a net advantage to be gained from delaying the widespread availability of strong encryption. But even these officials must realize that, for better or worse, current controls are not sustainable for long.

Notes

1. McCullagh, Declan, Wired News, 16 September 99, www.wired.com/news/business/story/21786.html.

2. Ted Bridis, Associated Press, 16 September 1999, 7:57 PM News item from Declan McCullagh at declan@well.com.

3. *EPIC CESA Text and Commentary,* 16 September 1999, 10:22 PM, www.epic.org/crypto/legislation/cesa.

4. Office of Technology Assessment, *Information Security and Privacy in Network Environment*, U.S. Government Printing Office, 1994, 115.

5. Schwartzstein, Stuart J.D. "Export Controls On Encryption Technologies," *SAIS Review*, Winter 1996, 15-16.

6. Ibid., 16.

7. Anthes, Gary H., "Feds Ease Crypto Rules, But with a `Key' Catch," *Computerworld,* 30, 7 October 1996, 32.

8. Anthes, Gary H., "Encryption Policies Still Under Fire," *Computerworld*, 30, 9 December 1996, 74.

9. Nuclear Regulatory Commission studies, "Global Trends in Computer Technology and Their Impact on Export Control," 1988; "Finding Common Ground: U.S. Export Controls in a Changed Global Environment," 1991.

10. United States, 106th Congress, The Security and Freedom through Encryption Act. H.R. 850.

11. Nichols, Randy, lecture delivered on 14 July 1999. Emgt. 289 IN: "Cryptography Systems Applications, Management and Policy."

12. Freedman, Alan, *The Computer Desktop Encyclopedia,* 2nd ed. (New York: The Computer Language Company Inc., 1999), 837.

13. Ibid.

14. Karn v. U.S. Dept. of State, 925 F. Supp. 1 (D.D.C. 1996).

15. Ibid.

16. Ibid.

17. Bernstein v. United States Department of State, 922 F. Supp 1426 (N.D. Cal. 1996).

18. Ibid.

19. Bernstein v. United States Department of State, 945 F. Supp. 1279 (N.D. Cal. 1996).

20. Bernstein v. United States Department of State, 974 F. Supp. 1288 (N.D. Cal. 1997).

21. Bernstein v. United States Department of Justice, Unites States Court of Appeals for the Ninth Circuit, Case Number 97-16686.

22. Bureau of Export Administration, U.S. Department of Commerce, BXA Statement on Encryption Case, available from www.bxa.doc.gov/factsheets/EncryptCase.html.

23. Junger v. Daley, F. Supp. (N.D. Ohio 1998).

24. Ibid.

25. Ibid.

26. Ibid.

27. Ibid.

28. Electronic Privacy Information Center, "Cryptography and Liberty 1999: An International Survey of Encryption Policy," available from http://www.gilc.org/crypto/crypto-survey-99.html.

29. Ibid.

30. "Guidelines for the Security of Information Systems," available from http://www.oecd.org/dsti/sti/it/secur/index.htm.

31. OECD letter, "OECD Adopts Guidelines for Cryptography," 4 June 1997, available from http://www.oecd.org//publications/letter/0604.html#A1.

32. Ibid.

33. Bert-Jaap Koops homepage, "Crypto Law Survey," Version 15.0, July 1999, available from http://cwis.kub.nl/frw/people/koops/cls2.htm#co.

34. Wassenaar Arrangement 1998, available from http://www.efa.org.au/Issues/Crypto/wass98.html.

APPENDIX A

Bits and Bytes—The Digital Revolution

Information takes many forms. Some are solely within the domain of the mind—ideas, concepts, and visualizations. Some are conveyed as sounds in speech or music. Some are written or typed or produced on laser printers in emulation of those rough scratch marks set down eons ago in the first efforts to preserve speech, or to influence the gods of the hunt through prayer, or to convey through poetry the awe and emotion of the artist in contemplating nature. Some information takes the form of photographs, pictures, or paintings. Of all of its possible forms, however, the most useful information is that which can be encoded as a stream of ones and zeroes—represented physically as higher or lower voltages, switches on or off, current flow or none—for such information is readily created, stored, compiled, analyzed, displayed, and communicated by the electronic computers that pervade our world today. Fortunately, a great deal, if not most, of information falls into this category.

Letters, Numbers, and Punctuation—The Digital Alphabet

Consider this: Any written material may be electronically encoded. A system that uses a sequence of only two conditions (e.g., off, on) or symbols (e.g., 0,1) to represent characters is known as a *binary system*. A sequence of at least five ones or zeroes is needed to describe any letter in the Roman alphabet widely used in western culture. These ones or zeroes are called binary digits, or "bits," and five bits can be arranged in 32 different ways as 00000, 00001, 00010, and 00011, up to 11111. With 26 letters to represent, we can assign 00000 to A, 00010 to B, 00011 to C and so forth, and still have six combinations left over when we've finished to serve as punctuation or for other uses. In such an encoding, numbers would have to be spelled out: "two" rather than "2" or "six hundred twenty-three" rather than "623."

If we wish to include the Arabic numbers and to differentiate between upper- and lowercase letters, more than 32 combinations are needed. With k bits we can, in theory, encode 2^k different characters. Thus, five bits yield 32 characters, six bits yield 64 characters, seven bits yield 128, and so on. Two primary standards have evolved. The International Consultative Committee on Telegraphy and Telephony (CCITT) offers a five-bit encoding widely used for Telex transmissions and called International Alphabet Number 2. The CCITT and the International Organization for Standardization (ISO) also recognize the seven-bit International Alphabet Number 5. Ten of the characters in International Alphabet Number 5 can be varied for local convenience, of which the American Standard Code for Information Interchange, or ASCII, character set described in Table A-1 is one example. Obviously, other encodings are possible, and several have been used in one application or another.

Modern computer and communication systems engineers have settled on eight bits or a multiple thereof—commonly called a "byte"—as a useful standard in sizing and arranging memory storage within computers. Encodings of eight bits can be arranged in any of 2^8 or 256 different ways. An example of an 8-bit encoding is given in Table A-2.

Numbers may be stored in computers in encoded form as a sequence of characters—in other words, counting number "1" as 00111001 in the 8-bit coding of Table A-2, or the real number "63.5" as 00111110 00111011 00110110 00111101. Alternatively, they may be stored as binary integers—the number "1" as 00000001, "2" as 00000010, "46" as 00101110, and so forth. To facilitate the use of negative numbers, like −5 or −114, computers use biased binary integers. In biased storage, if eight bits are available to store a number, the possible range may be chosen to be from −127 to +128, with 00000001 representing −127, 0000010 representing −126, and so forth up to 11111111 representing 128. The byte 00000000 is usually reserved for zero. This convention allows negative as well as positive integers to be used easily by the computer.

Of course, there is nothing to prevent us from using a larger number of bits than eight to represent numbers. In theory any number of bits can be used. Eight is often used because of its convenience in computers that have 8-bit storage registers or random access memories, but other values can and have been used. Some computers use storage lengths of up to 60 bits in each register or memory location, permitting binary representation of numbers as large as $2^{60} = 1152921504606845696$. Many computers have the capability of using double the number of bits needed by their registers and memory—16 bits, say, for an 8-bit machine—in what are called "double precision" calculations.

Appendix A

TABLE A-1

ASCII Encoding.

				Bits 5 to 7				
	000	100	010	110	001	101	011	111
0000	NUL	DLE	SP	0	@	P	`	p
1000	SOH	DC1	!	1	A	Q	a	q
0100	STX	DC2	"	2	B	R	b	r
1100	ETX	DC3	#	3	C	S	c	s
0010	EOT	DC4	$	4	D	T	d	t
1010	ENQ	NAK	%	5	E	U	e	u
0110	ACK	SYN	&	6	F	V	f	v
1110	BEL	ETB	'	7	G	W	g	w
				Bits 1 to 4				
0001	BS	CAN	(	8	H	X	h	x
1001	HT	EM	)	9	I	Y	i	y
0101	LF	SUB	*	:	J	Z	j	z
1101	VT	ESC	+	;	K		k	{
0011	FF	FS	,	<	L	\	l	
1011	CR	GS	-	=	M		m	}
0111	SO	RS	.	>	N	^	n	~
1111	SI	US	/	?	O	_	o	DEL

NUL = Null character	ENQ = Enquiry	LF = Line feed	SOH = Start of heading
ACK = Acknowledge	DLE = Date link escape	STX = Start of text	BEL = Bell
DCx = Device controls	ETX = End of text	BS = Backspace	NAK = Negative acknowledgment
EOT = End of transmission	HT = Horizontal tab	SYN = Synchronous/Idle	CAN = Cancel
EM = End of medium	ETB = End transmission block	SUB = Substitute	VT = Vertical tab
FF = Form feed	CR = Carriage return	SO = shift out	SI = Shift in
ESC = Escape	FS = File separator	GS = Group separator	RS = Record separator
US = United separator	SP = Space	DEL = Delete	

Another commonly used alternative form for storing numbers follows scientific notation, dividing the number to be stored into two parts called a "discriminant" and an "exponent." This works because any number can be written in the form:

TABLE A-2

An 8-Bit Character Set.

Null	00000000	+	00110011	V	01011110
CTRL A	00000001	,	00110100	W	01011111
CTRL B	00000010	-	00110101	X	01100000
CTRL C	00000011	.	00110110	Y	01100001
CTRL D	00000100	/	00110111	Z	01100010
CTRL E	00000101	0	00111000	[	01100011
CTRL F	00000110	1	00111001	\	01100100
CTRL G	00000111	2	00111010	]	01100101
CTRL H	00001000	3	00111011	^	01100110
CTRL I	00001001	4	00111100	_	01100111
CTRL J	00001010	5	00111101	`	01101000
CTRL K	00001011	6	00111110	a	01101001
CTRL L	00001100	7	00111111	b	01101010
CTRL M	00001101	8	01000000	c	01101011
CTRL N	00001110	9	01000001	d	01101100
CTRL O	00001111	:	01000010	e	01101101
CTRL P	00010000	;	01000011	f	01101110
CTRL Q	00010001	<	01000100	g	01101111
CTRL R	00010010	=	01000101	h	01110000
CTRL S	00010011	>	01000110	i	01110001
CTRL T	00010100	?	01000111	j	01110010
CTRL U	00010101	@	01001000	k	01110011
CTRL V	00010110	A	01001001	l	01110100
CTRL W	00010111	B	01001010	m	01110101
CTRL X	00011000	C	01001011	n	01110110
CTRL Y	00011001	D	01001100	o	01110111
CTRL Z	00011010	E	01001101	p	01111000
ESC	00011011	F	01001110	q	01111001
FS	00011100	G	01001111	r	01111010
GS	00011101	H	01010000	s	01111011
RS	00011110	I	01010001	t	01111100
US	00011111	J	01010010	u	01111101
SP	00100000	K	01010011	v	01111110

TABLE A-2
(*Continued*)

An 8-Bit Character
Set.

!	00100001	**L**	01010100	**w**	01111111
"	00100010	**M**	01010101	**x**	10000000
#	00100011	**N**	01010110	**y**	10000001
$	00100100	**O**	01010111	**z**	10000010
%	00100101	**P**	01011000	{	10000011
&	00100110	**Q**	01011001	|	10000100
"	00100111	**R**	01011010	}	10000101
(	00110000	**S**	01011011	~	10000110
)	00110001	**T**	01011100	**DEL**	10000111
?	00110010	**U**	01011101		

$$n_0 \times b^0 + n_1 \times b^1 + n_2 \times b^2 + >>> + n_k \times b^k, \text{ for some integer k.}$$

Of course, any number with a 0 exponent is just "1," and any number with an exponent of 1 is the number itself. In this formula, b is called the "base" and corresponds to the number of digits in the number system we are using. Our commonly used decimal system uses the base 10 and the digits 0, 1, 2, 3, 4, 5, 6, 7, 8, and 9. The numbers designated by n_i in the formula are single digits of the set composing the number system.

A few examples will help to make this clear:

$$5 = 5 \times 1 \qquad\qquad\qquad = 5 \times 10^0$$

$$50 = (0 \times 1) + (5 \times 10) \qquad\qquad = 0 \times 10^0 + 5 \times 10^1$$

$$523 = (3 \times 1) + (2 \times 10) + (5 \times 100) = 3 \times 10^0 + 2 \times 10^1 + 5 \times 10^2$$

We resort to negative exponents of the base to accommodate fractions expressed as decimals and other "real" numbers. By "real," mathematicians mean any number that can be expressed as a counting number followed by a decimal point and a sequence of digits. Fractions, that is, "rational" numbers, have digit sequences following the decimal point that eventually terminate or become a repeating sequence.

For example, the following numbers are rational:

$$1/2 = 0.5 \qquad\qquad 1/3 = 0.3333333333...$$

$$102\ 5/8 = 102.625 \qquad\qquad 9\ 1/9 = 9.1111111...$$

"Irrational" numbers never repeat or end. The best-known irrationals are the numbers:

$$\pi p = 3.1415926535\ldots$$

which is the ratio of the circumference of a circle to its diameter, and:

$$e = 2.71828\ldots$$

which is the base of the natural logarithms.

The irrational numbers and the rational numbers make up the real numbers. We use the convention b^{-k} to represent the number $1/b^k$ so that the expanded fractional part of a real number can be written as:

$$n_{-1} \times b^{-1} + n_{-2} \times b^{-2} + n_{-3} \times b^{-3} + >>>n_{-k} \times b^{-k} + >>>$$

Here are a couple more examples. Using the decimal system, $b = 10$, $b^\wedge -1 = 1/10$, $b^\wedge - 2 = 1/100$, or:

$$2.5 = 2 + 0.5 = 2 \times 10^0 + 5 \times 10^{-1}$$

$$\pi = 3 \times 10^0 + 1 \times 10^{-1} + 4 \times 10^{-2} + 1 \times 10^{-3} + 5 \times 10^{-4} + 9 \times 10^{-5} +$$

$$2 \times 10^{-6} + 6 \times 10^{-7} + 5 \times 10^{-8} + 3 \times 10^{-9} + 5 \times 10^{-10} + >>>$$

We can use this rather complex way of decomposing real numbers to facilitate the storage of really large numbers—larger than could be conveniently stored in binary or biased binary representations. In theory, we could just store the sequences of digits before and after the decimal point up to the limits of available memory, and for applications requiring great precision, we might have to resort to such an approach. Most of the time, however, we can rely on a variation of the decomposition described above to achieve convenient storage of large numbers in just a few words of memory. In doing so, however, we have to give up something. What we give up is precision.

A number requiring a large number of digits to represent more precisely can, of course, be approximated by a smaller number of digits together with a base to some power. Thus:

$$5{,}000{,}000{,}000 = 5 \times 10^9$$

and

$$5{,}238{,}675{,}412 \cong 5.24 \times 10^9$$

where $\cong$ means "is approximately equal to."

By storing only the two numbers 5.24, sometimes called the "characteristic," and 9, also called the "mantissa," we then have a close approximation of the original large number, and only two words of storage are consumed. The usual degree of accuracy is determined by the number of bits used in the registers and memory of the computer, but just as any number of bits can be chosen to represent a number in binary, any precision can be adopted by choosing an appropriate number of bits for storing the characteristic and mantissa.

Essentially, any letter, number, or punctuation mark can be stored as a sequence of ones and zeroes. Different encodings and formats are possible, and many variants have been used at one time or another. Engineers designing computers and communications systems often decide on the length of bit strings to be used in encodings and formats based on the convenience and economy dictated by the number of bits used in the registers and memories of their devices. In theory, however, any size can be chosen, and so any arbitrary degree of precision can be attained. And so much of the useful information in the world—accounting data and statistics, mathematics, love letters and business letters, nonfiction books, literature and biographies, posters, and e-mail, to name but a few forms—can be expressed as combinations of letter and numbers and punctuation marks, as any librarian can attest.

Pictures

Even if only letters and numbers could be stored and manipulated digitally, our computers would be immensely valuable. But they are yet more valuable because more than just textual characters can be reduced to bits and bytes. We are all familiar with the grainy quality of pictures in newspapers, yet the subjects of the pictures are recognizable. Such pictures are composed of arrays of many, many dots, each of which is, in turn, either black or white. The black and white may be therefore represented by a one or a zero. The dots or bits, called "pixels" by graphics technicians, are arranged in rectangular arrays. Given sufficient distance, the pattern recognition capabilities of the mind can integrate the dots into a picture, as shown in Figure A-1.

More-sophisticated systems use a byte rather than a single bit to describe each pixel, making shades of gray possible. The first pixel may be entirely black and may be represented by 00000000, while a nearby pixel may be completely white and may be represented by 11111111.

Figure A-1
Black and white dots
used to make
a picture.

Other pixels may be somewhere in between pure black and pure white—000101101, for example. Therefore, each pixel in the rectangular array of pixels can be any of 2^8, or 256 different shades of gray and thus will portray a more complex set of lights and shadows to the eye. (See Figure A-2.)

Even colors can be represented digitally. As in color television, basic colors can be combined to make a wide variety of hues sufficient to compose a color picture that is not only recognizable but also pleasing to the eye. Each pixel is composed of three basic colors: red, green, or blue. In a video display, each pixel location has three tiny dots of phosphor, each of which emits only one of the three colors when illuminated by a stream of electrons. The intensity of each dot is separately and individually controlled, so each can be represented by a byte of data, and each pixel is represented by three bytes, one for each phosphor dot. To get red, blue, or green, we illuminate only the red, blue, or green dot. To get white, we illuminate all three. Red and green without blue appears as yellow. Green and blue together appear as cyan, while red and blue are seen as magenta. All phosphors off (not illuminated) produce black color, appearing on the screen as no color at all.

Figure A-2
Grayscale representation makes a clearer picture.

Combining $2^8 = 256$ possibilities for each of the three colors in a common 8-bit computer, we get 256^3, or 16,777,216 possible different colors on the monitor display, more shades than the eye can readily differentiate. Of course, to store color pictures digitally requires three times as many bits as is required to store grayscale pictures, since one word of storage is required for each of the three primary colors as opposed to a single word of storage for the gray intensity of a grayscale pixel.

Sounds

Sounds, too, can be reduced to bits and bytes. Sounds are basically variations in the density of air that vibrate a membrane—the "eardrum"—inside our ears. These vibrations are translated mechanically by small bones to a liquid-filled chamber where nerve cells sensitive to specific frequencies detect the vibrations and translate them into nerve impulses to the brain. The sound vibrations can be viewed as variations in the density of the air over time. As the density changes more or less rapidly, the frequency we hear changes, and our mind translates the resulting nerve impulses into recognizable patterns. Faster vibrations are perceived as higher pitches or frequencies.

As with any graph, we can measure the height of the graph—in this case (Figure A-3), the amplitude—at specific time intervals and represent the measured values as numbers. The numbers representing the heights can, in turn, be encoded as bits and bytes. Figure A-4 shows the measured or "sampled" values over time. Obviously, if we sample more often the representation of the original graph is more accurate.

A "speaker" (or acoustic transducer) can reconvert the representation of sound as bytes into vibrations of air. Each byte results in a brief vibration of a diaphragm by a magnet in the speaker whose electromagnetic field is strengthened or weakened by changing the current in surrounding coils in accordance with the values of the stored bytes. If the duration of each frequency is small, the sequence of vibrations will approximate the original smoother shift in frequencies and the mind will compose the quantized variation into a recognizable pattern. As the frequency interval decreases, the reproduction gets better and better until it becomes indistinguishable from the original and we hear speech or music. See Figure A-5.

Figure A-3
Sound as a variation of air density over time.

Figure A-4
Measured or sampled values of sound frequency over time.

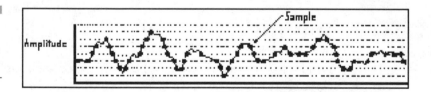

Figure A-5
Re-creating recognizable sound from digitized sound.

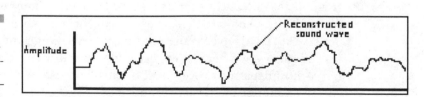

Digital Processing

Our ability to reduce words, pictures, sound, and other types of information to digital form as bits and bytes, and to reconvert the digital forms to approximations of their original forms that are close enough to be perceived as the originals by the mind, provides the basis for the digital revolution. Computers accept input in digital form, either because we enter it that way or because it is received from devices that convert data from other forms—analog sounds, pictures and paintings, and so forth—to digital form. The resulting bits and bytes are easily stored inside the computer system in either volatile memory that uses thousands of small circuits designed and built into random access memory chips, or on various kinds of magnetic media ranging from magnetic tapes to floppy disks to the stripes that adorn the nether sides of our credit and automated teller machine cards. We also use lasers to store and retrieve information in digital form on plastic or fiberglass disks (compact disk read-only memory, or CD-ROM). Other types of memory are also read-only memory (ROM) or are programmable read-only memory (PROM) and are widely used for such applications as startup instructions for personal computers. Flash memory provides a digital write-once capability.

The computer outputs digital information as characters or pictures on attached monitors or in the form of variations in voltage on a wire attached to an output port. These voltage variations can then be detected as digital input to other computers; or to devices such as modulators, which convert digital information to analog variations in sound for synthesizing voice or music or for transmission over telephone circuits; or to deviations of electron guns in cathode ray tubes for creation of picture displays; or to other uses.

Inside the computers, bits and bytes can be combined in arithmetical and mathematical operations. Logical operations—based on assignments of "true" and "false" conditions—are also possible. In combination, these operations permit the construction of algorithms or "programs"—sequences of instructions for the computer that combine, analyze, change, synthesize, and delete information. Such activities are so useful in our world, and computers have become so small and inexpensive, that today we find digital processing everywhere. The most obvious applications in science, mathematics, and warfare have led to wider application in engineering, accounting, word processing, and art. Information systems now control the basic functions of the nation's infrastructure, including the air traffic control system, power distribution and utilities, phone system, stock exchanges, the Federal Reserve monetary transfer system, credit and medical records, and a host of other services and activities.

Once computers were gigantic, room-sized devices that operated independently of one another. They were expensive and isolated in environmentally controlled facilities, and using them was an arcane art understood by few. As these systems evolved, they extended their connectivity, first to remote terminals and eventually to local and wide area networks, exchanging data with other computers and systems of computers over leased or shared links. More and more people learned to use them as the availability of programs made them easier to use, more "user-friendly." It is already apparent that productivity in the modern workplace depends directly on connectivity. Initiatives like the National Information Infrastructure (NII)—intended to be an "Information Superhighway" for our nation's commerce and government—are based on this emerging reality.

Communication Systems and Networks

When computers exchange information, we have the basis for modern communications systems. Sometimes, as with the telephone system, the computers act as switches to establish circuits over which analog or digital communications can be accomplished. Yesterday's and today's telephones are essentially analog devices, and once the phone companies' switching computers establish the circuit, the circuit stays in effect as long as the parties to the call wish to continue. When the call is terminated, the circuit is disestablished, freeing the switches to form other circuits for other calls. Since the circuits exist only for the duration of the call, they are called "virtual circuits" to distinguish them from hardwired dedicated circuits that continue in existence even when not in use.

Because computers work best with digital forms of information and the switches that compose our telephone systems are computers, our telephones now use tones to represent the information needed to establish virtual analog circuits, as shown in Figure A-6. These same tones enable us to use telephone circuits for the direct exchange of digital information between computers, facsimile machines, and other devices that are better suited to digital operations. To do so, we employ a "modu-

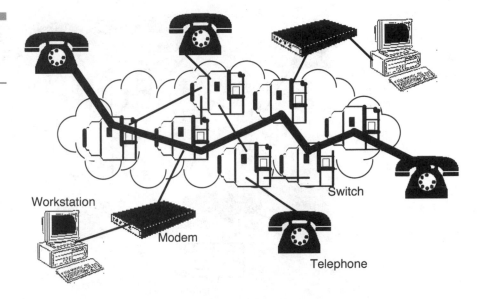

Workstation

Modem

Switch

Telephone

lator/demodulator," or modem, to convert digital representations of information to analog tones and vice versa.

Tomorrow's phones will undoubtedly be digital devices, eliminating in many cases the necessity for separate modems. Already some companies have installed Integrated Service Data Networks (ISDN) that combine digital voice and data capabilities in one system. A few entire countries have already converted to ISDN. Other types of digital phones use Frame Relay and Asynchronous Transfer Mode (ATM) protocols. Only the cost of replacing millions of dated analog devices prevents worldwide adoption of the more capable digital networks.

Packet Switching

The older analog virtual circuits have proven unsuitable for computer communications in other regards as well. In a typical phone call, much, if not most, of the time the virtual circuit is in existence, it is not actively in use! There are pauses between words and phrases, pauses at the end of sentences and paragraphs, and pauses while each party adjusts to the changeover from one speaker to the other. These pauses may seem brief to the parties engaging in a voice exchange, but to computers, which

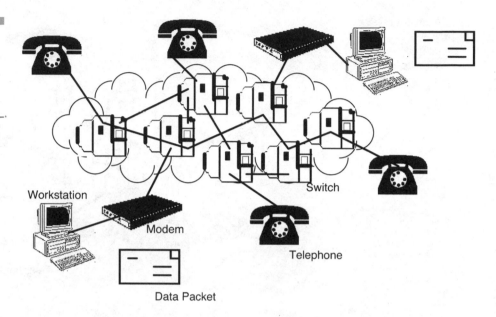

Workstation

Modem

Switch

Telephone

Data Packet

measure times in microseconds, they are vast wastelands of unused circuit capability.

To communicate efficiently and effectively over virtual circuits, computers need a different paradigm from that offered by human voice communications. A system more like the postal system than the phone system is required. Information to be transferred between computers is broken down into segments that are numbered for later reassembly. Each user computer, or host, attached to the network is given a unique network address so the sending computer can attach the intended recipient's address to each segment of the data to be transmitted, thus creating a "packet" consisting of the address, the segment number, and the data segment. Other information may be included for convenience and administrative purposes—for example, the address of the sending computer may be added to facilitate receipting for the information and checksums included to allow a determination as to whether the packet arrived unchanged or must be retransmitted.

In a "packet-switching" system, shown in Figure A-7, the computer switches that make up the network interconnecting the various host computers do not function as do the switches in a telephonelike, or "circuit-switching," system. Rather, they act as "store-and-forward" devices, receiving each packet from either a host or another switch and sending the packet along to another switch determined by the network management software. Basing its decision on circuit loading and other network parameters, the software determines the best next stop for the packet as it traverses the network on its way from sender to recipient. Thus, adjacent data segments in the original file or document may traverse very different paths before arriving at their destination host and being reassembled. While this packet switching systems approach to data communications is not at all like voice communications using circuit-switching systems, it nevertheless results in a perfect copy of the original file or document arriving at the correct destination. Such systems are very efficient in their use of scarce and expensive bandwidth.

Being able to represent almost any information in digital form and having circuit-switched and packet-switched networks available worldwide lets us use the powerful computers available today to create, store, and process information efficiently and inexpensively. This is the basis of the digital revolution.

APPENDIX B

DEFINITIONS OF ELECTRONIC SIGNATURES IN ENACTED STATE LEGISLATION

Source: Material condensed from ITEC with permission of McBride Baker & Coles (MBC) (last updated May 24,1999). Full text available from www.mbc.com. MBC is an excellent source of legal/IT information and is highly recommended.

This table provides the definition of the term "electronic signature" for each enacted statute, if available. Note the diversity of approaches. States without legislation or specific definitions not included.

State	Bill/Statute	Definition of Term "Electronic Signature"
Alaska	1997 AK SB 232	"An electronic or a digital method that is 1) executed or adopted by a person, including a state agency, with the intent to be bound by or to authenticate a record; (2) unique to the person using it; (3) capable of verification; (4) under the sole control of the person using it; and (5) linked to data in a manner that, if the data is changed, the electronic signature is invalidated."
Arizona	Ariz. Rev. Stat. Ann. s. 41-121	Uses the term "digital signatures" to refer to electronic Signatures.The term "electronic signature" is not defined in the act; however, the act uses the term "digital signature" in a manner that appears to refer to electronic signatures.
	AZ HB 2518	"An electronic or digital method of Identification that is executed or adopted by a person with the intent to be bound by or to authenticate a record." "An electronic signature shall be unique to the person using it, shall be capable of reliable verification and shall be linked to a record in a manner so that if the record is changed the electronic signature is invalidated."
California	CA Government Code s. 16.5	Uses the term "digital Signatures" to refer to electronic Signatures. The term "digital signature" is defined as "an electronic identifier, created by computer, intended by the party using it to have the same force and effect as the use of a manual signature."
Colorado	1997 CO SB 155	"An electronic signature may consist of an access code or any other identifying word or number assigned by a filing officer that is unique to a particular filer."

State	Bill/Statute	Definition of Term "Electronic Signature"
Florida	1996 FL SB 942	"Electronic signature means any letters, characters, or symbols, manifested by electronic or similar means, executed or adopted by a party with an intent to authenticate a writing. A writing is electronically signed if an electronic signature is logically associated with such writing."
Georgia	Georgia Electronic Records and Signatures Act (1997 GA SB 103)	"'Electronic signature' means an electronic or digital method executed or adopted by a party with the intent to be bound by or to authenticate a record, which is unique to the person using it, is capable of verification, is under the sole control of the person using it, and is linked to data in such a manner that if the data are changed the electronic signature is invalidated."
Idaho	Idaho Electronic Signature and Filing Act (1998 ID SB 1496)	"'Electronic signature' means any computer or electronically generated identifier that is intended by the person using it to have the same force and effect as a manual signature."
	1997 ID HB 221	This act amends the meaning of "sign" or "signature", as defined in the Idaho Business Corporation Act, to include "any manual, facsimile, conformed or electronic signature."
Illinois	Illinois Electronic Commerce Security Act; 1997 Illinois House Bill 3180	"'Electronic signature' means a signature in electronic form attached to or logically associated with an electronic record." Also uses the term "secure electronic signature": "If through the use of a qualified security procedure, it can be verified that an electronic signature is the signature of a specific person, then such electronic signature shall be considered to be a secure electronic signature at the time of verification, if the relying party establishes that the qualified security procedure was: (1) commercially reasonable under the circumstances; (2) applied by the relying party in a trustworthy manner; and (3) reasonably and in good faith relied upon by the relying party."
	Financial Institutions Digital Signatures Act (1997 IL HB 597)	Uses the term "digital signatures" to refer to encrypted electronic signatures. The term "digital signature" is defined as "an encrypted electronic identifier, created by computer, intended by the party using it to have the same force and effect as the use of a manual signature."
	15 ILCS 405/14.01—State Comptroller Act (1997 IL SB 516)	"An electronic identifier, created by computer, intended by the party using it to have the same force and effect as the use of a manual signature." (Uses the term "digital signature.")
Indiana	Electronic Digital Signature ActE (1997 IN SB 5a)	"An electronic identifier, created by computer, executed or adopted by the party using it with the intent to authenticate a writing."
	Electronic Digital Signature ActE (1997 IN HB 1945)	"An electronic identifier, created by computer, executed or adopted by the party using it with the intent to authenticate a writing."

State	Bill/Statute	Definition of Term "Electronic Signature"
Iowa	1997 IA SB 457	"A computer-created electronic identifier that is a) intended by the party using it to have the force and effect of a signature; (b) unique to the party using it; (c) capable of verification; (d) under the sole control of the party using it; (e) linked to the data in such a manner that it is invalidated if the data is changed.
Kansas	Kansas Digital Signature Act (1997 KA HB 2059)	"A computer-created electronic identifier that is: (a) intended by the party using it to have the force and effect of a signature; (b) unique to the party using it; (c) capable of verification; (d) under the sole control of the party using it; (e) linked to the data in such a manner that it is invalidated if the data is changed." (Statute uses the term "digital signature.")
Kentucky	1998 KY HB 708	"'Electronic signature' means an electronic identifier whose use is intended by the person using it to have the same force and effect as the use of a manual signature and containing the following characteristics: (a) It is unique to the person using it; (b) It is capable of verification; and (c) It is under the sole control of the person using it."
Louisiana	West's Louisiana Revised Statutes Annotated Section 40:2144 (1995)	Not specifically defined. However, the act provides for the use of "alphanumeric or similar codes, fingerprints, or other identifying methods" for medical records, subject to the guidelines promulgated by the Department of Health and Hospitals.
	1997 LA SB 609	Not specifically defined. However, the act defines "signature" and "sign(ed)" to include written of electronic signatures.
Maryland	Maryland Digital Signature Pilot Program, 1998 Md. Laws 482; (1998 MD HB 523)	Uses the term "digital signature" to refer to electronic signatures. Authorizes Electronic Signatures with specified authentication attributes only. "'Digital signature' means an electronic identifier created by a computer that (I) is intended by the party using it authorized signer to have the same use of a manual signature; (II) is unique to the authorized signer; (III) is capable of verification; (IV) is under the sole control of the authorized signer; (V) is linked to data in such a manner that if the data are changed, the signature is invalidated; and (VI) conforms to regulations adopted by the Secretary of State."
Mississippi	Digital Signature Act of 1997 (1997 MS HB 752)	"Any word, group of letters, name, including a trader assumed name, mark, characters or symbols made manually, by device, by machine, or manifested by electronic or similar means, executed or adopted by a party with the intent to the authenticate a writing."

State	Bill/Statute	Definition of Term "Electronic Signature"
Missouri	1998 MO SB 844 and 1998 MO SB 680	(The electronic and digital signature section of 1998 MO SB 680 mirrors 1998 MO SB 844.) The bill uses the term "electronically transmitted signature" rather than electronic signature. The term "electronically transmitted signature" is not defined. However, the act states that "any statutory requirement that a statement, document or notice be signed by any person shall be satisfied by an electronically transmitted signature that is: (1) unique to the person using it; (2) capable of verification; (3) under the sole control of the person using it; (4) linked to the document in such a manner that if the data is changed, the signature is invalidated; and (5) intended by the party using it to have the same force and effect as the use of a manual signature."
Nebraska	1997 NB LB 924	"An electronic identifier, created by computer, intended by the person using it to have the same force and effect as a manual signature." (Uses the term "digital signature.")
New Hampshire	1997 NH HB 290	"'Electronic signature' means a digital signature, executed or adopted by a party with an intent to authenticate a writing. A writing is electronically signed if a digital signature is logically associated with such writing."
	1997 NH SB 207	Not specifically defined, however, an electronic signature shall have the same force and effect as a manual signature if the signature is: (1) unique to the person using it; (2) capable of verification; (3) under the sole control of the person using it; (4) linked to the data in such a manner that if the data is changed the signature is invalidated; and (5) conforms to regulations adopted by the commissioner of administrative services.
North Carolina	1997 NC HB 1356	Authorizes electronic signatures with specified authentication attributes only. The term "electronic signature" is defined as "any identifier or authentication technique attached to or logically associated with an electronic record which is intended by the party using it to have the same force and effect as the party's manual signature." Further, "an electronic signature contained in a transaction between a person and a public agency, or between public agencies, shall have the same force and effect as a manual signature provided all of the following requirements are met: (1) The public agency involved in the transaction requests or requires the use of electronic signatures. (2) The electronic signature contained in the transaction embodies all of the following attributes: (a) It is unique to the person using it; (b) It is capable of certification; (c) It is under the sole control of the person using it; (d) It is linked to data in such a manner that if the data are changed, the electronic signature is invalidated; and (e) It conforms to rules adopted by the Secretary [of State] pursuant to this article."

State	Bill/Statute	Definition of Term "Electronic Signature"
Ohio	1997 OH HB 243	"Any of the following attached to or associated with an electronic record by an individual to authenticate the record: (a) a code consisting of a combination of letters, numbers, characters, or symbols that is adopted or executed by an individual as that individual's electronic signature; (b) a computer-generated signature code created for an individual; (c) an electronic image of an individual's handwritten signature created by using a pen computer."
Oklahoma	Electronic Records and Signature Act of 1998 (1997 OK HB 3287)	This act defines "electronic signature" as "any signature in electronic form attached to or logically associated with an electronic record executed or adopted by a person or its electronic agent with intent to sign the electronic record." The act also defines the term "signature" as "any symbol, sound, process, or encryption of a record in whole or in part executed or adopted by a person or the person's electronic agent with intent to: (a) identify the person, (b) adopt or accept a term or record, or (c) establish the informational integrity of a record or term that contains the signature or to which a record containing the signature refers."
Oregon	1997 OR HB 3046	"Any letters, characters or symbols, manifested by electronic or similar means, executed or adopted by a party with an intent to authenticate a writing."
Rhode Island	1997 RI HB 6118	"Any letters, characters, or symbols, manifested by electronic or similar means, executed or adopted by a party with the intent to authenticate a writing, and which is logically associated with such writing."
South Carolina	South Carolina Electronic Commerce Act (1997 SC SB 1167)	Electronic signature: "'Electronic signature' means any identifier or authentication technique attached to or logically associated with an electronic record that is intended by the party using it to have the same force and effect as a manual signature. Secure electronic signature: "'An electronic signature is deemed to be secure if: (1) it is created by application of a security procedure that is commercially reasonable and agreed to by the parties; (2) the electronic signature can be verified by use of a procedure that is recognized and approved [pursuant to statute]; or (3) when not previously agreed to by the parties, the electronic signature is: (a) unique to the party using it; (b) capable of identifying such party; (c) created in a manner or using a means under the sole control of the party using it; and (d) linked to the electronic record to which it relates, in a manner such that, if the record is changed, the electronic signature is invalidated."
Texas	1998 TX HB 984	"An electronic identifier, created by a computer, intended by the party using it to have the same force and effect as the use of a manual signature." (Uses term "digital signature.")

State	Bill/Statute	Definition of Term "Electronic Signature"
	1997 TX SB 645	Term not defined—presumably uses the term in same manner as 1997 TX HB 984 (which uses term "digital signature" to mean electronic signature)
	1997 TX SB 370	"An electronic identifier intended by the person using it to have the same force and effect as the use of a manual signature." (Statute use the term "digital signature.")
Utah	Utah Stat. Ann s. 46-1-16 (1998 UT SB 107)	Utah has passed legislation specifically addressing digital signatures.
	Utah Digital Signature Act (Utah Code Ann. 46-3-101 et seq.)	See above.
Virginia	Va. Code Ann. ss. 59.1-467 to 469 (1997 VA SB 923)	"An electronic identifier, created by a computer, intended by the party using it to have the same force and effect as the use of a manual signature." (Uses the term "digital signature.")
West Virginia	1998 WV HB 4293	"'Electronic signature' means any identifier or authentication technique attached to or logically associated with an electronic record that is intended by the person using it to have the same force and affect as a manual signature. Electronic signatures include, but are not limited to, the following: "(1) a "digitized signature," an electronically recorded handwritten signature; (2) a "digital mark," defined as a code indicating acceptance or approval which requires security protocols; or (3) a "digital signature."

APPENDIX C

Enacted Legislation Authorizing the Use of Electronic Signatures

Source: Material condensed from ITEC: McBride Baker & Coles (last updated May 24, 1999). Available from www.mbc.com.

State	Bill/Statute	Type of Signature	General Scope
Alabama	1997 AL HB 405	Electronic	Filing of tax returns
Alaska	1997 AK SB 232	Electronic	Public and private
Arizona	1998 AZ HB 2518	Electronic	State agencies
Arkansas	1999 AR SB 378	Digital Signature	All communications
California	1997 CA AB 521	Electronic	State colleges
	1997 CA AB 721	Electronic	Securities-related
	1997 CA SB 49	Electronic	Political Reform Act
	1995 CA AB 2755	Electronic	Certificates of death
	Code s. 16.5	Electronic	Public entities
Colorado	1997 CO SB 155	Electronic	UCC
Connecticut	1997 19a-25a	Electronic	Medical records
Delaware	Tit. 29, ss. 2706(a), 5942(a)	Electronic	State documents
Florida	1997 FL HB 1125	Digital/electronic	Notaries public
	1996 FL SB 942	Electronic	Public and private
	1997 FL HB 1413	Digital	Engineering documents
Georgia	1997 GA SB 103	Electronic	Public and private
	1998 §59-29-12	Electronic	O.C.G.A—all
	1997 GA HB 487	Electronic	Motor vehicles
	1997 GA HB 479	Electronic	Tax returns
	1997 GA HB 513	Digital signatures	Digital signature
	1999 GA SB 62	Electronic (specific)	All communications
Hawaii	1995 HI SB 2401	Electronic	Court documents
Idaho	1998 ID SB 1496	Electronic	State and local agencies
	1997 ID HB 221	Electronic	Idaho Business Corporation Act
Illinois	1997	IL HB 3180	Electronic Public and private

State	Bill/Statute	Type of Signature	General Scope
	1997 IL HB 597	Electronic	Financial institutions
	1997 IL SB 516	Electronic	State agencies
Indiana	1997 IN SB 5a	Digital	State agencies
	1997	IN HB 1945	Digital State agencies
Iowa	1995 48A.13	Electronic	Voter registration
	1997 IA SB 457	Electronic	Public and private
	1999 IA HF 624	Electronic	All communications
Kansas	1997 KA HB 2059	Electronic	Public and private
Kentucky	1998 KY HB 708	Electronic	Public and private
	1998 KY SB 390	Electronic	State agencies
Louisiana	1995 LA HB 2144	Electronic	Medical records
	1997 LA HB 1605	Electronic	Health care providers
1997	LA SB 609	Electronic	Vital medical records
1997	LA HB 294	Electronic	Financial instruments
Maine	1997 ME SB 473	Electronic	Motor Vehicle Code
Maryland	1998 MD HB 523	Electronic	Government agencies
Minnesota	1997 MN SB 2068	Digital	Public and private
	1997 MN HB 241	Electronic	Motor carriers
	1997 MN HB 325K	Digital	All communications
	1997 MN SB 1905	Digital	All communications
Mississippi	1997 MS HB 752	Digital	Public and private
	1997 MS HB 1313	Electronic	Secretary of State
Missouri	1998 MO SB 844	Digital	Secretary of State
	1997 MO SB 16	Electronic	Public office filings
	1998 MO SB 680	Digital	All communications
Montana	1997 MT HB 468	Electronic filing	Electronic filing
Nebraska	1997 NB LB 924	Electronic	Public and private
	1997 NB LB 622	Electronic	Architects/engineers
	1997 NB LB 1161	Electronic	Geologists
Nevada	1997 NV SB 42	Electronic	Financial transactions
	1997 NV AB 386	Electronic	State courts/public
New Hampshire	1997 NH HB 290	Electronic	Public and private

State	Bill/Statute	Type of Signature	General Scope
	1997 NH SB 472	Electronic	UCC statements
	1997 NH SB 207	Electronic	State instruments
New Mexico	1996 NM HB 516	Digital only	Public records
	1999 NM SB 146	Electronic/Digital	Public records
North Carolina	1997 NC HB 1356	Electronic	Public agencies
North Dakota	1997 ND SB 2071	Electronic	Public agencies
Ohio]	1997 OH HB 243	Electronic	Health care records
Oklahoma	1998 OK HB 3287	Electronic	Public and private
Oregon	1997 OR HB 3046	Electronic	Public and private
	1997 OR SB 125	Digital only	Trust co.—CAs
Rhode Island	1997 RI HB 6118	Electronic	Public agencies
South Carolina	1997 SC SB 1167	Electronic	All transactions
Tennessee	1997 TN SB 525	Electronic	Various transactions
	1997 TN HB 1718	Electronic	State courts
Texas	1998 TX HB 984	Electronic	Public agencies
	1997 TX SB 645	Electronic	State Comptroller
	1997 TX SB 370	Electronic	Motor vehicle licenses
Utah	1998 UT SB 107	Digital	Notary public
	46-3-101 et seq.	Digital	Public and private
	1998 SB 1	Digital only	Certificate authorities
Vermont	1997 VT SB 232	Electronic	Land records
Virginia	1997 VA SB 923	Electronic	Public and private
	1997 VA SB 153	Electronic	All communications
	1998 VA HB 794	Electronic	Court documents
	1998 VA SB 819	Electronic	All communications
Washington	1998 Chap 19.34	Digital	Public and private
	1997 WA HB 2931	Electronic	Public and private
West Virginia	1998 WV HB 4293	Electronic	Public and private
	WV Code 30-3-13	Electronic	Medical services
Wisconsin	1997 WI AB 811	Electronic	Public and private
	1997 WI AB 100	Electronic	State contractors
Wyoming	1997 9-1-306	Electronic	Secretary of State

APPENDIX D

Source: Thomas J. Smedinghoff of McBride Baker and Coles, *Summary of Electronic Commerce and Digital Signature Legislation*, Information and Technology and Electronic Commerce (ITEC) Law Department, Chicago, Illinois, September 22, 1999. Available from: ITEC Law Department, www.mbc.com/ecommerce/legis/congress.html

American Bar Association (ABA)

"ABA Digital Signature Guidelines," Information Security Committee of the Electronic Commerce Division, of the ABA Section on Science and Technology, August 1996.

Congress

- Government Paperwork Elimination Act; Senate Bill 2107 (Abraham)
- Digital Signature and Electronic Authentication Law (SEAL) of 1998; 1997 Senate Bill 1594 (Bennett)
- Computer Security Enhancement Act of 1997; 1997 House Bill 1903 (Sensenbrenner)
- Electronic Financial Services Efficiency Act of 1997; 1997 House Bill 2937 (Baker)
- Electronic Commerce Enhancement Act; 1997 House Bill 2991 (Eshoo)
- Internal Revenue Restructuring and Reform Bill; 1997 House Bill 2676 (Archer)
- The Millennium Commerce Act (1999 Senate Bill 761) (Abraham)
- Health Care Personal Information Nondisclosure Act of 1999 or Health Care PIN Act (1999 Senate Bill 578)
- Electronic Securities Transaction Act (1999 Senate Bill 921)
- Digital Signature Act of 1999 (House Bill 1572)
- Internet Growth and development Act of 1999 (House Bill 1685)
- Electronic Signatures in Global and National Commerce Act (1999 House Bill 1714)

- The Medical Information Privacy and Security Act (1999 Senate Bill 573)
- The Patients Bill of Rights Act (1999 Senate Bill 326)
- The Patients Bill of Rights Act (1999 Senate Bill 300)
- The Millennium Commerce Act (1999 House Bill 1320)
- The Medical Information Privacy and Security Act (1999 House Bill 1057)
- Security and Freedom through Encryption (SAFE) Act (1999 House Bill 850)
- Patient Protection Act of 1999 (1999 House Bill 448)
- Paperwork Elimination Act of 1999 (1999 House Bill 439)
- Secure Public Networks Act (1997 Senate Bill 909) (McCain/Kerrey)
- Electronic Data Security Act of 1997 (March 12 1997 draft)

Available from www.cdt.org/crypto/970312_admin.html and www.mbc.com/ecommerce/legis/congress.html from ITEC Law Department

Federal Reserve Board

Federal Reserve System Regulations on Electronic Fund Transfers; Regulation E—12 CFR 205 (March 20, 1998).

U.S. Food and Drug Administration

Regulations on Electronic Records; Electronic Signatures—21 CFR Part 11 (March 20, 1997)

Department of Health and Human Services

Health Care Financing Agency (HCFA) of the Department of Health and Human Services (HHS): Proposed Rule on Security and Electronic Signatures (August 12, 1998).

Treasury Department

U.S. Treasury Regulations on Sales of U.S. Savings Bond by Electronic Means; Changes to 31 CFR 370; Regulations Governing the Transfer of Funds by Electronic Means on Account of United States Securities.

Internal Revenue Service

Internal Revenue Service announces a pilot program for the use of PKI-based digital signatures for 1999 tax year.

National Conference of Commissioners on Uniform State Law (NCCUSL)

- Uniform Electronics Transactions Act, draft issued June 1998. Approved July 23 to 30 1999, at annual meeting.
- Uniform Computer Information Transactions Act (UCC Article 2B). Approved July 23 to 30, 1999, at annual meeting.

APPENDIX E

INTERNATIONAL—35 COUNTRIES AND POLITICAL ENTITIES ENACT DIGITAL SIGNATURE LEGISLATION

Sources: Stewart A Baker and Paul R. Hurst, *The Limits of Trust: Cryptography, Governments and Electronic Commerce* (New York: Kluwer Law International, 1998). Thomas J. Smedinghoff of McBride Baker and Coles, *Summary of Electronic Commerce and Digital Signature Legislation*, Information and Technology and Electronic Commerce (ITEC) Law Department, Chicago, Illinois, August 14, 1998. Available from www.mbc.com/ds_sum.html. Electronic Privacy Information Center, "Cryptography & Liberty 1999: An International Survey of Encryption Policy," EPIC 1999. Available from www.epic.org.

28 Countries Enact Digital Signature Legislation and Model Laws:

Argentina

- Presidential Decree No. 427/98.
- Resolution 45/97.
- Resolution AFIP No. 474/99 Federal Income Tax Administration, 1999.
- Resolution SFP No. 194/98 Secretary of Public Administration— Standards for Public Key Infrastructure for the National Public Sector of Presidential Decree.

Armenia

- Department of Information and Publications initiative on cryptography (July 31, 1997; study).

Australia

- Electronic Transactions Bill 1999.
- Gatekeeper—A Strategy for Public Key Technology Use in the Government (May 6, 1998).

- Victorian State Government E-Commerce Legislation.
- The Data Protection Bill 1999.
- Electronic Commerce Framework Bill (March 31, 1998).
- Selected Portions of Australia's Defense and Strategic Goods List, (1998).
- Category 5—Telecommunications and Part 2: Information Security, (1998).
- GSN—General Software Note (1998).
- General Technology Note (Part 3—Dual-Use List, 1998).
- Electronic Commerce: Building the Legal Framework (March 31, 1998).

Austria

Draft 2 Digital Signatures and Cryptography Act (July 9, 1998).

Canada

- Personal Information Protection and Electronic Documents Act; The House of Commons of Canada Bill C-54, 1st Session, 36th Parliament.
- Draft Uniform Electronic Commerce Act (March 15, 1999).
- Land Title Amendment Act 1999—1999 British Columbia Bill 93.
- Electronic Commerce Secretariat of the Department of Justice Canada (June 1995).
- Consultation paper by Government of Canada (GOC) Public Key Infrastructure (PKI).
- First Digitally Signed International Government Document Between Singapore, Canada, and Pennsylvania (June 5, 1998). Available from www.ec.gov.sg.

China

- The Notice of the General Administration of Customs of the People's Republic of China, Sec 50-305, of November 1, 1987 (List of Prohibited and Restricted Imports and Exports).
- Computer Information Network & Internet Security, Protection, and Management Regulations (December 30, 1997).

Colombia

Draft Proposal of Law on Electronic Commerce, Digital Signatures and Certification Authorities, 1998. Available from www.qmw.ac.uk/~16345/columbia_sp.htm.

Czech Republic

- Act No. 21/1997 Coll. (January 24, 1997) on Control of Exports and Imports of Goods and Technologies Subject to International Control Regimes.
- Decree 44/1997 (February 21, 1997), Granting a General License for Import of Controlled Goods.

Denmark

- Guidelines Concerning the National Cryptographic Policy and Statements on the Use of Cryptographic Products Issued by the Ministry of Transport and Communications (October 12, 1998).
- Draft Bill for an Act on Digital Signatures (1999).

European Union

- Europe's Way to the Information Society: An Action Plan (COM(94)347 Final).
- Europe and the Global Information Society, Recommendations to the European Council (the Bangemann Report).
- Draft Report of the European Electronic Signature Standardization Initiate (EESSI).
- PDF documents: DA,DE,EL,EN,ES,FI,FR,IT,NL,PT,SV (added May 20, 1999).
- Council Regulation (EQ No. 3381/94 (December 19, 1994).
- Council Decision No. 96/613/CFSP (October 22, 1996).
- Council Decision No. 97/419/CFSP (June 26, 1997).
- Directive on a Common Framework for Electronic Signatures—COM (1998) 297.
- Towards a European Framework for Digital Signatures and Encryption-COM (1997) 503.
- European Initiative in Electronic Commerce (COM (97) 157 final).

- Legal and Regulatory Issues Concerning the TTPs and Digital Signatures—Final Report.

Finland

- Announcement of the new Finnish Cryptographic Policy (January 5, 1999).
- Pre-Trial Investigation Act and Coercive Criminal Investigation Means Act (December 31, 1998).
- Letter by the Prime Minister to the Vice-President of the Council of State (Conseil d'Etat) and Accompanying Report by the Council of State: Conducting of a Study into the Legal Issues Raised by the Development of the Internet (September 22, 1997).
- Statute No. 562/1996 (July 26, 1996) on the Control of Exports of Dual-Use Goods (Unofficial Translation).
- Decree on Export Control of Certain Goods, No. 645/1996.
- Decision of the Ministry of Trade & Industry on the Goods & Technologies Subject to Export Licensing, No. 54/1997.

France

- Announcement of a dramatic change in cryptographic policy by Prime Minister Lionel Jospin (January 19, 1999) invalidating the 1996 laws.
- Article 17 of Law No. 96-659 (July 26,1996).
- Proposed Statutory Trusted Third-Party Rules for Encryption— Article 12—Proposed Telecommunications Law, 1998. Available from www.steptoe.com/france.htm.

Germany

- In 1999, Germany prevented key escrow from becoming part of the Wassenaar Arrangement.
- Germany's Digital Signature Act (August 1, 1997).
- Germany's Digital Signature Ordinance (November 1, 1997).
- Information and Communications Services Act 1997—requires licensing of certification authorities. Available from www.iid.de/rahmen (in German). Represents the most comprehensive digital signatures law in the world.

International Chamber of Commerce (ICC)
GUIDEC—General Usage in International Digitally Ensured Commerce (November 6, 1997).

India

■ Indian Information Technology Act (December 13, 1998).

■ Selected portions of India's Export Import Policy for 1997-2002:
  ■ Sections 1-16, NFEP Appendix, General Provisions, Sections 1 to 18.
  ■ Chapter 4 Certificates and Chapter: Imports.
  ■ Chapter 15.2 Restricted Items, A: Consumer Goods.

Ireland

■ President Bill Clinton and Irish Taioseach (Prime Minister) Bertie Ahern digitally sign joint communiqué on e-commerce (September 4, 1998).

■ Statutory Instrument No. 362 of 1996 implementing European Communities (Control of Exports of Dual-Use Goods) Regulations 1996 (December 3, 1996).

Also: Framework for Ireland's Policy on Cryptography and Electronic Signatures, Department of Public Enterprise.

Israel

■ Control of Products and Services Order (Engagement in Encryption) Decree 867 of 1974 ("Encryption Order").

■ Law for Control of Products and Services of 1957.

Italy

■ Italian technical rules on digital signature (April 15, 1999).

■ Regulations promulgated November 10, 1997. (Presidential Decree No. 513).

■ Legislation on Electronic Document and Digital Signature, Law No. 59 (March 1997).

■ Regulation on Criteria and Methods Concerning the Creation, Storage, and Transmission of Documents by Means of Computer-based or Telemetric Systems, Decree No. 513 (Nov. 10, 1997), (Presidential Decree No. 513). Available from www.interlex.com/testi/attielet.htm.

Japan

- Certificate Authority Guidelines (V. 1.0), (April 1997).
- Cross-Certification Guidelines (Alpha version), Electronic Commerce Promotion Council of Japan (ECOM), (June 1998).

Kazakhstan

- Resolution No. 967, Article 240, and Regulation No. 27
- Resolution No. 1037, Article 266, and Regulation No. 29.

Malaysia

- Table of Contents for the Digital Signature Act of 1997.
- MIMOS Berhad initiates Malaysia's first public key infrastructure pilot (December 23, 1997). (Modeled after Utah's law.)

Netherlands

- Netherlands Ministry of Economic Affairs, Information Technology: Electronic Commerce Action Plan, March 1998.
- National TTP (Trusted Third Party) Project Final Report (March 1, 1998). Available from www.minvenw.nl/hdtp/factsheets/trust1.html.

New Zealand

New Zealand Law Commission Publications: Electronic Commerce Part One: A Guide for the Legal and Business Community (October 1, 1998).

Norway

Regulation No. 51 (January 10, 1989).

Organization for Economic Cooperation and Development (OECD)

- Ministerial Conference on Electronic Commerce (October 7 to 9, 1998).
- 1997 Discussion Paper, "Dismantling the Barriers to Global Electronic Commerce."
- Recommendations of the Council Concerning "Guidelines for Cryptography Policy" (March 27, 1997). Available from www.oecd.org.

Pakistan

All encryption software and hardware must be inspected by and deposited with the Pakistan Telecommunications Authority, under the Pakistan Telecommunications Reorganization Act of 1999.

Russia

- Joint Decision No. 60 of the State technical Committee and Federal Agency for Government Communications and Information (FAPSI) (NSA equivalent; June 24, 1997).
- Edict No. 334 on Measures to Observe the Law in Development.
- Production, Sale, and Use of Encrypting Information (April 1995).
- Provision on the State Licensing of Activities in the Field of Information—Protection, FAPSI (1997).
- Russian Federation Information Act, Russian Federation Federal Act No. 24-Z; adopted by the State Duma (January 25, 1995).
- Russian Federation Federal Securities Market Commission Decree No. 9, Interim—Requirements on the Standards of Depository Activity (February 14, 1997).

Available in Westlaw: 1995 WL 139853, 1997 WL 241126, RUSLEGIS-LINE.

Singapore

- Singapore Electronic Transactions (Certificate Authority) Regulations (February 10, 1999).
- Singapore Security Guidelines for Certificate Authorities (February 10, 1999).
- Singapore Electronic Transactions Act, June 29, 1998.
- First Digitally Signed International Government Document Between Singapore, Canada, and Pennsylvania (June 5, 1998). Available from www.ec.gov.sg.

South Korea

The Basic Law on Electronic Commerce 1999.

Sweden

- Consultation Paper by the Swedish Interministerial Working Group on Digital Signatures—DS 1998:14.
- Report on Electronic Document handling, 1996.

Switzerland

Ordinance Concerning the Export, Import, and Transit of Dual-Use Goods and Specific Military Goods (June 25, 1997).

United Kingdom

- UK Building Confidence in Electronic Commerce—A consultation Document (March 5, 1999).
- UK Secure Electronic Commerce Proposal—Memorandum by Members of the Global Internet Liberty Campaign to the House of Commons Trade and Industry Committee.
- DTI (Department of Trade and Industry)—White paper on Strategic Export Controls (July 1998).
- DTI (Department of Trade and Industry)—Statement on the Legal Framework for Secure Electronic Commerce (April 27, 1998).
- Licensing of Trusted Third Parties for the Provision of Encryption Services—Public consultation paper on Detailed Proposals for Legislation (March 1997).
- DTI (Department of Trade and Industry)—Paper on Regulatory Intent Concerning Use of Encryption on Public Networks (June 1996).
- Paper on Securing Electronic Mail within HMG (Her Majesty's Government), (March 21, 1996). Available from www.dti.gov.uk/CII/respons.html.

United Nations Commission on International Trade Law (UNCITRAL)

- Draft Uniform Rules on Electronic Signatures (June 29, 1999), working paper 82.
- Draft Articles on Electronic Signatures (December 15, 1998).
- Draft Uniform Rules on Electronic Signatures (November 23, 1998).
- Draft Uniform Rules on Electronic Signatures (May 25, 1998).
- United States Proposal for Draft International Convention on Electronic Transactions.
- Draft Uniform Rules on Electronic Signatures (December 12, 1997).
- Model Digital Signature legislation, Draft Uniform Rules on Electronic Signatures (May 25, 1998).

- Report of Working Group on Electronic Commerce on Its Work of Its Thirty Fourth Session.

- Report of Working Group on Electronic Commerce on Its Work of Its Thirty Third Session.

- Report of Working Group on Electronic Commerce on Its Work of Its Thirty Second Session.

- Report of Working Group on Electronic Commerce on Its Work of Its Thirty First Session.

- Planning of Future Work on Electronic Commerce: Digital Signatures, Certification Authorities and Related Legal Issues.

- Model Law on Electronic Commerce. Adopted by General Assembly Resolution 51/162 (December 16, 1996).

United States

- Department of Commerce's Regulations on Encryption Items, 61 Fed. Reg. 68706 (December 30, 1996).

- Bureau of Export Administration (BXA): 15 CFR Parts 730,732,734,736,738,740,742,744,748,750,768,772, and 774. Docket No. 960918265-6366-03 RIN 0694-AB09

- Encryption Items Transferred from the U.S. Munitions List to the Commerce Control List AGENCY: Bureau of Export Administration, Commerce. Action: Interim Rule.

- Proposal for an International Convention on Electronic Transactions, UNCITRAL working group (May 25, 1998).

Wassenaar Agreement

Selected Portions of the Wassenaar Arrangement on Export Controls for Conventional Arms and Dual-Use Goods and Technologies.

Adopted by the Plenary of July 11-12, 1996.
(Sections 1-IX; Appendix 1-2; Category 5-Part 2 Information Security:5.B.2, 5.C.2, 5.E.2)

APPENDIX F

Premise

On May 6, 1999, the United States Court of Appeals for the Ninth Circuit ruled in favor of Daniel J. Bernstein in his case versus the United States Department of Justice. Bernstein challenged the government regulations, requiring that the source code of his "Snuffle" encryption software and various related papers be licensed for export. Bernstein argued that this constituted "prior restraint" of speech, which is protected by the First Amendment. This decision may be considered a small victory for two major groups: advocates for privacy on the Internet and the U.S. software industry.

However, it was major setback for the federal government, as it may lead (as the government argues) to a proliferation of strong encryption software getting into the hands of various potential bad guys (e.g., terrorists and drug dealers). Without laws to prevent strong encryption from getting into the hands of criminals, law enforcement and national security officials have argued publicly that they will have trouble intercepting and decrypting communications.

The findings in the Bernstein case decision were narrow, in that it allowed the free exportation of encryption source and object code. His source code was considered "expressive" and thus was protected under the First Amendment. The Bernstein decision is not just limited to source code. Although the analysis is about source code, the scope of the relief granted includes object code. Nevertheless, many people see this decision as the beginning of slippery slope that will eventually allow the free and open sale of strong encryption worldwide with no restrictions such as "key recovery." So far the software industry and the privacy and e-commerce advocates are winning, but that could change. This is just the beginning of what will prove to be a constant tug-of-war between the two sides, each side having strong arguments. The Justice Department may appeal this decision to the U.S. Supreme Court. In addition, Congress is taking up important legislation, which is directly related to this area of the law.

This appendix examines cryptographic controls, or the lack thereof, on privacy issues and on the software industry. As it relates to these areas, we will discuss how key recovery plays a role, how U.S. policy has evolved over the years, and where the government stands today. We will present how various foreign governments regulate cryptography and what effect it has on the global encryption industry. On the other side, we'll present the side of law and national security officials as to what potential problems they would experience if the current ruling stands.

Introduction

Daniel Bernstein is a professor at the University of Illinois at Chicago. Professor Bernstein teaches an undergraduate cryptography course under the Department of Mathematics, Statistics, and Computer Science. He teaches cryptography "for students to understand how to use encryption to protect information."[1] Prior to his job in Chicago, he was a Ph.D. candidate at the University of California at Berkeley, where he studied under the Department of Mathematics.

Approximately 12 years ago, he had a computer account that was attacked by a hacker. He spent a lot of time figuring out what the hacker had done, and this incident motivated Bernstein's involvement in computer security. Bernstein became more involved with computer security when he worked on a program that would track attacks by a hacker on university computers. During this project he saw how cryptography might have prevented a hacker's attack.

Bernstein pursued cryptography while at Berkeley. He developed an encryption system called "Snuffle" and wrote a mathematical description of the algorithm. Bernstein wanted to publish his work so that others may use it to "protect their computers from attack; communicate [his] ideas to others who may find them interesting or important contributions to the field; and subject Snuffle to outside review, testing, evaluation, and modification as part of the normal interchange of scientific and technological ideas."[2] At the time, the State Department administered regulations on encryption exports. He submitted a commodity jurisdiction request to determine if his work fell under the licensing jurisdiction of the State Department.

State Department's Response

Bernstein was informed that he needed to get a license to publish his Snuffle program. Bernstein was surprised to find this out because he thought his work was an expression of ideas, which would not be restricted due to his First Amendment rights. However, the State Department did not apply the public domain exception to Bernstein because they *do not allow the exception to apply to encryption at all.* In general, software that is placed into the public domain is exempted from the licensing processes, except when the subject is cryptography. If the subject is cryptography, the software *always* requires a license, even if it only is destined for the public domain. This meant that the State Department had a reason for restricting Bernstein from publishing his work. Bernstein requested that the State Department review/reclassify his work as a public domain exception because "technical data [in his work] related to a lot of software that was taken off the munitions list."[3] As is, his work was classified as munitions.

Bernstein then inquired if there were any publications in the public domain that were also on the munitions list. The State Department could not provide any examples of publications in the public domain that were on the list. According to Bernstein's interpretation of the State Department's public domain definition, nothing can be in the public domain unless it has already been published, and nothing can be legally published unless it is already in the public domain.[4] In former days, the authors called this a Catch-22 clause, after the popular book of the same name. The government controls classification of the information and therefore controls publication. This is contrary to what Bernstein believed, that publication should not to be controlled by the government.

Bernstein submitted a second request to the State Department and found that he would have to file his work as defense articles under a defense manufacturer. Bernstein appealed the State Department's decision on his first commodity jurisdiction request and did not receive a response. He filed suit against the State Department for restricting his First Amendment rights.

Background of the Case

The Bernstein Case argues that source code and description of source code (and object code) is speech entitled to protection under the First Amendment. The State Department argued that Snuffle was a munition subject to the International Traffic In Arms Regulations (ITAR), and a license would be needed to export the appendix describing the software.

Bernstein challenged the constitutionality of the ITAR regulations, specifically, as "on-the-face" invalid as a prior restraint of speech.

President Clinton made the Commerce Department responsible for the licensing of nonmilitary encryption and technologies in December 1996. The Commerce Department then created new Export Administration Regulations (EAR) to govern encryption technology under the Bureau of Export Administration (BXA). Bernstein had already filed the action challenging the constitutionality of the ITAR regulations administered by the State Department. He subsequently amended his complaint, adding the Commerce Department as a defendant making the same constitutional objections against Commerce as he had against the State Department.

Progress of the Case

Professor Bernstein filed the case in the Northern District of California, a federal district court. The case went before Judge Marilyn Patel in District court, and the District court made three rulings, all of which were favorable for Bernstein.

In the first ruling, the government attempted to have the case dismissed because it was out of the court's jurisdiction. According to Judge Patel, source code was speech protected by the First Amendment, which gave the court jurisdiction over the case. This first denied the government's motion to dismiss by holding that software was speech.

The second ruling, granting of summary judgment in favor of Bernstein because the ITAR regulations failed to meet the mandate of the First Amendment, came in December 1996. This was approximately eight months after the first ruling. Unrelated to this court ruling was an issue involving Bernstein's teaching of cryptography that was resolved by stipulation between parties and was not subject to judicial decision. As part of his class, Bernstein was permitted to publish encryption information on the Internet for his students to use without those students being penalized by the government (because it was encryption information).

The third and final ruling in the trial court dealt with the Commerce Department's regulations on encryption exports. The court found that the Commerce Department's regulation, which restricted speech before publication, was unconstitutional. This was a major decision in favor of Bernstein. The court decided it had the right to grant this injunction to everyone in the United States, but the court decided not to grant the injunction to everyone in the nation because the court expected an appeal from the government.

Immediately after the trial court's third ruling, the government submitted an emergency motion to place a stay on the Bernstein injunction. The court agreed to a partial stay, which placed a hold on the Bernstein injunction for approximately two weeks. The stay was intended to allow the Circuit Court of Appeals enough time to review the case. On September 8, 1997, two weeks after the stay was granted, Bernstein would be able to publish his work.

After September 8, the government requested another stay from the 9th Circuit Court of Appeals on the Bernstein injunction. On September 24, the court allowed the government's stay and request for a quick hearing date. The court set a date of December 8, 1997, for hearing Bernstein v. U.S. Department of Justice. The court heard oral arguments from both sides on December 8. Six months after the hearing, the Circuit Court ruled in favor of Bernstein by maintaining the District Court's decision. This was another decision in favor of Bernstein.

In June 1999, the government requested a judicial review of the 9th Circuit Courts decision. The Government in its petition requested the case be reviewed by the original 9th Circuit Court 11-judge panel. The government believed the original 9th Circuit Court judges should have "rewritten the regulations to make them Constitutional rather than strike them down."[5]

Arguments and Ruling in 9th Circuit Court of Appeals

The nub of the argument is whether the government export regulations were legal according to the First Amendment. The government's argument was that they did not have to defend themselves against violating the First Amendment rights if the item they are regulating requires "narrowly tailored" rules that are in the government's best interest. Bernstein's argument was whether the government has the right to regulate publication regardless of the government's intent and that current export regulations are unconstitutional.

The Circuit Court ruled that the government's export regulations were unconstitutional and violated the First Amendment. The court's ruling was grounded on the ambiguity of ITAR and EAR. The court found other issues that were not presented in this case and therefore could not provide a ruling on those issues. Some of these issues included the First

Amendment rights of anonymity and freedom, restrictions on the growth of encryption, and public denial to use encryption.

U.S. Policy, Law, and Opinions

Background

It is necessary to look at some of the other legislation and directives that form the basis for the U.S. government policy in the Bernstein case. The Computer Security Act of 1987 (CSA) provided the groundwork for government policy regarding the protection of the nation's computers, especially those used in national defense. This law provided the National Institute for Standards and Technology (NIST), a division of the Department of Commerce, responsibility for the nation's nonmilitary government computer systems. Under the law, the role of the National Security Agency was limited to providing technical assistance in the civilian security realm. Congress rightly felt that it was inappropriate for a military intelligence agency to have control over the dissemination of unclassified information.

However, the law was enacted after President Reagan issued the controversial National Security Decision Directive (NSDD) 145 in 1984, which gave NSA control over all government computer systems containing "sensitive but unclassified" information. A second directive, issued by National Security Advisor John Poindexter that extended NSA authority over nongovernment computer systems, followed this. In 1989, NSA signed a Memorandum of Understanding (MOU), which purported to transfer back to NSA the authority given to NIST. The MOU created a NIST/NSA technical working group that developed the controversial Clipper Chip and Digital Signature Standard. The NSA has also worked in other ways to weaken the mandate of the CSA. In 1994, President Clinton issued Presidential Decision Directive (PDD) 29. This directive created the Security Policy Board, which has recommended that all computer security functions for the government be merged under NSA control."[6] The agency has actively sought to maintain its monopoly and to suppress the private, nongovernmental development and dissemination of cryptography. The motivation behind NSA's and other agencies efforts to suppress cryptographic know-how is obvious—as the ability to securely encrypt information becomes more widespread, collection work becomes more difficult and time-consuming.

As discussed earlier, the ITAR was used to classify encryption algorithms and source code as part of the munitions list that is considered critical to the national defense. ITAR and other laws, directives, and agreements fall under the general classification of defense trade controls and was a product of the Cold War. These controls limit the export of critical materials, et al. to a selected group of nations.

The export of software products containing cryptographic features is governed by the ITAR, which is administered by the Office of Defense Trade Controls at the Department of State. In addition to software products specifically designed for military purposes, the ITAR "Munitions List" includes a wide range of commercial software containing encryption capabilities. Under the export-licensing scheme, the NSA reviews license applications for "information security technologies" covered by ITAR. While the agency denies the charges, industry representatives claim that NSA-imposed restrictions are stifling innovation in an area that is increasingly important to the computer industry.[7]

Current U.S. Export Regulations

In the last year, the U.S. government has eased restrictions on exporting encryption technology, but the regulations still are more restrictive than many other competing countries. Although they may look more liberal, some of these relaxed restrictions pertain to certain countries only. The following summarizes the current (1999) export regulations:[8]

- Release from the requirement of licensing of up to 56-bit DES and equivalent hardware and software
- Relaxed requirements for key recovery products to allow the export of higher strength products by U.S. company and their subsidiaries
- Export of strong encryption products to insurance companies and health and medical organizations and to online merchants for certain electronic commerce server applications
- License exceptions for export of strong encryption products if they contain key-recoverable or other plaintext access features that allow law enforcement access.

Some of the regulations appear less restrictive but come with strings attached, such as some strong encryption products must provide for key recovery. In addition, all encryption products that use keys up to 56 bits are still subject to a review by the BXA.

Several pieces of important legislation have been proposed since the mid-1990s. The focus of the proposed legislation is relaxation of the encryption regulations. These regulations and the impact on privacy and commerce will be discussed later in this document.

Major Encryption Legislation before the 105th Congress (1997 to 1998)

SAFE (H.R. 695)

SUMMARY   The Security and Freedom through Encryption Act (SAFE) was introduced by Reps. Bob Goodlatte (R-VA) and Zoe Lofgren (D-CA) on February 12, 1997. The original bill created a proprivacy approach to encryption by easing outdated export controls and prohibiting mandatory key escrow.

STATUS   Amendments to SAFE were passed by five committees but never received a full House vote. H.R. 695 died at the end of the 105th Congress. SAFE has been reintroduced in the 106th Congress as H.R. 850.

E-PRIVACY (S. 2067)

SUMMARY   The Encryption Protects the Rights of Individuals from Violation and Abuse in Cyberspace (E-Privacy) Act was introduced by Senators John Ashcroft (R-MO), Patrick Leahy (D-VT), and Conrad Burns (R-MT) on May 12, 1998. The E-PRIVACY Act created a proprivacy framework for computer security, protected the domestic use of strong encryption without key recovery, and eased export controls to allow export of strong encryption products overseas and limited government access to decryption keys.

STATUS   The E-PRIVACY Act was under consideration by the Senate Judiciary Committee but was never voted on. S. 2067 died at the end of the 105th Congress.

McCain/Kerrey (S. 909)

SUMMARY   Sponsored by Senators John McCain (R-AZ) and Robert Kerrey (D-NE), the Secure Public Networks Act forced encryption users to adopt risky key recovery mechanisms in order to participate in a certificate authority system. Meanwhile, McCain-Kerry provided only token relief from export controls.

STATUS The Secure Public Networks Act was introduced on June 16, 1997, by Senator John McCain (R-AZ). On June 19, 1997, McCain/Kerrey was amended and passed by the Senate Commerce Committee. S. 909 never received a full Senate vote and died at the end of the 105th Congress.

Pro-CODE (S. 377)

SUMMARY The Promotion of Commerce Online in the Digital Era (the "Pro-CODE") bill was introduced on January 28, 1997, by Senators Conrad Burns (R-MO), Patrick Leahy (D-VT), and Ron Wyden (D-OR). This bill prohibited domestic controls and eased export controls.

STATUS A hearing was held on Pro-CODE in the Senate Commerce Committee on March 19, 1997. The bill never received a full Committee vote, and died at the end of the 105th Congress.

Major Encryption Legislation before the 106th Congress (1999 to 2000)

SAFE (H.R. 850)

SUMMARY The Security and Freedom through Encryption Act (SAFE) was reintroduced by Reps. Bob Goodlatte (R-VA) and Zoe Lofgren (D-CA) on February 25th, 1999. Like H.R. 695 in the 105th Congress, H.R. 850 creates a proprivacy approach to encryption by easing outdated export controls and prohibiting mandatory key escrow.

STATUS Five committees in the House of Representatives have completed consideration of the SAFE Act, which would lift most export controls on strong encryption. Each of the five committees approved a different version of the bill: Three left it essentially intact, while two adopted gutting amendments. When the full House takes up the bill and amendments sometime after Labor Day, members will be presented with a choice between very different approaches to privacy and security on the Internet.

PROTECT (S. 798)

SUMMARY   The Promote Reliable Online Transactions to Encourage Commerce and Trade (PROTECT) Act of 1999 was introduced on April 14, 1999, by Senators John McCain (R-AZ), Conrad Burns (R-MT), Ron Wyden (D-OR), Patrick Leahy (D-VT), Spenser Abraham (R-MI), and John Kerry (D-MA). PROTECT allows immediate export of 64-bit encryption products, directs NIST to complete advanced encryption standards, allows export of AES products by 2002, and allows immediate export of "generally available" products over 64 bits. S. 798 was ordered on July 23, 1999, to report without amendment and placed on Calendar No. 263 for further action on August 5, 1999.

E-RIGHTS Act (S. 854)

SUMMARY   The Electronic Rights for the 21st Century Act (E-RIGHTS) was introduced by Senator Leahy (D-VT) on April 21, 1999. E-RIGHTS focuses on issues of governmental access, establishing or tightening privacy protections for many types of records. It covers, among a wide range of issues, wireless phone location information, satellite TV home viewing, book purchases, domain name registration information, records stored on networks, and decryption assistance. On April 21, 1999, the bill was referred to the committee of the Judiciary.

Privacy Concerns

The Bernstein case is more far-reaching than just a simple freedom of speech case. It has a profound effect on privacy. There are a variety of civil rights groups and individuals who see any restriction on encryption as a violation of the First Amendment and of the, now traditional, right of privacy. According to Michael Froomkin, Professor of Law at the University of Miami, Florida, "this decision, which I hope will be upheld by the Supreme Court, will be the first step towards greatly increased use of cryptography in domestic products and enhanced personal privacy for all Americans."[9] The privacy advocates maintain that any individual should be able to use cryptography to protect communication between themselves and the intended recipient. The community of law enforcement and intelligence organizations aligned against these advocates want "back doors" so they will be able to decrypt these messages, if need be.

One of the best reasons for the need for unrestricted access to strong encryption is to protect communication among human rights advocates. This is especially true of those brave souls who are in hostile countries reporting back to their home offices or even to the world on the Internet.

In an interview, Bernstein's attorney, Cindy Cohn, claims "if he (Bernstein) ultimately wins, we will see privacy over the Internet increase. If he loses, we will continue to experience a series of public incidents, in which computer messages were intercepted and read, causing damage to individuals and companies. The most serious incidents probably won't even be made public. The tools to gather, sift, and share such information (e-mail, etc.) are getting much stronger, so the public's privacy risk, without encryption, is increasing over time."[10]

Retarding the Use and Growth of Encryption in the U.S.

Professor Froomkin states in a interview on the Bernstein case that "the U.S. government has admitted that they have been using export control laws to retard the domestic use of cryptographic software."[11] For U.S. software companies to invest in the development of cryptographic products for everyday use, there must be a global market available. Export restrictions by the U.S. government increase the risk of not producing profitable encryption software. The software industry must make the choice between creating weak, exportable encryption software that the public will not want and strong encryption software that would be subject to export controls that limits the software to the U.S. only. This is consistent with the Cyberspace Policy Institute's study that claims that because of these export restrictions, "U.S. export controls may have discouraged U.S. software producers from enhancing security features of general-purpose software products to meet the anticipated demand by foreign markets."[12]

Stunting Research and Development

According to the Electronics Frontier Foundation, export controls of U.S.-developed encryption products have "hampered groundbreaking work in the field of cryptography."[13] Scientific development often depends on the free exchange of ideas among experts worldwide. Progress in cryptography is likewise affected. By limiting the publication of source code for cryptographic products, the U.S. has successfully blocked this international free exchange. "When undue regulation burdens and even prevents worldwide discourse concerning cryptography, new encryption methods cannot be tested adequately, workable international encryption standards cannot be developed, and cryptographers—unable to publish or obtain essential peer review without fear of prosecution—cannot be persuaded to enter the field of cryptography at all."[14] The 9th Circuit Court of Appeals commented on this but did not rule on it, since these arguments did not come before the court. However, the court did send a message to legislators and those in the Executive Branch asking for the easing of restrictions.

According to the Electronic Privacy Information Center (EPIC), export controls are the strongest tool used by governments to limit (the) development of encryption products. These restrictions make it difficult to develop international standards for encryption and interoperability of different programs. Compound this with Bernstein and others not being able to freely exchange new encryption algorithms globally and you get countries developing their own local programs which do not interoperate well (if at all) with other programs developed independently in other countries."[15] In addition, these products may not perform adequately or be secure due to the lack of peer review. Export restrictions make for smaller markets. U.S. companies and individuals are not interested in developing programs that would produce limited-potential profits. Thus, countries that have little or no export controls can take advantage of this. They can team with similar countries and develop marketable products, as well as international standards. Because of the tighter restrictions on the export of U.S. cryptographic products, some U.S. firms have actually moved their cryptographic development operations to their foreign subsidiaries in countries that have less restrictive or no export restrictions.[16]

According to Cindy Cohn, "export restrictions create a strong disincentive for individuals and companies to work in this area. When this is gone, the market demand for encryption will drive the industry and researchers."[17] Phil Zimmermann, the creator of Pretty Good Privacy (PGP), agrees. He claims that export controls on strong encryption "has depressed the quality and availability (of encryption software). It has the effect of suppressing domestic availability as well. The manufacturers make one form of software. MS Windows gets half its revenues from overseas. If they (Microsoft) made strong encryption, they could not sell it."[18]

Key Recovery—Another Bane to the U.S. Software Industry

Adding to the problem of export controls is the "encouragement" by the federal government for vendors to supply key recovery mechanisms with their encryption software. Key recovery encryption systems provide some form of access to plaintext outside of the normal channel of encryption and decryption.[19] The National Security Agency (NSA) proposed a type of key recovery, or key escrow, when it introduced the concept of the Clipper Chip in the early 1990s. Either term—recovery or key escrow—means that a third party is able to decrypt and encrypt messages and gain access to the plaintext. All key recovery systems share two essential elements:

- A mechanism by which a third party can obtain *covert* access to the plaintext of the encrypted data
- The existence of a highly sensitive key that must be secured for an extended period of time.[20]

Both the NSA and FBI would like to see this implemented in most, if not all, cryptographic systems to help ensure national security and to thwart criminal activity. One of the reasons Bernstein's algorithm would have been turned down by the BXA was that his strong encryption algorithm provided for no key recovery or escrow. However, it is arguable that key recovery systems create a less secure communications infrastructure and create a complexity that drives up the costs of using encryption.

The fear of government officials, of course, is that criminals will be able to communicate in secret without fear of their communications being tapped. However, government investigations of wiretapping represent a small fraction of the overall investigative techniques used to catch criminals. "In fact, the government's own records show that electronic surveillance is of marginal utility in preventing or solving serious crimes. In the past eleven years, less than 0.2 percent of all law enforcement wiretap requests were made in the investigation of bombings, arson, or firearms."[21] The FBI puts up a rather weak and unconvincing argument for the widespread use of key recovery. They resort to trying to scare the public by discussing the sensationalized consequences of imagined threats, instead of producing the kind of data needed to bring people over to their side. On the other hand, we can make the argument that from the criminal element's point of view, key recovery and escrow systems could just as easily be circumvented with about as much inconvenience as avoiding wiretaps. They can import the secure foreign algorithms, obtain criminally created U.S. secure systems without key recovery, and of course, resort to the most secure encryption device. The directions are quite complex.

In the end, key recovery becomes yet another obstacle that discourages the U.S. software industry from creating an encryption market that allows the U.S. to assert itself as the leader in encryption. Instead, foreign corporations, who have caught up in encryption technology, are leading the way. This is not because they have better technology, but because their government's policies are less restrictive than the United States especially on export controls and the demand for key recovery. Phil Zimmermann said in an interview "why would you build something that everyone knows has a trap door [key recovery system]. People would soon lack confidence in the product and no longer buy it."[22]

What the Rest of the World Is Doing

There are at least three things that the free world with the exception of the United States and United Kingdom appears to agree on:

- No domestic controls on cryptography
- No interest (let alone mandatory rules) in implementing "key escrow and recovery"
- Increase in intelligence and surveillance budgets to catch bad guys without invading the privacy of individuals.[23]

One of the more important agreements between the United States and the rest of the world came out of the Wassenaar Arrangement (WA). The WA is an agreement among 33 countries, including the U.S., to control dual-use technology, which includes cryptography. The WA was proposed in early 1998 and revised in December 1998 and includes some restrictions and some relaxation of existing agreements as follows:

- All cryptographic products of up to 56 bits are free for export.
- Mass-market cryptographic software and hardware of up to 64 bits are free for export.
- The export of products that use encryption to protect intellectual property (such as DVDs) is relaxed.
- Export of all other cryptographic products still requires a license. (This manifests itself very differently from country to country; i.e., it's easy in some countries, a real pain in others.)[24]

The WA did not address the issue of "public domain" encryption, such as that transferred via the Internet. An argument can be made that the source code to Bernstein's algorithm is in the public domain, since he certainly wasn't marketing it or embedding it in a commercial product. If indeed it is a public domain item, then the WA, at least, really has nothing to say about it. One could further argue that, if the WA did not address it, then it couldn't be that threatening from a national security perspective.

It appears that, despite lobbying by the United States, "key recovery" was intentionally left out of the WA, much to the dismay of the U.S. However, the United States has been active in advocating the use of key recovery in many other international forums with some success.

In 1997, the Organization for Economic Cooperation and Development (OECD) recently released their encryption policies. "The (OECD) Guidelines are intended to promote the use of cryptography, to develop electronic commerce through a variety of commercial applications, to bolster user confidence in networks, and to provide for data security and privacy protection."[25] It mainly focused on stressing international cooperation that will eventually lead to global standards on encryption. Surprisingly, Guideline Number 8 states, "Governments should cooperate to coordinate cryptography policies. As part of this effort governments should remove, or avoid creating in the name of cryptography policy, unjustified obstacles to trade."[26] To many people, "unjustified obstacles to trade" may describe U.S. cryptographic policies.

Furthermore, as stated by the Electronic Privacy Information Center (EPIC), "the European Union (EU) has played a key role in rejecting restrictions on encryption."[27] The EU seeks to dismantle intra-Union controls on commercial encryption products, and as a first step, they have imposed relatively weak restrictions on the export of cryptographic products, especially between member states. "(In effect) this amounts to EU domestic controls on products shipped among member states." Although weak, these restrictions still follow the principles agreed to in the Wassenaar Agreement for dual-use goods.[28]

There are several countries that are leaders in establishing encryption policies. Among these are the following two:

■ *Germany* This country has been on the forefront of opposing restrictions on encryption. Their export restrictions are not as severe as the United States' but are based on the EU regulation on dual-use products. In 1999, German efforts prevented key escrow from becoming part of the Wassenaar Arrangement.[29] Germany does not require, and has no plans to require, the use of key recovery systems in the sale of domestic encryption products.

■ *Switzerland* The Swiss abide by the EU and Wassenaar Arrangement. However, they make it clear that, although they will impose export restrictions on cryptography, these restrictions must not interfere with the advantages enjoyed by their domestic encryption industry. According to the EPIC International Cryptography report, "Switzerland will keep its efficient export permit process for cryptographic goods in order to encourage Swiss exports to increase their sales and share worldwide while being mindful of national security interests."[30]

U.S. as Laggard

The Cyberspace Policy Institute reported "the development of cryptographic products outside the U.S. is not only continuing but is expanding to additional countries" and that there are 805 products incorporating cryptography manufactured in 35 countries outside the United States. Of these, 167 use strong encryption, including triple DES and RC5, which are not necessarily inferior to U.S. products. The CPI claims that "the quality of foreign and U.S. products is comparable."[31] Finally, many of these foreign companies manufacturing cryptographic products use, as part of their marketing, a technique that creates "a perception that purchasing American products may involve significant red tape and the encryption may not be strong due to export controls."[32]

Since the U.S. has no import restrictions on cryptography, a U.S. citizen can import the "Privador System" from Estonia, but then would then have difficulty exporting it from the United States to someone in another country. (This is a corollary of "Catch 22.")

As seen above, many companies advertise the fact that U.S.-made strong cryptographic products have back doors that allow the U.S. government to gain access to the key and decrypt messages. However, perceptions can become reality. The United States' strong lobbying on the international stage for key recovery and its perceived strict export controls has received a lot of visibility globally. This has exacerbated the perception that U.S. cryptographic products must be weak, suspect, and difficult to obtain.

According to a report by the Cato Institute, "foreign-made encryption products are as good as, or better than, U.S.-made products. U.S. cryptographers have no monopoly on the mathematical knowledge and methods used to create strong encryption. Powerful encryption symmetric-key technologies developed in other countries include IDEA and GOST. Researchers in New Zealand have developed very strong public key encryption systems as well. As patents on strong algorithms of U.S. origin expire, researchers in other countries will gain additional opportunities to develop strong encryption technology based on those algorithms." Because of this, the report's conclusion is that export restrictions are futile and will not accomplish the goals that the United States is trying to pursue.

The report goes on to say that, theoretically, what the U.S. government has going for it is that U.S. software products, such Microsoft Word, are ubiquitous and have a very large share of the overseas market. Thus, the U.S. government feels that its policies will have an effect globally, since the imbedded cryptography in these products must abide by U.S. export laws. However, in one example, the report points out that within a short period of time, developers were able to take the exportable version of Netscape Navigator and imbed a strong encryption algorithm in place of the 40-bit key SSL. This algorithm was freely distributed worldwide via the Internet, and it worked on most Web sites.[32] As it is, you can almost draw the conclusion that Bernstein's algorithm would have been just another strong encryption algorithm on the international stage competing with all the others. Thus, if one didn't want to use his, others were certainly available from other countries.

Wrap-Up

Review

The Bernstein v. United States Department of Justice case argues that source code and description of source code and object code is speech entitled to protection under the First Amendment and cannot therefore be restricted by the government. Bernstein argues that the government needs to develop specific, clear, and enforceable rules and subject them to judicial review. Furthermore, the government must prove that those regulations are required to protect national security. The government argues that its current rules are sufficient and that that they don't need do anything more than recite a national security concern to support them. Bernstein insists that these rules are by any measure, unclear, nonspecific, and confusing. The 9th Circuit Court of Appeals decided in favor of Bernstein and ruled that the government export regulations on encryption violate the First Amendment.

EAR Violates First Amendment

The EAR closely guards the exportation of encryption software through a broad scope of regulations. The regulations as viewed by the circuit court "preclude the use of the Internet and other global mediums if such publication would allow passive or active access by a foreign national within the United States or anyone outside the United States."[33] The government continues by limiting exportation of source code that is printed on electronic media, such as CD-ROMs. The government has implied that it will use this regulation to limit encryption source code printed on paper that can be easily imported into a computer by such means as scanning. From Director of Export Policy for the BXA Jim Lewis's point of view, "I think that the interests of the U.S., from a security, law enforcement, and commercial perspective, would be best served by a decision that continued controls on source code."[34] The government regulation intends to restrict criminal and enemy access to encryption source code and products.

Basically, the government's EAR regulations are unconstitutional regardless of the regulations' intent to prevent enemies and criminals from illegally using encryption. The EAR regulations place prior restraint on encryption publication and restrict the expression of ideas. Under these regulations, an individual cannot publish encryption source code without approval from the government. According to the EAR and the Circuit Court of Appeals:

> BXA administrators are empowered to deny licenses whenever export might be inconsistent with "U.S. national security and foreign policy interests" No more specific guidance is provided. Obviously, this constraint on official discretion is little better than no constraint at all.[35]

Bernstein refrained from publishing encryption materials because he could not get government approval with specific reasoning and he was fearful of government prosecution. One of the encryption materials Bernstein refrained from publishing was the source code of his encryption system called Snuffle. Encryption source code and mathematical algorithms for many cryptographers are expressions of ideas. The government incorrectly interprets source code as a means to control the direct "operation of a computer without conveying information to the user."[36] Source code can be interpreted by people. Source code is another medium for expressing ideas. The government cannot restrict a person's right to express ideas without violating the First Amendment. From the findings above and by allowing Bernstein to publish his source code, we believe the 9th Circuit Court of Appeals made the correct ruling in the Bernstein v. Department of Justice case.

Will the Bernstein Case Impact U.S. Encryption in the Future?

The government uses export regulations as a control mechanism for encryption. The current regulations severely hamper the encryption efforts within the United States. Although Jim Lewis states that out of 1895 license applications in 1998, only 13 were denied, the firms must be willing to develop strong encryption for use within the United States. Firms can make weaker encryption systems for export outside the United States, but these systems would compete with stronger encryption products from other countries. The Bernstein case may be the case that loosens encryption regulations and opens the door for U.S. firms to export stronger encryption products in order to compete globally.

According to Cindy Cohn, if the Bernstein ruling is upheld as written, it will eliminate the current export restrictions on encryption software (both source code and object code) and hardware. Cohn continues her line of reasoning, "if it wanted to continue to regulate cryptography, the government would then have to promulgate new regulations that meet the configurational standards, meaning that the regulations will have to be altered dramatically and allow for quick judicial review. This will be a tremendous opportunity for U.S. businesses and others who want to use, develop, and promulgate strong cryptography, finally putting them on equal footing with their foreign competitors."[37]

However, Professor Froomkin is not as convinced as Bernstein's lead attorney. He perceives that a win for Bernstein may have a small impact on encryption regulations. He believes a win for Bernstein will force the government to rewrite the regulations in a manner that handles Bernstein as an exception instead of dealing with the entire issue.[38]

It is our opinion that the Bernstein case will have a significant impact on U.S. encryption. Assuming Bernstein stands in court, the government will rewrite the export regulations until the regulations qualify as constitutional. The government will continue to rewrite the regulations as long as it believes the nation's best interest is at stake. However, Phil Zimmermann summarizes the issue by stating, "Export control is rotting away."[39] At worst, the government's rewriting of any export policies will lead to civil disobedience. At best, the government will see the futility of it all, give up, and let freedom prevail.

Notes

1. Electronic Frontier Foundation (EFF), http://www.eff.org/bernstein
2. Ibid.
3. Ibid.
4. Ibid.
5. Ibid.
6. Electronic Privacy Information Center (EPIC), http://www.epic.org/crypto/csa
7. EPIC, http://www.epic.org/crypto/dss/sobel_dss_paper.htm
8. Bureau of Export Administration (BXA), http://bxa.doc.gov/Encryption/EncrypolicyUpdate.htm
9. Froomkin, www.law_miami.edu/froomkin/bernstein99.htm, p. 1.
10. Cohn interview by Rebecca Catey, submitted 8/16/99,Team 4, The George Washington University, Professor Randy Nichols, Information Security Certificate Program, Engineering Management 298.IN3, Cryptographic Systems: Application, Management and Policy, Summer 1999.
11. Froomkin interview by Joseph Wojszynski, submitted 8/16/99,Team 4, The George Washington University, Professor Randy Nichols, Information Security Certificate Program, Engineering Management. 298.IN3, Cryptographic Systems: Application, Management and Policy, Summer 1999.
12. Growing Development of Foreign Encryption Production in the Face of US Export Regulations, Cyberspace Policy Institute, www.cpi.seas.gwu.edu.
13. EFF, op. cit.
14. Ibid.
15. Cryptography and Liberty, EPIC, www.epic.org/reports/cyrpto1999.
16. Ibid.
17. Cohn interview, op. cit.
18. Zimmermann interview by Rebecca Catey, submitted 16 August 1999, Team 4, The George Washington University, Professor Randy Nichols, Information Security Certificate Program, Engineering Management 298.IN3, "Cryptographic Systems: Application, Management and Policy," Summer 1999.
19. "Risks of Key Recovery, Key Escrow and Trusted Third-Party Encryption," Hal Abelson, et al., http://www.cdt.org/crypto/risks98
20. Ibid.
21. Ibid.
22. Zimmermann interview, op. cit.
23. Cryptography and Liberty, EPIC, op. cit., 9-11.
24. Ibid.
25. Ibid, 14-15.
26. Ibid.

27. Ibid.

28. Ibid.

29. Ibid, EPIC, 39-40.

30. Ibid.

31. Growing Development of Foreign Encryption Production in the Face of US Export Regulations, Cyberspace Policy Institute, www.cpi.seas.gwu.edu.

32. "The Myth of Superiority of American Encryption Products," Henry B. Wolfe, Cato Institute, November 1998.

33. EFF, op. cit.

34. Lewis interview by Rebecca Catey, submitted 16 August 1999, Team 4, The George Washington University, Professor Randy Nichols, Information Security Certificate Program, Engineering Management 298.IN3, Cryptographic Systems: Application, Management and Policy, Summer 1999.

35. EFF, op. cit.

36. EFF, Ibid.

37. Cohn interview, op. cit.

38. Froomkin interview, op. cit.

39. Zimmermann interview, op. cit.

APPENDIX G

VPN COMPARISONS

Chapter 11 introduced the reader to virtual private networks (VPN). Appendix P further explores VPN countermeasures. *Information Security* is a superb source of practical information regarding practical INFOSEC applications. Both *Information Security* via Executive Editor Andy L. Briney (for free subscriptions contact www.infosecuritymag.com) and Christopher M. King, president of INFOSEC Engineering, in Chelmsford, MA, gave full permission to publish the VPN comparisons. Appendix P draws heavily on their *Information Security,* March 1999, VPN contributions. King eloquently describes challenges in deploying a VPN for an enterprise network in his *The 8 Hurdles to VPN Deployment*. The product comparison charts at the end of this appendix giving head-to-head comparisons of 42 VPN solutions are reprinted in this appendix. They are based on King's outstanding work. The information is believed to be accurate and updates are included. However, the authors neither endorse these products nor guarantee the accuracy of the information, which was vendor-supplied.

What Again Was a VPN?

A VPN is a way of using a public network transport (e.g., the Internet) to form a secure network connection, either between two enterprise sites (site-to-site) or between an individual and a site (remote access). The purpose of a VPN is to allow organizations to extend their network trust perimeter over public networks without sacrificing security. Using the Internet as a backbone, a VPN can securely and cost-effectively connect all of a company's offices, telecommuters, mobile workers, customers, partners, and suppliers. Companies can achieve substantial savings using Internet-based VPNs instead of private networks and corporate modem banks.

Type of Implementation

VPN implementations come in three primary forms:

- A special-purpose device consisting of two or more network interfaces, a real-time operating system, and hardware-based cryptographic support
- A pure software solution that either modifies the network kernel or runs above the transport layer
- A hybrid in which a VPN application runs on a standard computing platform that utilizes an outboard cryptographic processor to perform the VPN functions.

Gateway

A VPN gateway is a multihomed networking device that provides encryption and authentication services to a multitude of hosts behind it. The placement of the VPN gateway must be in-line, similar to that of a firewall. The network interface facing the public (untrusted) network is typically called the "black side," while the interface facing the internal (trusted) network is called the "red side." The VPN connection is transparent to users behind the gateway; the network connection appears to be a dedicated link but is actually occurring over the shared network.

Depending on the organization's security policy, outbound packets are encrypted, sent in the clear, or blocked. For inbound packets, the outer address is the VPN gateway, while the inner address is some host behind the gateway. The time-honored principle is to separate red-black for cryptographic purposes. Unencrypted packets should not be allowed in the black side of a VPN gateway, while encrypted packets from the untrusted network should not be allowed into the red side.

Client

A VPN client is a single-homed networking device, such as a PC, whose network transport software has been modified to perform encryption and authentication of traffic between VPN gateways and/or other VPN clients. The VPN client tunnels communications to the black address of the VPN gateway, authenticates the user, and then allows access to the red side of the gateway.

VPN Configurations

Three different VPN configurations are in use today: *enterprise, remote access*, and *extranet*.

Enterprise VPN

An enterprise or site-to-site VPN securely joins two networks (intranet or extranet) together (see Figure G-1). In most cases, the connection is

ENTERPRISE VPN ARCHITECTURE

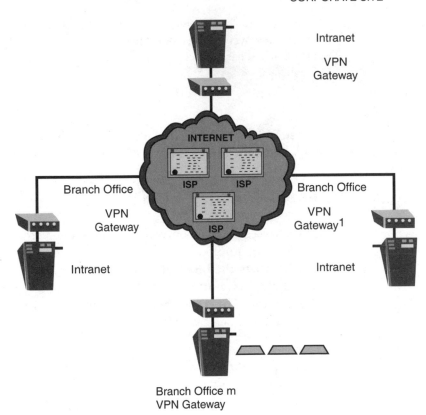

This figure depicts a typical corporation with three remote locations. Because it uses a public network, a site-to-site VPN can provide the same connectivity as leased lines at a much lower cost.

REMOTE-ACCESS VPN ARCHITECTURE

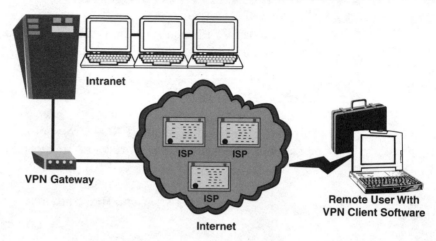

This figure provides a simplistic view of a VPN client. The client can access the VPN gateway over a dial-up or cable modem, or from a dedicated Internet connection. All packets destined for the protected intranet are encrypted and authenticated.

between a corporate site and a remote site over the Internet. Enterprise VPN technology is used in lieu of Frame Relay or leased lines.

Remote Access VPN

Remote access solutions involve use of expensive long-distance and toll-free telephone numbers to dial into corporate modems. An alternative to this is to utilize the Internet service provider's Post Office Protocol (POP) by dialing a local number and then setting up a secure connection into a VPN gateway. This involves VPN client software loaded on the remote user's machine (see Figure G2).

Extranet VPN

An extranet VPN is a subset of an enterprise VPN, with external business partners on the other side of the wire. An extranet allows a business to be its service provider, supplying a common network on which employees, partners, suppliers, and customers can share information and resources. Extranets have soared in popularity because they facilitate a seamless flow of information and commerce and they sharply reduce communication costs.

The security architecture necessary for extranet communication must not only protect corporate data but also facilitate various levels of user access control. The goal is to minimize risk to the corporate intranet while at the same time keeping the extranet configuration flexible.

There are two distinct types of extranets: one-to-many and many-to-many. A one-to-many extranet (see Figure G-3), which links many companies to a single resource, is more common today (e.g., home banking). Many-to-many extranets are less common, due in part to the immense scalability challenges of securely linking together a number of different company intranets. However, as large-scale VPN projects like the Automotive Network Exchange (ANX) gain momentum, many-to-many extranets will become more commonplace.

Extranet access control mechanisms generally fall into three categories:

■ Network access control mechanisms, such as VPNs, firewalls and network-level intrusion detection systems

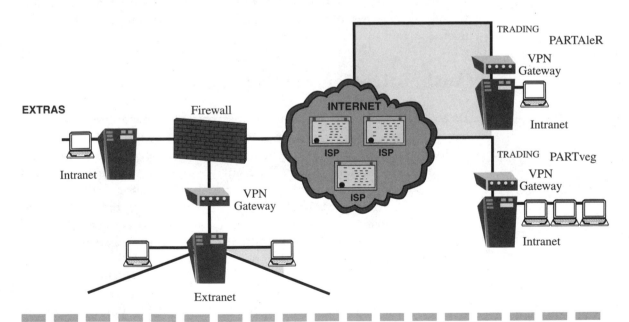

Figure G-3

- Authentication mechanisms, such as digital certificates or tokens
- Platform mechanisms, such as host-based intrusion detection systems and monitoring/auditing systems

As the network boundaries between intranets, extranets, and the Internet continue to erode, application-layer security will take on added importance. The problem is a lack of a common or standard protection scheme for applications. The need to provide an enhanced layer of security, reliability, and quality of service on top of the Internet will be the primary driver of VPNs as a subset of e-commerce extranet deployment.

The key to maximizing the extranet is to make it accessible to as many partners as possible regardless of their technical adeptness. The more participants there are, the greater the rates of return from the system.

Hurdles to VPN Deployment

No matter what its size, configuration, or architecture, deploying an enterprise VPN can be a complex process, with many hurdles to overcome. King presents eight prominent issues that must be addressed: authentication/key management, fault tolerance, performance, reliable transport, network placement, addressing/routing, administration/management, and interoperability.

Authentication/Key Management

Before VPN devices can communicate, they must negotiate a mutually agreeable way of securing their data (i.e., a security association). As part of this negotiation, each device has to verify that the other device is actually the entity it claims to be. Different VPN products support different authentication mechanisms, including shared secrets, (passwords), tokens, and digital certificates. However, *IPSec-compliant* VPN devices generally support only the use of a shared secret or digital certificate for authentication. Of the two, certificate-based authentication is more secure because it reduces the complexity of key distribution.

The problem with fielding certificate-based authentication systems is that public-key infrastructure (PKI) technology is in a state of flux. (Certificates were studied in Chapter 9 and PKI was reviewed in Chapter 19.) Most information technology vendors (e.g., Microsoft and

Netscape) have a solution that is tailored to their own specific PKI clients (e.g., Outlook and Navigator). The major drawback is that there aren't any agreed-upon standard protocols for requesting, validating, and cross-certifying certificates. However, the Internet Engineering Task Force (IETF's) PKIX (Public Key Infrastructure Working Group) continues to work on them.

Fault Tolerance

Enterprise-level solutions require a high level of availability. There are many ways to provide highly availability redundant hardware with full switching, redundancy components, dynamic load balancing, and so on. The challenge is to provide active session "failover protection" so that the communicating VPN device does not sense failures on the other end of the tunnel. The key is to synchronize all the information involved with the security association, such as the authentication header (AH), the encapsulating security payload (ESP), the size of cryptographic synchronization, and the source address of the security association and the level of sensitivity.

Fault tolerance has to exist between all VPN devices (gateways and clients). VPN clients form point-to-point connections between gateways. If the VPN client detects that the gateway is not responding, a secondary gateway can be defined. However, this is currently a manual process within the VPN client profile, though there's no reason it couldn't be automatic. Compounding the problem is the fact that the IPSec protocol currently does not support any fault-tolerant mechanisms. The IETF is addressing this problem.

Performance

IPSec cryptographic processing is computationally intensive. Diffie-Hellman and RSA public key cryptography require rapid multiplication and the production of the modulus of very large integers. This, coupled with the increasing speeds of network accesses and the need for simultaneous connections, makes it difficult for security-aware network devices. General-purpose computing platforms do not have the proper I/O capability to perform the necessary cryptographic and network processing. Offloading cryptographic functions to an outboard processor results in only minor gains in efficiency. Currently, the only viable solution is to combine the network interface card (NIC function) with the cryptographic functions.

Reliable Transport

VPNs are independent of the underlying transport network. But no matter how much security VPNs provide, if bottlenecks exist between VPN nodes, communications will suffer. Many enterprise network managers think the Internet is not yet capable of providing adequate, peak, or scaleable bandwidth. Moreover, bandwidth management prioritizes packets based on their attributes (e.g., protocol, IP address) and does not address the main problem of reliability. Vendors have designed their own protocols to address this problem; however, not all of the participating network devices support these technologies.

Network Placement

The placement of the VPN gateway in relation to the firewall is crucial, since firewalls cannot enforce network access control of encrypted packets. VPN technology is a newcomer to the network marketplace. Enterprises already overburdened with networking equipment—routers, firewalls, switches, and so forth—must now solve the problem of where to place a VPN gateway. The following are general VPN gateway placement rules:

- Do not compromise the overall network security policy.
- The VPN gateway placement must not be a single point of failure.
- The VPN gateway must accept only encrypted traffic from the untrusted network.
- The VPN gateway must accept nonencrypted and encrypted traffic from the trusted network.
- The VPN gateway must defend itself from Internet threats.
- The overall architecture must filter traffic after VPN decryption.

There are several placement options:

1. *In front of a firewall*   A VPN gateway in front of a firewall with a single connection to the untrusted network poses a single point of failure. Moreover, such a placement requires enterprises to pass both clear and encrypted text from the untrusted network, though in some cases, incoming unencrypted packets can be filtered after the decryption process. With such a setup it would never be known if the VPN gateways were compromised. This could be especially disastrous for extranet users.

2. *Behind a firewall*   If the VPN gateway is inside the firewall, the security protection is received from that firewall. Internet protocol (IP) packets of type 50 and 51 (authentication header and encapsulating security packet) would have to be allowed through the firewall. Universal datagram packets (UDPs) on port 500 for Internet key exchange protocol (IKE) would also have to be allowed in. As with gateways placed in front of a firewall, this placement also poses a single point of failure and requires that the VPN gateway accept both clear and encrypted traffic from the untrusted network.

3. *On a firewall*   Putting the VPN gateway on the firewall itself is, theoretically, a great idea, since such a placement would consolidate the administration and management of the network components. Although in time this technology will efficiently be put into a single box, it is not a viable solution today due to limitations in the ability to route, perform public key cryptography, and switch between encrypted sessions while performing access control and logging. Currently, it is much more efficient to maintain the VPN functions independently.

4. *Parallel to a firewall*   Most VPN vendors suggest two untrusted network connections, one for the firewall and the other for the VPN gateway. In this setup the VPN device is configured to accept encrypted traffic only. While such a placement avoids a single point of failure, the VPN device has to defend itself from threats on the untrusted network side. This architecture is dangerous considering that VPN devices have not proven themselves to be robust when directly connected over the Internet.

5. *VPN gateway on the firewall side*   A VPN gateway on a dedicated firewall interface is considered "on the side." This placement, shown in Figure G-4, protects the VPN device from threats on the untrusted network while filtering unencrypted traffic. The outside interface of the VPN gateway should be configured to accept only encrypted packets; all packets entering the inside interface should be encrypted before they're sent onto the Internet.

Addressing/Routing

Networks are not generally additive, and special attention must be paid to network addressing before joining two or more disparate networks. If the private address space of two or more networks overlaps, routing can

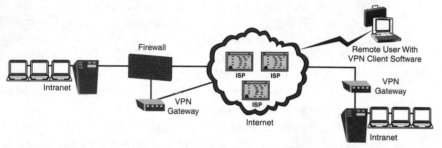

For many setups, the best placement of a VPN gateway is on the firewall side. Such a placement does not present a single point of failure, and both encrypted and cleartext packets are filtered using the exisiting firewall policy.

be a challenge. Tunneling potentially allows two illegal addresses to communicate with each other over a private network. Therefore, VPN devices need to communicate routing information to allow seamless communications.

VPN clients first have to establish a TCP/IP connection via an ISP, and then form a tunnel to the enterprise gateway. Once the tunnel is active, it is up to the VPN client security policy to allow traffic outside the tunnel. This setup is called "split tunneling," in which all packets destined for the enterprise are encrypted, while any packet that is not is sent over the Internet is in the clear. The downside to split tunneling is that a cracker who compromises your computer can use it to launch an attack on your intranet.

Currently, VPN LAN-to-LAN products form point-to-point tunnel connections in which routing tables have to be predefined. Some VPN vendors support "dynamic VPNs," which allow fully meshed network connections instead of' point-to-point tunnels with static routes.

Administration/Management

To be effective, VPN gateways and clients must perform several administration and management functions. Most VPN vendors provide a client/server graphical user interface (GUI) or Web interface for administration. Software updates can be performed using the management interfaces. Management platforms allow for the administration of single or multiple devices.

To provide more control for VPN administrators, some products support multiple privilege levels (e.g., grouping of devices or administrator privileges such as read-only, write, etc.). The management protocol that controls the devices must be performed through a secure channel. Management can be performed from the untrusted (black) side as long as it is in a secure fashion.

Interoperability

Because VPN technology uses encryption as the basis for its security, interoperability among vendors is a major concern. The IPSec specification was chosen to alleviate this problem. The term "IPSec-compliant" is what most VPN vendors use to mean that they meet the current IETF IPSec standards. The only true test of compliance, however, is an interoperability report among heterogeneous vendors. If all the vendors were IPSec-compliant, there would be no distinguishing factors. This is where IPSec extensions come in, including compression algorithms, non-IPSec cryptographic algorithms, non-IPSec authentication schemes, and multi-platform support (e.g., UNIX or Mac).

For VPNs to interoperate, the *VPN policy must be consistent throughout the enterprise*. VPN policies consist of authentication, authorization, and cryptographic attributes—for instance, key length negotiations and certificate validation. Outside clients must adhere to a subset of VPN policies to allow secure communications. King suggests that a combination of AH tunneling and ESP transport should be used between VPN endpoints. Inbound packets should use AH tunneling between VPN gateways to validate the originating site. Encrypted packets designated for a specific node would be inside the tunneled packet.

Wrap-Up

The major issues holding back VPNs is the reliability of the Internet, large-scale PKI deployment, gateway performance and VPN remote client software. The charts in Figures G-5 through G-8 try to address/compare responses to these hurdles in current VPN offerings.

Figure G-5

VPN COMPARISON CHART PART 1

	PRODUCT/DEVICE TYPE				CONFIGURATION/NETWORK PLACEMENT							CONTENT/BANDWIDTH MANAGEMENT				
Product	Hardware	Software	Cryptographic accelerator	# of platforms supported	Gateway-to-gateway	Client-to-gateway	Client-to-client	Placed on firewall	Placed in front of firewall	Placed behind firewall	Placed parallel with firewall	Content filtering: Packet filter/Application-level/None	Prioritizes traffic protocols by: Connection/Class/None/Other	Protocol support: PPTP/L2F/L2TP/IPSec/Other/All	Supports QOS features?
PathBuilder S500 Tunnel Switch — 3Com Corp — www.3com.com, 408-326-5000	✓			N/A	✓	✓			✓	✓		P, A	Co, Cl	P, L2TP, I	N/A
VPCom (Virtual Private Communications) — Ashley Laurent Inc — www.vpcom.com, 512-322-0676		✓	✓	3	✓	✓	✓	✓	✓	✓	✓	P, A	Q	L2TP, I	Y
Aventail ExtraNet Center — Aventail Corp — www.aventail.com, 206-215-0035		✓		N/A		✓		✓	✓	✓	✓	A	N	O	N
RaptorMobile — Axent Technologies Inc — www.axent.com, 800-44-AXENT		✓		6	✓	✓		✓				P, A	N	I	N
Pirma — Brivida Inc — www.brivida.com, 706-549-3200	✓			N/A	✓	✓			✓			N	N	P, L2F, L2TP, I	Y
SecurWare — Bull Worldwide Information Systems — www.bullsoft.com, 800-285-5727	✓	✓		2	✓	✓			✓			P	N	Q	Y
VPN-1 Gateway — Check Point Software Technologies Inc — www.checkpoint.com, 650-628-2000		✓	✓	5	✓	✓		✓				A	N	I	Y
IntraPort 2+ — Compatible Systems Corp — www.compatible.com, 303-444-9532	✓	✓		N/A	✓	✓			✓	✓		P, A	Co	I	Y
DiamondTEK — Cryptek Secure Communications LLC — www.cryptek.com, 703-802-9300	✓			N/A	✓	✓	✓		✓			P	N	I	N
RedCreek VPN for CyberGuard — CyberGuard Corp. — www.cyberguard.com, 800-666-4273	✓			N/A	✓	✓			✓		✓	N	N	I	N
Defensor — CyberSafe Corp. — www.cybersafe.com, 425-391-6000		✓		4	✓	✓		✓				P, A	N	O	N
PrivateWire — Cylink Corp — www.cylink.com, 408-328-5117		✓		N/A	✓	✓			✓	✓		P, A	N	O	N
F-Secure VPN+ — Data Fellows Inc. — www.datafellows.com, 408-938-6700		✓		2	✓	✓	✓	✓	✓	✓	✓	P	N	I	N
NetFortress VPN-10 — Fortress Technologies Inc — www.fortresstech.com, 813-288-7388	✓			N/A	✓	✓			✓	✓		N	N	O	N
OneGate 1000 — Freegate Corp. — www.freegate.com, 408-617-1000	✓	✓		N/A			✓					P	N	P, I	N
HP Praesidium Extranet VPN — Hewlett-Packard Co — www.hp.com, 408-447-5347		✓		5		✓		✓	✓	✓	✓	A	N	O	N
IBM eNetwork Firewall for AIX and NT — IBM Corp. — www.ibm.com, 919-543-8855		✓		2	✓	✓		✓				P, A	N	I	N
VTCP/Secure — InfoExpress Inc — www.infoexpress.com, 650-947-7880		✓		11	✓	✓			✓	✓		P, A	N	I, O	N
SafeNet 3.0 — Information Resource Engineering Inc. (IRE) — www.ire.com, 410-931-7500	✓	✓		N/A	✓	✓	✓		✓		✓	P	N	I	N
Fort Knox Policy Router — Internet Devices Inc. — www.internetdevices.com, 888-237-2244	✓			N/A	✓	✓		✓	✓	✓	✓	P, A	Co, Cl	I	Y
Conclave — Internet Dynamics — www.conclave.com, 805-370-2200		✓		N/A	✓	✓			✓			P, A	N	P, I	N

FOOTNOTES: [1]T1/E1 connections. [2]Four can be optionally added.

[3]Chrysalis-ITS (www.chrysalis-its.com) produces a cryptographic accelerator and key management product called Luna VPN which is integrated into Check Point's VPN solution.

Figure G-6

	FAULT TOLERANCE			ADDRESSING/ROUTING			AUTHENTICATION/KEY MANAGEMENT									ADMINISTRATION				PRICE
Redundancy	Heartbeat failover	Load balancing	Support for third-party FT products	Supports split/virtual tunneling	Supports dynamic/meshed connections	# of encrypted net. interfaces supported	Gateway access protected w/ authentication?	Authentication Type(s): Shared secret	Certificates	RADIUS	Tokens	LDAP	Supports cross-certification?	Max # of concurrent users supported	Supports remote administration	Supports central mgmt. from single station	Supports multiple administration levels	# of logging/alerting mechanisms	Price
✓				✓	✓	8¹	Y			✓		✓	N/A	2,048	✓		✓	N/A	$15,995–$29,995
✓	✓	✓		✓	✓	N/A	N/A	✓	✓		✓	✓	N	20,000		✓	✓	7	$1,295–$6,495
✓		✓			✓	N/A	Y	✓	✓	✓	✓	✓	N	N/A	✓	✓	✓	2	$7,995 for client/server bundle
		✓				N/A	Y	✓	✓	✓	✓	✓	Y	N/A	✓	✓	✓	N/A	$99
✓					✓	1¹	Y	✓	✓				Y	5,000	✓	✓	✓	1	$1,995/single tunnel device; $19,900/hub
		✓				2	Y	✓					N/A	N/A		✓		N/A	$16,000
✓		✓	✓	✓	✓	N/A	Y	✓	✓	✓	✓	✓	N	1,200		✓		N/A	starts at $2,495
	✓			✓	✓	32⁴	Y	✓	✓	✓	✓		Y	200	✓	✓	✓	N/A	$9,995
		✓				N/A	Y	✓					N	6,000	✓	✓	✓	2	$1,000/seat
✓	✓			✓		N/A	N/A	✓	✓	✓	✓		Y	N/A	✓	✓	✓	N/A	starts at $3,995
✓	✓	✓	✓	✓	✓	20	Y	✓		✓	✓	✓	Y	N/A	✓			N/A	$100/client; $25,000/trusted gateway
		✓			✓	10	Y	✓		✓			N	2,000	✓	✓	✓	2	$8,900
				✓	✓	N/A	Y	✓	✓	✓			Y	1,000	✓	✓		4	$99/client; $495/server; $2,495/gateway; $4,995/enterprise gateway
					✓	1	Y	✓					N	1,024	✓	✓		N/A	$5,995
✓				✓	✓	N/A	N/A	✓					Y	200	✓			N/A	$5,395
✓			✓	✓	✓	N/A	Y	✓	✓	✓	✓		N	N/A	✓	✓		2	starts at $8,495
	✓²	✓²	✓	✓		N/A	Y	✓			✓		N	N/A	✓	✓	✓	N/A	$2,500/25 users; $16,500/unlimited users
✓		✓	✓	✓	✓	1	Y	✓	✓	✓	✓	✓	N	N/A	✓	✓		3	$89/client; $1,495/server
✓	✓	✓	✓	✓	✓	2	Y	✓	✓	✓	✓		N	50,000	✓	✓	✓	N/A	$79–$250/client; $4,995/gateway; $15,995/central management
✓	✓			✓	✓	3	Y	✓	✓	✓	✓	✓	Y	5,000	✓	✓	✓	3	$1,995–$9,995
				✓	✓	8	Y	✓	✓	✓	✓	✓	Y	N/A	✓	✓	✓	6	$7,730 for a 2-node VPN with 100 users; $48,450 for a 10-node VPN with 1,000 users

¹ LAN-to-LAN connections.
² With add-on product.

NOTE: *Information Security* neither endorses these products nor guarantees the accuracy of the information, which was vendor-supplied.

Figure G-7

VPN
COMPARISON CHART PART 2

	PRODUCT/DEVICE TYPE				CONFIGURATION/NETWORK PLACEMENT							CONTENT/BANDWIDTH MANAGEMENT				
	Hardware	Software	Cryptographic accelerator	# of platforms supported	Gateway-to-gateway	Client-to-gateway	Client-to-client	Placed on firewall	Placed in front of firewall	Placed behind firewall	Placed parallel with firewall	Content filtering: Packet filter/application-level/None	Prioritizes traffic protocols by: Connection/Class/None/Other	Protocol support: PPTP/L2F/L2TP/IPSec/QOther/All	Supports QOS features?
The KyberPASS Security Server KyberPASS Corp. www.kyberpass.com, 800-845-1140		✓		5	✓	✓	✓	✓	✓	✓	✓	P, A	N		N/A
Netguard Control Center LanOptics Inc. www.ntfirewall.com, 972-738-6900		✓		N/A	✓		✓		✓		✓	P, A	Co, Cl	I, Q	Y
Lucent VPN Gateway Lucent Technologies www.lucent.com/security, 732-615-2759	✓	✓	✓	2	✓	✓	✓	✓	✓	✓	✓	P	N		N
NetScreen-100 NetScreen Technologies Inc. www.netscreen.com, 408-970-8889	✓			N/A	✓	✓		✓				P, A	Co, Cl		Y
VPN Server 5000 Network Alchemy Inc. www.network-alchemy.com, 831-460-3800	✓	✓		3	✓	✓		✓				P	N	P, L2TP, I	N
GVPN Network Associates Inc. www.nai.com, 408-988-3832		✓		7	✓	✓	✓	✓	✓	✓		A	N		N
Datacryptor 2000 Racal Security and Payments www.racalsec.com, 954-846-4700	✓			N/A	✓			✓	✓			N	Co	N/A	N/A
ciPro-VPN Radguard Inc. www.radguard.com, 877-RADGUARD	✓			N/A				✓	✓	✓	✓	P	N		N
NetSwift 1000 Rainbow Technologies Inc. www.rainbow.com, 888-667-4728			✓	N/A	✓			✓	✓			N	N	P, L2TP, I	N
Ravlin 10 RedCreek Communications Inc. www.redcreek.com, 510-745-3900	✓			N/A	✓	✓		✓	✓	✓		P	N/A		N
LanHover VPN Gateway Shiva Corp. www.shiva.com, 781-687-1000	✓			N/A	✓	✓		✓	✓	✓		P	N	I, Q	N
SonicWALL PRO Sonic Systems Inc. www.sonicsys.com, 408-844-9900	✓			N/A								P, A	N		N
SSH IPSec Express SSH Communications Security Ltd. www.ssh.fi, +358 9 4354 3221		✓		4	✓	✓	✓					P	N		N
Interceptor Firewall Appliance Technologic Inc. www.tlogic.com, 800-615-9911	✓			N/A	✓	✓		✓				P, A	N	P, Q	N
Permit Enterprise TimeStep Corp. www.timestep.com, 613-599-3610	✓	✓	✓	N/A[3]	✓	✓	✓	✓	✓	✓	✓	N	N		N
CryptoGate 3.0 Toshiba American Information Systems Inc. www.networks.toshiba.com, 888-422-6677		✓		N/A	✓	✓		✓	✓	✓	✓	P	N	I, Q	N
SmartGate VPN V-ONE Corp. www.v-one.com, 800-495-VONE		✓		N/A		✓		✓	✓	✓		A	Co	N/A	N
VPNware Systems VPNet Technologies Inc. www.vpnet.com, 408-445-6600	✓			N/A	✓	✓		✓	✓	✓		N	N		Y
Watchguard LiveSecurity System Watchguard Technologies Inc. www.watchguard.com, 206-521-8340	✓			N/A	✓	✓	✓					P, A	N	P, I, Q	N
Nortel Networks' Contivity Extranet Switch 2000[4] Westcon Inc. www.westcon.com, 914-829-7170	✓			N/A	✓	✓		✓	✓	✓		P, A	Co	P, L2F, L2TP	N/A
Omni S/R & OmniStack Xylan Corp. www.xylan.com, 800-999-9956	✓			2	✓			✓	✓	✓		P	Co, Cl	L2TP, I	Y

FOOTNOTES: [3] 4 Solaris, 2 NT.
[4] Westcon is a Nortel distributor.

Figure G-8

	FAULT TOLERANCE			ADDRESSING/ROUTING					AUTHENTICATION/KEY MANAGEMENT							ADMINISTRATION					PRICE
Redundancy	Heartbeat failover	Load balancing	Support for third-party FT products	Supports split/virtual tunneling	Supports dynamic/meshed connections	# of encrypted net. interfaces supported	Gateway access protect./w authentication?	Authentication Type(s): Shared secret	Certificates	RADIUS	Tokens	LDAP	Supports cross-certification?	Max. # of concurrent users supported	Supports remote administration	Supports central mgmt. from single station	Supports multiple administration levels	# of logging/alerting mechanisms	Price
			✓		N/A		Y		✓	✓	✓	✓	Y	N/A				N/A	$8,850
✓		✓	✓		1		Y	✓			✓	✓	N	N/A	✓	✓	✓	3	$5,000
✓		✓	✓		✓	4		Y	✓				N	2,000	✓	✓	✓	N/A	$24,980
	✓				3		Y	✓					N	1,000	✓	✓		3	$99.95
✓	✓	✓		✓	2		Y	✓	✓	✓			Y	20,000	✓	✓	✓	N/A	$50,000
✓	✓				N/A		Y		✓				Y	N/A	✓	✓	✓	N/A	N/A
	✓				31		N/A		✓					2,048	✓	✓	✓	2	starts at $1,595
✓	✓	✓	✓	✓	✓	4		N/A	✓	✓		✓	Y	N/A	✓	✓	✓	N/A	$8,450
✓	✓	✓		✓	✓	N/A		N/A					N	N/A				N/A	$1,299
			✓	✓	✓	2		N/A	✓	✓	✓	✓	N	1,000	✓	✓	✓	1	$3,500
✓		✓			2		N/A	✓	✓	✓	✓	✓	N	1,024	✓	✓	✓	3	$6,200-$9,950
					1		N/A			✓			N/A	N/A	✓	✓		2	$2,995
					N/A		N/A	✓	✓			✓	Y	N/A				N/A	N/A
			✓		3		Y	✓	✓				N	256	✓	✓		4	$3,745-$6,445
	✓		✓	✓	2		Y	✓	✓			✓	Y	2,000	✓	✓	✓	2	$3,995-$11,995
			✓		4		Y			✓			N	N/A	✓	✓		N/A	$995 (includes one management software, one server and 10 clients)
✓			✓	✓	N/A		N/A	✓	✓	✓	✓		Y	N/A	✓	✓	✓	1	$4,995/NT server software and two clients; $6,495/UNIX server software and two clients
✓	✓	✓		✓	N/A		Y	✓	✓	✓	✓		N/A	5,000	✓	✓		N/A	$3,995-$60,000
		✓	✓	✓	N/A		Y	✓			✓		✓	N	1,000	✓	✓	✓	1	$4,990
			✓		6		N/A			✓	✓	✓	N/A	200	✓	✓	✓	1	$20,000
✓				✓	N/A		Y	✓		✓	✓	✓	✓	N	N/A	✓	✓	✓	N/A	starts at $5,000

NOTE: *Information Security* neither endorses these products nor guarantees the accuracy of the information, which was vendor-supplied.
N/A–Not Available

APPENDIX H

LIABILITY OF CERTIFICATE AUTHORITIES PROVISIONS RELATING TO LIABILITY OF CERTIFICATION AUTHORITIES IN STATES THAT HAVE ENACTED LEGISLATION

(Last Updated September 26, 1999)

NOTE 1: This summary only lists states that have enacted statutes.

NOTE 2: Certification Authority means the person who authorizes and causes the issuance of certificate that verifies an electronic signature.

NOTE 3: The use of the term Liability refers to the responsibilities, warranties, and legal liabilities of a Certification Authority in issuing a certificate.

Only nine (9) States have addressed Certificate Authorities by enacting legislation. The acts have very different elements in each state and apply to different activities.

STATE   **BILL/STATUTE**
LIABILITY OF CERTIFICATION AUTHORITY

Illinois   Illinois Electronic Commerce Security Act;
1997 Illinois House Bill 3180 (5 ILCS 175/1-101 et seq.) .

Section 15-220. Unauthorized use if a signature device.

"No person shall knowingly access, alter, disclose, or use the signature device of a certification authority used to issue certificates without authorization, or in excess of lawful authorization, for the purpose of creating, or allowing or causing another person to create, an unauthorized electronic signature using such signature device. A person convicted of a violation of this Section shall be guilty of a Class 3 felony. A person who violates this Section in furtherance of any scheme or artifice to defraud shall be guilty of a Class 2 felony."

§15-301. Trustworthy services.

"Except as conspicuously set forth in its certification practice statement, a certification authority and a person maintaining a repository must maintain its operations and perform its services in a trustworthy manner."

§15-305. Disclosure.

"(a) For each certificate issued by a certification authority with the intention that it will be relied upon by third parties to verify digital signatures created by subscribers, a certification authority must publish or otherwise make available to the subscriber and all such relying parties: (1) its certification practice statement, if any, applicable thereto; and (2) its certificate that identifies the certification authority as a subscriber and that contains the public key corresponding to the private key used by the certification authority to digitally sign the certificate (its "certification authority certificate"). (b) In the event of an occurrence that materially and adversely affects a certification authority's operations or system, its certification authority certificate, or any other aspect of its ability to operate in a trustworthy manner, the certification authority must act in accordance with procedures governing such an occurrence specified in its certification practice statement, or in the absence of such procedures, must use reasonable efforts to notify any persons that the certification authority knows might foreseeably be damaged as a result of such occurrence."

§15-310 Issuance of certificate.

"A certification authority may issue a certificate to a prospective subscriber for the purpose of allowing third parties to verify digital signatures created by the subscriber only after: (1) the certification authority has received a request for issuance from the prospective subscriber; and (2) the certification authority has: (A) complied with all of the relevant practices and procedures set forth in its applicable certification practice statement, if any; or (B) in the absence of a certification practice statement addressing these issues, confirmed in a trustworthy manner that: (i) the prospective subscriber is the person to be listed in the certificate to be issued; (ii) the information in the certificate to be issued is accurate; and (iii) the prospective subscriber rightfully holds a private key capable of creating a digital signature, and the public key to be listed in the certificate can be used to verify a digital signature affixed by such private key."

§15-315. Representations upon issuance of certificate.

"(a) By issuing a certificate with the intention that it will be relied upon by third parties to verify digital signatures created by the subscriber, a certification authority represents to the subscriber, and to any person who reasonably relies on information contained in the certificate, in good faith and during its operational period, that: (1) the certification authority has processed, approved, and issued, and will manage and revoke if necessary, the certificate in accordance with its applicable certification practice statement stated or incorporated by reference in the certificate or of which such person has notice, or in lieu thereof, in accordance with this Act or the law of the jurisdiction governing issuance of the certificate; (2) the certification authority has verified the identity of the subscriber to the extent stated in the certificate or its applicable certification practice statement, or in lieu thereof, that the certification authority has verified the identity of the subscriber in a trustworthy manner; (3) the certification authority has verified that the person requesting the certificate holds the private key corresponding to the public key listed in the certificate; and (4) except as conspicuously set forth in the certificate or its applicable certification practice statement, to the certification authority's knowledge as of the date the certificate was issued, all other information in the certificate is accurate, and not materially misleading. (b) If a certification authority issued the certificate subject to the laws of another jurisdiction, the certification authority also makes all warranties and representations, if any, otherwise applicable under the law governing its issuance."

§15-320. Revocation of a certificate.

"(a) During the operational period of a certificate, the certification authority that issued the certificate must revoke the certificate in accordance with the policies and procedures governing revocation specified in its applicable certification practice statement, or in the absence of such policies and procedures, as soon as possible after: (1) receiving a request for revocation by the subscriber named in the certificate, and confirming that the person requesting revocation is the subscriber, or is an agent of the subscriber with authority to request the revocation; (2) receiving a certified copy of an individual subscriber's death certificate, or upon confirming by other reliable evidence that the subscriber is dead; (3) being presented with documents effecting a dissolution of a corporate subscriber, or confirmation by other evidence that the subscriber has been dissolved or has ceased to exist; (4) being served with an order requiring revocation that was issued by a court of competent jurisdiction; or (5) confirmation by the certification authority that: (A) a material fact represented in the certificate is false; (B) a material prerequisite to issuance of the certificate was not satisfied; (C) the certification authority's private key or system operations were compromised in a manner materially affecting the certificate's reliability; or (D) the subscriber's private key was compromised. (b) Upon affecting such a revocation, the certification authority must notify the subscriber and relying parties in accordance with the policies and procedures governing notice of revocation specified in its applicable certification practice statement, or in the absence of such policies and procedures, promptly notify the subscriber, promptly publish notice of the revocation in all repositories where the certification authority previously caused publication of the certificate, and otherwise disclose the fact of revocation on inquiry by a relying party."

Minnesota Minnesota Electronic Authentication Act (Minn. Stat. Ann. § 325K)

325K.03. Role of the secretary.

"The secretary shall be a certification authority. The secretary shall issue, suspend, and revoke certificates in the manner prescribed under section 325K.10 to applicants for licensure. The secretary may also issue, suspend, and revoke certificates for governmental entities."

325K.05. Licensure and qualifications of certification authorities.

"Subd. 1. Licensure Conditions. To obtain or retain a license, a certification authority must: (1) be the subscriber of a certificate published in a recognized repository; (2) employ as operative personnel only persons who have not been convicted within the past 15 years of a felony or a crime involving fraud, false statement, or deception; (3) employ as operative personnel only persons who have demonstrated knowledge and proficiency in following the requirements of this chapter; (4) file with the secretary a suitable guaranty, unless the certification authority is a department, office, or official of a federal, state, city, or county governmental entity, that is self-insured; (5) use a trustworthy system, including a secure means for limiting access to its private key; (6) present proof to the secretary of having working capital reasonably sufficient, according to rules adopted by the secretary, to enable the applicant to conduct business as a certification authority; (7) register its business organization with the secretary, unless the applicant is a governmental entity or is otherwise prohibited from registering; and (8) comply with all further licensing requirements established by rule by the secretary."

325K.08. Dangerous activities by certification authority prohibited.

"Subd. 1. Prohibition Generally. No certification authority, whether licensed or not, may conduct its business in a manner that creates an unreasonable risk of loss to subscribers of the certification authority, to persons relying on certificates issued by the certification authority, or to a repository."

"Subd. 2. Orders and Civil Actions. In the manner provided by the Administrative Procedure Act, chapter 14, the secretary may issue orders and obtain injunctions or other civil relief to prevent or restrain a certification authority from violating this section, regardless of whether the certification authority is licensed. This section does not create a right of action in a person other than the secretary."

325K.10. Issuance of Certificate.

"Subd. 1. Conditions. A licensed certification authority may issue a certificate to a subscriber only after all of the following conditions are satisfied: (1) the certification authority has received a request for issuance signed by the prospective subscriber; and (2) the certification authority has confirmed that: (i) the prospective subscriber is the person to be listed in the certificate to be issued; (ii) if the prospective subscriber is acting through one or more agents, the subscriber duly authorized each agent to have custody of the subscriber's private key and to request issuance of a certificate listing the corresponding public key; (iii) the information in the certificate to be issued is accurate; (iv) the prospective subscriber rightfully holds the private key corresponding to the public key to be listed in the certificate; (v) the prospective subscriber holds a private key capable of creating a digital signature; (vi) the public key to be listed in the certificate can be used to verify a digital signature affixed by the private key held by the prospective subscriber; and (vii) the certificate provides information sufficient to locate or identify one or more repositories in which notification of the revocation or suspension of the certificate will be listed if the certificate is suspended or revoked. The requirements of this subdivision may not be waived or disclaimed by either the licensed certification authority, the subscriber, or both."

325K.11. Warranties and obligations upon issuance of certificate.

"Subd. 1. Absolute Warranties to Subscribers. By issuing a certificate, a licensed certification authority warrants to the subscriber named in the certificate that: (1) the certificate contains no information known to the certification authority to be false; (2) the certificate satisfies all material requirements of this chapter; and (3) the certification authority has not exceeded any limits of its license in issuing the certificate. The certification authority may not disclaim or limit the warranties of this subdivision."

"Subd. 2. Negotiable warranties to subscribers. "Unless the subscriber and certification authority otherwise agree, a certification authority, by issuing a certificate, promises to the subscriber: (1) to act promptly to suspend or revoke a certificate in accordance with section 325K.14 or

325K.15; and (2) to notify the subscriber within a reasonable time of any facts known to the certification authority that significantly affect the validity or reliability of the certificate once it is issued."

"Subd. 3. Warranties to those who reasonably rely. By issuing a certificate, a licensed certification authority certifies to all who reasonably rely on the information contained in the certificate that: (1) the information in the certificate and listed as confirmed by the certification authority is accurate; (2) all information foreseeably material to the reliability of the certificate is stated or incorporated by reference within the certificate; (3) the subscriber has accepted the certificate; and (4) the licensed certification authority has complied with all applicable laws of this state governing issuance of the certificate."

"Subd. 4. Warranties following publication. By publishing a certificate, a licensed certification authority certifies to the repository in which the certificate is published and to all who reasonably rely on the information contained in the certificate that the certification authority has issued the certificate to the subscriber."

325K.13. Control of Private Key.

"Subd. 2a. Possession of a private key. A certification authority cannot hold a private key on behalf of a subscriber.

325K.14. Suspension of Certificate.

"Subd. 1. Suspension for 96 hours. Unless the certification authority and the subscriber agree otherwise, the licensed certification authority that issued a certificate that is not a transactional certificate must suspend the certificate for a period not to exceed 96 hours: (1) upon request by a person identifying himself or herself as the subscriber named in the certificate, or as a person in a position likely to know of a compromise of the security of a subscriber's private key, such as an agent, business associate, employee, or member of the immediate family of the subscriber; or (2) by order of the secretary under section 325K.10. The certification authority need not confirm the identity or agency of the person requesting suspension."

"Subd. 2. Suspension for 96 hours; other causes. The secretary may suspend a certificate issued by a licensed certification authority for a period of 96 hours, if: (1) a person identifying himself or herself as the subscriber named in the certificate or as an agent, business associate, employee, or member of the immediate family of the subscriber requests suspension; and (2) the requester represents that the certification authority that issued the certificate is unavailable. (b) The secretary may require the person requesting suspension to provide evidence, including a statement under oath or affirmation, regarding the requester's identity, authorization, or the unavailability of the issuing certification authority, and may decline to suspend the certificate in its discretion. The secretary or law enforcement agencies may investigate suspensions by the secretary for possible wrongdoing by persons requesting suspension."

"Subd. 3. Notice of suspension. Immediately upon suspension of a certificate by a licensed certification authority, the licensed certification authority shall give notice of the suspension according to the specification in the certificate. If one or more repositories are specified, then the licensed certification authority must publish a signed notice of the suspension in all the repositories. If a repository no longer exists or refuses to accept publication, or if no repository is recognized under section 325K.25, the licensed certification authority must also publish the notice in a recognized repository. If a certificate is suspended by the secretary, the secretary must give notice as required in this subdivision for a licensed certification authority, provided that the person requesting suspension pays in advance any fee required by a repository for publication of the notice of suspension."

325K.15. Certificate revocation.

"Subd. 3. After death or dissolution. A licensed certification authority must revoke a certificate that it issued: (1) upon receiving a certified copy of the subscriber's death certificate, or upon confirming by other evidence that the subscriber is dead; or (2) upon presentation of documents effecting a dissolution of the subscriber, or upon confirming by other evidence that the subscriber has been dissolved or has ceased to exist, except that if the subscriber is dissolved and is reinstated or restored before revocation is completed, the certification authority is not required to revoke the certificate."

Mississippi   Mississippi Digital Signature Act of 1997, Miss. Code 1972 Ann.

§ 25-63-1 (1997) (1997 MS HB 752)§ 25-63-7. Certification of digital signatures.

"(1) The Secretary of State shall serve as the certification authority to verify the digital signature of any public entity in Mississippi. (2) The Secretary of State shall license private certification authorities, conditioned upon their showing: (a) That they possess proficiency in encryption technology; (b) That they possess sufficient working capital; and (c)

That they maintain an office in this state or have established a registered agent for process in this state. (3) The Secretary of State shall have authority to revoke any license granted under the terms of this chapter upon notice for good cause shown."

Missouri   Missouri Digital Signature Act (1998 MO SB 680)

Section 8. 1.

"A certification authority, whether licensed or not, may not conduct its business in a manner that creates an unreasonable risk of loss to subscribers of the certification authority, to persons relying on certificates issued by the certification authority, or to a repository. 2. (1) The division may publish in one or more recognized repositories brief statements advising subscribers, persons relying on digital signatures, and repositories about any activities of a licensed or unlicensed certification authority, of which the division has actual knowledge, which create a risk prohibited by subsection 1 of this section; (2) The certification authority named in a statement as creating such a risk may protest the publication of the statement by filing a brief, written defense. Upon receipt of such a protest, the division shall: (a) Publish the written defense along with the division's statement; (b) Publish notice that a hearing has been scheduled to determine the facts and to decide the matter; and (c) Promptly give the protesting certification authority notice and a hearing as provided in chapter 536, RSMo; (3) Following the hearing, the division shall: (a) Rescind the advisory statement if its publication was unwarranted pursuant to this section; (b) Cancel the advisory statement if its publication is no longer warranted; (c) Continue or amend the advisory statement if it remains warranted; or (d) Take further legal action to eliminate or reduce a risk prohibited by subsection 1 of this section; (4) The division shall publish its decision in one or more recognized repositories."

Section 11. 1.

"(1) By issuing a certificate, a licensed certification authority warrants to the subscriber named in the certificate that: (a) The certificate contains no information known to the certification authority to be false; (b) The certificate satisfies all material requirements of sections 1 to 27 of this act; and (c) The certification authority has not exceeded any limits of its license in issuing the certificate; (2) The certification authority may not disclaim or limit the warranties of this subsection. 2. Unless the subscriber and certification authority otherwise agree, a certification authority, by issuing a certificate, shall: (1) Act promptly to suspend or revoke a certificate in accordance with sections 14 and 15 of this act; and

(2) Notify the subscriber within a reasonable time of any facts known to the certification authority which significantly affect the validity or reliability of the certificate once it is issued. 3. By issuing a certificate, a licensed certification authority certifies to all who reasonably rely on the information contained in the certificate that: (1) The information in the certificate and listed as confirmed by the certification authority is accurate; (2) All foreseeable information material to the reliability of the certificate is stated or incorporated by reference within the certificate; (3) The subscriber has accepted the certificate; and (4) The licensed certification authority has complied with all applicable laws of this state governing issuance of the certificate. 4. By publishing a certificate, a licensed certification authority certifies to the repository in which the certificate is published and to all who reasonably rely on the information contained in the certificate that the certification authority has issued the certificate to the subscriber."

North Carolina North Carolina Electronic Commerce Act, Session Law 1998-127

(1997 NC HB 1356)

§ 66-58.7. Civil penalty. "The Secretary may assess a civil penalty of not more than five thousand dollars ($5,000) per violation against any certification authority that violates a provision of this Article or any rules promulgated thereunder."

§ 66-58-8. Criminal penalty. "Any person who willfully violates any provision of this Article, or who willfully violates any rule or order under this Article, with intent to defraud, is guilty of a Class I felony."

Oregon The Electronic Signature Act, Oregon Revised Statutes §192.825 et seq. (1997 OR HB 3046)

§192.84. Certificates for verifying electronic signatures; registration of authentication authorities. "(3) The Director of the Department of Consumer and Business Services purposes of sections 1 to 7 of this Act, including the suspension or revocation of certificates or registrations issued by the director...."

Utah Digital Signature Act (Utah Code Ann. §46-3-101 et seq.)

§46-3-204 Dangerous activities by any certification authority prohibited. "(1) A certification authority, whether licensed or not, may not conduct its business in a manner that creates an unreasonable risk of loss to subscribers of the certification authority, to persons relying on certificates issued by the certification authority, or to a repository. (2) (a) The division may publish in one or more recognized repositories brief statements advising subscribers, persons relying on digital signatures, and repositories about any activities of a licensed or unlicensed certification authority, of which the division has actual knowledge, which create a risk prohibited by Subsection (1). (b) The certification authority named in a statement as creating such a risk may protest the publication of the statement by filing a brief, written defense. Upon receipt of such a protest, the division shall: (i) publish the written defense along with the division's statement; (ii) publish notice that a hearing has been scheduled to determine the facts and to decide the matter; and (iii) promptly give the protesting certification authority notice and a hearing as provided in Title 63, Chapter 46b, Administrative Procedures Act. (c) (i) Following the hearing, the division shall: (A) rescind the advisory statement if its publication was unwarranted pursuant to this section; (B) cancel the advisory statement if its publication is no longer warranted; (C) continue or amend the advisory statement if it remains warranted; or (D) take further legal action to eliminate or reduce a risk prohibited by Subsection (1). (ii) The division shall publish its decision in one or more recognized repositories. (3) As provided in Title 63, Chapter 46b, Administrative Procedures Act, the division may issue orders and obtain injunctions or other civil relief to prevent or restrain a certification authority from violating this section, regardless of whether the certification authority is licensed. This section does not create a right of action in any person other than the division."

§46-3-301 General requirements for certification authorities. "(1) A licensed certification authority or subscriber shall use only a trustworthy system: (a) to issue, suspend, or revoke a certificate; (b) to publish or give notice of the issuance, suspension, or revocation of a certificate; and (c) to create a private key. (2) A licensed certification authority shall disclose any material certification practice statement, and any fact material to either the reliability of a certificate which it has issued or its ability to perform its services. A certification authority may require a signed, written, and reasonably specific inquiry from an identified person, and payment of reasonable compensation, as conditions precedent to effecting a disclosure required in this subsection."

§46-3-303 Warranties and obligations of certification authority upon issuance of a certificate. "(1) (a) By issuing a certificate, a licensed certification authority warrants to the subscriber named in the certificate that: (i) the certificate contains no information known to the certification authority to be false; (ii) the certificate satisfies all material requirements of this chapter; and (iii) the certification authority has not exceeded any limits of its license in issuing the certificate. (b) The certification authority may not disclaim or limit the warranties of this subsection. (2) Unless the subscriber and certification authority otherwise agree, a certification authority, by issuing a certificate, shall: (a) act promptly to suspend or revoke a certificate in accordance with Sections 46-3-306 and 46-3-307; and (b) notify the subscriber within a reasonable time of any facts known to the certification authority which significantly affect the validity or reliability of the certificate once it is issued. (3) By issuing a certificate, a licensed certification authority certifies to all who reasonably rely on the information contained in the certificate that: (a) the information in the certificate and listed as confirmed by the certification authority is accurate; (b) all foreseeable information material to the reliability of the certificate is stated or incorporated by reference within the certificate; (c) the subscriber has accepted the certificate; and (d) the licensed certification authority has complied with all applicable laws of this state governing issuance of the certificate. (4) By publishing a certificate, a licensed certification authority certifies to the repository in which the certificate is published and to all who reasonably rely on the information contained in the certificate that the certification authority has issued the certificate to the subscriber.

§ 46-3-309 Recommended reliance limits and liability. "(1) By specifying a recommended reliance limit in a certificate, the issuing certification authority and the accepting subscriber recommend that persons rely on the certificate only to the extent that the total amount at risk does not exceed the recommended reliance limit. (2) Unless a licensed certification authority waives application of this subsection, a licensed certification authority is: (a) not liable for any loss caused by reliance on a false or forged digital signature of a subscriber, if, with respect to the false or forged digital signature, the certification authority complied with all material requirements of this chapter; (b) not liable in excess of the amount specified in the certificate as its recommended reliance limit for either: (i) a loss caused by reliance on a misrepresentation in the certificate of any fact that the licensed certification authority is required to confirm; or (ii) failure to comply with Section 46-3-302 in issuing the certificate; (c) liable only for direct, compensatory damages n any action to recover a loss due to reliance on the certificate, which damages do not include: (i) punitive or exemplary damages; (ii) damages for lost profits, savings, or opportunity; or (iii) damages for pain or suffering.

Washington   Washington Electronic Authentication Act (Chapter 19.34 RCW)

§19.34.220. Licensed certification authorities—Warranties, obligations upon issuance of certificate—Notice "(1) By issuing a certificate, a licensed certification authority warrants to the subscriber named in the certificate that: (a) The certificate contains no information known to the certification authority to be false; (b) The certificate satisfies all material requirements of this chapter; and (c) The certification authority has not exceeded any limits of its license in issuing the certificate. The certification authority may not disclaim or limit the warranties of this subsection. (2) Unless the subscriber and certification authority otherwise agree, a certification authority, by issuing a certificate, promises to the subscriber: (a) To act promptly to suspend or revoke a certificate in accordance with RCW 19.34.250 or 19.34.260; and (b) To notify the subscriber within a reasonable time of any facts known to the certification authority that significantly affect the validity or reliability of the certificate once it is issued. (3) By issuing a certificate, a licensed certification authority certifies to all who reasonably rely on the information contained in the certificate, or on a digital signature verifiable by the public key listed in the certificate, that: (a) The information in the certificate and listed as confirmed by the certification authority is accurate; (b) All information foreseeably material to the reliability of the certificate is stated or incorporated by reference within the certificate; (c) The subscriber has accepted the certificate; and (d) The licensed certification authority has complied with all applicable laws of this state governing issuance of the certificate. (4) By publishing a certificate, a licensed certification authority certifies to the repository in which the certificate is published and to all who reasonably rely on the information contained in the certificate that the certification authority has issued the certificate to the subscriber.

§19.34.280. Recommended reliance limit—Liability—Damages "(1) By specifying a recommended reliance limit in a certificate, the issuing certification authority recommends that persons rely on the certificate only to the extent that the total amount at risk does not exceed the recommended reliance limit. (2) Subject to subsection (3) of this section, unless a licensed certification authority waives application of this subsection, a licensed certification authority is: (a) Not liable for a loss caused by reliance on a false or forged digital signature of a subscriber, if, with respect to the false or forged digital signature, the certification authority complied with all material requirements of this chapter; (b) Not liable in excess of the amount specified in the certificate as its recommended reliance limit for either: (i) A loss caused by reliance on a misrepresentation in the certificate of a fact that the licensed certification authority is required to confirm; or (ii) Failure to comply with RCW 19.34.210 in issuing the certificate; (c) Not liable for: (i) Punitive or exemplary damages. Nothing in this chapter may be interpreted to permit punitive or exemplary damages that would not otherwise be permitted by the law of this state; or (ii) Damages for pain or suffering. (3) Nothing in subsection (2)(a) of this section relieves a licensed certification authority of its liability for breach of any of the warranties or certifications it gives under RCW 19.34.220 or for its lack of good faith, which warranties and obligation of good faith may not be disclaimed. However, the standards by which the performance of a licensed certification authority's obligation of good faith is to be measured may be determined by agreement or notification complying with subsection (4) of this section if the standards are not manifestly unreasonable. The liability of a licensed certification authority under this subsection is subject to the limitations in subsection (2)(b) and (c) of this section unless the licensed certification authority waives the limits. (4) Consequential or incidental damages may be liquidated, or may otherwise be limited, altered, or excluded unless the limitation, alteration, or exclusion is unconscionable. A licensed certification authority may liquidate, limit, alter, or exclude consequential or incidental damages as provided in this subsection by agreement or by notifying any person who will rely on a certificate of the liquidation, limitation, alteration, or exclusion before the person relies on the certificate.

West Virginia   Electronic Signatures Authorization Act (1998 WV HB 4293)

Section 39-5-4. Duties of the secretary of state and state auditor; state agencies use of electronic signature. (b). "The secretary of state is also designated the certification authority and repository for all governmental agencies which are subject to chapter twenty-nine-a of this code, and shall regulate transactions and digital signature verifications...."

Section 39-5-7. Secretary of state; liability. "The secretary of state, serving as authority and repository for governmental entities for signature keys, shall revoke any signature key when the secretary has reason to believe that the digital signature key has been stolen, fraudulently used or otherwise compromised. This article creates no liability upon the secretary of state for any transactions compromised by any illegal act or in appropriate uses associated with electronic signatures."

ALPHABET SOUP, CRYPTOTERMS, AND INTEROPERABILITY GLOSSARY

"Alphabet Soup, Cryptoterms, and Interoperability Glossary" includes frequently used acronyms, abbreviations, terms, phrases, buzzwords, and so on that one may hear in any conversation among security professionals. Various recognized sources (Menezes, Schneier, Smith, Stallings, Nichols, Kahn, and Breed) were tapped to obtain the definitions given here. We have drawn heavily on the NSTISSI 4009, *Information Systems Security Glossary*, published by NIST. The *Dictionary of Naval Abbreviations* compiled and Edited by Bill Wedertz, 3rd ed., was helpful. The *ICSA Glossary of Terms*, published for the ICSA Cryptography Consortium in 1998, rounded out the effort.

This section is divided into three sections. Section 1 presents the commonly used abbreviations and acronyms. Section 2 provides definitions for commonly used INFOSEC terms. Section 3 provides a glossary of well-known biometric countermeasure terms.

Section 1
Alphabet Soup

Commonly Used Abbreviations and Acronyms

ACL   Access Control List

ADP   Automated Data Processing

AIS   Automated Information System

AISS   Automated Information Systems Security

AK   Automatic Remote Rekeying

AKDC   Automatic Key Distribution Center

AKMC   Automated Key Management Center

AMS   (1) Auto-Manual System; (2) Autonomous Message Switch

ANSI   American National Standards Institute

ARPANET   Advanced Research Projects Agency Network

ASC   Accredited Standards Committee

ASCII   American Standard Code for Information Interchange

ASSIST   Program Automated Information System Security Incident Support Team

ATM   Asynchronous Transfer Mode

AUTODIN Automatic Digital Network

AVP Authorized Vendor Program

C2 (1) Command and Control; (2) Controlled Access Protection

C3 Command, Control, and Communications

C3I Command, Control, Communications, and Intelligence

C4I Command, Control, Communications, and Computers

CA Certification Authority

CAP Competitive Access Providers

CAW Certificate Authority Workstation

CCEP Commercial COMSEC Endorsement Program

CCI Controlled Cryptographic Item

CEPR Compromising Emanation Performance Requirement

CERT Computer Security Emergency Response Team

CIRT Computer Security Incident Response Team

CMCS COMSEC Material Control System

COMPUSEC Computer Security

COMSEC Communications Security

CONOP Concept of Operations

COTS Commercial Off-The-Shelf

CRL Certificate Revocation List

CRP COMSEC Resources Program (Budget) Crypt/Crypto Cryptographic-related

CSE Communications Security Element

CSSO Contractor Special Security Officer

CSTVRP Computer Security Technical Vulnerability Report Program

CT&E Certification Test and Evaluation

CTTA Certified TEMPEST Technical Authority

CUP COMSEC Utility Program

DAA Designated Approving Authority

DAC Discretionary Access Control

DAMA Demand Assigned Multiple Access

DCID Director Central Intelligence Directive

DCS (1) Defense Communications System; (2) Defense Courier Service

DES Data Encryption Standard

DISA Defense Information System Agency

DISN   Defense Information System Network

DoDTCSEC   Department of Defense Trusted Computer System Evaluation Criteria

DMA   Direct Memory Access

DMS   Defense Message System

DSA   Digital Signature Algorithm

DSN   Defense Switched Network

DSVT   Digital Subscriber Voice Terminal

DTD   Data Transfer Device

DTS   Diplomatic Telecommunications Service

DUA   Directory User Agent

EAM   Emergency Action Message

ECCM   Electronic Counter-Countermeasures

ECM   Electronic Countermeasures

EDAC   Error Detection and Correction

EDESPL   Endorsed Data Encryption Standard Products List

ELINT   Electronic Intelligence

ELSEC   Electronic Security

EMSEC   Emission Security

FDDI   Fiber Distributed Data Interface

FIPS   Federal Information Processing Standard

FOCI   Foreign-Owned, -Controlled, or -Influenced

FOUO   For Official Use Only

FSRS   Functional Security Requirements Specification

FTAM   File Transfer Access Management

GCCS   Global Command and Control System

GETS   Government Emergency Telecommunications Service

GPS   Global Positioning System

GTS   Global Telecommunications Service

GWEN   Ground Wave Emergency Network

IA   Information Assurance

I&A   Identification and Authentication

IATA   International Air Transport Association

IBAC   Identity Based Access Control
IDS   Intrusion Detection System
IFF   Identification, Friend or Foe
IFFN   Identification, Friend, Foe, or Neutral
INFOSEC   Information Systems Security
IO   Information Operations
IP   Internet Protocol
IPSO   Internet Protocol Security Option
IR   Information Ratio
IS   Information System
ISDN   Integrated Services Digital Network
ISO   International Standards Organization
ISS   Information Systems Security
ISSM   Information Systems Security Manager
ISSO   Information Systems Security Officer
ITAR   International Traffic in Arms Regulation

KAK   Key-Auto-Key
KDC   Key Distribution Center
KEK   Key Encryption Key
KMC   Key Management Center
KPK   Key Production Key
KSOS   Kernelized Secure Operating System
KVG   Key Variable Generator

LEAD   Low-Cost Encryption/Authentication Device
LEAF   Law Enforcement Access Field

MAC   (1) Message Authentication Code; (2) Mandatory Access Control
MAN   (1) Mandatory Modification; (2) Metropolitan Area Network
MEECN   Minimum Essential Emergency Communications Network
MEP   Management Engineering Plan
MER   Minimum Essential Requirements
MHS   Message Handling System
MI   Message Indicator
MIJI   Meaconing, Intrusion, Jamming, and Interference
MISSI   Multilevel Information Systems Security Initiative

MLS Multilevel Security

MRT Miniature Receiver Terminal

MSE Mobile Subscriber Equipment

NACAM National COMSEC Advisory Memorandum

NACSI National COMSEC Instruction

NACSIM National COMSEC Information Memorandum

NCCD Nuclear Command and Control Document

NCS (1) National Communications System; (2) National Cryptologic School; (3) Net Control Station

NCSC National Computer Security Center

NIST National Institute of Standards and Technology

NSA National Security Agency

NSAD Network Security Architecture and Design

NSD National Security Directive

NSDD National Security Decision Directive

NSEP National Security Emergency Preparedness

NSI National Security Information

NSO Network Security Officer

NSTAC National Security Telecommunications Advisory Committee

NSTISSAM National Security Telecommunications and Information Systems Security Advisory/Information Memorandum

NSTISSC National Security Telecommunications and Information Systems Security Committee

NSTISSD National Security Telecommunications and Information Systems Security Directive

NSTISSI National Security Telecommunications and Information Systems Security Instruction

NSTISSP National Security Telecommunications and Information Systems Security Policy

NTIA National Telecommunications and Information Administration

OPSEC Operations Security

ORA Organizational Registration Authority

OTP One-Time Pad

PAA Policy Approving Authority

PCMCIA Personal Computer Memory Card International Association

PKA   Public Key Algorithm

PKC   Public Key Cryptography

PKI   Public Key Infrastructure

PROPIN   Proprietary Information

PSL   Protected Services List

PWDS   Protected Wireline Distribution System

RACE   Rapid Automatic Cryptographic Equipment

SA   Systems Administrator

SAO   Special Access Office

SAP   (1) System Acquisition Plan; (2) Special Access Program

SBU   Sensitive But Unclassified

SCI   Sensitive Compartmented Information

SCIF   Sensitive Compartmented Information Facility

SDNS   Secure Data Network System

SDR   System Design Review

SHA   Secure Hash Algorithm

SI   Special Intelligence

SIGSEC   Signals Security

SISS   Subcommittee on Information Systems Security

SRA   Sub-Registration Authority

SSO   Special Security Officer

STE   Secure Terminal Equipment

STS   Subcommittee on Telecommunications Security

STU   Secure Telephone Unit

TA   Traffic Analysis

TAG   TEMPEST Advisory Group

TAISS   (CFD) Telecommunications and Automated Information Systems Security

TCB   Trusted Computing Base

TCSEC   DoD Trusted Computer System Evaluation Criteria

TEP   TEMPEST Endorsement Program

TPEP   Trusted Products Evaluation Program

TRANSEC   Transmission Security

TSCM   Technical Surveillance Countermeasures

TSEC   Telecommunications Security

**Section 2
Definitions**

A

A1   The highest level of trust defined in the Orange Book (Department of Defense Trusted Computer System Evaluation Criteria, DoD 5200.28-STD).

A5   The secret algorithm used in European cellular telephones.

ACA   The American Cryptogram Association has been the leader in the field of recreational and classical cryptography since 1929.

access   The opportunity to make use of an IS resource.

access control   Limiting access to information system resources only to authorized users, programs, processes, or other systems.

access control list (ACL)   A listing of users and their associated access rights. Used to implement discretionary and/or mandatory access control between subjects and objects.

access control mechanism   Security safeguard designed to detect and deny unauthorized access and permit authorized access in an IS.

access control officer (ACO)   The designated individual responsible for limiting access to information systems resources.

access level   A hierarchical portion of the security level used to identify the sensitivity of IS data and the clearance or authorization of users. Access level, in conjunction with the nonhierarchical categories, forms the sensitivity label of an object. *See also* category.

access list   (IS) A compilation of users, programs, or processes and the access levels and types to which each is authorized. (COMSEC) Roster of persons authorized admittance to a controlled area.

access period   A segment of time, generally expressed in days or weeks, during which access rights prevail.

access profile   Associates each user with a list of protected objects the user may access.

access type   The privilege to perform action on an object. Read, write, execute, append, modify, delete, and create are examples of access types.

accidental repetition   A repetition caused by chance, and not by the encipherment of identical plaintext characters by identical keying elements.

accountability   A property allowing auditing of IS activities to be traced to persons or processes that may then be held responsible for their actions. (COMSEC) Principle that an individual is entrusted to safeguard and control equipment, keying material, and information and is answerable to proper authority for the loss or misuse of that equipment or information.

accreditation   A formal declaration by a designated approving authority (DAA) that an IS is approved to operate in a particular security mode using a prescribed set of safeguards at an acceptable level of risk. *See also* designated approving authority; security safeguards.

accreditation package A product composed of a system security plan (SSP) and a report documenting the basis for the accreditation decision.

active attack An attack in which the attacker must create or modify information. This includes attacks by Henry the Forger, Play-It-Again Sam, and Bailey the Switcher.

additional servers Name servers, other than the primary and secondary name servers, that are available to identify a particular domain name with its corresponding Internet Protocol (IP) address or addresses.

additive A single digit or numerical group, or a series of digits, that for the purpose of encipherment, is added to a numerical cipher unit, code group, or plaintext, usually by cryptographic arithmetic.

additive method The method of encipherment wherein the cryptographic equations are $P + K = C$, and $P + K - C$.

additive system A cryptosystem in which encipherment is accomplished through the application of additives.

ADFGVX system A German high-command cipher system used in World War I. Essentially, a bilateral substitution system employing a 6×6 or 5×5 square to which columnar transposition was subsequently applied.

Advanced Encryption Standard (AES) To be approved by NIST for the next 20 to 30 years of use.

Advanced Research Projects Agency (ARPA) An agency of the U.S. Department of Defense that promotes exploratory research in areas that carry long-term promise for military applications. ARPA funded the major packet-switching experiments in the United States that led to the Internet.

adversary Person or organization that must be denied access to information.

agent In network management: That component of a system that responds to management requests and/or preprogrammed traps. In the client/server model: The system component that prepares information and exchanges it for a client or server application.

AH *See* Authentication header.

AKEP *See* Authentication Key Exchange Protocol.

algorithm A set of mathematical rules (logic) used in the processes of encryption and decryption. Also called *encryption algorithm* and *encryption engine*.

alias An assumed name (dummy) mail address that routes the message to all real addresses associated with the assumed name.

alternate COMSEC custodian A person designated by proper authority to perform the duties of the COMSEC custodian during the temporary absence of the COMSEC custodian.

American National Standards Institute (ANSI) Represents the U.S. in the ISO. A private standards body that develops, endorses, and publishes industry standards through various Accredited Standards Committees (ASC). The X9 committee focuses on security standards for the financial services industry.

anagram Plain language reconstructed from a transposition cipher by restoring the letters of the ciphertext to their original order.

anonymity Of unknown or undeclared origin or authorship, concealing an entity's identification.

ANSI *See* American Standards Institute.

aperiodic Characterized by absence of cyclic attributes or usage.

aperiodic system A system in which the method of keying does not bring about cyclic phenomena in the cryptographic text.

API *See* application programming interface.

application Information processing according to a set of instructions to accomplish a given end. Examples include electronic mail, credit card verification, electronic data interchange, database search, LAN/WAN connections, remote computing services, distributed data processing, information gateways, international access services, Frame Relay services, ATM networks, electronic publishing, electronic trading, authentication, database SQL, and so on.

application programming interface Provides means to take advantage of software features.

Archie A search utility program used to find files on the Internet.

ARP Address Resolution Protocol.

ARPANET A pioneering wide area packet-switched computer network developed by the U.S. Department of Defense Advanced Research Projects Agency (ARPA). The ARPANET was the original backbone for the modern Internet, and many of its protocols were adapted to work on the Internet, including those for e-mail, FTP, and remote terminal connections.

ASCII Acronym for American Standard Code for Information Interchange. The standard code, using a coded character set consisting of 7-bit coded characters (8 bits including parity check), used for information.

ASC Accredited Standards Committee.

ASN.1 Abbreviation for Abstract Syntax Notation One. ISO/IEC standard for encoding rules, DER (Distinguished Encoding Rules) and BER (Basic Encoding Rules).

assurance Measure of confidence that the security features and architecture of an IS accurately mediate and enforce the security policy.

asymmetric Does not need the same key on each end of a communication link.

asymmetric key encryption A separate but integrated user key pair composed of one public key and one private key. Each key is one way, meaning that the key used to encrypt information cannot be used to decrypt information. *See also* symmetric key encryption.

asynchronous Character-by-character or cell-by-cell or data unit-by-data unit transfer. Data units from any one source need not be periodically spaced within the overall data unit stream.

Asynchronous Transfer Mode *See* ATM.

ATM Acronym for Asynchronous Transfer Mode. A high-speed, cell-switching network technology that is capable of transmitting voice, video, data, and Frame Relay traffic in real time.

attack   An attempt to gain unauthorized access to an IS's services, resources, or information, or the attempt to compromise an IS's integrity, availability, or confidentiality, as applicable.

audit   (1) The process of examining the history of a transaction to find out what happened. An operational audit can be an examination of ongoing activities to determine what is happening. (2) An independent review and examination of records and activities to assess the adequacy of system controls, to ensure compliance with established policies and operational procedures, and to recommend necessary changes in controls, policies, or procedures.

audit trail   A chronological record of system activities to enable the reconstruction and examination of the sequence of events and/or changes in an event. The term *audit trail* may apply to information in an IS, to message-routing in a communications system, or to the transfer of COMSEC material.

authenticate   To verify the identity of a user, user device, or other entity, or the integrity of data stored, transmitted, or otherwise exposed to unauthorized modification in an IS, or to establish the validity of a transmission.

authentication   (1) The process of ensuring the identity of the connecting user or participants exchanging electronic data. Makes sure the person or server at either end of a connection is who he/she/it claim to be and not an impostor. (2) Security measure designed to establish the validity of a transmission, message, or originator, or a means of verifying an individual's authorization to receive specific categories of information.

authentication header   Provides authentication services at the IP layer on a packet-by-packet basis.

Authentication Key Exchange Protocol (AKEP)   Key transport based on symmetric encryption allowing two parties to end up with a shared secret key, secure against passive adversaries.

authentication system   A cryptosystem or process used for authentication.

authenticator   The means used to confirm the identity of a station, originator, or individual.

authorization   (1) To convey official sanction, access or legal power to an entity. (2) Access privileges granted to a user, program, or process.

Authorized Vendor Program   A program in which a vendor, producing an INFOSEC product under contract to the National Security Agency, is authorized to produce that product in numbers exceeding the contracted requirements for direct marketing and sale to eligible buyers. Eligible buyers are typically U.S. government organizations or U.S. government contractors. Products approved for marketing and sale through the Authorized Vendor Program are placed on the Endorsed Cryptographic Products List.

autoenchipherment   Encipherment by means of an autokey system.

autokey   The block cipher mode in which the cipher is used to generate the key stream. Also called *output feedback (OFB) mode*.

autokey system An aperiodic substitution system in which the key, following the application of a previously arranged initial key, is generated from elements of the plaintext or ciphertext of the message.

auto-manual system Programmable, handheld cryptoequipment used to perform encoding and decoding functions.

automated information systems (AIS) *See* information systems security.

automated security monitoring The use of automated procedures to ensure security controls are not circumvented or the use of these tools to track actions taken by subjects suspected of misusing the IS.

automatic remote rekeying A procedure to rekey distant cryptoequipment electronically without specific actions by the receiving terminal operator. Also called *noncooperative remote rekeying*.

availability (1) Requires that computer-system assets be available to authorized parties. (2) Timely, reliable access to data and information services for authorized users.

B

backbone A high-performance network of thick wire or fiber-optic cables that enables data transmission among networks that are connected to it.

backup A copy of files and programs made to facilitate recovery, if necessary.

benign The condition of cryptographic data that cannot be compromised by human access.

benign environment A nonhostile environment that may be protected from external hostile elements by physical, personnel, and procedural security countermeasures.

beyond A1 A level of trust defined by the DoD Trusted Computer System Evaluation Criteria to be beyond the state-of-the-art technology. It includes all the A1-level features plus additional ones not required at the A1-level.

binding The process of associating a specific communications terminal with a specific cryptographic key or of associating two related elements of information.

biometrics Automated methods of authenticating or verifying an individual based upon a physical or behavioral characteristic.

B-ISDN A high-speed communications standard for wide area networks that supports wide-bandwidth applications including voice, data, and graphics.

bit error rate The ratio between the number of bits incorrectly received and the total number of bits transmitted in a telecommunications system.

BLACK The designation applied to information systems, and to associated areas, circuits, components, and equipment, in which national security information is not processed.

blind signature   The ability to sign documents without the knowledge of content; notary public.

block   A string or group of bits that a block algorithm operates on; typical values are 40, 50, 64, 128, 512, 1024, and so on.

block cipher   Block algorithms—that is, algorithms that operate on plaintext in blocks (strings or groups) of bits.

blowfish   A symmetric block cipher system that can be used as a replacement for the DES or IDEA encryption algorithms. It takes a variable-length key, from 32 to 512 bits, making it ideal for both domestic and exportable use. It was designed in 1993 by Bruce Schneier as a fast alternative to the existing encryption algorithms.

boundary   A software, hardware, or physical barrier that limits access to a system or part of a system.

brevity list   A list containing words and phrases used to shorten messages.

browser   Client application software for accessing data on the World Wide Web.

browsing   The act of searching through IS storage to locate or acquire information, without necessarily knowing the existence or format of information being sought.

brute-force cracking   The process of trying to recover a crypto key by trying all reasonable possibilities.

bucket brigade   An attack against public key exchange in which attackers substitute their own public key for their requested public key. Also called a *man-in-the-middle attack*.

bulk encryption   The simultaneous encryption of all channels of a multichannel telecommunications link.

bypass   A flaw in a security device that allows messages to go around the security mechanisms. *Crypto bypass* refers to flaws that allow plaintext to leak out.

byte   A string of binary digits (usually 8, 16, 32, or 64 bits long) operated on as a basic unit by a digital computer.

C

CA   *See* certificate authority.

callback   A procedure for identifying and authenticating a remote IS terminal, whereby the host system disconnects the terminal and reestablishes contact. Synonymous with *dialback*.

call sign cipher   A cryptosystem used to encipher/decipher call signs, address groups, and address-indicating groups.

category   A restrictive label applied to classified or unclassified information to limit access.

CBC *See* Cipher Block Chaining.

CCITT Abbreviation for Consultative Committee for International Telegraphy and Telephony.

CDK Abbreviation for crypto developer kit. A documented environment, including an API for third parties to write secure applications using a specific vendors cryptographic library.

cell Fixed-sized packets (the ATM standard is 53 octets, but proprietary lengths—for instance, 16 and 24 octets—have been used). Cells are identified and switched by means of a 5-byte header.

CERT Acronym for Computer Emergency Response Team. Security clearinghouse that promotes security awareness. CERT provides 24-hour technical assistance for computer and network security incidents. CERT is located at the Software Engineering Institute at Carnegie Mellon University in Pittsburgh, Pennsylvania.

certificate An electronic document attached to a public key by a trusted third party that provides proof that the public key belongs to a legitimate owner and has not been compromised. Also called *digital certificate*.

certificate authority (CA) A trusted third party who issues, revokes, and manages certificates, validating that public keys are not compromised and that they belong to the correct owners. Specifically, the third level of the public key infrastructure (PKI) certification management authority responsible for issuing and revoking user certificates, and exacting compliance to the PKI policy as defined by the parent policy creation authority (PCA). Also called *certification authority*.

certificate management The process whereby certificates (as defined above) are generated, stored, protected, transferred, loaded, used, and destroyed.

certificate revocation list (CRL) A list of certificates that have been revoked before their scheduled expiration date.

certification The administrative act of approving a computer system, component, product, and so forth for use in a particular application; the endorsement of information by a trusted entity. The comprehensive evaluation of the technical and nontechnical security features of an IS and other safeguards, made in support of the accreditation process, to establish the extent to which a particular design and implementation meets a set of specified security requirements.

certification agent The individual responsible for making a technical judgment of the system's compliance with stated requirements, identifying and assessing the risks associated with operating the system, coordinating the certification activities, and consolidating the final certification and accreditation packages.

certification authority (CA) *See* certificate authority.

certification authority workstation (CAW) A commercial off-the-shelf (COTS) workstation with a trusted operating system and special-purpose application software that is used to issue certificates.

certification test and evaluation (CT&E)   Software and hardware security tests conducted during development of an IS.

certified TEMPEST technical authority (CTTA)   An experienced, technically qualified U.S. government employee who has met established certification requirements in accordance with NSTISSC-approved criteria and has been appointed by a U.S. government department or agency to fulfill CTTA responsibilities.

CFM (Cipher Feedback Mode)   A block cipher that has been implemented as a self-synchronizing stream cipher.

challenge-and-reply authentication   Prearranged procedure in which a subject requests authentication of another and the latter establishes validity with a correct reply.

CHAP (Challenge Authentication Protocol)   A session-based, two-way password authentication scheme.

checksum   A numeric value used to verify the integrity of a block of data. The value is computed using a checksum procedure. A crypto checksum incorporates secret information in the checksum procedure so that it can't be reproduced by third parties that don't know the secret information. *See also* hash total.

check word   Ciphertext generated by cryptographic logic to detect failures in cryptography.

Chi-square test   A statistical test used for determining the likelihood that two distributions derive from the same source.

cipher   Any cryptographic system in which arbitrary symbols or groups of symbols represent units of plaintext or in which units of plain text are rearranged, or both.

ciphertext   Encrypted plaintext.

cipher alphabet   An ordered arrangement of the letters of a written language and the characters to replace them in a cryptographic process of substitution.

Cipher Block Chaining (CBC)   A block cipher mode that combines the previous block of ciphertext with the current block of plaintext before encrypting it; very widely used.

cipher feedback   A block cipher mode that feeds previously encrypted ciphertext through the block cipher to generate the key that encrypts the next block of ciphertext; also called *CTAK*.

cipher system   The hardware and/or software making up the means to encrypt and decrypt plaintext. Encryption and decryption can be implemented in software on the host computer or in hardware devices placed on the links between computers. Also called *cryptosystem*.

ciphertext   Data that has been encrypted with a cipher, as opposed to plaintext.

ciphony   Process of enciphering audio information, resulting in encrypted speech.

circuit switching A method of handling traffic through a switching center, either from local users or from other switching centers, whereby a connection is established between the calling and called parties.

classified information Information that has been determined pursuant to Executive Order 12958 or any predecessor order, or by the Atomic Energy Act of 1954, as amended, to require protection against unauthorized disclosure and is marked to indicate its classified status.

clearing The Removal of data from an IS, its storage devices, and other peripheral devices with storage capacity in such a way that the data may not be reconstructed using common system capabilities (i.e., keyboard strokes); however, the data may be reconstructed using laboratory methods. Cleared media may be reused at the same classification level or at a higher level. Overwriting is one method of clearing. *See also* magnetic remanence.

cleartext Characters in a human-readable form or bits in a machine-readable form. Also called *plaintext*.

client A device or application that makes use of the services provided by a server in a client/server architecture.

code (1) A system of instructions making up software. A system of symbols making up ciphertext. (2) A system of communication in which arbitrary groups of letters, numbers, or symbols represent units of plaintext of varying length.

code book A document containing plaintext and code equivalents in a systematic arrangement, or a technique of machine encryption using a word substitution technique.

code group (1) A group of symbols assigned to represent a plaintext element. (2) A group of letters, numbers, or both in a code system used to represent a plaintext word, phrase, or sentence.

code vocabulary A set of plaintext words, numerals, phrases, or sentences for which code equivalents are assigned in a code system.

coincidence A recurrence of textual elements occurring within a message or between messages.

coincidence test The Kappa test, applied to two ciphertext messages to determine whether or not they both involve cipherment by the same sequence or cipher alphabets.

command authority Individual responsible for the appointment of user representatives for a department, agency, or organization and their key-ordering privileges.

Commercial COMSEC Endorsement Program (CCEP) A relationship between NSA and industry in which NSA provides the COMSEC expertise (i.e, standards, algorithms, evaluations, and guidance) and industry provides design, development, and production capabilities to produce a type 1 or type 2 product. Products developed under the CCEP may include modules, subsystems, equipment, systems, and ancillary devices.

communications cover The concealing or altering of characteristic communications patterns to hide information that could be of value to an adversary.

communications deception The deliberate transmission, retransmission, or alteration of communications to mislead an adversary's interpretation of the communications.

communications profile An analytic model of communications associated with an organization or activity. The model is prepared from a systematic examination of communications content and patterns, the functions they reflect, and the communications security measures applied.

communications security Measures and controls taken to deny unauthorized persons information derived from telecommunications and to ensure the authenticity of such telecommunications. Communications security includes cryptosecurity, transmission security, emission security, and physical security of COMSEC material.

compartmentalization A nonhierarchical grouping of sensitive information used to control access to data more finely than with hierarchical security classification alone.

compartmented mode INFOSEC mode of operation wherein each user with direct or indirect access to a system, its peripherals, remote terminals, or remote hosts has all of the following: (a) valid security clearance for the most restricted information processed in the system, (b) formal access approval and signed nondisclosure agreements for that information to which a user is to have access, and (c) valid need-to-know for information to which a user is to have access.

compromise Disclosure of information to unauthorized persons or a violation of the security policy of a system in which unauthorized intentional or unintentional disclosure, modification, destruction, or loss of an object may have occurred.

computer abuse Intentional or reckless misuse, alteration, disruption, or destruction of information-processing resources.

computer cryptography The use of a crypto-algorithm program by a computer to authenticate or encrypt/decrypt information.

computer security Measures and controls that ensure confidentiality, integrity, and availability of IS assets including hardware, software, firmware, and information being processed, stored, and communicated.

computer security incident Attempted or actual compromise of the confidentiality, integrity, or availability of a computer system or its information.

COMSEC (communications security) Protection of all measures designed to deny to unauthorized persons information of value that might be derived from a study of communications.

COMSEC equipment Equipment designed to provide security to telecommunications by converting information to a form unintelligible to an unauthorized interceptor and, subsequently, by reconverting such information to its original form for authorized recipients; also, equipment designed specifically to aid in, or as an essential element of, the conversion process. COMSEC equipment includes crypto-equipment, cryptoancillary equipment, cryptoproduction equipment, and authentication equipment.

COMSEC incident   An occurrence that potentially jeopardizes the security of COMSEC material or the secure transmission of national security information.

COMSEC insecurity   COMSEC incident that has been investigated, evaluated, and determined to jeopardize the security of COMSEC material or the secure transmission of information.

COMSEC manager   The person who manages the COMSEC resources of an organization.

COMSEC material   An item designed to secure or authenticate telecommunications. COMSEC material includes, but is not limited to key, equipment, devices, documents, firmware, or software that embodies or describes cryptographic logic and other items that perform COMSEC functions.

COMSEC Material Control System (CMCS)   Logistics and accounting system through which COMSEC material marked "CRYPTO" is distributed, controlled, and safeguarded. Included are the COMSEC central offices of record, cryptologistic depots, and COMSEC accounts. COMSEC material other than keys may be handled through the COMSEC Material Control System.

COMSEC monitoring   The act of listening to, copying, or recording transmissions of one's own official telecommunications to analyze the degree of security.

COMSEC profile   A statement of COMSEC measures and materials used to protect a given operation, system, or organization.

COMSEC system data   Information required by a COMSEC equipment or system to enable it to properly handle and control key.

COMSEC training   The teaching of skills relating to COMSEC accounting, use of COMSEC aids, or installation, use, maintenance, and repair of COMSEC equipment.

concept of operations (CONOP)   A document detailing the method, act, process, or effect of using an IS.

confidentiality   (1) Assurance that data is not read or accessed by unauthorized persons. (2) Assurance that information is not disclosed to unauthorized persons, processes, or devices.

configuration control   The process of controlling modifications to hardware, firmware, software, and documentation to ensure the IS is protected against improper modifications prior to, during, and after system implementation.

configuration management   The management of security features and assurances through control of changes made to hardware, software, firmware, documentation, test, test fixtures, and test documentation throughout the life cycle of an IS.

connection integrity   Assurance that the connection is not modified by unauthorized entities.

connectionless integrity   Detecting modification to an individual IP datagram regardless of the sequence or order of the datagram in a stream of traffic.

connectionless mode　A technology where each data unit (packet) is independently routed to the destination; no connection establishment activities are required.

contamination　The introduction of data of one security classification or security category into data of a lower security classification or different security category.

contingency plan　A plan maintained for emergency response, backup operations, and post-disaster recovery for an IS, to ensure the availability of critical resources and to facilitate the continuity of operations in an emergency situation.

controlling authority　The official responsible for directing the operation of a cryptonet and for managing the operational use and control of keying material assigned to the cryptonet.

cookie　A file or token of sorts passed from the Web server to the Web client (your browser) that is used to identify you and could record personal information such as ID and password, mailing address, credit card number, and so on. Also called *persistent client state HTTP cookie*.

cost-benefit analysis　An assessment of the cost of providing protection or security commensurate with the risk and magnitude of asset loss or damage.

countermeasure　An action, device, procedure, technique, or other measure that reduces the vulnerability of an IS.

covert channel　An unintended and/or unauthorized communications path that can be used to transfer information in a manner that violates an IS security policy. *See* overt channel and exploitable channel.

covert channel analysis　The determination of the extent to which the security policy model and subsequent lower-level program descriptions may allow unauthorized access to information.

covert storage channel　A covert channel involving the direct or indirect writing to a storage location by one process and the direct or indirect reading of the storage location by another process. Covert storage channels typically involve a finite resource (e.g, sectors on a disk) that is shared by two subjects at different security levels.

covert timing channel　A covert channel in which one process signals information to another process by modulating its own use of system resources (e.g, central processing unit time) in such a way that this manipulation affects the real response time observed by the second process.

cracking　The process of overcoming a security measure. Cracking a key means attempting to recover the key's value; cracking some ciphertext means attempting to recover the corresponding plaintext.

credentials　(1) Something that provides a basis for credit or confidence. (2) Information, passed from one entity to another, used to establish the sending entity's access rights.

critical application　A computing application in which an attacker could cause incredibly serious damage, including loss of life.

CRL　*See* Certificate revocation list.

cross-certification When two or more organizations or certificate authorities that share some level of trust.

cryptanalysis The art or science of transferring ciphertext into plaintext without initial knowledge of the key used to encrypt the plaintext. Operations performed in converting encrypted messages to plain text without initial knowledge of the crypto algorithm and/or the key the employed in the encryption.

CRYPTO Marking or designator identifying COMSEC keying material used to secure or authenticate telecommunications carrying classified or sensitive U.S. government or U.S. government-derived information.

crypto-algorithm A well-defined procedure or sequence of rules or steps, or a series of mathematical equations used to describe cryptographic processes such as encryption/decryption, key generation, authentication, signatures, and so on.

crypto-equipment Equipment that embodies a cryptographic logic.

cryptographic Pertaining to, or concerned with, cryptography.

cryptographic component The hardware or firmware embodiment of the cryptographic logic. The cryptographic component may be a modular assembly, a printed wiring assembly, a microcircuit, or a combination of these items.

cryptographic initialization A function used to set the state of a cryptographic logic prior to key generation, encryption, or other operating mode.

cryptographic logic The embodiment of one or more crypto-algorithms, along with alarms, checks, and other processes, essential to effective and secure performance of the cryptographic process(es).

cryptographic randomization A function that randomly determines the transmit state of a cryptographic logic.

cryptography The art or science concerning the principles, means, and methods for rendering plain information unintelligible and for restoring encrypted information to intelligible form.

cryptogram An encrypted message, file, and so on; a simple word/character substitution cipher.

cryptography The branch of cryptographic science that deals with the means, methods, and apparatus of converting plain text messages into secret messages and vice versa.

cryptolinguistics The study of characteristics of languages that have some application in cryptology, for example, frequency data, letter combinations, universal patterns, and so on.

cryptologic Pertaining to cryptology.

cryptology The field that encompasses both cryptography and cryptanalysis.

cryptonet Stations holding a common key.

cryptoperiod The time span during which each key setting remains in effect; sometimes refers to the amount of data encrypted with it.

cryptosecurity A component of COMSEC resulting from the provision of technically sound cryptosystems and their proper use.

cryptosynchronization The process by which a receiving decrypting cryptographic logic attains the same internal state as the transmitting encrypting log.

cryptosystem The hardware and software making up the means to encrypt and decrypt plaintext. Encryption and decryption can be implemented in software on computers or in hardware devices placed on the links between computers. Also called *cipher system*.

cryptosystem assessment The process of establishing the exploitability of a cryptosystem, normally by reviewing transmitted traffic protected or secured by the system under study.

cryptosystem evaluation The process of determining vulnerabilities of a cryptosystem.

cryptosystem review The examination of a cryptosystem by the controlling authority, ensuring its adequacy of design and content, continued need, and proper distribution.

cyclic phenomena Periodic ciphertext repetitions in a cryptogram enciphered with a repeating key.

cyclic redundancy check An error-checking mechanism that checks data integrity by computing a polynomial algorithm-based checksum.

D

DAA *See* designated approving authority.

dangling threat A set of properties about the external environment for which there is no corresponding vulnerability and therefore no implied risk.

dangling vulnerability A set of properties about the internal environment for which there is no corresponding threat and therefore no implied risk.

data Digital information or just plain information depending on the context.

Data Encryption Standard (DES) A cryptographic algorithm designed for the protection of unclassified data and published by the National Institute of Standards and Technology in Federal Information Processing Standard (FIPS) Publication 46.

data integrity Condition existing when data is unchanged from its source and has not been accidentally or maliciously modified, altered, or destroyed.

data key A crypto key that encrypts data as opposed to a key that encrypts other keys.

data link The portion of a system of computers that transfers data between them, including wiring, hardware, interfaces, and device driver software.

data origin authentication Corroborating the source of data is as claimed.

data security The protection of data from unauthorized (accidental or intentional) modification, destruction, or disclosure.

datagram A packet individually routed through a network and reassembled at the receiving end.

DBS Abbreviation for direct broadcast satellite.

decertification The revocation of the certification of an IS item or equipment for cause.

decimation The process of selecting members of a series by counting off at an arbitrary interval with the original series being treated as cyclic.

decipher To convert enciphered text to plaintext by means of a cryptographic system.

decode (1) That section of a code book in which the code groups are in alphabetical order, or other systematic order. (2) To convert encoded text to plaintext by means of a code, not by cryptanalysis.

decrypt (1) To convert ciphertext into the original plaintext using a cryptosystem. Decryption (and encryption) can be implemented in software on computers or in hardware devices placed on the links between computers. (2) A generic term encompassing both *decode* and *decipher*.

dedicated mode An IS security mode of operation wherein each user, with direct or indirect access to the system, its peripherals, remote terminals, or remote hosts, has all of the following: (a) valid security clearance for all information within the system, (*b.*) formal access approval and signed nondisclosure agreements for all the information stored and/or processed (including all compartments, subcompartments, and/or special access programs), and (c) valid need-to-know for all information contained within the IS. When in the dedicated security mode, a system is specifically and exclusively dedicated to and controlled for the processing of one particular type or classification of information, either for full-time operation or for a specified period of time.

denial of service (DoS) The result of any action or series of actions that prevents any part of an IS from functioning.

DES Acronym for Data Encryption Standard. A U.S. data encryption standard adopted in 1976 as FIPS 46.

design documentation A set of documents, required for Trusted Computer System Evaluation Criteria (TCSEC) classes C1 and above (as defined in the Orange Book, Department of Defense Trusted Computer System Evaluation Criteria, DoD 5200.28-STD), whose primary purpose is to define and describe the properties of a system. As it relates to TCSEC, design documentation provides an explanation of how the security policy of a system is translated into a technical solution via the Trusted Computing Base (TCB) hardware, software, and firmware.

designated approving authority (DAA) An official with the authority to formally assume responsibility for operating a system at an acceptable level of risk. This term is synonymous with *designated accrediting authority* and *delegated accrediting authority*.

dictionary attack A calculated, brute-force attack to reveal a password by trying obvious combinations.

Diffie-Hellman The first public key algorithm, using discrete logarithms in a finite field, invented in 1976.

digital cash Electronic money that is stored and transferred through a variety of complex protocols.

digital certificate A signed electronic document (digital ID) that notarizes and binds the connection between a public key and its legitimate owner. Similar to how a drivers license or passport proves the owner's identify. Its purpose is to prevent unauthorized impersonation and provide confidence in public keys.

digital signature 1 An electronic identification of a person or thing created by using a public key algorithm, intended to verify to a recipient the integrity of the data and the identity of the sender of the data.

digital signature 2 A cryptographic process used to ensure message originator authenticity, integrity, and nonrepudiation. Also called *electronic signature*.

digital signature algorithm A procedure that appends data to, or performs a cryptographic transformation of, a data unit. The appended data or cryptographic transformation allows reception of the data unit and protects against forgery—for example, by the recipient.

discrete logarithm The underlying mathematical problem used in asymmetric algorithms like Diffie-Hellman and Elliptic Curve, the inverse problem of modular exponentiation, which is a one-way function.

distinguished name Globally unique identifier representing an individual's identity.

DMS Abbreviation for Defense Messaging System. Standards designed by the U.S. Department of Defense to provide a secure and reliable enterprisewide messaging infrastructure for government and military agencies.

DN Abbreviation for (1) domain name, indicates the general domain of the activity or user and could represent many IP addresses, whereas the fully qualified domain name (FQDN) corresponds to one IP address. (2) Abbreviation for distinguished name.

DNS *See* Domain Name Server, Domain Name Space, and Domain Name System.

DNSSEC Acronym for Domain Name System Security. An IETF working group-proposed draft that will specify enhancements to the DNS protocol to protect the DNS against unauthorized modification of data and against masquerading of data origin; adds data integrity and authentication capabilities to the DNS via digital signatures.

DoD Trusted Computer System Evaluation Criteria A document containing basic requirements and (TCSEC) evaluation classes for assessing degrees of effectiveness of hardware and software security controls built into an IS. This document, DoD 5200.28 STD, is frequently referred to as "the Orange Book."

domain A domain represents a level of the hierarchy in the Domain Name Space and is represented by a domain name. For example, the domain name "icsa.net" represents the second-level domain "icsa," which is a subset, or sub-domain, of the top-level domain "net," which is, in turn, a larger subset of the total Domain Name Space.

domain name   The textual name assigned to a host on the Internet. The Domain Name Service (DNS) protocol translates between domain names and numerical IP addresses.

Domain Name Server   *See* name server.

Domain Name Space   All the domain names that currently represent the networks, computers, and other network devices that can be described and represented by the Domain Name System (DNS).

Domain Name System (DNS)   A distributed database of information used to translate domain names into Internet Protocol (IP) addresses.

domain   The unique context (e.g, access control parameters) in which a program is operating; in effect, the set of objects a subject has the privilege to access.

DSA   Abbreviation for Digital Signature Algorithm. A public-key digital signature algorithm proposed by NIST for use in DSS.

DSS   Abbreviation for Digital Signature Standard. An NIST-proposed standard (FIPS) for digital standards using DSA.

due diligence   Such a measure of prudence, activity, or assiduity, as is properly to be expected from, and ordinarily exercised by, a reasonable and prudent person under the particular circumstances; not measured by any absolute standard, but depending on the relative facts of the special case.

E

e-cash   Electronically transferred money.

EC   Abbreviation for electronic commerce or for elliptic curve.

ECC   Abbreviation for elliptic curve cryptography/cryptosystem. A technology that uses the algebraic system defined by the points of an elliptic curve to provide public-key cryptographic algorithms.

EDI   Abbreviation for electronic data interchange. This refers to the direct, standardized computer-to-computer exchange of business documents (purchase orders, invoices, payments, inventory analyses, and others) between your organization and your suppliers and customers.

EES   Abbreviation for Escrowed Encryption Standard. A U.S. government-proposed standard for escrowing private keys.

Electronic Codebook (ECB)   A block cipher mode that consists of simply applying the cipher to blocks of data in sequence.

electronic messaging services   Services providing interpersonal messaging capability; meeting specific functional, management, and technical requirements; and yielding a business-quality electronic mail service suitable for the conduct of official government business.

electronic security Protection resulting from measures designed to deny unauthorized persons information derived from the interception and analysis of noncommunications electromagnetic radiations.

electronic signature *See* digital signature.

ElGamal Scheme Used for both digital signatures and encryption based on discrete logarithms in a finite field; can be used with the DSA function.

element A removable item of COMSEC equipment, assembly, or subassembly, normally consisting of a single piece or group of replaceable parts.

e-mail Electronic mail.

emissions security Protection resulting from measures taken to deny unauthorized persons information derived from interception and analysis of compromising emanations from crypto-equipment or an IS.

encipher (1) To convert a plaintext into unintelligible language or signals by means of cipher system. (2) To convert plaintext to ciphertext by means of a cryptographic system.

encode To convert plaintext to ciphertext by means of a code.

encryption algorithm (1) Used for both digital signatures and encryption based on discrete logarithms in a finite field; can be used with the DSA function. (2) A set of mathematically expressed rules for rendering data unintelligible by executing a series of conversions controlled by a key.

encrypt (1) To convert plaintext into unintelligible forms by means of a cipher system (cryptosystem). Encryption (and decryption) can be implemented in software on computers or in hardware—the set of mathematical logic that actually converts (encrypts/decrypts) data. (2) Generic term encompassing both *encipher* and *encode*.

end-to-end (hardware) encryption (1) A technology where the data is disguised throughout its path, the encoding and decoding devices are synchronized, the data is encrypted at its source and decrypted at its destination, and the data-link header is in cleartext. In addition, the source and destination need not be kept secret or transparent to the hardware. The hardware must detect start/stop instructions and/or be sensitive to data communications procedures. (2) Encryption of information at its origin and decryption as its intended destination without intermediate decryption.

end-to-end security The safeguarding of information in an IS from point of origin to point of destination.

endorsement NSA approval of a commercially developed product for safeguarding national security Information.

entering wedge A weakness in a cryptosystem or other security system that gives an attacker a way to break down some of the system's protections.

enterprise The collection of systems, computers, networks, and so on that society depends upon for information transfer, processing, and management.

entrapment The deliberate planting of apparent flaws in an IS for the purpose of detecting attempted penetrations.

entropy A mathematical measurement of the amount of uncertainty or randomness.

environment An aggregate of external procedures, conditions, and objects affecting the development, operation, and maintenance of an IS.

erasure A process intended to render magnetically stored information irretrievable by normal means.

ESP Abbreviation for encapsulating security payload.

Evaluated Products List (EPL) Equipment, hardware, software, and/or firmware evaluated by the NCSC in accordance with DoD TCSEC and found to be technically compliant at a particular level of trust. The EPL is included in the NSA Information Systems Security Products and Services Catalog.

executable contents Data with contents that represent an executable computer program that is capable of modifying persistent data on a host computer.

executive state One of several states in which an IS may operate, and the only one in which certain privileged instructions may be executed. Such privileged instructions cannot be executed when the system is operating in other (e.g, user) states. Also called *supervisor state*.

exploitable channel A channel that allows the violation of the security policy governing an IS and is usable or detectable by subjects external to the trusted computing base. *See also* covert channel.

extraction resistance Capability of crypto-equipment or secure telecommunications equipment to resist efforts to extract keys.

F

fail-safe An automatic protection of programs and/or processing systems when hardware or software failure is detected.

failure access Unauthorized access to data resulting from hardware or software failure.

failure control A methodology used to detect imminent hardware or software failure and provide fail-safe or fail-soft recovery.

FDDI Abbreviation for fiber distributed data interface. An ANSI standard specifying a packet-switched LAN-to-LAN backbone for transporting data at high throughput rates over a variety of multimode fibers. FDDI addresses the bottom two layers of the OSI model.

file A collection of data stored and dealt with as a single, named unit.

file protection Aggregate of processes and procedures designed to inhibit unauthorized access, contamination, elimination, modification, or destruction of a file or any of its contents.

file security Means by which access to computer files is limited to authorized users only.

file transfer   The electrical transfer of a file from one storage or processing unit to another.

FIPS   Acronym for Federal Information Processing Standards. U.S. government standards published by NIST.

firewall   (1) A device, installed at the point where network connections enter a site, that applies rules to control the type of networking traffic that flows in and out. Most commercial firewalls are built to handle Internet protocols. (2) A gateway, bridge, router, or front-end processor that limits access between networks in accordance with local security policy. Also called a *front-end security filter*.

firmware   A program recorded in permanent or semipermanent computer memory.

flaw   An error of commission, omission, or oversight in an IS that may allow protection mechanisms to be bypassed.

flaw hypothesis methodology   A system analysis and penetration technique in which the specification and documentation for an IS are analyzed to produce a list of hypothetical flaws. This list is prioritized on the basis of the estimated probability that a flaw exists on the ease of exploiting it, and on the extent of control or compromise it would provide. The prioritized list is used to perform penetration testing of a system.

flooding   The insertion of a large volume of data resulting in denial of service.

flow ID traffic   A flow identifier used in host-to-host traffic to differentiate traffic flow types.

forgery   A data item with contents that mislead the recipient to believe the item and its contents were produced by someone other than the actual author.

formal verification   The process of using formal proofs to demonstrate the consistency between formal specification of a system and formal security policy model (design verification) or between formal specification and its high-level program implementation (implementation verification).

Fortezza   Formerly known as Tessera. A PCMCIA card used by the U.S. government's Capstone project.

FPGA   Abbreviation for field-programmable gate arrays.

FQDN   Abbreviation for fully qualified domain name. Corresponds or maps to one IP address. An FQDN is registered with one of the international NICs or the InterNIC—a registered, identified user site.

Frame Relay (FR)   Packet-mode switching interface for handling high-speed data and interconnecting LANs and WANs in low error-rate environments. A streamlined version of X.25, Frame Relay uses variable packets (frames) as the transfer format with less overhead and sequence checking. Error checks occur only at the destination point..

frequency   The number of actual occurrences of a textual element within a given text.

frequency distribution   A tabulation of the frequency of occurrence of plaintext or ciphertext; a frequency count.

frequency hopping   The repeated switching of frequencies during radio transmission according to a specified algorithm, in order to minimize unauthorized interception or jamming of telecommunications.

FTP   Abbreviation for file transfer protocol.

G

GAK   Acronym for Government Access to Keys. A method for the government to escrow individual's private keys.

gateway   (1) A major relay station that receives, switches, relays, and transmits ILC traffic. A gateway converts one protocol suite to another, when necessary, to allow different computer systems to communicate. A gateway can operate at any OSI layer above OSI level 3, the network layer. (2) An interface providing a compatibility between networks by converting transmission speeds, protocols, codes or security measures.

general solution   A solution dependent on exploiting the inherent weaknesses of the cryptographic system arising from its own mechanics, without the presence of any specialized circumstances.

granularity   The relative fineness to which an access control mechanism can be adjusted.

GSS   An abbreviation for generic security services.

guard   The process limiting the exchange of information between systems.

H

hacker   An unauthorized user who attempts or gains access to an IS.

handshaking procedures   The dialog between two IS's for synchronizing, identifying, and authenticating themselves to one another.

hardware encryption   A technology where plaintext is encrypted by hardware devices online between the host computers. There are two approaches to hardware encryption: end-to-end and link. *See also* end-to-end encryption and link encryption.

hash code   *See* message digest.

hash function   A function that produces a message digest that cannot be reversed to produced the original. Also called a *one-way hash function*.

hash total   The value computed on data to detect error or manipulation. *See also* checksum.

hashing   The computation of a hash total.

headers   Formatted information attached to the front of data sent through a computer network containing information used to deliver and process correctly the data being sent.

hierarchical trust A graded series of entities that distribute trust in an organized fashion, commonly used in X.509 issuing certifying authorities.

high-risk application A computer application in which the enterprise operating it can suffer a significant loss through a computer incident.

high-risk environment Specific location or geographic area where there are insufficient friendly security forces to ensure the safeguarding of information systems security equipment. Also called *high-threat environment*.

hijacking An attack in which the attacker takes over a live connection between two entities so that he or she can masquerade as one of the entities.

HMAC A mechanism for message authentication that combines an iterative cryptographic hash function such as MD5 or SHA-1 with a secret shared key.

host A computer system that resides on a network and is capable of independently communicating with other systems on the network.

host address The address used by others on the network to communicate with a particular host.

HTML Abbreviation for hypertext markup language.

HTTP Abbreviation for Hypertext Transfer Protocol. The protocol used by WWW servers and clients to exchange hypertext data.

hypertext Associated with information on the World Wide Web. Any text that contains "links" to other documents. Specifically, words or phrases in one document that are user-selectable and that cause another document to be retrieved and displayed. These "links" usually appear in a different color than the main text and are underlined.

I

IBM SKMP-IBM secure A key management protocol.

ICE An acronym for integrated cryptographic engine.

ICMP An abbreviation for Internet Control Message Protocol. An IP protocol used for monitoring and control of an IP network.

IDEA An acronym for International Data Encryption Algorithm. An algorithm designed by Lai and Massey in 1991. Patented internationally, offered by ACSOM, a Swiss company. IDEA uses a 128-bit key and is considered strong.

identification (1) The determination of the plaintext value of a cipher element of code group. (2) The process an IS uses to recognize an entity.

identity certificate A signed statement that binds a key to the name of an individual and has the intended meaning of delegating authority from that named individual to the public key.

identity token A smart card, metal key, or other physical object used to authenticate identity.

identity validation A process composed of tests that enable an information system to authenticate users or resources.

IEEE Abbreviation for the Institute of Electrical and Electronics Engineers.

IKE The Internet Key Exchange protocol is planned to establish IPSec-based virtual private networks on the Internet. When used together in the IKE hybrid protocol, a subset of the Oakley key exchange, modes are used in the ISAKMP framework to negotiate and provide authenticated keying material for security associations in a protected manner.

imitative communications deception The introduction of deceptive messages or signals into an adversary's telecommunications signals. *See* communications deception and manipulative communications deception.

impersonating A form of spoofing.

inadvertent disclosure The accidental exposure of information to a person not authorized access.

incident An event having actual or potentially adverse effects on an IS.

Index of Coincidence (IC) The ratio of observed number of coincidences in a given body of text to the number of coincidences expected in a sample of random text of the same size.

indicator An element inserted within the text or heading of the message to serve as a guide tot the selection of derivation and application of the correct system and key for the prompt decryption of the message.

individual accountability The ability to associate positively the identity of a user with the time, method, and degree of access to an IS.

information assurance (IA) Information operations (IO) that protect and defend information and information systems by ensuring their availability, integrity, authentication, confidentiality, and nonrepudiation. This includes providing for restoration of information systems by incorporating protection, detection, and reaction capabilities.

information operations (IO) Actions taken to affect adversary information and information systems while defending one's own information and information systems.

information system (IS) The entire infrastructure, organization, personnel, and components for the collection, processing, storage, transmission, display, dissemination, and disposition of information.

information systems security Protection of information systems against (INFOSEC and/or ISS) unauthorized access to or modification of information, whether in storage, processing, or transit, and against the denial of service to authorized users, including those measures necessary to detect, document, and counter such threats. Also called *telecommunciations security* (TSEC).

information systems security officer (ISSO) The person responsible to the designated approving authority for ensuring the security of an information system throughout its life cycle, from design through disposal. Also called *system security officer. See also* network security manager.

initialize To set the state of a cryptographic logic prior to key generation, encryption, or other operating mode.

in-line encryptor A product that plies encryption automatically to all data passing along a data link.

integrity   (1) Assurance that data is transmitted from source to destination without undetected alteration. (2) The quality of an IS reflecting the logical correctness and reliability of the operating system; the logical completeness of the hardware and software implementing the protection mechanisms; and the consistency of the data structures and occurrence of the stored data. Note that, in a formal security mode, integrity is interpreted more narrowly to mean protection against unauthorized modification or destruction of information. (3) Assurance that data is not modified (by unauthorized persons) during storage or transmittal.

interface   The common boundary between independent systems or modules where interactions take place.

internal security controls   Hardware, firmware, or software features within an IS that restrict access to resources only to authorized subjects.

Internet Architecture Board (IAB)   An organization that oversees the development of Internet standards and protocols and acts as a liaison between the Internet Society (ISOC) and other standards bodies.

Internet Assigned Numbers Authority (IANA)   Located at the Information Sciences Institute at the University of Southern California in Marina del Rey, California, the IANA oversees registration for various Internet Protocol parameters, such as port numbers, protocol and enterprise numbers, options, codes, and types.

Internet Engineering Steering Group (IESG)   The operational management arm of the Internet Engineering Task Force (IETF).

Internet Engineering Task Force (IETF)   Formed by the Internet Architecture Board, the IETF is an international, voluntary body of network designers, engineers, researchers, vendors, and so on who work together to resolve technical and operational problems on the Internet and develop Internet standards and protocols. The IETF meets three times a year; however, the bulk of the collaboration and work takes place on the various mailing lists maintained by its participants.

Internet stack layers   These include the physical layer (copper wire, fiber-optic cable), the network access layer (Ethernet, ATM), the Internet Protocol (IP) layer, the transport (TCP, UDP) layer, and the application layer (HTTP, NNTP, POP, IMAP).

InterNIC   Abbreviation for Internet Network Information Center. Under a cooperative agreement with the National Science Foundation (NSF), certain companies (called InterNICs) administer second-level domain name registration services in the top-level domains (e.g., com, net, mil, org). Some also provide information and education services. AT&T provides directory and database services.

information security   Technical security measures that involve communications security, cryptography, and computer security.

Internet   The global set of networks interconnected using TCP/IP.

interoperability   The condition achieved among communications-electronics systems or equipment when information or services can be exchanged directly and satisfactorily between them and their users.

interval A distance between two points or occurrences, especially between recurrent conditions or states. The number of units between a letter, digraph, or code group, and the recurrence of the same letter, digraph, or code group, counting either the first or second occurrence of both.

intranet A private network, usually within an organization, that uses the Internet protocols but is not directly connected to the global Internet.

IP Abbreviation for Internet protocol. (1) A protocol that moves packets of data from node to node. Works above layer 3 (network) of the OSI reference model, like an OSI layer 3[fr1/2]. (2) The standard protocol for transmission of data from source to destinations in packet-switched communications networks and interconnected systems of such networks.

IP address The standard way to identify a computer connected to the Internet. Each IP address consists of eight octets expressed as four numbers between 0 and 255, separated by periods, for example: 176.31.23.13.

IPPCP Abbreviation for Internet Protocol Payload Compression Protocol.

IPSec Abbreviation for IP Security Protocol. A way that businesses can open up an encrypted link to a trading partner's network.

IPX Abbreviation for Internet Packet Exchange.

IS Abbreviation for information systems.

ISAKMP The Internet Security Association and Key Management Protocol defines procedures and packet formats to establish, negotiate, modify, and delete security associations (SAs). ISAKMP defines payloads for exchanging key generation and authentication data. These formats provide a consistent framework for transferring key and authentication data that is independent of the key generation technique, encryption algorithm, and authentication mechanism. ISAKMP is designed to support many different key exchange protocols, but does not establish session keys itself.

ISDN Abbreviation for Integrated Services Digital Network. A network that supports transmission of voice, data, and image-based communications in an integrated form.

ISO Abbreviation for International Organization for Standardization. The organization that created the seven-layer OSI structure for telecommunications.

ISP Abbreviation for Internet service providers.

IT Abbreviation for information technology.

ITAR Abbreviation for International Traffic in Arms Regulations.

K

Kerberos A trusted-third-party authentication protocol developed at MIT.

key (1) A sequence of symbols that when used with a cryptographic algorithm enables encryption and decryption. The security of the cryptosystem is dependent on the security of the key. (2) Usually a sequence of random or pseudorandom bits used initially to set up and periodically change the operations performed in crypto-equipment for the purpose of encrypting or decrypting electronic signals, or for determining electronic counter-countermeasure patterns (e.g, frequency hopping or spread spectrum), or for producing another key. Also called *keyword* or *key sequence*.

key-auto-key   Cryptographic logic using a previous key to produce a new key.

key distribution center (KDC)   A device that provides secret keys to allow pairs of hosts to encrypt traffic directly between themselves.

key encrypting key (KEK)   A crypto key used to encrypt session or data keys and never used to encrypt the data itself.

key escrow   A mechanism for storing copies of crypto keys so that third parties can recover them if necessary to read information encrypted by others.

key exchange   The process for getting session keys into the hands of the conversants.

key length   The number of bits representing the key size; the longer the key, the stronger it is.

key list   A printed series of key settings for a specific cryptonet. Key lists may be produced in list, pad, or printed tape format.

key management   (1) The overall process of generating and distributing cryptographic key to authorized recipients in a secure manner. (2) The supervision and control of the process whereby a key is generated, stored, protected, transferred, loaded, used, and destroyed.

key management proxy   A node implementing a key management protocol on behalf of some other node.

key pair   A public key and its corresponding private key as used in public key cryptography.

key production key (KPK)   A key used to initialize a key-stream generator for the production of other electronically generated key.

key recovery   A mechanism for determining the key used to encrypt some data.

key splitting   A process for dividing portions of a single key between multiple parties, none having the ability to reconstruct the whole key.

key size   The number of bits in a key.

key stream   The sequence of symbols (or their electrical or mechanical equivalents) produced in a machine or auto-manual cryptosystem to combine with plaintext to produce ciphertext, to control transmission security processes, or to produce a key.

key updating   An irreversible cryptographic process for modifying a key.

keying material   Key, code, or authentication information in physical or magnetic form.

Knapsack algorithm   The first generalize public-key encryption algorithm, developed by Ralph Merkle and Martin Hellman.

L

Label   *See* security label.

labeled security protections   An elementary-level mandatory access control protection features and intermediate-level discretionary access control features in a trusted computing base (TCB) that uses sensitivity labels to make access control decisions.

laboratory attack   The use of sophisticated signal recovery equipment in a laboratory environment to recover information from data storage media.

layer   Usually referring to one of the OSI basic reference-model levels.

least privilege   A principle requiring that each subject be granted the most restrictive set of privileges needed for the performance of authorized tasks. Application of this principle limits the damage that can result from accident, error, or unauthorized use of an IS.

lightweight crypto   A set of crypto capabilities that is as strong as possible but still sufficiently weak to qualify for favorable treatment under U.S. export regulations.

link   The existence of communications facilities between two points.

link encryption   The encryption of information between nodes of communications system.

link (hardware) encryption   Performed through a series of switches (nodes) before the data reaches its destination. An encryption device is needed at each node, the source and destination are kept secret, the header need not be in cleartext, the encryption devices are transparent to the data on the line, and the data does not affect the processors at each end.

local area network (LAN)   A network that consists of a single type of data link and that can reside entirely within a physically protected area.

local authority   An organization responsible for generating and signing user certificates.

logic bomb   A resident computer program that triggers an unauthorized act when particular states of an IS are realized.

low probability of detection   The result of measures used to hide or disguise intentional electromagnetic transmissions.

low probability of intercept   The result of measures to prevent the interception of intentional electromagnetic transmissions.

low-risk application   Computer applications that, if penetrated or disrupted, would not cause a serious loss for an enterprise.

LSB   Abbreviation for least-significant bit.

M

malicious logic   Hardware, software, or firmware intentionally included in an IS for an unauthorized purpose.

man-in-the-middle (MIM)   An attack against a public key exchange in which the attacker substitutes his or her own public key for the requested public key; also called a *bucket brigade attack*.

mandatory access control (MAC)   A means of restricting access to objects based on the sensitivity of the information contained in the objects and the formal authorization (i.e, clearance, formal access approvals, and need-to-know) of subjects to access information of such sensitivity. *See also* discretionary access control.

mandatory protection   A security mechanism in a computer that unconditionally blocks particular types of activities. For example, most multiuser systems have a "user mode" that unconditionally blocks users from directly accessing shared peripherals. In networking applications, some vendors use mandatory protection to prevent attacks on Internet servers from penetrating other portions of the host system.

manipulative communications deception   The alteration or simulation of friendly telecommunications deception for the purpose of deception.

manual cryptosystem   A cryptosystem in which the cryptographic processes are performed without the use of crypto-equipment or auto-manual devices.

masquerade   An attack in which an entity takes on the identity of a different entity without authorization. A form of spoofing.

MD2   Message digest algorithm 2.

MD4   Message digest algorithm 4.

MD5   Message digest algorithm 5.

medium-risk application   A computer application in which a disruption or other security problems could cause losses to the enterprise, some of which are an acceptable cost of doing business.

medium-strength crypto   A set of crypto capabilities that may qualify for favorable export treatment by the U.S. government if the vendor is actively developing crypto products that contain key escrow features.

memory scavenging   The collection of residual information from data storage.

message   Information sent from one entity to another on the network. A single message may be divided into several packets for delivery to the destination and then reassembled by the receiving host.

message authentication code (MAC)   Data associated with an authenticated message allowing a receiver to verify the integrity of the message.

message digest   A unique snapshot image of data that can be used for alter comparison. Change a single character in the message and the message will have a different message digest. Also called a *hash code*.

Message Security Protocol (MSP) An e-mail crypto protocol developed as part of the Secure Data Network System and used in the Defense Message System.

MIC Abbreviation for Message Integrity Code. Originally defined in PEM for authentication using MD2 or MD5. Micalg (message integrity calculation) is used in secure MIME implementations.

MIME Acronym for Multipurpose Internet Mail Extensions. A standard that lets a user transfer nontexual data—for example, graphics.

mimicking A form of spoofing.

MLS Abbreviation for multilevel security.

mode One of several ways to apply a block cipher to a data stream; includes CBC, CFB, and OFB.

mode of operation A description of the conditions under which an IS operates based on the sensitivity of information processed and the clearance levels, formal access approvals, and need-to-know of its users. Four modes of operation are authorized for processing or transmitting information: dedicated mode, system-high mode, compartmented/partitioned mode, and multilevel mode.

modulus In public key cryptography, part of the public key.

monoalphabetically A characteristic of encrypted text that indicates that it has been produced by means of a single cipher alphabet. The frequency distribution is characterized by troughs and peaks that are announced.

MSP Abbreviation for Message Security Protocol. The military equivalent of PEM; an X.400-compatible application level protocol for securing e-mail, developed by NSA in late 1980.

MTU Abbreviation for message transfer unit.

multilevel device Equipment trusted to properly maintain and separate data of different security categories.

multilevel mode An INFOSEC mode of operation wherein all the following statements are satisfied concerning the users who have direct or indirect access to the system, its peripherals, remote terminals, or remote hosts: (a) some users do not have a valid security clearance for all the information processed in the IS, (b) all users have the proper security clearance and appropriate formal access approval for that information to which they have access, and (c) all users have a valid need-to-know only for information to which they have access.

multilevel security (MLS) The concept of processing information with different classifications and categories that simultaneously permits access by users with different security clearances and denies access to users who lack authorization.

munition Anything that is useful in warfare. According to U.S. law, cryptosystems are munitions. This is the rationale behind export controls on cryptosystems.

mutual suspicion The condition in which two ISs need to rely upon each other to perform a service, yet neither trusts the other to properly protect shared data.

N

name server A computer that has both the software and the data (zone files) needed to match domain names to IP addresses.

name service A service that provides individuals or organizations with domain name-to-IP address matching by maintaining and making available the hardware, software, and data needed to perform this function.

NAT Abbreviation for Network Address Translator. As specified in RFC 1631, a router connecting two networks together; one designated as "inside" is addressed with either private or obsolete addresses that need to be converted into legal addresses before packets are forwarded onto the other network, designated as "outside."

National Computer Security Center (NCSC) A U.S. government organization that evaluates computing equipment for high-security applications.

National Institute of Standards and Technology (NIST) An agency of the U.S. government that establishes national standards.

National Security Agency (NSA) An agency of the U.S. government responsible for intercepting foreign communications for intelligence reasons and for developing cryptosystems to protect U.S. government communications.

national security information Information that has been determined, pursuant to (NSI) Executive Order 12958 or any predecessor order, to require protection against unauthorized disclosure.

national security system Any telecommunications or information system operated by the United States government, the function, operation, or use of which: (a) involves intelligence activities; (b) involves cryptologic activities related to national security; (c) involves command and control of military forces; (d) involves equipment that is an integral part of a weapon or weapon system; or (e) is critical to the direct fulfillment of military or intelligence missions and does not include a system that is to be used for routine administrative and business applications (including payroll, finance, logistics, and personnel management applications). Specified in Title 40 USC Section 1452, Information Technology Management Reform Act of 1996.

need-to-know The necessity for access to, or knowledge or possession of, specific information required to carry out official duties.

network (1) An organization of stations capable of intercommunication; a combination of circuits and terminals serviced by a single switching or processing center. (2) IS implemented with a collection of interconnected network nodes.

network encryption Crypto services applied to information above the data-link level but below the application software level. This allows crypto protections to use existing networking services and existing application software transparently.

network front end A device implementing protocols that allow attachment of a computer system to a network.

network protocol attack A software package that provides general-purpose networking services to application software, independent of the particular type of data link being used.

network reference monitor   An access control concept referring to an abstract machine that mediates all access to objects within a network by subjects within the network.

network security   The protection of networks and their services from unauthorized modification, destruction, or disclosure. It provides assurance the network performs its critical functions correctly and there are no harmful side effects.

network security architecture   A subset of network architecture specifically addressing security-relevant issues.

network security officer   An individual designated to ensure network security.

network system   A system implemented with a collection of interconnected components. A network system is based on a coherent security architecture and design.

network trusted computing base (NTCB)   The totality of protection mechanisms within a network, including hardware, firmware, and software, the combination of which is responsible for enforcing a security policy. *See also* trusted computing base.

network weaving   A penetration technique in which different communication networks are linked to access an IS to avoid detection and trace-back.

NIC   Abbreviation for Network Information Center. The organizational authority that administers the registration of domain names on the Internet; aka InterNIC in the United States.

NLSP   Abbreviation for Network Layer Security Protocol.

NNTP   Abbreviation for Network News Transfer Protocol.

node   A point of concentrated communications; a central point of communications. Switching devices are often called *nodes* because they form the junctions between routes or trunks in a data network.

nonce   A random value sent in a communications protocol exchange; often used to detect replay attacks.

nonrepudiation   The condition when a receiver knows or has assurance that the sender of some data did in fact send the data, even though the sender later may desire to deny ever having sent the data.

nonsecret encryption   *See* public key cryptography.

normal frequency   The standard frequency of a textual unit or letter, as disclosed by a statistical study of a large volume of homogeneous text.

NSP   Abbreviation for network service provider .

NSTAC   Abbreviation for the President's National Security Telecom-munications Advisory Committee.

null   A dummy letter, letter symbol, or code group inserted into an encrypted message to delay or prevent its decryption or to complete encrypted groups for transmission or transmission security purposes.

O

Oakley A protocol by which two authenticated parties can agree on secure and secret keying material. The basic mechanism is the Diffie-Hellman key exchange algorithm. The Oakley protocol supports perfect-forward security, compatibility with the ISAKMP protocol for managing security associations, user-defined abstract group structures for use with the Diffie-Hellman algorithm, key updates, and incorporation of keys distributed via out-of-band mechanisms.

offline cryptosystem A cryptosystem in which encryption and decryption are performed independently of the transmission and reception functions.

one-time cryptosystem A cryptosystem employing a key used only once.

one-time pad A Vernam cipher in which one bit of a new, purely random key is used for every bit of data being used.

online cryptosystem A cryptosystem in which encryption and decryption are performed in association with the transmitting and receiving functions.

one-time password A password that can only be used once; usually produced by special password-generating software or by a hardware token.

one-way hash A hash function for which it is extremely difficult to construct tow blocks of data that yield exactly the same hash result. Ideally, it should require a brute-force search to find two data blocks that yield the same result.

Open System Interconnection (OSI) A system capable of transparently operating in telecommunications environments of dissimilar computers.

operational data security The protection of data from either accidental or unauthorized intentional modification, destruction, or disclosure during input, processing, storage, transmission, or output operations.

operations security (OPSEC) The process of denying information to potential adversaries about capabilities and/or intentions by identifying, controlling, and protecting unclassified generic activities.

Orange Book (1) The National Computer Security Center book entitled "Department of Defense Trusted Computer Systems Evaluation Criteria" that defines security requirements. (2) The DoD Trusted Computer System Evaluation Criteria (DoD 5200.28-STD).

organizational registration authority (ORA) An entity within the public key infrastructure (PKI) that authenticates the identity and the organizational affiliation of the users.

OSI Abbreviation for Open Systems Interconnection (interface). Usually refers to the International Standard Organization (ISO) seven-layered protocol model for the exchange of information between open systems—a model for the connection of generalized data systems through communications networks. The seven layers are physical, data-link, network, transport, session, presentation, and application.

output feedback A block cipher mode in which the cipher is used to generate the key stream; also called *autokey mode*.

over-the-air key distribution   Providing electronic keys via over-the-air rekeying, over-the-air key transfer, or cooperative key generation.

over-the-air key transfer   Electronically distributing a key without changing the traffic encryption key used on the secured communications path over which the transfer is accomplished.

over-the-air rekeying (OTAR)   Changing the traffic encryption key or transmission security key in remote crypto-equipment by sending a new key directly to the remote crypto-equipment over the communications path it secures.

overt channel   A communications path within a computer system or network designed for the authorized transfer of data. *See* covert channel.

overwrite procedure   The process of writing patterns of data on top of the data stored on a magnetic medium.

P

packet   A sequence of data and control characters (binary digits) in a specified format that is switched/transferred as a whole.

packet switching   The process of routing and transferring data by means of addressed packets so that a channel is occupied only during the transmission of the packet. No physical connection is necessary. The packets are routed throughout the network towards their destination, where the entire message is reconstructed. Upon completion of the transmission, the channel is made available for the transmission of other traffic.

PAD   Acronym for packet assembler/disassembler. A device that assembles character strings into packets, including routing information, and that later dissembles the packets.

PAP   Acronym for Password Authentication Protocol. An authentication protocol that allows PPP peers to authenticate one another; it does not prevent unauthorized access but merely identifies the remote end.

parity   Bit(s) used to determine whether a block of data has been altered.

partitioned security mode   IS security mode of operation wherein all personnel have the clearance, but not necessarily formal access approval and need-to-know, for all information handled by an IS.

passive attack   An attack in which data is observed but not modified. This is the type of attack performed by Peeping Tom.

passphrase   A sequence of characters, longer than the acceptable length of a password, that is transformed by a password system into a virtual password of acceptable length.

password   A sequence of characters or words that a subject submits to a system for purposes of authentication, validation, or verification. Also called *pass code*.

password sniffing An attack in which someone examines data traffic that includes secret passwords in order to recover the passwords, presumably to use them in masquerades.

PCMCIA card A credit card-size memory or PC Card that meets the PC Card Standard developed jointly by the Personal Computer Memory Card International Association (PCMCIA) and the Japan Electronic Industry Development Association (JEIDA).

PEM Acronym for Privacy Enhanced Mail. A protocol to provide secure Internet mail (RFC 1421-1424), including services for encryption, authentication, message integrity, and key management; PEM uses X.509 certificates.

penetration The unauthorized act of bypassing the security mechanisms of a system.

penetration testing Security testing in which evaluators attempt to circumvent the security features of a system based on their understanding of the system design and implementation.

perfect forward secrecy (PFS) The concept by which the compromise of a single key will permit access only to data protected by that key. For PFS to exist, the key used to protect transmission of data must not be used to derive any additional keys, and if the key used to protect transmission of data is derived from some other keying material, that material must not be used to derive any more keys.

perimeter The physical boundary between the inside and the outside. Security measures rely on being able to trust individuals within a perimeter, at least to some degree.

physical network address A host address on a data link.

PKCS Abbreviation for Public-Key Cryptography Standards. A set of standards for public key cryptography developed in cooperation with an informal consortium (Apple, DEC, Lotus, Microsoft, MIT, RSA, and Sun) that includes algorithm specific and algorithm independent implementation standards.

plaintext (1) The readable data or message before it is encrypted. (2) Unencrypted information. Also called *chartext*.

policy-approving authority (PAA) The first level of the PKI certification management authority that approves the security policy of each PCA.

policy creation authority (PCA) The second level of the PKI certification management authority that formulates the security policy under which it and its subordinate CAs will issue public key certificates. Also known as a *policy certification authority*.

POP Abbreviation for Post Office Protocol. An Internet protocol for retrieving e-mail from a severe host.

port number A number carried in Internet transport protocols to identify which service or program is supposed to receive an incoming packet. Certain port numbers are permanently assigned to particular protocols by the IANA. For example, e-mail generally uses port 25 and Web services traditionally use port 80.

PPP An abbreviation for Point-to-Point Protocol. A protocol that provides router-to-router and host-to-network connections over synchronous and asynchronous communications links. The preferred standard for TCP/IP connections to the Internet.

Pretty Good Privacy (PGP) An e-mail crypto protocol designed by Phil Zimmerman that used RSA and IDEA, implemented in a software package widely distributed on the Internet.

PRF Abbreviation for pseudorandom function.

private key (1) The privately held "secret" component of an integrated asymmetric key pair. (2) An encryption methodology in which the encryptor and decryptor use the same key, which must be kept secret.

privileged access Explicitly authorized access of a specific user, process, or computer to a computer resource.

proprietary information Material and information relating to or associated with a company's products, business, or activities, including but not limited to financial information; data or statements; trade secrets; product research and development; existing and future product designs and performance specifications; marketing plans or techniques; schematics; client lists; computer programs; processes; and know-how that have been clearly identified and properly marked by the company as proprietary information, trade secrets, or company confidential information. The information must have been developed by the company and not be available to the government or to the public without restriction from another source.

protective packaging Packaging techniques for COMSEC material that discourage penetration, reveal a penetration has occurred or was attempted, or inhibit viewing or copying of keying material prior to the time it is exposed for use.

protocol (1) The procedures that are used by two or more computer systems so they can communicate with each other. (2) A set of rules and formats, semantic and syntactic, permitting ISs to exchange information.

proxy A facility that indirectly provides some service. Proxy crypto applies crypto services to network traffic without individual hosts having to support the services themselves. Firewall proxies provide access to Internet services that are on the other side of the firewall while controlling access to services in either direction.

pseudorandom number generator (PRNG) A procedure that generates a sequence of numerical values that appear random. Cryptographic PRNGs strive to generate sequences that are almost impossible to predict. Most PRNGs in commercial software are statistical PRNGs that strive to produce randomly distributed data with a sequence that may, in fact, be somewhat predictable.

public cryptography Body of cryptographic and related knowledge, study, techniques, and applications that is, or intended to be, in the public domain.

public key A key used in public key cryptography that belongs to an individual entity and is distributed publicly. Others can use the public key to encrypt data that only the key's owner can decrypt.

public key algorithm   A cipher that uses a pair of keys—a public key and private key—for encryption and decryption; also called an *asymmetric algorithm*.

public key certificate   Contains the name of a user, the public key component of the user, and the name of the issuer who vouches that the public key component is bound to the named user.

public key cryptography (PKC)   An encryption system using a linked pair of keys. What one pair of keys encrypts, the other pair decrypts. Also called *non-secret encryption*.

public key infrastructure (PKI)   The framework established to issue, maintain, and revoke public key certificates.

purging   Rendering stored information unrecoverable by laboratory attack.

R

Rainbow Series   A set of publications that interpret Orange Book requirements for trusted systems.

random   In mathematics, pertaining to the chance variations from an expected norm.

random number   A number with a value that cannot be predicted. Truly random numbers are often generated by physical events that are believed to occur randomly.

randomizer   An analog or digital source of unpredictable, unbiased, and usually independent bits. Randomizers can be used for several different functions, including key generation or to provide a starting state for a key generator.

RC4   Rivest Cipher 4, a proprietary algorithm of RSA Data Security, Inc.

RC5   Rivest Cipher 5.

real-time reaction   An immediate response to a penetration attempt that is detected and diagnosed in time to prevent access.

recovery procedures   Actions necessary to restore data files of an IS and computational capability after a system failure.

RED   A designation applied to information systems, along with associated areas, circuits, components, and equipment in which national security information is being processed.

red/black separation   A design concept for cryptosystems that keeps the portions of the system that handle plaintext rigidly separate from portions that handle ciphertext. Portions that handle both are vigorously minimized and then very carefully implemented.

RED/BLACK concept   The separation of electrical and electronic circuits, components, equipment, and systems that handle national security information (RED), in electrical form, from those that handle nonnational security information (BLACK) in the same form.

RED signal   Any electronic emission (e.g, plaintext, key, key stream, subkey stream, initial fill, or control signal) that would divulge national security information if recovered.

reference monitor   Access control concept referring to an abstract machine that mediates all accesses to objects by subjects. *See also* network reference monitor.

reference validation mechanism   The portion of a trusted computing base whose normal function is to control access between subjects and objects and whose correct operation is essential to the protection of data in the system.

replay   An attack that attempts to trick the system by retransmitting a legitimate message.

Request for Comments (RFCs)   The official document series of the Internet Engineering Task Force (IETF) that discusses computing, computer communication, networking, Internet protocols, procedures, programs, and concepts.

residual risk   The portion of risk remaining after security measures have been applied.

risk   The likelihood that a vulnerability may be exploited or that a threat may become harmful.

risk assessment   The process of analyzing threats to and vulnerabilities of an IS and the potential impact the loss of information or capabilities of a system would have on national security. The resulting analysis is used as a basis for identifying appropriate and cost-effective countermeasures.

risk management   The process concerned with the identification, measurement, control, and minimization of security risks in information systems to a level commensurate with the value of the assets protected.

role   The set of transactions a user is authorized to perform.

root   The top of the Domain Name System (DNS) hierarchy. Examples include .com, .net, .mil.

root server   Name servers that contain authoritative data for the very top of the Domain Name System (DNS) hierarchy. Technical specifications currently limit the number of root servers to 13, located in the U.S., the U.K., Sweden, and Japan.

router   An internetworking switch operating at the OSI level 3, the network layer.

routing host   A host that routes IP packets between networks, as well as providing other services.

RSA (RSA Data Security, Inc.)   Referring to the principles: Ron Rivest, Adi Shamir, and Len Adleman, or to the algorithm they invented. The RSA algorithm is used in public key cryptography and is based on the fact that it is easy to multiply two large prime numbers together, but hard to factor them out of the product.

RSADSI   Abbreviation for RSA Data Security, Inc.

S

SA *See* security association.

SAFE Acronym for Security and Freedom through Encryption. A congressional act to ease export controls on encryption products.

SALT Acronym for a random string that is concatenated with passwords before operated on by a one-way function; helps prevent against successful dictionary attacks.

sanitize Removing information from media such that data recovery is not possible. It includes removing all classified labels, markings, and activity logs.

scavenging Searching through object residue to acquire data.

SDSI Abbreviation for Simple Distributed Security Infrastructure. A new PKI proposal from Ronald L. Rivest (MIT) and Butler Lampson (Microsoft). A means of defining groups and issuing group membership, access control lists, and security policies. SDSI's design emphasizes like local name spaces rather than a hierarchical global name space.

second-level domain In the Domain Name System (DNS), the level of the hierarchy immediately underneath the top-level domains. In a domain name, that portion of the domain name that appears immediately to the left of the top-level domain. For example, the "icsa" in "icsa.net."

secret key A crypto key that is used in a secret key (symmetric) algorithm. The secrecy of encrypted data depends solely on the secrecy of the secret key.

secret key algorithm A crypto algorithm that uses the same key to encrypt data and to decrypt data; also called a *symmetric algorithm*.

secure Safe, protected, free from attack or damage.

secure channel A means of conveying information from one entity to another such that an adversary does not have the ability to reorder, delete, insert or read (SSL, IPSEC, whispering in someone's ear, etc.).

secure communications Telecommunications deriving security through the use of type 1 products and/or protected distribution systems.

secure hash standard A specification for a secure hash algorithm that can generate a condensed message representation called a *message digest*.

secure operating system The resident software-controlling hardware and other software functions in an IS to provide a level of protection or security appropriate to the classification, sensitivity, and/or criticality of the data and resources it manages.

secure state The condition in which no subject can access any object in an unauthorized manner.

secure subsystem A subsystem containing its own implementation of the reference monitor concept for those resources it controls. A secure subsystem must depend on other controls and the base operating system for the control of subjects and the more primitive system objects.

security association (SA) The set of security information relating to a given network connection or set of connections. SAs contain all the information required for execution of various network security services such as the IP-layer services of header authentication, payload encapsulation, and transport, or application-layer services such as self-protection of negotiation traffic.

security association bundle A sequence of SAs through which traffic must be processed to satisfy a security policy that is not achievable with a single SA.

security fault analysis An assessment, usually performed on IS hardware, to determine the security properties of a device when hardware fault is encountered.

security filter An IS trusted subsystem that enforces the security policy on the data passing through it.

security flaw An error of commission or omission in an IS that may allow protection mechanisms to be bypassed.

security inspection The examination of an IS to determine compliance with security policy, procedures, and practices.

security kernel Hardware, firmware, and software elements of a trusted computing base (TCB) implementing the reference monitor concept. The security kernel must mediate all accesses, be protected from modification, and be verifiable as correct.

security label Information representing the sensitivity of a subject or object, such as its hierarchical classification (CONFIDENTIAL, SECRET, TOP SECRET) together with any applicable nonhierarchical security categories (e.g, sensitive compartmented information, critical nuclear weapon design information).

security perimeter Includes all components/devices of an IS to be accredited. Separately accredited components generally are not included within the perimeter.

security range The highest and lowest security levels that are permitted in or on an IS, system component, subsystem, or network.

security requirements The types and levels of protection necessary for equipment, data, information, applications, and facilities to meet security policy.

security requirements baseline A description of the minimum requirements necessary for an IS to maintain an acceptable level of security.

security safeguards Protective measures and controls prescribed to meet the security requirements specified for an IS. Safeguards may include security features, management constraints, personnel security, and security of physical structures, areas, and devices. *See* accreditation.

security services Includes authentication, privacy, confidentiality, integrity, nonrepudiation, authorization, administration, audit, and so on.

security specification A detailed description of the safeguards required to protect an IS.

security test and evaluation The examination and analysis of the safeguards required to protect an IS, as they have been applied in an operational environment, to determine the security posture of that system.

seed, random A random data value used when generating a random sequence of data values with a pseudorandom number generator (PRNG).

self-authentication The implicit authentication, to a predetermined level, of all transmissions on a secure communications system.

sensitive information Information, the loss, misuse, or unauthorized access to or modification of which could adversely affect the national interest or the conduct of federal programs, or the privacy to which individuals are entitled under 5 USC Section 552a (the Privacy Act), but that has not been specifically authorized under criteria established by an executive order or an act of Congress to be kept secret in the interest of national defense or foreign policy. (Systems that are not national security systems, but contain sensitive information, are to be protected in accordance with the requirements of the Computer Security Act of 1987, PL 100-235.)

sensitivity label Information representing elements of the security label(s) of a subject and an object. Sensitivity labels are used by the trusted computing base (TCB) as the basis for mandatory access control decisions.

SEPP Acronym for Secure Electronic Payment Protocol. An open specification for secure bank card transactions over the Internet. Developed by IBM, Netscape, GTE, CyberCash, and MasterCard.

sequence An ordered arrangement of symbols (letter, digits, etc.) having continuity. The members of a component of a cipher alphabet; the symbols in a row, column, or diagonal of the cipher square in order; key letters or key figures in order.

server Computers, devices, or processes that provide service to clients in a client/server architecture.

session A single communication transaction.

session key The secret (symmetric) key used to encrypt each set of data on a transaction basis. A different session key or set of session keys is used for each communication session.

SET Acronym for secure electronic transaction. Provides for the secure exchange of credit card numbers over the Internet.

SHA Abbreviation for Secure Hash Algorithm. A specified secure hash standard developed by the National Institute for Standards and Technology (NIST).

SHA-1 The 1994 revision to SHA, which is considered more secure.

signals security A generic term encompassing COMSEC and electronic security.

Simple Key Interchange Protocol (SKIP) A protocol that establishes session keys to use with IPSEC protocol headers. SKIP data is carried in packet headers and travels in every IPSEC-protected packet.

Simple Mail Transfer Protocol (SMTP) An Internet protocol for transmitting e-mail between e-mail servers.

SKIP Acronym for Simple Key-management for Internet Protocols, developed by Sun Microsystems, Inc.

skipjack   The 80-bit key encryption algorithm contained in NSA's Clipper Chip. The algorithm is classified; NSA will not release information on how it works.

smart card   Tamper-resistant hardware devices that store private keys and other sensitive information.

S/MIME   A standard e-mail protocol developed by RSA Data Security. It enables a secure e-mail environment that authenticates the identity of the sender and receiver, verifies message integrity, and ensures privacy of the message contents and all attachments.

SNA   Abbreviation for System Network Architecture (IBM).

sniffer   A software tool for auditing and identifying network traffic packets.

sniffing   An attack that collects information from network messages by making copies of their contents. Password sniffing is the most widely publicized example.

SNMP   Abbreviation for Simple Network Management Protocol.

Sockets   The package of subroutines that provide access to TCP/IP on most systems.

software encryption   Encryption accomplished by software operations.

software system test and evaluation   A procedure that plans, develops, and documents the process of the fulfillment of all baseline functional performance, operational, and interface requirements.

solution   (1) The process or result of solving a cryptogram or cryptosystems by cryptanalysis, aka *cracking*. (2) The approach to solving a network connection or security problem.

speech privacy   Techniques using fixed-sequence permutations or voice/speech inversion to render speech unintelligible to the casual listener.

split knowledge   The separation of data or information into two or more parts, each part constantly kept under control of separate authorized individuals or teams so that no one individual or team will know the whole data.

splitting   The process of dividing a crypto key into two separate keys so that an attacker cannot reconstruct the actual crypto key even if one of the split keys is intercepted.

spoofing   The attempt to gain access to an IS by pretending to be an authorized user. Impersonating, masquerading, and mimicking are forms of spoofing.

spread spectrum   Telecommunications techniques in which a signal is transmitted in a bandwidth considerably greater than the frequency content of the original information. Frequency hopping, direct sequence spreading, time scrambling, and combinations of these techniques are forms of spread spectrum.

SSL   Abbreviation for Secure Sockets Layer. Developed by Netscape to provide security and privacy over the Internet. Supports server and client authentication and maintains the security and integrity of the transmission channel. Operates at the transport layer and mimics the "sockets library," allowing it to be application independent. Encrypts the entire communication channel and does not support digital signatures at the message level.

SSO Abbreviation for single sign on. A system where one logon provides access to all resources of the network, LAN, WAN, and so on.

SST Abbreviation for Secure Transaction Technology. A secure payment protocol developed by Microsoft and Visa as a companion to the PCT protocol.

state variable A variable representing either the state of an IS or the state of some system resource.

stream cipher A cipher that operates on a continuous data stream instead of processing a block of data at a time.

strong crypto Crypto facilities that exceed the standards for lightweight or medium-strength cryptography and therefore face significant restrictions under U.S. export rules.

STU-III Stands for Secure Telephone Unit. An NSA-designed phone for secure voice and low-speed data communications for use by the U.S. Department of Defense and its contractors.

subject security level Sensitivity label(s) of the objects to which the subject has both read and write access. The security level of a subject must always be dominated by the clearance level of the user associated with the subject.

subregistration authority (SRA) An individual with primary responsibility for managing the distinguished name process.

subroutines A set of instructions, appearing within a computer program, for performing a specific task.

substitution cipher The process when the characters of the plaintext are substituted with other characters to form the ciphertext.

superencryption (1) A further encryption of the text of a cryptogram for increased security. (2) The process of encrypting encrypted information. Occurs when a message, encrypted off line, is transmitted over a secured, online circuit, or when information encrypted by the originator is multiplexed onto a communications trunk, which is then bulk-encrypted.

superuser A special user who can perform the control of processes, devices, networks, and file systems.

suppression measure An action, procedure, modification, or device that reduces the level of, or inhibits the generation of, compromising emanations in an IS.

symmetric algorithm *See* secret key algorithm.

symmetric key When the same key is used to encrypt and decrypt data, it is termed *symmetric*.

symmetric key encryption The process of using one and only one key to perform both the encryption and decryption processes. *See also* asymmetric key encryption.

synchronous transmission The entire message is sent with control information surrounding the text portion of the transmission.

system administrator (SA) The individual responsible for the installation and maintenance of an information system, providing effective IS utilization, adequate security parameters, and sound implementation of established INFOSEC policy and procedures.

system assets   Any software, hardware, data, administrative, physical, communications, or personnel resource within an IS.

system development   Methodologies developed through software engineering methodologies to manage the complexity of system development. Development methodologies include software engineering aids and high-level design analysis tools.

system high   The highest security level supported by an IS.

system-high mode   An IS security mode of operation wherein each user, with direct or indirect access to the IS, its peripherals, remote terminals, or remote hosts, has all of the following: (a) valid security clearance for all information within an IS, (b) formal access approval and signed nondisclosure agreements for all the information stored and/or processed (including all compartments, subcompartments, and/or special-access programs), and (c) valid need-to-know for some of the information contained within the IS. *See also* compartmented mode, dedicated mode, and multilevel mode.

system indicator   A symbol or group of symbols in an offline encrypted message identifying the specific cryptosystem or key used in the encryption.

system integrity   The quality of an IS when it performs its intended function in an unimpaired manner, free from deliberate or inadvertent unauthorized manipulation of the system.

system low   The lowest security level supported by an IS.

system profile   A detailed security description of the physical structure, equipment component, location, relationships, and general operating environment of an IS.

system security   The degree of security as determined by evaluation of the totality of all system elements and INFOSEC countermeasures.

system security engineering   The effort to achieve and maintain optimal security and survivability of a system throughout its life cycle.

system security evaluation   A risk assessment of a system, considering its vulnerabilities and perceived security threat.

system security officer   *See* information systems security officer.

system security plan   A formal document fully describing the planned security tasks required to meet system security requirements.

T

TCP   Abbreviation for Transmission Control Protocol. Verifies correct delivery of data from client to server; uses virtual circuit routing. Occupies layer 4 (transport) of the OSI reference model. Electronic mail uses TCP as its transmission control.

TCP/IP   Abbreviation for Transmission Control Protocol/Internet Protocol.

TDM   Abbreviation for Time Division Multiplexing.

TDMA   Time Division Multiple Access.

telecommunications   Preparation, transmission, communication, or related processing of information (writing, images, sounds, or other data) by electrical, electromagnetic, electromechanical, electro-optical, or electronic means.

Telnet   A virtual terminal protocol that enables remote logons to computers across a network.

TEMPEST   A short name referring to investigation, study, and control of compromising emanations from IS equipment.

text   The part of the message containing the basic information that the originator desires to be communicated.

threat   Any circumstance or event with the potential to cause harm to an IS in the form of destruction, disclosure, adverse modification of data, and/or denial of service.

threat analysis   The examination of information to identify the elements comprising a threat.

threat assessment   A formal description and evaluation of threat to an IS.

threat monitoring   Analysis, assessment, and review of audit trails and other information collected for the purpose of searching out system events that may constitute violations of system security.

time bomb   A resident computer program that triggers an unauthorized act at a predefined time.

time-stamping   Recording the time of creation or existence of information.

TLS   Abbreviation for Transport Layer Security. A software-based security protocol based on minor changes to Netscape's Secure Sockets Layer version 3.0. Provides data source authentication, data integrity, and confidentiality. Submitted to the IETF for change control in 1996.

token, authentication   A hardware device that generates a one-time password to authenticate its owner; also sometimes applied to software programs that generate one-time passwords.

token, e-mail   A data item in the header of an encrypted e-mail message that holds an encrypted copy of the secret key used to encrypt the message; usually encrypted with the recipient's public key so that only the recipient can decrypt it.

token ring   Networking using token-passing on a ring configuration.

token passing   A deterministic access method that allows only one station at a time the right to access the network. A special data structure called a *token* passes from station to station in sequence. A station that has data to transmit grabs the token and changes a bit, making the token into a packet header. When the data is received, the altered token is placed back on the ring as an acknowledgment from the intended recipient that the data was received without error. The transmitting station then generates a new token and passes it to the next station on the network.

traffic analysis   A branch of cryptology that deals with the external characteristics of signal communications and related materials for the purpose of obtaining information concerning the organization and operation of a communication system.

traffic encryption key   A key used to encrypt plaintext, to superencrypt previously encrypted text, or to decrypt ciphertext.

traffic-flow confidentiality   Involves concealing the existence of the traffic flowing through a connection.

traffic-flow security   A measure used to conceal the presence of valid messages in an online cryptosystem or secure communications system.

traffic padding   The generation of spurious communications or data units to disguise the amount of real data units being sent.

transmission security   A component of COMSEC resulting from the application (TRANSEC) of measures designed to protect transmissions from interception and exploitation by means other than cryptanalysis.

transport   To carry from one place to another, especially over long distances.

transposition cipher   In this cipher type, the plaintext remains the same but the order of the characters is transposed.

trapdoor   Hidden software or hardware mechanism used to circumvent security controls.

triple DES (3DES)   An encryption configuration in which the DES algorithm is used three times with three different keys.

Trojan horse   (1) A program with secret functions that surreptitiously access information without the operator's knowledge, usually to circumvent security protections. (2) A program containing hidden code allowing the unauthorized collection, falsification, or destruction of information.

trust   A firm belief or confidence in the honesty, integrity, reliability, and so forth of a person or company.

trusted computer system   An IS employing sufficient hardware and software assurance measures to allow simultaneous processing of a range of classified or sensitive information. *See also* network trusted computing base.

trusted computing base (TCB)   The totality of protection mechanisms within a computer system, including hardware, firmware, and software; the combination responsible for enforcing a security policy.

trusted distribution   A method for distributing trusted computing base (TCB) hardware, software, and firmware components that protects the TCB from modification during distribution.

trusted facility management   Administrative procedures, roles, functions, privileges, and databases used for secure system configuration, administration, and operation.

trusted identification   The identification method used in IS networks whereby the forwarding sending host can verify that an authorized user on its system is attempting a connection to another host. The sending host transmits the required user authentication information to the receiving host.

trusted path A mechanism by which a person using a terminal can communicate directly with the trusted computing base (TCB). A trusted path can only be activated by the person or the TCB and cannot be imitated by untrusted software.

trusted process A process that has privileges to circumvent the system security policy and has been tested and verified to operate only as intended.

trusted recovery The ability to ensure recovery without compromise after a system failure.

trusted software The software portion of a trusted computing base (TCB).

TTL Abbreviation for Time to Live. The lifetime in seconds or number of transmissions of a packet.

TTP Abbreviation for trust third party. A responsible party, upon which all participants involved agree in advance, that provides a service or function, such as certification by binding a public key to an entity, time-stamping, or key escrow.

tunnel A secure virtual connection through the Internet.

U

Unauthorized disclosure The exposure of information to individuals not authorized to receive it.

unclassified Information that has not been determined pursuant to EO 12958 or any predecessor order to require protection against unauthorized disclosure and that is not designated as classified.

UDP Abbreviation for User Datagram Protocol.

untrusted process A process that has not been evaluated or examined for adherence to the security policy. It may include incorrect or malicious code that attempts to circumvent the security mechanisms.

updating An automatic or manual cryptographic process that irreversibly modifies the state of a COMSEC key, equipment, device, or system.

user (1) A person or process authorized to access an IS. (2) (PKI) An Individual defined, registered, and bound to a public key structure by a certification authority (CA).

user ID A unique symbol or character string used by an IS to identify a specific user.

User Partnership Program A partnership between the NSA and a U.S. government agency to facilitate the development of secure IS equipment incorporating NSA-approved cryptography. The result of this program is the authorization of the product or system to safeguard national security information in the user's specific application.

user profile   Patterns of a user's activity that can show changes from normal behavior.

U.S.-controlled facility   A base or building to which access is physically controlled by U.S. persons who are authorized U.S government or U.S government contractor employees.

V

validation   (1) A means to provide timeliness of authorization to use or manipulate information or resources. (2) The process of applying specialized security test and evaluation procedures, tools, and equipment needed to establish acceptance for joint usage of an IS by one or more departments or agencies and their contractors.

VAN   Acronym for value-added network.

verification   (1) The process of authenticating, confirming, or establishing accuracy. (2) The process of comparing two levels of an IS specification for proper correspondence (e.g, a security policy model with top-level specification, top-level specification with source code, or source code with object code).

virtual private network (VPN)   A private network built atop a public network. Hosts within the private network use encryption to talk to other hosts. The encryption excludes hosts from outside the private network even if they are on the public network.

virus   (1) A small program that attaches itself to a legitimate program. When the legitimate program runs, the virus copies itself onto other legitimate programs in a form of reproduction. (2) A self-replicating, malicious program segment that attaches itself to an application program or other executable system component and leaves no obvious signs of its presence.

vulnerability   A weakness in an IS, cryptographic system, or components (e.g, system security procedures, hardware design, internal controls) that could be exploited.

vulnerability analysis   A systematic examination of an IS or product to determine the adequacy of security measures, to identify security deficiencies, to provide data from which to predict the effectiveness of proposed security measures, and to confirm the adequacy of such measures after implementation.

W

web of trust   A distributed trust model used by PGP to validate the ownership of a public key where the level of trust is cumulative based on the individuals knowledge of the "introducers."

word pattern   The characteristic arrangement of repeated letters in a word that tends to make it readily identifiable when enciphered monoalphabetically.

work factor (1) The amount of work an attacker must perform to overcome security measures. (2) An estimate of the effort or time needed by a potential perpetrator, with specified expertise and resources, to overcome a protective measure.

worm (1) A computer program that copies itself into other host computers across a network. In 1988 the Internet Worm infected several thousand hosts. (2) An independent program that replicates from machine to machine across network connections, often clogging networks and computer systems as it spreads.

X

X.25 A recommendation of the CCITT (now ITU-T) that outlines procedures for switching data through a packet-switched network.

X.400 An ITU-T recommendation known as the Message Handling System, one of two standard architectures used for providing e-mail services and interconnecting propriety e-mail systems. The other is Simple Mail Transfer Protocol (SMTP).

X.500 A specification of the directory services required to support X.400 e-mail.

X.509v3 An ITU-T digital certificate, which is the internationally recognized electronic document used to prove identity and public key ownership over a communication network. It contains the issuer's name, user's identifying information, and issuer's digital signature.

XOR Abbreviation for the exclusive OR operation. A mathematical bit operation to represent different additive states.

Section 3
Biometric Terms

A

active impostor acceptance Occurs when an impostor submits a modified, simulated, or reproduced biometric sample, intentionally attempting to relate it to another person who is an enrollee, and he or she is incorrectly identified or verified by a biometric system as being that enrollee.

acoustic emission A proprietary technique used in signature verification. As a user writes on a paper surface, the movement of the pen tip over the paper fibers generates acoustic emissions that are transmitted in the form of stress waves within the material of a writing block beneath the document being signed. The structure-borne elastic waves behave in materials in a similar way to sound waves in air and can be detected by a sensor attached to the writing block.

API Abbreviation for application program interface. A set of services or instructions used to standardize an application. An API is computer code used by an application developer. Any biometric system that is compatible with the API can be added or interchanged by the application developer.

AFIS Acronym for Automated Fingerprint Identification System. A highly specialized biometric system that compares a single finger image with a database of finger images. AFIS is predominantly used for law enforcement, but it is also being put to use in civil applications. For law enforcement, finger images are collected from crime scenes (in which case they are known as "latents"), or they are taken from criminal suspects when they are arrested. In civilian applications, finger images may be captured by placing a finger on a scanner or by electronically scanning inked impressions on paper.

algorithm (biometric) A sequence of instructions that tell a biometric system how to solve a particular problem. An algorithm will have a finite number of steps and is typically used by the biometric engine to compute whether a biometric sample and template are a match.

artificial neural network A method of computing a problem. An artificial neural network uses artificial intelligence to learn by past experience and compute whether a biometric sample and template are a match.

ASIC Acronym for application-specific integrated circuit. An integrated circuit (silicon chip) that is specially produced for a biometric system to improve performance.

attempt The submission of a biometric sample to a biometric system for identification or verification. A biometric system may allow more than one attempt to identify or verify.

authentication *See* verification.

automatic ID/auto ID An umbrella term for any biometric system or other security technology that uses automatic means to check identity. This applies to both one-to-one verification and one-to-many identification.

B

behavioral biometric A biometric characterized by a behavioral trait rather than a physiological characteristic that is learned and acquired over time.

bifurcation A branch made by more than one finger image ridge.

binning A specialized technique used by some AFIS vendors. Binning is the process of classifying finger images according to finger image patterns. This predominantly takes place in law enforcement applications. Here, finger images are categorized by characteristics such as arches, loops, and whorls and held in smaller, separate databases (or bins) according to their category.

Searches can be made against particular bins, thus speeding up the response time and accuracy of the AFIS search.

biometric A measurable, physical characteristic or personal behavioral trait used to recognize the identity, or verify the claimed identity, of an enrollee.

biometric data The extracted information taken from the biometric sample and used either to build a reference template or to compare against a previously created reference template.

biometric engine The software element of the biometric system, which processes biometric data during the stages of enrollment and capture, extraction, comparison, and matching.

biometric sample Data representing a biometric characteristic of an end user as captured by a biometric system.

biometric system An automated system capable of:

1. Capturing a biometric sample from an end user
2. Extracting biometric data from that sample
3. Comparing the biometric data with that contained in one or more reference templates
4. Deciding how well they match
5. Indicating whether or not an identification or verification of identity has been achieved

biometric taxonomy A method of classifying biometrics. Sample classifications might be as follows:

Cooperative versus Non-Cooperative User

Overt versus Covert Biometric System

Habituated versus Non-Habituated User

Supervised versus Unsupervised User

Standard Environment versus Nonstandard Environment

biometric technology A classification of a biometric system by the type of biometric.

body odor A physical biometric that analyzes the unique chemical pattern made up by human body smell.

booking The process of capturing inked finger images on paper for subsequent processing by an AFIS.

C

capacitance A finger image capture technique that senses an electrical charge, from the contact of ridges, when a finger is placed on the surface of a sensor.

capture The method of taking a biometric sample from the end user.

certification   The process of testing a biometric system to ensure that it meets certain performance criteria. Systems that meet the testing criteria are said to have passed and are certified by the testing organization.

comparison   The process of comparing a biometric sample with a previously stored reference template or templates. *See also* one-to-many and one-to-one.

claim of identity   When a biometric sample is submitted to a biometric system to verify a claimed identity.

claimant   A person submitting a biometric sample for verification or identification while claiming a legitimate or false identity.

closed-set identification   When an unidentified end user is known to be enrolled in the biometric system.

D

D Prime   A statistical measure of how well a biometric system can discriminate between different individuals. The larger the D Prime value, the better a biometric system is at discriminating between individuals.

degrees of freedom   The number of statistically independent features in biometric data.

discriminant training   A means of refining the extraction algorithm so that biometric data from different individuals are as distinct as possible.

DNA   A unique, measurable human characteristic. However, current DNA technology is not automatic and cannot currently rank alongside other biometric technologies.

DPI   Abbreviation for dots per inch. A measurement of resolution for finger image biometrics.

E

ear shape   A lesser-known physical biometric that is characterized by the shape of the outer ear, lobes, and bone structure.

Eigenface   A method of representing a human face as a linear deviation from a mean or average face.

Eigenhead   The three-dimensional version of Eigenface that also analyzes the shape of the head.

encryption (biometric)   The act of converting biometric data into a code so that people will be unable to read it. A key or a password is used to decrypt (decode) the encrypted biometric data.

end user   A person who interacts with a biometric system to enroll or have his or her identity checked.

end user adaptation   The process of adjustment whereby a participant in a test becomes familiar with what is required and alters his or her responses accordingly.

enrollee   A person who has a biometric reference template on file.

enrollment   The process of collecting biometric samples from a person and the subsequent preparation and storage of biometric reference templates representing that person's identity.

enrollment time   The time period a person must spend to have his or her biometric reference template successfully created.

equal error rate   When the decision threshold of a system is set so that the proportion of false rejections will be approximately equal to the proportion of false acceptances. Also called *crossover rate*.

extraction   The process of converting a captured biometric sample into biometric data so that it can be compared to a reference template.

F

face recognition   A physical biometric that analyzes facial features.

face monitoring   A biometric application of face recognition technology where the biometric system monitors the attendance of an end user at a desktop.

facial thermogram   A specialized face recognition technique that senses heat in the face caused by the flow of blood under the skin.

failure to acquire   The failure of a biometric system to capture and extract biometric data.

failure to acquire rate   The frequency of a failure to acquire.

false acceptance   When a biometric system incorrectly identifies an individual or incorrectly verifies an impostor against a claimed identity. Also known as a *Type II error*.

False acceptance rate (FAR)   The probability that a biometric system will incorrectly identify an individual or will fail to reject an impostor. Also known as the *Type II error rate*. It is stated as follows:

$$FAR = NFA/NIIA$$

or

$$FAR = NFA/NIVA$$

Where: FAR is the false acceptance rate

NFA is the number of false acceptances

NIIA is the number of impostor identification attempts

NIVA is the number of impostor verification attempts

false match rate   An alternative to false acceptance rate. Used to avoid confusion in applications that reject the claimant if their biometric data matches that of an enrollee. In such applications, the concepts of acceptance and rejection are reversed, thus reversing the meaning of false acceptance and false rejection.

False nonmatch rate An alternative to false rejection rate. Used to avoid confusion in applications that reject the claimant if their biometric data matches that of an enrollee. In such applications, the concepts of acceptance and rejection are reversed, thus reversing the meaning of false acceptance and false rejection.

false rejection When a biometric system fails to identify an enrollee or fails to verify the legitimate claimed identity of an enrollee. Also known as a *Type I error*.

false rejection rate (FRR) The probability that a biometric system will fail to identify an enrollee, or verify the legitimate claimed identity of an enrollee. Also known as a *Type I error rate*. It is stated as follows:

$$FRR = NFR/NEIA$$

or

$$FRR = NFR/NEVA$$

Where: FRR is the false rejection rate

NFR is the number of false rejections

NEIA is the number of enrollee identification attempts

NEVA is the number of enrollee verification attempts

field test A trial of a biometric application in real-world as opposed to laboratory conditions.

filtering A specialized technique used by some AFIS vendors. Filtering is the process of classifying finger images according to data that is unrelated to the finger image itself. This may involve filtering by sex, age, hair color, or other distinguishing factors.

finger geometry A physical biometric that analyzes the shape and dimensions of one or more fingers.

finger image A physical biometric that looks at the patterns found in the tip of the finger.

fingerprint/fingerprinting The preferred terms are *finger image* and *finger scanning*.

finger scanning The process of finger image capture.

H

hamming distance The number of disagreeing bits between two binary vectors. Used as measure of dissimilarity.

hand geometry   A physical biometric that involves analyzing and measuring the shape of the hand. Also called *hand recognition*.

I

identification   The one-to-many process of comparing a submitted biometric sample against all of the biometric reference templates on file to determine whether it matches any of the templates, and if so, the identity of the enrollee whose template was matched. The biometric system using the one-to-many approach is seeking to find an identity amongst a database rather than verify a claimed identity. Also called *recognition*.

impostor   A person who submits a biometric sample in either an intentional or inadvertent attempt to pass him or herself off as another person who is an enrollee.

iris recognition   A physical biometric that analyzes iris features found in the colored ring of tissue that surrounds the pupil.

iris features   A number of features can be found in the iris, including corona, crypts, filaments, freckles, pits, radial furrows, and striations.

IrisCode   The biometric data that is generated for each live iris presented. The code is a mathematical representation of the features of the iris.

K

keystroke dynamics   A behavioral biometric under development that analyzes typing rhythm when an end user types onto a keyboard.

L

latent   An impression of a finger image collected from a crime scene.

live capture   The process of capturing a biometric sample by an interaction between an end user and a biometric system.

live scan   The term *live scan* is typically used in conjunction with finger image technology.

M

match/matching   The process of comparing a biometric sample against a previously stored template and scoring the level of similarity. An accept or reject decision is then based upon whether this score exceeds the given threshold.

minutiae   Small details found in finger images such as ridge endings or bifurcations.

P

palm A physical biometric that analyzes the palm of the hand. Typically, this will involve an analysis of minutiae data.

passive impostor acceptance When an impostor submits his or her own biometric sample, claiming the identity of another person (either intentionally or inadvertently). The person is then incorrectly identified or verified by a biometric system.

performance criteria Predetermined criteria established to evaluate the performance of the biometric system under test.

physical/physiological biometric A biometric that is characterized by a physical characteristic rather than a behavioral trait.

PIN Acronym for personal identification number. A security method whereby a (usually) four-digit number is entered by an individual to gain access to a particular system or area.

platen The surface on which a finger is placed during optical finger image capture.

R

receiver operating curves A graph showing how the false rejection rate and false acceptance rate vary according to the threshold.

response time The time period required by a biometric system to return a decision on identification or verification of a biometric sample.

retina A physical biometric that analyzes the layer of blood vessels situated at the back of the eye.

ridge The raised markings found across the fingertip.

ridge ending The point at which a finger image ridge ends.

S

signature verification A behavioral biometric that analyzes the way an end user signs his or her name. The signing features such as speed, velocity, and pressure exerted by a hand-holding a pen are as important as the static shape of the finished signature. Also called *dynamic signature verification (DSV)*.

speaker-dependent A term sometimes used by speaker verification vendors to emphasize the fact their technology is designed to distinguish among voices.

speaker separation A technology that separates overlapping voices from each other and from other background noises.

speech recognition   This is not a specific biometric. Often confused with speaker verification, speech recognition involves recognizing words as they are spoken and does not identify the speaker.

speaker verification   A part physical, part behavioral biometric that analyzes patterns in speech. Also called *voice verification*.

SVAPI   Abbreviation for Speaker Verification Application Program Interface. A biometric API for speaker verification systems.

T

template/reference template   Data that represents the biometric measurement of an enrollee used by a biometric system for comparison against subsequently submitted biometric samples.

thermal   A finger image capture technique that uses a sensor to sense heat from the finger and thus capture a finger image pattern.

third-party test   An objective test, independent of a biometric vendor, usually carried out entirely within a test laboratory in controlled environmental conditions.

threshold/decision threshold   The acceptance or rejection of biometric data is dependent on the match score falling above or below the threshold. The threshold is adjustable so that the biometric system can be more or less strict, depending on the requirements of any given biometric application.

throughput rate   The number of end users that a biometric system can process within a stated time interval.

Type I error   *See* false rejection.

Type II error   *See* false acceptance.

U

ultrasound   A technique for finger image capture that uses acoustic waves to measure the density of a finger image pattern.

user   The client to any biometric vendor. The user must be differentiated from the end user and is responsible for managing and implementing the biometric application rather than actually interacting with the biometric system.

V

validation   The process of demonstrating that the system under consideration meets in all respects the specification of that system.

valley   The corresponding marks found on either side of a finger image ridge.

veincheck/vein tree A physical biometric under development that analyzes the pattern of veins in the back of the hand.

verification The process of comparing a submitted biometric sample against the biometric reference template of a single enrollee whose identity is being claimed, in order to determine whether it matches the enrollee's template. Also called *authentication*.

voiceprint A representation of the acoustic information found in the voice of a speaker.

W

WSQ Abbreviation for Wavelet Transform/Scalar Quantization. A compression algorithm used to reduce the size of reference templates.

Z

zero-effort forgery An arbitrary attack on a specific enrollee identity in which the impostor masquerades as the claimed enrollee using his or her own biometric sample.

ANNOTATED REFERENCES AND RESOURCES

Presented below are resources for further study. In addition to the cited sources, the reader may find research papers and practical material through the following sources/Internet links:

Algonquin College: www.infosyssec.com/infosyssec/index.html

COMSEC Solutions Resource Page: www.comsec-solutions.com

Counterpane Systems Database of Papers: www.counterpane.com

Professor Dorothy Denning Links: www.cs.georgetown.edu/~denning/

Lecture Notes in Computer Science 1440: Advances in Cryptology 1981 to 1997, Springer-Verlag, 1998 (with CD-ROM of all proceedings)

NIST: Computer Security Resources Clearing House: http://csrc.nist.gov/topics/welcome.html

White House Archive: http://www.pub.whitehouse.gov/search/everything.html

Algorithms

Brickell, E., D. Denning, S. Kent, D. Maher, and W. Tuchman. SKIPJACK Review: Interim Report, "The SKIPJACK Algorithm," 28 July 1993.

Blum, M. and S. Micali. "How to Generate Cryptographically Strong Sequences of Pseudo-Random Bits." *SIAM Journal on Computing*, 13, no. 4 (November 1984): 850-864.

Garon, G. and R. Outerbridge. "DES Watch: An Examination of the Sufficiency of the Data Encryption Standard for Financial Institutions in the 1990s." *Cryptologia*, XV, no. 3 (1991): 177-193.

Goldreich, O. *Modern Cryptography: Probabilistic Proofs and Pseudo-Randomness*. Berlin: Springer-Verlag, 1999.

Lai, Xuejia. "On the Design and Security of Block Ciphers." *ETH Series in Information Processing* 1 (1992). Article defines the IDEA cipher.

Lai, Xuejia and James L. Massey. "A Proposal for a New Block Encryption Standard." *Advances in Cryptology*. Eurocrypt '90 Proceedings (1992): 55-70.

Menezes, Alfred J., Paul van Oorschot, and Scott A. Vanstone. *Handbook of Applied Cryptography*. Boca Raton, Fla.: 1998.

Micali, S. "Fair Cryptosystems." *Report MIT/LCS/TR-579.b*, MIT Laboratory for Computer Science, Cambridge, Mass., November 1993.

Patterson, Wayne. *Mathematical Cryptology for Computer Scientists and Mathematicians*. Lanham, Md.: Rowman & Littlefield, 1987.

Rhee, Man Young. *Cryptography and Secure Communications*. New York: McGraw-Hill, 1994.

Schneier, Bruce. *Applied Cryptography*, 2nd ed. New York: Wiley, 1996.

Schroeder, M. R. *Number Theory in Science and Communications: With Applications in Cryptography, Physics, Digital Information, Computing, and Self Similarity*, 3rd ed. Berlin: Springer-Verlag, 1999.

Authentication and Digital Signatures

American Bar Association. "Digital Signature Guidelines, Information Security Committee, Science and Technology Section." Draft, 5 October 1995.

Camenisch, Jan L., Jean-Marc Piveteau, and Markus A. Stadler. "Blind Signatures Based on the Discrete Logarithm Problem." Eurocrypt '94. In *Lecture Notes in Computer Science*. Vol 950. Berlin: Springer-Verlag, 428-432.

CCITT (International Consultative Committee on Telegraphy and Telephony) Recommendation X.509: "The Directory-Authentication Framework." 1988.

CCITT. Draft Recommendation X.509: "The Directory-Authentication Framework." Gloucester, November 1987.

Chaum, David. "Designated Confirmer Signatures." Eurocrypt '94. In *Lecture Notes in Computer Science*. Vol. 950. Berlin: Springer-Verlag, 1995, 86-91.

Chen, Lidong and Torben P. Pedersen. "New Group Signature Schemes." Eurocrypt '94. In *Lecture Notes in Computer Science*. Vol 950. Berlin: Springer-Verlag, 1995, 171-181.

Cramer, Ronald and Ivan Damgard. "Secure Signature Schemes Base on Interactive Protocols." Crypto '95. In *Lecture Notes in Computer Science*. Vol. 963. Berlin: Springer-Verlag, 1995, 297-310.

Diffie, W., P. Van Oorschot, and M. Wiener. "Authentication and Authenticated Key Exchanges." *Designs, Codes, and Cryptography* 2, no. 2 (1992): 107-125.

Feghhi, Jahal, Jahil Feghhi, and Peter Williams. *Digital Certificates: Applied Internet Security*. Reading, Mass.: Addison-Wesley, 1998.

Fiat, A. and A. Shamir. "How to Prove Yourself: Practical Solutions to Identification and Signature Problems." Crypto '86. In *Lecture Notes in Computer Science*. vol. 263. Berlin: Springer-Verlag, 1987, 186-194.

Grant, Gail L. *Understanding Digital Signatures: Establishing Trust over the Internet and Other Networks*. Berkeley, Calif.: McGraw-Hill, 1998.

Kabay, M. E., "Identification, Authentication and Authorization on the World Wide Web: An ICSA White Paper." June 1997.

Kent, S. and R. Atkinson. "IP Authentication Header." draft-ietf-ipsec-auth-header-06.txt, February 1998.

Krawczyk, H., et al. "HMAC: Keyed-Hashing for Message Authentication." RFC 2104, February 1997.

Langford, Susan K. "Threshold DSS Signatures without a Trusted Party." Crypto '95. In *Lecture Notes in Computer Science*. Vol. 963. Berlin: Springer-Verlag, 1995, 397-409.

Naccache, David, David M'Raihi, Dan Raphaeli, and Serge Vaudenay. "Can D.S.A. Be Improved? Complexity Trade-Offs with the Digital Signature Standard." Eurocrypt '94. In *Lecture Notes in Computer Science*. Vol. 950. Berlin: Springer-Verlag, 1995, 77-85.

Nichols, Randall K. and Hart Degrafft. "Digital Signatures." Chap. 10 in *The ICSA Guide to Cryptography and Commercial Computer Security Systems*. McGraw Hill, 1998.

Nyberg, Kaisa and Rainer R. Rueppel. "Message Recovery for Signature Schemes Based on the Discrete Logarithm Problem." Eurocrypt '94. In *Lecture Notes in Computer Science*. Vol. 950. Berlin: Springer-Verlag, 1995, 182-193.

Oppliger, Rolf. *Authentication Systems for Secure Networks*. Boston: Artech House, 1996.

Pfitzmann, Andreas, Birgit Pfitzmann, Matthias Schunter, and Michael Waidner. "Mobile User Devices and Security Modules: Design for Trustworthiness." *IBM Research Report RZ 2784 (#89262) 02/05/96*, IBM Research Division, Zilfich, February 1996.

Pfitzmann, Andreas, Birgit Pfitzmann, Matthias Schunter, and Michael Waidner. "Vertrauens-wfirdiger Entwurf portabler BenutzerendgerAte und Sicherheitsmodule." *VerIABliche IT-Systeme* (VIS '95); Dul FachbeitrAge, Vieweg, Wiesbaden, 1995, 329-350.

Pfitzmann, Birgit. *Digital Signature Schemes: General Framework and Fail-Stop Signatures*. Berlin: Springer-Verlag, 1996.

Reiter, M. and S. Stubblebine. "Toward Acceptable Metrics of Authentication." *Proceedings of the 1997 IEEE Symposium on Security and Privacy*, May 1997.

Rivest, Ron, A. Shamir, and L. Adleman. "A Method for Obtaining Digital Signatures and Public Key Cryptosystems." *Communications of the ACM* 21, 1978.

Rogers, B. "Use of Block Ciphers for Message Authentication." draft-rogers-cbe-mac-OO.txt, 12 February 1998.

Schnorr, C. *Procedures for the Identification of Participants as Well as the Generation and Verification of Electronic Signatures in a Digital Exchange System*. German Patent Number 9010348.1. Patent applied for 24 February 1989. Patent received 29 August 1990.

Solms, S. Von and D. Naccache. "On Blind Signatures and Perfect Crimes." *Computers and Security*, 11, no. 6 (October 1992): 581-583.

Yen, Sung-Ming and Chi-Sung Laih. "Improved Digital Signature Suitable for Batch Verification." *IEEE Transactions on Computers* 44, no. 7 (1995): 957-959.

Biometric Encryption

Bodo, Albert. *Method for Producing a Digital Signature with Aid of a Biometric Feature*. German Patent Number DE 42 43 908 A1, 1994.

Clarke, R. "Human Identification in Information Systems: Management Challenges and Public Policy Issues." *Information Technology & People*, 7, no. 4 (1994): 6-37.

Colombi, Major John, Ph.D., USAF. *Human-Authentication API, Interface Specification*. U.S. Biometrics Consortium. http:/www.biometrix.org/meetings/bc10/tilton/ppframe.htm.

Daugman, J. "High Confidence Visual Recognition of Persons by a Test of Statistical Independence." *IEEE Trans. on Pattern Analysis and Machine Intelligence* 15 (1993): 1148-1161.

Hahn, W. B. Jr. and K. A. Bauchert. "Optical Correlation Algorithm development for the Transfer of Optical Processing to Systems (TOPS) Program." *Proc. SPIE* 1959 (1993): 48-54.

Jain, Anil, Ruud Bolle, and Sharath Pankanti. *Biometrics: Personal Identification in Networked Society*. Dordrecht, Netherlands: Kluwer Academic Publishers, 1999.

Kumar, B. V. K. Vijaya. "Tutorial Survey of Composite Filter Designs for Optical Correlators." *Applied Optics* 31 (1992): 4773-4801.

Kumar, B. V. K. Vijaya and L. Hassebrook. "Performance Measures for Correlation Filters." *Applied Optics* (1990): 2997-3006.

Lange, L. and G. Leopold. "Digital Identification: It's Now at Our Fingertips." *EEtimes* 946 (March 24, 1997). Available at http://techweb.cmp.com/eet/823.

Lee, H. C. and R. E. Gaensslen, eds. *Advances in Fingerprint Technology*. Boca Raton, Fla.: CRC Press, 1991.

Newham, E. *The Biometrics Report*. SJB Research, Langport, U.K. 1998. Available from http://www.sjbresearch.com.

Parks, J. R. "Personal Identification—Biometrics." In *Information Security*, edited by D. T. Lindsay and W. L. Price. North Holland: Elsevier Science, 1991, 181-191.

Réfrégier, P. H. "Optimal Trade-Off Filters for Noise Robustness, Sharpness of the Correlation Peak, and Horner Efficiency," *Opt. Lett.* 16 (1991): 829-831.

Roethenbaugh, Gary and James L. Wayman. "Technical Testing and Evaluation of Biometric Identification Devices." Biometrics: National Biometric Test Center, San Jose State University, San Jose, Calif., 1999.

Roethenbaugh, Gary. "Biometrics Explained." NCSA, Draft v2.0, 1997. In 1998, NCSA changed to ICSA, and a new version of this document was filed at the ICSA library at www.icsa.net.

Roberge, Danny, Colin Soutar, and B. V. K. Vijaya Kumar. "Optimal Correlation Filter for Fingerprint Verification." *Proc. SPIE* 3386 (1998): 123-133.

Soutar, Colin, Danny Roberge, Alex Stoianov, Rene Gilroy, and B. V. K. Vijaya Kumar. "Biometric Encryption Using Image Processing." *Proc. SPIE* 3314 (1998): 178-188.

Soutar, Colin, Danny Roberge, Alex Stoianov, Rene Gilroy, and B. V. K. Vijaya Kumar. "Biometric Encryption—Enrollment and Verification Procedures." *Proc. SPIE* 3386 (1998): 24-35.

Steward, E. G. *Fourier Optics: An Introduction*. Hemel Hempstead, U.K.: Ellis Horwood Limited, 1983.

Stoianov, Alex, Colin Soutar, and Al Graham. "High-Speed Fingerprint Verification Using an Optical Correlator." *Proc. SPIE* 3386 (1998): 242-252.

VanderLugt, A. *Optical Signal Processing*. New York: Wiley, 1992.

Certificate Authorities

Baker, Stewart A. and Paul R. Hurst. *The Limits of Trust: Cryptography, Governments, and Electronic Commerce*. Washington, D.C.: Kluwer Law International, 1998. Baker's analysis is brilliant and his book is highly recommended to all readers.

Beguin, Phillippe, Jean-Jasques Quisquater. "Fast Server-Aided RSA Signatures Secure Against Active Attacks." Crypto '95. In *Lecture Notes in Computer Science*. Vol. 963. Berlin: Springer-Verlag, 1995, 57-69.

Blaze, M., J. Feigenbaum, and J. Lacy. "Decentralized Trust Management." *Proceedings of the 1996 IEEE Symposium on Security and Privacy*, May 1996.

Kent, Stephen. "Reasoning about Public-Key Certification." Presentation at RSA Data Security Conference, January 1996.

Kent, Stephen. "Let a Thousand (10,000?) CAs Reign." Keynote for Defense Information Management Seminar (DIMACS) Workshop on Trust Management, September 1996.

Stephen Kent. "How Many Certification Authorities Are Enough?" BBN Technologies, unclassified presentation, Cambridge, Mass., 1997. Presentations at RSA Data Conference, 1996, and DIMACS Workshop on Trust Management, 1996.

Moeller, M. "Digital IDs: Offering an Expanded View of Users: VeriSign's Next Digital Certificates Extend Electronic IDs to Include Personal Data." *PC Week* 14, no. 5: 2 (3 February 1997).

Rapoza, J. "Sentry CA Crosschecks Certificates; Review: Xcert Uses LDAP Directory Secured via SSL for Flexible Authentication between Authorities." *PC Week* 14 no. 15:46 (14 April 1997).

Schunter, Matthias. *Vertrauen als Integraler Bestandteil Kryptografischer Spezifikationen*. Rust Center, Grundlagen, Rechtliche Aspekte, Standardisierung, Realisierung, DuD achbeitrAge, Vieweg, Wiesbaden 1995, 173-179.

Citations/Legal/Testimony

Administrative Office of the United States Courts, Report on Applications for Orders Authorizing or Approving the Interception of Wire, Oral, or Electronic Communications (Wiretap Report) 1993.

Bernstein v. United States Department of State, 922 F. Supp 1426 (N.D. Cal. 1996).

Bernstein v. United States Department of State, 945 F. Supp. 1279 (N.D. Cal. 1996).

Bernstein v. United States Department of State, 974 F. Supp. 1288 (N.D. Cal. 1997).

Bernstein v. United States Department of Justice, United States Court of Appeals for the Ninth Circuit, Case Number 97-16686.

Charney, Scott. Testimony to the Secretary, Federal Trade Commission. Published electronically 21 October 1997, http://www.usdoj.gov/criminal/cyber-crime/comment1ftc.html.

Computer Security Act of 1987. Public Law 100-235 (H.R. 145), 101 Stat., 1724-1730.

Foreign Intelligence Surveillance Act, 50 U.S.C. Sec.1801, et seq.

Global Internet Liberty Campaign (GILC). "An International Survey Of Encryption Policy." Published electronically February 1998, http://www.gilc.org/crypto/crypto-survey.html.

House Report 100-153, "Part 2: The Committee on Government Operations' Report on the Computer Security Act of 1987." Washington, D.C., 1987.

H.R. 3627, *A Bill to Amend the Export Administration Act of 1979 with Respect to the Control of Computer and Related Equipment*, 1993.

Junger v. Daley, F. Supp., (N.D. Ohio 1998).

Karn v. U.S. Dept. of State, 925 R. Supp. 1 (D.D.C. 1996).

Koops, Bert-Jaap. "Crypto Law Survey." Version 15.0, July 1999. Available from http://cwis.kub.nl/~frw/people/koops/cls2.htm#co, Internet.

Kuner, Christopher. "Cryptography Regulation in Germany: Present and Future." *3 Computer & Telecommunications L. Rev.* 116 (June 1997).

Letter of 15 October 1996 from Senators and Representatives Conrad Burns, Ron Wyden, Trent Lott, Lauch Faircloth, Larry Pressler, Larry Craig, Barbara Boxer, Al Simpson, Craig Thomas, Pete Domenici, Patty Murray, Kay Bailey Hutchison, John Ashcroft, Don Nickles, Bob Goodlatte, Zoe Lofgren, Howard Cable, Bill Barr, Sonny Bono, Steve Chabot, and Tom Campbell to Michael Kantor, Secretary of Commerce. Published electronically at http://www.epic.org/crypto/clipper/white_house_ state-ment_4_93.html.

Letter of April 25, 1997, from the Software Publishers Association to Tom Bliley and Rick White, Committee on Commerce, House of Representatives. Published electronically at 1997http://www.house. gov/white/press/105/19970425waschre-sponse.html.

Litt, Robert S., Deputy Assistant Attorney General, U.S. Department of Justice, Criminal Division, before the Subcommittee on Social Security, Senate Ways and Means Committee, United States Senate, Washington, D.C., 20530, 6 May 1997.

Reidenberg, Joel R. and Schwartz, Paul M. *Data Privacy Law: A Study of United States Data Protection*. Charlottesville, Va.: Lexis Law Publishers, 1996.

Security and Freedom through Encryption Act, 106th Cong. H.R. 850.

18 U.S.C. 1030: http://mailer.fsu.edu/~btf1553/ccrr/federal.htm.

18 U.S.C. 1831 - 1839: http://mailer.fsu.edu/~btf1553/ccrr/federal.htm.

18 U.S.C. 1029: http://mailer.fsu.edu/~btf1553/ccrr/federal.htm.

18 U.S.C. 1343: http://mailer.fsu.edu/~btf1553/ccrr/federal.htm.

18 U.S.C. 2511: http://mailer.fsu.edu/~btf1553/ccrr/federal.htm.

18 U.S.C. 2701: http://mailer.fsu.edu/~btf1553/ccrr/federal.htm.

United States v. Peterson, 98 F. 3d 502, 504, Ninth Circuit, 1996. Upholds two-level enhancement under sentencing guidelines for the use of special skills to facilitate crimes, including crime described in text.

Wassenaar Arrangement 1998. Available at http://www.efa.org.au/issues/crypto/wass98.h.

Classical Cryptography

American Cryptogram Association. *ACA and You: Handbook for Members of the American Cryptogram Association*, 1995.

Bauer, F. L. *Decrypted Secrets: Methods and Maxims of Cryptology*. Berlin: Springer-Verlag, 1997.

Doyle, Arthur Conan. "The Adventure of the Dancing Men." *The Strand Magazine* 26, no. 156 (December 1903). Available at http://etext.lib.virginia.edu/cgibin/browse-mixed?id=DoyDanc&tag= public&images=images/modeng&data=/lv1/Archive/eng-parsed.

Friedman, William F. *Elements of Cryptanalysis*. Laguna Hills, Calif.: Aegean Park Press, 1976.

Friedman, William F. *Advanced Military Cryptography*. Laguna Hills, Calif.: Aegean Park Press, 1976.

Friedman, William F. and Lambros D. Callimahos. *Military Cryptanalytics—Part I*. Vol. 1. Laguna Hills, Calif.: Aegean Park Press, 1985.

Friedman, William F. and Lambros D. Callimahos. *Military Cryptanalytics—Part I*. Vol. 2, Laguna Hills, Calif.: Aegean Park Press, 1985.

Friedman, William F. and Lambros D. Callimahos. *Military Cryptanalytics—Part III*. Laguna Hills, Calif.: Aegean Park Press, 1995.

Friedman, William F. and Lambros D. Callimahos. *Cryptanalytics—Part IV*. Laguna Hills, Calif.: Laguna Hills, Calif.: Aegean Park Press, 1995.

Follet, Ken. *The Key To Rebecca*. New York: Signet, 1980.

Gaines, Helen Fouche. *Elementary Cryptanalysis*. New York: Dover, 1956.

Kahn, David. *The Codebreakers: The Story of Secret Writing*. 2nd ed., New York:

Macmillan, 1967.

Kippenhahn, Rudolf. *Code Breaking: A History and Exploration*. New York: Overlook Press, 1999.

National Security Agency. *Friedman Legacy: A Tribute to William and Elizabeth Friedman*. Central Security Service, Center for Cryptological History, 1995.

Nichols, Randall K. *Classical Cryptography Course*. Vol. I, Laguna Hills, Calif.: Aegean Park Press, 1995.

Nichols, Randall K. *Classical Cryptography Course*. Vol. II, Laguna Hills, Calif.: Aegean Park Press, 1996.

Rowlett, Frank B. *The Story of Magic: Memoirs of an American Cryptologic Pioneer*. Laguna Hills, Calif.: Aegean Park Press, 1998.

Singh, Simon. *The Code Book: The Evolution of Secrecy from Mary, Queen of Scots, to Quantum Cryptography*. New York: Doubleday, 1999.

Shulman, David. *An Annotated Bibliography of Cryptography*. New York: Garland Publishing, 1976.

Weber, Ralph Edward. *United States Diplomatic Codes and Ciphers, 1775-1938*. Chicago: Precedent Publishing, 1979.

Computer Crime

Associated Press. "Swedish Hacker Pleads Guilty." New York, 8 March 1997.

Barlow, J. P., et al. "Is Computer Hacking a Crime?" *Harper's Magazine* (March 1990) 46-57.

Bunch, Brian and Alexander Hellemans. *The Timetables of Technology: A Chronology of the Most Important People and Events in the History of Technology*. New York: Simon & Schuster, 1993, 23.

Clanchy, M.T. *From Memory to Written Record*. Oxford, U.K.: Blackwell Publishers, 1993.

Denning, Dorothy E. "Who's Stealing Your Information?" *Information Security* (April 1999) 29.

DeYoung, H. Garrett. "Thieves Among Us." *Industry Week* 245 (June 1996): 12-16.

Edwards, Owen. "Hackers from Hell." *Forbes ASAP Supplement* (October 1995): 182.

Eells, Richard and Peter Nehemkis. *Corporate Intelligence and Espionage*. New York: Macmillan, 1984.

ICSA. *Fifth Annual ICSA Labs Computer Virus Prevalence Survey*. August 1999. Available from http://www.ICSA.net.

Layton, RADM Edwin T. "And I Was There." New York: William Morrow, 1985, 448.

Levine, Diane E. "Viruses and Related Threats To Computer Security." Chap. 19

in *Computer Security Handbook*. 3rd ed., edited by Arthur E. Hutt, Seymour Bosworth, and Douglas B. Hoyt, eds. New York: Wiley, 1995.

Parker, Donn B. *Fighting Computer Crime*. New York: Wiley, 1999.

Ritchey, Barbara D. DISC6341, Professor Hirschheim. "Computer Crimes and How to Prevent Them." 23 September 1996. Available at http://disc.cba.uh.edu/~rhirsch/fall96/barba.htm.

Rosenblatt, Kenneth S. *High-Technology Crime: Investigating Cases Involving Computers*. San Jose, Calif.: KSK Publications, 1995.

Thompson, Cheryl W. "Arrested, Charged, and AWOL." *The Washington Post*, 10 March 1999, B1.

U.S. Senate. "Security in Cyberspace." Hearings before the Permanent Subcommittee on Investigation, 22 May 1996.

Winkler, Ira. *Corporate Espionage*. Rocklin, Calif.: Prima Publishing, 1997.

Violino, Bob. "Your Worst Nightmare." *Information Week* (February 1996): 34-36.

Zwillinger, Marc J. *Investigation and Prosecution of Computer Crime*. Computer Crime and Intellectual Property Section Criminal Division, U.S. Department of Justice, 4 November 1998. Available at http://www.amc.army.mil/amc/ci/nov4a/tsld005.htm.

Cryptanalysis

Biham, E. and A. Shamir. "Differential Cryptanalysis of DES-Like Cryptosystems." *Journal of Cryptology*. 4, no. 1 (1991), 3-72.

Biham, E. and Shamir, A. *Differential Cryptanalysis of the Data Encryption Standard*. Berlin: Springer-Verlag, 1993.

Biham, E. A. Shamir. "Differential Cryptanalysis of Snefru, Khafre, REDOC-II, LOKI, and LUCIFER." *Proceedings of Crypto '91*, edited by J. Feigenbaum, 1992, 156-171.

Brickell, E. F. and A. M. Odlyzko. "Cryptanalysis: A Survey of Recent Results." *Proceedings of the IEEE* 76, no. 5 (May 1988): 578-593.

Cracking DES: Secrets of Research, Wiretap Politics & Chip Design. Sebastopol, Calif.: Electronic Frontier Foundation. O'Reilly & Associates, 1998.

Kumar, I. J.. *Cryptology: System Identification and Key-Clustering*. Laguna Hills, Calif.: Aegean Park Press, 1997.

Lewis, Frank W. *Solving Cipher Problems—Cryptanalysis, Probabilities, and Diagnostics*. Laguna Hills, Calif.: Aegean Park Press, 1992.

Matsui, M. "Linear Cryptanalysis of DES Cipher." in *Proceedings of Eurocrypt '93*, 1993.

Rueppel, R. *Design and Analysis of Stream Ciphers*. Berlin: Springer-Verlag, 1986.

Wiener, W., "Efficient DES Key Search." Presentation at Rump Session of Crypto, August 1993, Santa Barbara, Calif. Available as TR-244, School of

Computer Science, Carleton University, Ottawa, Canada.

Wiener, M. "Efficient DES Key Search—An Update." *RSA Laboratories Cryptobytes* (Autumn 1997).

Yair, Frankel and Moţi Yung. "Cryptanalysis of the Immunized LL Public-Key Systems." Crypto '95. In *Lecture Notes in Computer Science*. Vol. 963. Berlin: Springer-Verlag, 1995, 287-296.

Elliptic Curve Cryptography

Adleman, L., J. DeMarrais, and M. Huang. "A Subexponential Algorithm for Discrete Logarithms over the Rational Subgroup of the Jacobians of Large Genus Hyperelliptic Curves over Finite Fields." In *Lecture Notes in Computer Science*. Vol. 877. Berlin: Springer-Verlag, 1994, 28-40.

Agnew, G., R. Mullin, and S. Vanstone. "An Implementation of Elliptic Curve Cryptosystems over F_2155." *IEEE Journal on Selected Areas in Communications* 11 (1993): 804-813.

Blaze, M., W. Diffie, R. Rivest, B. Schneier, T. Shimomura, E. Thompson, and M. Wiener. "Minimal Key Lengths for Symmetric Ciphers to Provide Adequate Commercial Security." Report of adhoc panel of cryptogrphers and computer scientists, January 1996, http://www.crypto.com/papers.

Boneh, D. and R. Lipton. "Algorithms for Black-Box Fields and Their Applications to Cryptography." Crypto '96. In *Lecture Notes in Computer Science*. Vol. 1109. Berlin: Springer-Verlag, 1996, 283-297.

Certicom, "The Elliptic Curve Cryptosystem for Smart Cards." White paper, May 1998.

Certicom, "Remarks on the Security of The Elliptic Curve Cryptosystem." White paper. September 1997.

FIPS 186, Digital Signature Standard. National Institute for Standards and Technology, 1993. Available at http://csrc.ncsl.nist.gov/fips/.

Koblitz, N. *Algebraic Aspects of Cryptography*. Berlin: Springer-Verlag, 1999.

Koblitz, N. "Elliptic Curve Cryptosystems." *Mathematics of Computation* 48 (1987): 203-209.

Koblitz, N. *A Course in Number Theory and Cryptography*. 2nd ed., Berlin: Springer-Verlag, 1994.

Koblitz, N. "CM-Curves with Good Cryptographic Properties." Crypto '91. In *Lecture Notes in Computer Science*. Vol. 576. Berlin: Springer-Verlag, 1992, 279-287.

LaMacchia, B. A. and A. M. Odlyzko. "Computation of Discrete Logarithms in Prime Fields." *Designs, Codes, and Cryptography* (1991): 47-62.

Menezes, A., T. Okamoto, and S. Vanstone. "Reducing Elliptic Curve Logarithms to Logarithms in a Finite Field." *IEEE Transactions on Information Theory* 39 (1993): 1639-1646.

Menezes, A. *Elliptic Curve Public Key Cryptosystems*. Dordrecht, The Netherlands: Kluwer Academic Publishers, 1993.

Menezes, A., P. Van Oorschot, and S. Vanstone. *Handbook of Applied Cryptography*. Boca Raton, Fla.: CRC Press, 1997.

Miller, V. "Uses of Elliptic Curves In Cryptography." Crypto '85. In *Lecture Notes in Computer Science*. Vol. 218. Berlin: Springer-Verlag, 1986, 417-426.

Miyaji, A. "On Ordinary Elliptic Curve Cryptosystems." Asiacrypt '91, In *Lecture Notes in Computer Science*. Vol. 218. Berlin: Springer-Verlag, 1993, 460-469.

Nyberg, K. and R. Rueppel. " Message Recovery for Signature Schemes Based on the Discrete Logarithm Problem." *Designs, Codes, and Cryptography* 7, 1996, 61-81.

Rosing, Michael. *Implementing Elliptic Curve Cryptography*. Greenwich, Ct.: Manning Publications, 1999.

Schirokauer, O. "Discrete logarithms and local units." *Philosophical Transactions of the Royal Society of London* , 345 (1993): 409-423.

Shoup, V. "Lower Bounds for Discrete Logarithms and Related Problems." Eurocrypt '97. In *Lecture Notes in Computer Science*. Vol. 1233. Berlin: Springer-Verlag, 1997, 256-266.

Solinas, J. "An Improved Algorithm for Arithmetic on a Family of Elliptic Curves." Crypto '97. In *Lecture Notes in Computer Science*. Vol. 1294. Berlin: Springer-Verlag, 1997, 357-371.

Zuccherato, R. "New Applications of Elliptic Curves and Function Fields in Cryptography." Ph.D. thesis, University of Waterloo, Canada, 1997.

E-Mail

Crocker, S. "Internet Privacy Enhanced Mail." In *The Third CPSR Cryptography and Privacy Conference Source Book*, edited by David Banisar. Upland, Pa.: Diane Publishing Co.

Garfinkel, Simon. *PGP: Pretty Good Privacy*. Sebastopol, Calif.: O'Reilly & Associates, 1995.

Kent, S. "Internet Privacy Enhanced Mail." *Communications of the ACM* 36, no. 8 (August 1993), 48-59.

Linn, J. and S. T. Kent. "Privacy for DARPA-Internet Mail." In *Proceedings of the 12th National Computer Security Conference*. Baltimore, Md., October 10 to 13, 1989, 215-229.

Linn, J. "Privacy Enhancement for Internet Electronic Mail: Part I: Message Encryption and Authentication Procedures." RFC 1421, February 1993.

Rescorla, E., and A. Schiffman, "The Secure Hypertext Transfer Protocol." Internal draft. Enterprise Integration Technologies, December 1994.

Schneier, Bruce. *E-mail Security*. New York: Wiley, 1995.

Stallings, William. *Protect Your Privacy: A Guide for PGP Users*. Upper Saddle River, N.J.: Prentice-Hall, 1995.

INFOSEC

Amoroso, Edward. *Fundamentals of Computer Security Technology*. Upper Saddle River, N.J.: Prentice-Hall, 1994.

AXENT Technologies. *Security Briefcase Handbook*. Rockville, Md., 1998. Available from www.axent.com.

Blackstock, Paul W. and Frank L. Schaf Jr. "Intelligence, Espionage, Counterespionage and Covert Operations." Gale Research Co., Detroit, Mich., 1978.

Bologna, J., *Handbook of Corporate Fraud: Prevention, Detection, Investigation*. Boston: Butterworth-Heinemann, 1993.

Bosworth, Bruce. *Codes, Ciphers, and Computers: An Introduction to Information Security*. Rochelle Park, N.J.: Hayden Books, 1990.

Carroll, John M. *Computer Security*. 3rd ed. Boston: Butterworth-Heinemann, 1996.

Copeland, Guy L. and Frederick G. Tompkins. "A New Paradigm for the Development of U.S. Information Security Policy, Computer Science and Corporation." White paper. Herndon, Va., September 1995.

CSI, the Computer Security Institute, a leading security training organization that publishes surveys and reports such as computer crime and information security program assessment. It jointly works with the FBI on its annual surveys. Web address is http://www.gocsi.com/homepage.shtml.

Dam, Kenneth W. (preface) and Herbert S. Lin (ed.) *Cryptography's Role in Securing the Information Society*. Computer Science and Telecommunications Board, National Research Council. Washington, D.C.: National Academy Press, 1996.

Davies, D. W. and W. L. Price. *Security for Computer Networks: An Introduction to Data Security in Teleprocessing and Electronic Funds Transfer*. 2nd ed. New York: Wiley, 1989.

Denning, Dorothy. *Information Warfare and Security*. Reading, Mass.: Addison-Wesley, 1999.

Denning, D. E. R. *Cryptography and Data Security*. Reading, Mass.: Addison-Wesley, 1983.

Department of the Army. *Counterintelligence*. FM 34-60. February 1990.

Department of Defense Directive 5200.28-STD, "Trusted Computer System Evaluation Criteria." Included in the *National Security Agency Information Systems Security Products and Services Catalog*.

Eloff, Jan H. P. and Sebastiaan H. Von Solms. *Information Security: The Next Decade*. London: Chapman and Hall, 1995.

Freedman, Alan. *The Computer Desktop Encyclopedia*. 2nd ed. CD-ROM. Point Pleasant, Pa.: The Computer Language Company Inc., 1999, 837.

Garfinkel, Simon and G. Spafford. *Practical UNIX Security*. Sebastopol, Calif.: O'Reilly & Associates. 1991.

Gasser, M. *Building a Secure Computer System*. New York: Van Nostrand Reinhold, 1988.

OECD. "Guidelines for the Security of Information Systems." 1 July 1997. Available at http://www.oecd.org/dsti/sti/it/secur/index.htm. OECD stands for Organisation for Economic Co-operation and Development.

Hutt, A. E., S. Bosworth, and D. B. Hoyt, eds. *Computer Security Handbook*. 3rd ed. New York: Wiley, 1995.

"Introduction to Data Mining." Published electronically August 1997 at http://www.cs.bham.ac.uk/~anp/dm_docs/dm_intro.html.

Kabay, Michel E. *The NCSA Guide to Enterprise Security: Protecting Information Assets*. New York: McGraw-Hill, 1996.

Koblitz, Neal. *A Course in Number Theory and Cryptography*. 2nd ed. Berlin: Springer-Verlag, 1994.

Kovacich, Gerald L. *Information Systems Security Officer's Guide: Establishing and Managing an Information Protection Program*. Boston: Butterworth-Heinemann, 1998.

Leach, Harold H. "Storage." Published electronically March 1998 at http://lcsweb.com/News/storage.htm.

Lubar, Steven. *Infoculture: The Smithsonian Book of Information Age Inventions*. Boston: Houghton Mifflin, 1993, 320.

Karger, P. A. and R. R. Schell, "Multics Security Evaluation: Vulnerability Analysis," (ESD-TR-74-193), Electronics Systems Division, USAF, Hanscom Air Force Base, Bedford, Mass., 1974 (NTIS:AD A001120).

National Security Agency. "Multilevel Information Systems Security Initiative (MISSI)." *Key Management Concepts*, Rev. 2.5, February 1995.

Neumann, Peter G. *Computer-Related Risks*. Reading, Mass.: Addison-Wesley, 1995.

Nichols, Randall K. *ICSA Guide to Cryptography and Commercial Computer Security Systems*. New York: McGraw-Hill. Available at www.comsec-solutions.com.

Nichols, Randall K. "Common Industry Practices for Implementing Cryptography." White paper, ICSA, May 1997. Available at http://www.icsa.net.

Pfleeger, C. P. *Security in Computing*. Englewood Cliffs, N.J.: Prentice-Hall, 1989.

Rosenblatt, K. S. *High-Technology Crime: Investigating Cases Involving Computers*. San Jose, Calif.: KSK Publications, 1995.

Russell, D. and G. T. Gangemi Sr. *Computer Security Basics*. Sebastopol, Calif.: O'Reilly & Associates, 1991.

Schwartau, W. *Information Warfare*. 2nd ed. New York: Thunder's Mouth Press, 1997.

Schou, Corey. *Handbook of INFOSEC Terms*. Version 2.0, CD-ROM, Idaho State University & Information Systems Security Organization, 1996. Available from glossary@sdsc.isu.edu.

Shannon, C. E. "The Communication Theory of Secrecy Systems." *Bell System Technical Journal* 28 (October 1949).

Sippey, Michael. "The One-to-One Future—Part II." *Stating the Obvious*. (2 February 1998). Available at http://stating.theobvious.com/archives/020298.html.

National Security Agency. *Solutions for A Safer World*. Four-part video, Unclassified, Information Systems Security Organization, 1996.

Stang, D. J., et al. *Network Security Secrets*. Boston: IDG Book, 1993.

Torrieri, Don J. *Principles of Military Communication Systems*. Norwood, Mass.: Artech, 1981.

Vacca, John. *Internet Security Secrets*. Boston: IDG Books, 1996.

Wayner, Peter. *Disappearing Cryptography*. San Diego: Academic Press, 1996.

Welsh, Dominic. *Codes and Cryptography*. New York: Oxford Science Publications, 1993.

Information Warfare (Infowar)

Campen, Alan D., Douglas H. Dearth, and R. Thomas Goodden, ed. *Cyberwar: Security, Strategy, And Conflict in the Information Age*. Fairfax, Va.: AFCEA Press, 1996.

Collins, John M. *Military Space Forces—The Next 50 Years*. New York, NY, Pergamon-Brassey's, 1989. Commissioned by the U.S. Congress.

Denning, Dorothy E. *Information Warfare and Security*. Reading, Mass.: Addison-Wesley, 1999.

Emmett, Peter C. "Software War: The Militarization of Logic." *Joint Forces Quarterly* (Summer 1994). Prepared by the Reliability and Vulnerability Working Group of the Information Infrastructure Task Force, IITF, Telecommunications Policy Committee, "National Information Infrastructure (NII) Risk Assessment: A Nation's Information At Risk." 29 February 1996.

Keegan, John. *A History of Warfare*. New York: Alfred A. Knopf, 1993, 377.

Kelly, Kevin. *Out of Control: The Rise of Neo-Biological Civilization*. Reading, Mass.: Addison-Wesley, 1994, 8-9.

Montalbano, William D. "For Dissident, Just the Fax Causes British-Saudi Rift." *Los Angeles Times*. (Originally published Saturday, April 27, 1996, Home Edition Part A, Page 1.) Available at http://www.saudhouse.com/news/april/1.htm.

Nichols, Randy. "Cryptography Systems Applications, Management and Policy." Lecture held on 14 July 1999. Emgt 289 IN. Slides available at www.comsec-solutions.com.

Nichols, Randall K., COMSEC Solutions presentation to FBI Security CIITA agents. Quantico, Va., 27 May 1999. COMSEC Solutions is a leading cryptographic, antivirus, and biometric countermeasures firm (http://www.comsec-solutions.com).

Niksic, Alexandra. "Serbia's Digital Demos." *The Irish Times: Computimes* (Monday, 10 February 1997). Available at http://www.irish-times.com/irish-times/paper/1997/0210/cmp2.html.

Nuclear Regulatory Commission studies. "Global Trends in Computer Technology and Their Impact on Export Control" (1988); "Finding Common Ground: U.S. Export Controls in a Changed Global Environment" (1991).

Parker, D. B. *Proceedings of the 14th National Computer Security Conference*, 1991.

Joint Security Commission. "Redefining Security." Report to the Secretary of Defense and the Director of Central Intelligence, 28 February 1994, 103.

Schwartau, W. *Information Warfare*. 2nd ed. New York: Thunder's Mouth Press, 1997.

Tompkins, Fred G. "U.S. Information Security Policy: How Should the Government Approach the Post-Cold War Environment?" Eastern Michigan University, Ypsilanti, Mich., 22 September 1995.

U.S. Senate. "Vulnerability of Telecommunications and Energy Resources to Terrorism." Hearings before the Committee on Governmental Affairs, Senate Hearing 101-73, 7-8 February 1989, Washington, D.C.: U.S. Government Printing Office, 1989.

Intelligence

Church, William, man. ed. "CIWARS Intelligence Report—13 September 1998: 1997-1998 Infrastructure Vulnerability Report." *Journal of Infrastructural Warfare and the Center for Infrastructural Warfare Studies*, 2, no. 23, 5, 13-17. Available from http://www.iwar.org.

Codevilla, Angelo. *Informing Statecraft: Intelligence for a New Century*. New York, Maxwell Millian International, 1992, 192.

Kennedy, Colonel William V. *Intelligence Warfare*. New York: Crescent Books, 1983.

Martin, Frederick Thomas. *Top Secret Intranet: How the U.S. Intelligence Built INTELINK—The World's Largest, Most Secure Network*. Upper Saddle River, N.J.: Prentice-Hall, 1997.

Pitorri, Peter. *Counterespionage for American Business*. Butterworth-Heinemann, 1998.

Richelson, Jeffrey T. *The U.S. Intelligence Community*. 3rd ed., Boulder, Col.: Westview Press, 1995.

Internet/VPN

Note: The Internet drafts are at ftp://ftp.ietf.org/internet-drafts/XXXX, and the RFCs are at ftp://ds.internic.net/rfc/rfcXXXX.txt. Also, both the Internet drafts and RFCs are evolving documents and may have different revision numbers.

Anonymous. *Maximum Security: A Hacker's Guide to Protecting Your Internet Site and Network*. Indianapolis: SAMS, 1997.

Ahuja, Vijay. *Network and Internet Security*. San Diego: Academic Press, 1996.

Atkins, Derik, et al., *Internet Security: Professional Reference.* Indianapolis: New Riders Publishing, 1996.

Avolio, Frederick M. "Firewalls and Virtual Private Networks." TIS white paper, 1998. Available at www.tis.com.

Bates, R. J. Jr. *Disaster Recovery Planning: Networks, Telecommunications, and Data Communications.* New York: McGraw-Hill, 1992.

Bernstein, T. A., B. Bhimani, E. Schultz, and C. A. Siegel. *Internet Security for Business.* New York: Wiley, 1996.

Chapman, D. B. and E. D. Zwicky. *Building Internet Firewalls.* Sebastopol, Calif.: O'Reilly & Associates, 1995.

Cheswick, W. and S. Bellovin. *Firewalls and Internet Security: Repelling the Wily Hacker.* Reading, Mass.: Addison-Wesley, 1994. Cheswick and Bellovin list 40 weak points in this book.

CiPro Conceptual Guide: A Theoretical Guide to the Virtual Private Network (VPN). RADGUARD, Ltd., 1998. Available at www.radguard.com.concept.html.

Cisco Systems. "IP Security." 1998. Available at www.cisco.com.

Cisco Systems, "Solutions for Virtual Private Dial-up Networks." 1998. Available at www.cisco.com.

Cisco Systems. "VPN Solutions: Understanding Today's Choices for Building Service Provider Virtual Private Networks." Cisco systems, 1998. Available at www.cisco.com.

Cisco Systems. "VPN Solutions: IP VPN Frequently Asked Questions." Cisco Systems, 1998. Available at www.cisco.com.

Cobb, Stephen. "Security Issues in Internet Commerce." NCSA white paper, Version 2.0, 1997. Available at www.ICSA.net.

Cobb, Stephen. *NCSA Guide to PC and LAN Security.* McGraw-Hill, New York: 1996

Cooper, Frederick J., et al. *Implementing Internet Security.* Indianapolis: New Riders Publishing, 1995.

Cryptosystem White Paper. "The Secured Solution for the Internetworking Revolution." RADGUARD, Ltd., 1998. Available at www.radguard.com.

Faurer, Lincoln D. "Computer Security Goals of the Department of Defense." *Computer Security Journal* (Summer, 1984).

Ford, Warwick and Michael S. Baum. *Secure Electronic Commerce: Building the Infrastructure for Digital Signatures and Encryption.* Upper Saddle River, N.J.: Prentice-Hall, 1997.

Gates, Bill. *Business @ The Speed of Thought: Using a Digital Nervous System.* New York: Warner Books, 1999.

Harkins, D. and D. Carrel. "The Internet Key Exchange." draft-ietf-ipsec-isakmp-oakley-07.txt, February 1998.

Herscovitz, Eli. "Secure Virtual Private Networks: The Future of Data Communications." RADGUARD, Ltd., 1998. Available at www.radguard.com./VPNmrkt.html.

Hughes, L. J. Jr. *Actually Useful Internet Security Techniques.* Indianapolis: New Riders Publishing, 1995.

IAB Privacy and Security Research Group. "Privacy Enhancement for Internet Electronic Mail—Part I: Message Encipherment and Authentication Procedures." RFC 1113B, 18 December 1990.

IBM. *IBM Comprehensive Guide to Virtual Private Networks*. Vol. I, IBM Redbooks, 1999. Available at www.redbooks.ibm.com/sg245201/sg240006.htm.

Kam, P., et al. "The ESP DES-CBC Transform." RFC 1829, August 1995.

Kantor, Andrew and Michael Neubarth. "Off the Charts: The Internet 1996." *Internet World* (December 1996).

Kent, S. and R. Atkinson. "IP Authentication Header." draft-ietf-ipsec-auth-header-06.txt, February 1998.

Kent, S. "IP Encapsulating Security Payload." draft-ietf-ipsec-esp-v2-05.txt, February 1998.

Klander, Lars. *Hacker Proof: The Ultimate Guide to Network Security*. Las Vegas: JAMSA Press, 1997.

Maugiam, Douglas, et al. "Internet Security Association and Key Management Protocol (ISAKMP)." draft-ietf-ipsec-isakmp-09Axt, 26 July 1997.

McCarthy, Vance. "Web Security: How Much Is Enough?" *Datamation*, 43, no. 1 (January 1997).

Nichols, Randall K. "Virtual Private Networks (VPNs)." White paper, ICSA, August 1998. Available at www.comsec-solutions.com.

Orrnan, H. K. "The OAKLEY Key Determination Protocol." draft-ietf-ipsec-oakley-02.txt, undated.

Phillips, Lee Anne. *Using HTML 4*. 4th ed. New York: QUE Publications, 1998.

Piper, Derrell. "The Internet IP Security Domain of Interpretation for ISAKMP." draft-ietf-ipsec-ipsec-doi-09.txt

PyroWall White Paper. "The Secured Solution for the Internetworking Revolution." RADGUARD, Ltd., 1998. Available at www.radguard.com.

Ramo, Joshua Cooper. "Welcome to the Wired World." *Time Magazine* (5 December 1997). Available at http://mouth.pathfinder.com/time/magazine/1997/int/970203/special.welcome_to.html.

Rimer, Daniel, H. "Stepping into the Internet Era: The Transition of Enterprise Computing." *iWord* 2, no. 2 (April 1997). Available at http://www.hamquist.com/iword/iword22/istory22.html.

Rose, L. J. *NetLaw: Your Rights in the Online World*. Berkeley, Calif.: Osborne/McGraw-Hill, 1994.

Russell, Deborah and G.T. Gangemi Sr. *Computer Security Basics*. Sebastopol, Calif.: O'Reilly & Associates, Inc., 1991.

Sage, Karen M. "Network Management Solutions for IP-VPN Services." Cisco Systems, 1998. Available at www.cisco.com.

Scott, Charlie, Paul Wolfe, and Mike Erwin. *Virtual Private Networks*. Sebastopol, Calif.,: O'Reilly & Associates, 1998.

"SET Secure Electronic Transaction Specification." Book 3: Format Protocol Definition. Version 1.0, May 1997. http://www.mastercard.com/shoponline/set/

Smith, Richard. *Internet Cryptography*. Reading, Mass.: Addison-Wesley, 1997.

Stallings, William. "A Secure Foundation For VPNs." *Information Security* (March 1998).

Stallings, William. *Cryptography and Networking Security: Principles and Practice.* 2nd ed. Upper Saddle River, N.J.: Prentice-Hall, 1998.

Strategic Research Corporation. *PC Magazine's Network Buyers Guide.* Emeryville, Calif.: PC Magazine, 1996.

TimeStep Corporation. "Business Case for Secure VPNs." TimeStep Corporation, Kanata, Ontario, 1998. Available at www.gimestep.com.

TimeStep Corporation. "Understanding the IPSec Protocol Suite." Kanata, Ontario, 1998. Available at www.timestep.com.

Vacca, John. *Internet Security Secrets.* Foster City, Calif.: IDG Books, 1995.

Vacca, John. *Internet Security.* Rockland, Mass.: Charles River Media, 1997.

VPNET Technologies. "What's a VPN Anyway? Or, the Cloud's Silver Lining in Your Net. VPNET Technologies, 1998. Available at www.vpnet.com.

Wayner, Peter. *Digital Cash: Commerce on the Net.* New York: AP Professional, 1995.

Key Management

Ehrsam, W. F., S. M. Matyas, C. H. Meyer, and W. L. Tuchman. "A Cryptographic Key Management Scheme for Implementing the Data Encryption Standard." *IBM Systems Journal* 17, no. 2 (1978) 106—125.

Flynn, R. and A. S. Campasano. "Data Dependent Keys for a Selective Encryption Terminal." In *AFIPS Conference Proceedings.* Vol. 47, Edited by S. P. Ghosh and L. Y. Liu. National Computer Conference, Anaheim, Calif., 5-8 June 1978. Montvale, N.J.: AFIPS Press, 1978, 1127-1129.

Gordon, J. "Strong RSA Keys." *Electronics Letters.* 20, no. 12 (7 June 1984): 514-516.

Matyas, S. M. and C. H. Meyer. "Generation, Distribution, and Installation of Cryptographic Keys." *IBM Systems Journal.* 17, no. 2 (1978): 126-137.

Menke, S. M., K. Power, and S. Graves. "New FIPS Defines Key Use." *Government Computer News.* 16 no. (7):3 (17 March 1997).

Smith, Michael, P. C. Van Oorschot, and M. Willett. "Cryptographic Information Recovery Using Key Recovery." White paper, Key Recovery Alliance, 17 June 1997.

Orman, H. K., "The OAKLEY Key Determination Protocol." draft-ietf-ipsec-oakley-02.txt, undated.

Network and Protocols

Panel on Crisis Management of the CSIS, CSIS Science and Technology Committee. "America's Hidden Vulnerabilities: Crisis Management in a Society of Networks." Report. Center for Strategic and International Studies. Georgetown University, Washington, D.C., 1984.

Austin, Tom. "Tunnel Vision." *Infosecurity News* (May 1997) 34 ff.

Blaze, M. "Protocol Failure in the Escrowed Encryption Standard." White paper, 31 May 1994.

Committee on Review of Switching, Synchronization, and Network Control in National Security Telecommunications, National Research Council. "Growing Vulnerability of the Public Switched Networks: Implications for National Security Emergency Preparedness." Washington, D.C.: National Academy Press, 1989.

Diffie, W. "Network Security Problems and Approaches." *Proceedings of the National Electronics Conference* 38 (1984): 292-314.

Kaufman, Charlie, Radia Perlman, and Mike Spenser. *Network Security: Private Communication in a Public World.* Upper Saddle River, N.J.: Prentice-Hall, 1995.

Lyons, Frank. "A Network Security Review." *Infosecurity* 8, no. 2, News (March/April 1997).

Moore, J. H. "Protocol Failures in Cryptosystems," *Proceedings of the IEEE* 76, no. 5 (May 1988): 594-602.

Price, W. and D. Davies. *Security for Computer Networks.* New York: Wiley, 1984.

Rescorla, E. and A. Schiffmann. "The Secure Hypertext Transport Protocol." Version 1.1, Internet-Draft, Enterprise Integration Technologies." July 1995. Available at http://www.eit.conV/ projects/s-http/draft-ietf-wts-shttp-OO.txt.

Rotenberg, M. "Communications Privacy: Implications for Network Design." *Communications of the ACM* 36, no. 8 (August 1993): 61-68.

SANS Institute. "1999 Network Security Roadmap." Available at www.sans.org.

Tanenbaum, A. *Computer Networks.* 3rd ed. Upper Saddle River, N.J.: Prentice-Hall, 1996.

Policy

Association For Computing Machinery. "Codes, Keys and Conflicts: Issues in U.S. Crypto Policy." Report of a Special Panel of ACM U.S. Public Policy Committee (USACM), June 1994.

Abelson, Hal, et al. "The Risks of Key Recovery, Key Escrow, and Trusted Third-Party Encryption." 21 May 1997. Available at http://www.info-sec.com/crypto/report.html-ssi.

Anthes, Gary H. "Feds Ease Crypto Rules, but with a `Key' Catch." *Computerworld* 30 (7 October 1996): 32.

Anthes, Gary H. "Encryption Policies Still Under Fire." *Computerworld* 30 (9 December 1996): 74.

Baker, Stewart A. and Michael D. Hintze. "United States Government Policy on Encryption Technology." 3 *Computer & Telecommunications L. Rev. 109* (June 1997).

Hoffman, Lance J. et al., "Cryptography Policy." *Communications of the ACM 37* (1994): 109-117.

Bureau of Export Administration, U.S. Department of Commerce. BXA Statement on Encryption Case. 7 May 1999. Available at www.bxa.doc.gov/factsheets/EncryptCase.html.

Hoffman, Lance, Faraz A. Ali, Steven L. Heckler, and Ann Huybrechts. "Cryptography: Policy and Technology Trends." December 1993. Revised 30 January 1994, under contract DE-AC05-84OR21400.

Hoffman, Lance J., et al. "Growing Development of Foreign Encryption Products in the Face of U.S. Export Regulations. "Report no. GWU-CPI-1999-02, 10 June 1999.

Hoffman, Lance J., ed. *Building in Big Brother: The Cryptographic Policy Debate.* Berlin: Springer-Verlag, 1995.

International Organization for Standards. "Information Processing Systems— Open Systems Interconnection Model—Part 2: Security Architecture." Draft International Standard ISO/DIS 7498-2, 1987.

International Traffic in Arms Regulation (ITAR), 22 CFR 120-130.

Leonard, Peter and Natalia Yastreboff. "Encryption and Australian Government Policy." *3 Computer & Telecommunications L. Rev. 119* (June 1997).

OECD. "OECD Adopts Guidelines for Cryptography." Letter of 4 June 1997. Available at http://www.oecd.org//publications/letter/0604.html#A1.

Pozhitkov, Igor. "State Policy on Encryption in the Russian Federation." *3 Computer & Telecommunications L. Rev. 123* (June 1997).

Schwartzstein, Stuart J. D. "Export Contols On Encryption Technologies." *SAIS Review* (Winter 1996): 15-16.

Seminerio, Maria. "Is Government-Mandated Key Recovery `Inevitable?'" *ZDNN* (10 July 1997).

Singleton, Solveig. "Policy Analysis: Encryption Policy for the 21st Century." Available at http://www.cato.org/pubs/pas/pa-325es.html.

U.S. Department of Commerce and U.S. National Security Agency. *A Study of the International Market for Computer Software with Encryption.* Prepared for the Interagency Working Group on Encryption and Telecommunications Policy (July 1995).

Ward, Conor. "Regulation of the Use of Cryptography and Cryptographic Systems in the United Kingdom: The Policy and the Practice." *3 Computer & Telecommunications L. Rev. 105* (June 1997).

Privacy

Alderman, Ellen and Caroline Kennedy. *The Right to Privacy.* New York: Alfred Knopf, 1997, 323.

D. Banisar. "Statistical Analysis of Electronic Surveillance." Presentation at the National Institute of Standards and Technology, Computer System Security and Privacy Advisory Board, 3 June 1993.

Chandler, J., D. Arrington, and L. Gill. *Foreign Encryption Technology Controls.* Washington, D.C.: The George Washington University, National Law Center, 1993.

Chandler, J., D. Arrington, and L. Gill. *Issues Regarding the Use of Cryptographic Technologies in the Commercial Sector.* Washington, D.C.: The George Washington University, National Law Center, 1993.

Chaum, David. "Achieving Electronic Privacy." *Scientific American* (August 1992): 96-101.

Communications Security Establishment. "Trusted Systems Environment Guideline." CID/09/17 (Ottawa), 1992.

Department of Defense. "Public Key Infrastructure Roadmap for the Department of Defense." Version 2.0, Revision C, February 1999.

Diffie, W. "Communication Security and National Security Business, Technology, and Politics." *Proceedings of the National Communications Forum* 40 (1986): 734-751.

Diffie, Whitfield and Susan Landau. *Privacy on the Line: The Politics of Wiretapping and Encryption.* Cambridge, Mass.: MIT Press, 1998, 6.

Electronic Privacy Information Center. *Cryptography and Liberty 1999: An International Survey of Encryption Policy.* Available from http://www.gilc.org/crypto/crypto-survey-99.html.

Elledge, D. "Keep Out Prying Eyes." *Information Week* 629, no. 102 (5 May 1997).

Entrust. "Making PKI Pay for Itself." 1999. Available at www.entrust.com.

Franklin, Charles E. H., ed. Business *Guide to Privacy and Data Protection Legislation.* The Hague, Netherlands: ICC Publishing S.A., Kluwer Law International, 1996.

Privacy Rights Clearing House. "Fact Sheet #4: Reducing Junk Mail." Available at http://www.privacyrights.org/fs/fs4-junk.htm.

Sarris, Christina. "Summary of the FTC Public Workshop, 'Consumer Privacy on the Global Information Infrastructure' on June 4-5, 1996," Arent Fox, 2 July 1996. Available at http://www.webcom.com/lewrose/arcticle/privacy2.html.

Smith, N. Jeff. *Managing Privacy.* Chapel Hill, N.C.: The University of North Carolina Press, 1994, 7-9.

U.S. Congress Office of Technology Assessment. "Protecting Privacy in Computerized Medical Information." #OTA-TCT-576. Washington, D.C.: U.S. Government Printing Office, 1993.

Vogel, Jennifer. "Getting to Know All About You: Attention Shoppers—What You Tell Supermarket Clubs May Be Used Against You." *Salon Magazine* (14 October 1998).

Public Key Cryptography

Beth, T., M. Frisch, and G. Simmons, "Public Key Cryptography: State of the Art and Future Directions." In *Lecture Notes in Computer Science.* Vol. 578. Berlin: Springer-Verlag, 1992.

Beth, T. "Algorithm Engineering for Public Key Algorithms." *IEEE Selected Areas of Communication* 1 no. 4 (1990): 458—466.

Bhimani, Anish. "All Eyes on PKI." *Information Security* (October 1998). Available at http://www.infosecuritymag.com.

Breed, Charles. "PKI: The Myth, the Magic, and the Reality." *Information Security* (June 1999): 20-27.

Brickell, E. F. "A Survey of Hardware Implementations of RSA." In *Lecture Notes in Computer Science*. Vol. 435, edited by G. Brassard. Crypto '89. Berlin: Springer-Verlag, 1990, 368-370.

Briney, Andy. "Pioneers...or Guinea Pigs?" *Information Security* (June 1999): 34-40.

Cobb, Stephen. *NCSA Guide to PC and LAN Security*. New York: McGraw-Hill, 1995.

Certicom. "Current Public-Key Cryptographic Systems." White paper, April 1997. Available at http://www.certicom.com.

Datapro, Inc. "Datapro Report on Encryption Devices." Delran, N.J., March 1993.

DeMaio, Harry. "Getting Started with PKI." *Information Systems Security* (Summer 1999): 27-36.

Department of Defense (DoD). "Medium-Assurance Public Key Infrastructure (PKI) Functional Specification." Draft, Version 0.3, 20 Oct 98.

Diffie, W. "Conventional versus Public Key Cryptosystems." In *Secure Communications and Asymmetric Cryptosystems*, edited by G. J. Simmons. Boulder, Colo.: Westview Press, 1982, 41-72.

Diffie, W., "The First Ten Years of Public-Key Cryptography," *Proceedings of the IEEE*, 76, no. 5 (May 1988): 560-577.

Diffie, W. and M. Hellman. "Privacy and Authentication: An Introduction to Cryptography." *IEEE Proceedings* 67, no. 3 (1979): 397-427.

Diffie, W. and M. Hellman. "New Directions in Cryptography." *IEEE Transactions on Information Theory* 22 (1976): 644-654.

"DoD Information Infrastructure Public Key Infrastructure (PKI) Concept of Operations." Third draft, 24 October 1997, Mitre/Disa/NSA.

ElGamal, T. "A Public-Key Cryptosystem and a Signature Scheme Based on Discrete Logarithms." *IEEE Transactions on Information Theory* 31 (1985): 469-472.

Gustafson, H., E. Dawson, and W. Caelli. "Comparison of Block Ciphers." In *Proceedings of Auscrypt '90*, edited by J. Seberry and J. Pieprzyk, 1990, 208-220.

Haykin, M. E. and R. B. J. Warnar. *Smart Card Technology: New Methods for Computer Access Control*. NIST Special Publication 500-157, September 1988.

ICSA. "ICSA Program for IPSec Product Certification." Version 1.0, 15 May 1998. Available at www.ICSA.net.

Kinch, Lynn, John Allen, Sami Mousa, Terry May, and Harry Watson. "Public Key Infrastructure: Building Trust Online" for the course Cryptographic Systems: Application, Management and Policy (EMGT 298IN3). Team paper for Professor Nichols, SEAS, at The George Washington University, 16 August 1999.

Kohls, D. and Lance J. Hoffman. "TurboTrade: A National Information Infrastructure Cost/Risk/Benefit Model." Report GWU-IIST-93-17, Department of Electrical Engineering and Computer Science, The George Washington University, Washington, D.C., September 1993.

Massey, J. "An Introduction to Contemporary Cryptology." *IEEE Proceedings* 76, no. 5 (1988): 533-549.

Merkle, R. C. *Secrecy, Authentication, and Public Key Systems*. Ann Arbor: UMI Research Press, 1982.

Menezes, Alfred J., P. C. Van Oorschot, and S. A. Vanstone. *Handbook of Applied Cryptography*, Boca Raton, Fla.: CRC Press, 1997.

Merkle, R. "Fast Software Encryption Functions." *Proceedings of Crypto '90*. Menezes and Scott A. Vanstone, eds. (1991): 476-501.

Murray, William. "You Can't Buy PKI." *Information Security* (June 1999): 28-29.

National Research Council. *Computers at Risk: Safe Computing in the Information Age*. Washington, D.C.: National Academy Press, 1991.

Neumann, P. *Computer-Related Risks*. Reading, Mass.: Addison-Wesley, 1994.

Nechvatal, James. "Public-Key Cryptography." Security Technology Group, National Computer Systems Laboratory, National Institute of Standards and Technology, Gaithersburg, Md.: 1989.

Oppliger, Ralph. "Case Study: How to Build a Corporate PKI." *Computer Security Alert* (May 1998). Available at www.gocsi.com/crypto.htm.

"PKI Evolution to Application." *SC Info Security Magazine*. (August 1999): 19-22.

Rhee, Man Young. *Cryptography and Secure Communications*. New York: McGraw-Hill, 1994.

Rivest, Ron. "Ciphertext." *The RSA Newsletter* 1 (1993).

Rivest, R. "The MD5 Message-Digest Algorithm." RFC1321, April 1992.

Rivest, R. L. and A. T. Sherman. "Randomized Encryption Techniques." *Advances in Cryptology: Proceedings of Crypto '82*. D. Chaum, R. L. Rivest, and A. T. Sherman, eds., New York: Plenum Press, 1983, 145-163.

Rivest, R. "Responses to NIST's Proposal." *Communications of the ACM* 35, no. 7 (July 1992): 41-47.

Ryska, Norbert and Siegfried Herda. *Kryptographische Verfahren in der Datenverarbeitung—Gesellschaft für Informatik*. Berlin: Springer-Verlag, 1980.

Salomaa, A. *Public-Key Cryptography*. Berlin: Springer-Verlag, 1990.

Schneier, Bruce. *Applied Cryptography: Protocols, Algorithms, and Source Code C*. 2nd ed. New York: Wiley, 1995.

Schnorr, C. "Efficient Identification and Signatures for Smart Cards." *Advances in Cryptology—Crypto '89*, Berlin: Springer-Verlag, 1990, 239-251.

RSA. "Understanding Public Key Infrastructure (PKI)." RSA Data Security white paper, August 1999.

Office of Technology Assessment. *Information Security and Privacy in Network Environment*. Washington, D.C., U.S. Government Printing Office, 1994, 115.

VeriSign, "PKI Enterprise Solutions." White paper, 1999. Available at www.verisign.com.

Wayner, Peter. *Digital Copyright Protection*. San Diego: Academic Press, 1997.

Standards

Communications Security Establishment, The Canadian Trusted Computer Product Evaluation Criteria Version 3.0e. Canadian System Security Centre, CSE, 1993.
Available from Criteria Coordinator
S5B InfoSec Standards and Evaluations/Communications Security Establishment

P.O. Box 9703 Terminal
Ottawa K1G 3Z4
Phone: 613-991-7331
Fax: 613-991-7323
E-mail: criteria@manitou.cse.dnd.ca

Datapro Networking Report 2783. "ISO Reference Model for Open Systems Interconnection (OSI)." August 1991, 7.

FIPS 186, Digital Signature Standard (DSS). Specifies a digital signature algorithm appropriate for applications requiring a digital rather than a written signature.

FIPS 185, Escrowed Encryption Standard (EES). Specifies a voluntary technology available for protecting telephone communications (e.g., voice, fax, modem).

FIPS 180, Secure Hash Standard (SHS). Specifies a secure hash algorithm (SHA) for use with the Digital Signature Standard. Additionally, for applications not requiring a digital signature, the SHA is to be used whenever a secure hash algorithm is required for federal applications.

FIPS 46-2, Data Encryption Standard (DES). Provides the technical specifications for the DES.

FIPS 113, Computer Data Authentication. Specifies a data authentication algorithm, based upon the DES, which may be used to detect unauthorized modifications to data, both intentional and accidental. The message authentication code as specified in ANSI X9.9 is computed in the same manner as the data authentication code as specified in this standard.

FIPS PUB 190, Guideline For the Use of Advanced Authentication Technology Alternatives. September 1994. See http://csrc.ncsl.nist.gov/fips/fip190.txt.

FIPS 140-1, Security Requirements for Cryptographic Modules. Establishes the physical and logical security requirements for the design and manufacture of modules implementing NIST-approved cryptographic algorithms.

FIPS 171, Key Management Using ANSI X9.17. Adopts ANSI X9.17 and specifies a particular selection of options for the automated distribution of keying material by the federal government using the protocols of ANSI X9.17.

National Bureau of Standards, Federal Information Processing Standards Publication 46: Data Encryption Standard. 15 January 1977.

National Bureau of Standards, Federal Information Processing Standards Publication 81: DES Modes of Operation. 2 December 1980.

National Bureau of Standards, Federal Information Processing Standards Publication 74: Guidelines for Implementing and Using the NBS Data Encryption Standard. 1 April 1981.

National Bureau of Standards, Federal Information Processing Standards Publication 46-1: Data Encryption Standard, 1987.

National Computer Security Center (1983-). Rainbow Series. Monographs on many aspects of information systems security.

National Institute of Standards and Technology, Publication XX: Announcement and Specifications for a Digital Signature Standard (DSS), 19 August 1991.

National Institute of Standards and Technology, Federal Information Processing Standards Publication 185, Escrowed Encryption Standard, 9 February 1994.

National Institute of Standards and Technology, Federal Information Processing Standards Publication 186: Digital Signature Standard (DSS), 19 May 1994.

National Institute of Standards and Technology, Approval of Federal Information Processing Standards Publication 185, Escrowed Encryption Standard, Federal Register, Vol. 59, No. 27, 9 February 1994.

National Institute of Standards and Technology and National Security Agency, Memorandum of Understanding between the

Director of the National Institute of Standards and Technology and the Director of the National Security Agency Concerning the Implementation of Public Law 100-235, 24 March 1989.

The Orange Book is DOD 520 0.28-STD, published December 1985 as part of the Rainbow Series. For a copy of the "Trusted Computer System Evaluation Criteria," contact:

Department of Defense
National Security Agency
ATTN: S332
9800 Savage Road
Fort Meade, MD 20755-6000
Phone: 301-766-8729.

RSA Data Security, Inc., Cryptographic Message Syntax Standard, PKCS-7, 1 November 1993.

Stallings, William. *Networking Standards: A Guide to OSI, ISDN, LAN, and MAN Standards*. Reading, Mass.: Addison-Wesley, 1993.

Telecommunications

Dreher, Richard, Lawrence Harte, Steven Kellogg, and Tom Schaffnit. *The Comprehensive Guide to Wireless Technologies: Cellular, PCS, Paging, SMR, and Satellite*. Fuquay-Varina, N.C.: APDG Publishing, 1999.

Gibilisco, Stan. *Handbook of Radio and Wireless Technology*. New York: McGraw-Hill, 1999.

Harte, Lawrence, Steve Prokup, and Richard Levine. *Cellular and PCS: The Big Picture*. New York: McGraw-Hill, 1997.

Harte, Lawrence, Richard Levine, and Geoff Livingston. *GSM Superphones*. New York: McGraw-Hill, 1999.

Inglis, Andrew F. and Arch C. Luther. *Satellite Technology: An Introduction*. 2nd ed., Boston: Focal Press, 1997.

Pelton, Joseph N. *Wireless and Satellite Telecommunications*. Upper Saddle River, N.J.: Prentice-Hall, 1995.

Rhee, Man Young. *CDMA Network Security*. Upper Saddle River, N.J.: Prentice-Hall, 1998.

Vacca, John. *Satellite Encryption*. Academic Press, 1999.

INDEX

About RSA Security Inc.

RSA Security Inc. is the most trusted name in e-security, helping organizations build secure, trusted foundations for e-business through its two-factor authentication, encryption and public key management systems. As the global integration of Security Dynamics and RSA Data Security, RSA Security has the market reach, proven leadership and unrivaled technical and systems experience to address the changing security needs of e-business and bring trust to the new, online economy.

A truly global company with more than 5,000 customers, RSA Security is renowned for providing technologies that help organizations conduct e-business with confidence. The company's RSA SecurID Æ enterprise authentication products are protecting information in the majority of the Fortune 100 today, addressing the important need for easy, hacker-proof user authentication both inside and outside the corporate network. These same products are similarly used by leading electronic commerce businesses, including securities trading and banking applications, to protect against external attack and fraudulent activity. The company's RSA BSAFE Æ line of encryption-based security technologies are embedded in over 450 million copies of today's most successful Internet applications, including Web browsers, commerce servers, e-mail systems and virtual private network products. The majority of all secure electronic commerce and communication on the Internet today are conducted using RSA Security technologies. Both RSA SecurID and RSA BSAFE are considered de facto standards worldwide.

RSA Security now offers its customers the RSA Keon"! family of PKI products, a solution for enabling, managing and simplifying the public key authentication and encryption security in today's leading e-mail, Web browser, Web server and VPN applications. Elements of RSA Keon are available on an OEM basis to allow application designers to build many core RSA Keon benefits into new applications, and other options are available to adapt existing, installed applications to gain RSA Keon security and management benefits. RSA Keon is the first product to combine the expertise of the entire company, from public key technology to large systems scalability and management.

Headquartered in Bedford, Mass. and with offices around the world, RSA Security is a public company (NASDAQ: RSAS) with yearly revenues in excess of $200 million.

The Markets and Products

With the proliferation of the Internet and revolutionary new e-business practices, there has never been a more critical need for sophisticated security technologies and solutions. Today, as public and private networks merge and organizations increasingly expand their businesses to the Internet, RSA Security's core offerings are continually evolving to address the critical need for e-security. As the inventor of leading security technologies, RSA Security is focused on three core disciplines of e-security, including:

Public Key Infrastructure RSA Keon is a family of interoperable, standards-based PKI products for managing digital certificates and providing an environment for authenticated, private and legally binding electronic communications and transactions. The RSA Keon family ñ from a robust certificate authority to developer components and turn-key enterprise solutions ñ provides a common foundation for securing Internet and e-business applications. In addition, through an exclusive reseller relationship with VeriSign, RSA Security offers organizations a solution with the choice of an outsourced core certificate authority with VeriSign OnSite, the industry's leading managed CA service, or through fully in-house software deployments using the RSA Keon Certificate Server.

Authentication RSA SecurID solutions provide centrally managed, strong, two-factor user authentication services for enterprise networks, operating systems, e-commerce Web sites and other IT infrastructure, ensuring that only authorized users access data, applications and communications. Supporting a range of authentication devices, including hardware tokens, key fobs, smart cards and software tokens, RSA SecurID solutions create a virtually impenetrable barrier against unauthorized access, protecting network and data resources from potentially devastating accidental or malicious intrusion. RSA SecurID installations are managed through RSA ACE/Server authentication management software, providing the ability to scale deployments in the hundreds of thousands of users.

Encryption RSA BSAFE is a family of platform-independent crypto-security development tools that enable corporate and commercial software developers to reliably incorporate security into a wide variety of applications. These encryption components are used to secure applications for electronic commerce and services over the Internet and intranets, enterprise security, entertainment, wireless communications, delivery of digital information over cable, and other uses. Built to provide implementations of standards like SSL, SMIME, RSA and the PKCS family of open standards, RSA BSAFE products can save developers man-years of time and risk in their development schedules.

Commitment to Interoperability

RSA Security's offerings represent a set of open, standards-based products and technologies that integrate easily into organizations' IT environments, with minimal modification to existing applications and network systems. These solutions and technologies are designed to help organizations deploy new applications securely, while maintaining corporate investments in existing infrastructure. In addition, the RSA Security maintains active, strategic partnerships with other leading IT vendors to promote interoperability and enhanced functionality.

Strategic Partnerships

RSA Security has built its business through its commitment to interoperability. Today, through its various partnering programs, the company has strategic relationships with more than 500 industry-leading companies ñ including 3COM, AOL/Netscape, Apple Computer, Ascend, AT&T, Nortel Networks, Cisco Systems, Compaq, IBM, Oracle, Microsoft, Novell and Intel ñ who are delivering integrated, RSA Security technology in more than 1,000 products.

Customers

RSA Security customers span a wide range of industries, including an extensive presence in the e-commerce, banking, government, telecommunications, aerospace, university and healthcare arenas. Today, more that 5 million users across 4,500 organizations (including more than half of the Fortune 100) use RSA SecurID authentication products to protect corporate data, and over 500 companies embed RSA BSAFE software in some 1,000 applications, with a combined distribution of over 450 million units worldwide.

Worldwide Service and Support

RSA Security offers a full complement of world-class service and support offerings to ensure the success of each customer's project or deployment through a range of ongoing customer support and professional services including assessments, project consulting, implementation, education and training, and developer support. RSA Security's Technical Support organization is known for resolving requests in the shortest possible time, gaining customers' confidence and exceeding expectations.

Global Presence

RSA Security is a truly global e-security provider with major offices in the U.S., United Kingdom, Singapore and Tokyo, and representation in more than 45 countries with additional international expansion underway. In May 1998, the Company established a Japanese subsidiary to capitalize on the significant opportunity in the Japanese security market. In January 1999, the Company opened an international development center in Brisbane, Australia, where RSA Security will develop and distribute strong encryption products to global markets. The RSA SecurWorld channel program brings RSA Security's products to value-added resellers and distributors worldwide, including locations in Europe, the Middle East, Africa, the Americas and Asia-Pacific.